Nature's Nation

An Environmental History
of the United States

John Opie
New Jersey Institute of Technology

Harcourt Brace College Publishers

Fort Worth   Philadelphia   San Diego   New York   Orlando   Austin   San Antonio
Toronto   Montreal   London   Sydney   Tokyo

Publisher	Earl McPeek
Acquisitions Editor	David C. Tatom
Developmental Editor	Pam Hatley
Project Editor	Sandy Walton
Art Designer	Candice Johnson Clifford
Production Manager	Diane Gray

Cover image credit: New York State, Office of Parks, Recreation and Historic Preservation, Olana State Historic Site

ISBN: 0-15-500219-8
Library of Congress Catalog Card Number: 97–73575

Address for Orders
Harcourt Brace College Publishers, 6277 Sea Harbor Drive, Orlando, Florida 32887-6777
1-800-782-4479

Address for Editorial Correspondence
Harcourt Brace College Publishers, 301 Commerce Street, Suite 3700, Fort Worth, TX 76102

Web Site Address
http://www.hbcollege.com

Harcourt Brace College Publishers will provide complimentary supplements or supplement packages to those adopters qualified under our adoption policy. Please contact your sales representative to learn how you qualify. If as an adopter or potential user you receive supplements you do not need, please return them to your sales representative or send them to: Attn: Returns Department, Troy Warehouse, 465 South Lincoln Drive, Troy, MO 63379.

Printed in the United States of America

8 9 0 1 2 3 4 5 6 7   039   9 8 7 6 5 4 3 2 1

Harcourt Brace College Publishers

PREFACE

Note to the Instructor (and Students)

This history book is written with measured passion. It raises questions about an American success story that depleted the nation's (and world's) natural capital without factoring in the environmental costs. Though accounting for a mere 5 percent of the world's population, Americans today consume more than 30 percent of the world's resources and produce 40 percent of its wastes and pollution. However, *Nature's Nation* was not written to damn the past or vilify the present, but to explore how Americans first perceived and then took charge of their seemingly limitless forests, deep soils, and rich veins of minerals. As a result, Americans acquired a mastery over nature that encouraged a democratic, industrial, capitalist, and consumer-based society. This approach does not try to repudiate the move toward human dominance of the American environment in order to return to some idyllic pastoral age in the past (which never existed). More realistically, it informs contemporary environmental conflicts (and, with luck, future trends) by uncovering their historic foundations.

Nature's Nation examines several important features of American history that have been largely ignored, played down, or misunderstood. One is that colonial and frontier history is not a story of the conquest of an empty wilderness, but the meeting of two cultures. Europeans and Native Americans began to compete for the same geography, and this resulted in a sweeping European domination. Another is that the first major European reshaping of the American environment was not a factory system, but an agriculture that responded to habitual human scarcity with tremendous food surpluses. Without an understanding of agricultural abundance based on soil and water consumption—today's farmer feeds 97 others—it is difficult to explain the rest of the American experience.

When resource-based industrialization appeared, it quickly became a dominating juggernaut over the physical world and its inhabitants that is now inescapable. Industrialization saw the natural world as obsolete until that natural world was absorbed into the factory system. Industrialization is very alluring—the continuous and cumulative production of a wide array of material goods that creates a growing and prosperous middle class. Only a small minority, such as New England's Transcendentalists and the utopian enthusiasts of New York's Burnt-Over District, turned to natural forces to find fundamental values.

Yet another feature was the fabrication of a Second Nature—a constructed infrastructure of metropolitan islands defined by systems of water, electricity, fuels, public transportation, and automobiles. The islands were connected across a rural landscape first by roads, canals, and railroads, and later by superhighways, airline routes, and electronic highways. These human constructs were also a means to surpass the messy and inconvenient natural world. We also learn the risks of environmental mismanagement and collapse, as in Appalachia and the High Plains.

Nature's Nation concludes with an examination of the modern environmental revolution, including new science and the vigorous application of law and regulation. Americans rediscovered their plundered and polluted geography, and, to their credit, aggressively moved to clean up, protect, and refresh the nonhuman world around them.

When environmental awareness and protection are highlighted, it is easy to slip into historical hindsight. Our attention to our gradually unfolding history will hopefully caution us from improperly judging each generation for what it did not know about nature's embrace. If we insist that future generations understand us today on our own terms, we ourselves must have the same respectful attitude toward the past. Yet, this history also emphasizes that we have only recently learned to look at our surrounding world through the fresh eyes of ecological science. Environmental history learns "the rules of the game" from the contemporary study of biomes, ecosystems, and hydrological cycles.

We also discover that America is still mostly an unknown in environmental terms; our environment is the most neglected aspect of our history. Still, many aspects of American life are unintelligible except in the framework of nature's forces. Regardless of our contemporary separation from raw nature, all people are still located in a specific place that can be marked out on a map. Economists have long spoken of the "invisible hand" of the marketplace in shaping material life. In this book we will come to understand that the natural world is a powerful "visible hand" that only *seemed* invisible because we ignored it. This book intends to bring America's environment from the invisible background and highlight it as a central force in American history. What if we turned the tables and made the environment the dominant feature of our history, and then tried to relate politics, economics, science, technology, society, and culture to it? The result is environmental history that is inherently multidisciplinary.

An environmental approach makes both the natural world and its human habitation much more complex, challenging, and interesting. We learn, for example, that America's geography is not a fixed material base. It is perpetually dynamic with its own diverse agendas, a continuously moving point on a moving line. This approach also suits the open-ended nature of democracy, because both nature and democracy are quite unpredictable, filled with unrepeatable events, and their intermingled futures are continuously diverted into new channels.

While the book is roughly chronological, it is also topical. Readers will see that there are significant chronological overlaps among chapters. I believe this is unavoidable and even desirable. History is not tidy.

As my colleague, Norbert Elliot, a seasoned textbook writer, argues, no textbook is neutral. It should have voice that offers a carefully thought-out point of view. An effective textbook should also make adventuresome statements, be provocative to educate the student and make the instructor think about his or her field in a new way. In addition, the author should synthesize and crystallize the subject matter, even in the thicket of historical detail. Elliot adds that the author should make the reader feel like he or she can deal with the subject. That is, the reader can begin to feel confident about making hypotheses about the subject and offering opinions. Not the least, the author should make the reader feel as if the material can be of use within his or her own life. The material should not remain "inert" but become something about which the reader can claim a level of ownership, not just for another course, not just on the job, but within the landscape of his or her own mind.

This textbook is intended for undergraduate courses and graduate programs not only in history and American studies, but also as a supporting volume wherever environmental issues are raised: biology, public policy, environmental science, chemical and civil engineering, anthropology, geography, economics, political science, sociology, literature, law, architecture, and planning, and elsewhere in the humanities and sciences.

Several features have been added to the book to make the material accessible and useful to a wide range of students. Frequent sidebars highlight personalities, issues, and debates in the environmental arena or examine a particular aspect of a technological or environmental problem. Maps, charts, diagrams, and photos also appear throughout the text, and annotated bibliographies end each chapter and provide ample resources for further study in the field.

Many friends and colleagues helped me in a process that began in 1991 and did not conclude until 1997 (at least this time around). Special thanks to Norbert Elliot, John Perkins, Donald Worster, Chris Sellers, Pete Lederman, Keith Kloor, and Lise Sedrez. For their careful reading of the manuscript and encouraging commentary throughout its development, I would like to thank J. Donald Hughes, University of Denver; Martin V. Melosi, University of Houston; John H. Perkins, The Evergreen State College; and Hal K. Rothman, University of Nevada, Las Vegas. My wife Barbara exercised her prodigious patience, and I tested it.

BRIEF CONTENTS

Preface   ix

Introduction: What Is American Environmental History?   1

PART ONE   EUROPEANS TAKE COMMAND   9

CHAPTER ONE   "O STRANGE NEW WORLD!"   10

CHAPTER TWO   THE WORLD WE HAVE LOST: PEOPLE OF THE LAND   55

PART TWO   SHAPING THE NATIONAL LANDSCAPE   83

CHAPTER THREE   THE FEDERAL GEOGRAPHY   84

CHAPTER FOUR   WHEN THE UNITED STATES WAS AN UNDEVELOPED COUNTRY   114

CHAPTER FIVE   UNIFYING AMERICAN SPACE   154

CHAPTER SIX   ROMANTIC AMERICA AND UTOPIANISM: LAYING CLAIM TO PARADISE   186

PART THREE   CREATING THE INDUSTRIAL INFRASTRUCTURE   215

CHAPTER SEVEN   DETERMINING AMERICA'S ENVIRONMENTAL FUTURE: THE RUSH TO INDUSTRIALIZE   216

CHAPTER EIGHT   RESHAPING THE NATION: THE BUILT ENVIRONMENT AND PUBLIC WORKS   242

CHAPTER NINE   THE ENVIRONMENTAL COSTS OF INDUSTRIAL AMERICA: CITIES AND LANDSCAPES IN TROUBLE   269

CHAPTER TEN   FROM NATURE'S WATER TO PUBLIC WORKS WATER: AMERICA BECOMES A HYDRAULIC CIVILIZATION   304

CHAPTER ELEVEN   HITTING THE WALL: ENVIRONMENTAL LIMITS IN APPALACHIA AND ON THE HIGH PLAINS   344

PART FOUR   RETHINKING AMERICA: THE MAKING OF ENVIRONMENTALISM   369

CHAPTER TWELVE   RECOVERING "ORIGINAL AMERICA": THE WILDERNESS MOVEMENT   370

CHAPTER THIRTEEN   ENVIRONMENTALISM ENTERS THE AMERICAN MAINSTREAM: ENVIRONMENTAL SCIENCE, RACHEL CARSON'S *SILENT SPRING*, AND PUBLIC AWARENESS   404

CHAPTER FOURTEEN   RISK AND REGULATION: ENVIRONMENTALISM ENTERS THE MODERN ERA   434

CHAPTER FIFTEEN   INTO THE TWENTY-FIRST CENTURY: THE UNITED STATES AND THE GLOBAL ENVIRONMENT   464

Index   495

Credits   517

CONTENTS IN DETAIL

Preface   ix

Introduction: What Is American Environmental History?   1
The Environmental Challenge to American Triumphalism   *2*
Three Views on the American Environment   *3*
Keeping a Historical and Geographical Perspective   *4*
Contemporary Environmental Issues   *5*
What Is the Plan for This Book?   *5*
For Further Reading   *6*

PART ONE   EUROPEANS TAKE COMMAND   9

CHAPTER ONE   **"O STRANGE NEW WORLD!"**   **10**
The Encounter Was a Unique, Unrepeatable and Fatal Event   *10*
Europeans Did Not Discover America, They Invented It   *11*
The Reality Behind the Myths   *13*
    The Unexpected Continent   13
    Easy European Entry into the New World   14
    America's Startling Natural Abundance   15
The Unexpected Peoples: The First Nations   *18*
    Successful Native Farming in the Face of Climate Adversity   19
    Indian Regions of the Future United States   22
    Conflicting Environmental Worlds: European Separation from Nature
        and Indian Interdependence with Nature   24
Imperial Alternatives   *25*
    Colonialism and Mercantilism: Their Environmental
        Consequences   25
    The Spanish Way in Florida   27
    Water Pathways into the Interior   28
    Seeking a Balance: The French Alternative Would Have Changed
        American History   28
    The English Gain a Foothold and Begin to Domesticate the
        Landscape   31
Native Americans Fall into Harm's Way   *35*
    The European View: "Savages" Were Enemies Who Had No Rights   35
    European Dependency on Natives   37
    Why Did the Indians Lose?   37
    Indian-White Relations through U.S. History   39
Why Was the New World So Easy to Conquer? The European
   Advantage   *40*
    Europe's Ecological Strength   41
    The Aggressive European Mentality: A Passion for Conquest   41

Technology as a Focused Skill   42
Disease   43
The Force of Numbers   43
Was America Uniquely Vulnerable to European Conquest?   45
The Biological Exchange   46
*Conclusion: A One-Time Experiment Changes Human and
    Environmental History   48*
For Further Reading   49

CHAPTER TWO   THE WORLD WE HAVE LOST: PEOPLE OF THE LAND   55
The Forgotten World of Farming   56
Today Few Americans Know What Was Once Common to All   56
The Agrarian Challenge of Early America   57
Undertooled   57
Undercapitalized   58
Labor Intensive   58
Autonomous Homestead and the Psychology of Isolation   59
Early Rural America: The Passing of the Frontier   60
Constructing Useful Farmland Out of Wilderness   61
From a Forest Environment to a Familiar Landscape   61
Clearing the Land   64
Animal Management   66
Plants   68
*Farming Was Not Enough for Europeans: Property, Ownership,
    Sovereignty   70*
The Geography of Abundance   73
New England   73
Southeastern Pennsylvania   75
The South   76
The Great Valley of Virginia   77
Conclusion: Life Newly Defined by Abundance   79
For Further Reading   80

PART TWO   SHAPING THE NATIONAL LANDSCAPE   83

CHAPTER THREE   THE FEDERAL GEOGRAPHY   84
The Dilemma of Independence: Inventing a Geography   85
The Geography of Revolution and Independence   85
Foreign Threats to a Federal Geography   90
Who Owns the Land? Inventing and Building a Public Domain   91
The Geography of the Constitutional Debates   94
The Northwest Ordinance of 1787   96
*The Great American Experiment in Land Reform: Selling the Public
    Domain   98*
Getting a Grip on the Land: The Land Survey Ordinance of 1785   99
The Privatization of America's Geography: Rush to Wealth   106
Ohio as the Speculator's Battlefield   106
Correcting the System to Suit the Land Rush   108
The Problem with Squatters   110
Conclusion: From Public Domain to Private Property   112
For Further Reading   113

CHAPTER FOUR   WHEN THE UNITED STATES WAS AN UNDEVELOPED COUNTRY   **114**
Overview   115
    What Is an Undeveloped Country?   115
America in 1790: The Threat of Economic Failure   116
American Advantages, Environmental and Otherwise   119
Space: America's Environmental Challenge   122
    Constructing America's Cities: Preindustrial Infrastructures   123
    Conquest of the Heartland: Creation of a Transportation
        Infrastructure   128
    Gaps and Passes, Trails and Roads: People on the Move   133
Modernization from a Primitive Geography: Setting Goals for
    Material Life   136
    The Ideology of Material "Progress"   136
    The Rising Tide: Movement toward a Higher Standard of Living   137
Prosperity in the Age of Wood   141
America's New Mission: The Rush Toward Industrialization   145
    The Demand for Labor-Saving Devices, Goods, and National
        Security   145
    The First Revolution in Mechanization: Textiles   146
    The Limits to Industrialization   147
Conclusion: America by 1840   148
For Further Reading   152

CHAPTER FIVE   UNIFYING AMERICAN SPACE   **154**
Toward a Continent-Size Nation: "A Restless, Sometimes Lawless,
    Landgrabbing People"   156
Swallowing Up the Wild West   158
    The Trapper's "Original West"   158
    The Explorer's West—Scientific, Military, and Commercial   161
    Invasion Routes to Americanize the West   162
    The Southwest Takeover   163
    Invasion Route to the Pacific Northwest   165
    Railroads and the Engineered West   173
Conclusion: What the West Might Have Been, and What It Became   183
For Further Reading   185

CHAPTER SIX   ROMANTIC AMERICA AND UTOPIANISM: LAYING CLAIM
             TO PARADISE   **186**
The Changing Face of Nature   187
    The Ambitious Goal of Natural History: Total Knowledge of the
        New World   188
    The Strange New World Must Conform with the Old World   188
Everything in Its Place: The Enlightenment Catalogs the
    New World   189
    Natural History, A Utilitarian Science   189
    Natural History Applied to the Unknown Western Wilderness   191
Everything a Divine Correspondence: The Romantic Revolt   193
    Reason and Science Alone Cannot Explain Nature: The
        Transcendentalist Vision   193
    A Hothouse Movement?   194
    New Ways of Sensing, Perceiving, and Knowing: Nature Becomes
        Spirit   196

Henry David Thoreau as an Environmentalist   197

*The Artist Takes Charge: Thomas Cole and the National
    Landscape   198*

Romantic Landscape Painting as the Medium to Know Nature   198

How the Artists Conveyed Their Message: The Sublime   201

The Social Message of Landscape Painting: Thomas Cole   202

Nature's Nation: America's Environmental Advantage   204

*The Geography of Hope: Utopian Communities in the
    Wilderness   205*

"Utopia in Our Time": Its Inevitability   206

Utopia Uniquely Set on America's Land   207

The Environment of the Human Body   208

The Technological Sublime: Romancing the Machine   210

The America—Nouveau Europe—of Man-Made Monuments   210

Conclusion: The Transcendentalist Failure of Nerve   212

For Further Reading   213

PART THREE   CREATING THE INDUSTRIAL
                       INFRASTRUCTURE   215

**CHAPTER SEVEN   DETERMINING AMERICA'S ENVIRONMENTAL FUTURE:
                              THE RUSH TO INDUSTRIALIZE   216**

The Attractions of Industrialization   217

Why Work in a Factory?   217

Mechanization Takes Command   218

The Dramatic Example of Steel   220

Extractive Industries and Nonrenewable Resources   221

A Nation of Natural Resources   221

*Another Raw Material for the Factories: 40 Million
    Immigrants   228*

*The American Corporation: Making Industrialization
    Permanent   229*

*The Second Industrial Revolution: The Progressives and Social
    Efficiency through the Technological "System"   234*

Industrialization in the Twentieth Century   236

Coming Full Circle: Industrializing the Farm   237

Conclusion   240

For Further Reading   241

**CHAPTER EIGHT   RESHAPING THE NATION: THE BUILT ENVIRONMENT AND
                              PUBLIC WORKS   242**

*The Way Americans Saw It: From Geographical Determinism
    to Technological Liberation   243*

A Network of Cities Captures the Inland Landscape   243

The Building of an Infrastructure System   244

The South Finds Its Own Well-Worn Path   246

The Profession of Engineering   248

Public Works for Private Cities   250

Infrastructure in the City: Public Utilities   250

The Industrial City Spreads across the Landscape   251

The Transformation of America by the Railroads   251

America's Love Affair with Mobility   253

Roads and Highway Improvement   260
The Collapse of the Cities   264
Urban Decay and Failed Renewal   264
Flaws in the Infrastructure System   266
Conclusion   267
For Further Reading   268

**CHAPTER NINE   THE ENVIRONMENTAL COSTS OF INDUSTRIAL AMERICA:
CITIES AND LANDSCAPES IN TROUBLE   269**

Daily Life and Work in the Factory Cities   270
Pollution, Waste, and Human Degradation Undermine the Industrial
Revolution: The Negative Infrastructure   270
After the Factory, Everything Else Was an Afterthought   271
A Public Debate: Was Industrialization Inherently Flawed?   272
Social Darwinism: An Intellectual Debate   273
The People Rebel: Disillusionment about Industrialization   275
Pittsburgh, Unfortunately, Had It All   276
The Russell Sage Foundation Report of 1914: "The Pittsburgh
Survey"   277
Pittsburgh's Plague of Typhoid: Human Costs   278
Contrasts: The Tenement and the City Park   279
A "Double Standard of Civil Morality"   281
"We Are Manufacturers, Not Real Estate Dealers"   282
Pittsburgh: "Public Moral Adolescence"   283
The Struggle for Urban Reform: An Uphill Battle   284
The Beginnings of Urban Cleanup   285
George Waring, Water Flushing, and Sanitary Engineering   285
Alice Hamilton, Occupational Disease, and Early
Environmentalism   286
Conquering Industrial Diseases   288
Chicago: "Hog Butcher to the World"   290
Preindustrial Meat Processing   290
Railroads, Chicago's Stockyards, and Refrigerator Cars   291
Mechanization in the Meatpacking Factory: The Disassembly
Line   292
The Interconnected Meat Industry   294
Cityscapes and Landscapes in Trouble   296
Three Case Studies   296
Conclusion   301
For Further Reading   302

**CHAPTER TEN   FROM NATURE'S WATER TO PUBLIC WORKS WATER: AMERICA
BECOMES A HYDRAULIC CIVILIZATION   304**

Introduction: The Water Network Is Another Infrastructure   304
Engineering Urban Water Systems in the East   306
The Army Corps of Engineers in Charge of Waterways   308
The Problem of the West: Not Enough Water   309
The Federal Land System Worsens the Situation   310
Roads Not Taken: Alternative Settlement Patterns   311
*The American Answer to the Problem of the West: Reclamation and
Irrigation   316*

The Irrigation Crusade   316
The Government Takes Charge: Federal Reclamation Reinvents the
    West   318
The Newlands Act: Reclamation Act of 1902   319
The Reclamation Service   320
Reclamation in the Late Twentieth Century: Rethinking Dams   322
Hydrological Giantism in California   324
California Water Wars: The Problem with Los Angeles   325
Agriculture, Cities, and Environmental Impact: California Water
    Projects   328
Reclamation Takes Over the West   332
Harnessing the Colorado River   332
Taming the Columbia Basin: The Hydroelectric Infrastructure   334
The Central Arizona Project   336
Reconstructing Appalachia   338
The Tennessee Valley Authority   338
The Corps of Engineers and the Tennessee-Tombigbee
    Connection   340
Conclusion   342
For Further Reading   343

**CHAPTER ELEVEN   HITTING THE WALL: ENVIRONMENTAL LIMITS IN APPALACHIA
AND ON THE HIGH PLAINS   344**

*Introduction: Environmental Challenges, Human Mistakes, and
    Industrial Misuse   345*
The Demolition of Appalachia   346
Appalachia, Like the Plains, Was First a Barrier   346
A Prolonged Frontier History: The Appalachian "Mountaineer"   347
Wasting the Birthright: Bad Farming   348
Selling the Birthright: The Great Appalachian Forest   348
The Birthright Denied: Coal Mining and Stripping the Land   349
The High Plains   355
Semiarid Climate: The Environmental Challenge of the High
    Plains   355
Early History of the Plains   357
Irrigation: The Technological Answer to the Plains Climate   361
Conclusion   366
For Further Reading   367

PART FOUR   RETHINKING AMERICA: THE MAKING
                OF ENVIRONMENTALISM   369

**CHAPTER TWELVE   RECOVERING "ORIGINAL AMERICA": THE WILDERNESS
MOVEMENT   370**

George Catlin and the Idea of National Parks   370
*"Preserve the Wilderness!" The Disappearance of Original
    America   371*
Nature in the Cities: The Parks Movement   374
The Fragmented Wilderness: Natural Wonders and Curiosities   375
America's "Crown Jewels": The National Park System   375
Yosemite   376
Yellowstone   378

Other National Parks and the National Park Service   379
Changing Agendas for the National Parks   381
Battle over National Park Concessions   383
John Muir, Yosemite, and the Sierra Club   *386*
From the Defeat at Hetch Hetchy to the Victory at Echo Park   *389*
From Scenery to Ecosystem: The Modern Wilderness Movement   *391*
The Wilderness Act of 1964   391
Battling the Bureau of Reclamation   393
Alaska: The Last Great Wilderness   *394*
Aldo Leopold, Ecological Science, and the Land Ethic   *396*
The Impact of Tourism on Wilderness   *398*
Conclusion: Deep Ecology—Toward a Wilderness Philosophy   *401*
For Further Reading   *403*

**CHAPTER THIRTEEN   ENVIRONMENTALISM ENTERS THE AMERICAN MAINSTREAM:
ENVIRONMENTAL SCIENCE, RACHEL CARSON'S *SILENT
SPRING*, AND PUBLIC AWARENESS   404**

*New Environmental Conditions: Human Action Dominates the
    American Earth*   *405*
The New Science of Ecology   *406*
Emergence of Ecology   407
Ecology as a Modern Science: Eugene P. Odum's Textbook   412
From an Applied Science to a Visionary "Subversive" Science   413
Ecology Becomes "Big Science"   416
Has Science Failed to Keep Its Promise to Discover and Solve
    Environmental Problems?   417
NGOs: The Empowerment of Nongovernmental Organizations   *417*
The Remarkable Role of the NGOs   418
Traditional Environmental Organizations   418
Professionalization of the NGOs   422
Local Action Organizations: PIRGs and NIMBYs   424
Citizen Access to Environmental Policy   425
Radical Environmental NGOs   426
The Antienvironmentalist Movement   429
*Conclusion: Environmental Science, Public Activism, and Earth
    Day 1970*   *431*
For Further Reading   *433*

**CHAPTER FOURTEEN   RISK AND REGULATION: ENVIRONMENTALISM ENTERS
THE MODERN ERA   434**

The Impossible Dream: Making a Risk-Free Environment   *435*
Industrial Breakdowns: "The Big Technological Letdown"   *435*
Battling the Chemical Industry   436
Regulating the Risks: America's "Environmental Era"   *436*
Public Perception of Risk and Scientific Evidence: The Dilemma   *439*
Fear of Cancer Shapes Two Decades of Environmental Debate   441
Environmentalism's Newfound Weapons: Law and Regulation   *443*
Law and the Making of Environmental Policy   443
The "Public Trust" Is a Precedent for Environmental Protection   443
Limits to Protection through the Marketplace   444
EPA: The Environmental Protection Agency   *446*
Historic Regulatory Agencies and "Big Government"   446
The Politics of Environmental Regulation, 1970 to 1996   447

The Power of Administrative Law   451
  A Powerful Tool: The Environmental Impact Statement (EIS)   452
*The Clean Air Act of 1970 Sets Rigorous Standards and
  Procedures*   454
  Example: Automobile Emissions   456
The 1972 Clean Water Act Pushes Technological Innovation   457
*Superfund and the Controversial Control of Dangerous Land
  Sites*   458
Conclusion: Three Cultures—Science, Law, and Economics   461
For Further Reading   462

**CHAPTER FIFTEEN   INTO THE TWENTY-FIRST CENTURY: THE UNITED STATES AND
          THE GLOBAL ENVIRONMENT**   **464**

The Tragedy of the Commons   465
America's Environmental Isolationism   467
  The Lost Opportunity   467
  Postwar American Indifference to Global Environmental
    Scarcity   469
Oil Makes the World Go Round . . . for a Time   469
  Risky Dependency on Oil   470
  Is Oil the Major Source of Environmental Harm?   471
  Responses to the 1970s Oil Crisis   472
Rethinking Industrialization   474
  1972 Report to the Club of Rome: The Limits to Growth   474
  The International Agenda: Shift from Growth to Sustainability   478
  The New Economics: Uncoupling Growth and Quality of Life   479
*Global Environmentalism and the Demonizing of the United
  States*   480
  It Took 20 Years to Get from Stockholm to Rio (via Nairobi)   480
  June 1992 Earth Summit at Rio: UN Conference on Environment and
    Development   482
*Response: The "Greening" of Corporate America and the Rise of
  Industrial Ecology*   484
An Environmental Worldview: The Gaia Hypothesis   487
Environmentalism Enters the Mainstream   489
A Final Word   490
For Further Reading   493

Index   495

Credits   517

Nature's Nation

An Environmental History
of the United States

WHAT IS AMERICAN ENVIRONMENTAL HISTORY?

There is a difference between the way a European perceives nature and the way an American does. . . . When a European . . . encounters a tree, it's a tree made familiar by history, to which it's been a witness. This or that king sat underneath it, laying down this or that law—something of that sort. A tree stands there rustling, as it were, with allusions. Pleased and somewhat pensive, our man, refreshed but unchanged by that encounter, returns to his inn or cottage . . . and proceeds to have a good merry time. Whereas when an American walks out of his house and encounters a tree it is a meeting of equals. Man and tree face each other in their respective primal power, free of references: neither has a past, and as to whose future is greater, it is a toss-up. Basically, it's epidermis meeting bark. Our man returns to his cabin in a state of bewilderment, to say the least, if not in actual shock or terror.

—JOSEPH BRODSKY (1994)

There is a lot of truth in the immigrant poet Joseph Brodsky's statement. When his American scrapes epidermis against bark on the primitive frontier, Brodsky describes a profound incompatibility that induced Americans to see themselves belligerently at war with nature. Americans used industrial technology to isolate themselves from the raw threat of wilderness by fabricating a second nature—our steel-beamed, concrete-walled, and polystyrene world. This isolation deepened because industrial America redefined wilderness into utilitarian natural resources, useful only when exploited by technology, and otherwise valueless. Brodsky concludes, "This utter autonomy strikes me as utterly American."

The Environmental Challenge to American Triumphalism

As the result of this utter autonomy, Americans believed in a history of national triumphalism. It is a tantalizing concept. Triumphalism shows up in most American history textbooks. The lack of supplies, tools, and shelter made the first settlers painfully vulnerable to nature's starving times and bitter winters. America's first conquest of nature was to cut down forests and plow soils for food surpluses that became the basis for all future improvements. The nineteenth-century Industrial Revolution consumed natural resources like coal, iron ore, and limestone to raise American living standards to levels that Roman emperors would have envied. Thus American triumphalism depends on an environmental imperialism: We learned to twist nature any way we wished and turned the world into our artifacts. The tenets of triumphalism are very hypnotizing: The power of science and technology is unlimited, nature is to be tamed to serve humanity, material progress is inevitable, and enlightened humans like Americans represent the pinnacle of all creation.

Environmental history doesn't exactly see it this way. Instead, without denying the enormous benefits of industrial productivity, an environmental approach to American history takes a bolder look behind the scenes, finding that American triumphalism is fast draining the nation's (and world's) natural resources, which are inevitably limited. With a mere 5 percent of the world's population, today Americans consume over 30 percent of the world's resources and produce 40 percent of its waste and pollution. Beginning with the first settlements, Americans began to lay waste to the continent's seemingly limitless forests, deep soils, and rich veins of minerals. An environmental view also directs our attention to the prodigal use of fuels like coal or oil whose noxious burnings and smoking threaten the right to breathe good air, the multiplication of dumps of long-lasting synthetic chemicals that poison cities and towns, and the creation of nuclear wastes that demand an unthinkable 40,000 generations of careful monitoring to reach their half-life in 12,000 years.

Part of the problem is that we have only recently learned to look at our surrounding world in ways that may possibly be appropriate to its survival. It can be argued that no one knew what America's geography was like until ecologists began applying ideas of biomes, ecosystems, and interdependency to the landscape. Regions like the Atlantic Coast wetlands, all of Appalachia and the Great Plains, the Sacramento Valley, and myriad other places have been misunderstood. America is still mostly an unknown in environmental terms. We are only beginning to understand how profoundly human affairs are intertwined with the entire history of climates, forests, soils, and energy systems as well as our more familiar surroundings of electronic media, consumer goods, sports figures, and ways of behaving based on religion and politics and the marketplace. The single most important contribution of environmental history is to remember that we humans spring from nature, continuously live in it, must live with the changes we force on it, and, finally, must work to sustain it, if for nothing else than our own sakes.

Three Views on the American Environment

There are at least three ways in which our views of the American environment can affect how we see American history. First, most American history textbooks treat the nation's physical setting as an unchanging backdrop, a fixed material base for the study of more essential subjects such as politics, war, and society and culture. Hence most history textbooks may use one physiographic map as a frontispiece and hardly refer to the nation's physical environment again except in simple maps of continental expansion. In contrast, environmental history insists on a clear understanding that America has a unique geography, climate, vegetation, and wildlife that continuously shapes and reshapes our daily lives. One not-so-surprising result is that the nonhuman world becomes much more interesting. It is infinitely lavish and fertile, and perpetually dynamic, a continuously moving point on a moving line. The human invasion of the American wilderness first by Native Americans and recently by Europeans, together with its settlement, domestication, and emergence into an urban industrial landscape, is a historic process that goes through fascinating multifold changes.

Second, an environmental viewpoint is often seen as a revisionist critique that says most historians, preoccupied with geographical expansion, political democracy, gross national product, and manifest destiny (e.g., triumphalism), ignore the exploitation and waste of the nation's resources. The problem with the traditional templates of American history, say environmental historians, is that they have generally discounted environmental problems such as resource depletion, the real costs of toxic waste dumps, the creation of unhealthy cities, and the continuous loss of wilderness reserves. Yet environmental history is more than noisy criticisms.

A third approach describes a continuous and open-ended interaction between Americans and their environment. Human affairs also become much more interesting. This view suits the dynamic nature of democracy. Both nature and democracy are quite unpredictable, filled with unrepeatable events, and their intermingled futures are continuously diverted into new channels. Cultural historian Perry Miller was exactly on target when in 1967 he described democratic America as nature's nation. This approach does not try to return to some idyllic pastoral age in the past (which never existed). More realistically, it informs contemporary environmental conflicts (and, with luck, future trends) by uncovering their historic foundations. The advantage of a historical approach is that by learning how environmental problems appeared, and how they came out, we can also learn how to prevent future environmental problems. We will also see that environmental history enlarges some aspects of the American experience—Jefferson's natural history, Thoreau's transcendentalism, grassroots participatory democracy, government regulation—and energetically denounces other aspects—wastefulness, pollution, and exploitation of both humans and nature.

This third approach is the frame for this book; it could simultaneously create an attractive reinterpretation of American history. The American environment has been the most neglected aspect of American history. This book intends to bring America's environment from the invisible background and highlight it as a central force in American history. What if we turned the tables and made it the dominant feature of our history, and then tried to relate politics, economics, technology, and society and culture to the environment? True, environmental history cannot be understood except in the contexts of economic, political, and social and cultural history. At the same time, these other histories truly cannot be understood except in the context of environmental history.

Keeping a Historical and Geographical Perspective

We will try to be fair to the past and see the New World environment as each successive generation of Americans saw it. That is, the American environment will open up before us as it did for the first European visitors, beginning as an unknown eastern edge of an unknown "barrier island" to the fabled Orient. Just as colonial Americans did not know that a revolution and independence were coming, they had no idea that the new nation might include a Midwest over the horizon or a West to the distant Pacific, nor that industry and a cornucopia of consumer goods would exploit unimagined raw materials, nor that an interstate highway system would allow them quickly to traverse the nation in tens of millions of private vehicles simultaneously clouding and poisoning the air.

Our attention to this gradually unfolding environment will caution us from improperly judging each generation for what it did not know about nature's embrace. How do I judge my own father, a metal fabricator in Chicago, who knew no better than to dump scrap metals and burn waste chemicals in the back lot? Hindsight can also create its own blinders: Fifty years ago historians and anthropologists concluded that the Indians lived in an untouched primeval forest; today we know Native Americans did much to shape their environment for their benefit by fire and other devices, although their touch remained lighter than Europeans. If we insist that future generations understand us today on our own terms, we ourselves must have the same respectful attitude toward the past.

We are speaking of what some experts call the social construction of history. Nature is not simply "out there"; instead we construct mental, political, economic, and social pictures of the structures and actions of nature. Environmental history must give special attention to the continuously shifting images, myths, visions, and perceptions that Americans have devised to view their geography. We will see the American environment through many different lenses, including romantic mysticism, pragmatic usefulness, and ecological science. The result is a paradox: Human communities are inside nature, yet nature can be viewed only from the perspective of human communities.

Nevertheless, environmental history is definitively grounded in "place." Each moment exists in a particular geography where individual people live and work and play, and that can be marked out on a map. A bioregional history that connects ecological place and human culture is a drastic move away from politically drawn borders of township and county, state and nation, which are mostly useless in understanding nature. It is not that the local environment determines the course of human affairs, but that its features offer a range of possibilities which human ingenuity can shape to enjoy the good life or fail miserably.

Contemporary Environmental Issues

Together with this sensitivity to the past on its own terms, we will also look at the forces that created today's staggering environmental problems (and an array of solutions). History is not only what mattered in the past, but also what matters to us today. The United States has a major responsibility for the following:

- ◆ uncontrolled human population growth
- ◆ world hunger
- ◆ exploitation of soil and water by industrial agriculture
- ◆ waste of renewable resources: rangeland and forests
- ◆ exploitation of nonrenewable mineral resources: coal and petroleum
- ◆ protection of declining wilderness areas
- ◆ decline of genetic diversity and the extinction of species
- ◆ accelerated urban growth and degradation
- ◆ growing energy needs requiring fossil fuel consumption
- ◆ nuclear energy and renewable alternative energy sources
- ◆ air and water pollution
- ◆ solid, hazardous, and toxic wastes
- ◆ global atmospheric and other worldwide environmental changes
- ◆ recent exploitive industries: tourism and recreation.

It is difficult to sympathize with America's environmental problems. They are self-induced wounds. Americans knew they were risking destruction, pollution, and waste. Or did they?

What Is the Plan for This Book?

What happened to America's environment? Obviously, the land, soil, water, air, plants, trees, animals, and scenic wonders are not today what they were when Christopher Columbus landed on a Caribbean island in 1492. In Chapter 1 we focus our attention on the first European explorers and settlers who lived on the edges of a frightening wilderness. The Indians they encountered and sought to destroy had, as we shall see, their own environmental impact. Chapter 2 tells the story of a remarkable step by which Americans began to domesticate the natural forces of soil, water, and plants into the most productive agricultural system in world history. Farming is an intensely environmental world mysterious to most of us that deserves to be highlighted as a major and essential feature of our history. Chapters 3, 4, and 5 look at the knotty problem of America's westward movement. It is more than the romantic frontier story that climaxed in the Marlboro cowboy. Western expansion is above all a story about private property, which has since dominated America's environmental prospects. Chapter 6 looks at the beginnings of an alternative view from American Transcendentalists that put far higher value on nature, especially on the spiritual value of wilderness, than did the emerging capitalist viewpoint.

In the second half of the book, we make an all-important shift into the built environment of towns and cities connected by railroads, highways, and airline links. Chapter 7 describes the powerful shift to industrialism and capitalism that has decisively shaped how Americans treated their landscape and built their cities. In Chapter 8 the operative word becomes *infrastructure* (instead of ecosystem), to describe not only the buildings and roads, but also electric power grids, telephone and communications connections, water and sewage systems, and all the other structures and connections we live with. The goal of this industrial and consumer society was to push the natural world as far into the background as possible. Chapter 9 fleshes out the now familiar story of industrial pollution. Chapter 10 reminds us that most of the West, in particular, is a water-dependent "hydraulic civilization." Chapter 11 is an excursion into two large regions, Appalachia and the High Plains, which were decisively harmed by industrial exploitation.

The last part of the book describes the environmental revolution. Chapter 12 describes why Americans can take credit for being the first modern people to recognize the importance of wilderness enough to set small pieces aside in national parks and monuments. Chapter 13 describes the environmental movement over the last 30 years, including the rise of ecology as the science of the environment, the impact of Rachel Carson's *Silent Spring* in 1962, and the growing power of nongovernmental organizations (NGOs) such as the Sierra Club, the Environmental Defense Fund, and Earth First! Chapter 14 enters the maze of environmental legislation and regulation that is a belated attempt to overcome the chilling side effects of uncontrolled industrialization. We discover the full force of a vast array of environmental laws and bureaucracies that now have changed American history. The book closes with Chapter 15, which reviews major international environmental issues, such as a global dependence on petroleum and the conflict-filled role of the United States in shaping international environmental policies.

Throughout the book we discover that many aspects of American life are unintelligible except in the framework of nature's forces. Economists have long spoken of the invisible hand of the marketplace in shaping material life. In this book we will come to understand that the natural world is a powerful visible hand that only seemed invisible because we ignored it. The concept of this book—to see a raucous humanity integrated in the bubbling ferment of nature—is not an easy one. Nor is it easy to find a new American dream in a new environmentalism. We must redefine ourselves in our response to our primal geography. Because America's experience with its new geography is historically brief, its natural qualities—its scale, its newness, its variety—carry even greater importance. This was Joseph Brodsky's insight as he scraped tree bark against epidermis.

For Further Reading

An environmental approach has forced a new look at how American historians practice their craft. A good starting point are two essays by Elizabeth Ann R. Bird, "The Social Construction of Nature: Theoretical Approaches to the History of Environmental Problems," and

Carolyn Merchant, "The Theoretical Structure of Ecological Revolutions," in a special issue of *Environmental Review* in 1987 (Vol. 11, No. 4). Then see the lively debate between Donald Worster, William Cronon, and Richard White in the March 1990 issue (76:1087–1147) of the *Journal of American History,* as well as White's provocative essay, "American Environmental History: The Development of a New Historical Field," *Pacific Historical Review* 54 (August 1985): 297–335. See also Cronon's "A Place for Stories: Nature, History, and Narrative," *Journal of American History* 78 (March 1992): 1347–76, and "The Uses of Environmental History," *Environmental History Review* 17 (Fall 1993): 1–22. Worster continues to write about the meaning of environmental history in two books, *The Ends of the Earth: Perspectives on Modern Environmental History* (1988) and *The Wealth of Nature: Environmental History and the Ecological Imagination* (1993). See also the contrasting views by Dan Flores, "Place: An Argument for Bioregional History," *Environmental History Review,* 18, No. 4 (Winter 1994): 1–18, compared to Donald Worster, "Nature and the Disorder of History," *Environmental History Review* 18, No. 2 (Summer 1994): 1-16. See also J. Donald Hughes, "Ecology and Development as Narrative Themes of World History," *Environmental History Review* 19 (Spring 1995): 1–16, Duncan R. Jamieson, "American Environmental History." *Choice* 32, No. 1 (September 1994): 49–60, Barbara Leibhardt, "Interpretation and Causal Analysis: Theories in Environmental History," *Environmental Review* 12, No. 1 (1988): 23–36, and Chris H. Lewis, "Telling Stories About the Future: Environmental History and Apocalyptic Science," *Environmental History Review* 17 (Fall 1993): 43–60.

PART ONE

EUROPEANS
TAKE COMMAND

CHAPTER ONE

"O STRANGE NEW WORLD!"

—Shakespeare, *The Tempest*

*God forbid that we should give out a dream of our own imagination for
a pattern of the world.*

—Francis Bacon (1561–1626), A Pioneer in Scientific Method

*For the last time man came face to face with something commensurate to
his capacity for wonder.*

—F. Scott Fitzgerald (1896–1940),
The American Novelist on the European Discovery of the New World

The Encounter Was a
Unique, Unrepeatable, and Fatal Event

In the grand sweep of global history, the European conquest of the Americas was a unique encounter between worlds that earlier had known nothing of each other. Elsewhere, even such distant peoples as the Chinese and Romans had observed, admired, and feared each other. Contact between different peoples was usually not a sudden flash of discovery, but a gradual process. This surprise meeting between the New and Old Worlds was dramatically different. Nothing remotely similar had happened before in history, and it could not happen again. Even contemporaries quickly realized that the European meeting with the New World was one of the great turning points in human affairs. Spanish historian Francisco Lopez de Gomara in 1551 flamboyantly called it "the greatest event since the creation of the world, excluding the incarnation and death of Him who created it." Later the seventeenth-century philosopher John Locke concluded, "In the beginning everything was America." Today the comparison is often made with the first moon landing on July 20, 1969.

The scale of the environmental, cultural, and psychological exchange is almost beyond comprehension. The encounter was shaped by strong European prejudices, none of which matched the real thing. Some saw riches beyond belief and a utopian realm that suggested a second Garden of Eden. To others America was a deranged experience of chaos, an "other world" of satanic origins where humans lost self-control and descended into the abyss. European zealousness to enforce its prejudices may have wasted the opportunity for mutual understanding between Europeans and natives and the founding of a truly new human society. Instead, Europeans lumped together New World native peoples under the derisive label "savages" and the New World's geography was entirely "wilderness." They concluded that both were useless in themselves and empty of intrinsic value. Europeans carried with them their long-standing habit of not investing much value in nature, beginning with the man-nature dualism of Greek philosophy, the Christian belief that humans made in the image of God were far superior to a soulless nature, and the inflated humanism of the Renaissance, which sought to dominate nature through art and science. As a result, Europeans saw only an empty continent, ready to be licked into any shape they decided. They neither responded sympathetically to the New World ecology nor to its successful Indian societies. In a vivid modern analogy historian Alfred Crosby writes that the ships carrying explorers, soldiers, and settlers as well as European animals, plants, and diseases, "were like giant viruses fastening to the sides of gigantic bacterium and injecting into it their DNA, usurping its internal processes for their own purposes."

As we shall see, Europeans became, for better or for worse, the dominant human group in the New World. To be more specific, they were primarily white male Europeans of a particularly avaricious type willing to endure enormous hardships for wealth and power. Back home, European women were often treated as little more than chattel, defined as property and molded by a male-dominated society. Native American peoples, thrown into shock by the intrusion of such violent thugs, were unable to cope with European weapons, disease, habits, and numbers, and soon learned that they faced a bleak and oppressed future. The black Africans whom Europeans tore away from their homes and turned into slaves were forced into a particularly vicious mode of servitude. Europeans did not have the foggiest idea of the scale by which they were reshaping the rest of human history and the global environment, but they were not innocent of the results.

Europeans Did Not Discover America, They Invented It

The European encounter with the American continent teaches us an immediate and daunting lesson: We must accept the notion that all people view the world around them through various filters of ideas, beliefs, and assumptions that color their perceptions. There is no such thing as a strictly objective experience; even a scientific viewpoint is fluid and changeable.

When Europeans invaded the New World, their heads were already filled with dreams of mastering the people and geography of the entire globe. This passion was sparked by imperialism, the Christian missionary impulse, a Renaissance compulsion for personal glory, a warlike spirit tending toward butchery, a bundle of old myths about what lay beyond the Western Sea, and plain and simple greed for gold, silver, jewels, spices, and other riches. Such unique filters shut out alternative views and prevented Europeans from seeing the New World on its own terms as a natural environment coupled with long-standing native cultures.

Before the western voyages of discovery, the Atlantic horizon that Europeans faced was as blank an unknown as the back side of the moon. To fill this void Europeans had long spun a fantastic geography in their heads that encouraged extravagant adventure. The mythical Atlantis was a vague and misty land beyond the western sea. Antilla was an equally mysterious western place where Christians had fled from Muslims invading Spain; there they built seven perfect cities (one supposedly located on the site of today's town of Liberal, Kansas). This was reinforced by the washing ashore at Ireland, the Hebrides, or the Canaries of the remains of men of unknown races, strange and frightening pieces of carved wood, branches of unfamiliar trees, and other dismaying objects. Even after contact, America remained a piecemeal fabrication. His head filled with preconceived notions, Christopher Columbus did not comprehend his landfall for what it finally turned out to be. He denied that he had found a New World, since this would go against all his expectations. At first he insisted that it must be eastern Asia, but he sensed that something was wildly wrong. Columbus remains a metaphor for all Americans: We still don't comprehend what we found. Thus it is essential to call the opening years the "invention" of America instead of the "discovery" of America. After European discovery America never enjoyed its own environmental identity. Europeans were primarily interested in defining its usefulness according to their needs. The new nation-states of Spain, France, England, and the Netherlands were in a life-and-death struggle for power that required not only gold and silver, but also strategic goods that ranged from trees for ship masts to indigo for dyes.

Columbus shrewdly told his sponsors what they wanted to hear. He reported that Spain could capture for its exclusive enjoyment a great colonial empire of pure air, sweet water, fertile land, vast forests, and infinite mineral riches. The Church would enjoy millions of new converts. Above all, Columbus's investors would enjoy strongboxes overflowing with gold. A mistaken report of gold in interior Cuba, which Columbus thought was part of the Asian mainland, led him to send a diplomatic mission to meet "El Gran Can," the Great Khan of China. One anecdote is particularly revealing: When a native tribe tried to escape an attack by Columbus's force, one chief left as a temptation his stunningly beautiful daughter, tied to a stake and wearing nothing but a gold ring in her nose. Columbus, arriving with his men, stopped suddenly at the sight of the young woman, stared at her for a long moment, pointed a trembling finger, and demanded, "Where did you get that ring?"

After Europeans realized they had found a New World, they expected it to be unblemished and ready to be plucked, like Paradise before the Fall. This vision was reinforced by unclothed native peoples of the Caribbean and Central America. They were described as innocent and timid, generous to a fault to their visitors, sharing their food and gold and women. But the new landfall was also confusing. The natives practiced cannibalism and routinely tortured their captives. Europeans concluded that the natives were instead savages, an inexplicable curse inside the new Eden. There were also strange and dangerous animals and plants: rattlesnakes, alligators, vampire bats, maddening swarms of mosquitoes, and poison ivy. The tapir was strangely formed and the iguana a truly ugly lizard, larger than any European reptile. Instead of a new Paradise, was America the place where Europeans had to their horror stumbled on God's hidden laboratory to test new untried creations? Or was it his dumping ground for mistakes? Should Europeans have taken more seriously their realization that America offered no grapes to make the wine needed to celebrate the Lord's Supper? If Eden and Mount Ararat were both in the Eurasian continent, then how could humans and animals be in America? A biologically unique America was a very troublesome enigma.

Yet there was an indisputable reality—a specific geography—beyond the myths, the misunderstandings, and the distorted exploitation. When Europeans first skirted along the puzzling western shorelines of the stormy Atlantic, they believed they were amid a group of islands vaguely off the eastern coast of Asia. Only later did they reluctantly admit to the unexpected existence of a shockingly enormous free-standing continent. The first explorers bumped into real rocky shores in the wrong places, a never-ending forest wilderness instead of cities of gold, and strange but tangible plants, animals, and humans instead of placid welcoming Chinese in flowing robes. John Smith was not writing fantasy when he described New England streams that really did boil with smelts, salmon, shad, and alewives, and the coast offered lobsters weighing 25 pounds. He insisted that "one hundred men may in two or three hours make their provisions for a day, of good corn, fish and flesh." The New World was startlingly concrete, a physical reality out of nowhere, an astonishing place beyond the wildest fictions, impossibly outside the closed world created in Genesis and described by Aristotle.

The Reality Behind the Myths

The Unexpected Continent

What was the American environment like before Europeans took charge? America's fifteenth-century landscape—plants and animals, native peoples, terrain and climate—had gradually emerged from the fourth ice age 12,500 years earlier. This was only the most recent transformation of a 60-million-year climate process that created a world we can still find familiar. America's environment is in perpetual slow motion, but at different rates of speed. Slowest is geological change. Along the eastern coastline this includes "drowned" river valleys such as Chesapeake Bay and New York City's harbor and "submerged platforms" or shallow banks above Cape Cod that created one of the greatest fisheries in the world. The continent rises to the surface as the Coastal Plain, itself the youngest visible geology in the East, made up of marshes and sandhills in Maryland, southern New Jersey, Long Island, and Cape Cod. Further inland stands the Piedmont, made up of compressed fragments of continents and islands pushed onto the edge of North America by plate tectonics. This includes New England, highlighted by resistant metamorphic and igneous rocks of the White Mountains, Mount Monadnock, and Mount Katahdin. The most spectacular mountain building in the East remains the Appalachian Mountains, originally the eastern edge of old North America, built up by faulting, folding, and crumpling of thick sediments, the result of an early Paleozoic collision with a large landmass from the east. Among the oldest rocks are the "Precambrian Basement" under the Midwest, a region that spent long periods of time under shallow Paleozoic seas with thick layers of sediment combined with the flow of erosion from the western slopes of the Appalachians.

A far faster force was glacial impact from climate change, as we shift from millions of years to tens of thousands of years. In the past, the thick, heavy frozen mass of the glacier scraped everything down to bedrock and then slowly retreated over millennia. The ice sheet reached down almost to the Mason-Dixon line, covering all of New England, New York, and the northern halves of New Jersey and Pennsylvania, and spread across the Midwest (except for the famous driftless region in southwestern Wisconsin) into Kansas and Missouri to swing upward across the northern Rockies and end at the Pacific slightly south of the Canadian border. Ice also covered the northern half of Europe and cut across Asia. Glaciers left behind piles of gravel known as moraines as the edges melted back. Cape Cod and Long Island are merely gravel ridges piled and shaped by glacial movement. Today's major rivers, including the Hudson, Ohio, Mississippi, Missouri, Colorado, and Columbia, were diverted from earlier geological tracks. The five midcontinent Great Lakes resulted from the glacial invasion that scraped off as much as 100 feet of Paleozoic sedimentary rock that was ground to sand, silt, and clay and redeposited to become the flat plains of Ohio, Indiana, Illinois, and Iowa. One difference between North and South in the United States is that the history of the landscape can be measured in the North by the thousands of years since the last retreat of the glaciers, whereas in the South the landscape on the coastal plain has a prehistory that is 180 million years old.

The glaciers slowly but inexorably forced southward a broad variety of trees, shrubs, grasses from the north, as well as grazing animals and their carnivores, birds and fishes. These crowded against the plants and creatures of the warmer southern climate. Many of these are still crowded together today in the Great Smoky Mountains in southern Appalachia where the borders meet of eastern Kentucky and Tennessee, western North Carolina and Virginia. The region is a "relict forest," largely unchanged while dinosaurs waned, mammals grew into mammoths, and, much more recently, humans learned to hunt deer, gather nuts, and plant maize. It is also one of the world's great variety forests. Northern hemlock and spruce stand, separated only by altitude, exposure, or soil, close by temperate beech, walnut, and elm trees, as well as southern tulip trees, linden, and sassafras. The modern American naturalist May T. Watts writes of this southern Appalachian region, "Here no vacationer need be homesick long. If he comes from eastern Asia he can sit in a heath under great rhododendrons; if he comes from the Great Lakes area, he can find his forest of beech-maple-hemlock; if he comes from the prairie's edge, he can seek out a dry southerly slope and hobnob with oaks and hickories; if he longs for Canada, he can climb up among the spruces and firs." As the ice drew back into the Arctic, native plants and animals ventured north again, and the southerners gradually crept northward as well. By 7,000 to 5,000 years ago, New England's forests turned from spruce and pine back into oak and chestnut. North America had reached the ecological condition—soil, plants, eastern forests, deer and buffalo, streams filled with fish, dense groves of canebrakes, vast midcontinent grasslands, western mountains and deserts—in which sixteenth-century Europeans found it as they edged warily inland.

Easy European Entry into the New World

After the early explorers cruised the Atlantic border of the future United States, they made a critical discovery. A ragged coast of islands, inlets, sounds, and bays offered a string of safe anchorages, notably Boston Harbor, Narragansett Bay, New York Harbor, Delaware Bay, and Chesapeake Bay. Although the explorers' ships loomed enormous to the natives, they were small enough to find haven from Atlantic storms in bays and estuaries. Equally important, the relatively empty continent, and the low-mortality fighting tactics of the natives, meant that Europeans were not challenged by rains of arrows from fortified castles or a swirling cavalry as they had been during the Crusades against Islam. Nor were they threatened by bands of armed warriors in outrigger canoes as in the Pacific Ocean. The rivers would also become the first highways into the unknown land. The broad, gently sloping, coastal plain meant ships could sometimes sail against the easy river current when the wind was right. Nevertheless, the coast of North America lay undisturbed by Europeans for another 100 years. The Grand Banks along several hundred miles of Canadian and New England coast was one of the world's greatest fisheries. Each season 200 or more private cod fishing boats crossed from England, France, Spain, Portugal, and Basque country to cast their nets along the shore. Fishermen were indifferent to the inland geography, feared and avoided the natives, and worried more about running aground along uncharted shores than about geopolitics. They were satisfied with scattered onshore posts for resupply, repair, fish drying, and temporary shelter. Each boat returned home before the stormy winter season with a cargo of up to 25,000 beheaded, partly cleaned, and heavily salted fish. Fishing settlements at Cape Breton, the Gaspé Peninsula, and a few temporary shelters at Salem were not the advance guard for European settlement. A few French fishermen were more marooned than settled on Sable Island, 150 miles east of Nova Scotia.

America's Startling Natural Abundance

Sixteenth-century Europeans had just survived and risen above the disasters of plague, starvation, and the little ice age of the fourteenth century. Thus they were enthralled about first reports that the New World enjoyed an extraordinary natural abundance of wildlife and plants. In 1776 the Scottish economist Adam Smith advised that history proved "that whichever nation seizes the territory will advance more rapidly to wealth and greatness than any other human society."

The Great Forest

If the Atlantic coastline of North America had been dry prairie instead of an extended forest, settlement might never have taken place. Europeans would have imagined only a wasteland and contented themselves with fishing its shores. Instead, one of the world's great mixed forests covered 360 million acres that included most of the eastern third of the future United States. To European settlers, forest land had its own embedded mythology. Settlers arrived with an extensive set of old folk legends. The forest was the home of werewolves, ogres, witches, and child-eating monsters. So-called fairy tales of Hansel and Gretel, Little Red Riding Hood, Sleeping Beauty, and Snow White warned children (and adults) of demonic forest enemies that grasped body and soul. It was a Christian virtue to rid the world of such pagan groves. These fears were reinforced by the real frontier world, where danger and death lurked for anyone who got lost in America's primeval forest. Panthers, bobcats, wolves, black bears, porcupines, and skunks made real life dangerous and unpleasant.

Despite these deeply felt threats, out of the forest also came the "best poor man's country." Europeans were delighted to discover that North America's forest vegetation was familiar (unlike their early experience with the west coast of Africa). They recognized oaks, beech, maple, ash, popular, willow, and pines and other conifers. They easily spotted nut trees like walnut and chestnut. Fleshy wild fruits that were familiar included southern dewberry, persimmon, wild plums (widely praised as "better than Castile plums"), cherries, and red mulberry. Oak, walnut, and hickory hardwoods made the best firewood providing the most heat, the least smoke, and the longest lasting fire. Europeans also knew that huge oaks and hickories grew in prime alluvial (river-deposited) soils that received drenching rains. This bonanza land "produced from fifty to seventy bushels of Indian corn to each acre."

Yet the first settlers did not encounter a truly ancient primeval climax forest. The perceptive Swedish natural historian Per Kalm noted in 1772 that by the time most eastern trees stood for 150 years, they began to decay and became more vulnerable to inevitable climate disturbances like tornadoes and hurricanes as well as natural and human-made fires, all of which questioned great age. True, white pines were reported from 150 to 200 feet tall, sycamore trunks up to 15 feet in diameter, together with tulip trees and cottonwoods 5 feet in diameter. Such plant communities were stable and self-replicating ecosystems but also faced dynamic processes of fire, wind damage, disease, insects, and human activity. Nor was the forest as dense as described in some early reports; there were large open patches and thinly spread stands of trees. Since most Europeans, aside from far-ranging trappers, depended on Indian help for their survival, they stayed close to native encampments and did not often encounter landscapes untouched by human hands. Wherever permanent native villages consumed wood in their immediate vicinity, a secondary forest appeared. In such native-modified forests, deer populations thrived and populations of rabbits, quail, and wild turkey increased. Indians even encouraged black bears in close range for their store of fat; bear grease was used in food and ointments.

Despite their reliance on the Indians, Europeans found Indian use of the forest incomprehensible, since it did not fully exploit desirable resources. Especially among the English, the European objective was never to retain the environmental status quo, but to clear the land (other than utilitarian woodlots) for farming, roads, and towns. This made the existing forest into an economic deficit. It had negative value because of the time and labor required for clearing. The large-scale elimination of the continuous eastern forest was one of history's great deforestations, comparable to Italy of the late Roman Empire, to India during the British raj, and in modern times to the devastation of Brazil's rain forest. As we see in more detail in Chapter 5, the prodigal consumption of apparently limitless wood substituted for stone and iron to build not only houses and fences, but also plank roads and canal locks. It provided chemicals such as potash, pitch, tar and turpentine, as well as maple sugar. Only later would the forests be protected to save watersheds and harbor scarce wildlife, and offer to the general public recreation and a haven for spiritual renewal.

Wildlife

Early European visitors to any part of the future United States were struck with awe at the abundance of wildlife. Waterfowl filled the shore sky from horizon to horizon. In 1534 the French explorer Jacques Cartier sighted a single rocky island off the Canadian coast, and he was astounded over the large and fat seabirds that swarmed in such numbers that "all the ships of France might load a cargo of them without once perceiving that any had been removed."

Was it sportsmanlike, Cartier wondered, if he clubbed his food supply, or even trampled it to death? New England fishermen tore their nets on thousands of salmon in their streams. Fishing along the coastline yielded boiling masses of codfish, sea bass, haddock, herring, lobster, mullet, crab, oysters, clams, and mussels. Flocks of passenger pigeons by the million (out of a total of 2 billion and now extinct for almost 100 years) literally blotted out the sun over the eastern landscape. European explorers and trappers may have struggled through dense underbrush and chest-deep swamps, but they comfortably feasted on salmon and shad in northern streams, eels and catfish in the Mississippi and Gulf rivers, and found oyster beds and freshwater mussels in unspoiled bays and estuaries. The Spanish adventurer Hernando De Soto gave the first real report on whoppingly large buffalo herds that ranged into the Carolinas. He also described extraordinary wild turkeys that stood 3 feet tall and weighed as much as 40 pounds. So many plump turkeys roosted in trees across Pennsylvania, Virginia, Kentucky, and Tennessee that their numbers broke large branches. In 1595, when French explorer Samuel de Champlain went into unknown territory to seek the water route to the Pacific, his people caught pikes and muskies 8 feet long and 4-foot lake trout because the fish had a chance to grow to their maximum mature size. The fishermen were also tortured by clouds of mosquitoes that drove them near to insanity. In the 1720s and 1730s, when independent explorers Pierre Vérendrye and his sons followed rumors of a great river flowing west into the Pacific, they entered the Dakotas, where on the open plains the Mandan Indians prospered on buffalo, antelope, deer, and bear, and grew corn, squash, and pumpkins. In 1742 these Frenchmen trekked as far as Nebraska, Montana, and even into Wyoming, where they reported very few natives but "plenty of wild beasts." Later, in 1804, American explorers Meriwether Lewis and William Clark, as they struggled up the Missouri River, reported uncountable herds of deer and antelope, industrious beavers, and hundreds of flocks of duck and geese. Reports of 60 million Plains buffalo that took days to pass one spot were not tall tales.

Food from the Soil

More important than game, and equally impressive, was the land's capacity to grow food. Europeans brought with them familiar wheat and oats that easily took hold and prospered in America's soil. Imports included the fast-growing peach tree, which pioneers planted first because it yielded fruit within five years. Settlers also ate native corn, pumpkins, beans, and potatoes, but their customary diet introduced Old World plants: onions, radishes, cauliflowers, cabbages, and salad greens. Food scarcity was not an American problem. Early in the nineteenth century one French traveler wrote, "There is no settler, however poor, whose family does not take coffee or chocolate for breakfast, and always a little salt meat; at dinner, salt meat, or salt fish, and eggs; at supper again salt meat and coffee." The salt was to keep the meat edible without refrigeration, but the Frenchman was amazed because back in Europe a peasant farmer considered himself fortunate to have meat once or twice a month. Such abundance of food provided an unusually deep and secure base for European-style civilization. There is a critical period in American history of agricultural dominance that deserves more recognition. It is described in more detail in Chapter 2. This agricultural phase of an American farm society covered almost 200 years, approximately 1670 to 1870, before the rise of industrialization. Poverty and deprivation were rare in the early American agricultural environment. Farming was not a burden but an opportunity. Land often was a greater attraction to the growing swarm of immigrants than political rights or religious liberty.

The Confusing American Climate

Europeans complained that they had been misled about the continent's climate. Most early migrants arrived from Britain, the Netherlands, and western Germany, where they enjoyed a climate without extreme seasonal changes. Even though northwestern Europe was considerably further north than the eastern coast of the future United States, American winters were often extremely cold, fed by air masses from north-central Canada, and hot humid summers resulted from tropical air masses from the Gulf of Mexico. London stood at the same latitude as Newfoundland, but the English homeland had milder winters. Climate watchers began to lean toward Virginia as "suited to the English temper" compared to bitter Massachusetts winters. Because Virginia was on the same latitude as Spain and the Holy Land, Roanoke colonists attempted in vain to grow sugarcane, oranges, and lemons as well as traditional English wheat, barley, and oats.

Pessimists began to believe that apart from a few isolated spots, most of America was a land of summers so hot as to be unbearable, and of frigid winters that brought unexpected suffering. Later, climate historians recognized that North America's colder weather and extreme weather fluctuations had been aggravated by the little ice age that coincided with the first two centuries of discovery. Benjamin Franklin may have been

The Unexpected Peoples: The First Nations

Whatever Europeans may have believed, they did not find a wilderness in the New World. They reoccupied a land along the eastern coast that native peoples had already occupied successfully for at least 5,000 years. In reality, the European invaders, by laying waste to the native peoples by disease, war, alcohol, habitat loss, and demoralization, conquered not a wilderness but their own invented wasteland imposed on what had once been a civilized region. Then they attempted to turn this emptiness into another Europe. Europeans squandered the native accomplishments and prevented further independent development by the Indians. One can only speculate about what other original contributions the Indians might have offered to humanity. As a result, after this chapter our historical narrative pays little attention to the Indians.

Overall the location of inhabited regions of North America are approximately the same today as they were in A.D. 1492. The major cities of the eastern United States are located on old Indian settlements. The High Plains were sparsely populated in the native era. In some cases, the land was truly vacant. North America contained empty areas, "bloody hunting grounds," such as Kentucky, where competing tribes made it too dangerous to inhabit.

Humans other than Europeans had made their homes in the New World certainly by 10,000 B.C. and possibly as early as 40,000 B.C. Humans are the most adaptable and therefore the most widely distributed of today's large land animals. Most humans trekked from Siberia to Alaska across a land bridge during an ice age that occurred at some point after 26,000 B.C.

right when he observed that during his lifetime in the eighteenth century the winters were getting warmer as the climate began to abate. In this early version of global warming, Jefferson, Franklin, and the leading American doctor Benjamin Rush all concluded that humankind played a decisive role. They desperately wanted to demonstrate the power of civilized human intervention to modify the raw wilderness and challenging climate. They happily decided that America's extreme winters and summers were becoming more habitable because European settlers were cutting down the continent's forests. Noah Webster, usually a scientific skeptic, nevertheless believed in 1799 that the clearing of the forests caused the air to "vibrate" more intensely and make winters warmer. In 1806 he reported that the heat accumulated in the ground during the summer was released during the winter if the ground had been cleared of trees.

Colonial leaders insisted that superior civilizations emerged primarily in temperate climates. Such civilizations, by improving the temperature when they cleared forest lands, could control their own futures. Erratic climate extremes would presumably soften as America's landscape progressed from an immature wilderness—an inferior environment for the building of civilization—to a mature domesticated landscape. It was a powerful argument for speedy development by draining swamps, burning underbrush, cutting forests, and replacing them with crops of grains and vegetables in a pastoral landscape. Both nature and humankind, it seemed, would benefit from this mutually fulfilling interaction.

It was much as 1,000 miles wide where the ocean bottom at the Bering Strait today is still only about 120 feet below the surface. But until about 11,000 B.C., an ice barrier just south of Alaska hampered further movement except through a few ice-free corridors. The earliest migrants were not Eskimos, but a type of Mongoloid who had the advantage of being genetically broader than most Asians and thus more adaptable to new conditions over broad periods of time. They were joined in the crossing by woolly mammoth, caribou, and other species. The Arctic tundra environment, without trees, was little different than it is today, a climate so cold that it required innovations in tailored fur clothing and pit houses to survive. The opportunistic migrants also survived by hunting in teams to cut down the enormous mammoths, mastodons, and bisons. As the glaciers receded and the climate and animal life changed, humans spread rapidly with evidence of early humans in Tierra del Fuego at the southern tip of South America by 8,000 B.C. The geographic and climatic conditions of North America have been about what they are today since 7,500 B.C.

Successful Native Farming in the Face of Climate Adversity

Some time between 7,000 to 5,000 B.C., New World people added farming to hunting when they entered temperate and tropical climates. They first learned to cultivate the bottle gourd, chili pepper, and summer squash or pumpkin. Farming arrived about 1,000 years later than in the Old World but as an independent discovery. Maize (corn) came under cultivation about 5,000 to 2,500 B.C. (wild corn had existed since about 80,000 B.C.) and squash about 2,000 B.C. Between about 5,000 B.C. and 2,500 B.C. these human farmers coped remarkably well with a major climate upheaval that we would describe as a large-scale global warming—a hot and dry period (the altithermal era) that would be agriculturally challenging even in modern terms. But the demands of this long climate adversity may also have delayed cultural advances in technology and social organization, which in turn prevented Native Americans from responding successfully to the European invasion. This is a controversial view proposed by anthropologist Harold Driver who wrote, "By the time the Indians began to farm, about 7,000 B.C., they were only about two thousand years behind the earliest farming in the Old World, about 9,000 B.C. From this time on, however, the Indians fell behind, and remained in a stage of incipient agriculture for about five thousand years. It was not until after 2,000 B.C. that their farming provided more food than did their hunting and gathering [and in some places hunting and gathering remained dominant]." Driver added, "In the Old World, in contrast, permanent villages and towns with wall-to-wall adobe brick rooms were achieved by 6,000 B.C., suggesting that farming was already the dominant means of subsistence. Cities with populations in the tens of thousands do not appear in the New World until about the beginning of the Christian era, while in the Old World there were a number of such cities by 3,000 B.C." The question here is whether it is a Western conceit that Europeans were "advanced" and Indian cultures were "backward." Or were they simply different?

Despite their so-called lack of development, most American Indian societies achieved a high level of cultural sophistication while they lived off hunting and wild food gathering. Even Driver admitted that "primitive" hunting deserves admiration as a sophisticated skill. Successful hunting depended on subtle knowledge about the habits and ranges of dozens, even hundreds, of species of animals, hard earned by wounds and near brushes with violent death. Ethnohistorian Francis Jennings wrote, "Even in a land lush with wild life, a hunter has to know the habits of his prey in that locality; he has to know the salt licks and water holes and breeding places, the peculiarities of local climate and weather. Without such specialized information, even the most skillfully trained user of weapons can go hungry in the woods or lose himself and die of exposure." To the bow and arrow were added the thrusting lance and the sling, all of which had to be used with skill. Visual disguises, auditory decoys, and other deceptions required sophisticated know-how of animal habits. Blowing on a leaf or piece of grass held in the hands imitated the cry of a fawn to draw a doe. Moose hunters during the rutting season poured water a few feet above a stream or lake to imitate the sound of a urinating female moose in order to draw a male. Native Americans learned to be particularly adept at driving game with fire. Fishermen used fences or barriers called weirs as well as a variety of spears, nets, and traps, but they found fishhooks ineffective.

The sophisticated expansion of their food supply was as remarkable as Native American prowess as hunters. Most Indian foods north of the Rio Grande were not originally native, but were deliberately transferred from a lusher Central America. Central America still nurtures the vast majority of wild plants and plants that potentially could become domestic crops. Large varieties of native edible plants decline dramatically as one moves north and the possibilities become virtually zero on the prairies and in the eastern forest. The Hopewell people were among the most successful to combine hunting and farming. They lived in villages over a broad area ranging from Kansas to Ohio and from the Great Lakes to the Gulf of Mexico. They flourished from 200 B.C. to A.D. 400 (an era almost three times longer lived thus far than the United States), cultivating maize and living principally on game and wild plants. Further east, agriculture in the great eastern woodlands of North America by about 1,000 B.C. included squashes, pumpkins, gourds, sunflower, black beans, kidney beans, and domesticated turkeys, dogs, and bees. The all-important maize appeared slightly later in this region. Beans and corn, whether the Indians knew it or not, gave them a balanced diet of vegetable protein. An acre or two of corn provided 25 to 60 bushels of corn, half the caloric intake needed for a family of five. In New England, natives used clamshell hoes to plant five or six grains of corn and three or four kidney beans each in mounds like molehills, about a yard apart. When the grains and beans germinated and grew together, the beans interlaced with the corn as it grew to 5 to 6 feet. The combination kept the ground quite free from weeds and held ground moisture during dry spells. This was not the orderly single-crop farming of European monoculture: The soil was not disturbed by plowing in the European way, its organic nutrition remained intact, and it was safe from erosion. Contrary to myth, the natives did not fertilize their fields with fish—the work would have been too hard and unpleasant. They simply abandoned their fields every eight to ten years when the soil lost its fertility.

Admittedly, the Indians suffered under technological limits that restricted their ability to expand farming or repel European-style agriculture. The plow and draft animals were unknown. We would call most Native American farming a form of horticulture or garden cultivation. The natives labored over small local plots using a straight pointed stick, an implement with a blade attached, a rake, and the hoe. This also meant they could not work the tough sod and heavy grasses of the prairie ranging from Illinois to Colorado and left it as hunting grounds. Thus the central third of the continent was not available to them for farming, a region that became the future "breadbasket of the world." Even in the eastern forest their stone axes could not fell large trees, which natives simply girdled by pounding with their axes. As a result of such limitations, the Indians only farmed 1 percent of the available land, an area so small it would have failed to provide for European-style farming and European-sized populations. But for the Indians, it was sufficient and gave them ecological security. Small-scale and light horticulture did not mean worse farming. According to one seventeenth-century Jesuit report, "From the month of May up to the middle of September, they are free from all anxiety about their food; for the cod are upon the coast, and all kinds of fish and shellfish." Admittedly, the rest of year was difficult, with families sometimes going without food for as much as ten days; yet they did not starve. Despite agricultural success, hunting and gathering were never abandoned. Women worked the fields and men ranged wide for hunting and fishing. This combination allowed the natives to establish their own ecological balance with the forests, fisheries, or meadows, one that was not integrated into any larger "civilized" commercial marketplace or dependent on ownership of land that Europeans demanded. Wild foods always supplemented farming for American Indians: acorns, chestnuts, and walnuts in the east, pecans to the west, as well as grapes and plums, mulberries and persimmons. Raw acorns were poisonous and had to be ground up and soaked to remove tannic acid before they could be eaten for their starches and fats. The native peoples enjoyed a finely balanced hunting and fishing life connected to a fundamental agricultural rhythm and adaptable to the challenge of a long-term ecological change such as warming and drought.

Tested by climate fluctuations during 5,000 years, natives along the east coast of North America had devised a series of successful ways of life based on collaboration with the local environment. In a real way, the Americans were more successful adapters, since they stayed with local resources while Europeans chose to import external resources. Europeans would "solve" a local environmental challenge by overwhelming it rather than relearning how to use it more effectively for survival. They had no respect for the natives' mobile communities that lived successfully off seasonal changes in the land. Europeans disbelieved, for example, any sophistication or civilization among the Iroquois of New York State because they moved their towns about twice in a generation due to exhaustion of the soil, scarcity of firewood and timber for building, and depletion of game. Europeans forgot that the tobacco they planted consumed soil resources in less than a decade and that most pioneer farmers moved onto new land repeatedly.

Indian Regions of the Future United States

We have seen that in most regions of the future United States, the Native Americans enjoyed healthy subsistence societies and usually produced food surpluses for barter or to lay away for the hard times that would inevitably reappear. This was outside the Old World pattern of monoculture crops, large domestic animals, and a market economy. Their material subsistence and cultural patterns were closely limited by regional geography, whereas Europeans strove to break out of any narrow regionalism. A satisfying and enduring material life of the Indians was incorporated into local ecologies instead of standing separately from them, as Europeans tended to do. This was not a simple environmental determinism, since the Indians were leading participants in the dynamics of their local ecological system.

It is convenient to briefly identify eight Native American geographical regions:

1. The Pacific Northwest Coast offered the most distinctive aboriginal North American society, rich in art and innovative in community relations. Although their world ranged from glaciers in the north to sandy beaches in the south, it can be characterized as a varied coast of islands and waterways, heavy forests, many streams, and heavy rainfall in a temperate climate. Convenient water travel encouraged communications between villages. The staple food was fish like salmon, halibut, and cod, although natives also caught sea mammals and shellfish, dried sea plants, and consumed wild land plants like berries and roots. The people enjoyed an excess of protein, an abundance of fat, starch from roots, and sugar from berries. Such abundance encouraged local population growth and leisure time for a complex social structure, ceremonial life, art forms, and an unusually high level of material possessions.

2. Closely related were people of the Plateau, the Columbia River system, whose environment was a forested world cut by streams and rivers, but with less rainfall and increasing aridity. These were democratic and peaceful peoples for whom moose, other large game, and fish (salmon) made meat the staple food. Villages had their own territories for fishing, hunting, and gathering, but not exclusively. Most famous were the Nez Perce, who in the 1870s were tragically wiped out by Europeans at the time they were led by Chief Joseph.

3. Aboriginal California was not a powerful or influential Indian region, although it was one of the more heavily populated regions of the continent at 275,000 to 300,000 people. The native people were dispersed and diverse. The indulgent climate supplied sufficient shellfish, small game, and nuts without plant cultivation. With Spanish invasion the natives declined to a few struggling tribes. These were virtually enslaved by the Spanish and nearly disappeared under U.S. rule after 1848, particularly during the white population explosion of the Gold Rush of 1849. Small backwoods tribes that remained were scorned by whites and other Indians alike. They lived on acorns, small game such as rodents and birds, invertebrates such as earthworms, grasshoppers, and caterpillars, and some seafood along the coast.

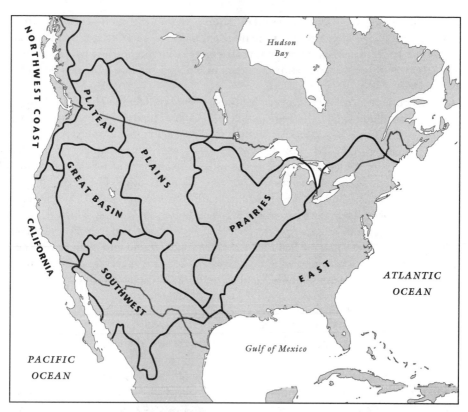

Native American Geographical Regions. This map is only suggestive, since native peoples believed that they belonged to the land, not that the land belonged to them. However the different regions define general environmental conditions under which native peoples lived. The eastern region could readily be divided into northeastern and southeastern.

4. The Great Basin and Southwest Desert, then and now, provided a meager living at isolated oases in a general desert environment. The Mongollan culture, which first appeared in eastern Arizona about 100 B.C., combined food collecting, small-game hunting, and cultivation of maize, squash, and beans. Similar were the Hohokam (to about A.D. 1400), as well as the cliff-dwelling Anasazi (until nearly the fifteenth century). But endemic famine wore the natives down; in good times they subsisted on wild plants such as piñon pine nuts, and on the rare deer, antelope, and rabbit. Farming was seasonal in part-time settlements. Life for arid-lands natives such as the Apaches was transformed with horses and techniques learned from Plains Indians.

5. Plains Indians are the best known to most people in the United States today. The Blackfoot, Crow, Dakota Sioux, Cheyenne, and Comanches were as aggressive meat eaters as the English. Even though fish were abundant in the Plains streams, they were not eaten by the Plains Indians. They ate buffalo meat, rode horses after about A.D. 1600, lived in conical tipis, and did not farm. After they acquired horses from the Spanish, they became the most

nomadic of all Indians, their lives centering on bison hunts on the open plains and winter camps in stream valleys. They remained the most competitive warriors against Europeans until late in the 1870s. Their abundant meat protein gave them physical strength and powerful stature, but their societies collapsed when the buffalo were exterminated down to a few hundred by 1890.

6. The Prairie Indians of the modern Midwest hunted buffalo like the Plains Indians, but they also farmed and lived in permanent villages. Farming (maize, beans, squashes, sunflowers) furnished less than half their diet; hunting remained a dominant feature of their lives.

7. and 8. Indians in the East, from Ohio to the coast, were more sedentary peoples than those of the Prairies, more dependent on farm crops, and creators of the two largest political organizations north of Mexico: (7) the Iroquois of New York and (8) the Five Civilized Tribes of the South. Eastern Indians were the first to teach Europeans how to raise corn, beans, pumpkins, and tobacco. They received perhaps half their food from farming, which was dominated by great maize, bean, and squash fields, but they never abandoned hunting and gathering in the extensive eastern forest. Their diet was nutritionally sound and famines were rare. Even when a community was compelled to flee its village because of attack by a superior force, it managed to get a living from its knowledge of the supportive woods environment.

Conflicting Environmental Worlds: European Separation from Nature and Indian Interdependence with Nature

To European thinking, human beings were superior to nature because they enjoyed the faculties of mind and spirit. Both Greek philosophy and the Christian tradition preached a dualistic separation from nature. In the arrangement, nature possessed no intrinsic meaning or worth. Indeed, it was designed for human benefit. The difference could not have been greater for American Indians. To them, the natural world was not separate but instead continuously dissolved into the realm of persons and personal relations. The world was peopled with nonhuman persons often endowed with mysterious powers. These persons channeled the life force, widely called Manitou, that animated nature. Sacred ties of tribal and family kinship connected to the vital forces of nature itself. Animals embodied the power of the earth: hare, moose, bear, coyote. The primal task of each individual Indian was to connect himself or herself to them. The Native American did not seek mastery over nature. The controlling ethic of native life was a valid correspondence between the self and sacred nature. The result was an ecological perspective. All the world was seen to be of the same substance, which allowed movement between realms, shifts from animal to human form, the change of humans into animals. A paddler of a canoe might see in the distance the head of a bear in the lake's water, only to find when he got closer it was a tree stump, but for him it was the bear that had changed itself into a tree stump. The same interaction was true with time, with events outside ordinary time having the power to shape daily existence. There were no boundaries between self and the sacred, nor among animals, spirits, and humans. An intricate, subtle, and sophisticated network flowed among the social, natural, and supernatural worlds, continuously seeking balance. Healers or shamans used magic and miracle to establish correspondence between the Indian and nature. They claimed extraordinary powers that could call up, for example, the guardian spirit of an animal that the hunter killed, in order to apologize for taking its life. Through shamans and guardian spirits, the Algonkians, for example, could connect to the Manitou to participate in its universal supernatural power. The Indian placed great value on sacramental ceremonies to enter into this balance with nature. The "numinous" world of spirits was always very close, and the land itself contained ceremonial places inhabited by sacred powers and persons.

If we can apply a European construct, the end result was an Apollonian person, characterized by modest, gentle, and cooperative behavior. The anthropologist Laura Thompson wrote of the ideal Hopi man:

> Thus the Hopi individual is: (1) strong (in the Hopi sense, i.e., he is psychically strong—self-controlled, intelligent, and wise—and he is physically strong); (2) poised (in the Hopi sense, i.e., he is balanced, free of anxiety, tranquil, "quiet of heart" and concentrated on "good" thoughts); (3) law-abiding (i.e., responsible, actively cooperative, kind and unselfish); (4) peaceful (i.e., non-aggressive, non-quarrelsome, modest); (5) protective (i.e., fertility-promoting and life-preserving, rather than injurious or destructive to life in any of its manifestations, including human beings, animals, and plants); (6) free of illness.

This ethic of harmony also reduced crime and violence. Illness crossed the lines between physical and mental states and could be cured psychosomatically. Warfare rigorously avoided bloodshed; tribal massacres were rare before the white man came.

Imperial Alternatives

Colonialism and Mercantilism: Their Environmental Consequences

In 1584 the English planner Richard Hakluyt urged the policy of transformation of the landscape from Florida to Nova Scotia into a European model by importing hardy and experienced farmers to cultivate the virgin land, stocking the land with domestic animals, planting Old World grains and legumes, marketing the commodities, and thus extending the benefits of English civilization to the sparsely populated continent. The plan was part of a large empire-building strategy called mercantilism. It dominated European thinking about the New World environment from the fifteenth to the mid-nineteenth centuries. Mercantilism demanded stiff controls of strategic raw materials to supply the mother country and deliberately stifled the internal development of conquered regions. If the future United States had remained a coastline string of English colonies under mercantilism, it would have stayed economically subordinate and undeveloped, a supplier of raw materials for England, and forced to depend on the mother country for finished or manufactured goods. Colonials were forbidden to enhance (value-added) raw materials: They were not to fabricate wool textiles from raw wool or fur hats from beaver pelts. Enforcement of mercantilist controls, such as England's repressive Navigation Acts, was a major factor that encouraged colonials to turn to armed intervention and seek independence in 1776.

Another important strategy was that of colonialism itself. Colonialism is the result of conquest, usually military, in which a labor force and local resources suffer long-term exploitation. In the future United States, however, an exception became the rule because the native peoples were largely eliminated despite their potential as a labor force. As a result the

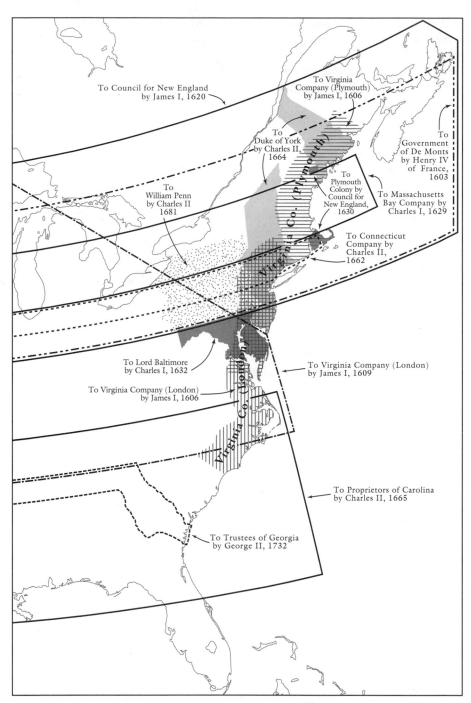

To Council for New England
by James I, 1620

To Virginia
Company (Plymouth)
by James I, 1606

To
Duke of York
by Charles II,
1664

To
Government
of De Monts
by Henry IV
of France,
1603

To
Plymouth
Colony by
Council for
New England,
1630

To Massachusetts
Bay Company by
Charles I, 1629

To
William Penn
by Charles II
1681

To Connecticut
Company by
Charles II,
1662

Virginia Co. (Plymouth)

Virginia Co. (London)

To Lord Baltimore
by Charles I, 1632

To Virginia Company (London)
by James I, 1609

To Virginia Company (London)
by James I, 1606

To Proprietors of Carolina
by Charles II, 1665

To Trustees of Georgia
by George II, 1732

Colonial Land Grants. In acts of remarkable hubris, European states, particularly England, claimed ownership (often with overlapping claims) of the entire east coast of the future United States. Ignorance of geography impelled them to extend the claims indefinitely westward. Settlers and land speculators usually acquired farms and estates not from the native peoples, but gained title from the crown-designated companies, proprietors, trustees, and individual landlords such as William Penn. Native "rights" were generally ignored, acquired at a pittance, and misleading to the Indians.

actual colonials by the eighteenth century were not Indians, but fellow Englishmen and a scattering of Dutch, Germans, and French.

The Spanish Way in Florida

Since the North American coastline produced no gold, silver, jewels, or spices, the Spanish treated it as a border region outside the rich Mayan civilization in Mexico.* In the early 1500s, using a small ragtag garrison at St. Augustine on the Atlantic coast of Florida, the Spanish only sketchily mapped Florida, Georgia, and the Carolinas. Spanish absolutism and centralized control inhibited the self-reliance and independent action by adventurous frontiersmen that might have enlarged their territories. One motivation, not well supported, was to convert the local Indians to Roman Catholic Christianity. The Spanish encountered fierce resistance from native Indians and were unable to generate colonial wealth from the inhospitable soil and debilitating climate (South Florida was not truly developed until the 1920s). One example was an exploratory expedition in 1528 led by the notoriously brutal Captain Panfile de Narvaez toward a rumored wealthy Kingdom of Apalachee. Landing on the Gulf Coast of Florida his soldiers slowly worked northward through stagnant freshwater swamps. Huge alligators cruised around and under their boats, terrified them with mating roars, and attacked their catches of fish. Narvaez's venture found no rich cities and crowds of welcoming citizens in flowing robes. After eating their own horses, Narvaez and his men began to starve in some of the most abundant fishing country in the world. One of Narvaez's men, Alvar Núñez Cabeza de Vaca, described how the struggling soldiers often waded across rivers, "treading on oysters, which cut our feet badly," only to encounter frightening perils such as rattlesnakes and coral snakes. Vaca reported the challenge of "vast forests, the trees being astonishingly high" and the expedition's slow travel through tangles of fallen timber. Vaca and three others were the only members of the expedition who were rescued hundreds of miles away in west Texas. Another expeditionary force of 600 soldiers led by Hernando De Soto solved the apparent food problem not by living off the prodigious land, but by bringing 13 hogs who over the next four years became 500 meat-on-the-hoof as well as efficient snake killers. Between 1539 and 1543, De Soto's men blindly zigzagged through 350,000 square miles of still unknown parts of Florida, together with Georgia, Alabama, Mississippi, Arkansas, Oklahoma, and Texas, in search of another Aztec civilization. Instead he found, and ignored, Florida country that was "low, very wet, pondy, and thickly covered with trees." Georgia's longleaf pine country was "abundant, picturesque, and luxuriant, well watered, and having good river margins," but produced no gold or gems. De Soto, with only a handful of pearls for his efforts, refused to report on his failure.

The Spanish reconnaissance into Florida and the Gulf Coast stayed blind to the luxuriant, semitropical, uncultivated mixed forests, lakes, and marshes because its only mission was to find another Aztec or Inca gold-filled civilization. Gold paid for wars and empire building. When Spanish power began to collapse internationally in the eighteenth century, so did two centuries of Spanish influence in the Florida region. At best, Florida was a defensive frontier against French and English threats. The Spanish would soon lose interest in devoting manpower to such an apparent wasteland. Nevertheless, Florida persisted as Spanish territory

---

* Spanish colonization and imperialism experienced a different path in the future American Southwest, a subject covered in Chapter 11.

from 1565 until its acquisition by the United States in 1821, except for a brief period of British control from 1763 to 1783.

Water Pathways into the Interior

As they moved inland into the future United States, European explorers mostly traveled along rivers and on lakes. The major exceptions were the laborious land treks of Coronado across the empty plains and De Soto through southern swamps and forest. These were not followed up. Rather, the broad rivers of America invited exploration; each great sweeping bend might complete the perpetual search for the Northwest Passage. Although the passage eluded the explorers, the rivers offered the most convenient pathways through the eastern forest, made connections with powerful Indian tribes, allowed trade for precious furs, and linked regions together that equaled the scale of large empires. For example, the entire history of the French in Canada is tied to the great passageway to the interior, the St. Lawrence River. The St. Lawrence gave them access to the five interior Great Lakes, which in turn permitted domination of the heartland of the continent from the Arctic to the Rocky Mountains. The French connected the heartland with the Gulf of Mexico and immediately seized Louisiana from the Spanish to secure the mouth of the Mississippi River. The French had the best opportunity to build a vast empire in North America because they were the first to learn the geography of the continent's water connections. But, as we see later, French policies toward the New World did not encourage them to exploit their early knowledge of America's waterways.

On a much lesser scale, the Dutch by 1615 began to work their way up the broad Hudson. They secured their claim by building a trading post just below present-day Albany. The Hudson River in turn gave access to the Mohawk River, the only major gap in the Appalachian mountain barrier. But this passageway toward the interior heartland was barred until the middle of the eighteenth century by a major native military and economic alliance, the confederacy of the five Iroquois nations. A hundred miles south, when the Dutch entered the Delaware River, they were hampered by shoals in the bay and halted by a river falls upstream. They and the Swedes satisfied themselves with Indian trading. The Chesapeake Bay provided one of the best points of access to the interior. It ran north by northwest for almost 200 miles, 10 to 20 miles wide, with almost 50 streams and rivers running into it, including the Susquehanna at the top, the Potomac flowing midway down from the west, and also the Rappahannock, York, and James rivers. By 1627 explorers from Virginia's Jamestown began to search up the Potomac and Susquehanna rivers. In the Deep South explorers spoke primarily of streams, bayous, lagoons, sounds, estuaries, marshes, and swamps, and named them the Alabama, Coosa, Tombigbee, and Savannah rivers, the sounds of Albemarle, Pamlico, and the Sea Islands.

Seeking a Balance: The French
Alternative Would Have Changed American History

Beginning with the navigator Jacques Cartier's expedition in 1534, the French searched up the St. Lawrence River for the elusive Northwest Passage. Like the Spanish, at first they also sought gold, silver, jewels, and spices, and hungrily listened to sly Indian rumors of the fabulous "Kingdom of the Saguenay," always vaguely in the distant west. Although Cartier failed to find the passage or jewel-encrusted kingdoms, he described a vast interior where the land was well forested, and fur-bearing animals abounded. On Canada's Gaspé Peninsula, Cartier was impressed with the towering trees of the primeval forest, "as excellent for making masts for ships of three hundred tons and more, as it is possible to find." And since he had not yet encountered any natives, the land seemed open for the taking. Bryon Island, in the middle of the bay leading to the St. Lawrence River, was "covered with fine trees and meadows, fields of wild oats, and of peas in flower, as thick and fine as ever I saw in Brittany, which might have been sown by husbandmen." During his second expedition in 1535, Cartier moved up the St. Lawrence River and opened the way for French explorers, who would be the first Europeans to enter the Great Lakes, the Ohio and Mississippi river valleys, and reach toward the Rockies. He admired the riverbanks, saying, "This region is a fine land as it is possible to see, being very fertile and covered with magnificent trees of the same varieties as in France, such as oaks, elms, ash, walnut, plum-trees, yew-trees, cedars, vines, hawthorns, bearing fruit as large as a damson." However, he warned that the weather was far more arctic than around Paris, with a much longer season of bitter cold. Between 1604 and 1607 the cartographer, soldier, and explorer Samuel de Champlain reinforced Cartier's earlier opportunistic assessment of the St. Lawrence River valley.

The French established Quebec and Montreal on the St. Lawrence River as trading posts adjacent to a few strategic Indian settlements. The rest of the St. Lawrence valley was mostly empty of Indian tribes, but the French did not attempt to fill the void with settlers. The land suitable for cultivation stretched in a narrow band along the St. Lawrence; much of the interior landscape was the barrens of the ancient granite Laurentian Shield that had been scraped clean by the most recent glaciers. Wealthy young gentlemen adventurers arrived to seek their fortunes, but fell ill and learned that the Canadian winter was impossibly harsh. Missionaries described New France as mostly an empty land, in large part because "the winter generally lasts here five months and a half; the snow is three or four feet deep." The European population of New France was only 360 in 1640 and 675 in 1650. The successful fur trade increased this to 2,500 in 1663 and 6,500 by 1668. By 1672 the French government discouraged organized immigration. Settlement was also limited by the difficulty of getting past rapids on both the St. Lawrence and Ottawa rivers.

French missionaries such as Father Jacques Marquette in 1674, joined by fur trappers, rapidly made connections between the Great Lakes and the Mississippi. They learned to piece together local Indian information, use lightweight native canoes to follow shallow streams, portage over low land barriers, and map lucrative trade routes. In contrast, no single Indian tribe had ever learned the large-scale geography of America as would the French. By 1673 the French entered Lake Michigan to Green Bay where they followed the Fox River to a 2-mile portage to the Wisconsin River that fed into the Mississippi River. Crucial connections between the Great Lakes and the Gulf of Mexico included the 5-mile portage from the Chicago River at the southwestern corner of Lake Michigan that led to the Illinois and Mississippi rivers. Several links connected western Lake Superior to the upper reaches of the Mississippi. By 1700 the French learned that the Maumee River at the west end of Lake Erie allowed a 30-mile portage to the Wabash River, which flowed into the Mississippi. A Jesuit priest, Pierre François Xavier de Charlevoix, was among the first to take a company of men along the entire route in 1721 from the St. Lawrence through the Great Lakes and down the Mississippi to Natchez. While he sought the ever-elusive passage to the Pacific and Cathay, he also described wonders such as Niagara Falls, "the noblest cascade perhaps in the world," and told anecdotes about Indian ceremonies that turned them into admirable people instead of savages. Charlevoix also reported that the inner continent was a pastoral landscape with untouched agricultural opportunities. The Illinois country was "beautiful, unbounded meadows where buffaloes are to be seen grazing in herds of two or three hundred." The Arkansas region had "forests which almost entirely cover this immense country. There is nothing, perhaps, in nature comparable to the size and height of the trees, or to their variety." About the same time, a Dutchman in French employ, Le Page du Pratz, described Louisiana as a resource treasure trove of animal hides, timber, cotton, tobacco, indigo, maize, peas, and rice. He pragmatically recommended that "a country fertile in men, in productions of the earth, and in the necessary metals, is infinitely preferable to countries from which men draw gold, silver, and diamonds." America was becoming a more tempting place than Asia.

If René-Robert Cavelier, Sieur de La Salle, an intimate of Colbert, had had his way, he would have shipped furs to France by way of the Mississippi River and the Gulf of Mexico, and not by way of Montreal on the St. Lawrence, ice bound for five months of the year. The result might have been a powerful fur-trading empire in the middle of the continent that would have transformed North America's history. A combination of factors discouraged the French from taking advantage of their early firsthand information to wrest control of North America. The French, far more than the English or Spanish, allowed geography and native peoples to shape their colonization. Not the least, European wars prevented capital and supplies from being allocated to the enormous geography of New France. The climate, increased conflict with Indians, and other hardships discouraged new settlers. Above all, the French established an alternative policy that recognized several powerful Indian tribes as equals and made them partners in an international trade in furs. This included recognition of de facto native land title to the interior of North America, unlike the brutal takeaways by the English. In reality, the French were far more dependent on the Indians than the Indians were on them. Merchants in Canada found it more important to accommodate the Iroquois than obey colonial officials and policy set in distant Versailles. The modern Canadian historian W. J. Eccles writes that the French were not interested in occupying land: "In North America in the late seventeenth century the French merely voyaged through the lands to trade with the Indians, obtain a cargo of furs, then transport it back to Montreal. The Indians were the important factor." The French had the military resources to drive the natives into submission, but instead they worked out careful agreements with the Algonkins, the Hurons, and the Iroquois as equals and as allies. While the English rushed to conquer, remove the Indians, clear the trees, and settle, French policy was to retain the Canadian wilderness as a vast income-producing preserve, managed by the Indians, with the fur trade its cash crop. Small numbers of French traders and settlers stayed along the St. Lawrence and Ottawa rivers, paddled onto the Great Lakes, lived off abundant game and fish, and hardly touched the landscape or interfered with native societies.

Settlements in the St. Lawrence valley were also inhibited by large land grants beginning in 1634 that directly transplanted the European feudal system of aristocratic overlords and peasant vassals. Title to land rested with the king, who granted land as concessions that were like long-term leases. One advantage of this arrangement is that it curbed speculation, but it would not produce privately owned small farms, as in the English colonies. Nor did the traditional small villages of France appear because farms lined up along the St. Lawrence River, sometimes in a single narrow ribbon that backed directly onto an uninhabited virgin wilderness. As Eccles put it, "The Canadians insisted on having river frontage and living apart, lords of their own little domains, with access to the wider world beyond by way of the river." The land is still laid out in the same manner today. In contrast with the English colonies, the French on the St. Lawrence used the river almost exclusively as their highway and did not embark on road building until the eighteenth century. Even in winter they traveled, shipped cargoes, and communicated by sleighs and wagons on the river and lake ice.

The French gradually lost hold because of their style of feudal landholding, noncompetitive fur-trading monopolies, and settlement restricted to Catholics only. The English created an expansionist juggernaut based on the buildup of population and the spread of agricultural settlement to replace the Indian wildlands-based environment. The French lacked a settlement frontier that advanced steadily westward in a rough line marked by cleared land. The French frontier in Canada was several small military outposts, sometimes fortified and manned by professional soldiers to control the Indians and keep the British away, but mostly designed to protect the fur trade. By 1757 only 70,000 Europeans in New France faced 1.5 million English colonists. If French policy had dedicated men and resources to secure the full length of the Mississippi River and thus the interior valley of the continent, the French rather than the English or Americans might have decisively shaped the rest of North America's history and geography. A uniquely different civilization would have emerged, based on French sympathy toward the native peoples, their manorial land use system, and their cautious approach to existing environmental conditions.

In summary, by the late seventeenth century Europeans moved inland and staked out the entire continent between France, England, and Spain, each with different land use strategies. In the north, the stakes were high—the continental fur trade, the fisheries of Newfoundland and Acadia, control of the Great Lakes for access to the western fur trade, the midwestern exploitation of the deerskin trade, and control of the Mississippi valley in the mysterious heartland. Whoever controlled the midcontinent would box in the English and hold off the Spanish; the French established strongholds at Detroit, Fort Duquesne, Michilimackinac, and in the Illinois country. But they failed to build enough strength in numbers to hold on to the heartland. Subsequently they lost Canada to the English with the Peace of Paris in 1763 following the French and Indian Wars. To close out the French story, they abandoned any remaining opportunity when Napoleon sold the entire midcontinent—the Louisiana Purchase—to Thomas Jefferson in 1803. After the War of 1812, the new United States turned its view westward and would deliberately replace both French and Indians with tens of thousands of English-style agricultural settlers who crossed the Appalachians, spread into the Ohio River valley, and shortly after, reshaped the Mississippi valley. "The axe and the plow finally defeated the canoe and the musket." The opportunity for the French alternative had been lost.

The English Gain a Foothold and Begin to Domesticate the Landscape

When Sir Francis Drake successfully raided the Spanish fort at St. Augustine, it was clear that the English, although latecomers, were emerging as a force to be reckoned with along the North American coast. The English had shifted their interest from immediate plunder to permanent colonies. They had little competition along a 1,000-mile coastline because to the south the Spanish were preoccupied in Mexico and the Caribbean and to the north French fur traders stayed with beaver trapping in a wilderness environment. Queen Elizabeth's favorite, Humphrey Gilbert, failed to establish a settlement on the barren coast of Newfoundland in two attempts, one in 1578 and again in 1583. Another royal favorite, Walter Raleigh, Gilbert's half brother, led two ships that reached Roanoke Island off North Carolina in 1584. Native hospitality to the struggling English settlement served up venison, fish, melons, roots,

A Wild Animal, the American Beaver, Shapes Both Nature and History

Europeans were adept at turning animals into wealth. This was true not only with domesticated animals like the horse, cow, sheep and pig, but also with wild animals like the American beaver. Beaver populations ranged across most of the future United States, making them a powerful environmental force across stream-fed landscapes. Beaver dams captured and held water, soil, and sediment that created fertile meadows and reduced erosion. Beaver ponds, including their surrounding marshes and clumps of brush, offered habitats for birds, fish, and plants. This molding of the natural habitat stored floodwaters in reservoirs, slowed seasonal runoff, and preserved watersheds. Even when a beaver colony exhausted its food supply and abandoned a dam that broke, the exposed deep muck provided the basis for meadow grasses which fed moose and deer. Frontier settlers used such "natural" meadows for mowing hay and grazing cattle. Because the beaver was an active agent in nature, both Indians and Europeans gave it human qualities of engineering know-how (building dams) and a work ethic ("busy as a beaver"). Only humans would be a greater force for environmental modification, beginning with fires deliberately set by the Indians to clear underbrush and encourage wildlife populations.

Beaver hats were first reported in the 1580s and did not go out of style until early in the nineteenth century. The beaver was the first step in a system of links between it as a renewable resource in the wilderness, between two distinctively different human societies, climate change in Europe, a clothing technology, and fashion. Canada's abysmally cold and long winters advantageously produced these luxuriantly furred animals. Hardy natives trapped and skinned them to trade by the thousands. Furs were light in weight, with high value relative to their bulk, and easy to transport. The connection between source and market was simple—a ship and crew to cross the Atlantic with trading goods, a few agents who knew Indian language and customs, and a return trip laden with furs. No heavy clearing of trees for settlement and difficult construction of house and barn and fences, and no costly slaves to gather and process the goods were necessary. In 1627, 90 years after Cartier had first explored deep into the continent and learned to make a rich trade in furs, the French established the trading Company of New France, which received exclusive authority to explore and manage North America from Louisiana to the Arctic Circle, and to hold tightly a monopoly of the fur trade and Atlantic fisheries. Back in the Old World, the market potential became enormous when Europeans demanded warm fur-lined clothing for indoor and outdoor use following the little ice age of the fifteenth century. This was an era when the heating of buildings was practically nonexistent. To this need can be added a wildly popular fash-

and fruits, but Raleigh's people needlessly stirred up conflict with local tribesmen. These first English settlers attempted to live off the land without native assistance, apparently failed, and simply disappeared.

ion that required beaver pelts to make felt hats. Beaver hats were produced in a wide variety of popular cocked, flat-topped, flat-crowned, slouch, plumed shovel, and sporting "beavers." Hatters used the soft inner barbed hairs of a beaver's fur that stuck to a felt base made of rabbit hair, a combination for which there was no alternative. By the early 1600s the French exported tens of thousands of beaver skins, making fur trading second only to fishing as a profitable New World business. Between 1700 and 1775 over half of England's total fur imports were beaver pelts. Demand in Europe eventually collapsed because of changes in style toward a narrower brim and the switch to blended felts using rabbit or Peruvian llama wool.

The fur business depended on legendary frontier trappers, the *coureurs de bois* or *voyageurs,* usually about 200 at a time in the backcountry. They appropriated Indian ways of clothing, diet, language, travel by foot or canoe, living off the land, Indian fighting, and stoic endurance of privation. They retained European weapons, greed for wealth, entrepreneurial zeal, and exploration into the unknown. A returning canoe load, paddled by two or three men, would bring in 20 hundredweight, or 40 packs of beaver skins, each worth 100 crowns. They made no attempt to destroy the wilderness because their way of life required its preservation. The modern Canadian historian W.C. Eccles writes, "They changed the face of the land hardly at all. Their canoes left no marks on the rivers and lakes as they passed. A few trees were cut at a campsite or along a portage, or a larger clearing was made and a log house built where a post was established, but when abandoned in favor of a better and usually more distant site, only a few years were needed to erase all signs of its existence. Yet a few hundred such men held the west in fee for France." They were more similar to Georges Banks' fishermen than to English frontier settlers. They did not occupy the western wilderness; they merely established collection stations—"factories"—for the return to Montreal. They were always a tiny minority among the Indian nations, largely dependent on them and therefore highly responsive to Indian interests. English (and later U.S.) settlers by contrast did not see the Indians as commercial partners, but as a major obstacle to "progress" that must be removed. The great nineteenth-century historian Francis Parkman wrote, "The English borders regarded the Indians less as men than as vicious and dangerous wild animals." This was far different from the mutual respect between *voyageur* and Indian.

Because of intensive trapping and killing to satisfy a European fashion, the American naturalist Benjamin Smith Barton by 1792 accurately predicted the disappearance of the beaver from its northeastern habitats. Such extinction had an unanticipated ripple effect because of the beaver's environmental impact: the decline of ducks who used beaver ponds for breeding, shrinkage of ponds and disappearance of brush that meant reduction in the numbers of muskrats, otters, mink, and raccoon, the loss of browse places for moose, deer, and black bear, as well as fewer meadows and greater soil erosion.

Only temporarily deterred by early disasters, the English kept on coming. In 1606 a motley company of wealthy young men moved up the James River in Virginia. Passage to the Pacific was said to be merely ten days overland travel beyond the headwaters. The arriving lace-cuffed gentlemen, whose servants did the hard work, did not bring a single farmer or fisherman with them. However, a few became enthralled with the vast plenty of the land, including crowds of egrets, herons, ducks, wild geese, woodcock, beaver, otter, and muskrats in the wetlands. Everywhere inland were masses of edible turkeys, partridges, pigeons, deer, elk, rabbit, raccoons, and even bison. Nonhuman predators included bear, panther, wildcats, and foxes. Fruit and nuts fell from the trees in layers on the ground. Familiar strawberries were "four times bigger and better than ours in England." They found wild sweet potatoes "as big as a boy's leg, and sometimes about as long and as big as both the leg and thigh of a young child." The rivers ran with shad and the coastal waters abounded with sturgeon and sea bass of sizes unknown today. They relished oysters that grew to such enormous sizes of 9 to 13 inches that they had to be served up in pieces before they could be swallowed. Twenty-five years later on the same Virginia coast, Capt. John Smith added his report of a primeval fragrant forest of pine, oak, cedar, and sassafras. He described oak trees that could be sawed into single timbers 2½ feet square and 60 feet long. America gradually became less a barrier to Asian riches and more its own world of untapped natural resources available to the first conqueror.

In the next several chapters we will see how westward expansion across North America would mostly follow British development patterns characterized by land ownership, Indian removal, and massive agricultural settlement. From an English point of view, for example, it could hardly be said that the French occupied the West, and thus the English believed that the French had wasted their colonial opportunity. One prospective English settler crossed the Appalachians, looked at the enticing Midwest, larger than all of France, Germany, and Poland, and found it, "all well provided with rivers, a very fine wholesome air, a rich soil, capable of producing food and all things necessary. In fine, the Garden of the World!" Enjoying middle-class mobility and ambition, the English were not tied down to the formalized less flexible societies of Spain and France. The Spanish were blinded by gold and enslaved the natives, the French were better at wilderness skills and Indian relations, the English instead imported more people, transformed the land into private property, and domesticated the wilderness into farmland. In New England they even duplicated the compact villages of Old England. Such English interests were in direct conflict with the Indians. The English refused to consider alternative approaches to the New World. Their actions were shaped by their passion for land as private property. Unlike the French, they saw the natives as obstacles to economic development and the progress of civilization. They cut down the forest and drove both animal and human life westward before them. They were determined to create a different, domesticated farmland. The English had also learned lessons from their bitter attempt to subdue, colonize, and assimilate the Irish, which they would apply to New World colonies. A major Irish rebellion in 1556 led the English to begin a systematic colonization on that island that turned over "plantations" to English landlords, imported loyal English settlers, and separated the natives into isolated "reservations." The same policies of ruthless repression of natives, acquisition of land, and settlement would be transferred to colonial North America.

Like a human version of a biological population that took advantage of an "empty niche," the English colonies enjoyed a birthrate of 3 percent per year, something never before seen in history. In a combination of births and immigration, Massachusetts alone went from

2,000 in 1632 to 16,000 in 1643 and 30,000 in 1665. This population explosion was aided by an abundance of food that brought an improved diet and better health. There was no colonial underclass that lived in abject poverty and near starvation. Instead, as in Old England, the colonies had an emerging middle class not tied down to feudalism and willingly mobile. As we see in Chapter 2, the English settlements were based on an efficient exploitive agriculture that in turn allowed the rise of a merchant class, the interconnections of trade, urbanization, and the multiplication of wealth. Disposable wealth in its turn allowed an accelerated expansion into the interior and technologies to exploit natural resources. As a result, the English (later Americans) simply overwhelmed the native peoples, drove off their European competitors, took over the continent, and learned how to use its wealth. But we are getting ahead of our story.

Native Americans Fall into Harm's Way

There was a sort of legal valve controlling the conveyance of land so that it always moved from Indian to Englishman and never reversed direction. This situation was peculiar to colonialism; it did not apply between the subjects of different European nations.

—ETHNOGRAPHER FRANCIS JENNINGS (1975)

Whatever ecological balance the native peoples of the eastern forest had achieved up to the appearance of Europeans became irrelevant, since it was about to be irrevocably ended. Every protective measure the Indians had possessed over hundreds of years to insulate themselves and their environment was matched and overmatched by a European alternative. Not many people—anywhere, anytime—could stand up to a deadly combination that hit Native Americans simultaneously: the jolt of foreign invasion, the collapse of indigenous ecologies, the catastrophe of biological scourge, the total infusion of an overweening market economy, the population explosion of the foreigners, and incorporation into a European biological complex of animals, people, plants, and pathogens.

The European View: "Savages" Were Enemies Who Had No Rights

Since classical times, Europeans had described the peoples on the edges of their civilization as "barbarians" and "savages." The ancient Greeks saw the Persians as morally inferior, lower on the evolutionary or civilizational scale; this was a view repeated by the Romans toward the Huns and Franks, and by the Germans and French toward the Celts and Vikings. For the English, their own savages were the upland Scots in the rugged north, and especially the "wild

Irish" who inhabited the island next door to England. Not that England was much better off in farming, herding, language, literature, metal and weaving technologies, and urbanization. A contemporary Italian from Florence or Venice would have see them both as inferiors. But severe repression of Irish tribesmen hardened the English for their unusually harsh treatment of Native Americans. The English concluded that a native lifestyle was mostly worthless: The Indians were incapable of wresting a generally satisfactory living, much less a civilization, from the wilderness. The natives offered little or nothing of value to Europeans. A "Drug List" prepared for use of Massachusetts troops in King Philip's War contained not a single medicinal product of American origin. Europeans in America looked on themselves as bearers of civilization who would be ennobled by overcoming the dark powers of the wilderness. Hence European military expeditions received from their home governments total sovereignty over foreign lands and peoples, regardless of the native peoples' interests. To resist white Europeans was the same as resisting God. One long-standing viewpoint was that the New World peoples were neolithic societies still struggling to find their way on the next step beyond the Stone Age, a thousand years behind the Old World. Was it "primitive" to say, in the words of one native wise man, after he saw the first European plow at work, "You ask me to plow the ground? Shall I take a knife and tear my mother's bosom?" From the Indian point of view, the European was the brutal savage. Most English colonists concluded that they were free to act without scruples. Savages, whether in Ireland, America (or later, Africa), were in a no-man's-land, literally "off the map" of any known geography. Therefore the usual humanitarian rules about morality, civility, and decency were judged irrelevant until introduced as part of a settled society. In historian Francis Jennings's words about European treatment of the Indians, "No slaughter was impermissible, no lie dishonorable, no breach of trust shameful, if it advantaged the champions of true religion." Jennings concluded, "To call a man savage is to warrant his death and to leave him unknown and unmourned." English colonizers never adopted the concept of the noble savage that Rousseau and the Romantics devised in the eighteenth century. At best the Indian was a pet. But mostly he was prey, cattle, or vermin, and never citizen (U.S. citizenship did not come to American Indians until 1924). Natives could be ignored, forced to assimilate into "civilization," or be removed.

In most cases Europeans lumped together about 40 different native cultures along the Atlantic Coast of North America. Geographer Donald Meinig observed, "What Europeans labelled as an Indian 'nation' might vary from an independent band of a hundred people to a loose confederation of many thousands." Indians lived in independent tribes and clans—shaped by kinship and ceremony—that could not be reconciled with the laws and traditions that governed Old World lord-vassal relationships. The most decisive differences between European and Indian had to do with concepts of individuality, privately owned property, territorial sovereignty, and attitudes toward nature based on radically divergent religious and economic worldviews. Europeans construed native ways to reflect a barbaric incapacity to master the wilderness. Meinig described the mutual woe of this dysfunctional relationship between the English and Indians: "Grievances and misunderstandings begat quarrels, quarrels begat violence, local violence begat more systematic coercion, and successful coercion in one locality was aggressively extended to other localities. Much of the violence was gratuitous, powered by a brutal opportunism that in turn engendered hatreds and retaliations." The result was, said Meinig, "a vast collision of cultures that produced chaos." He described the Old World-New World encounter as "a long period of harassment, expulsions, wanton killings, warfare, destruction, punishments, executions, enslavements, and subjugations that sooner or later engulfed every seaboard region and radiated ever more deeply into the continent. It was chaotic because no power could control it, because there was no authority on either side capable of halting it."

European Dependency on Natives

Thus European explorers and invaders had discovered an inhabited world. They did not settle a virgin land. It is bitterly ironic that most initial European intrusions were by small companies of lightly armed and poorly disciplined adventurers who would have starved and been lost without native generosity. They depended at first on Indian handouts and by raiding Indian gardens. Every European "discoverer" had Indian guides. Early settlers avoided heavy labor to clear woods by acquiring the lands already cleared by Indians. When the Indians demonstrated maize to the struggling European settlers, the Indians were amused and revolted by the invader's sloppy, even lazy, weeding and cultivation compared to neat, clean Indian fields. Historian Arthur C. Parker concluded that Indian maize "was the bridge over which English civilization crept, tremblingly and uncertainly, at first, then boldly and surely to a foothold and a permanent occupation of America." Francis Jennings added, "What America owes to Indian society as much as to any other source, is the mere fact of its existence." Europeans may have even been incapable of conquering true wilderness without Indian help; the natives had been pioneering the land for 1,000 years. Where Indians enjoyed hunting "parks," Europeans saw lethal wildernesses. Europeans were poorer frontiersmen, trappers, hunters, and farmers than the Indians, but they had developed techniques for managing other peoples. The true European competency was their skill in conquering others. Europeans were able to hold on to their precarious beachheads only because of their military prowess in firearms, armor, horses, ships, and strong forts.

Why Did the Indians Lose?

Indians quickly learned to prefer European metal implements and wool cloth to the product of their own crafts. This preference created a fatal connection with the European market economy. Soon Indians became dependent clients for European supplies of steel awls and axes, brass rings and iron wire, guns, bullets and shot, fishhooks, copper or brass kettles, steel knives (including special scalping knives), iron pickaxes, needles, scissors and shears, steels and flints to make fires, iron and steel hatchets, tomahawks and hatchets. They became habituated to European food and drink: sugar, molasses, rice, wheat flour, coffee, tea, whiskey, and rum. Such trade with Europeans insinuated subtle but deep changes in Indian society that brought it under the control of the marketplace. When the natives learned that the Europeans wanted animal skins in trade, they enlarged their traditional subsistence hunting into commercial hunting. This drove a wedge between their traditional religious view of animal powers and spirits and their new needs. Indians were pulled away from their own agricultural and hunting traditions to serve in a wider European economy. In contrast, European acquisitions from the Indians were culturally benign. Europeans benefited by learning to grow new

Who Exterminated the Buffalo? Were the Indians Really Ecologists?

Buffaloes once ranged virtually across the continent from Canada's Yukon to the Atlantic coast of Georgia. Modern estimates of the carrying capacity of the vast range suggests a population of 75 million in 1500 and 40 million in 1800, still far more than the human population of North America. They "blackened the plains," "roared like distant thunder," "drank up a river dry," "turned the grass to dust." They died naturally in large numbers in heavy blizzards, swollen rivers, and swampy bogs. Buffalo were described by Meriwether Lewis as "extremely gentle." His fellow explorers "frequently throw sticks and stones at them in order to drive them out of the way." Buffalo may have been "stupid," but relied on their size and strength and herds for security. Their only truly dangerous enemy was man, but not only the white man. The Indians, using the buffalo as a source of universal supplies, were opportunistic in capturing and killing them. They ran them onto soft ice or deep snow, into box canyons and over cliffs. They treated them ritualistically as fellow creatures in spirit and flesh, with preparatory dances and pipe smoking, sacred stones, red-painted skulls, and ceremonies: "Be not angry at us; we are obliged to destroy you to make ourselves live." The communal hunts that followed sometimes produced enormous surpluses of meat, hides, and bone that was wasted. In one trader's words in 1809, the dead "bulls were mostly entire, none but good cows having been cut up," and another counted only 1 in 20 carcasses touched, "so that thousands are left to rot where they fell." At one so-called jump site in southern Colorado, evidence shows a kill of 200 buffalo 8,500 years ago. It produced over 50,000 pounds of meat that would sustain a tribe of 100 people with 100 dogs for a month, if half was dried for future use. But still a quarter of the carcasses had not been touched and many others barely butchered.

The Plains Indians had used buffalo as the mainstay of their material lives: "meat, bone, fat, most organs, testicles, nose gristle, nipples, blood, milk, marrow and fetus" for food, with tongues and humps as special delicacies, and skins for robes, bedding, gloves, winter clothing, ceremonial and decoy costumes, spoons and drinking cups, carrying bags and containers, kettles, shields, moccasins, leggings, rope, bowstrings, and many other uses including children's rattles. One modern interpreter called the buffalo the Indians' "department store, builder's emporium, furniture mart, drugstore, and supermarket rolled into one." Nevertheless the Indians shopped selectively; they found it far easier to consume more tender buffalo cow meat, edible in all seasons, and softer hides than the tougher bulls, who were virtually inedible in rutting season. The

productive crops, to wear buckskin clothing and moccasins, to paddle canoes, to explore the wilderness on Indian trails, to survive in the wilderness, to take over Indian clearings, and generally to acquire the Indian's continent. But despite the heaviest pressures and widest opportunities, Indians showed little interest in becoming Europeans, living in European houses and wearing European clothes in European towns, working the fields in European ways, and fighting European wars.

Indians also craved white man's horses for hunting, travel, and warfare. They first became available about 1680 and turned into a universal Plains animal, tamed or wild, by 1800. Horses, like white man's cattle, became wide-ranging competitors for grazing on the short grasses of the semiarid High Plains.

So many buffalo would perish in a single drive, and the meat was so difficult to preserve that the Indians would only take the tongues and humps of some of the animals, or only the fetus as a special delicacy, and leave the rest to rot and decay. Elsewhere, one early trapper in 1792 reported "an intolerable stench of the great number of putrified carcasses" at the bottom of a cliff where Indians had driven 250 buffalo now dead piled six deep. In 1804 Meriwether Lewis saw a Mandan Indian "buffalo jump" with "the remains of a vast many mangled carcasses of buffalo which had been driven over a precipice of 120 feet." These reports led the modern anthropologist Shedard Krech to conclude that the native peoples of the New World were often neither noble savage or ecological Indian. According to Krech, the Plains Indians, and others, may have lived more lightly on the land than greedy Europeans, but they were not the intensive ecologists that modern Americans thought them to be. Native peoples must share the blame for ecological destruction and species extinctions, but the scale and speed accelerated vastly with the appearance of white Europeans.

In Shedard Krech's words, "Today there is almost universal agreement that the near-extinction of the buffalo [by human slaughter] is one of the grimmest narratives in the history of wildlife." No doubt white men were the grimmest exterminators when beginning in 1867 they turned buffalo hunting into a remarkably vicious popular entertainment that captured the public eye. After the Civil War they rode train excursions in which "sportsmen" blasted away at herds with six-shooters and repeating rifles. For every buffalo killed, five limped away wounded to die in agony. In one 3-year period, between 4 and 5 million buffalo were shot and left rotting on the Plains, although there was some market for their skins as cheap alternatives to cowhides for leather products, but buffalo meat was not popular. Indians were excluded from this sport to starve in arid reservations. Railroad lines soon divided forever the once-far-ranging buffaloes into northern and southern herds that splintered into ecologically untenable populations. Cattle ranchers took over historic buffalo range in Texas and Kansas, and farmers invaded the Plains after unusually heavy rains in the 1870s made the land temporarily more attractive. Commercial hunting of buffalo was finished by the fall of 1883, ended by a combination of drought, blizzards, and the virtual disappearance of herds wiped out by the slaughter. A few hundred in remnant herds found refuge in the new Yellowstone National Park and a few dozen joined Buffalo Bill Cody's traveling wild west show.

Indian-White Relations through U.S. History

The Indians often had little choice between enslavement by the Spanish or extermination by the English. The encounter with Europeans became a painfully familiar pattern of predictable events: First, an Indian tribe became connected to English advances through trade in furs, firearms, and metal tools. This peaceful trading relationship opened the door to a rapid increase in local European settlement. The Indians found themselves under pressure to "sell" their land—often under coercion, often unknowingly. Slow to anger, but finally enraged, the Indians turned to violence to protect their sacred Mother Earth. By force of superior arms and often with superior numbers, the Europeans crushed Indian resistance. Massacres took place on both sides, but the Indian numbers suffered disproportionately. Defeated, humiliated, and helpless, the natives were absorbed into other tribes or endured a forced migration westward onto strange land controlled by hostile tribes or were located on a reservation (or a combination of these). The result was inevitably the death of 5,000-year-old cultures.

The white man indeed spoke with forked tongue. The Northwest Ordinance of 1787 guaranteed land rights to Indians, with property not to be taken without Indian consent. It soon proved to be an empty promise as Indians were driven westward, fought bitter and bloody battles, and tried to settle across the Mississippi. The Louisiana Purchase of 1803 was believed to offer plenty of room for all Indians who formerly lived east of the Mississippi. When so-called Civilized Tribes of the Southeast endeavored to adapt to European ways, including business enterprise, Congress considered forming an Indian state and admitting it to the Union. But white man's land rushes led to the notorious Indian Removal Act of 1830 to move all Indians east of the Mississippi westward. Congress appropriated only $500,000 for compensation. The not surprising result was the Cherokee "Trail of Tears," a march on foot westward, prodded by army soldiers, of 100,000 men, women, and children to Indian Territory in Oklahoma. But land in the west was not empty, and tribes there resented the invasion of their hunting grounds by eastern tribes.

There were more troubles over territory after the Mexican War, when the United States took from Mexico the lands of large and aggressive Navaho tribes. Together with the Apaches, Navahos stole over 450,000 sheep as damages for their lost sheep, homes, and other goods. The Navahos entered their own reservation in 1868, which was on such arid land in Arizona and New Mexico that few whites were attracted to it. In 1871 Congress passed a law putting an end to further treaties with Indian tribes. After the Civil War, Indian-white relations were characterized by vicious warfare, climaxing in the capture of Geronimo and rebel Apaches in 1886 and the wanton massacre of over 300 Sioux men, women, and children at Wounded Knee, South Dakota, in 1890. This was the last major bloodshed involving Indians in the United States. Since then the original native peoples of the New World—sometimes called the "First Nations"—have been absorbed into the white people's mainstream, set aside on reservations, or allowed to succumb to disease, unemployment, and moral disillusionment. Ironically, in 1928 the "Meriam Survey" stressed that Indian assimilation should not be forced, and urged a change of policy. Not until 40 years later did Indians receive special attention in the 1968 civil rights bill.

Why Was the New World So Easy to Conquer? The European Advantage

One reason Europeans held Native Americans in such contempt was the natives' inability to stand up against European ferocity. We cannot discount the difficulties and hardships that individual persons endured to win the continent, but in general Europeans quickly overwhelmed both Native Americans and North America's geographical challenges.

Contrary to the classic textbook description of European "discovery," the future history of the New World was not primarily the conquest of primeval wilderness by European civilization, but instead it was the interaction between two human ways of living and two responses to the same ecosystems. To Europeans, each regional environment, in this case the eastern forest ecosystem, was treated as a negative force until it could be demolished and replaced by the farmland and centers of commerce. The local peoples were never understood in their own terms, but only through the eyes of European covetousness. One of the most remarkable aspects of the Old World-New World encounter was the capacity of Europeans to continuously focus and enlarge their technological, economic, and psychological powers to meet the task. A great deal of American history can be explained by understanding these powers.

Europe's Ecological Strength

Geographically, western Europe is merely a large peninsula jutting out at the extreme western fringe of the immense landmass of Asia. Fewer and fewer solid blocks of land exist as one moves westward; the continent becomes more peninsulas and broken coastlines. Western Europeans were biased toward the interplay of sea and land, unlike landlocked peoples. Trade and travel were relatively easy using many waterways and the flat central plain. Europeans also enjoyed a benevolent climate of rainfall of not less than 20 inches or more than 40 inches, as well as temperatures that avoided extremes, neither too little or too much sunlight, and a growing season of approximately eight months. Their soil was fertile and productive across the great plain that extended from Spain across France, the Low Countries, northern Germany, and into Poland. European farmers were good stewards who increased the fertility of their land by creating loam through crop rotation, composting, and manuring. In particular, they enjoyed reliable food surpluses to feed an enlarging population even while exporting to acquire exotic goods from Arabs and Asians.

Because of this ecological strength, European society could recover from disasters and reach new levels of material well-being while also growing rapidly in numbers. Human failure, whether from political errors or military defeats, plagues or local famines, did not mean Europe's downfall as it would for societies in the Sahel desert of east Africa, or monsoon-burdened Bangladesh. Neither was European civilization tied down to constant management of irrigation as in central Asia nor did it depend on continuous hard labor to maintain rice fields and fend off an ever-encroaching jungle. Europeans could thus turn their attention to matters other than daily survival. European invaders and settlers would also enjoy the extraordinary good fortune that they could cross the great western ocean and find so much that was familiar on the opposite side. As we shall see, the attractions of the New World were very often "biogeographical"—access to fertile land under a temperate climate—as much as they were political or religious.

The Aggressive European Mentality: A Passion for Conquest

Other factors gave Europeans easy access to the rest of the world. One was psychological. Asians, Africans, and Native Americans were astonished by European single-minded aggressiveness. No peaceable people these, but noisy, brawling, enthusiastic, militant, and demanding, uncontrolled like a hyperactive child. They were brutal and daring men with demonic energy. One contemporary explanation was that the English were beefeaters who burned off their excess protein through their boisterousness. Other peoples saw Europeans as uncivilized and dangerous, a race of bullies. The natives of the New World believed they were madmen. This belligerence also resulted from Europe's pack of contentious nationalistic states, all racing for more land, power, and wealth. Previously, ancient and medieval civilizations had almost invariably sought stability; fifteenth-century Europeans instead were unique in their belief in the continuous, cumulative expansion of human power over the environment and even over human destiny. "Progress" was the most powerful idea that Europeans carried with them when they went abroad. Other influences came from emerging competitive capitalism, which valued material growth, the swashbuckling individualism of the Renaissance; and, not the least, Christian missionary zeal to convert all of humanity exclusively to its faith. The result was a strange mixture of the "Four G's": greed, glory, gunpowder, and gospel. Ironically, Europeans sincerely hoped not only to exploit the world, but to build a better world.

Sixteenth-century Europeans were also unusual in their fascination with the outside world, be it for adventure, curiosity, piety, or plunder. Other civilizations, such as the Chinese, had equal ability, and occasionally ventured outward, but they had no compelling desire to conquer strange and presumably inferior peoples. Europeans, in contrast, held the concept that they inhabited a rich planet, which it was their divinely ordained destiny to conquer. For almost 400 years Europeans had already driven eastward in the Crusades to recapture the Holy Land. Christian missionaries were known in India and China. The Vikings had wandered several times across the Atlantic beyond Iceland and Greenland to land on the North American continent. The Venetians built their power largely around venturesome expeditions, as later would the Dutch. Rowers in galleys invaded the Canary Islands and the Azores, and they reached the west coast of Africa. Europeans knew how to "Europeanize" the New World because they had already dropped rabbits, burros, sheep, cattle, and goats as well as human settlers on the unsuspecting lushly forested Azores islands (soon almost treeless), the Madieras islands (soon little more than a sugar colony powered by slaves), and the Canary islands (whose Stone Age population wilted before disease, technology, and alien culture).

Technology as a Focused Skill

To non-Europeans, this aggressive warlike posture was made worse because of the overwhelming military technology of the invaders. Their armor and muskets and frightening mounted horsemen were only part of the story. No one could compete with European supremacy at sea. They commanded the waters in large squareriggers: ships made more manageable by three or four masts, with up to four sails on each mast, controllable by ingenious rigging, and guided by the sternpost rudder instead of a steering oar. These monuments to the shipbuilder's craft could efficiently tack into the wind and avoid disaster from storms. Europeans turned their vessels into powerful weapons platforms (the first major military innovation since the ancient chariot and the medieval stirrup and part of a long tradition that would include the machine gun, the tank, the submarine, and the guided missile) carrying heavy cannon in an age when most people still fought with spear, club, and arrow.

Europeans dared to cross open waters by means of the miraculous guidance of the compass (since the thirteenth century), better mariner's charts, and the astrolabe (since the fifteenth century) to measure latitude (measurement of longitude waited 200 more years), as well as sheer bravado. Europeans could run their ships beyond the sight of land for weeks to catch a better wind or current. They were practiced in steering to within a few miles of the desired landfall. They could also return home, a fact at least as important as discovery. In the fifteenth and sixteenth centuries, European seamen learned that all the seas are one, allowing them to reach any country in the world that had a coastline. Columbus traveled 2,600 miles in 36 days without sight of land; Vasco da Gama did the same for 96 days over 4,500 miles. Before this, humanity was slow moving, and seldom crossed long distances overland, much less across the great oceans.

Disease

The greatest weapon in the European arsenal was probably disease. Commonplace European crowd diseases like smallpox and measles became lethal weapons among native populations that had no acquired immunity to them. The Indians, according to one witness, "died like fish in a bucket." A German missionary wrote in 1699, "The Indians die so easily that the bare look and smell of a Spaniard causes them to give up the ghost." An epidemic of smallpox began in 1519 in Central America and raced down to Peru. Historian Alfred Crosby writes that smallpox caused "in all likelihood the most severe single loss of aboriginal population that ever occurred." The microorganisms might as well have come from outer space. Although the natives' immune systems and mentality tolerated their own burdens of yaws, syphilis, hepatitis, encephalitis, polio, and tuberculosis, they were decimated by smallpox (now extinct worldwide), nuisance or childhood diseases like measles, scarlet fever, chicken pox, and whooping cough, and serious threats like bubonic plague, malaria, typhoid fever, amoebic dysentery, diphtheria, cholera, yellow fever, dengue fever, and influenza. A modern Amazon rain forest tribal chief concluded, "White men cause illness; if the whites had never existed, disease would never have existed either." Most native peoples believed that epidemic diseases were supernatural in origin; carriers of disease thus were destroying angels from the gods. One seventeenth-century French adventurer agreed, "It appears visibly that God wishes that these savages yield their place to new peoples." Europeans seemed immune to the decimation. Natives even kneaded infected blood into their master's bread, and dumped smallpox corpses in their wells, with no success. For several centuries, the New World endured the combined effects of a war zone and charnel house.

The Force of Numbers

Compared to crowded, bustling Europe, anywhere between 1 million and 2.5 million natives were bunched across the vast landscape of the future United States. A landscape containing an average of about one person per 4 square miles must have appeared empty to Europeans who had just experienced a population explosion after the plagues and famines of the fourteenth century. This eerie emptiness was reinforced by European discovery of vacated Indian fields due to disease or tribal warfare. Some large interior places such as the Kentucky canebrakes or the Shenandoah Valley were wholly uninhabited. Even where powerful tribes controlled a strategic region, like the Iroquois across New York, the land seemed lush but vacant to

SMALLPOX WAS PARTICULARLY terrifying not only because it was deadly, but also because it was hideous and unfamiliar. Symptoms included a high fever, vomiting blood, skin eruptions that turned into suppurating abscesses, ugly oozing smelly scabs, or blindness and disfiguring pocks if one survived. This scourge fulfilled prophecies in native mythology about the arrival of white gods. The incubation period of 12 days made it even more mysterious. Natives, reeling before the onslaught of these "gods," were often demoralized when not annihilated.

The smallpox epidemic among Mexico's Aztec in 1520 had more to do with their collapse than the military prowess of Cortez and his small band of men. One contemporary reported that 29 of every 30 men, women, and children perished. By 1600 the population of Mexico's central valley was down 80 percent. Of 2 million Incas in Peru, only 20,000 survived the appearance of the pest-bearing white gods. There were not enough able-bodied men to work Inca irrigation ditches or bury the dead, much less oppose new Spanish masters. New England was strangely, and providentially, mostly empty when Puritan settlers arrived because a pestilence had already swept through it in 1616 and 1617. John Winthrop, first governor of Massachusetts Bay Colony, reported in 1634, three years after the first Boston settlement, that the natives "are near dead of smallpox, so as the Lord hath cleared our title to what we possess." In 1738 smallpox destroyed half the Cherokee Nation; 21 years later, half the Catawbas, two-thirds of the Omaha Indians a half century later, and nearly half the entire native population between the Missouri River and New Mexico.

The plains Kiowa, after several epidemics, made smallpox part of their mythology: "Who are you?" "I'm smallpox." "Where do you come from and what do you do and why are you here?" "I am one with the white men. I am always their companion and you will find me in their camps and in their houses." "What do you do?" "I bring death. My breath causes children to wither like young plants in the spring snow. I bring destruction. No matter how beautiful a woman is, once she has looked at me she becomes as ugly as death. And to men I bring not death alone but the destruction of their children and the blighting of their wives. The strongest warriors go down before me. No people who have looked at me will ever be the same."

European settlers as they edged along the rivers and valleys into unknown forests. They believed they truly entered an empty continent.

Immediately after discovery, Europeans came in overwhelmingly large numbers, more than 1,200 in Columbus's second voyage alone, not the skimpy 100 that the Vikings landed in Vineland, nor the few hardy individuals in rafts and outriggers from Polynesia. Along the eastern coast, the densest native populations lived in southern New England and at the Chesapeake Bay. From what we have seen about European advantages, it is not surprising that over the next 400 years the European invaders to the future United States successfully reduced Indian competitors from 2.5 million in 1492 to a tenth that number, 250,000, in 1890. Yet successful English settlement of the future United States was not a forgone conclusion despite advanced technology, intensive agriculture, and unusual willpower. It would take a century for the English to match in numbers the 72,000 natives estimated to live in New England in 1600. Algonkian populations that covered much of the Northeast had reached 140,000 by the early 1600s. Rather quickly afterward, however, they were decimated by epidemics from 1616–18 and 1633–34 that wiped out 90 percent of their people. European inhabitants of New England would not reach 100,000 until well into the eighteenth century, 90 percent of them farmers dedicated to reconstructing the landscape. This was a one-way migration that would swell into the world's greatest movement of peoples. The actual immigrants were self-selecting. Immigrants were not a cross section of society. The nobles, the wealthy, the established, and the contented stayed at home. Those who became Americans were the aggrieved middle classes and religious minorities, the impoverished who had few alternatives but migration, and the ambitious and energetic entrepreneurs willing to risk life, limb, and their future. These were people motivated to migrate long distances to Old World port cities, willing to cross the dangerous Atlantic, who deliberately took the risk of frontier isolation, separation from family and friends, and the abandonment of traditions. After about two centuries of European occupation, North and South America in 1800 had 5 million white settlers and 1 million black slaves.

Was America Uniquely Vulnerable to European Conquest?

Did America have weaknesses or outright defects that made it more vulnerable to successful invasion? A few historians and anthropologists, such as Albert Crosby and Harold Driver, take a provocative stand that Americans were highly vulnerable to European-style conquest. According to this view, the New World had been tardily civilized and was thus presumably less developed. Crosby also argues that "the Western Hemisphere was somehow less hospitable to the techniques and arts of civilization than Eurasia. When the conquistadors arrived with iron and steel, the peoples of the high Amerindian cultures were still in the early stages of metallurgy. They used metals for ornaments and idols, not for tools."

In addition, in the Old World, the staple crops, such as wheat, spread east and west through similar climate zones. But in the Americas, a geography of mountain ranges that ran north and south inhibited the spread of crops. Also, early maize was not originally a good provider, with a few scrawny kernels on a stubby ear, whereas Old World wheat was highly productive from the first. A society could not build large populations, or many cities, on ears of early corn, but in the Near East, and in Europe, people could, and did, build civilizations on grains of wheat. Europeans were forced to introduce their own grasses and crops—clover and hay as well as wheat and barley—to support the animals they brought with them. From the first, European plants aggressively filled niches where there had been no identical grasses and crops earlier. The quick-fruiting peach tree seemed as energetic a conqueror as the pig, carp, starling, or English sparrow. Entire economies depended on the introduction of foreign cotton, rice, and sugar plants. By 1600 the important European food plants were well established and even dominant. They tripled the number of grains, fruits, and vegetables that humans in the New World could farm for food. Overall, we must admit that humanity's food basket is all the better since the encounter between Old and New Worlds. Counting calories and nutritional quality, New World crops like maize and the potato improved the human future. Acre for acre, beans, maize, and potatoes provide more sustenance than rice and wheat.

Western Hemisphere people had tamed only dogs, llamas, guinea pigs, and some fowl, whereas Europeans enjoyed domesticated dogs, cats, pigs, sheep, goats, cattle, horses, donkeys, reindeer, chickens, geese, ducks, and honeybees. In the Old World, large animals like cattle and horses had joined with humans since before the Sumerians 5,000 years before. This offered an immense advantage over people who drew on little more than the strength of their own muscle. Cattle also provided essential protein from milk or meat from forage grasses or leaves that humans cannot digest. The omnivorous pig thrived on virtually any barnyard scraps or forest food. By contrast, the large animals of the New World were extinct, other than the Plains buffalo: no more mammoths, giant ground sloths, saber-toothed tigers, giant buffalo, prehistoric horses, or camels. North America did not, unlike Africa, have the vast populations of gazelles, zebras, wildebeest, oxen, and elephants, or predators like lions and tigers. Charles Darwin's American contemporary, Alfred Russel Wallace, called the New World "a zoologically impoverished world, from which all the hugest, and fiercest, and strongest forms have recently disappeared." This offered an ecological niche, ready and waiting, which European horses and cattle filled by their transformation into feral mustangs and mean-spirited longhorns.

The Biological Exchange

The traditional story of human conquests and institutional changes looks trivial if Europeans instead are described as carriers of uncontrollable biological forces. Historian Alfred Crosby opened this issue in 1972 when he argued that European entry into the New World—the Columbian Exchange—resulted in vast redistribution of life-forms. The European invasion changed the biota of the earth more thoroughly than at any time since the end of the Permian Period 280 million years ago. During the ancient Permian Period, all the continents were fused as one great supercontinent, Pangaea, in which all living things competed and evolved together. About 180 million years ago Pangaea began to split and drift apart to gradually shape our modern continents. Life-forms on each continent began to develop independently, such as two kinds of South American camel (llama and alpaca). But there was no animal compared to the horse, ass, or ox. In a mere geological twitch of time, Europeans forged a remarkable technological reconnection of the different parts of Pangaea. True, the world's oceans had occasionally carried drifting specimens from one place to another, or rare connections were made by venturesome Polynesians or Vikings. But a deliberate and massive interchange was forged by Spaniards, Frenchmen, Dutchmen, and Englishmen. Columbus's second voyage in 1493, which carried the first known shipload of horses, dogs, pigs, cattle, chickens, sheep, and goats, was the forerunner of the worldwide reconnection. Their transplanted animals, such as pigs and cattle, invaded and altered the new environments with dramatic speed and deadly efficiency. Such actions forced extinctions and alterations of species at a speed and on a scale never before experienced.

Horses found most of the New World extremely hospitable. They thrived and went wild in northern Mexico. Herds of these mustangs entered the central continental steppes to recover the old niche of their ancient long-gone forebears. Soon there were more horses in the Americas than anywhere else in the world. Wild horses extended as far as the California coast, north onto the Canadian plains, and east across the Mississippi. The familiar stories that describe how nomadic Plains Indians took readily to the horse, and the rise of the horse-mounted cowboy, need not be repeated here. In Europe horses were very expensive, demanded costly care, and belonged to the wealthy. Lower classes walked. In the United States, horses ran free, provided a cheap mode of transportation, could be harnessed to pull a plow or wagonload, and lived in backyard barns even in the cities. The horse was the most familiar and widespread means of transportation that Americans knew until the rise of its replacement, the automobile.

From Europe came wheat, rice, barley, oats, chickpeas, onions, radishes, salad greens, garden crops (cauliflowers and cabbages), sugarcane, melons, peaches, apples, pears, and hemp. By the early twentieth century in California's San Joaquin Valley, such "introduced" plants made up 63 percent of the grassland, 66 percent of the woodland, and 54 percent of its chaparral. Places that once had no wheat, such as America's High Plains, became "the breadbasket of the world." The New World provided nonfood items like tobacco, rubber, and American cotton. Its native foods included pumpkins, sweet potatoes, peanuts, squashes, tomatoes, beans, potatoes, and cocoa, and, of course, corn. What Americans call corn and Europeans call maize (they use the word *corn* for all grains) is debatably the most important food contribution of the New World to the rest of the globe. Varieties of corn existed widely across many climate zones in the New World. It can be eaten by humans and their livestock, offering essential carbohydrates, sugars, and fats. A saying went, "Whoever grows corn will never experience famine." It can prosper in places too dry for rice and too wet for wheat. The famous stories in which Indians saved starving settlers by showing them how to grow corn are mostly true. Its yield per acre is double that of wheat. The potato, which became at least as valuable as wheat in the temperate zones of the Old World, offers several times more food value per acre than wheat or corn. Its advantage is that it grows in poor land and prospers from sea level to well over 10,000 feet. Even the least adept farmer can grow potatoes. In a short time it became the primary staple across Europe, from Ireland to Russia. Beans, "the poor man's meat," exist worldwide in more than a thousand species. They concentrate protein, oils, and carbohydrates. The Old World gave America the all-important soybean, and America returned the favor with the lima, butter, pole, kidney, navy, snap, string, and frijole bean, among others.

Not every import was beneficial. Europeans, as we noted, also brought parasites and pathogens on their bodies, their animals (including brown and black rats), and their plants. The biological exchanges inexorably continue through today and into the indefinite future. Cholera, malaria, and now AIDS arrived from the Old World. Humans have not been the only victims. Aggressive birds like the starling dispossessed millions of American birds. Carp entered American waters in 1877 and immediately spread against native fish. Colonial farmers carried the Hessian fly to the New World, where it depleted their own wheat fields so much that in Connecticut farmers who had exported 10,000 bushels of wheat soon had to import 3,000 bushels. Other unhealthy imports were the black stem rust ("blast") that attacked wheat and rye, the ordinary black fly, Japanese beetles, and the ubiquitous cockroach. Dutch elm disease and chestnut tree fungus virtually wiped out two wonderful native trees. Aggressive and tiresome weeds included the dandelion, nettles, nightshade, black henbane, ragweed, and crabgrass. The fast-growing noxious kudzu came from Asia. In return, the American vine aphid nearly destroyed the French wine industry in the 1860s. From America came the muskrat, which became a European pest. American gray squirrels have nearly eliminated Britain's red squirrels. Extremely aggressive African bees entered the New World through Brazil 30 years ago and have already mated with and displaced the docile native bee in all of South and Central America, with conquest of North America in their sight.

Conclusion: A One-Time Experiment
Changes Human and Environmental History

Invasion of North America was part of a global picture. Europeans, more specifically the Spanish, English, French, and for a brief time the Portuguese and Dutch, spread irresistibly beyond their borders in a fashion unprecedented in the history of the world. They dominated—economically, politically, culturally—every other society they touched. This gave Europeans wealth and power previously unimaginable. Yet the European reconnaissance of North America during the sixteenth century was at first disappointing and distracting. There were no cities with golden treasure as in Mexico or Peru. The gateway to the riches of Cathay was unexpectedly elusive, although Europeans did not easily abandon their search for the Northwest Passage. Exploration along the coastline and nervous dashes into bays and estuaries, together with almost random crossings of the landscape, instead revealed a richly diverse forest densely filled with wild animals, clouds of birds, and streams thick with fish. This report, because it was not gold, remained difficult for Europeans to comprehend. Their geographical knowledge was limited, stereotyped, and misunderstood. The French came closest to an accommodation with the environment and the natives, the English the least.

Europeans claimed to own the continent before they knew what they had. They thought in terms of nation-states and empires, and therefore saw the New World as a map determined by imperial boundary lines, regardless of alternative possibilities and Native American refusal to accept ownership of land. Most Europeans could not fathom the so-called savage mind in its belief, ritual, and lifestyle. Their interpretive viewpoint remained a combination of biblical and Greek mythology in which the demonic Indian emerged as a familiar of the devil. The modern essayist Alastaire Reid wrote, "First seen as Ariel, the Indian is soon turned into Caliban: beast, slave, less than human." The contrast became more severe over time. The European intellectual heritage grew more mechanistic, abstract, and rational, whereas Indians were more tolerant, more personal, and more directly in touch with nature. As a result of European blinders, the Indian contribution to American culture, like the African or Asian, remained a mere accretion without substantially transforming Europeans in any fundamental way. Francis Jennings writes,

> Indian agriculture contributed new crops, but it did not cause Europe to forsake the plow. Indian herbs were added to the European pharmacopoeia without changing the physician into a powwow. Indian warriors fought with and against European soldiers and taught the value of guerrilla tactics in certain circumstances; but drill, discipline, and a hierarchical command structure remain basic to modern military forces. Indian voluntarism and equalitarianism struck the European political imagination, but the nation-state grew ever more centralized and bureaucratic and acquired new techniques for compelling its subjects to obedience and conformity.

Very little of an original Indian environmentalism survived to modern times.

The European conquest of the New World was a relatively easy task, even before Europeans realized what they had. Europeans, like most peoples would, applied to the utmost their superior naval and military technologies to have their way. They soon learned the stunning power of disease, and in some cases they deliberately infected the natives. To them, their own high aggressiveness was simply human intelligence applied in a superior way. European imperialism, despite its grand designs, was nevertheless a puny result compared to the dramatic and immediate biological disruptions caused by discovery and transplantations of plants, animals, and diseases. The flora (wheat, corn, cotton) and fauna (horses, cattle, pigs, chickens) that now dominate the New World because of the human hand are so narrowly specialized that they create genetic constraints instead of the multifold opportunities that the New World once offered. More irreplaceable species have been threatened and extinguished in the last 500 years because of human action than in a million years of the usual processes of evolution. Usually, when paleontologists and evolutionary biologists speak of "explosive evolution," they mean a change over several million years. In this sense we cannot yet have the foggiest idea about the long-term consequences of the Columbian Exchange.

For Further Reading

The best places to continue exploration of an environmental approach to Europe's encounter with the New World are in Alfred W. Crosby's pathbreaking books, *The Columbian Exchange: Biological and Cultural Consequences of 1492* (1972), and *Ecological Imperialism: The Biological Expansion of Europe, 900–1900* (1986). Early European responses to the American environment can be found in Kirkpatrick Sale, *The Conquest of Paradise: Christopher Columbus and the Columbian Legacy* (1990). Readers should also dip into the influential essays by Frederick Turner in *Beyond Geography: The Western Spirit Against the Wilderness* (1980) and Henry Savage, Jr., *Discovering America: 1700–1875* (1979). The best place to begin a review that treats Native Americans with dignity is Dee Brown's classic *Bury My Heart at Wounded Knee: An Indian History of the American West* (1981). For environmental issues, see J. Donald Hughes, *American Indian Ecology* (1983), and R. Douglas Hurt, *Indian Agriculture in America: Prehistory to the Present* (1987). The misunderstanding and mistreatment of Indians is also trenchantly reported by Francis Jennings, *The Invasion of America: Indians, Colonialism, and the Cant of Conquest* (1975) and *The Founders of America: How Indians Discovered the Land, Pioneered in It, and Created Great Classical Civilizations; How They Were Plunged into a Dark Age by Invasion and Conquest, and How They Are Reviving* (1993). The preceding can be contrasted with the comprehensive anthropological study by Harold E. Driver, *Indians of North America* (2nd ed., rev., 1969), and T.D. Stewart, *The People of America* (1973). For two pathfinding environmental approaches, see William Cronon, *Changes in the Land: Indians, Colonists, and the Ecology of New England* (1983), and Carolyn Merchant, *Ecological Revolutions: Nature, Gender, and Science in New England* (1989). The connections between the natural world and Indian spirituality are effectively described in Calvin Martin, *Keepers of the Game: Indian-Animal Relations and the Fur Trade* (1978), Catherine L. Albanese, *Nature Religion in America: From the Algonkian Indians to the New Age* (1990), and the marvelous portrayal of a single New England tract of land in John Hanson Mitchell, *Ceremonial Time: Fifteen Thousand Years on One Square Mile* (1984). The connection between Indians, whites, and buffalo extermination is examined by Shedard Krech in "Ecology and the American Indian," in *Ideas from the National Humanities Center* 3, No. 1 (Summer 1994): pp. 4–22. These and other major issues are also addressed in Christopher Vecsey and Robert W. Venables (eds.), *Ecological Issues in Native American History* (1980), and by Richard White, "Native Americans and the Environment," in *Scholars and the Indian Experience*, edited by W.R. Swagerty, pp. 179–204 (1984).

Environmental impacts are also part of three comprehensive studies, one by geographer Donald W. Meinig, *The Shaping of America: A Geographical Perspective on 500 Years of History, Vol. 1: Atlantic America, 1492–1800* (1986), another by social historian Daniel J. Boorstin, *The Discoverers: A History of Man's Search to Know His World and Himself* (1983), and the classic by the traditional historian Samuel Elliot Morison, *The European Discovery of America. The Northern Voyages, A.D. 500–1600* (1971). The French partnership with the Indians is depicted in W. J. Eccles's revisionist *The Canadian Frontier: 1534–1760* (1969), and the Spanish transplantation covered in John Francis Bannon's *The Spanish Borderlands Frontier, 1513–1821* (1970). See also the collection of essays in John J. TePaske's *Three American Empires* (1967). An excellent set of firsthand accounts is collected in John Bakeless, *America as Seen by Its First Explorers: The Eyes of Discovery* (1950). The first data-based study of environmental change since 1500 is Gorden G. Whitney's *From Coastal Wilderness to Fruited Plain* (1994). It focuses on the dynamics of the presettlement eastern forest, but also provides important coverage of the midwestern tallgrass prairie and the changes wrought by pre–Civil War agriculture. An overall environmental approach to world history, which gives a context to the Columbian Exchange although it does not specifically cover it, are in William H. McNeill's broad essays in two collections, *The Global Condition: Conquerors, Catastrophes, and Community* (1992) and *Mythistory and Other Essays* (1986). McNeill also summarizes the important environmental framework offered by the French historian Fernand Braudel in his magisterial multivolume works on the Mediterranean and on early modern capitalism. See also George Gaylord Simpson, *The Geography of Evolution* (1965). For a critical and detailed look at the impact of technology on European expansion, see the underrated classic by William Woodruff, *Impact of Western Man: A Study of Europe's Role in the World Economy, 1750–1960* (1967).

Was the Discovery of America a Mistake?
An Eighteenth-Century Debate

One of the great and mostly forgotten controversies of the eighteenth century was whether the discovery of America was a mistake. That is, would humanity have been better, and happier, if the New World had never been discovered? A corollary was whether America itself was so badly flawed to be itself God's, or nature's, mistake. Critics argued that America's environment created thin and wan failures in its plants, animals, and people that could not compete with Europe's robust versions. Furthermore, after the discovery, something went fundamentally wrong and out of place in human affairs worldwide. The laws of nature that tidily governed the Old World seemed to be contradicted by the unbearably hot and cold lands of the New World, its terrifying natural forces, and its truly strange plants and animals. The known world prior to America could be organized and understood, but America remained puzzlingly different. It was unpredictable, abnormal, and sometimes downright perverse.

The Frenchman Guillaume-Thomas, Abbé de Raynal (1713–1796), an intellectual giant of the eighteenth century, philosopher and economist, churchman and social reformer, argued in the 1770s that Europeans' bad and vulgar habits went out of control when they entered the strange environs of America: fighting ceaseless wars, building empires on the bodies of captive native peoples, extending the blasphemous institution of slavery, and carrying disease to blot out the lives of innocent natives by the millions.* Raynal organized an essay contest to debate the subject, "Was America a Mistake?" He thought the New World was beyond improvement and remained primitive, chaotic, degenerate, and beyond hope. The American wilderness fostered native peoples who were malformed, feeble, and contemptible creatures: "Men who have little more hair than eunuchs cannot abound in generating principles. The blood of these people is watery and cold. The males have sometimes milk in their breasts. Hence arises their tardy inclination to the sex. Hence hath proceeded that want of population which hath always been observed in them." Apparently powerless before the striding Europeans, the natives were also spiritually impoverished.

Raynal reasoned that both Europeans and natives were better off before they chanced on each other. Europeans degenerated once they settled in the New World, a dramatic assertion of environmental determinism. Spain and Portugal built empires in the New World, and then went into decline. France and England could be next. It would have been better not only for Columbus to have returned empty-handed, but also for the Spanish conquistadores to have failed against the Aztecs and the Incas. Then there would not have been 20 million natives dead, whole regions emptied of people, wiping out great Aztec and Inca civilizations. In this argument, the Atlantic

(continued)

---

* Much later the same theme of Europeans going bad would appear in Joseph Conrad's novella *Heart of Darkness* and be the issue of the Vietnam War.

Ocean best served as a wall to guard the Old World from physical and spiritual infection. When it became an avenue of commerce, the critics complained all of Europe became infected by addictive and enervating substances: tobacco, coffee, and chocolate—not to mention syphillis. Raynal's gratuitous advice to degenerate Americans was not to seek genius and so never to be disappointed, "to know how to make themselves happy by economy and with mediocrity."

The greatest natural scientist of the eighteenth century, the Frenchman Georges-Louis Leclerc, Comte de Buffon (1707–1788), explained the backwardness of America by arguing it had emerged late from Noah's flood. Indeed, he noted, some of the waters were only now draining from wetlands. And because humans came late, the land had been barely improved by cultivation. Beneficial sunlight didn't break through the dense forests. Nature withdrew into itself, and life-forms were stunted. The native American lived a primitive scattered existence with no society or culture. Besides lacking sexual drive, "his sensations are less acute . . . he is more cowardly and timid. He has no vivacity, no activity of mind." Buffon argued that when America had been settled for several more centuries, the marshes drained, forests cleared, and land cultivated, it might be received into the company of the world's great civilizations. Until then America contained "weak" species, not only beardless Indians uninterested in procreation (hence their small population) but also lesser creatures than the horses, cattle, and pigs that Europeans had to import.

More malicious than Raynal or Buffon was Abbé de Pauw, an aggressive encyclopedist of the 1760s, who looked on America as so recent a creation from the primordial ooze that it was unfit for human habitation. Only lower sorts of crawling and dangerous things, like huge stinking toads and monstrous evil bats, spread themselves thinly over an immense and forbidding landscape. When America's humans descended from the high places where they had take refuge from the Flood, they tried to settle on "vast prairies still covered with slough and slime" where the dank air took away their natural powers. The least vigorous European is more than a match for the strongest American. The men were so hairless they didn't even have eyebrows. De Pauw argued that Europeans would fail to bring the benefits of Christian civilization to America. Europeans who had the misfortune to intermarry with native peoples, he noted, produced Creoles, who, however well educated, "have never produced a single book through the whole extent of America. From Cape Horn to Hudson's Bay, there has never appeared a philosopher, an artist, a man of learning, whose name has found a place in the history of science or whose talents have been of any use to others." At Harvard College, already 130 years old, de Pauw concluded that "the professors have not as yet produced a single scholar capable of adding anything whatever to the literature of the world." He said nothing about Yale or Princeton.

America had a few friends. The most authoritative European champion of America was the Marquis de Chastellux, soldier for the American Revolution, philosopher on taste and happiness, member of the Academy, and a cosmopolite. To him America was the most enviable of societies, both pastoral and sophisticated, symbolized in the sturdy independence of the American farmer. America's new resources and new markets stimulated the fundamental force of civilization: commerce, which now boomed to new heights. The aristocratic Marie-Jean-Antoine-Nicholas de Caritat, Marquis de Condorcet (1743–1794), was equally optimistic about progress toward a new democratic society in the New World. He made his mark as an economist and a humanitarian. His defense offered a typical geographical explanation of America's greatness: It enjoyed a vast extent of empty land, inexhaustible resources, and generations of happy farmers, living on the benevolent soil, who would bring betterment to the rest of the world by trading their products for the manufactures of Europe. "America will, in a few generations, double the progress of Mankind and make that progress doubly swift," he claimed. "That progress will embrace both the useful arts and the speculative sciences."

The New World had defenders among its citizens, too, of course. Thomas Jefferson, in Paris as representative of the new United States to France, collided sharply with Buffon over his statements about smaller and fewer animals in the New World. Jefferson had already written a long refutation of Buffon and Raynal in his *Notes on the State of Virginia* (1785). The New World's air and water, he said, provided better health and longer life to the European settlers than they would have found had they stayed home. In a remarkable statistic, the first settlers of Andover, Massachusetts, he claimed, lived on the average of 72 years before they died, or approximately double the normal life span of the day. This was possible because of improved diet with maize as a staple, and a higher standard of living that selected the best European resources.

A dinner party story that Thomas Jefferson told about Benjamin Franklin debunked the notion that transplanted Europeans tended to degenerate:

> The Doctor [Franklin] . . . had a party to dine with him one day at Passy [near Paris, France], of whom one half were Americans, the other half French, and among the last was the Abbé [Raynal]. During the dinner he got on his favorite theory of the degeneracy of animals, and even of man, in America, and urged it with his usual eloquence. The Doctor at length noticing the accidental stature and position of his guests, at table, "Come," says he, "M. l'Abbé, let us try this question by the fact before us. We are here one half Americans, and one half French, and it happens that the Americans have placed themselves on one side of the table, and our French friends are on the other. Let both parties rise, and we will see on which side nature has degenerated." It happened that his American guests were Carmichael, Harmer, Humphreys, and others of the finest stature and form, while those of the other side were remarkably diminutive, and the Abbé himself particularly, was a mere shrimp. He parried the appeal, however, by a complimentary admission of exceptions, among which the Doctor himself was a conspicuous one.

Franklin was not only pragmatic but also had a quick wit. The surprising part of the story is that Jefferson got it at all, since he never showed much of a sense of humor in all his earnestness.

Jefferson also confronted Raynal about the contributions of Americans to civilization. Give Americans as much time as the Greeks, he said, and they will produce a

(continued)

Homer, as much time as the Romans a Virgil, the French a Racine and Voltaire, and the English a Shakespeare and Milton. As to the natives, Jefferson wrote, "Monsieur Buffon has indeed given an afflicting picture of human nature in his description of the man of America. He might have admitted, that the Iroquois were larger, and the Lenopi, or Delawares, taller than people in Europe generally are. 'They have no ardor for their females.' It is true they do not indulge those excesses, nor discover that fondness which is customary in Europe; but this is not owning to a defect in nature but to manners." At Jefferson's request, the American general John Sullivan sent Buffon huge elk antlers from Maine larger than any in Europe. Jefferson sent Buffon skins of beaver, panther, and eagle, and he wrote of the giant elephant bones—mastodon remains—found in Hudson River cliffs, creatures who must still roam the mysterious inner continent. To Jefferson, America was a blessing to humanity; the New Man of the New World would advance to greater heights of civilization and happiness. Buffon showed his greatness by confessing his mistake to Jefferson and writing a revision to his classic natural history. Indeed, the higher humidity and heavier moisture in the New World, which Buffon claimed was the reason, actually produced more and better food, so "we see animals not only multiplied in their numbers, but improved in their bulk, as far as the laws of their nature will admit."

CHAPTER TWO

THE WORLD WE HAVE LOST: PEOPLE OF THE LAND

As much land as a man tills, plants, improves, cultivates, and can use the product of, so much is his property. He by his labor does, as it were, enclose it from the common.

—John Locke, 1690

Man lives on nature—[this] means that nature is his body, with which he must remain in continuous interchange if he is not to die. That man's physical and spiritual life is linked to nature means simply that nature is linked to itself, for man is part of nature. To say that man is a corporeal, living, real, sensuous, objective being full of natural vigor, is to say that he has real, sensuous, objects as objects of his life, or that he can only express his life in real, sensuous objects.

—Karl Marx, ca. 1850

After Europeans recognized that the New World was not the Indies, but a fresh geography, they began to advance on it with an expanded curiosity and hungry greed. Europeans were not interested in adapting to a surprising new world, but only in Europeanizing it as quickly as possible. The first signs of prosperity in the English colonies came not from industrialization, but from food production. Factory production amounted to less than 1 percent of

55

colonial economic growth between 1700 and the American Revolution. America's first environmental transformation reconstructed the landscape into the most productive farming in world history; industrialization would come later (see Chapters 4 and 7).

The Forgotten World of Farming

Today Few Americans Know What Was Once Common to All

Most immigrants held in common a knowledge of agriculture more than their religious motivation, social status, or even a desire for personal liberty. Each person—boy or girl, man or woman, white or native, slave or free—knew how to milk a cow, kill a chicken, or plant a field. The cycles of ordinary life were controlled by the demands of spring planting and fall harvesting. They watched for freezing cold and scorching heat and worried over muddy fields and diseased animals.

The United States was for more than half its history a nation of farmers. For most immigrants the main attraction was private ownership of 40 or more acres of good farmland, enough to make them self-sufficient with potential for a cash crop. In the context of world history, this was a rare opportunity for ordinary people. Such a scale of ownership of productive farmland was unprecedented. They put all their primary energies in manipulating and reshaping their immediate environment to make it familiar and supportive. Their first task was to survive; America promised these immigrants that they could also prosper. The 1810 census, 35 years after independence, identified 7 million Americans, of whom only about 6 percent lived in towns of over 5,000 inhabitants; 90 percent lived directly on their farms. Not until the beginning of the twentieth century did the census report that more than half of America had moved away from a life of plowing fields and milking cows. They became factory and office workers who lived in city apartments and, eventually, suburban ranch houses, although most remembered their farm origins. Later, in the blink of an eye between 1930 and 1960, the 30 percent still on the farm became a scant 3 percent. Today farm people make up less than 2 percent of the population—only 1 in 50 Americans, the lowest percentage in the world—and half of these work part time in off-farm jobs. This move away from the land involved a greater revolution than we have previously understood; it has separated virtually all Americans from the way most all other humans have lived—nestled within a local ecosystem—for the last 10,000 years.

Private ownership of farmland and productive food production became a dominant way of life across America's geography. Reliable food surpluses meant a victory over food scarcity for the first time in human history. This was revolutionary. The fear of food scarcity had shaped human consciousness since the dawn of history. The English economist Thomas Malthus had already raised the specter that humanity's population growth would eventually outstrip its global food resources. In the American colonies, and later the new United States, the combination of virgin soil, the skilled farmer, and new tools and machines created an unprecedented surge in food supplies. It had taken Europeans 2,500 years to build a durable agriculture on a supportive soil. In contrast, Americans went in a hectic 250 years between

1620 and 1870 from native American hunting and horticulture through the agricultural revolution and into the surplus revolution. Today it is claimed that each American farmer feeds 97 other people; in 1800 he produced enough food for 5 other people.

America's agricultural success story is so remarkable that its long-term negative costs have been largely ignored. Was individual farming, based on private property and market economics, the best way to channel the New World's soil and water? Even Thomas Jefferson wondered, for example, whether the nation's public lands ought to be rented or leased, not sold into private hands, and thus kept as a public treasure. Ecological stresses, such as depleted soil, would multiply under the demands of capitalism. This chapter tells the story of farming as it emerged as a dominant and long-standing national way of life. American society was for a long time uniquely and deeply tied to good soil in a temperate climate, of which it possessed more than any other people in the world. In Chapter 11, when we look at the Dust Bowl of the 1930s, we will also learn how the American way of farming, for all its benefits, went far in destroying an entire region.

The Agrarian Challenge of Early America

Despite the extraordinary victory over food scarcity that American abundance soon provided, at first farmers were not able to take full advantage of the New World's vast virgin soils. They were undertooled, undercapitalized, and short on labor-saving technologies. They also created a difficult burden when, unlike agrarian villagers around the world, they chose to live alone directly on their land and abandoned the age-old advantage of cooperative production.

Undertooled

The farm tools used on the frontier had not changed since the Middle Ages. The great nineteenth-century historian Henry Adams wrote of the primitive conditions: "The plough was rude and clumsy; the sickle as old as Tubal Cain, and even the cradle not in general use; the flail was unchanged since the Aryan exodus; in Virginia grain was still commonly trodden out by horses." Methods were ancient. Farmers were still broadcasting (scattering by hand) seeds and harvesting grain by hand. Thus the frontiersman lived an "undertooled" existence. The frontier farmer's technology did not suit his needs, and it was prone to partial or total failure. A broken metal plow tip or a split rifle barrel brought everything to a halt. He might have to plow with a wooden tip or trap wild animals to carry him through a winter. He had no easy way to pull tree stumps or carry his surplus bushels of wheat to market. Adams reminds us the immigrant farmer "worked harder and suffered greater discomforts" than back in Surrey or Devonshire:

> The climate was trying; fever was common; the crops ran new risks from strange insects, drought, and violent weather; the weeds were annoying; the flies and mosquitoes tormented him and his

cattle; laborers were scarce and indifferent; the slow and magisterial ways of England, where everything was made easy, must be exchanged for quick and energetic action; the farmer's own eye must see to every detail, his own hand must hold the plow and the scythe. Life was more exacting, and every such man in America was required to do, and actually did, the work of two such men in Europe.

Pioneer farm people tried to compensate by hard physical work under dangerous conditions. Frontier farmers lived under what behavioral psychologists today would call high-risk conditions as they wavered between survival and failure. Their life was hazardous because wilderness circumstances meant difficult situations happened more frequently and tested their peak abilities constantly. When one faced one crisis after another on a daily basis, the inevitable failures took their toll. Coping with an unknown, dangerous, and hostile environment, life for the American farmer involved more difficult work, more critical decisions, and more uncontrollable factors than in long-settled regions.

Undercapitalized

The pioneer farmer also lacked capital to fully exploit his opportunities. A farmer was lucky if he arrived at a wilderness site with the physical resources of a cow, a few pigs, "indifferent horses" or tired oxen, a few hand tools, and a supply of seed corn, flour, and cider. In 1789 the aristocratic French traveler Chastellux estimated that the average pioneer farmer began with about $125 in hard-earned cash, most of which he used to make a small down payment on 40 acres. Free land, or even cheap land, was a myth. If the farmer kept his health, worked continuously, and was a skilled axeman, carpenter, blacksmith, and husbandman, he might carry himself along for three years on $500, including payments on the land. By then he might have cleared and planted 20 acres. To overcome problems of bad health or low skill or simple bad luck, he would need an unthinkable $1,000. If any cash became available it would usually go for a down payment for more land (the interest rate was 12 to 20 percent) to enlarge the farm. The occasional luckier farmer who had cash in his mattress could hire "set-up men" for 50 cents a day (typical minimum wage for unskilled labor) to do the heaviest clearing. Basic materials that he could not produce—salt, iron, sugar—remained scarce and relatively costly. Adams writes, "The money for which he sold his wheat and chickens was of the Old World; he reckoned in shillings or pistareens, and rarely handled an American coin more valuable than a larger copper cent." Since capital was "scarce as hen's teeth," the American farmer lived mostly in a self-sufficient barter economy. In the early 1780s South Carolina farmers paid their state tax in indigo, and the state government was grateful to receive it.

Labor Intensive

Agriculture was still based on traditional European hand-tool dirt farming. The clearing and working of land depended on muscle power, skill at all basic agricultural activities, and seven simple tools, most of which had not changed substantially since the dawn of agriculture: axe, grubbing hoe, spade, rake, sheath knife, wedge, and mallet. The ever-present rifle was actually a recently introduced device, and many new immigrants wasted ammunition through inexperience. The technological revolution with its labor-saving and efficient mechanical equipment would come later. Nevertheless, small technical changes offered small incremental improvements: Grain was better harvested with the sweeping motion of the scythe instead of the short cuts of a hand sickle. More efficient was the newfangled cradle, which was a scythe fastened to a lightweight wooden frame that laid the stalks in regular rows. Plows began to have metal edging and were now sometimes pulled by stronger, quicker horses instead of slow oxen. But roads, grinding mills, and metalworking were as primitive as in Roman times. All materials were natural, from tanned leather to woven cloth. All energy came from animal and human muscle, water and wind power, and wood fires. The labor force was the entire farm family (and an occasional unreliable hired hand). Too often the family lacked draft animals and the husband pulled the plow, which the wife guided. Children were expected early to do the milking, haying, plowing, planting, and harvesting.

Autonomous Homestead and the Psychology of Isolation

The frontier farm family labored through its days and nights in intense isolation on a lonely separate site, distant from neighbors. The French naturalist André Michaux remembers in 1803 the excited hospitality of isolated Kentucky farm families as he gathered exotic plants on the southern and western frontiers. They had seen no one else in months, and then only if their farm was near a road or path or river. One Ohio farmer told the English traveler Frances Trollope in 1828, "'Tis strange to us to see company in a partial clearing in the very heart of the forest. I expect the sun may rise and set a hundred times before I shall see another human that does not belong to the family." These settler clearings seemed scattered at random, far from neighbors, further hidden across northern Ohio flatlands by widespread swampiness and impassable roads. Despite this isolation, Americans have historically taken for granted that the best approach to frontier farming was the distinctive separate family homestead. The lonely homestead stands in pointed contrast to the rural village communities based on feudalism in Europe and tribal or ethnic relationships in Africa and Asia. New England folk started out in compact farming villages and half of the South on plantation communities, but the first farmers to move westward into the Appalachians and the Midwest found they lived where they could not see their nearest neighbor's house or at night the faint glow of candles from a neighbor's windows. "We have no villages in America," said Albert Gallatin, Jefferson's secretary of the treasury. This unusual isolation came from the necessity of living on the cleared land to protect it from squatters and hold it for private ownership. The obvious advantages of community property—cooperative labor, safety against enemies, support in hard times—was lost to settlers who demanded private title to land. More often than not the farmer and his family were literally off the map, having settled on land that had not been explored, mapped, or surveyed. They were compelled to live independently, untouched by major events, many of them not profoundly affected by the American Revolution or the War of 1812. In a real sense they were historyless, their existence based on nature's cycles. Folks feared for themselves and the conditions of their souls in an unearthly environment that seemed filled with the "silence of God." The strangeness of the wilderness led some frontiersfolk to believe they lived in the absence of God. No wonder frontier accounts tell of the madness of wives and the violence of husbands. The strongest sense of security may have been the farmer's psychological bond with his tract of land.

Early Rural America: The Passing of the Frontier

Even as farmers advanced from risky frontier subsistence to a more substantial rural life, farm life remained local, tied to the individual farmstead and the nearby town. Life was controlled by bad roads, the restricted loads that sleighs or oxcarts might bear, and unpredictable weather. The maximum distance a loaded wagon behind two horses could travel in one day on a bumpy road was a round trip of 14 miles. Travel was determined by the weather and the seasons. Winter months were too cold for safe travel and the spring and fall rains turned roads into quagmires. If an inland town, for example in New England, was more than 25 miles from a port or a navigable river, it remained isolated from commercial markets. The farmer who got his corn to town had it ground at the local mill and converted some of it into whiskey at the local distillery. At the country store he bartered potash, cordwood, livestock, vegetables, furs, skins, even feathers and beeswax for what food, fuel, clothing, and tools he did not make: tea, coffee, salt, ammunition, hardware, pottery, tableware, and drygoods. The stores were remarkable institutions. One traveler in 1806 noted that a western Pennsylvania store carried "both a needle and an anchor, a tin pot and a large copper boiler, a child's whistle and a pianoforte, a ring dial and clock, a skein of thread and trimmings of lace, a check frock and a muslin gown, a frieze coat and a superfine cloth, a glass of whiskey and barrel of brandy, a gill of vinegar and a hogshead of Madeira wine." Where the country store was too distant, the farm family looked forward to the peddler, who carried small goods—tinware, scissors, pins and needles, buttons and ribbons, cheap shoes and cotton goods, even children's books. Hundreds of these itinerants worked the countryside, traveling up to 25 miles a day.

Nevertheless, for the common man and woman, farming in America marked a dramatic advance beyond Britain and Europe in satisfying basic material needs and building confidence in the future. The acquisition and development of fertile land became attainable; one could invest one's life in such a goal. Limited markets, lack of capital, labor-intensive farming, and poor transportation held farmers to a subsistence level, but this was a significant achievement compared to a European peasantry. As early as 1790 farmers in the famous Kentucky bluegrass country sent animals eastward long distances along "the Kaintuck Hawg Road," better known as Daniel Boone's Wilderness Road. A 150-pound hog might gain weight on the way but a steer weighing 900 pounds would lose 100 pounds on a long drive. Fresh meat was sold in city markets or cured into salt meat for sailors or exported. More fortunate frontier farmers could float grain, lumber, and flour, as well as whiskey and pork, down the Ohio River, meet the Mississippi, and be carried to Natchez for the plantation trade or to New Orleans for foreign or eastern markets. Some lucky farmers grew tobacco in the Old South, because it could be cured, packed into large 1,400-pound hogsheads, and shipped by wagon or small boat to Richmond for export. The hogsheads could even be rolled to market towns. By 1800 many American farmers set themselves on a commercial track, growing wheat to be milled into flour and baked into bread, raising livestock to be driven to city slaughterhouses, and growing broomcorn for brooms. Hundreds of thousands of farmers would advance beyond subsistence by connecting themselves to the wider market economy by producing grain, rice, tobacco, and indigo specifically from sale.

The unusual combination of prosperity and isolation in early American agriculture may have forced political democracy on the European settlers. Political fragmentation and pluralism emerged out of the spatial and psychological autonomy that began to characterize the geography of the English colonies. Geographical expansion westward were rarely organized moves by entire communities, but instead depended on individual initiative, which in turn encouraged scattered settlement. The old sense of community was lost, to be replaced not by another community, but by near-anarchic democracy. In addition, without domination by the rigid social and economic structures of either feudalism or centralized authority, mercantile power became the primary network or infrastructure spread like a net across the agricultural society. The colonies may have been varied in their religion, society, and politics, but they had a common participation in a rural economy based on agricultural abundance. The grand dimensions of American space, and its uniquely dispersed settlement by enterprising Europeans, may go far to explain American history. The role of commerce and cities is explored in Chapter 13.

Constructing Useful Farmland Out of Wilderness

From a Forest Environment to a Familiar Landscape

In 1785 the French observer Hector St. John de Crèvecoeur reported that settlers believed the domestication of a forest into a farmland was a good deed: It conquered wild nature and thus reduced the domain of evil forces. Decent settlers transformed "hitherto barbarous country" into a "fine, fertile, and well-regulated district." When many settlers spoke of America as the new Garden of Eden, they meant not the raw wilderness, but the human-made garden carved out of the forest. Had not John Locke said that a piece of raw land, once it receives human labor, becomes the property of the laborer? In their mind's eye, early settlers looked beyond their isolated farmsteads and saw an idealized replication of English country life: a rustic village, where a cluster of houses formed its own ordered world, a village common, orchards and vegetable plots close by, grain fields in a ring, hay fields beyond, and outlying pastures extending into a dark forest wilderness. Home was in the clearing, not deep in the woods. Farmers in New England believed they could identify stages of transition from wilderness to "made land." They distinguished between "wastes" (untouched wilderness, barren rocks, and swamps), "unbroken" (fields surveyed and titled, but unfenced and untouched by plows), "broken" (plowed land but unplanted), and "improved" or "dressed" land (planted and often fenced). Frederick Jackson Turner claimed in his famous 1893 "frontier thesis" that such stages of the transition from wilderness to settlement explained American history. From this vantage point, the story of America was a simple tale of progressive achievements that together built a superior human society. Andrew Jackson voiced this rural paradise in his second inaugural address in 1833: "What good man would prefer a country covered with forests, and ranged by a few thousand savages to our extensive Republic, studded with cities, towns, and prosperous farms, embellished with all the improvements which art can devise of industry execute, occupied by more than 12,000,000 happy people, and filled with all the blessings of liberty, civilization, and religion." Thirty years later, this process was made the law of the land by passage of the famous Homestead Act that Abraham Lincoln signed in 1862. It offered 160 acres of land free for those who "improved" the land and lived on it. Such expansion was judged necessary and inevitable, a physical demonstration of citizen participation in Manifest Destiny, at first symbolized by clearing away the trees.

THE AMERICAN FRONTIER went through predictable "stages" of development. When the great French essayist Alexis de Tocqueville visited frontier regions in 1836, he reported that he could find "the history of the whole of humanity framed within a few degrees of longitude."

Orasmus Turner's 1849 "Four sketches and descriptions of the pioneer in Western New York frontier lands"

The First Six Months (Orasmus Turner, *A Pioneer History of the Holland Purchase of Western New York*).

The Second Year (Turner, *Pioneer History of the Holland Purchase*).

Ten Years Later (Turner, *Pioneer History of the Holland Purchase*).

The Work of a Lifetime (Turner, *Pioneer History of the Holland Purchase*).

Clearing the Land

How different was the real experience? Forest clearing was hard labor with inadequate tools and did not lend itself to sentimental feelings about wilderness. One frontier traveler complained that Americans "have an unconquerable aversion to trees; and whenever a settlement is made, they cut away all before them without mercy. To them the sight of a wheat field or a cabbage garden would convey pleasure far greater than that of the most romantic woodland views." The problem of initial clearing was so great that Plymouth Colony itself had been established in 1620 on an open Indian field, a pattern often repeated in New England. The first Dutch settlers in 1646 in the lower Hudson River valley deliberately searched out deserted Indian clearings to grow wheat and oats, as did pioneers in the wilds of New Jersey and Pennsylvania. Europeans also learned from the Indians that they might survive by first planting quick-maturing crops like squash, pumpkins, corn, and beans, grown easily in small mounds or wherever a small patch of roughly cleared ground could be found. In most cases, there was no convenient clearing.

Newly arrived settlers with no time to spare before facing cold weather might attack the forest by cutting away the undergrowth and digging out small trees to clear enough land for a food plot. People depended on the surrounding woods so extensively for game, berries, and nuts that frontier farming should be seen as a combination of primitive hunter-gathering and agriculture. Only later, during the slow winter season, when a settler was not frantically planting and cultivating his small patches of corn and vegetables, would he attempt to cut down larger trees and dig out their roots for a cleaner field to plow the soil and sow the grain. This was attempted with a few tools and often without draft animals. As early as the 1630s, John Smith in Virginia told pioneers that girdling trees was easier and effective—"a notch in the bark a hand broad about the tree and the tree will sprout no more." Then the farmer could pile cleared shrubs and small trees around the tree and burn the lot. He quickly learned that the burn spot would be too potash rich and force his critical first crop of corn to grow too tall with tiny ears. Otherwise, corn virtually grew itself for immediate food for family and livestock, whereas European wheat, barley, rye, or oats needed to be planted in rows and receive disciplined cultivation. A tree-free clearing might not appear for two years or more because clear-cutting was so demanding that it was done only where open land was needed for houses, orchards, or roadways. Stumps were usually left to rot for five to ten years before the remains were hand-levered out or pulled out chained to oxen. Farmers simply planted their maize or potatoes in the open spaces between stumps. The result was often a scrubby collection of fields for corn, hay, and pasture.

The move toward permanence—the shift from a frontier to a rural economy—remained a critical next step. Having built a rude cabin for the family and a shed for the animals, most farmers were pleased if they cleared as much as 5 acres in the first year. A skilled and energetic woodsman, working full time with his family, might axe an acre a week even where the trees were large and dense. Three to four weeks per acre was more typical. It might take another three weeks of full-time labor, with the help of neighbors, to pull the stumps from a single acre. Simultaneously the farmer would also be busy improving the crude log house, outbuildings, and the all-important fences to protect his crops. He would also be building beds, tables, chairs, and storage chests. He cut tens of cords of wood for fuel and hoarded provisions for the winter. In time he dug a shallow well and joined his neighbors to clear and level a road to the river or market town. By the second year, 8 to 10 acres were more or less open, to be planted again in corn or at best half corn and vegetables, and half wheat for some cash. Within three to five years an energetic family might be settled on 80 acres, half cleared at best. Most families could support themselves on as little as 25 acres, but needed 100 acres to prosper. The transition into a post-frontier Middle American rural farm took at least ten years.

Pioneering European settlers began to create continuous openings to break up the forest for permanent and stable settlement. The English traveler Andrew Burnaby was impressed that half of his 100-mile trip in 1759 between Annapolis to Philadelphia went through large stretches of cleared country. The enthusiastic French traveler, the Marquis de Chastellux, in 1789 saw hundreds of energetic settlers each erecting a house and barn and fences in a new clearing: "I have never traveled three miles without meeting a new settlement either beginning to take form or already in cultivation." Another Englishman, Henry Tudor, as he crossed upstate New York in the early 1830s, saw "literally a new creation only to be witnessed in America," since Europe had for centuries been a landscape built by human hands. But he found the result ugly and depressing, a landscape of deadened forests that "offered to the eye an aspect of desolation, that excited rather a painful and melancholy feeling. [Girdling was] a wanton mode of destroying the tree by cutting its throat." Pioneer farmers faced the difficult challenge to clear away trees until about 1840, when westward movement finally reached the open midwestern prairie at roughly today's Indiana-Illinois state line. By 1850 almost 114 million acres of land had been "improved" in the United States, mostly carved out of the eastern forests during two centuries of pioneering. Despite Tudor's complaint, the result was widely acclaimed as a victory over the forest, the successful outcome of a continuous warfare by which civilization would prevail against forces of barbaric chaos and evil.

Wood and Waste

In this widespread ecological shift from Indian forest culture to European-style farms, few Americans showed any early environmental concern. William Cronon writes, "Colonial farmers treated their land as a resource to be mined until it was exhausted, rather than one to be conserved for less intense but more perennial use." Ironically, as more land was opened to crops or pasture, woodlots became scarce and their cash value went up because of the demand for wood for heating, building, and fencing, as well as forage for pigs. Individual woodlots ran from 10 to 20 acres, a size that allowed for a workable 45-year rotation in northern and central climate between cutting old growth and growing new trees. But a series of cold winters that burned more fuel or the unanticipated replacement of rotted fences could press hard on the individual farmer and his woodlot. Wood for fuel far exceeded any other consumption of the eastern forest. Most wood, even cherry hardwoods, were piled up and burned or cast off after clearing land or building a cabin or a fence. A skilled axman could cut, split, and stack more than a cord of wood a day (4 x 4 x 8 feet). But in one winter season he might consume 20 or 30 cords and cut down 10 to 20 acres of woodland to keep one fire burning in the inefficient and cavernous fireplaces of the day.

By 1850 Connecticut and Rhode Island had consumed 70 percent of their forests; Massachusetts, 60 percent; Vermont, 55 percent; New Hampshire, 50 percent; and Maine, 25 percent. Log cabin construction used wood extravagantly, as did the zigzag "Virginia fences" on the frontier. The gradual switch to wood-burning stoves instead of drafty fireplaces offered a real saving in wood and labor. Later, coal fires and brick houses reduced the demand for wood. As early as 1818 President James Madison warned that "the injurious and excessive destruction of timber and firewood" threatened rural America. Some of this indifference is understandable. Americans developed the bad habit of intensive forest cutting and soil exploitation to compensate for severe shortages of labor and capital. Trees and soil were part of a "free" commons, available to all. Americans worried little about sustainability on the land because the American landscape seemed to constantly enlarge as the new nation acquired territory from France, Britain, and Mexico. Farmland became a version of endless venture capital that could be readily risked. Cronon adds, "The Americans' tendency to farm overlarge tracts of land, their 'rage for commerce,' their investment of little capital in their farmlands, and their wasteful practices in feeding livestock brought permanent damage to the landscape."

Animal Management

Besides reshaping the land, farming also involved the management of horses, cows, sheep, pigs, chickens, ducks, and geese. Settlers brought these livestock and barnyard animals from England on the first ships. Sheep were imported for their wool and meat, but they were the most vulnerable to frontier threats like wolves and frigid weather. Pigs, cattle, and horses quickly learned to adapt, and when let loose often reverted to the wild as feral animals. Even the varieties of trees changed as grazing drove out oaks and white pines and allowed increased numbers of red cedars and hemlocks. Large animals not only ate their way through field and forest, but they mangled the ground, compacted the soil, and lowered its nutrients and ability to hold water. A major difference between Indian and European farming was this management of large animals—cattle, pigs, and horses—including herding them in fields and pastures, harnessing them to pull plows and carry loads, and consuming them for milk and meat. Oxen were the strongest creatures to pull a plow through rocky hilly soil. In turn, the plow allowed the spread of intensive single-crop farming. Plowing may be the single most important step of environmental change beyond what the Indians could do. Second was the introduction of English grasses to pasture large animals: blue grass, rye grass, bents, and red and white clover. Open places that had been deer browse were turned into concentrated animal pasture. New England's environment, for example, was so transformed that the Indians' traditional interaction with their geography became impossible.

Cattle

Three heifers and a bull arrived at Plymouth Colony in 1624, and the wealthier Massachusetts Bay Colony began regular imports in the 1630s. To the south, already 100 cattle were unloaded at Jamestown in 1611, and with more arrivals and natural increase Virginia may have had herds totaling 30,000 by 1639. The animals were of mixed breeds and small, less than 350 pounds in most cases. Cattle provided proteins in milk, cheese and butter, and meat as well as hides for leather goods. Ownership of large numbers of domestic animals symbolized wealth and abundance in Massachusetts Bay as early as 1634. One astonished visitor wrote, "Can Americans be very poor, where for four thousand souls there are fifteen hundred head of cattle, besides four thousand goats and swine innumerable?" Cattle often pulled plows and wagons. They foraged in the fields and woods of the countryside, as well as salt and fresh-water marshes. In the winter, cattle were kept in small one-story barns and fed cornhusks, cornstalks, and marsh-grass hay. In many seasons they were half starved and scrawny until the introduction of European forage, such as red clover and rye. The great advantage of cattle was that they could walk to market. By 1650 large herds from Lynn, Watertown, and Roxbury were marketed in Boston. Cattle drives took herds into downtown Boston and Philadelphia well into the nineteenth century.

Pigs

Porkers especially prospered in the New World. Alfred Crosby writes, "Once ashore in America [the pig] became a fast, tough, lean, self-sufficient greyhound of a hog much closer in appearance and personality to a wild boar than to one of our twentieth-century hogs." Settlers clipped their ears to identify ownership, turned their pigs loose into the woods, and hoped to capture and slaughter the fatted animals later. Salt pork, ham, and bacon were national staples before refrigeration. With the fat from the hogs, frontiersfolk could deep-fry doughnuts and crullers for a welcome change in their diet. William Cronon reports that swine became "the weed creatures of New England, breeding so quickly that a sow might farrow three times in a year, with each litter containing twelve to sixteen piglets." They multiplied so rapidly that swine laws allowed open hunting season to keep them under control. Turned loose in the American eastern forest, these omnivorous beasts quickly multiplied as they learned to forage on acorns, chestnuts, walnuts, persimmons, apples, berries, young shoots and roots known as "mast," and occasionally, unwary small animals. Fast, aggressive, and hungry, the wilderness pig was something to be avoided on the trail. The Massachusetts Court in 1658 warned that "many children are exposed to great dangers of loss of life or limb through the ravenousness of swine, and elder persons to no small inconveniences." Swine were also able to hold their own against bears and wolves. Cronon concludes, "Pigs thus became both the agents and the emblems for a European colonialism that was systematically reorganizing Indian ecological

HISTORIAN LOUIS B. WRIGHT wrote of pigs on the frontier,

The coming of cold weather meant hog-killing time, with additional work for everyone—men, women, and children. Fat porkers were rounded up, knocked on the head with an ax, and their throats cut. They were dipped in a barrel of boiling water to loosen bristles so they could be scraped clean. Then the white carcass was hung from a limb, gutted, and the edible parts (almost everything) saved. Liver, lungs (called lights), kidneys, and brains were highly prized. The small intestines were emptied, scraped, washed, and saved to be used for stuffed sausage. Some intestines were cleaned and eaten as chitterlings. Fat was placed in pots over a fire to try out (render) the lard. The residue from the fatty pieces, called cracklings, made shortening for cornbread. Lean trimmings were ground into sausage. Spareribs and backbone, regarded as especially tasty fresh meat, were eaten first. Shoulders, hams, and sides were put down in salt to season awhile before final curing in the smokehouse. All this preparation required immense labor, but a supply of pork products served as the main meat diet of most farm families, since far more pork was consumed than beef.

relationships." The Indians had never seen anything like them. Pigs actually competed with the Indians for food, including oyster banks and other Indian shellfish gathering grounds.

Plants

Europeans extensively farmed two New World plants, corn and tobacco, in ways that had major environmental impacts. Tobacco as a single-crop plant was particularly destructive. Corn was so useful to Europeans that they shifted its planting from an Indian polyculture combination with beans and squash into high-yield monoculture. Back in the Old World farmers had planted wheat or rye that alternated with barley or oats or nitrogen-fixing legumes (peas or beans) on manured fields that lay fallow half the time for recovery. The result was a durable environmental balance that had lasted almost a thousand years. The same was not often true for European farms in the New World.

The list of European imported plants is long and impressive. European grain crops included rye, barley, oats, and wheat. Root crops and vegetables included carrots, red beets, radishes, turnips, peas, cabbage, lettuce, garden beans, cucumbers, and naked oats. Garden herbs were sorrel, parsley, marigold, French mallow, chervil, burnet, winter and summer savory, thyme, sage, spearmint, fetherfew, coriander, and dill. Flowers and garden plants included ground ivy, houseleek, hollyhock, garden sorrel, impatience, English roses, and tansy. Unfortunately, Old World weeds, including dandelions, thistles, nettles, nightshade, ironwort, and henbane, came with the new plants. One needs only to observe how these grasses and weeds dominate America's meadows and fields today to understand the dramatic ecological transformation that ensued.

Tobacco in the South

Tobacco does not build soil; instead, it consumes the nutrients of the soil at an unusually broad scale and heavy rate. Europeans first learned from the Indians that tobacco leaves, once dried into a powder, burned a medicinal smoke that supposedly cleared up phlegm and "other gross humors." It soon became a "poor man's luxury" sought by all classes in England. The tobacco business boomed with enormous profits. Like corn, tobacco could be grown in almost any soil, even on second-rate hills, and in barely cleared fields between trees, stumps, and wood trash. It spread quickly from Virginia as new colonies rose in Maryland and North Carolina. However, colonial planters soon discovered that a farm dedicated to tobacco production is a farm whose soil quickly becomes toxic. The land is exhausted and the farm abandoned even before stumps would be rotted out. With luck, three or four crops of tobacco might be followed by a few seasons of corn or wheat before the land entirely gave out. It turned to weeds and eventually reverted to the pine forest it once had been. The entire cycle might take only 20 years. This was intensive farming, a damaging process that many southern farmers admitted was "a scourging tillage." Jefferson was not alone when he said of his own farm in Virginia, "We can buy an acre of new land cheaper than we can manure an old one." Most tobacco farmers did exactly that, and moved inland to fresh untouched soil. Most planters admitted that this was not stewardship, but gross exploitation that wore down the southern coastal land. The cycle was repeated in the backcountry. But, as long as tobacco was treated as a commodity on the marketplace and not a crop that would protect the farm's future, it was the crop of choice because it yielded six times more profit than any other crop. This exploitation was cynically called "the Virginia mode of cultivation."

Corn Everywhere, but Especially on the Frontier

For hundreds of years the Indians depended on their combined field of corn, beans, and squash (three-plant polyculture). This, they had learned, maintained soil quality at superior and long-lasting levels. It is not surprising that corn was sacred to the Indians, its origin tied to a legend involving the dragging of a woman's body over the fields. Planting time was set by the disappearance over the horizon of a cluster of stars known to Europeans as the Pleiades, by spring runs of alewives up the rivers, and by the springtime appearance of the leaves on the white oak "to the size of a mouse's ear." Native women planted four grains of corn and two pole bean seeds in hand-shaped individual soil mounds, 360 to an acre, and between these hills would go the squash and pumpkins. Such cultivation mimicked natural ecological polyculture patterns, together with periodic burning of the fields that produced ash as a natural fertilizer. The harvests of about 18 bushels per acre must have been colorful; in Carolyn Merchant's words, "Corn was black, red, yellow, blue, and white, speckled and striped. Bush and pole beans were red, white, yellow, and blue. Crane and crooknecked squash and pumpkins appeared in several colors and varieties as well." Fresh corn and beans produced a succotash—an excellent mixed protein—seasoned with fish, ground nuts, and Jerusalem artichokes. But, as southern environmental historian Timothy Silver observed, corn is the most soil-depleting crop of all the major grains. It is a large plant, its thick stem and big leaves reaching up to 10 feet. It has a large spreading root and must be far more widely spaced than other grains. Corn took almost as heavy a toll of soil as tobacco, but at least provided food instead of a smoke. This was recognized relatively early. In 1775 one writer worried, "Maize is a very exhausting crop; scarce any thing exhausts the land more." Under monoculture planting, the soil yielded less after two years and gave up the ghost in six years. Farmers eventually learned to extend corn production through crop rotation and to fertilize using ashes (potash) and cow manure.

The first crop of corn often made the difference for pioneer survival. When in the late summer of 1789 an early frost along the Ohio valley ruined the young corn crop, it meant a long hungry winter for settlers. Frontier dependence on corn cannot be overstated. It could be grown almost anywhere, with little tending, on partially cleared land and even in sandy soil. Corn did not shatter when it ripened, so harvesting could wait until autumn after the other crops were gathered. It did not need threshing like wheat, barley, or oats, nor did it have to be ground up at a water mill often distant from the isolated frontier farm clearing. White settlers sometimes used a hand mill made of two small millstones, the top with a center hole into which the corn was poured. The grain could also be pounded into cornmeal with a simple mortar and pestle. It could also be cooked and eaten on the cob. Pioneers on the primitive frontier ate a carbohydrate-rich soupy milk-and-corn mush out of a big bowl at every meal, dipping cups or even their hands. Corn mush could be alternated with corn boiled with meat and beans, or made into hominy and johnnycakes. On a more settled table, corn mush or cornbread remained a staple with salt pork or venison or squirrel meat. The diet also included turnips, pickles, peach preserves, wild nuts, and molasses made from pumpkins. Roasted or burnt corn could also be mixed with water and courageously drunk as a substitute for coffee. Most settlers, except teetotalling Baptists and Methodists, believed that a better use was a quick and rough whiskey made from corn.

Farming Was Not Enough for Europeans: Property, Ownership, Sovereignty

Native Americans could show a grim, sardonic humor. In the 1780s European settlers killed by the Indians were sometimes found with their mouths stuffed with dirt because they always wanted land. Native peoples found incomprehensible the European passion for private ownership of land. Along most of the Atlantic coastline, the mobile Indians sought free access to land to find game or new farm fields. Their "property" was no more than what they carried— their clothing, fishing gear, wooden, stone and shell tools, and baskets for corn, beans, and smoked meat. Europeans thus believed that the natives lived in foolish poverty like English beggars amid the plenty of the New World. The Puritan leader Francis Higginson concluded that the natives squandered their opportunities for wealth and civilization because they "are not able to make use of the one fourth part of the land, neither have they any settled places, as towns to dwell in, nor any ground as they challenge for their own possession." Thus for Europeans, Indian land was a no-man's-land until an English government assumed jurisdiction to insert it into a European scheme of things. In 1633, for example, Massachusetts Bay's Jonathan Winthrop asserted that most land in America was *vacuum domicilium*—legally "waste"—because the Indians had not cleared, cultivated, or settled it as defined by English law. Virginians, for example, did not get property from the natives; they got it from the Virginia Company. The Indians expressed surprise that anyone could claim the land, which was sacred, and use it for their personal and permanent property. They found it difficult to believe that "fair purchase" of land extinguished their ineffable right to hunt or farm.

The settlement of North America came at a time when land in the British Isles and western Europe (France, the Netherlands, Spain, Sweden, the Germanies) was in the midst of a long transition from the open fields surrounding the medieval manor—ownership by a local nobleman with farmers as his tenants—to the individual ownership of free-standing farm tracts. This involved a revolutionary switch to sole control in single parcels of farmland. In this context, America's "empty" land was an extraordinarily tempting opportunity to extend the new system of individual ownership. The English philosopher John Locke, in his 1690 *Second Treatise on Government*, reinforced Old World attitudes when he argued that the right to property is based on labor. English settlers thus felt themselves justified (and were authorized by local governments) to take sole possession of any land they could "improve" by their labor, whereas the natives were too lazy, "so as they had rather starve than work." If natives left the land underused, they abandoned their right to it, even for hunting and gathering. Improved land was defined as land that was fenced, planted with crops, and pastured for cattle and horses. Cronon concludes, "Colonists thus rationalized their conquest of New England. By refusing to extend the rights of property to the Indians, they both trivialized the ecology of Indian life and paved the way for destroying it." Sir William Samuel Johnson in the 1770s added, "This notion of their being free states is perfectly ridiculous and absurd. Without policy, laws, etc. there can be no such thing as a State. The Indians had neither in any proper sense of the words." Americans institutionalized this alienation of Native Americans in 1823, when Chief Justice John Marshall, in *Johnson and Graham's Lessee* v. *William McIntosh*, concluded that the rule of law was not applicable to people who were warlike and lived in the forest. They existed outside the codes of both morality and law. The logic, said modern historian Francis Jennings, was simple, compelling, and faulty.

As a result, when Europeans indulged their passion for territorial ownership, the opportunity was permanently lost for creative alternatives of land division and disposal. European territoriality confused and frustrated the Indians. Thomas Morton and Roger Williams, both outcasts from the Puritans for their radical utopian views, were among the few to question Lockean property rights. Wasn't the land's natural abundance on which the natives feasted a truer form of wealth because it liberated the spirit? The Indians followed more complex rules. They attached different values and rights that distinguished between unimproved hunting land, improved hunting sites (with game fences, traps, pitfalls, etc.), fishing sites, wild-plant-gathering tracts, and farm plots. Indian hunters worked in well-defined territories in which they claimed varieties of land use rights: trap lines, subsistence huntings, fishing locations, weirs, and shellfish beds. There were "best places" for snaring and trapping land animals, and for gathering roots and berries. Indians burned away the underbrush to maintain large parks for hunting, thus turning a common wilderness into a managed hunting ground. Indeed, after contact with Europeans, some Indians came to speak of deer as their version of sheep. Kinship relations among the Indians was the context for such land "ownership." Among some eastern tribes, cultivated land was parceled out to households led by women. On the northwest coast, title to a fishing weir was inherited by the eldest son. On the wide-open midcontinent plains and prairie, hunting territory was managed by the entire band or tribe. Kinship played down individualism and private property; such concepts were incomprehensible to most Indians (and to most peoples worldwide other than Europeans). Instead, kinship fostered a strong sense of community among small groups. It offered a collective understanding of land tenure. It was reinforced by a rich ceremonial life of mutuality and community best reflected in the potlatches of tribes of the Pacific Northwest. Eastern tribes like the Powhatan and Iroquois divided hunting land and fishing sites by kinship groups. There was no distinction between communal property, family property, and personal property. "Sale" of a tract of land in the Indian's mind meant the admission of the white man to a sachem's (medicine man) authority within the area specified, not its transfer as private property. In contrast, the concept of Indian kinship could not be integrated into individual property rights. Kinship resisted written laws and feudal hierarchy, and was thus seen as an Indian incapacity for civilization. This put Europeans on a collision course with Indian kinship.

Land was the principal wealth of the colonies for an extended time, and it became their primary business. No English colony in America was originally settled under the direct management of the royal government; instead, royal charters allowed privatization from the first. English claims along the eastern coast of the future United States were legal, it was said, because John Cabot was the first to reconnoiter in 1497 in Henry VII's name, and this was followed up by Humphrey Gilbert in Elizabeth's name in 1583. Thus the English monarch not only was sovereign but could deed to anyone. The rush was on. Huge land grants launched most of the American colonies. In 1639 Sir Ferdinand Gorges received a crown grant for what is now the entire state of Maine. Sir William Alexander exceeded this with all of Nova Scotia. In the mid-1600s, both kings Charles I and Charles II were particularly active with lavish gifts to their favorites. For example, when Sir William Berkeley became governor of Virginia, he gave himself thousands of acres and joined seven others to receive the grant of the Carolinas. William Penn, as son of Admiral Sir William Penn and under royal patronage,

Quitrents, Primogeniture, and Entail

Except in New England, the landlords also benefited from old medieval income schemes. Even after they deeded smaller tracts of land to actual settlers, they continued to collect annual dues called quitrents. (Quitrents originally were cash payments to avoid medieval military service.) Written into all the colonial charters except for Massachusetts Bay, Connecticut, and Rhode Island, quitrents usually were 2 to 4 shillings per 100 acres a year, although sometimes rates went up two or three times higher. Colonial quitrents reached into tens of thousands of pounds of additional income, especially when actively sought by individual proprietors as a major source of income. Quitrents were charged alongside normal property taxes, and most settlers believed they were repressive and stinging throwbacks to ancient tyranny. When Massachusetts became a royal colony in 1691, its new charter called for quitrents, but the uproar was so great that collection was ignored. Sometimes a quitrent was a token payment, in one case, with obvious irony, one raccoon skin each year for thousands of acres taken from an Indian tribe. Quitrents should have drained the colonies of cash, but they were not widely collected or enforced. They remained a source of tension during the entire colonial era and were cited as one of the reasons to seek redress from the king or to justify independence. Americans worried about the 1774 reforms of colonial land laws, which would have set a consistent and vigorously enforced collection of a half-penny quitrent per acre, with no exceptions. Primogeniture was the ancient means of keeping a tract of land undivided, by the oldest son inheriting a family's holdings to preserve feudal property. It was applied in colonial Virginia and other southern regions. Entail was similar to primogeniture. It restricted inheritance to a limited number of descendants for several generations, in order to preserve large estates from disintegration by equal inheritance. Only a few cases of entail are known in the colonies, mostly to keep tobacco plantations intact.

received all of Pennsylvania and Delaware from Charles II. Most of what is now Pennsylvania, Maryland, Delaware, West Virginia, North Carolina, and parts of Virginia was controlled by just four favored families.

The importance of this privatization cannot be overemphasized for the future of all American history. (The only exception in the current United States were some Spanish colonies.) The momentum to treat the colonial landscape as "a great game board on which property may be traded or rented, subdivided or consolidated, improved or neglected" (the words of geographer Edward T. Price) never changed. Virginia, New Hampshire, New York, New Jersey, the Carolinas, and Georgia reverted to crown status, but land division never let up; whereas Maryland, Pennsylvania, Massachusetts, Connecticut, and Rhode Island kept their corporate status. Nor can it be overemphasized that government-controlled land distribution systems soon failed in the face of distance, an inadequate bureaucracy, and the survival needs of the on-site settlers. New England only for a time controlled land division into church-based townships until commercial interests swamped the system; in all the colonies south of New York, so-called indiscriminate location meant that individuals freely picked out the choicest land on which to build a home and farm for subsistence and a surplus to sell. This could be profitably developed and sold to later migrants. Land in America was always a marketable commodity and seen as a highly desirable investment as well as a place of settlement. Individual self-interest, at the price of community, was an American norm from the earliest days. To put it generously, social goals fell to expediency.

The Geography of Abundance

New England

Early explorers and potential settlers had concluded that New England, like Canada, was uninhabitable except during the summer because the winters were too harsh. The Plymouth Colony venture had originally planned to land in Virginia before its ships went off course. They and the Puritans of Massachusetts Bay discovered New England was habitable in a limited way. The soil was famously stony, made up of debris left by retreating glaciers. Farmers complained that they harvested rocks more than corn and beans. The podzol soil, like that under most forest canopies, was composed of 2- to 4-inch layers of humus and leaf litter and soon turned acid under cultivation. Just below it was a reddish clay subsoil, full of iron. Farmers had to augment the soils with calcium from lime, nitrogen from animal manure or legumes like peas and clover, potassium from charcoal, and phosphorus from fish or animal bones.

Despite the climate and soil handicaps, a transplanted European ecosystem of animals, plants, pathogens, and people displaced native ecosystems. These latter became isolated into impossibly small units doomed to failure. The Narragansett sachem Miantonomo lamented in 1642, "Our fathers had plenty of deer and skins, our plains were full of deer, as also our woods, and of turkeys, and our coves full of fish and fowl. But these English have gotten our land, they with scythes cut down the grass, and with axes fell the trees; their cows and horses eat the grass, and their hogs spoil our clam banks, and we shall all be starved." The Puritan Edward Johnson responded, "The Lord hath been pleased to turn all the wigwams, huts, and homes the English dwelt in at their first coming, into orderly, fair, and well-built houses, well furnished many of them, together with orchards filled with goodly fruit trees, and gardens with variety of flowers." Forest clearings and fenced monoculture fields had replaced the native three-plant polyculture corn, bean, and squash complex. Indians needed thousands of upland and forest acres to hunt animal meat, but competing English cattle and pigs thrived on much less. European timber trade also invaded forested land formerly occupied by deer, elk, and moose. Europeans ended extensive river fishing by damming streams and polluting waters. The fur trade decimated beaver, muskrat, fox, lynx, and bear populations. Competition with the Indians for space was solved not only by ecosystem collapse and disease, but also in the 1670s by the elimination of up to 3,000 natives in King Philip's War and the migration of the disheartened remnant to New York and Canada.

European spread into New England's wilderness was surprisingly disciplined. Colonial authorities turned over parcels of land to companies of settlers—usually like-minded Puritans

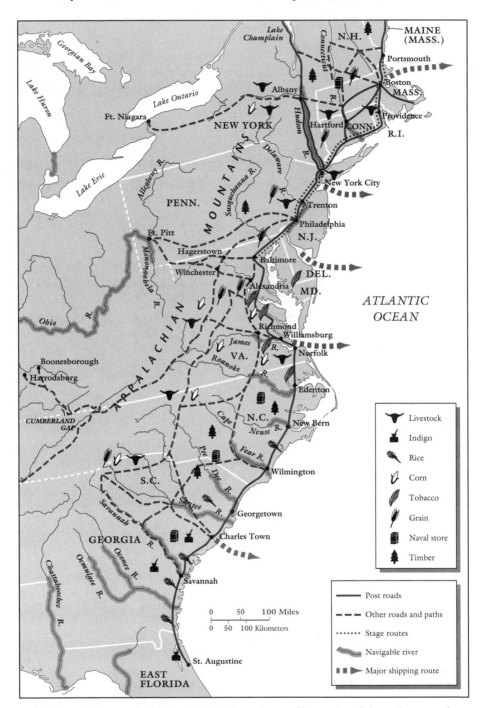

Food Production in the Late Eighteenth Century. Colonial agriculture quickly earned a well-deserved reputation for its abundance and attractiveness to new immigrants. This was despite considerable handicaps in getting surplus grains and animals to market over the primitive roads of the day. Most transportation went along waterways.

in a religious community—who created entire towns on former wilderness land. Ideally, these townships were 36 miles square with rectangular lots of 50 to 100 acres, containing abundant land larger than most could properly farm. Local geography controlled the actual layout. New England townships resembled traditional English farming villages or manors: blocks of house lots facing a common green, surrounded by open fields divided into strips, and common pastures and woods. In the central part of a new town, house lots and space for gardens and orchards were allocated to individuals based on their wealth, number of servants and cattle, and social status. Each family's house was the center of food processing, toolmaking, and the spinning of cloth. Immediately behind it stood the vegetable and herb gardens together with a barnyard full of chickens and geese, and stables for a cow and horse. Within a century, New England farms that began with 200 to 300 acres were divided into units as small as 30 acres whenever descendants divided the land. Cleared fields that were relatively flat could be planted in a three-field crop rotation of corn the first year, rye the second, and the third with oats, barley, or spring wheat, or fallow the third to recover fertility. Livestock included oxen and horses for carrying loads, plowing, and travel, and cows and goats for milk, butter, and cheese, sheep for mutton and wool, and pigs and elderly cattle for salt meat. Farmers constantly worried whether they would have enough hay for winter feed. Even salt marshes became a valued source of hay.

By 1700 agriculture in New England was not the path to prosperity. Farmers could not overcome too many rock-strewn fields, stone outcrops, and soils of marginal fertility. The region also experienced the invasion of a destructive wheat blast (fungous black stem rust). Exhausted farmland returned to its preagricultural state by reverting back to brushy meadows and the second-growth forest that began to cover much of New England. By the revolutionary era New England was no longer food sufficient and imported its wheat for bread from the Chesapeake Bay region. In less than a century New Englanders turned from farming to land speculation; Puritans were transformed into Yankees. It was easy to see that there was more profit in fishing and trade than wresting a living from thin rocky soil in a perilous climate. They connected themselves to trade routes with Spain, Madeira, the Azores, the Canary Islands, Newfoundland, and the West Indies. A marketplace economy dominated the region's timber, crops, and animals. It was fixed to a network of gristmills and sawmills, connected by roads, footpaths, river travel, and market towns. Since early settlement, New England merchants had traded natural resources (furs, lumber, fish, agricultural cows, sheep, wheat, corn, oats) for necessary manufactured items from England (cloth, blankets, stockings, leather goods, iron pots, pottery, weapons, gunpowder, salt). Less successful farmers who stayed on the land would soon join the first wave of migrants westward.

Southeastern Pennsylvania

The northeastern top of the Great Valley of Virginia stood in southeastern Pennsylvania. It quickly gained the title "the best poor man's country in the world" because even "poor servants have become very rich" in food, cash, and land. These three were the ingredients for a superior standard of living and quality of life. The region offered a temperate climate, good soil supporting a vast forest, flat or gently rolling terrain, and good rainfall. After farmers cleared trees from the land, they planted corn, wheat, and rye and took pride in their cattle, horses, and pigs. The difference was Pennsylvania "Deutsch" from the Palatinate who settled around Lancaster and York and established a superior rural farm life as early as 1750. (This is the still profitable farmland of today's Amish and Mennonites.) These eastern Pennsylvania farmers soon entered a rural market infrastructure because they generated more cash than usual from the sale of wheat, corn, livestock, and lumber. The typical southeastern Pennsylvania farmer held about 150 acres of prime farmland, with about 35 acres in crops, 13 in meadow for hay, 20 for pasture, 3 for the farmstead, and the rest (55–60 acres) in fallow to rebuild the soil, or in woodlots. Apple, peach, or cherry orchards grew 100 to 150 trees on 2 acres. Acreage planted in wheat gave 20 to 40 bushels per acre, compared to "old (worn-out) land" producing 8 to 12 bushes per acre. The pride of most farmers was their livestock, especially cattle and horses, as well as the universal free-running pigs. Overall this Pennsylvania farmer developed the most productive agricultural skills of early America, including knowledge of fertilizers and crop rotation. The rotation sequence was usually corn-hemp-flax (or hops or potatoes) to wheat (if the land was too rich the wheat would go to straw). Bad fields were improved by leaving them fallow in grass and clover. By 1800 the fields were worked by the famous "Bucks County" light plow and plowed "thrice-over" in a typically labor-intensive fashion. Surprisingly, these farmers did much superficial plowing that only scratched the surface of the soil, but low yields satisfied them because the land holdings were large. This southeastern Pennsylvania farming was still a low-technology, high-labor system. It was extensive not intensive agriculture. Nevertheless it produced an extremely good life, far better than in England or Europe. It astonished European visitors, still accustomed to scarcity and subsistence, to learn that an eighteenth-century Pennsylvania Dutch family of five consumed 750 pounds of meat a year and could sacrifice 300 bushels of grain for domestic animals.

The South

Europeans first found the region from Maryland to Georgia inhospitable. It was a zone of warm summers over 90° F and mild winters rarely below 50° F, with sandy soils watered by 40 to 60 inches of rain. The climate was too often hot and muggy, the air filled with mosquitoes, gnats, and bugs, the swampy places full of disease. Georgia's Okefenokee Swamp covered hundreds of square miles. The 2,200-square-mile tract below the lower James River was rightly called the Great Dismal Swamp. Where the land was dry, it was a flat world of "useless" loblolly pines and junipers that colonists wrongly labeled cedars. These "barrens" stretched far west into Texas.

The English outpost at Jamestown in 1607 nearly failed through incompetence and was almost wiped out by an Indian massacre in 1622, but prevailed to become the base for an expanding English settlement. In 1624 the English turned the corner when they began to distribute free land to promote widespread planting of the new luxury product, tobacco. The scramble for good tobacco land and the "headright" of immigrants to 50 acres, together with casual or indifferent land sale laws, created a maze of contention over titles and land boundaries. This, together with settlements built up in likely estuaries and river mouths, made the South, particularly Virginia, look formless. The South lacked the centralizing force of major cities and ports and was barely connected by rough trails. It was a land of large plantations, virtually like Europe's feudal principalities, less from a deliberate land policy than by aggressive planters seizing large estates of the best land along rivers, inlets, and creeks. Rights to large blocks of land were acquired from royal or commercial grants. They started at 250 acres maximum but quickly went over 1,000 acres to soar to 10,000 acres or more. (Yet most people did not live on plantations, but on marginal farms, and for them the basic geographical unit was the county, centered on the county seat of government and commerce.) This plantation system kept farming costs high, held settlers in even more profound isolation, and depended on high-profit tobacco in order to stay self-sufficient. Tobacco crops required higher capital investment than northern corn or wheat. Tobacco also required specialized buildings and curing houses. Especially it depended on a slave economy, detached and dismembered from its African origins. The European population reached 20,000 in 1650, with a few hundred African slaves, and this skyrocketed to 400,000 inhabitants by 1750, of whom a high percentage were slaves. Southerners learned that the southern pine forests were not "waste" trees of extensive coastal "pine barrens" as first believed, but provided wood and naval supplies of pitch, tar, and turpentine. Timber production is still one of the major alternative sources of income in the South. A rural landscape emerged in the South, unlike the rest of the United States because it lacked cities as trading centers and did not have the promise of nascent industry. It remained a thinly dispersed rural society with features—plantations, slavery, tobacco, and rice crops—unlike the rest of colonial America, and frozen in time. The South prospered as long as tobacco, and later cotton, brought high value in Europe. But this European connection positioned the region more on the edge or periphery of European markets, rather than a vanguard for unique wilderness expansion. The South looked eastward rather than westward.

Another successful transplant was the rice economy of the Carolinas. The Chinese called rice the "good grain of life," and many Asian societies regarded it as a sacred plant. It was introduced into the Carolinas in 1647, probably by slaves from West Africa, many of whom knew rice planting, cultivation, and harvesting. Rice stands apart from other major foods like wheat, corn, or potatoes because it is cultivated in ponds of water, or paddies. Thus it did not spread inland like tobacco or cotton. Cultivation required absolutely level paddies, which are planted by broadcasting dry seed or transplanting seedlings from a nursery bed. Rice crops centered on the river lands around Charleston, South Carolina, although other intensive rice districts were around Wilmington, North Carolina; Beaufort, South Carolina; and Savannah, Georgia. Rice production also requires intensive human labor, which encouraged the use of black slaves as the "free" resource. As early as 1704, a census around Charleston listed 4,080 whites, 4,100 blacks, and 1,400 Indian slaves. By the 1730s South Carolina's population was estimated at 30,000, of whom 20,000 were blacks, and one estimate puts the black slave population at over 40,000 by 1745 and over 80,000 by 1765, living among 40,000 whites. Local whites feared for their security, especially as they were scattered thinly and bordered by a vast wilderness into which slaves could escape. But black slavery was essential to rice production. In some parts of the world it still takes one person 1,000 hours to grow and harvest a single acre of rice. Tending the paddies is backbreaking work that requires much stooping, especially to weed and to prune the tops and roots to stimulate higher yields. Harvesting was done with sickles or knives, and threshing and winnowing was similar to wheat.

The Great Valley of Virginia

The environment of tree-covered hills and hollows that characterized the southern Appalachians may have been the greatest and most varied deciduous forest European settlers had encountered since Roman times. A long history of climate and glacial movement, together with rich soil and wide range of altitude (900–6,000 feet) compressed into this region an extraordinary treasure of 2,500 varieties of trees, shrubs, and other plants. No wonder the early

SLAVERY WAS AN age-old practice going back to prehistoric times, and a common feature of ancient Near Eastern societies as well as classical Greece and Rome. It declined in medieval Europe, but was prevalent in the Muslim world. The Portuguese first made contact with an existing African slave market in the 1440s in their quest for gold and the passage around Africa to India. Muslim slave caravans supplied several hundred black West African slaves a year who were shipped to Portugal and Spain. By 1550, 50,000 slaves were laboring in the Portuguese sugar industry off the west coast of Africa, and perhaps 100,000 African slaves were opening sugar fields in Brazil and the Caribbean. Even before their arrival in the future United States, slaves were considered a primary source for mass labor, a commodity on the marketplace, and a sign of personal wealth by white slave owners. Colonial slave owners used blacks as another form of capital alongside land, machines, and livestock, and their numbers permitted the rapid expansion of export of tobacco, rice, and cotton.

When the South's tobacco and rice plantations of the South began to expand in the early nineteenth century, slaves made up almost half of the South's labor force. They became indispensable when the numbers of white indentured servants from Britain fell dramatically by the time of American independence. It was believed slaves could endure the southern climate because they originally came from hot and humid sub-Sahara Africa. These slaves became essential both as a free labor force and for their agricultural skills from West Africa. Southerners believed that each slave could be held responsible for 3 acres of tobacco or cotton, but in fact the real number may have been the reverse. An entire rural economy depended on the risky institution of slavery for its commercial success. Raw land had once been the "free" resource on which the economy depended; it soon shifted to humans, or slaves, as the "free" resource.

By the era of the English colonization of the Atlantic coast, slavery had come under attack as vicious and immoral, especially by the English, Dutch, and French. Slavery was "even more drastic and rigid than [the treatment] given Native Americans." Slavery in the United States is now recognized as one of the world's worst because it divided families, restricted education and religion, and gave slaves no protection from abuse and murder, unlike a relatively more "humane" slavery in Brazil. The rich regional, ethnic, and cultural differences that characterized African blacks were deliberately destroyed in their shipment, sale, and enslavement in America.

American botanist William Bartram wrote in 1791 of the "sublime forest" with black oaks 30 feet in circumference, massive chestnut trees 13 feet thick at the base, and beeches and gum trees that towered to 150 feet. The valley lacked permanent Indian settlements and was difficult to reach from the settled coast. Earlier native burning and hunting created a region with many open grass-covered meadows. Well-watered and fertile limestone soils at low prices drew boisterous Scots-Irish and efficient German immigrants. A farmer-hunter could pay for 100 acres in one good season if he produced 7 elk hides or 30 deerskins. Nevertheless, limited access to markets, lack of capital, and labor-intensive farming kept valley farmers on a subsistence level into the 1760s. Typical Great Valley farmsteads began on 10 acres, planted in corn, wheat, or rye, yielding 10 to 17 bushels per acre. Eventually, by the 1760s most settlers owned between 100 and 400 acres. Because of mountain barriers between them and the coast, settlers had difficulty finding manufactured goods, such as salt, sugar, iron, nails, and clothes. Only a few products paid their transportation costs east: furs, ginseng, and whiskey. Farmers in more remote areas of the valley, unable to transport grain to market (wheat would become moldy or infested before wagons carried it 150 miles), raised cattle and hogs who could walk long distances on the Great Philadelphia Wagon Road. Herds could be seen blocking the streets of Philadelphia well into the nineteenth century. By 1800 a network of roads and trails made the valley more accessible and helped it shift into a cash crop economy based on wheat. It changed from frontier conditions to a rural society, but unlike most of the South was mostly slave free. The valley also provided a vital migration link from the East Coast, across the Appalachian Mountains, and into the American heartland.

Conclusion: Life Newly Defined by Abundance

One of the world's great agricultural success stories took hold when the independent property-owning farmer appeared on the American frontier landscape. This legendary figure dominated American expansion westward. European agriculture simplified the ecosystem, exploited the soil, saw crops only as commodities, and set sights on short-term profits. This agricultural tradition was not a happy combination of European and Native American farming. Rather it overwhelmed the Indian ecology of the New World through a combination of large domestic animals, the plow and monoculture crops, and ownership of the land as private property. Jefferson, Franklin, Crèvecoeur, and others believed this version of farming guaranteed westward progress, improved economic development, and spread the benefits of civilization.

The frontier farmer remained undertooled, undercapitalized, and isolated, but the American landscape, with its fertile soil and forgiving climate, was the foundation for a remarkable shift from scarcity to an abundance of food. Americans improved on their beef-eating and mutton-filled British cousins by consuming enormous amounts of deer, bear, and squirrel as well as turkeys, wild ducks, partridge, woodcocks, snipes, and millions of pigeons. There was "no better eating than a good fat woodchuck" stuffed and baked with herbs. A seventeenth-century list of farm foods included corn, wheat, rye, barley for beer, salt pork and beef and fish, butter, cheese, peas, vegetables, cider, potatoes, turnips, and fruit. James Fenimore Cooper describes "American poverty" in 1784: "As for bread [said the mother in a story] I count that for nothing. We always have bread and potatoes enough; but I hold a family to be in a desperate way when the mother can see the bottom of the pork-barrel." At an Ohio inn in 1807, a traveler could sit down to "good coffee, roast fowls, chicken pie, potatoes, bread and butter, and cucumbers," and other menus featured turnips, peas, beans, apples, cherries, strawberries, and melons, as well as pork, beef, and abundant game. One traveler in 1818, near Wheeling on the upper Ohio River, summed up,

> I believe I saw more peaches and apples rotting on the ground than would sink the British fleet. I was at many plantations in Ohio where they no more knew the number of their hogs than myself. . . . they have such flocks of turkeys, geese, ducks and hens, as would surprise you: they live

principally upon fowls and eggs; and in summer upon apple and peach pies. The poorest family has a cow or two and some sheep...and adorns the table three times a day like a wedding dinner—tea, coffee, beef, fowls, pigs, eggs, pickles, good bread; and their favorite beverage is whiskey or peach brandy. Say, is it so in England?

Agricultural abundance became an American hallmark that attracted settlers westward onto and beyond the frontier. It would allow settlers to look confidently into the wilderness of the Ohio and Mississippi valleys for still greater prosperity. Ohio settlement was so successful that it set a national example for family farming. Farming beyond Ohio into Illinois and Iowa prospered as improved technology, commercial markets, and better capitalization offered more opportunity. At one time Thomas Jefferson believed it would take a hundred generations for Americans to possess the continent to the Pacific Ocean; in reality it took five generations. Few farmers settled for long on their own land, unlike the permanence of Europe's peasant villages. Instead, most farmers, no matter how dedicated, were also speculators. They cleared a site, brought the land under tillage, and sold it for a profit to move on to the next plot still under forest cover. In 1802 a New Yorker wrote, "It is considered here a small affair for a man to sell, take his family and some provisions and go into the woods upon a new farm, erect a house, and begin anew." Naturalist John Muir remembers his dismay as a boy in the 1850s, when, just as the worst backbreaking work was done to establish the family farm, his father sold out and moved the Muirs to begin again in a new raw wilderness site.

In worldwide terms, this shift toward abundance was as dramatic as widespread ownership of land. The perpetual flow of surplus food was quickly recognized internationally as America's most obvious accomplishment, and it was envied by all classes of European society. Even the immigrant mechanic or carpenter, once he acquired some savings, would buy a piece of land and become a farmer. Most remarkable to contemporaries was the notion that agricultural surpluses might be sustained over the long run and were not merely a spurt in growth between starving times. Farming in America created unusually high living conditions compared to elsewhere. This standard of living in turn would become the standard of measure, unusually high, for successful industrialization. Nevertheless, to most Americans farming is now a lost world.

For Further Reading

No single comprehensive study of the impact of agriculture on American development places it within an environmental and global context. The closest is Edward Hyams's classic 1952 *Soil and Civilization*. Similar cross-cultural studies worth a look at are Charles B. Heiser's *Seed to Civilization: The Story of Food* (1990) and Henry Hobhouse's *Seeds of Change: Five Plants That Transformed Mankind* (1986). One of the most thoughtful surveys remains Willard W. Cochrane's *The Development of American Agriculture: A Historical Analysis* (1979), but agricultural history in an environmental context has not yet found a voice. Other useful resources for colonial agriculture remain P. W. Bidwell and J. I. Falconer, *History of Agriculture in the Northern United States, 1620–1860* (1925), L. C. Gray, *History of Agriculture in the Southern United States to 1860* (1933), Howard S. Russell, *A Long Deep Furrow: Three Centuries of Farming in New England* (1976), and James A. Henretta, *The Evolution of American Society, 1700–1815* (1973). For further reading on agricultural symbol and myth, go to Mircea Eliade's two classics, *The Sacred and the Profane* (1957, 1959) and *Myth and Reality*

(1963). Regional environmental history of the colonial era has benefited from the pathbreaking work of William Cronon in his *Changes in the Land: Indians, Colonists, and the Ecology of New England* (1983), which is matched by Carolyn Merchant's *Ecological Revolutions: Nature, Gender, and Science in New England* (1989). Compare these to Douglas R. McManis's more traditional but detailed *Colonial New England: A Historical Geography* (1975). As for eastern Pennsylvania farming, James T. Lemon's classic, *The Best Poor Man's Country: A Geographical Study of Early Southeastern Pennsylvania* (1972), is still definitive. As to the South, Timothy Silver acknowledges his debt to Cronon in the provocative and revisionist study, *A New Face on the Countryside: Indians, Colonists, and Slaves in South Atlantic Forests, 1500–1800* (1990). One unheralded masterpiece about the relationship between plants and humans across America is May Theilgaard Watts, *Reading the Landscape of America* (1975). For individual crops, see the definitive and detailed work by Redcliffe Salaman, *The History and Social Influence of the Potato* (1949; rev. 1985), and the popular but informative essays by Betty Fussell, *The Story of Corn: The Myths and History, the Culture and Agriculture, the Art and Science of America's Quintessential Crop* (1992). A stab at colonial agricultural standard of living and quality of life is made in two popular histories, David Freeman Hawke's *Everyday Life in Early America* (1989) and Stephanie Grauman Wolf's *As Various as Their Land: The Everyday Lives of Eighteenth-Century Americans* (1993). A rewarding geographical perspective is in Donald W. Meinig's *The Shaping of America: A Geographical Perspective on 500 Years of History, Vol. 1: Atlantic America, 1492–1800.* (1986).

PART TWO

SHAPING THE
NATIONAL LANDSCAPE

CHAPTER THREE

THE FEDERAL GEOGRAPHY

If the cause of the happiness of this country was examined into, it would be found to arise as much from the great plenty of land in proportion to the inhabitants, which their citizens enjoyed, as from the wisdom of their political institutions.

—Albert Gallatin, Jefferson's Swiss-Born Secretary of the Treasury
(and a Western Land Speculator), 1796

The whole country is agog for land, and almost every man who can procure money is thus investing in it.

—New Orleans Courier, July 25, 1836

Americans will always lie when tempted by a land deal.

—The Great American Maxim

In less than 150 years, the United States became one of the world's largest countries. With 3.68 million square miles, the United States today ranks fourth after Russia (5.2 million square miles), Canada (3.8 million square miles), and the People's Republic of China (3.7 million square miles). For most of American history, an apparent surplus of empty land led Americans to believe that virtually no control was necessary. In 1800 only 5 million inhabitants were spread thinly east of the Mississippi. By 1900 the population coast to coast had exploded to 76 million due to massive migration and a high birthrate. But there were still nearly

30 acres of land for every man, woman, and child in the country. In 1980 each of 250 million Americas still enjoyed the equivalent of 10 acres, divided into 3⅓ acres of forest land, 2 acres of cropland, 1⅓ acres of wasteland, ½ acre for recreation and wildlife, ⅔ acres of grass pasture and rangeland, and ¼ acre of roads, airports, and urban land. By A.D. 2000 the figure will still be high when compared to under 2 acres per person in China or less than 1 acre per person in another large nation, India.

This chapter describes how European colonials looked inward at the bountiful North American continent from their perch along the eastern seaboard. When the English colonies split into an independent United States and a loyalist Canada, the new Americans had few precedents by which to define their enormous new geography or determine its best use. The outcome was one of the world's great experiments in land use—driving off the native peoples, surveying the undivided geography into mathematical segments, and "alienating" most of the new public domain into private hands. Ever since, land reform around the world has used the American experiment as a model for successful geographical development.

The Dilemma of Independence: Inventing a Geography

The Geography of Revolution and Independence

The geography of the Revolutionary War is confusing. Different regions shifted their loyalty and became temporary battlegrounds. Only in Massachusetts, Connecticut, Maryland, and Virginia did rebels control the government. Loyalists formed the majority in New York, New Jersey, South Carolina, and Georgia. The people of Pennsylvania, Delaware, and the Carolinas showed little interest in the conflict except when troops marched, bivouacked, and fought in the neighborhood. General Nathanael Greene, when he moved troops into the Carolinas and Georgia, wrote that he seemed to be operating in enemy country. Nevertheless, one major American advantage was that the rebels were often fighting for their homes. In contrast, the British faced a logistical nightmare. Although troops could be brought overland from Canada or by ship from the Caribbean, most military supplies and the cash to finance the overseas war had to come from London. British responses thus involved a geographic time delay of three weeks to three months. The Continental Congress used geographical space to threaten Britain: "We admit that your fleets could destroy our towns, and ravage our seacoasts. These are inconsiderable objects, things of no moment to men whose bosoms glow with the ardor of liberty. We can retreat beyond the reach of your navy, and, without any sensible diminution of the necessities of life, enjoy the luxury of being free." The English dreaded that the Americans might retreat into the interior of the continent and become transformed into "hordes of English tartars, pouring down an irresistible cavalry on the unfortified frontiers." In fact, the geographical space of the colonies had a different impact: Self-sufficient and isolated back-country settlers were unaffected by skirmishes for ports and cities. Terrain and distance kept local agricultural people far from warfare or other world events. One revolutionary army recruiter at Fort Pitt complained that even in wartime settlers migrated "chiefly to avoid militia duty and taxes." In the heat of the patriotic conflict, they still talked "of nothing but killing

HUDSON BAY COMPANY

Lake Superior

Ft. Michilimackinac

Chippewa

Mississippi R.

Lake Michigan

Lake Huron

PROVINCE OF QUEBEC

St. Lawrence R.

NOVA SCOTIA

MAINE (part of Mass.)

N.H.

Albany   MASS.

Boston

L. Ontario

Ft. Niagara   Iroquois

NEW YORK   CONN.

R.I.

Fox

Ft. Detroit

Lake Erie

New York

N.J.

Potowatoml

Ft. Miami   Delaware

PENN.

Philadelphia

MD.   DEL.

Ft. Chartres

Vincennes

St. Louis

Ohio R.

Shawnee

VIRGINIA

Williamsburg

Kaskaskia

INDIAN RESERVE

Cherokee

NORTH CAROLINA

ATLANTIC OCEAN

SPANISH LOUISIANA

Mississippi R.

Chickasaw

Creek

SOUTH CAROLINA

Augusta   Charles Town

Choctaw

GEORGIA

Savannah

WEST FLORIDA

Mobile   Pensacola

New Orleans

EAST FLORIDA

St. Augustine

Gulf of Mexico

—— Proclamation Line, 1763

- - - The Indian Boundary Line

||||| Adjusted Territory, 1781

0   150   300 Miles

0   150   300 Kilometers

Competition for the Heartland of the Continent. British North America had a turbulent western frontier composed of Indian tribes, an uncontrolled rush of settlers onto unmapped and unsurveyed land, and competing French interests. By 1763, the French lost their North American interests to the British, but the Proclamation Line of 1773 to separate fractious settlers and native people became one of the major inducements to American independence and revolution.

Indians and taking possession of their lands." Fighting on the western front was limited because the British, to avoid unnecessary expense, had in early 1776 withdrawn their regular troops from the far western Illinois country. The oft-repeated view still holds: The Americans did not win the Revolution so much as the British lost it. British strategy was sound—conquer the cities and the countryside will fold—but a lack of leadership from political generals defeated the strategy. The truth remains that although the Americans used their geography to military advantage, they only avoided defeat because of timely French naval assistance.

Land played another critical role during the conflict. It was a form of wealth far more stable than inflated paper money that became virtually worthless regardless whether it was from Congress or issued by the states. Often the only way for Washington and his generals to keep a minimum of soldiers in the field was to pay them in warrants for untitled western land as far as the distant Mississippi River. Military service thus created a special class of citizens who would be paid off in pieces of public geography instead of from the public treasury. George Rogers Clark rewarded his western troops with 300 acres each of western land they had just conquered. New York offered bounties beginning at 600 acres, depending on military rank, Pennsylvania from 200 to 2,000 acres, Virginia from 100 to 5,000 acres, and North Carolina from 200 to 12,000 acres. Land in lieu of cash also assured that rich patriots like Jefferson and the Lees in Virginia, and John Hancock and the Adamses in Massachusetts, would not be taxed to pay the troops. The passion for land-ownership was so great that Congress lured deserters from among Hessian mercenaries as well as British officers and soldiers with promises of free land. State authorities rationalized that because the Indians mostly allied themselves with the British, their western lands were spoils of war. After the war, Congress in 1796 belatedly set aside a large Military District in the Northwest Territory to compensate veterans angry at long delays in receiving land. Few veterans ever saw the land, since most sold their warrants at deep discounts to speculators. In the Military District over 2 million acres were patented, with 1.5 million acres going to less than 100 speculators.

The resulting geography of the 13 independent states, formed vaguely into a single nation, was truly fuzzy over boundaries, state sovereignty, and land ownership. By its unshackling from Britain had the new nation also undone social contracts and legal bonds? In 1787 Noah Webster admitted, "the present situation of our American states is very little better than a state of nature," in which land titles, surveys, ownership, and payments must be reinvented, as if it were a new Creation. Separatists who disputed important regions of New York, Pennsylvania, Maryland, and Virginia threatened fragmentation into a myriad of ill-formed political units. Americans feared they might descend into a chronic state of internal war. To avoid chaos, the 13 new states claimed sovereignty within their borders based on the rights they had held as colonies. Private title to land was still fully accepted as legal, except when it was Tory property. By the end of the war, a third of all land in the colonies had been confiscated as Tory and British. It soon would be thrown on the market. This forced one of history's major displacements when between 80,000 and 100,000 loyalist civilians abandoned their rights and property. Aside from these Tory losses, most everyone was relieved when legal authorities stated that colonial laws, land sales, and property contracts were not dissolved with the Revolution. After all, it was argued, the Revolution was fought to protect property rights from illegal and excessive intrusion. This eventually became legal doctrine confirmed by the U.S. Supreme Court in 1834: The people may "change their allegiance but their rights of property remain undisturbed." In the fateful 16 years between 1775 and 1791, the debate over land claims and ownership did much to shape the new nation's government as it moved from the raw independence of the decentralized Articles of Confederation and toward a federal and constitutional system with a public domain. Americans invented their own territorial future.

Two cases in particular helped define America's future, one over the integrity of Pennsylvania's territory within its borders, the other over the right of Vermont to secede from New York.

The Struggle over Pennsylvania's "Empty Land"

Unlike other colonies, which claimed land coast to coast, Pennsylvania had a western boundary set at 5° west (about 300 miles) from the Delaware River. Pennsylvania's northern and southern boundaries covered the territory between 40° and 43° (about 100 miles). William Penn also bought a smaller parcel of land from the Duke of York that extended down the Delaware River, but this confused the southern boundary with Maryland, and a settlement in 1769 became the famous Mason-Dixon line. It seemed that Pennsylvania's territorial integrity was clearer than most colonies. Not so. The problem was that most of Pennsylvania, aside from the southeastern prosperous farmland centered around Lancaster and near Philadelphia, remained virtually untouched. The empty spaces of western Pennsylvania in particular received more attention from settlers and speculators from Virginia than from eastern Pennsylvanians. As a result, Virginia's governor John Murray, notorious for his greed for land, argued that the Pittsburgh region belonged to Virginia because of royal grants, "pre-occupancy" by Virginian settlers, its defense by Virginians during the war, and the "general acquiescence of all persons," even Pennsylvania officials. He warned Pennsylvania authorities that it would "be in vain to contend [with Virginia interests] in the way of force." Armed men from Virginia walked the streets of Pittsburgh. Finally, after a noisy debate that climaxed in a raucous meeting in Baltimore, the 1769 Mason-Dixon Line was extended westward in 1779 to run south of Pittsburgh, as long as existing Virginia landowners were guaranteed their land titles north of the line.

Little Connecticut, already crowded with people, also lusted after the Pennsylvania wilderness. Connecticut people formed themselves into the Susquehanna Company and simply took over the lush but empty Wyoming Valley in north central Pennsylvania. In 1774 the Connecticut Assembly formally annexed the district and its willing 2,000 settlers, a move legally based on vague colonial charters and land company purchases from Indians. The implication was that if Pennsylvanians were so foolish not to develop their land, and farmers arrived from Connecticut to improve it, then it belonged to Connecticut. Would not a settler from Connecticut who cleared the land and made it produce wheat have more of a right to it than local Indians or a distant land owner or state? Wyoming Valley settlers began to run their own affairs and ignore state officials. In response, a group of wealthy Pennsylvanians raised a private army to march against the intruders from Connecticut. The notorious hothead Ethan Allen, fresh from his victorious separation of Vermont from New York, arrived to tell settlers in Wyoming Valley, "You have been greatly oppressed by the land schemers of Pennsylvania. . . . Crowd your settlements, add to your numbers and strength; procure firearms and ammunition, be united among yourselves." Simultaneously, Shays' Rebellion by disaffected separatist farmers in western Massachusetts was expected to spread to the angry settlers in the Wyoming Valley. Pennsylvania reluctantly created Luzerne County in 1786 to offer a degree of self-government and in 1787 confirmed bona fide land titles that legitimized landholders from Connecticut.

Pennsylvanians probably would not have had enough military force to combat the claims of either Virginia or Connecticut, and the state would have begun to fall apart. Pennsylvania's problems, to the surprise of many, did not induce a bloody civil war between the states, but were settled peaceably. Few Americans wanted any further conflict between fellow countrymen. This set an important precedent for interstate relations in America. These struggles concerning private capture of "empty" land and the authority of a state to control its territory helped bring on a national debate that soon led to the Constitutional Convention in 1787. Settlers in both western Pennsylvania and the Wyoming Valley began to think of themselves less as belonging to Virginia or Connecticut or Pennsylvania, and more as American citizens. Connecticut settlers told Pennsylvania officials after the settlement, "We care not under what state we live, if we can live protected and happy." The peaceful resolution was part of a growing sense among the inhabitants of the states that they were citizens of a new nation and joint owners of a national geography.

New York's Vermont

New York was in trouble over both its undeveloped western claims and its northeastern boundary. Bounty land for veterans, the "New Military Tract," covered 1.5 million acres in the western Finger Lakes country. This land became a money tree for speculators, who bought up the soldiers' scrip for only $8 per 600 acres and turned around and sold it for $3 to $6 per acre. One observer wrote, "Immigrants are swarming into this fertile region in shoals like the ancient Israelites seeking the land of promise." By 1804 about 30,000 people decided to live in the tract. Further west, Europeans forced their way onto the lands of the Onondaga and Mohawk Indians, who were subdued by military force and shipped west to reservations. By 1810 almost 60,000 settlers had rushed into the region. A large territory of 2.25 million acres—"Genesee country"—had been in the hands of a wealthy Scotsman, Sir William Pulteney, since 1791. He advertised it in Britain and France, as well as the United States. An overall plan for the Genesee country anticipated the later Homestead Act by limiting the

Nature Does Not Go Away: Shays' Rebellion as a Climate Incident

In 1786-87 farmers in western Massachusetts took up arms against what they believed were unjust misfortunes. They were ridden with debt, hard cash was virtually nonexistent, lawyers charged exorbitant fees, Boston lenders seemed callous, and the state legislature appeared indifferent. Daniel Shays and his followers ran into financial trouble partly because they were traditional farmers who remained committed to personal self-sufficiency. They felt themselves losing out to more commercial farmers who were connected to wider markets. The farmers forcibly prevented county courts from sending them to debtors' prison. They were soon dispersed by a state militia, and Shays and other rebels pardoned. The rebellion gained wide attention as a signal that the new United States might fall into social splintering and the chaos of repeated insurrections unless the new Constitution was ratified soon, which it was in 1789.

A turning point for the failure of such traditional farmers in western Massachusetts may have been a period of particularly unpredictable weather, against which they could not protect themselves nearly as well as the market-connected farmers. Before 1750 New England's weather had been cool—"neoglacial"—but quite stable and reliable, and farmers could plan their farming with some assurance. But the century between 1750 and 1850 was a transitional "change-over" period with large climate fluctuations. The isolated farmers in western Massachusetts found themselves confused and harmed by unusual variations in growing season, by unpredictable storms, snowfalls, and droughts, and by extremes in temperature. They ran into serious debt when the "growing degree days" of 13 out of 24 years between 1750 and 1774 were too few for corn to mature at all. In their anger and frustration, they took up arms.

acreage that one individual could buy and by requiring residence and improvement of the property on a timetable. The promise of access to world markets through a future canal between the Hudson River and Lake Ontario made this rich farmland particularly attractive. In contrast to westward expansion, New York's desolate far north frontier, "a dreary scene," included the Ten Towns that Indians still used for hunting deer and beaver. When a single wealthy speculator, Alexander Macomb, bought virtually all of the region and kept it off the market, it remained a wilderness into the next century.

Back east at the New England border, several New York counties split off in 1777 to form an independent region called Vermont. All the states feared such "floating" borders and looked to Congress to protect their territorial integrity. Congress worried that Vermont's "poisonous serpents" would encourage malcontents elsewhere to break the United States into a hundred bickering neighborhoods, like a Balkans in the New World. One Vermont supporter said of the relations with New York, "The hatred subsisting between us, is equivalent to that which subsists between the independent states of America and Great Britain." Congressman John Sullivan cautioned, "It was not a time for America to court new enemies or add to the number of the disaffected." Gouverneur Morris warned that it was not "agreeable to see Americans embruing their hands in the blood of each other." While Congress wavered, New York blustered about armed intervention, and New Hampshire and Massachusetts began to look hungrily at pieces of the Vermont pie. Vermont's crafty mountaineers began to annex adjacent towns, 35 in New Hampshire to the east and 12 in New York, actions that made resolution of the case urgent before violence boiled over several borders. Everyone feared a civil war in which other New Englanders would back up the rebels and spread the conflict. It seemed clear that Vermont separatism could be suppressed only by a show of force. Skirmishes between New York militia and Vermont irregulars proved embarrassing to New York, and no one else sought to intervene. The stakes were not trivial. Vermont spent 13 years as an independent entity. As historian Peter Onuf observed, the United States could not tolerate this independence; it might allow the British to gain a foothold in northern New England. It also became clear that Vermont could not survive as an autonomous nation. Nor could it be coerced back into New York without subverting principles of self-determination over which the Revolution was being fought. Most Vermonters considered themselves loyal Americans as well as Vermonters. They saw themselves as inhabitants of a territory inherited from the colonial period, but their loyalty rested with the new nation and the war being fought to secure its independence. Vermont joined the union as a separate state in 1791.

Foreign Threats to a Federal Geography

In 1783 the peace treaty signed in Paris gave the new United States sovereignty over territory from Maine to the Mississippi, a landmass of more than 900,000 square miles, greater than any nation in all of Europe other than czarist Russia. When Americans scouted the new space, they often found British or Spanish officials backed by soldiers disputing claim to U.S. territory. Great Britain, anticipating a rapid geographical breakup of the fragile new United States, held on to several strategic forts in the land south of the Great Lakes and north of the Ohio River. It even built a new fort on Ohio's Maumee River to control the fur trade and keep the Indians friendly to British interests. The forts would not be abandoned until 1796, the intrusion settled by Jay's Treaty of 1794, which also made the 49th parallel, rather than the 45th parallel, the boundary between the United States and British Canada. Equally troublesome was Spanish intervention on the Mississippi River. Spain had only reluctantly recognized American independence. Now it closed the river to American traffic wherever it flowed through Spanish territory centered around Louisiana. It also declared that the region south of the Ohio River was to be held forever for exclusive Indian use even while the new nation was beginning to make territorial claims on what would become Alabama and Mississippi. The Spanish rightfully feared the inevitable invasion of its territory by land-hungry American pioneers. Much of this was sorted out temporarily by Pinckney's Treaty with Spain in 1795, which gave the United States a southern boundary at the 31st parallel as well as American rights to trade on the Mississippi and shipment overseas from New Orleans. As to the French, they had been America's ally during the Revolution, but in 1793, a diplomat, Citizen (Edmond Charles) Genet, roamed the backcountry to spy out American intentions toward the Mississippi region until he was discovered and expelled. The French also benefited from Spanish weakness. The entire Spanish province of Louisiana that included the vast midcontinent prairie and plains had been left to manage its own affairs. By 1800, threatened by the rise of the energetic Napoleon, the Spanish traded all of Louisiana to France for some small Italian holdings. Americans discovered an ambitious and aggressive nation on its weak backside. The young nation seemed beset by threats from every quarter by powerful challengers who expected its collapse. Although Americans initially seemed hopelessly lost in their experimental Confederation, which was on the verge of collapse into fragmented states, they soon built a union that emerged as one of the most durable institutions in all of modern world history. The task of creating a sovereign geography, however, was not easy.

Who Owns the Land? Inventing and Building a Public Domain

In the 1780s the "West" meant the large territory along the spine of the Appalachian Mountains that stretched as far as the Mississippi River. Did it belong to the states, the nation at large, aggressive land companies, or to individual farmers who were already planting fields and building homes? Quarrels over public and private ownership of open territory had previously undermined the Revolutionary War effort. In addition, no one was certain of the rights of western populations. Could they demand to become new states? Or would they become, as past history suggested, colonies of the original 13 states? The problem was made worse because newly independent Americans were not certain of the borders, divisions, or terrain of the nation's western geography. Accurate maps did not exist, and relatively few Americans had yet traveled to the Forks of the Ohio, much less beyond. Indian rights were being pushed aside by invading settlers, unequal warfare, and forced treaties. Groups of war veterans demanded hundreds of thousands of acres in compensation for lost pay. Thousands of unauthorized squatters swarmed across the Ohio River into the disputed landscape. Speculators took over much of what would later become West Virginia, Kentucky, Tennessee, Alabama, and Mississippi. For example, Georgia endured its "Yazoo frauds," in which three private companies acquired over 25 million acres of western land in the Yazoo region around Natchez for less than a cent an acre, soon followed by four more companies that received 21.5 million acres for a cent and a quarter an acre. Some common understanding had to be reached to avoid confusion and possible violence. Knowing the reckless passion Americans had for smart dealing in land, the lack of a reliable survey or legal title had become a serious problem.

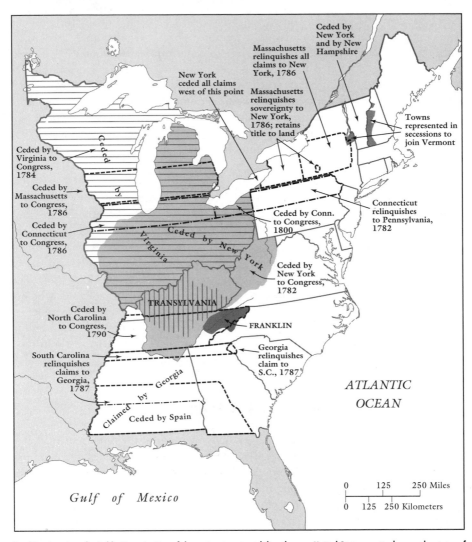

Land Cessions into the Public Domain. One of the major steps to stabilize the new United States was to clear up the status of its uncertain western lands that were more extensive than the original thirteen states. These were criss-crossed by claims of ownership by competing states, private speculative empires, war veterans with land warrants, and new settlers, together with the existence of entire native nations and British and Spanish interventions. The western lands were secured as public domain between 1785 and 1815 in a remarkable series of legislative acts, economic policies, diplomatic negotiations, and warfare.

There was nothing intrinsically illegal about speculation: The rewards were often so astronomical that many otherwise decent citizens rushed to stretch the rules. This included schemes to avoid paying any official price. One early example in the 1780s involved a Pennsylvania backcountry farmer-speculator, William Findlay. He said a man could borrow $100 from the state on a tract he already owned, then exercise the right to buy state paper securities on the open market at a third of their face value. He then traded these public securities back to the state at full value for more land, thus generating an instant paper profit of 200 percent. Findlay said it was "magical." The state also benefited because it received 6 percent interest on the original $100 and had sold off a $300 parcel of land to reduce its public debt. In 1783 many law-abiding citizens of North Carolina made themselves rich by selling western untitled state lands to themselves at outrageously low prices. This self-delivered gift became the state of Tennessee.

The situation was so fluid that pragmatic local action overwhelmed general laws and old traditions. Speculators, who were often also public officials, bought time for their machinations by delaying as long as possible the ratification of the Articles of Confederation from November 1777 to February 1781. The states battled each other. Smaller states energetically sought to cut pieces out of the large states (Connecticut's Wyoming Valley in the heart of Pennsylvania) while simultaneously keeping them from expanding westward. Maryland refused to ratify the Articles of Confederation until Congress fixed the western boundaries of all the states. "Back lands," it said, should be "common property" and sold to pay for the Revolutionary War. The use of old colonial charters by individual states such as Virginia, to claim ownership of the entire West, it said, were "so extravagant, so repugnant to every principle of justice, so incompatible with the general welfare of all the states." Maryland reminded its fellow states that the West had been "wrested from the common enemy by the blood and treasure of the thirteen states." New Jersey, Delaware, and Rhode Island joined in insisting that no state, particularly Virginia, had exclusive claim "to the soil of the back lands." The New Jersey assembly argued that "the property which existed in the crown of Great Britain . . . ought now to belong to the Congress, in trust for the use and benefit of the United States." Large states energetically campaigned for even larger regions based on colonial charters. Historian Merrill Jensen writes, "The landed states may be pardoned their refusal to sacrifice their interests to the 'good of the whole' when it is recognized that they saw nothing in such phrases but the program of the speculators of the landless states." As long as states disputed land boundaries, the new United States was a paper document and a geographical horror. Threats of armed conflict sometimes became actual fighting, as in the case of New York and Vermont. Fortunately, individual states, worn down by the Revolution, did not make it general policy to march soldiers across state borders to enforce claims. It became clear that a stronger central government would help guarantee boundaries, administer the public domain, and peacefully establish new western states.

Virginia's Reluctant Gift

One of the greatest acts of goodwill in American history was the Virginia cession of 1784, in which the most powerful state of all the original 13 surrendered its enormous western claims that went back to its 1609 charter. Virginia could have divided most of the midwestern heartland—a massive 283 million acres—into as many as 12 of her own colonies and controlled the emerging United States (like Russia had dominated the old Soviet Union in the twentieth century). Instead, when Virginians looked westward after the war, they reluctantly admitted that the state's borders should follow the Ohio River and not stretch across it. They concluded they could not govern such a large and distant territory. They already discovered that the Indiana, Illinois, and Wabash land companies "owned" massive tracts of its claims north of the Ohio River. South of the Ohio River, Virginians also saw trouble in the appearance of Vandalia, which enclosed most of today's West Virginia. Separatists had also created the principality of Transylvania in the Kentucky country. Virginians concluded that Kentucky frontiersmen were "turbulent and unruly"—an "infamous company of land pirates"—and thus a different sort than eastern Virginia plantation farmers and not loyal to Virginia's interests. In addition, more than 100 years of careless surveying and sales, together with uncontrollable squatters, created overlapping properties, spawned endless litigation, and left an impossible confusion in Virginia's western lands. The Virginia Assembly ceded its land claims north of the Ohio River to the United States on January 2, 1781, although the actual transfer did not take place until March 1, 1784. Probably Virginians did not realize they were giving up 220,000 square miles of the world's most fertile soils. Virginians accepted the inevitability of the fifteenth new state of Kentucky in 1792, a rare instance in which a new state was birthed directly from an old state (the only other cases were Vermont from a recalcitrant New York and eventually Maine from Massachusetts). Kentucky covered over 40,000 square miles, almost 26 million acres, larger than 8 of the original 13 colonies. Kentucky's separation was not entirely a giveaway. Virginia had already ceded to the May family almost a million acres in Kentucky, and turned over 200,000 to 300,000 acres to dummy names for later payouts. Overall, powerful Virginians took about 6.5 million acres, more than a quarter of the entire state, a region greater than Massachusetts and Delaware combined.

Of the other states with western interests, Georgia was second only to Virginia. Had all its claims been recognized, it could have become the second largest state, with 94 million acres, or 19 times the size of New Jersey and 15 times bigger than Maryland. North Carolina claimed 53 million acres, almost the size of New York and Pennsylvania combined. Massachusetts and Connecticut could have quadrupled their size with over 25 million acres if their unconnected western lands had been retained. Instead, the states knuckled under Virginia's lead to create the public domain in which the states collectively had a common interest. Preceded by New York's limited cession in 1782, Virginia's action in 1784 was followed by Massachusetts in 1785, Connecticut in 1786, and North Carolina in 1790. By 1780 Congress confirmed that the western lands were territory held in common, to be "settled and formed into distinct republican states, which shall become members of the federal union, and shall have the same rights of sovereignty, freedom and independence, as the other states." Cessions of the western lands provided 233.4 million acres of public domain, not including 3.8 million acres of the Connecticut Western Reserve and over 4.2 million acres of the Virginia Military Tract. This was slightly more than the entire area of the original 13 states. Public domain historian Paul W. Gates wrote, "Since it had taken the population of the 13 colonies more than 170 years to spread lightly over the area east of the Alleghenies, leaving great areas still untouched, and to begin to break through into Kentucky and Tennessee, one might have expected that this huge area of public land would satisfy American needs for many years." Such was not the case.

The Geography of the Constitutional Debates

By modern standards, the Constitutional Convention took little time, from May 25 to September 17 of 1787. (It took far longer—until 1789—for enough states to ratify the Constitution.) Philadelphia's summer was steamy and the doors and windows of the hall were kept closed away from the peering eyes of lobbyists, the public, and the press. The delegates who gathered wearily were prepared for the collapse of the infant United States of America. A strong central government with true geographical sovereignty seemed a distant dream. Few people expected a move toward 13 small nations, but three independent nations might have been a workable outcome—New England, a middle state dominated by New York and Pennsylvania, and a southern nation dominated by Virginia. No one took seriously one delegate's suggestion to erase all existing states and start out afresh with new borders, geographies, and populations. Past history stood against a strong central government: As a colony each state had a stronger political and economic link with London across 3,000 miles of stormy Atlantic Ocean than with its neighboring colonies. Earlier colonial attempts at formal political bonds, such as the Albany Plan of Union enthusiastically promoted by Benjamin Franklin, had already failed. Many colonial leaders had admitted the need for common policies toward the Indians, western expansion, and military readiness, but bitter rivalries over trade, territory, and special privileges from London made colonies like Massachusetts, New York, and Virginia fiercely jealous of each other. And everyone disliked the irascible people of Rhode Island so much that it was often whispered that the colony should be dismembered and split between Connecticut and Massachusetts. Those who expected large fortunes out of western lands realized they were often thwarted by the frailty of the Confederation government and the uncertainty caused by the constant wrangling between it and the states. Large states sought to pay off debts and build their treasuries by owning and selling the land. Small states complained they too had debts, had fought as vigorously for independence as any state, and must not be cut off from a profitable national domain.

Land—enormous unimaginable wilderness—was the silent partner in the negotiations in Philadelphia for a new government. The Constitutional Convention was in large part a national real estate debate. In Philadelphia the delegates realized that hundreds of millions of acres were at stake. Not so silent a partner to the constitutional debates was the impudent and opportunistic Ohio Company. Its actions forcefully demonstrated the need for orderly land distributions. Even during the closed-door discussions in Philadelphia, the Ohio Company successfully lobbied the Confederation Congress in session in New York City to sell a million acres of Ohio land for a paltry $100,000. The new territory was one-third the size of Connecticut. The Constitutional Convention can be construed as a conclave of conniving land barons. Land-hungry delegates and the speculator lobby worked to make certain the new government would continue the lucrative policy of trading land for distressed or discounted government scrip, at one-fourth to one-eighth its dollar face value. Speculators also knew well that a strong national government would raise the real value of government paper that they had bought cheaply. Before 1787 public land worth at face value $10,000 could be negotiated for $2,000 in scrip. But if the proposed Constitution was adopted, the same deal might cost $6,000 or even the full $10,000. American land barons and large-scale speculators took care to be named delegates from their states. Land-rich George Washington was elected president of the convention. Thirty-three of the 55 delegates were landed rich men. Despite Thomas Jefferson's obvious self-interest, he was stuck in Paris as the American minister. Hugh Williamson, a delegate from North Carolina, spoke for his colleagues when he dissembled, "For myself, I conceive that my opinions are not biased by private interest, but having claims to a considerable quantity of land in the western country, I am fully persuaded that the value of those lands must be increased by an efficient federal government." If we put aside the lofty idealistic statements made by the delegates at Philadelphia, many constitutional provisions aided land speculation by the wealthy. These included centralization of legal and regulatory authority over land, preservation of the sanctity of private property, protection of contract obligation, support for internal improvements, and ownership of property as a condition for the right to vote. Many of the Founding Fathers worked hard to guarantee that the Constitution was a pro-entrepreneur document. Article I, Section 10, reads, "No State shall . . . pass any . . . law impairing the Obligation of Contracts," seemed a deliberate step to protect private enterprise. The Constitution sanctified private property, but did not promote it outside of agriculture. The 1785 Land Survey Act already implied the speedy transfer of public land into private farmland. Charles Beard's 1913 economic interpretation of the Constitution still carries weight: "Speculation in western lands was one of the leading activities of capitalists in those days. The chief obstacle in the way of the rapid appreciation of these lands was the weakness of the national government which prevented the complete subjugation of the Indians, the destruction of old Indian claims, and the orderly settlement of the frontier. Every leading capitalist of the time thoroughly understood the relation of a new constitution to the rise in land values beyond the Alleghenies." The Confederation government had neither the funds nor the authority to raise and send troops into open regions to protect settlers and the interests of speculators. In other words, the stronger the federal government, the safer the western lands, and the bigger the profits.

The Northwest Ordinance of 1787

In less than four years, between 1784 and 1787, Congress had gained control of the public domain and guaranteed that new western states would have full equality with the old original states. In a short time, Americans attempted to absorb the meaning of their large-scale geography from Maine to the Great Lakes and down the Mississippi Valley to Louisiana, much of it uncharted country. In the late 1700s no one was clear whether the interior of the continent was of value beyond fur trapping and trade with Indians. In 1787 James Monroe flatly told Thomas Jefferson that the United States west of the Appalachians was no bargain: "A great part of the territory is miserably poor [and] consists of extensive plains which have not had from appearances, and will not have, a single bush upon them for ages. The districts therefore within which these fall will perhaps never contain a sufficient number of inhabitants to entitle them" to become new and equal states. No wonder Jefferson, despite his usual optimism, concluded that it would take 100 generations before Americans would settle the continent to the western sea. (The actual total would be less than five generations.) Despite these misgivings, opportunists like Alexander Hamilton wondered how to gain control over "the amazing extent of the country." Doubters worried that "no extensive empire [could ever] be governed upon republican principles." Once the people of the United States marched across the mountains toward the Mississippi River, would their nation become so large to "degenerate to a despotism"? There were no historic precedents for a democracy of such size. Had not the great political philosopher, Plato, decreed that only small republics could ensure universal citizen participation? Would Americans keep either their liberties or an extensive geography, but not both? Was it "impossible for one code of laws to suit Georgia and Massachusetts?" In 1786 Jefferson cautiously affirmed, "Our present federal limits are not too large for good government." James Madison added that bigger was better, since "the greater number of citizens and extent of territory renders factious combinations less to be dreaded" because they could be dispersed into the countryside and not rub against each other. The doubling and tripling of the nation's size would swamp interstate rivalries and enhance the authority of the federal government as the giver of land and interstate peacemaker. Yet, could it be seriously believed "that this vast country including the western territory will 150 years hence remain one nation"? Would not the West become a separate and rival nation centered on the Mississippi

River? The question of western independence loomed large. If westerners got free navigation on the Mississippi, would they have little interest in remaining with the old Atlantic coast–oriented union? Jefferson wrote that, unless Congress held firm, "our several states will crumble to atoms by the spirit of establishing every little canton into a separate state." Congress confirmed that states would be created for westerners, but it insisted that westerners could not make their own states.

One modern English historian, J. H. Plumb, concluded that the geographical expansion of the United States as a single nation was one of world history's major achievements. The American experience is remarkable, he said, because it avoided balkanization into several different conflicting nations. Settlers in Virginia's Kentucky region, separated from the state government by 100 miles of trackless mountains and forests, wrote blistering reports that they had fewer rights than British colonials once had. Kentucky's frontier politicians insisted that their isolating geography "precludes every idea of a connection on republican principles, and originates many grievances." Separatists threatened to take North Carolina's Franklin region out of the state to free themselves from the "aristocratical spirit" in the east. John Jay advised New Yorkers that "we have unquestionably more territory than we can govern." James Lovell of Massachusetts acknowledged that his state's "extent of territory" made government unwieldy. Determining the future status of the western region was not merely a theoretical exercise. British and Spanish agents were rumored to be behind separatist claims in the West. Was it not inevitable that the rapidly expanding United States would break up into factions and become vulnerable to takeover by one of the great imperial powers? A Maine separatist threatened switching to Britain. It was still feared that the British would snap up weak New Hampshire in the north and South Carolina would be stripped away by Spain.

Would western regions become colonies of the old states? Would they be treated like Ireland and Scotland had been by the English? Political philosophers agreed that the original 13 states must hold no monopoly of statehood. Yet agitation for new states led into the unknown political and legal thickets of sovereignty, territoriality, and ownership. How large, or small, in its geography and its population, should a self-governing state be? In 1784 Jefferson proposed to a congressional committee an idealistic plan for a nation of small states, each between 100 and 150 miles square. Behind the scene also stood an opportunistic Massachusetts clergyman, the Reverend Manasseh Cutler, a principal backer of the Ohio Company, and intimate with investors of the rapacious Scioto Company. When Cutler showed up in New York City in July 1787 to lobby Congress, he had already hatched a shady scheme to acquire 3 to 5 million acres in Ohio, "all for the cost," said historian Ray Billington, "of one oyster dinner and a loan of $200,000 in depreciated currency." To Congress's credit, considering its need to generate quick money by selling land, it realized that it must not allow the public domain, a region larger than the original 13 states, to become either a vast colony or a number of troublesome private kingdoms. Nor could western settlers take matters into their own hands and undermine the authority of the central government.

A few days after Cutler's ominous appearance, Congress unanimously passed the Northwest Ordinance of 1787. It was a great and definitive piece of Confederation legislation. Even George Washington, a real estate enthusiast, had warned, "We are fast verging to anarchy and confusion." The ordinance transformed the "Territory North West of the Ohio" into a federal district that would become three to five territories, each to be administered by a governor, secretary, and three judges named by Congress. When the adult male population reached 5,000, they could elect a legislature to share power with a council of five chosen by the governor and

Congress. At this stage the territory could send a nonvoting delegate to Congress. The final stage of statehood would be reached when the total population reached 60,000. They could then write their own state constitution and apply for admission to the Union on equal terms with all other states. The ordinance included its own bill of rights guaranteeing freedom of worship, proportional representation, trial by jury, the common law, writ of habeas corpus, and right of private contracts, all in anticipation of the 1791 federal Bill of Rights. Slavery was prohibited and feudal inheritance laws were forbidden. All of these steps were to take place under the friendly guidance of Congress, which thereby confirmed its power over the public domain and the state-making process.

The stakes had been immeasurably high. The public domain created between 1784 and 1787 attracted floods of white settlers and fostered the growth of the entire nation. The large and attractive region, with deep soils, abundant rain, and a temperate climate, gave prestige to the central government versus the competing interests of individual states. The government proceeded to drain wet areas, irrigate dry places, and manage the forests. Federal land created demand for internal improvements including transportation ties connecting the old East and the new West. Roads, turnpikes, canals, and railroads followed (and sometimes anticipated) farmers who settled on the public domain.

The Great American Experiment in Land Reform: Selling the Public Domain

Some of the most important maps depicting American society are cadastral maps that show a fragmented private ownership of land over more than two-thirds of the present United States. Looking back, colonial land distribution had been a series of extensive experiments that encouraged population growth by attracting land-hungry immigrants. It promoted rapid but sketchy settlement of a continuously expanding geography. Back in their country of origin, be it in Britain or in Europe, the most economically depressed people in the eighteenth century had been landless farmers, insecure tenants, and those who worked marginal land; they lived amid poverty, hunger, and death with little hope for future improvement. A central tenet of most immigrants' dreams was to own a plot of land on which to grow one's own food crops, husband a few domestic animals, and house and feed a family. To most Europeans this meant 5 or 10 acres of arable land; ownership of 100 acres was like a realized fantasy. Successful farming created individual economic security and produced a society that shared economic progress on the broadest possible basis.

After independence, excited Americans peered westward over the top ridges of Appalachian mountains. But what did they see? They no longer were impeded by the loathsome Proclamation Line and Quebec Act, by which England attempted to shut down western expansion, but they feared the justifiable anger of the Indians and worried about speculators who held out the best farmland while waiting for high prices. They also enjoyed unparalleled geographical mobility. For the freedman, no internal controls, such as customs offices, border patrols, identity documents, migration regulations, or constraints on river navigation or road travel, existed between states and territories and undesignated regions. Movement across the nation's geography was taken to be a basic natural right and personal freedom in the United

States. In Donald Meinig's words, a powerful combination of "Liberty, property, and mobility lay intertwined at the base of America culture," together with "a special fusion of capitalism, individualism, and nationalism."

The American dream was defined by private property: A man (few women enjoyed such rights) could buy the land he wanted, use it profitably or wastefully, sell what he wanted, divide it, or simply hold it indefinitely. Once the government sold a parcel of land, it stepped out of the picture to allow the marketplace to take control. It was widely believed that private ownership was the wellspring of individual rights and free enterprise by allowing virtually unconstrained use by the landowner. Nor could anyone who owned land, it was believed, experience personal failure, since ownership of good farmland, combined with agricultural skill, promised abundance and prosperity. But it is important to add that private land became a vested interest that defended the social and economic status quo in which it was created. Land ownership is thus troublesome to reshape (e.g., land reform). Ironically, private property made the revolutionary United States into one of the most conservative nations on earth.

The issues surrounding the western lands must be seen in the context of explosive land reform soon to come in Mexico, Chile, Egypt, and other nations as well as the United States. Land reform historically meant the guaranteed right of an increasing number of ordinary people to hold land. Such possession was an incentive to improve the land and raise productivity. This included authoritative property surveys supported by government authority and kept as public record. Titles to land also created reliable markets for the sale of land between private parties. In the United States most land reform that began in 1785 was a form of centralized national planning that promoted optimum-scale operation of farmland. Through public land offices, it created and managed regional markets by setting prices, holding auctions, and limiting the power of middlemen. Six hundred forty acres (later 160 acres) was defined as a correct size for full and efficient utilization of resources under given technological conditions. Government also controlled so-called externalities, such as the cost and availability of low-interest loans and long-term credit. Where farmer-citizens were still unable to prosper, it offered subsidies and other incentives. Overall, government actions had as much impact on the relative cost of farming as any existing "free market." There were inherent problems in the American land reform system. It was usually a long-term investment, sometimes with rewards so distant they could not satisfy immediate survival needs. Hamilton correctly feared that a stake in the land tended to reduce the incentive to seek opportunity elsewhere, such as in industry. Jefferson's emphasis on the family farm also created one of America's most unique and troublesome features: the isolated farm of a single family, instead of farmers congregated together in the Old World agrarian village. This made the American farmer's life more vulnerable when prices were low or the climate went bad.

Getting a Grip on the Land: The Land Survey Ordinance of 1785

Following the Revolution, with a weak central government and state authority in disarray, speculation ran wild over tremendous tracts in central and western New York, in western Pennsylvania, and across western Virginia that would become Kentucky and western North Carolina that would become Tennessee. The constantly shifting "Indian line" of safe settlement, together with uncontrolled activity by land companies, turned remote western regions into fluid territories where established eastern practices simply disappeared like wild shots into a dense forest. This was further complicated by free land distributed to veterans by warrants that they frequently sold at large discounts. Nor were matters helped by the "Land Grab Act" of 1783 that offered 100 acres of public land at 10 pounds in radically depreciated paper currency. It became increasingly clear that the newly independent Americans needed a plan for land survey and public sale that would establish orderly land distribution and settlement. Otherwise they were risking the loss of control over the public domain. They had learned from their colonial experience that a geometric land pattern was at best troublesome to impose after settlement and probably impossible. It sold poor land with the good and entirely ignored rivers, mountains, swamps, and dry places. Yet in 1785 Timothy Pickering worried, "If adventurers should be permitted to ramble over that extensive country, and take up all the most valuable tracts, the best lands would be in a manner given away; and the settler thus dispersed it will be impossible to govern; they will soon excite the resentments of the natives."

Nevertheless, a geometric pattern was chosen as the law of the land. Thomas Jefferson was the mastermind behind the land grid survey and sale of the public domain. He was determined to abolish feudal hereditary rights and peasantlike tenancy that had been carried over from England. He first suggested not sale of the public domain into private hands, but long-term leases. Leases might avoid the dangers of private misuse, reduce continuous conflict on overlapping titles, and prohibit speculation by the wealthy. Getting nowhere with leasing, Jefferson rode a tide of popular opinion when he advocated low-cost sale as the hard-earned natural right of Americans. He rebuked George Washington and Robert Morris when they kept good land off the market while waiting for higher prices. Alexander Hamilton, Jefferson's conservative protagonist, had a crustier opinion. He retorted that the western land was the nation's one great asset and should not be squandered but sold for the best possible price to raise funds to pay the national debt and run the government. Other opinions were equally divided. Should the rest of the land be sold to deserving settlers as cheaply as possible? Or should it go for the highest possible price to raise cash for the struggling new government? The Jeffersonian dream was of the yeoman farmer on a small secure tract of 40 to 160 acres, a grand estate by any definition elsewhere in the world. Jefferson was not the only one who fervently believed that smallholder land ownership made poverty and pauperism practically nonexistent. This freehold farming intentionally sought to redistribute income and wealth in favor of ordinary citizens.

Jefferson chaired the congressional committee to draft the land distribution plan, and he used the opportunity to recommend the orderly Massachusetts township surveys in combination with the southern system of government land offices to administer title claims, registrations, and payments. Jefferson's creative intellect, to the exasperation of his co-workers, laid out three alternative tract plans on the committee—1,000 acres, 850 acres, and 640 acres. The first would have revolutionized surveying by eliminating the traditional Gunther's surveyor's chain of 66 feet and applying the rational 100 feet (just as Jefferson would persuade the new nation to settle on 100 cents to the dollar). But Jefferson could not budge his committee from Gunther's chain, of which landscape historian John R. Stilgoe says, "no mathematical ratio is more important in the American Enlightenment landscape." An acre was 10 square chains, each tract to be called a "hundred." Jefferson also fiddled with the mile, sometimes using the geographical mile of 6,086 feet, giving 850 acres per square mile, but eventually he agreed to the statute mile of 5,280 feet, generating 640 acres. In 1784 Jefferson provided his committee with specific details for the survey. A base line or surveyor's line that ran east to west would be crossed by north-south meridian lines at mathematically regular intervals. The survey must be "plainly marked by chaps or marks on the trees [and] exactly described on a plat [map]." Ever the practical farmer, he hedged his geometrical approach by insisting that useful terrain descriptions be marked on the plat, with "all water-courses, mountains, and other remarkable and permanent things" located in distances from base and meridian lines.

Congress dithered, and Jefferson reluctantly left the committee's unfinished business to others when he was appointed ambassador to France. There he became a more determined advocate of a federal land system to serve the freehold farmer after he visited Versailles's formal gardens, a playground of the aristocracy that excluded ordinary people. In 1785 a new committee tinkered lightly with Jefferson's scheme before sending it to Congress for debate and vote. The ordinance had one primary objective: "The western territory . . . ceded by individual states to the United States" and "purchased of the Indian inhabitants" was to be "disposed" into private hands as quickly as possible. The geometric pattern held, with townships set at 6 square statute miles. The first township was to be sold whole, the second by lots or sections, "and thus in alternate order through the whole of the first range." Lots number 8, 11, 26, and 29 were held out for the national government, without explanation. Lot 16 was protected for the maintenance of a public school in each township. The plan brushed aside several existing land ownership patterns: the traditional metes-and-bounds, the French "long-lot" *ranges* measured by 192-foot *arpents,* and the irregular "blazed" lots of "indiscriminate location and subsequent survey," often measured in 39-inch "perches," that had confounded land titles in Virginia and Pennsylvania. No one could agree on an ideal farm size. The new landscape geometry varied from 640-acre mile-square sections to 23,040-acre 6-square-mile townships. Later, corrective legislation worked the minimum size down to half sections of 320 acres, followed by the fabled "quarter section" of 160 acres, and eventually quarter-quarter sections covering only 40 acres. The debate has never subsided. A midcontinent plains farmer on 640 acres complained in 1880 that he was "starvin' to death on [his] gov't claim." "Irrigation crusaders" around 1900 claimed that in California an industrious and efficient farmer would on 40 acres earn four times more than his brother factory worker toiling in an industrial city.

The Land Ordinance, passed on May 20, 1785, set sales at public auction, with a standard price of a dollar an acre. This was the going price for land in much of prerevolutionary America, but it remained too expensive for most small farmers. If a buyer was lucky enough to hold veterans' scrip or other depreciated paper, he could get land at pennies an acre. The ordinance was intended to prevent speculators, individually or in companies, from rambling over the public domain and picking up the most valuable land at the lowest possible prices. In reality, the ordinance attracted wealthy speculators across the country, as some congressmen probably intended. Protection from speculation broke down immediately by misuse of discounted warrants and depreciated certificates to acquire land for pennies an acre regardless of the official price. Most troublesome was that there were no limits set on the number of tracts an individual or a single private company could acquire, nor was any requirement made for settlement or improvement. Yet had the Land Survey Ordinance of 1785 not been passed, Americans might have spent the rest of their history buying land solely from a series of powerful and autonomous private land companies with virtual feudal powers over personal fiefdoms.

By passage of the land ordinance, the struggling Confederation Congress shaped the rest of America's history, environmental and otherwise. This was two years *before* the delegates met in Philadelphia and wrote the Constitution. The land ordinance created the right-angled geometric pattern of continuous land survey and public sale that would eventually crisscross the western two-thirds of the emerging United States. Like an over-the-horizon radar, the survey looked into new regions—known, unknown, unseen and sometimes only imagined—forests, plains, mountains, deserts, and gardens to the Pacific shore. The survey provided a means to rationalize and control the American land, buy it and sell it, even while it did not yet have a recognizable geography or final boundary line. It changed the entire national domain west of Pennsylvania and north of the Ohio River from a formless wilderness into a national geometry of gigantic squares and rectangles. It was also a highly efficient way to generate public funds and guarantee private property.

The Seven Ranges

For want of enough good surveys, a frontier was nearly lost. The Confederation Congress could groan and birth a good law, but it fell into its usual inept ways in the simple discharge of the ordinance of 1785. Skilled surveyors were hard to find; they were most often self-taught measurers who learned to use instruments by platting the perimeters of their own farms and those of a few neighbors. In addition, the Ohio terrain of the Seven Ranges is chopped up into myriad stream hollows and hills. Surveyors repeatedly complained about "swamps, flies, and fever" as well as angry Indians. A small stone monument near East Liverpool, Ohio, where the north side of the Ohio River crosses from Pennsylvania, marks the beginning point of the Seven Ranges survey. It was to run up to the Indian lands in Ohio's northwest quarter set by the Greenville treaty (discussed later in this chapter). The impact cannot be overestimated. Over the next 50 years a newly arrived farmer could show up at the regional land office (the first established at Zanesville in Ohio) and identify his geometric right-angled quarter section by a location and number on a map. He would pay $1 per acre to have absolute personal ownership. The rationality of the system, with precise location of townships and sections, made it possible to buy a specific tract without seeing it, a real boon for speculators. The nation's official geographer, Thomas Hutchins, who had already surveyed the southern boundary of Pennsylvania, was personally to run the first base line westward. He used a sextant, an ordinary compass, and circumferentors to establish a true astronomic meridian. He reported a latitude of 40°38'02", which was 25 seconds off the actual 40°38'27" (additionally his compass readings did not compensate for magnetic variation). The west end of his survey angled about a mile south of the intended latitude.

With 8 other surveyors and 30 chainmen and axmen, Hutchins was to measure seven townships (42 miles) westward and his surveyors to work at right angles south to create 6-mile-square townships down to the Ohio River near Marietta. Because of the meander of the Ohio River, the eastern border of the Seven Ranges was irregular, but the rest was geometric. Over ten days in the early fall of 1785, Hutchins ran his line 4 miles west, using a compass and a two-pole (33 foot) Gunther's chain. A wood post marked the end of each mile, and trees were blazed (marked by the chop of an ax) along the way. Hutchins stopped work prematurely because of rumors of nearby Indian troubles. He also complained that the pay rate for his men of $2 a day was inadequate for accurate work; Congress replied by taking him off the true meridian requirement. Surveying did not resume until August 1786. After completing his base line, his team started range lines south to the Ohio River, until Indian troubles once more stopped work at the end of October. Work resumed slowly amid Indian threats through June 1787. Hutchins forwarded his legal plats and descriptive field notes to the Board of Treasury in New York in July 1788. The interior lines of each township, to divide each into 36 equal square miles, were not surveyed in the field, but drawn on the plat map that the

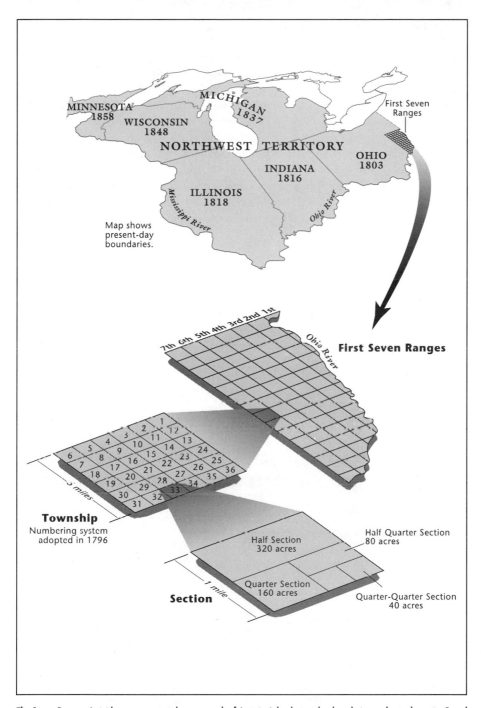

The Seven Ranges. A rigid geometry spread across much of America's landscape that largely ignored actual terrain. Based on the Land Survey Ordinance of 1785, it began with the mapping and survey of the Seven Ranges in southeastern Ohio. To the east and south, the land remained in irregular patterns of ownership and settlement. The far southwest and the Texas region were covered by separate sale and survey systems. But the rest of the United States, and its future expansion, would come under the rectangular (cadastral) survey and private sale system. It was a powerful system of land reform.

geographer provided to the federal Board of Treasury. Different groups, such as religious community, could buy a whole township to subdivide and settle. Or individuals could buy lots in the alternative townships.

Congress had put the survey on an impossibly accelerated timetable because it desperately needed money out of the land sales. By 1787, after 20 months of work, the field surveyors, much to the dismay of Congress, had surveyed and located on plat maps only four of the Seven Ranges. The four surveyed ranges were put on the market immediately. The first patent was sold for $640 to a John Martin in New York City on March 4, 1788, for Lot 20, Township 7, Range 4, an unmarked piece of land because it was inside a township. Martin himself would have had to locate his tract, which would have to be "stubbed in" from the nearest corner on the township line. This showed a large flaw in the survey system. Only about 73,000

Public Land Laws, 1785–1916

Year	Price (per acre)	Size (acres)	Conditions
1785	$1 minimum	640 or more	Cash sale; amended in 1787 to provide for payment of one third in cash, the remainder in three months
1796	$2 minimum	640 or more	One half of purchase price paid within 30 days, the remainder within one year
1800	$2 minimum	320 or more	One fourth of purchase price paid within 30 days, then annual installments of one fourth for three years, at 6 percent interest
1804	$2 minimum ($1.64 for cash)	160 or more	Credit as in act of 1800; discount to $1.64 per acre for cash payment
1820	$1.25 minimum	80 or more	End of credit system; cash payment only
1830	$1.25 minimum	160 maximum	Squatters on public domain land allowed to purchase their tracts at the minimum price (preemption); temporary act, had to be renewed biennially
1832	$1.25 minimum	40 or more; 160 limit on preemption	Cash purchase only; right of preemption reaffirmed
1841	$1.25 minimum	40 or more; 160 limit on preemption	Cash purchase only; established right of preemption, doing away with necessity of renewing legislation
1854 (Graduation Act)	12.5 cents minimum	40 or more	Reduction of the sale price of land in proportion to the length of time it had been on the market; price ranged from $1 for land unsold for ten years to 12.5 cents for land unsold for thirty years

acres were sold for $117,000, all to small purchasers, and no entire townships had been sold. The survey of the same land cost only $14,876.34, but Congress was disappointed. In one of its last major acts in early 1789, the Confederation Congress ordered the Board of the Treasury to complete the survey and sale of the rest of the Seven Ranges under the original conditions. This was a second attempt to revive small-size land sales. But sales ground to a halt as Americans waited anxiously for the outcome of the Constitutional Convention and approval of the new Constitution by the original 13 states. Not until seven years later, in 1796, would the new federal Congress amend the land survey legislation in an attempt to resolve the muddled interests, priorities, and policies that controlled the public domain. As late as 1800 only 50,000 acres were actually titled into private hands because of flawed legislation and bureaucratic delays.

Public Land Laws, 1785–1916 (continued)

Year	Price (per acre)	Size (acres)	Conditions
1862 (Homestead Act)	Free	160 or less	Payment of an entry fee and five years continuous residence; land could be preempted after six months' residence for $1.25 per acre cash
1873 (Timber Culture Act)	Free	160	Cultivation of trees on one quarter of a 160-acre plot gave the settler title to the whole 160 acres; amended in 1878 to require the cultivation of trees on only one sixteenth of the plot
1878 (Timber and Stone Act)	$2.50	160 or less	Sale of lands chiefly valuable for timber or stone resources to bona fide settlers and mining interests
1877 (Desert Land Act)	$1.25	640; reduced to 320 maximum in 1890	Sale of a section of land to a settler on condition that it be irrigated within three years; amended in 1891 to increase the amount of improvements required, with one eighth of the land to be under cultivation; payment to be 25 cents at time of entry, $1 at the time of making proof of compliance with the law
1909 (Enlarged Homestead Act)	Free	320 acres	Five years' residence with continuous cultivation; designed for semiarid lands that were nonirrigable and had no minerals or merchantable timber
1916 (Stock-Raising Homestead Act)	Free	640 acres	Designed for land useful only for grazing; conditions similar to previous Homestead laws

---

The Privatization of America's Geography: Rush to Wealth

Buying land on speculation became a national preoccupation. The public domain was like an expanding universe as long as the territory of the United States grew and the Land Office released more land for sale. A speculator was often one's next-door neighbor. Most local "poor" farmers openly bought more land than they could possibly plant, took advantage of their firsthand information, and craftily sold to newcomers, or waited until prime soil became scarce. Land office agents tended to look the other way and themselves used inside information to snatch good farmland.

Ohio as the Speculator's Battlefield

Nothing excited George Washington, normally a very reserved man, more than a good land deal. Even when he was a struggling young militia officer assigned to the Forks of the Ohio country, he opportunistically scouted and bought land. In 1783 Washington admitted that the western lands must not be suffered "to be overrun with land jobbers, speculators, and monopolisers or even with scattered settlers." Americans must not abandon the public domain "to aggrandize a few avaricious men to the prejudice of many." In 1784 he might have described himself when he wrote, "Men in these times talk with as much facility of 50,000, 100,000, even 500,000 acres as a gentleman formerly would of 1,000 acres. In defiance of the proclamation of Congress, they roam over the country on the Indian side of Ohio, mark out lands, survey, and even settlement." By 1796 Washington owned 32,373 acres in the Ohio Country alone. "Any person who neglects the present opportunity of hunting out good lands, and marking and distinguishing them for his own (in order to keep others from settling them)," he said, "will never regain it." He also publicly vouched for the new Ohio Company, said to be composed of veterans who had served with him. In one breathtaking move in 1787 Congress sold over a million acres to the Ohio Company. The company paid with depreciated (discounted) land certificates it had been quietly accumulating at less than 10 cents an acre. If anyone complained that with such a deal the nation was squandering its capital resources to pay daily bills, it seemed minor in light of the vast stretches of real estate still untouched north of the Ohio River. Within a week Congress enhanced the value of the company's new holdings when it passed the Northwest Ordinance. By the fall of 1787 Congress authorized other large sales of "not less than one million of acres in one body." This resulted in a land grab in 1788 by the wealthy and clever New Jersey politician John Cleves Symmes. He found and took land that had tens of miles of valuable frontage on the north side of the Ohio River (including today's Cincinnati). He complained that freshly arrived settlers "almost laugh me full in the face when I ask them one dollar per acre for first-rate land, and tell me they will soon have as good for thirty cents" from the government. Symmes distorted his surveys so much and paid so little attention to the well-being of settlers while charging the highest possible prices for doubtful property titles that Congress, embarrassed by his scheming, killed further large land sales.

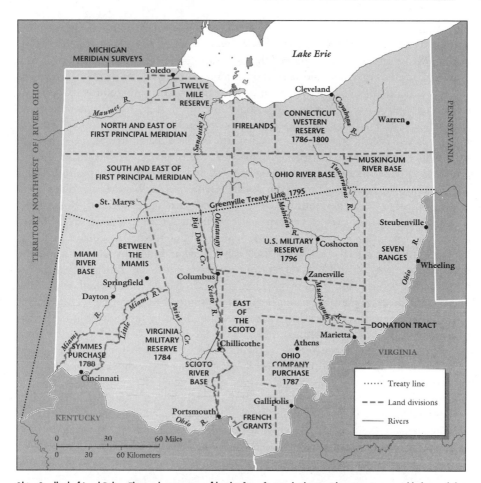

Ohio: Seedbed of Land Policy. The implementation of land reform first took place in Ohio. Americans quickly learned that the public lands went into private hands through often-conflicting actions involving the official survey and sale system, claims by determined local squatters, veterans with warrants, outright large-scale grants to speculators, and conquest and removal of native peoples.

Connecticut demanded its Western Reserve carved out of the Ohio country to compensate victims and veterans of the Revolutionary War. After the British had burned New Haven, Greenwich, Norwalk, Fairfield, and New London, the legislature granted 500,000 acres of "Firelands" at the western end of the reserve. It sold the rest of the reserve to the Connecticut Land Company, ignoring Indian land claims that were not finally overcome until 1805. A private survey was more than 1° off at its western border, giving it hundreds more acres, but Surveyor General Jared Mansfield accepted the mistake to avoid resurveying trouble and litigation. His reward was a local town in his name. With the setting apart of veterans' lands in Connecticut's Western Reserve (including today's Cleveland) and the Virginia Military Tract (another large veterans' reserve), less than half of Ohio's land, much of it in the inaccessible center of the state, was available for the government to sell to ordinary settlers.

The Indians watched ferocious white land-grabbers with disbelief; they seemed less than human. In 1783 nearly half of the new nation was unceded Indian land, legally off limits to settlers. White settlers took for granted that American policy intended to clear the entire Ohio Valley of Indians to foster land sales and settlement. The Indians were not treated as equals, but as inhabitants of a protectorate of dependent peoples, ambiguously called "resident foreign nations." George Washington said nothing out of the ordinary when he wrote that the new United States acquired its territorial sovereignty in 1783 not from the native peoples but because "Great Britain has ceded all of the lands of the United States within the limits described by the provisional treaty." In this view, the land was not taken from the natives but from the English king. The Indians deserved little sympathy, it was said, because they had been brutal allies of the British during the Revolutionary War. Most Indians obviously saw the British as better neighbors than the surly and rapacious Americans. Not surprisingly, Indians turned violent toward the perpetually intruding settlers and twice, in 1790 and 1791, badly mauled a large force of U.S. militia sent to subdue them. An Indian confederation demanded that the survey of the Seven Ranges be halted and the Ohio River become the southern boundary of tribal lands. The Americans had no interest in creating a permanent Indian buffer state. In 1794 troops led by Gen. "Mad Anthony" Wayne defeated an unusual combined Indian force at the Battle of Fallen Timbers in northwestern Ohio. Nearly two-thirds of Ohio and part of Indiana were reluctantly surrendered by the Indians at the Treaty of Greenville in 1795. They were promised that the white soldiers would keep settlers from intruding onto the remaining native soil, nor would white men come for more land again. Settlers enthusiastically rushed into the new empty Ohio country without waiting for legal niceties, like survey and public sale, from an eastern government. The population of the new state, Ohio, mushroomed twelvefold from 50,000 to 600,000 between 1803 and 1820. Similar promises were made, and broken, with Cherokee, Creek, Choctaw, and Chickasaw tribes who inhabited most of the southern backcountry from Tennessee to the Gulf Coast and would find themselves driven westward to clear the land for white settlers.

Correcting the System to Suit the Land Rush

Congress revived on-site surveying in Ohio in 1790. President Washington named Rufus Putnam, territorial judge in Ohio and also chief agent for the notorious Ohio Company, as the new surveyor general. It was like letting the fox into the chicken coop, but the president hoped Putnam's familiarity with Ohio development would give the government a shrewd and knowledgeable negotiator to make the best of the public domain. To his credit, Putnam put experienced surveyors at work in the field and kept scrupulous records. By 1797 he had surveyed to Indian territory at the Greenville treaty line in the northwest quarter of the state. In 1803 Jared Mansfield would become the first professional surveyor general. He had taught mathematics at West Point, wrote basic textbooks in algebra, geometry, calculus, and astronomy, and acquired superior field equipment from England. Survey historian C. Albert White said, "It was during Mansfield's tenure of office that the rectangular system of surveys was developed into a system closely approaching that in use today." The combination of an efficient survey, Indian removal, tens of thousands of trespassing squatters, a few thousand bona fide farm owners, and a speculative economy brought new public land states into the Union:

Indiana in 1816, Mississippi in 1817, Illinois in 1818, Alabama in 1819, and Missouri in 1821.

Congress amended the ordinance of 1785 by the more "liberal" Land Act of 1796. It focused on "the sale of the lands of the United States, in the territory northwest of the river Ohio, and above the mouth of the Kentucky River." The price went up to $2 an acre, which put land costs far out of reach for most farm families, but offered land on credit. Credit, however, was so limited in the new law as to be virtually meaningless—based on a 5 percent immediate down payment, with payment of 50 percent within 30 days and the balance within a year. It became clear that settlers could not afford to buy full 640-acre sections, much less entire townships. In an era of a barter economy, when poor farmers rarely saw $100 cash in a year, only a few farm families had $64 on hand for the down payment on the minimum 640-acre tract, and they would be most unlikely to come up with an additional $574 within 30 days, much less the balance of $640 at the end of a year. Congress showed its true colors by granting a substantial 10 percent discount to cash-rich buyers who paid in a lump sum. No wonder many small farmers simply settled as squatters on unclaimed (and usually unsurveyed) but fertile land. They hoped that possession and improvements would allow them to keep the land.

If Congress intended to sell land to pay the national debt, the sales were so small, or so deeply discounted, that by May 1800 only a total of 121,540 acres had been sold averaging much less than $1 an acre, partly because of the cash-on-the-barrelhead discount. Deeply depreciated government securities, 12 to 15 cents on the dollar, were widely applied at face value to land purchase. One official complained that at this rate the national debt for 1796 alone would not be paid off for 100 years. The older states for a time were selling their land much cheaper and in small lots. New York sold on credit for as little as 20 cents an acre and no more than a dollar. Massachusetts was selling its Maine land for 50 cents an acre. Pennsylvania auctioned land in its northwest corner at an average of 34 cents, and squatters in Virginia could make their farm legal for 25 cents an acre. As a corrective, the Land Act of 1800 allowed sale of 320-acre half sections, and opened credit slightly. In 1800 a farmer could put down $160 to buy 320 acres. After two years another $160 was due, plus $57.60 interest. A year later another $160 plus $19.20 interest came due. The final payment was $160, with $9.60 interest, by the fourth year, for a total of $726.40, compared to $1,280 within one year as required by the act of 1796 four years earlier. For the frontier settler who needed five years to carve out a productive farm and who might need many years to overcome a mortgage of a few hundred dollars, the new terms were still beyond reach. But the new terms kept Ohio a speculator's dream. Cash-rich senators and judges fulfilled Alexander Hamilton's prophecy that the nation's land expansion belonged to the big investor. In 1801 almost 397,000 acres were transferred into private hands and by 1804 it reached 1.3 million acres. Ohio's public domain had largely disappeared by 1820. This "Ohio fever" soon became "Illinois and Missouri feever."

The Act of 1800 also introduced a major change by establishing local land offices in Ohio. Before this all surveys and sales had been operated directly from the department of the treasury in Washington, with impossible delays. Local land offices now became the outposts for surveying new land and adjudicating boundary disputes. They produced the all-important survey plat maps and kept records of ownership. Government management still fell behind. The officer at Shawneetown in Indiana complained, "There are nearly a thousand improved places in this district that are not located." In response to such complaints, Congress passed the Act of 1812, which created the all-important General Land Office. It continued in operation

wherever public land was being sold until 1935, when the Taylor Grazing Act finally terminated public land sales. The General Land Office immediately did a "land office business" because it directed orderly, consistent, and uncomplicated surveys, published field reports marked
clearly on plat maps, ran public auctions of new empty lands, sold leftover land at minimum
government prices, and confronted squatters over the best land. Commissioner Josiah Meigs
wrote in 1818 that "so wise, beautiful and perfect a system was never before adopted by any
government or nation on earth." One land registrar complained that everyone comes "like the
locusts of Egypt, and darken the office, with clouds of smoke and dust, and an uproar occa-
sioned by whiskey and avarice." The notice of an auction attracted crowds of speculators "in
their ruffled shirts" carrying wads of discounted paper warrants. Anxious squatters struggled to
purchase their own farmland as cheaply as possible. Land office historian Malcolm J.
Rohrbough wrote, "A public land sale ranked with birth, marriage, and death among the most
significant events in the life of any frontiersman. Here, in a few seconds, decisions were made
that had a lifelong impact on the men who were present."

Complaints still poured in the land offices about erroneous surveying by incompetent
surveyors and platters, as well as backlogs in field notes, records of sales, private land claims,
and settlement of disputes in land offices. The problems produced a businesslike restructuring of the Land Office in 1836. A Senate committee in 1840 belatedly admitted that "few
places afford such ready and certain means of acquiring fortunes, and of extending favors and
accommodation to a large and influential portion of the community, as those attached to the
land system." Farmers reacted to speculators by forming themselves into claims clubs to intimidate outside buyers. In northern Illinois, "If a speculator should bid on a settler's [e.g.,
squatter's] farm, he was knocked down and dragged out of the office, and if the striker was
prosecuted and fined, the settlers paid the expense." Claims clubs subverted the law across
some of the nation's best farmland in the Midwest. One Michigan group wrote its own constitution, set up its own private vigilante government to control land sales and title transfers,
and even ran its own surveys and boundaries from township lines.

As the survey blanketed the landscape, the land offices grew from 36 in 1831 to 62 in
1837. Land officers on all levels emerged as some of the most powerful officials in the nation,
and were often free to interpret the laws as they saw fit. Some contemporaries feared a class
war between government agents, individual preempting farmers, capitalistic speculators, and
manipulative congressmen. In 1830 and 1831 overall land office sales covered 4.7 million
acres. The years 1834 and 1835 saw 19.2 million acres passed from public to private hands
through the land office. In 1836 over 20 million acres were sold for over $25 million. One of
Congress's goals was reached and surpassed: Within 50 years after passage of the 1785 land
ordinance more than 4.5 million people poured into the vast public domain west of the Appalachians. One modern historian concluded that the operations of the land office at Marietta or at Zanesville were as important to American history as the battle of Bunker Hill and
the taking of Fort Ticonderoga.

The Problem with Squatters

The ordinance of 1785 did not, in fact, create the first historical settlement pattern on western public lands. Squatters came first. Once the Indians were driven off, the first surveying
teams would not find empty territory but instead a landscape peppered with irregular fields
and homesites. Tens of thousands of squatters had quickly hunkered down on the best farm-

land of the region to build homes and barns and fences and cultivate the land, regardless of the land claims of speculators or legal settlers. When it came to possession of a specific piece of land, established law and official policy sometimes meant little. In 1815, when farmer Daniel Ashby settled in Missouri's Howard County, he wrote, "I drove out 375 head of stock hogs, and squatted in the west part of the settlement of Howard County. There I lived as happy as Lord Selkirk [Robinson Crusoe] on his island. I was monarch of all I surveyed." These squatters—"preemptors"—dared anyone to push them off. Jefferson despised them as much as speculators. He complained of rough and ready Scots-Irish, a lawless breed of "bold and indigent strangers," who moved onto unsettled tracts in "an audacious manner." Responsible settlers, he believed, would not choose to live on "the verge of anarchy," left unprotected by "the influence of the law." The federal government continued to insist that the western domain was closed and empty land. Government proclamations and the laws of 1785, 1796, and 1800 legally sealed off western territory until the Indians were removed, the survey made, and auction opened. The Land Act of 1804 emphasized that squatting was illegal, with penalties as high as $1,000 and a year in jail. While an exasperated President James Madison threatened military force against squatters in 1815, Congress contrarily granted new exemptions to Ohio trespassers in order to avoid possible land wars. Government officials like treasury secretary Albert Gallatin and General Land Office commissioner Josiah Meigs were convinced that the crowds of illegal settlers were beyond control. If they succeeded in staying on the land, they threatened the last chance for orderly distribution of the public lands under the survey system. Nevertheless, Meigs also wrote that "peaceable bona fide settlers, who are only waiting for an opportunity to become legal proprietors of the soil they now harmlessly occupy," should be encouraged.

The debate over preemption became a struggle over the government's control of its own public domain. Squatting was illegal but was it not, the squatters answered, a patriotic duty to develop the public domain by clearing the wilderness, turn it into prime farmland through hard labor, and build farms and towns? To them, the arrival of the survey team was not an opportunity for clear title and official registration, but another source of serious trouble because it could mean someone else owned the land. Forcible removal went against public opinion because squatters improved the land. Such uprooting was too similar to Indian removal. One Ohio congressman wrote in 1816 in defense of squatters, "They have fought [in the War of 1812], and some of them have bled, in defense of their homes. Does policy require that the arm of the government should be lifted against them? Shall they, with their wives and children, at an inclement season of the year, by military force, be driven from their possessions? This to them will be more terrible than the whoop of the remorseless enemy. Shall their government, now, visit them with more certain ruin?" Louisiana surveyor Gideon Fitz proposed that it was far better to give the land to the poor farmer rather than to rapacious speculators.

The western land boom had in fact abruptly ended in 1820, during the nation's banking crisis, when paper money inflated and commodity prices collapsed. The Land Act of 1820 abolished the credit system and virtually brought an end to land sales. Perhaps to muffle protest, the base price was reduced to $1.25 an acre and the minimum purchase to 80 acres. The act also got the General Land Office out of the messy mortgage banking business and difficult repossession of land after farmers failed to keep up their payments. However, land sales collapsed so deeply that Congress for the next 12 years could not fix the problem with more legislation. Nevertheless, the squatter problem festered through most of the nineteenth century. In 1828 the House Committee on Public Lands urged preferential treatment for squatters: "It is right and proper that the first settlers, who have made roads and bridges over the public lands at their expense and with great labor and toil, should be allowed a privilege greater than other purchasers." In 1830 the Land Office Commissioner was accurate when he reported, "If the poorer occupants have not the present means of paying ($1.25 per acre) for (the now-minimum) 80 acres of land, it is not to be expected that in twelve months they would generally have the means of paying for 160 or 320 acres." Preemption acts in the 1830s and 1840s caved in to reality when they condoned trespass on public land. They gave sole first rights to buy up to 160 acres to settlers who fulfilled "the fact of cultivation and possession" on land scheduled for surveying.

Conclusion: From Public Domain to Private Property

White Europeans did not conquer America's territory east of the Mississippi by marching armies of troops and cavalry through mountain passes and across open plains. The closest thing to a traditional battle was at Fallen Timbers in north central Ohio in 1794, a disaster for the Indians that encouraged them to avoid in the future such direct confrontations on European terms. Instead, the conquest was an infiltration by trappers and traders that weakened Indian self-reliance. These were followed by white settlers, in fact an armed citizenry that tolerated no opposition from Indians. Often squatters on untitled government land, they were also willing to use arms to defend themselves and their farms against federal land agents. Geographer Donald Meining concludes, "Throughout the history of Atlantic America, conquering was mainly a folk movement; the fighting that paved the way for and protected White settlers was done by frontiersmen working in local gangs or self-appointed militia (George Washington referred to them as 'a parcel of Banditti') rather than by regular military forces." As settlers cut away the forests and planted single-crop fields, we begin to see a shift from frontier life within natural ecosystems of a forest or river valley to a rural existence within a human-made infrastucture of houses, barns, fences, corn and wheat fields, roads, towns, and markets. The natural environment became the mere background to economic development. Land became a commodity to be bought and sold instead of a cherished resource to be owned for generations. Farmers prospered less by growing crops than by buying land cheaply, developing it by clearing trees, plowing, and fencing, and selling it at a higher price. As early as 1790, James T. Callender, one of Jefferson's political allies, complained that the whole continent had been converted "into an immense gaming table." Land speculation usually paid off handsomely. Movement to the frontier was not into the wilderness, but to the promised land. In Forrest McDonald's words, "Now when the Republic was young all Americans knew what to do when they got real money: If you gave an American a dollar, he would buy something costing ten. This was only good sense, the American knew, because soon the ten would, by the sheer magic of America, become a hundred. The instrument of this magic, the touchstone, was land."

In the eyes of land historian Malcolm J. Rohrbough, the land system never worked very well because Congress did not understand the significance of the public domain, the power of its distribution into private hands, large and small, and the layers of confusion created by contradictory survey laws, public sale legislation, and relief acts. Rohrbough added that "one of the principal objects of the rectangular survey was a usable system of land description, and here the surveys proved successful. But much of the surveying was bad, and all of it was tardy." In fact, the survey and sale grid, by its standardized rectangular character, made no environmental, agricultural, social, or economic sense except for convenient and efficient distribution of public property into the hands of autonomous individuals. Western settlers did not entirely trust the survey, nor the institution of public sale. Settlers took the view that the land was there to be taken, and the rules and regulations of the government did not change their natural rights as citizens to engage in squatting. Land costs remained out of reach for many farm families. When thwarted, citizens resorted to fraud, violence, and intimidation against the soulless government and soulless speculators. Few Americans believed it was fraud to search out a tract of land, occupy it by blazing its perimeters, setting up a tent, a rude lean-to, or at most a cabin and fence, and assume that proper title would be obtained in a vague future.

In the process of capturing the western lands, and settling them, the diverse people of the United States had a common experience that made them self-consciously "Americans" with primary loyalty no longer to an individual colony or state, but to the federal government that seemed particularly determined to enhance their opportunities for a better life (see also Chapter 5). Thomas Jefferson in his first inaugural address in 1801 emphasized a government that would leave the people "free to regulate their own pursuits of industry and improvement, and shall not take from the mouth of labor the bread it has earned." Because it allowed its inhabitants to keep the fruits of their labor, the federal government found an ally in the ordinary citizen. By 1800 a million Americans had settled beyond the mountains. But, as noted, independent farmers could still not afford $1 or $1.50 per acre on federal land.

For Further Reading

One of the most detailed summaries of the beginnings of westward movement onto "empty land" is still by Ray A. Billington, *Westward Expansion: A History of the American Frontier* (1949). Even more magisterial is Paul W. Gates's unmatched study *History of Public Land Law Development* (1968). Gates's study of the selling of the public domain should be compared with William D. Pattison, *Beginnings of the American Rectangular Land Survey System, 1784–1800* (1957), Malcolm J. Rohrbough, *The Land Office Business: The Settlement and Administration of American Public Lands, 1789–1837* (1968), and John Opie, *The Law of the Land: 200 Years of American Farmland Policy* (1987). Edward T. Price's *Dividing the Land: Early American Beginnings of Our Private Property Mosaic* (1995) is a definitive and comprehensive study of pre-1785 Survey land distribution. For the broader context of land reform, environmental land use, public versus private interest, and the role of government, see Richard H. Jackson, *Land Use in America* (1981), and Richard N.L. Andrews (ed.) *Land in America: Commodity or Natural Resource?* (1979). Two outspoken critiques of European-based land reform in the United States and elsewhere are Erik Eckholm, *The Dispossessed of the Earth: Land Reform and Sustainable Development* (1979), and Daniel M. Friedenberg, *Life, Liberty, and the Pursuit of Land: The Plunder of Early America* (1992). Peter Onuf's *The Origins of the Federal Republic* (1983) is a brilliant assessment of early American expansionism.

CHAPTER FOUR

WHEN THE UNITED STATES
WAS AN UNDEVELOPED COUNTRY

*The physical texture of American life [around 1800] was far closer to
that in the villages of many third-world countries today than to anything
in the present-day United States. Everywhere the nights were intensely
dark and the stars intensely bright. Most houses were small and poorly
lit. Americans were usually dirty and often insect-ridden. Smells—of the
barnyard and stable, tannery and tavern, house and hearth, privy and
chamber pot—were pungent and profuse. Food was often heavy and
coarse; most meat was heavily salted, tastes were harsh. Hard physical
exertion was an ordinary and unremarkable part of life for all but a
few. Disease and bodily discomfort could rarely be cured, only endured,
and death was an early and frequent visitor. Childbirth posed significant
risks to health and life.*

—Historian Jack Larkin, *The Reshaping of Everyday Life, 1790–1840* (1988)

Overview

The newly independent Americans feared their immature nation would fall into economic collapse. As late as 1800 the nation's overall prospect was not good. The per capita earning power of the people did not grow between 1799 and 1819. This bleak prospect deeply threatened the fresh-faced American dream that merged material prosperity with personal liberty. Yet Americans knew they owned a vast geography chock full of wealth if they could only acquire the right tools. Their answer was to imitate England's successful Industrial Revolution by introducing mechanization to the American continent. Americans rushed to modernize to overcome low levels of communications, transportation, and production. Only such "internal improvements" (a term written into federal powers by the Constitution) would, they believed, bring economic prosperity and perpetuate their fledgling nation. By 1815 at least the political future of the union seemed assured as it held together despite a nearly fatal war with Britain. When involvement in European affairs slipped below their eastern horizon, Americans began to pay more attention to internal development of their territory, mostly across the Appalachian Mountains. The challenge became greater still after 1803 because the new Louisiana Purchase was a largely unknown region that doubled the size of the United States and carried its western boundary from the Mississippi River to the Rocky Mountains (see Chapter 5). Simultaneously the nation's population grew from 4 million in 1790 to 17 million in 1840.

The United States emerged as the first example of a so-called undeveloped nation. American history is still often seen simplistically as an inevitable progression that climaxed in our contemporary consumer society. This chapter argues that the process of industrialization in the fledgling United States was not spontaneous but resulted from a complex of deliberate choices among a wealth of alternatives. It must be remembered that the concepts of progress, modernization, and industrialization are not neutral terms, but are components of an economic program—capitalism—that depends on increasingly rapid consumption of natural resources. Nor was America's success guaranteed, since many human and geographical obstacles had to be overcome. Nevertheless, the results were so rewarding that environmental costs, no matter how severe, were rarely questioned. Environmental protection was far from people's minds. The concept of a human society within environmental constraints had to wait for another century. Americans did not urge appropriate and sustainable development that included accommodation to local ecosystems.

What Is an Undeveloped Country?

Widely accepted modern definitions of an undeveloped country (UDC) are apt descriptions of the condition of the early United States, such as poor communications, inadequate transportation, and weak industrial production, as well as a low level of capital for investment, underdeveloped factory skills, a small labor pool, no large middle class that ambitiously sought material goods, and the resistant customs, institutions, and values of a predominantly agricultural society. The new United States was comparatively free of several major debilitating UDC characteristics: overall poverty, illiteracy, overpopulation, and poor health. Above all, the new nation enjoyed a superior and forgiving environment. Much of the development of a UDC depends on environmental advantages. How well is the nation endowed with a temperate climate, good soil and water, trees above ground and minerals below? Does it have ocean ports for access to the international trade network? Do its rivers provide easy transport? Can its frontiers be defended militarily? The United States may have prospered only because its environmental systems—soils, minerals, and forests—were immediately responsive to low-level development that served most social and economic needs (compared with the labor-intensive rice culture of Southeast Asia or the chronic destruction from annual monsoons in Bangladesh). In America a landscape depleted of wood from a forest, a low tobacco harvest from overused soil, or the end of a vein of iron ore could also be remedied by a fresh start in the western wilderness. Not the least, an emerging nation could sustain its growth only if it possessed the political stability that was uppermost in the Founding Fathers' minds. This required successful transitions of power without extreme swings in the political climate, and effective government administration. Military security required stable borders and internal safety. Americans began to enjoy a level of political, economic, and personal security that was one of the main attractions of immigration. Except on the frontier borderlands, Americans (aside from slaves) had relief from violence and war, particularly compared to the class cruelty, legalized looting, and continuous nation-state military skirmishing of Europe. In addition, a reasonably stable government offered a solid base for the risky experiment of industrialization, which threw aside most traditional values and institutions.

America in 1790: The Threat of Economic Failure

Often forgotten is the historic reality that the new United States was in grave economic shape for its first 35 years. Americans had already struggled against at least four limiting factors.

1. One limitation was being removed by independence. Americans had breathed a great sigh of relief when the Revolutionary War had freed them from the colonial status of imperialism and mercantilism. Imperial Britain had restrained its North American colonials by the Proclamation Line of 1763, customs duties, colonial taxation, and the Quebec Act of 1784. However, unlike the resulting political fireworks of the Declaration of Independence, the Constitution, and the Bill of Rights, the new United States did not explode on the scene economically. Americans had anticipated a rush of prosperity after independence. Instead, the postrevolutionary economy went through a deep depression and then stagnated. Americans feared a vicious circle of low income, low savings, and economic stagnation. The struggling new nation nearly fell into 13 little economies, each with conflicting policies toward land ownership and business enterprise. To overcome this chaos and the threat of national collapse, the Constitutional Convention met in Philadelphia to construct a Constitution that actively favored business enterprise. It provided rigorous protection of private property (e.g., unrestricted profits) and assured government participation in economic development. The Bill of Rights in 1798 prevented the federal government from arbitrarily invading private rights, including property.

THOMAS JEFFERSON'S 1787 *Notes on the State of Virginia* was a report to the French government on America's potential to exploit its natural resource for economic development. During the Revolution, the French asked him to justify their support for the new nation. Was it likely to survive as an independent state? Was their commitment, with its serious international repercussions, likely to become a wasteful embarrassment? Beginning with Virginia as his centerpiece because he knew it best, Jefferson told the French of the immensely rich and virgin geography, its potential for a flourishing culture, and the virtuous dedication of the population to build a superior nation. Following a detailed description of soils, climate, terrain, plants, and animals, Jefferson described the emergence of a societal infrastructure characterized by private ownership of property, and transformation of the wilderness into buildings, roads, agriculture, manufacturing, and commerce. A short list of the elements that Jefferson believed would control the future material development of the new nation included the following:

- *geography* (terrain, soil, water, climate)
- *type of land use* (pastoral high-yield farming)
- *level of technological development* (hand labor and appropriate mechanization)
- *economic structures* (capital and credit for farmers, as well as access to markets, and public investment for internal improvements)
- *political organization* (participatory local, state, and federal government)
- *infrastructure* (roads, communications, rural-urban connections)
- *government policy* (land use, natural resource management)
- *social institutions* (family, community)
- *cultural milieu* (personal freedom, entrepreneurial opportunity)

Jefferson's report, despite its enthusiasm, admitted that the new nation had far to go, partly because its agricultural technology was primitive even by the low standards of the late eighteenth century.

2. A second restraining force was geography. It controlled the daily pattern of life that seemed as unhealthy, hazardous, uncomfortable, and monotonous as it had been since the Middle Ages. Living conditions in the new country were overwhelmingly primitive and seemingly a backward step. The great historian Henry Adams, looking backward to 1800 from his vantage point in 1890, wrote, "America was backward even after two centuries of struggle, the land was still untamed; forest covered every portion, except here and there a strip of cultivated soil; the minerals lay undisturbed in their rocky beds, and more than two thirds of the people clung to the seaboard within fifty miles of tide-water, where alone the wants of civilized life could be supplied. The interior was little more civilized than in 1750." He added, "No civilized country had yet been required to deal with physical difficulties so serious, nor did experience warrant conviction that such difficulties could be overcome."

3. A third restraining force was that Americans were undertooled to meet their challenges. They lived in a handmade world. Manufacturing was small in scale and unmechanized.

Work, or energy, still stood within age-old limits—muscle power of humans and animals, and some help from waterwheels. The means to overcome environmental constraints had not changed significantly, wrote Adams, since rudimentary farming by the Jutes and Angles in the fifth century A.D. The modern economic historian Curtis Nettles judged that the farmer's tools in 1800 "would have been familiar in ancient Babylonia." Even the best farmers, the German immigrants around Lancaster, Pennsylvania, did only light top-of-the-soil plowing, which was labor intensive and got low yields. Not much had improved by 1815. Nettels added, "A bird's-eye view of the United States in 1815 would have revealed a vast, busy land inhabited by 8,500,000 people. A great majority of them were farm folk who used simple tools and processes to manufacture large quantities of the goods they needed. In villages and towns and at mill sites one could have found many small shops and mills in which the proprietors, each working alone or with a few hands, made specialized products for surrounding farms, urban markets, and export trade." "A Rip Van Winkle awakening in 1815 after a forty years' sleep," he continued, "would have found many things unaltered. The rural family still made most of the manufactured goods it used."

4. A fourth constraint resulted ironically from prosperity through farming. Unusually high returns on agriculture meant that alternative investment in industry moved slowly. Alexander Hamilton, George Washington's first secretary of the treasury, complained bitterly about the diversion of scarce federal money to support settlement of the western wilderness, funds which instead should be devoted to building industry and commerce. The English economist Adam Smith wrote in 1776 about the unique tug of land for farming: "When an artificer has acquired a little more than is necessary for carrying on his own business, he does not, in North America, attempt to establish a manufacture but employs it in the improvement and purchase of uncultivated land." As late as 1800, a quarter century after independence, the United States appeared destined to be best known as a highly successful agricultural nation. Swiss-born Albert Gallatin, Thomas Jefferson's new secretary of the treasury, reported that between April and October, Indian corn made the penniless immigrant into a capitalist. The initial material transformation of the United States came not through industrialization, but through the widely held belief among nineteenth-century Americans that a higher standard of living and a more desirable quality of life originated in the rich farmlands of southeastern Pennsylvania, the Great (Shenandoah) Valley of Virginia, and especially the newly acquired midwestern deep black (chernozoan) soils. This challenges the common notion that industrialization was America's first engine of prosperity.

Nevertheless, most Americans looked to industrialization for some form of economic "takeoff." They looked enviously to the iron forges and textile mills that gave Old England a new prosperity. As early as 1775, the famous medical spokesman Benjamin Rush gave five reasons for industrialization in an address to the newly formed United Company of Philadelphia for Promoting American Manufactures: (1) It is cheaper to manufacture goods at home than pay import prices; (2) industrial invention will improve agriculture; (3) industry provides employment for the poor and indigent; (4) the best immigrants are skilled workers seeking employment; and (5) dependence on English goods, regulations, and uncertain colonial policy would be reduced. By 1840 Americans began to follow the path toward industrialization, which they believed would free them from the direct control of nature, allow them to master their expanding geographical territory, and overcome environmental obstacles to prosperity.

American Advantages, Environmental and Otherwise

The new Americans possessed environmental and social advantages that would be envied today by a Third World nation. Americans had no fear of starvation; the virgin soil practically threw food at them. Few people lived in actual poverty. The average standard of living was much higher than in Britain or Europe. Henry Adams would write that by the early nineteenth century, "In the United States, except among the slaves, the laboring class enjoyed an ample supply of the necessaries of life. They claimed superiority over the laboring class in Europe."

One of the great advantages of the United States was its geographical newness. Income from fresh land, unavailable in Europe to the vast majority of people, made America's geography seem like a gigantic money tree. Nor did old feudal rules about owning, fencing, and using the land have to be overthrown. The modern historian Russel Blaine Nye reported on a land-centered optimism: "The fertility of the American soil, the enormous variety and fecundity of its plant and animal life, the vast reaches and unlimited resources of its waters and wood, the salubrity and balance of its climate, all made the United States a mighty stage . . . to put into practice basic principles of society and government impossible to test elsewhere." Historian David Potter described the special nature of the United States in 1800: "A country with inadequate wealth could not safely promise its citizens more than security of status—at a low level in the social hierarchy and with a meager living. But this promise is, in its denial of equality, by definition, undemocratic. A democracy, by contrast, setting equality as its goal, must promise opportunity, for the goal of equality becomes a mockery unless there is some means of attaining it." Americans believed that a standard of living well above poverty and subsistence was an essential ingredient of American democracy.

Americans amazed Europeans with their geographical adventuresomeness (see later discussion on the great migration into the Midwest). Freedom of choice, especially to enter new occupations and move into new regions with little restriction, was quickly and enthusiastically endorsed. The geographical mobility permitted in America was unheard of in human history. This was particularly true between 1790 and 1820, with the creation of ten new states. "In just thirty years a million square miles were transformed from a hunter's paradise to a farmer's domain," concluded historian Richard D. Brown. "Americans appear to have accepted with little anxiety the traumas involved in pulling up stakes and moving. Their confidence in the future and their desire to share in the general improvement outweighed their local and familial attachments." This new freedom of movement belonged primarily to white males: Slaves had as little mobility as prisoners, and wives especially and women generally were under the legal domination of men.

Another great advantage was American mechanical skills. A man who dirtied his hands had a place of honor in American society, where in Europe the ordinary laborer was held in disdain. This know-how ranged from the simple use of a hammer, chisel, saw, and plane to the development and use of more sophisticated and complex machines such as the iron forge, grist mill, potter's wheel, spinning wheel, land loom, and fulling machine. Frontier settlers had to repair their tools and machines and often fabricated them. "Mechanicks" worked "with the memory of their hands and three-dimensional, visual thinking and the cultivation of imagination." A farmer-hosteler in New Jersey told a German visitor, "I am a mover, a

Jefferson and Hamilton Debate the Nation's Future Course

Over the past 250 years some nations have experienced rapid economic growth while others have not. What explains this? What do faster developing countries have that is lacking in others? In America the debate goes back more than 200 years. Thomas Jefferson, who saw himself as the nation's intellectual leader, and Alexander Hamilton, George Washington's right-hand man, who saw himself as America's economic savior, debated in the 1780s and 1790s about the nation's future development. Which could provide more adequately for the material well-being of Americans: agriculture or manufacturing? One economic historian, Marvin Fisher, called the debate between agriculture and industry "a morality play, not an economic dispute" because of its wide-ranging social implications.

Jefferson urged caution. British factories hummed profitably because they used pauper labor. The unnatural working and living conditions of the factory towns did not build better people; it broke them down physically and spiritually. England's factories were surrounded by dingy slums that produced debilitated and slavish humans. One Englishman warned Americans, "The present state of our manufacturing population ought to be a lesson and a warning to them to avoid, as long as possible, touching the accursed thing." Other observers reported that England's industrial cities fostered not only filth and waste, but also crime, poverty, and helplessness. Early in the century Americans had powerful scruples against noxious working conditions that 50 years later they would accept as necessary by-products of industrial prosperity.

In place of hopeless factory workers, Jefferson professed the yeoman farmer who owned his piece of land and worked on it as a free independent person. This was the first enduring American hero. In 1787 Jefferson earnestly argued that "those who labor in the earth are the chosen people of God." He said, "Corruption of morals in the mass of cultivators is a phenomenon of which no age nor nation has furnished an example. . . . While we have land to labor then, let us never wish to see our citizens occupied at a work-bench, or twirling a distaff. . . . Let our work-shops remain in Europe." Small landholders were also the most important prop to the new republic because they strengthened local economies and kept wealth from being concentrated in the hands of a few. All the people, Jefferson insisted, had a right to America's bountiful landscape. James Madison added that independent family farmers were "the best basis of public liberty and the strongest bulwark of public safety."

In fact, Jefferson's idealized yeoman farmer was largely a myth. Most American farmers acted more in Hamilton's pragmatic mode. They had little reverence for the land. They were interested in transferring the limited nutrients of a forest soil directly into corn, tobacco, or wheat until the soil wore out. Then they moved on, without a backward regretful look. Farmers were wiping out America's primeval eastern forests in a twinkling. Equally mythical was the claim to virtue by early industrialists. One group of Massachusetts venture capitalists promised "to give employment to a great number of persons, especially females who now eat the bread of idleness. . . . Our design [in building a factory] is not to enrich ourselves." Surely this was disingenuous.

In 1779 Alexander Hamilton complained that the nation was on the wrong course: "The farmers have the game in their hands. If they do not like the price [they] are not obliged to sell because they have almost every necessary within themselves, salt and one or two more excepted, which bear a small proportion to what is wanted from them and which they can obtain by barter for other articles equally indispensable." Farming, Hamilton argued, might allow a broad and extensive use of America's natural wealth, but industrialization would bring an opportunity for more efficient exploitation. Industrialism provided dynamism, a capacity to manipulate natural resources, and an increase in the scale of wealth four times that of farming. In 1787 Hamilton's associate Tench Coxe pleaded for immediate industrialization:

> It will consume our native productions now increasing to super-abundance—it will improve our agriculture and teach us to explore the fossil and vegetable kingdoms into which few researches have heretofore been made—it will accelerate the improvement of our internal navigation and bring into action the dormant powers of nature and the elements—it will give us real independence by rescuing us from the tyranny of foreign fashions, and the destructive torrent of luxury.

Hamilton's 1791 *Report on Manufacturers* has ever since made him the darling of capitalists and the prophet of America's future economic success. The new United States, he said, in order to compete with the world's nations, desperately needed an economic miracle, which only industrialization could bring. He promoted mechanization as "an artificial force brought in aid of the natural force of man; and, to all the purposes of labor, is an increase of hands, an accessing of strength." Hamilton urged a "big-push" approach with major government interventions to jump-start industrialization, including protective tariffs for infant businesses and patents to encourage innovations. These would move the United States out of its deadening stagnation. Hamilton also responded to Jefferson's high-minded moralizing when he argued that manufacturing was superior to agricultural work because it was "constant" not "seasonal," "uniform" not "careless." It was more ingenious and efficient and hence more productive. Overall, manufacturing was essential to national security and prosperity, a "populous, thriving, and powerful nation."

Hamilton's critics saw not stagnation but a balanced humane economy in a yeoman producer republic. The conflict between Jefferson and Hamilton was not between a premodern and modern nation, nor even between a nonmarket or marketplace-based economy, but which course of action would take the United States out of a restrictive mercantilism dominated by England. Hamilton ran into a chorus of angry criticism when he argued that national planning, directed by the central government, should force industrialization on the agricultural nation. This seemed a return to a tyrannical government ruling a downtrodden people, but Hamilton trusted more in a right-thinking elite than in ordinary people. He argued that the western territories should not be opened up; instead, expansion should be strictly controlled if not halted. Expansionist policies were diverting the nation's limited investment resources. The nation already had an oversupply of farmers and farmland; what it needed was more factories and machinery, and more businessmen and industrial workers, to turn out more goods. Government support for rapid industrialization, Hamilton argued, must include tariffs to exclude foreign goods, controls over the export of raw materials, subsidies for new industries, rewards for American inventions and protection of industrial secrets, and a national supra-governmental agency to direct and manage the process. Not the least, Hamilton saw himself at the head of the operation.

shoemaker, furrier, wheelwright, farmer, gardener, and when it can't be helped, a soldier. I make my bread, brew my beer, kill my pigs; I grind my axes and knives; I built those stalls and that shed there; I am barber, leech, and doctor." If the workmanship was good, he could sell or barter his creations. Such artisans were remarkably accurate in shaping watertight wooden barrels, forging straight rifle barrels, and constructing squared houses. So comfortable with basic tools and machines, Americans took readily to receive, adapt, and use the new textile equipment of England's Industrial Revolution. A simple drawing, or even the description of the basic concept of a machine, would allow reproduction and improvement of inventions first developed in Britain. This was a rude but highly successful form of technology transfer, which meant not only getting the device, but relating it to local needs. The process involved invention, development, and innovation by which a device is put to productive and profitable use.

Space: America's Environmental Challenge

Despite the advantages of a temperate climate and good soil and water, Americans nevertheless faced serious handicaps because of the vast expanses of wilderness. This constricted inter-

THE ITALIAN NAVIGATOR Verrazano in 1524 entered New York harbor but made no effort to go up the Hudson River; the Englishman Henry Hudson searched up the river toward Albany in the employ of Dutch speculators in 1609. The Dutch, who were from the first aggressive merchants riding exceptional ships, looked at the broad Hudson as an American Rhine, and they envisioned a regional network of canals and rivers serving a rich agricultural farmland in imitation of the Netherlands. True to the legend, Peter Minuit, director general of the Dutch West India Company, did purchase Manhattan Island in 1626 from the local Algonquin-speaking Lenape Indians. He paid about 60 guilders worth of cloth, trinkets, and beads for all 20,000 acres of the island. It was a good investment because it commanded the point where the Hudson River flowed into an excellent anchorage protected from Atlantic storms.

The island was called by the natives Manhattan, or Island of the Hills. It is composed of solid granite bedrock, Manhattan schist, mostly scraped clean by the edge of the last great glacier. Where Manhattan schist is the strongest, it now supports the Empire State Building and the Chrysler Building at midtown and the twin towers of the World Trade Center at the downtown tip, as part of New York City's famous skyscraper skyline. The lower tip of the island had many hills that would be leveled down in later years. Upper Manhattan was higher, with rocky outcroppings, and where giant oaks once flourished in "very good woodland." There were "many brooks of fresh water affording cool and pleasant resting places" among ponds and swamps. A great open meadow stretched along the East Side, a stream and marsh where Canal Street now runs, and land east of Fifth Avenue and west of Greenwich Street was under water. Above 40th Street the island was dense forest, "useless except for hunting." The inhabitants were hordes of birds, deer, and a few native clans of 100 to 200 people each, who hunted, gathered wild nuts, tubers, and berries and tended fields of corn, beans, squash,

nal trade, made it expensive, and kept the nation undeveloped. Improvements in the speed and extent of internal transportation were far more important to the United States than to European nations. Population centers were far more separated than in Britain or France. Port cities were more distant from their hinterland and cargo-laden vessels had to cross a difficult span of ocean to participate in international trade. A road and canal system was virtually nonexistent. Only rivers allowed for early travel to the interior. The new nation's people were few and disconnected. Isolated farmsteads had small cash crops and made few purchases. The new states remained as isolated as when they were colonies. The problem deepened because private enterprise or a state legislature could not support the investment to construct a canal or turnpike. The United States was profoundly a capital-scarcity country, in which the federal government eventually took over costly internal improvements.

Constructing America's Cities: Preindustrial Infrastructures

Wharves and Docks Create the Earliest Patterns: Boston, New York, Philadelphia, and Baltimore

When a company of colonists first set ashore, they did not rush into the forbidding forest. Their first impulse was to cluster a settlement near water, which served as a lifeline back to

and pumpkins. They enjoyed an abundance of fish, oysters, and clams from the Hudson and East rivers, and New York Bay. Some Indian trails would become roadways such as the Bowery and Broadway. Staten Island and Long Island were mixed meadows and forest, well watered and filled with wild turkeys, geese, and deer. New Jersey across the Hudson was a myriad of wetlands and swamps inhabited by 40-pound wild turkeys that could be caught by hand. The waters served up 9-foot-long sturgeon as well as messes of oysters, clams, lobsters, and crabs. Gowanus oysters, "the best in the country," grew a foot long and had to be cut up into three or four mouthfuls. By the 1670s this was being overlaid by a commercial outpost.

Although Manhattan was 12.5 miles long and 2.5 miles at its widest point, the Dutch settlement called New Amsterdam covered only the southernmost tip of the island. It was protected by a northern defensive wall that ran in a straight line from river to river, alongside of which was "Wall Street." A canal dug by the Dutch in early years would be filled in and called Broad Street for its width. The Dutch remained more capable at trade than in settlement; the seal of the town of New Amsterdam displays a beaver. By 1655 it had 17 streets on an orderly grid where 1,000 people lived in about 120 houses, surrounded by vegetable gardens and fields for grazing domestic animals. When Dutch rule was replaced by the English in 1664, only 2,000 Europeans inhabited Manhattan. A hundred years later it would be near 25,000 people, one of the larger cities of the British Empire. New York City surpassed Boston and Philadelphia as the most vigorous and cosmopolitan city of the English colonies. Crowding at the lower end of town encouraged merchants to buy lots under the East River, fill them with dirt and rubble, and create new business districts. Water Street, now two blocks inland, was once underwater.

Europe where ships could reach them with military support, trading goods, food, clothing, and supplies. Behind them, a wooden wall protected their few crude huts from the dangers lurking in the forest. The earliest American public works project was often a common wooden wharf built by merchants for unloading and loading arriving ships. They soon added planked sidewalks to avoid deep mud on the streets. Private merchants would band together to plan, finance, and pave a street with bricks or cobblestones or build a connecting bridge over a swamp or stream. Cargoes were transferred to wagons to catch a dirt road into the country-side or loaded onto a smaller boat that could travel upstream into the interior. Warehouses, mercantile offices, processing operations, shipbuilding, and ropewalks soon appeared as auxiliary enterprises to shipping. Employment depended on the waterfront: coopers, sailmakers, carpenters, blacksmiths, and places for food, drink, and lodging. Clustered nearby each waterfront, in an unplanned, haphazard way, were public buildings: customs houses, banks, shops, hotels, and churches. Residential houses appeared on the outskirts, but within walking distance of the waterfront.

Boston was founded in 1631 on an unpleasant marshy peninsula because of its natural harbor. Within two decades Boston's life bustled around the town dock, the adjacent market-place, a great park called the Common, and the Puritan meetinghouses. Gradually over the next 50 years, the dock expanded into a row of wharves that dominated the peninsula, "the masts of the sailing ships challenging the height of majestic church spires." The earliest settlement on Manhattan Island was planted at its southern extreme about 1625, a cluster of buildings around a Dutch fort that overlooked the harbor. A wooden wall separated the raw settlement from the mysterious woods, dangerous natives, and wild animals on the rest of the island. From the first, New Amsterdam's wharf was the dominant feature of "this outpost of one of the most developed commercial societies in the Old World" (see accompanying feature). City life centered on the rows of wharves that spread northward on both sides of the island. In the southern colonies, a number of small tobacco ports were dominated by their wharves and adjacent warehouses. One of them, Baltimore, founded in 1729, began to outdistance its competitors because it became the overseas shipping point, from an expanding row of wharves, that served a wheat and grain farming region in its hinterland.

Philadelphia started very differently, but experienced the same result. When the wealthy Quaker businessman William Penn became proprietor of Pennsylvania in 1681, his first step was to lay out a large, well-proportioned, and orderly city. To dreamers like Penn during the Age of Reason, the landscape of paradise was not a romanticized wilderness, but a utopian city. The site of Philadelphia just north of the convergence of the Schuylkill and Delaware rivers took the shape of a formal geometric gridiron containing five main squares, one at the city's center as a focal point. Philadelphia was intended to be a great uncrowded city of wide avenues, large private houses, and the squares as public parks, for the sake of improved urban well-being. Penn foresaw that Philadelphia's commercial growth depended on the Delaware River as an ideal overseas shipping point. The river anchorage was deep enough for ships of heavy tonnage, well protected from ocean storms and salty enough from tides that it rarely froze. What Penn did not anticipate was that most of the city's activity would take place not in the squares he had laid out so carefully, but in the dynamic and diverse activities of warehouses, wharves, retail stores, and artisan workshops that soon spread more than a mile along the Delaware shore. Philadelphia abandoned its orderly, centralized plan to become a "linear city" along the riverfront, with virtually all settlement less than half a mile from its bustling wharves. Do-good reform-minded residents such as Ben Franklin complained that the benefits of Philadelphia's plan were overwhelmed by street noise, air pollution, and congestion like that of a densely packed medieval city.

Land connections between the cities were so poor that most goods went by coastal ship or boat. Roads rarely made cities. Boston, without a navigable river that connected it with the West, began to stagnate. The only city to prosper without a working river was Lancaster, Pennsylvania, because it aggressively built an important turnpike to connect it with the western part of the state. But in this case there was no competing river that ran east and west across the Allegheny Mountains. New York City prospered on the movement of flour, salted meat, and other agricultural goods. Philadelphia's large hinterland offered grain, meat, lumber, and flour and sent manufactured goods far west into the Ohio Valley. Baltimore's fleet of new clipper ships made it the flour center of the nation. An inland city like Albany shipped furs, Trenton and Lancaster served farmers, and western towns at the terminus of eastern roads like Pittsburgh and Wheeling outfitted families rafting down the Ohio River to seek their fortunes. Overall, Boston, New York, Philadelphia, and Baltimore grew from small trading posts on the ocean edge of the wilderness into the urban centers of the British colonies because they were transportation connections between inland farms and the markets of England. The wharves and the cities that sprung up around them were "hubs of a growing network that made the idea of an independent America, as a group of united states, plausible and perhaps possible by 1776."

Private Land-Ownership Shapes the American City

For the ordinary immigrant, the opportunity to own land was a civil right that promised superior personal freedom. Private property could not be seized by the government except under due process of law. And as we saw earlier, land ownership was the critical step in the fulfillment of the American dream of personal liberty and material prosperity. The autonomy of the property owner was extraordinary. Fee-simple ownership meant that no one had the right to dictate to the owner what he might do with his property, to whom he might or might not sell his land, or who might inherit his property. America's major cities were mostly in private hands. This would change little in the 50 years between colonial times and the first decades of the nineteenth century. The coastal cities were primarily highly profitable commercial outlets that collected goods and channeled them to overseas and interstate trade.

When public works were desperately needed, the best most colonial cities could do was to require from each householder a number of days each year to labor on public works. In 1644 New Haven insisted that all men between 16 and 60 give four days of work to deepen the channel of a town creek. Newark promised that its able-bodied men would each work three days to help anyone who would build a corn mill. Given human nature, these arrangements were unsatisfactory. Early city people lived more self-contained and self-sufficiently than today. Their private life took place in a heavily timbered house with a small barn behind for the horses, a cow, and pigs (who foraged on garbage in the streets), as well as a vegetable plot and a fruit tree or two. Much later, in 1889, an observer wrote, "When a man lives by himself, he can do as he pleases and let others do the same, but when 125,000 people are gathered on 10 square miles of land they must of necessity give up certain of their liberties. It is the sacrifice they make for the sake of the advantages of city life. The denser the population the more stringent and exacting must be sanitary regulations and indeed all other regulations." A modern historian added, "In the country a man might construct his home, build his fire, dig his well, erect his privy, and dispose of his rubbish without thought for the well-being of his neighbors, but in town these became objects of community concern."

Urban historian Sam Bass Warner argued that this freedom from interference led to distortions in city life that dehumanized it and caused the city to fall into disorder and chaos. The physical territory of a city, he said, should instead have been treated as a social resource that needed to serve many public needs. Instead, America's private property traditions, despite the personal benefits they showered on landowners, blocked the common welfare. For example, municipal improvements often stopped at the edge of the street. Warner added, "If toilets, lights, fire barriers, windows, stairs, and central heating were to be installed, the landowner had to do it, and execution therefore was dependent upon his financial capabilities and his personal willingness to modernize. Within the boundaries of the private lot itself, the city could only admonish, harass, and fine; it could not install or repair on its own initiative." When Philadelphia pioneered public waterworks in the late eighteenth century, it discovered that a city water pipe in the sidewalk did not guarantee that taps, toilets, and tubs were installed inside the house. Despite Boston's disastrous fire in 1872, its city statutes did not allow public funds to aid owners to rebuild private buildings, even to redevelop the city's downtown. In the nineteenth century municipal building improvements continued to be blocked because the land remained largely in private hands. When cities grew into giant systems that spread over many miles, urban social demands changed, but each bit of land stayed private. Warner argued that this "alienation" has been a prominent and harmful feature of the cities through all of American history. He compared this unfavorably with the public reform of European cities during the nineteenth and twentieth centuries. He concluded, "We have steadfastly protected the privileges of millions of small owners and have refused to provide decent protection against rats, cold, disease, overcrowding, and fire for millions more."

The primary exception to urbanization was the South. Even when slave owners were not in the majority, they dominated economic life, agricultural technologies, and attitudes toward nature. Most southerners lived isolated from knowledge of the world outside the plantation or county. Physical movement was legally restricted for slaves, and difficult for whites on all levels. The plantation way of life was self-sufficient in the old ways. It produced most of its own food, livestock, clothing, and equipment. It remained as hierarchical as a medieval manor; family connections meant more than business contacts. The lack of new ideas from foreign immigrants also constrained change. Overland roads and commercial centers did not appear to replace the old direct connection between plantation wharf and distant market. Geographical mobility, so important to northern development, was discouraged. By 1860 the South did have 604 miles of canals and 10,900 miles of railroads, but by then the North had 3,950 miles of canals and 20,700 miles of railroads, and the gap was widening. In addition, southern canals and railroads were not intended to carry people, mail, or newspapers, but to bring cotton to market. The South was a world of great landed estates, devoted to luxury and leisure, more like England and Europe than the rest of the United States.

Safety, Convenience, and Health

Many of the physical problems that nag modern urban society—transport, health, and crowding—appeared early in American cities. Proximity—measured by walking distance—to the city's lifeline and hub of wharves, warehouses, and markets, turned America's early cities into dense medieval-like mixtures of businesses and residences. In Boston, the streets and alleys became a crowded jumble as they followed the terrain and old animal trails and cowpaths.

Housing shortages and high real estate prices left two or three families living in a single small house. Wooden sheds and shacks took up every odd corner or open space. Even in spacious Philadelphia, Penn's blocks were soon divided by alleys as property values rose. Over time, Philadelphians built smaller houses, often no more than 800 square feet, set in attached rows, on tiny plots 17 feet wide and 25 feet deep, that were once backyards of larger houses.

The threat of fire constantly frightened city dwellers because most buildings were constructed of wood on crowded streets and alleys. One simple mistake—an errant ember from a fireplace, a spark from a lantern, a careless smoker—led to fast-spreading, out-of-control conflagrations that consumed the congestion of wooden buildings and sheds. If a wind came up, it carried a fire quickly across entire neighborhoods. Boston burned in 1653, 1676, 1679, and 1711. Four hundred buildings of the city core turned into smoldering rubble in 1760. Fire-control technology was primitive and access to water was unpredictable. Outdoor smoking was forbidden in Boston, gunpowder was put under careful storage, and night watches were created to alert townspeople in case of fire. Boston required that all household fires be covered or extinguished between 9 P.M. at night and 4:30 A.M. Fire departments were made up of volunteers. The first building codes regulated the construction of roofs (no reed or straw roofing), chimneys (still often wood and plaster), and dumps for brush or rubbish. Philadelphia had urged building with brick and stone from the first, but wood was much cheaper and remained the primary building material. When major fires struck several cities, the widespread rebuilding helped to modernize and reshape them. Yet no city gave significant thought to an overall plan to restructure the streets, alleys, and neighborhoods of a burned-out area. Even later, when Chicago rebuilt in 1871, Boston in 1872, and Baltimore in 1904, they all continued their earlier haphazard development.

Epidemic disease was the second major fear. America's most crowded cities were also its seaport cities, where international connections introduced dangerous organisms from far afield. Smallpox, cholera, and yellow fever spread illness, disfigurement, and death to most city families. A yellow fever epidemic took 5,000 lives in Philadelphia in 1793, or 1 in 10 of its inhabitants. Mortality from infectious diseases was particularly high among infants and young children. Most city people were also exposed to tuberculosis, influenza, and dysentery. Poor public health was aggravated by poverty, bad sanitation, and misguided medical care.

The devastating smallpox epidemic in Boston in 1721 caused medical authorities to introduce inoculation protection, but other medical "cures" included large doses of mercury, bleeding and the application of leeches, spoonfuls of strychnine, and tobacco-smoke enemas. One plague survivor wrote, "Cholera kills and doctors slay." Most early American physicians believed that epidemics and infectious diseases were caused by bad city air or "miasma," foul odors that drifted carrying sickness from the corpses of dogs and horses, from the excrement of privies, and from garbage in the streets. America's most famous revolutionary era doctor, Benjamin Rush, was ahead of his time when in 1799 he refused to lay blame for epidemics and "pestilential maladies" on climate. Instead, he argued that scientific evidence showed "sources of disease and death may be found among Americans created by their own negligence. Until they learn this, they will still wallow in filth, crowd their cities with low direct houses and narrow streets; neglect the use of bathing and washing; and live like savages, devouring in hot seasons undue quantities of animal food at their tables, and reeling home after midnight debauches."

Drinking water came from public and private wells that were often polluted by seepage from waste dumps, privies, and even graves. Some of these problems were not new, especially in the cities. Since the Middle Ages, household garbage and human excrement had often been disposed of by dumping it out the handiest window onto the public street below. The urban outdoors was treated by everyone as a commons—belonging to no one. An early New York City ordinance forced householders to scrape the mess up twice a week between April and December and pile it into the center of the street. In winter it lay where it landed. This "Corporation Pudding" got kicked around by horses, wagons, and pedestrians until it more or less disappeared. A good rain, or scavenging by a feral pack of dogs or pigs, would help in the cleanup. New Yorkers also dumped their slop buckets into the East River or Hudson River, and into Lower Manhattan's Collect Pond, in which often floated dead dogs and cats, and that was also the source of water for the city's major well, called the Tea Water Pump in Chatham Street (Park Row). Where a family had its own privy in the backyard, they dumped wastewater and garbage into its cesspool or "vault" as well as out the window. Sewage problems became especially serious when American cities became sizable. At the time of the Revolution, for example, Philadelphia at 40,000 people was second in population only to London in the British Empire, and Boston, New York, and Baltimore had begun to expand rapidly. Even if several merchants joined together to hire a scavenger service, one might walk past chicken or pig entrails outside a butcher shop and dead dogs or horses anywhere. An English sanitary engineer, Edwin Chadwick, created a revolution when in 1842 he perfected a sewer that flushed itself with water to remove solid waste. Cities began to use this "water-carriage sewer" as a means to control disease and remove waste. Yet as late as 1857 New York City provided sewers for only 158 of its 500 miles of streets. Most cities began to recognize the importance of sanitation and eventually passed regulations about the location and depth of privies and graves, tanneries and slaughterhouses, as well as pollution of streams and ponds. City pride and business interests also called for clean streets paved with gravel and cobblestones. Even under the best circumstances, only main thoroughfares were paved in most American cities until late in the nineteenth century. Side streets remained dusty or muddy and layered with filth. A famous tall tale told of a citizen who offered help to a man embedded to his neck in a mud hole on a city street. "No need to worry," he said, "I have a horse underneath me." Drainage was helped when Boston, for example, began to grade streets so they were "crowned"—sloped from a high middle to side gutters that drained off stagnant water and decaying refuse. By the early twentieth century, most American cities were believed safer and healthier than their European counterparts.

Conquest of the Heartland:
Creation of a Transportation Infrastructure

In colonial and early national times, the farmer or merchant suffered from a meager commercial infrastructure that was little different from that of medieval Europe. One rule of thumb used by settlers deep in the countryside was they could not profitably send a wagonload of surplus corn or grain more than 40 or 50 miles—about a three day ride—to a navigable river or passable dirt and plank road. When new sources of raw materials were discovered—better grades of coal in western Pennsylvania and Virginia, saltpeter from Appalachian caves, lead from the mines around Galena in Illinois—they were too remote from each other to assemble them easily for manufacturing until the transportation infrastructure expanded. It was a stretch when iron bars, purposely bent to fit over the backs of packhorses, were carried across the Alleghenies. Such limitations severely restricted a European-style

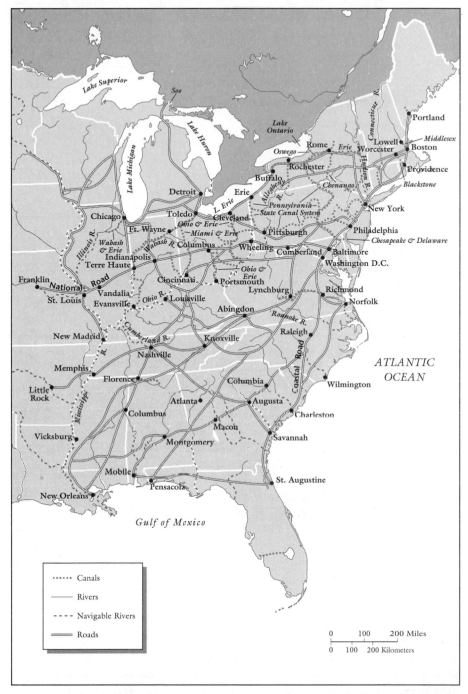

Building an Infrastructure. Americans dedicated themselves in the era between independence and the Civil War to the construction of a European-style transportation system. A series of public roads and canals connected towns and cities; linked rivers, lakes, and the Atlantic coastline; connected rural farmers with their markets; and encouraged entry into the western wilderness. Where in 1800 it took a traveler six weeks from New York City to St. Louis, by 1840 the distance could be covered in a remarkable two weeks.

expansion into the native environment. The solution was to expand America's infant infrastructure to promote the movement of people, goods, and information.

Jefferson, Gallatin, and the Constitution's "Internal Improvements"

In the 1830s English traveler Harriet Martineau exclaimed how much nature had done for the United States, and yet now much "remained for human hands to do." Thirty years earlier, Jefferson told Congress in his state of the union address that the federal government must be responsible for "roads, rivers, canals and such other objects of public improvement." In addition, government-sponsored public works would also unite a very large nation. But not until 1808 did Jefferson's Swiss-born secretary of the treasury, Albert Gallatin, propose a national network of canals and roads as a means to take farm products to markets and bring manufactured goods to the farm. The difficulties of transportation and access to local coal beds and water power added to early limits. Both Gallatin and Jefferson concluded that private capital could not profitably build roads or canals for great distances in regions of low populations. Gallatin's famous 1808 *Report of the Secretary of the Treasury on the Subject of Public Roads and Canals* spelled out a comprehensive system of internal improvements using "direct aid from government," a then astounding $20 million over the next ten years. He offered a definition for internal improvements: "the adoption by government or community of deliberate and concerted policies which are designed to promote economic expansion or prosperity and in which positive action to provide favorable conditions for economic activity is emphasized more strongly than negative regulation or the correction of abuses." His responsiblity, he concluded, was to make the nation's natural resources accessible, not to protect them. Gallatin established government policy to open "speedy and easy communications through all its [the nation's] parts. Good roads and canals will shorten distances," he argued, "facilitate commercial and personal intercourse, and unite, by a still more intimate community of interests, the most remote quarters of the United States." He concluded, "No other single operation, within the power of government, can more effectively tend to strengthen and perpetuate that union which secures external independence, domestic peace, and internal liberty." Gallatin's first project sought to simplify coastline navigation by cutting canals through four necks of land across Cape Cod, between the Raritan and Delaware rivers in New Jersey, across the peninsula between the Delaware and the Chesapeake, and to channelize the "marshy tract which divides the Chesapeake from Albemarle Sound." He also pieced together dozens of ambitious proposals, including a road between Baltimore and Cumberland, Maryland, and a canal across New York from the Hudson to Lake Ontario that anticipated the Erie Canal. Congress tabled the budget request as too costly, but both projects would be eventually completed.

Were massive public expenditures constitutional? The Constitution saw the importance of a national marketplace system when it granted to Congress authority over interstate commerce, which included navigation and thus water projects. It sought to stabilize the economy by controlling the coinage of money, but left all-important credit and borrowing to the states and private interests. It ran its own business when it took over the mails and postal roads. Yet the Constitution made no attempt to support scientific research, engineering training, or subsidies for manufacturing. Big-government Federalists said that government had "implied powers" to create financial institutions, taxing authorities, and appropriate agencies to serve the general welfare and public safety. Jefferson, spokesman for the Democratic-Republicans, acknowledged the need to open agricultural markets and manage internal improvements as the nation expanded westward. A broad network of roads and canals would "enable every industrious citizen to become a freeholder, to secure indisputable titles to the purchasers, to obtain a natural revenue, and above all to suppress monopoly." Nevertheless, the Democratic-Republicans feared pork-barrel legislation and the inevitability of corruption. When in 1796 the House endorsed a postal road from Maine to Georgia, Jefferson complained, "I view it as a source of boundless patronage, a bottomless abyss of public money." Thirty years later, a path-breaking decision in 1824 by Chief Justice John Marshall's Supreme Court, *Gibbons* v. *Ogden,* ruled against a steamboat monopoly between New York and New Jersey and put inland navigation under federal jurisdiction. It opened up federal planning and budgeting to establish a network of waterways, launched an era of fierce competition among hundreds of steamboat lines, and created demand for public works. Congress did not waste time: The General Survey Act of 1824 was "to procure the necessary surveys, plans, and estimates upon the subject of roads and canals," beginning with the Chesapeake and Ohio Canal, clearing sand by dredging and debris by removing snags from the Ohio and Mississippi rivers, and improving harbors. "Revenue was a secondary object" compared to public benefit; cost effectiveness became less a factor than national development.

The Network of Man-Made Canals

In the early days of the nation, travel and trade was chiefly conducted by way of water. Overland travel took weeks of brutal effort through hazardous terrain. For example, produce from a farm along the Hudson River could be put on a boat and two or three men could navigate the load downstream to the markets at New York City. To carry the same load, but overland from the Pennsylvania backcountry to a Philadelphia market, required 40 wagons, 160 horses, and 80 men. The result was that a New York farmer easily made 30 percent more profit than a landlocked Pennsylvania farmer. Along the Atlantic coast, sloops, shallops, ketches, schooners, and brigs carried tobacco, rice, and indigo, as well as mail and travelers. Some boosters who looked at the rough maps of the heartland were justified in believing that the future of the United States lay with the Ohio and Mississippi and Missouri river valleys. The Mississippi, they said, would function like the Rhine or Danube in Europe, the Yellow River in China, or the Ganges in India.

Government officials and private entrepreneurs also sought to cover the nation with an elaborate network of laboriously excavated canals. Progress was slow. In the first quarter of the nineteenth century, waterway improvement consisted mostly of short canals with locks around falls and rapids of otherwise navigable rivers. The span of relative peace between the War of 1812 and the Mexican War encouraged public interest in internal development. Part of Henry Clay's "American System" included a transportation network together with high tariffs on imports and a strong federal bank. Nevertheless, the Bonus Bill of 1817 that would have created "a good system of roads and canals," including a connection between Lake Michigan to the Mississippi River, was rejected as pork barrel. This second failure (after Gallatin's proposal) at national planning was partially bypassed by indirect financing by Congress and by state and municipal ventures, such as $7 million raised to begin the waterway from the Hudson River to Lake Erie.

The highly successful Erie Canal project had to skirt through a northern breach of the Appalachians. When digging first began in 1817, the goal was to improve on two turnpikes originally built between the Hudson and Buffalo in 1802. When completed in 1825, the Erie

Canal offered a 363-mile-long water route between New York City and the Great Lakes. The improvement in travel made the Erie Canal an international attraction. One work animal could haul as much freight by pulling a canal boat as 50 mules pulling 12 loaded wagons on a good turnpike. Westbound settlers traveled not at 20 cents but at less than 2 cents per mile and a ton of freight dropped from $100 by road to $20 by canal. A barrel of salt pork, which cost $10 to bring from Cincinnati over the Appalachians to New York, could be shipped by canal boat for $3.50. The 20-day journey by wagon from Albany to Buffalo dropped to 8 days by canal boat. Before the canal opened, it cost over $5 per hundredweight to convey goods from New York City to the frontier town of Columbus, Ohio. After the Erie Canal opened, the hundredweight cost fell to $2.50 while it still cost $4 from Philadelphia to Columbus by way of Pittsburgh. A far less successful link than the Erie Canal was attempted between Philadelphia and the strategic Ohio River by lifting loaded boats through a series of locks and moving them on skids across the Appalachians. The Chesapeake and Ohio Canal, planned as another east-west link by means of the Potomac and Ohio rivers, outraced costs. An enormous $11 million was consumed to reach Cumberland, Maryland, nearly three times the estimate with the most difficult construction to come. The project may have been more than available technology could accomplish. Delays opened the door to fatal competition from a new technological juggernaut, the railroads. The C&O Canal never made it to the Ohio River.

After the success of the Erie Canal, engineered waterways filled the dreams of Americans. Fantastic schemes and mistaken geography induced visions that joined the Missouri or Colorado rivers through the Rocky Mountains to the Columbia River. An 1824 pamphlet claimed that "seventy-five miles of canals is all that is needed to give us full water communication with the Pacific Ocean" and the long-sought passage to Asia. Between 1815 and 1840 transportation was transformed by a network of canals totaling 3,300 miles and soon plyed by steamboats. With relatively straight canals, travel by water need not depend on the misdirection and meanders of natural waterways. Man-made navigable waterways opened previously inaccessible parts of the public domain across central Ohio and Indiana. Congress commissioned the Illinois-Michigan canal in 1827 to connect the Great Lakes with the Mississippi River. But long canals covering hundreds of miles were the largest and most costly engineering projects of their time and had to be economically justified by spreading huge fixed construction costs over years of profitable trade. Once a canal was built, however, its operating costs were quite low. Bulky freight moved cheaply and quickly between formerly isolated river systems. By 1861 Congress had spent more than $43 million, the equivalent of six Erie Canals, on waterway projects. It had also put the Army Corps of Engineers in control of large-scale civil works. The era of the canal system was brief, however, overwhelmed by 1840 with the arrival of the railroads.

Steamboats

The most dramatic technological advance on America's waterways came with steam power. It truly revolutionized the capacity of Americans to conquer their vast geography. Steamboats (and later the steam locomotive, discussed in Chapter 6) effectively networked the nation from the Atlantic Ocean to the foothills of the Rocky Mountains. It is difficult today to imagine the dramatic change American travelers and merchants felt when the steamboat allowed them to move *upstream* against the powerful currents of the Ohio, Mississippi, or Missouri rivers. Before steam power, boatmen carrying merchandise on the long trip from Pittsburgh down the Ohio and Mississippi to New Orleans had no means to return up the rivers. They broke up their flatboats for lumber or firewood and either stayed in the South or trekked laboriously more than 1,500 miles north along the Natchez Trace and Zane's Trace. The first steamboat launched in Pittsburgh in 1809 made her maiden journey to Louisville in 70 hours. By comparison, in 1782 the French traveler Crèvecoeur took 212 hours to make the same journey. By 1825 people thought it miraculous that a steamboat could travel from New Orleans to New York City by steaming up the Mississippi River, enter the Ohio River, follow canals to Lake Erie, take the Erie Canal and the Hudson River, all upstream in 24 days. Ten years before, it took 24 days to float one-way downstream, the distance only from Pittsburgh to the mouth of the Ohio. Steamboats allowed settlers and businessmen to ply the Great Lakes, to push upstream into the once mysterious Upper Missouri Valley, to probe into the Plains along the Arkansas and Republican rivers, and from the Pacific Coast to search eastward along the Sacramento and Columbia rivers. The steamboat did as much to open up the West as it did during the European conquest of the heart of Africa's darkness. It converted the Mississippi into a national highway system. Steamboat travel remains a historic conquest that accelerated the long-sought control over geography and resources.

Gaps and Passes, Trails and Roads: People on the Move

Despite the convenience of the Hudson, Ohio, and Mississippi rivers, and the expanding network of canals, they did not reach all regions. The problem of passable overland travel was not new and would not get better for many decades. Until the coming of the railroads in midcentury, no method of land technology matched travel on the rivers and canals. In colonial days only a few post roads paralleled the coastline to carry mail and newspapers between Boston and Baltimore and as far inland as Richmond. To this can be added a limited network of wagon roads that connected farmers and towns. It was difficult labor to remove large rocks and tree stumps from a pathway. Maintenance required continuous filling of ruts. Even the best roads still became impassable quagmires during a spring thaw or a rainy spell. The best time to travel to avoid mud or snow was in April or September. As late as 1800 a stagecoach ride from Baltimore to Philadelphia cost a workman a month's salary (70 years later, in 1870, a month's wages would have bought him rail fare to Omaha). Into the early nineteenth century, minor improvements included metal tires on wooden wheels, wider wheels that did not cut roadbeds so badly, teeth-jamming corduroy roads of crisscross tree trunks especially in swampy lowlands, and occasionally laborious and expensive road grading for drainage and less steep grades.

Most travelers still walked. A smaller number rode horseback. When a hill was too steep, people would walk alongside their horses or trudge uphill beside the struggling oxen or horses pulling a wagon or stagecoach. Migrating families slept in the wagons and spent scarce cash to buy fodder for their horses and provisions for themselves. One English traveler around 1820 tells of a family with a cart, horse, packs, and bare feet. Another with a little money used "a small wagon (so light you might almost carry it) that carried bedding and utensils and small children." Migrating farm families also used the famously reliable Conestoga wagons, drawn by six horses or four oxen. This sway-topped, canvas-covered, heavy wooden wagon could haul a ton or more over the rough stump-strewn unimproved "roads" that broke the undercarriages of ordinary vehicles. Most migrants were wise to carry spare axles and wheels because even the best wagons broke down and overturned at an alarmingly frequent rate.

The Great Settler Migration: Across the Appalachian Mountains, into the Ohio Valley, and onto the Midwestern Prairie

The Appalachian Mountains had always been a daunting 200-mile-wide barrier to the flat midwestern prairie. It extended in a sweeping 1,300-mile arc from upstate New York to eastern Georgia. At first, individual families and small companies of settlers using only pack animals filtered westward through dense forest and over rugged mountain-and-valley terrain along animal traces and Indian paths. Travel by wagon was impossible until two military roads, the old Braddock's and Forbes's, forced their way to the Ohio River at the new Fort Pitt. Beginning in 1804, after more clearing and widening, stagecoaches made regular runs between New York and Pittsburgh, covering the ground in a week of bone-jarring and dusty travel. The horse-drawn vehicles carried 12 people in a leather-slung carriage at a maximum of 10 miles an hour. One traveler reported that "the pain of riding exceeded the fatigue of walking," but at least went faster. The English traveler Morris Birkbeck wrote in 1818, "We find ourselves in the very stream of emigration. Old America seems to be breaking up, and moving westward. We are seldom out of sight, as we travel on this grand track [Pennsylvania's Forbes Road] towards the Ohio, of family groups, behind and before us. Add to these the numerous stages loaded to the utmost, and the innumerable travelers on horseback, on foot, and in light wagons, and you have before you a scene of bustle and business, extending over three hundred miles, which is truly wonderful." One early advantage that migrants had at the Forks of the Ohio was that it was free of Indian settlements, having been a centuries-old no-man's-land for hunting and occasional raiding parties. In this peaceful setting, one migrant had the freedom to pause and marvel that "the hills are clothed with a thick forest of trees, consisting of white, red and black oak, hickory, ash, chestnut, poplar, sassafras, dogwood and grapevine."

With the Ohio Valley opened for settlement, it meant that for the first time in American history a great natural highway was open in the general direction of westward movement. As a traveler continued west from the hills around Pittsburgh, he encountered a broad floodplain that opened onto the Ohio River Valley, one of the world's great fertile regions. One traveler reported a farmer's paradise: "In spring heavy rains; in summer an almost cloudless sky, with heavy dews at night; in autumn some rain followed by the Indian summer; and the winter from ten weeks to three months long, which is dry, sharp, and pleasant." After arriving at Pittsburgh for recovery and resupply, a man on a good horse needed four more weeks of travel across the roadless midwestern countryside to reach the Mississippi. River travel was far more practical. Migrants unloaded their packs and wagons onto shallow draft flatboats (to avoid sandbars, rocks, and tree snags in the turbulent river). The going price was high: $75 plus the cost of an experienced crew of four men. It took ten days to get to the Falls of the Ohio at Louisville, where the river fell 26 feet in 2 miles over jagged rocks. In 1828 a canal opened around the Falls. Now a boat could reach the Mississippi in 15 days and reach New Orleans in a month. In the second quarter of the nineteenth century, the Ohio River churned with barges, schooners, keelboats, skiffs, rowboats, and log and plank rafts carrying a single family down river, and as many as 3,000 flatboats a year. Unless river travelers were traders carrying goods to St. Louis or New Orleans, most migrants left the river at Cincinnati or Louisville. They would continue overland by wagon or simply walk into western Ohio, Indi-

ana, and Illinois. In some cases, shallow boats or rafts would be floated to follow smaller connecting rivers like the Muskingum, Scioto, Wabash, Licking, and Kentucky.

Settlers also used the natural passage through the mountains in upstate New York to
reach Buffalo. From there they sailed west on Lake Erie, or took the Great Ridge Road, which
followed the Lake Erie shoreline from Buffalo to Cleveland. Central Ohio, the Scioto Basin
from Chillicothe to Columbus, offered the first large open prairie. Such open land had once
been avoided as an infertile "barrens." But one immigrant reflected growing optimism when
he said he willingly traveled 603 miles from Virginia to find his fortune on such good and accessible soil. But Ohio flatness also meant low muddy bottom lands or thick "gloomy" forests.
An impassable "fearsome" region called the Black Swamp stopped travel westward from Connecticut's Western Reserve. (One of the nation's biggest early civil engineering projects was
the construction of a military road across the swamp in the 1830s, followed in the 1850s by
swamp drainage.) Beyond the dense forests that covered the fertile soils of Ohio and Indiana
were millions of acres of prairie country, covered with grass so thick and tall that government
surveyors could barely mark out section lines. The first wave of settlers arrived before the land
was surveyed and mapped, and became instant "squatters" (preemptors).

According to the census of 1800, the Ohio territory, which had 45,365 inhabitants,
gained statehood in 1803, and grew 20-fold by 1830 to 937,903 people. The Indiana territory (statehood in 1816) grew from 5,641 in 1800 to 343,031 in 1830. Kentucky, a state
since 1792, counted an increase from 220,955 in 1800 to 687,417 in 1830. In 1800 only
1 percent of Americans lived in the Midwest; by 1840 the Midwest had 3 million settlers, or
17 percent of all Americans. Americans had embarked on one of the great land migrations in
history. Still, no one faced the dangers of travel to the west, the arduous work of settlement,
and the risk of failure and death on the frontier for frivolous reasons. For at least the first ten
years of settlement, the average midwesterner earned barely half as much as the average north-
easterner (but almost as much as a southerner if the deliberately impoverished slave is included). The pioneer farm family was far from markets and lacked cash for the latest farm
inventions. Nevertheless, between 1820 and 1840, western farm life improved because of a
combination of bountiful land and grain prices that doubled as eastern production declined
and overseas exports skyrocketed. By 1860, with the threat of civil war, grain prices rose to
triple their price in 1820. The surplus of corn or wheat or livestock that the frontier farmer
traded for goods or cash allowed him to acquire items that belonged only to the well-off
in Europe: tea, pepper, chocolate, cotton goods, gunpowder, tobacco, ironware, boots, hats,
a stove, window glass. During the first half of the nineteenth century, Americans probably came close to the maximum level of material culture that ordinary people could enjoy
anywhere.

Another entryway that paralleled the Forbes Road was the Cumberland Road (earlier
called Braddock's Road), which followed an old Indian path along the Potomac and traveled
through southwestern Pennsylvania to Redstone on the Monogahela. It became the second
stretch of Albert Gallatin's controversial federally financed National Road (now U.S. 40) from
Baltimore to Cumberland, which began construction in 1811. It reached Wheeling by 1818,
Zanesville in central Ohio by 1826, Columbus by 1833, and eventually Indianapolis and
Vandalia in southern Illinois. Paved with the new macadamizing process, the National Road
was, as described by frontier historian Francis Philbrick, "Four rods wide, slightly crowned,
with drainage ditches at the sides, its bed a varying mixture of earth, crushed stone, sand, and
gravel, with sound bridges, and no grade exceeding five percent, the road was a freighter's

dream come true—and an emigrant's. It was, moreover, constantly improved." Such improvements cut the cost of moving heavy freight by half. By 1830 the overland trip to the Mississippi River had been halved to two weeks. (In comparison, it still took five times longer than the first manned trip to the moon in 1969, thus making the time of travel equivalent today to a very far trip into space.) The local impact of a new road was spectacular. Transportation costs in roadless parts of Indiana and Ohio were so high that a wheat surplus was uncompetitive. As a road or canal neared, the value of wheat and corn doubled.

Further south stood what American historians have called one of the great mountain passes in human affairs, the Cumberland Gap, an ancient geological notch 1,600 feet deep through Cumberland Mountain near the southern end of today's Virginia-Kentucky boundary. The Cumberland Gap has probably been overrated when it has been compared to Europe's Brenner Pass through the southern Alps or the Khyber Pass at the eastern limit of Alexander the Great's expeditions to India. The Gap's famous Wilderness Road, although an important connection to the famed Kentucky Bluegrass country, did not carry as great a mass of westward migrants as did New York's Mohawk Valley or the Forks of the Ohio. First reported in 1750, its fame is tied to the near-mythic figure Daniel Boone, who in truth was hired by the wealthy North Carolina speculator Richard Henderson to lead a rough gang of axmen to cut a road to his western claims. Migrants embarked at Harper's Ferry on the Potomac River, found their way past the prosperous farmers of the Shenandoah Valley, struggled across the ridges between the Holston and Powell rivers, to reach the Gap, which opened onto the rich Indian-free farmlands of a planned large proprietary colony, Transylvania, in the Kentucky region. Another more southerly path to the Gap came through the relatively easy way along the valley of east Tennessee, but migrants from the South were far fewer in number.

The United States still had far to go in basic transportation. Most roads were unsurfaced, even in cities. In 1804 the Ohio legislature decreed that stumps left in a public roadway must be less than a foot high, and in Indiana the specifications of the National Road permitted stumps as big as 15 inches high by 18 inches wide. Many rivers and inlets were bridged, with private ferries only at most traveled points. Many fords at shallow water crossings were impassable at high water times. Private turnpikes only partly compensated for a few public works and rarely entered regions of low populations that needed them the most. Whereas steamboats transformed river travel, a few prototype steam-powered overland carriages failed because they could not cope with steep grades, muddy roads, and fords across rivers.

Modernization from a Primitive Geography: Setting Goals for Material Life

The Ideology of Material "Progress"

The famous English scientist Joseph Priestly, discoverer of oxygen, migrated to the new United States in 1794 because he was convinced it had the right combination of economic opportunity and political freedom. Average Europeans were peasants tied down by material scarcity, compelled to work a plot of their master's land, locked into the same hard physical work their ancestors did, restricted by laws and customs, and devoid of hope for improvement. The American Tench Coxe, fervent advocate of industrialization, agreed that only in the United States could one find civil liberty, religious liberty, freedom from government oppression, high employment, the anticipation of profit, domestic happiness, and lack of internal warfare (despite the Indians) that fostered material improvement.

To Americans the rise to modernity meant following the precepts of the Enlightenment, which emphasized the free individual. On the one hand, the individual must be free from the tyranny of a king. On the other hand, the individual should be free from the bonds of the natural world. Enlightenment thinkers believed the path to human prosperity was through scientific discovery, technological innovation, capitalism, factory production, and the efficient use of nature. These Enlightenment precepts marked the beginnings of the modern belief that human happiness could be measured by an improved material life—better health, shelter, and consumer goods—rather than heavenly spirituality or military glory. The Enlightenment rationalists saw themselves as newly sensitive to human suffering; thoughtful people could not be indifferent to poor living conditions even for the lowliest of citizens. Pain, suffering, poverty, and deprivation were not humanity's eternal lot, but long-standing difficulties that could be overcome. In 1776, the same year as the Declaration of Independence, the economic philosopher Adam Smith published his *Wealth of Nations,* a manifesto claiming that industrial capitalism would liberate humanity from material oppression. Smith's ideas fit into American plans because he defined individual freedom as the capacity to pursue one's own business or economic goals, constrained only by the forces of the marketplace. Earlier, in 1758, Franklin's Poor Richard had already written, "Sloth makes all things difficult, but industry all easy. . . . We may make these times better if we bestir ourselves. . . . There are no gains, without pains. . . . Diligence is the mother of good luck . . . and God gives all things to industry." Government was not to interfere; nature was not to be protected; the Industrial Revolution must be welcomed because it meant the continuous retooling of nature to serve ever-increasing human demands. George Washington, in his 1783 circular letter to the governors of the 13 states, wrote that the rational mind does not dwell on matters of the soul's salvation, but on the natural world where "the treasures of knowledge are laid open for our use." John Adams and Thomas Jefferson joined Franklin in the conviction that Americans should not simply endure their lot in life, as had the world's people for untold centuries. The natural world around them was intended for their benefit. Had not Newton's science revealed its laws for them to manipulate? Franklin spoke of "the growing felicity of mankind even in the conveniences of daily living," and wished he could enjoy life in two or three centuries. The modern philosopher Alfred North Whitehead, looking back from 100 years later, said that the first 50 years of American independence was an era "when even wise men hoped." In more mundane terms, historian Richard Hofstadter wrote, "Here [in America], more than elsewhere, the poor man, if white, could really hope to edge his way into the middle class."

The Rising Tide: Movement toward a Higher Standard of Living

American skilled workers were paid two or three times more than they would have been in England, Germany, or France. At the same time, food prices were substantially lower, as were other consumer goods, such as textiles, which created more disposable income for land and labor-saving devices. All these factors attracted immigrants and intensified the hopes among

Physical Stature as a Measure of Material Well-Being

Thomas Jefferson insisted that a large part of human misery was the oppression induced by poverty: "If we can bring it about that men are on the average an inch taller in the next generation than in this; if they are an inch larger round the chest; if their brain is an ounce or two heavier, and their life a year or two longer—that is progress." Jefferson was wrong on brain weight, and we have no data on male chest circumference, but he was on target on height and longevity as useful measures for an improved standard of living.

Individual height or stature certainly is genetically based, but can be improved through diet, personal hygiene, public health measures, the intensity of work, working conditions, and the disease environment, which in turn can also reflect changing income and social and economic conditions. Data based on records of military recruits, convicts, runaway slave ads, firemen and policemen, oath takers, a few skeletal remains, and others, show that Americans (at least, young adult males) were on the average during the Revolutionary War significantly taller than the English in the same era, suggesting a negative impact of England's industrial workplace and slum living conditions. British troop measurements showed that they did not reach American stature (approximately 172 centimeters) until the late nineteenth century. Historically, immigrants to the United States showed improvement over one generation of 2 to 4 centimeters, mostly connected to improved diet and health. Americans themselves experienced a slight decline of average height during the 1830s when the nation adjusted to the shift from farming to factories.

Better height was also linked to access to land use. When a less than wealthy family did not have access to land, they were hard put to maintain good levels of diet and

working peoples for greater benefits in the future. However, historian Walter Licht cautioned, "American workers may on average have received greater compensation and benefited from lower food prices to allow them to live at higher standards than laboring men and women in Europe, but this may have also come at the cost of longer hours of work and an intensified pace of work." Indeed, at the bottom of the economic scale, an unskilled worker earned 80 cents a day or $250 a year; most contemporary estimates required at least $400 a year to support the basic necessities for a family of four. Most such families required multiple breadwinners in wife and children.

Food as a Symbol of Prosperity

Americans in part defined progress by the variety, palatability, and convenience of their diets. Family consumption of beef became a symbol of prosperity because it was purchased with cash and eaten fresh rather than preserved. Like their English forebears, Americans were beefeaters. It was two-thirds of their meat diet and pork a quarter, the rest being mutton or fowl and virtually no fish or shellfish. The status of fresh beef contrasted with the easy avail-

diversity of food. The quantity of their work increased and the quality of their food went down. This was also true of laborers, slaves, and poor families in cities, where higher rent and fuel costs probably prevented improvements in diet. Economist Richard H. Steckel wrote in 1992,

> The abundance of good land in America enabled farmers to choose only the most productive plots for cultivation, possibly allowing them to exert less physical effort, after clearing the land, for a given amount of output compared with [shorter] European farmers. The land was lightly populated in America, which tended to reduce the spread of communicable diseases that lessened the ability to work and that claimed nutrition from the diet. Income and wealth were more equally distributed in the United States during the late colonial period than at any time except the mid-twentieth century. A move toward equality in access to resources at a given level of income tends to increase the average height of a population.

Jefferson may have indeed been justified in emphasizing farming because it provided the health benefits of isolation from communicable disease, low population density that allowed food surpluses, and little industrial development. Steckel concludes that the decline in stature during the second quarter of the nineteenth century—when factory production took off—means that the validity of the usual economic measures of material well-being can be challenged, such as real wages, productivity, and capital stock. "A particular type of prosperity may have accompanied industrialization while other aspects of the standard of living deteriorated," he observed, because of dense urban housing, poor diet, exposure to infectious diseases (cholera), child labor, and severe working conditions (a long workday, heavy labor, polluted air). In the late nineteenth century, military recruits from urban slums were shorter than farm boys.

ability of salt pork. Because fresh meat could not be stored for long, it required organized market outlets in an established and secure society. Before that, most families ate fresh beef only occasionally when they joined several families and shared a fast-spoiling carcass. Only calves and pigs were sometimes butchered at home. Even then, internal organs spoiled too quickly to be palatable; heads, feet, and tallow went to nonfood use.

The more food a family did not produce or process itself, but purchased from the outside, the more it considered itself "modern." Wheat flour was a luxury item in farmland America until the 1840s. Earlier the family ate loaves of "Injun [corn] and rye." New flour-milling technology made wheat flour more affordable and available, but lowered its nutritional value by extracting the wheat germ and adding adulterants. Buying at the local market also showed that the family earned enough cash to indulge itself. It was still rare in the 1820s to find fresh meat, milk, butter, eggs, vegetables, and fish for sale in town shops. Farmers complained that they could not count on selling enough to justify the time and effort required to haul the goods to town and hawk them about. A country store or town marketplace was more likely to sell preserved (salted) meat, live animals, grains, cheeses, nuts, herbs, and seasonable fruits and vegetables. Overall, easier cooking and improved food preservation did not change significantly until the 1830s. Home food processing still included meat salting and packing, baking, cheese-making, brewing, and butchering. Preservation through canning and refrigeration only became common after the Civil War. As for sweets, in 1772 Americans consumed about 17 pounds of sugar and 5 gallons of molasses. Sugar consumption soared to 35 pounds per person in 1860. It was used mostly to sweeten coffee and tea given to the sick; only the middle and upper class ate sugared desserts.

As for spirits, Americans were notorious for their alcoholism. After 1790 American men switched from traditional rum to cheap western whiskey. Per capita consumption of alcohol reached 4 gallons by the late 1820s, but dropped overall to 1.5 gallons by 1840 with the rise of the temperance movement. Neither beer nor wine were popular beverages until after 1850. Two-thirds of white adult Americans drank tea in 1773; ownership of a formal tea service was a symbol of status. By 1800 more than half the households had a fine set. Coffee overtook tea drinking by 1830, helped by falling coffee bean prices. Both tea and coffee were often beyond the means of poor people, which made their use a symbol of material improvement. However, some poor people may have used them as hunger suppressants.

In general, the wealthy and middle class ate better and more diverse diets, frontier set-tlers ate probably the same as early colonial inhabitants, and poor city dwellers may have ex-perienced a real decline in nutritional value, quantity, and variety in their diet. The city poor, burdened by crowding and industrial pollution, did not have their own chickens or pigs or milk from their own cow. This was at a time when they faced higher bodily needs because of long hours of hard labor in the factories. They were living closer to the nutritional edge.

Domestic Lifestyle

One frontier traveler reported on the material possessions and practices by which wilderness settlers believed they had reached domestic respectability: individual knives and forks for all members of the family to eat with instead of shared implements, drinking glasses or cups for all, "fancy" chairs for all to sit on, a feather bed instead of straw ticking, solid wooden bed-steads, a chest for clothes and valuables, candlesticks and expensive candles, a mirror, a shelf clock, and even a set of English ceramic plates. Where once household furnishings had been fabricated mostly in the home, a new "parlor culture" required the outside purchase of win-dow glass, window curtains, walls with lithographed pictures on factory-manufactured wall-paper, machine-woven carpets, mass-produced clocks, upholstered furniture, electroplated silverware, heating stoves, and eventually gas lights. A family was judged lower class and un-successful if it had little or no furniture, no artificial light (even candles were costly), no in-door toilets or running water, and when the whole family, male and female, worked in the fields and barn.

The more the adult woman in a family worked strictly in a gender-specific domestic setting—cooking, gardening, food preserving, cleaning, sewing, washing, child raising, church-going, and moral uplift—the more a family believed it had moved upward on the scale of success. Americans enthusiastically joined the "ideology of domesticity" as a sign of upward mobility. The switch may have been progressive, as in the Northeast, where many young farm-bred women, who had for a time left home to work in the textile factories, put long hours into dairying back on the farm, but began to see themselves in the desirable posi-tion of "housewives"—full-time domestic workers—by the mid-nineteenth century.

The impact of great external events, such as presidential elections or overseas wars, was minor compared to the significance of work, meals, family life, and sleep. For farmers, the changing seasons of the year and the fickle climate controlled their lives far more than any government administration. The flow of their lives through sickness and health, marriage and family, were their primary concerns. The everyday spaces of home and neighborhood, regular travel to town, the feel of the familiar axe or plow or kitchen knife or broom, even the furnishings of their houses, established a consistent sense of well-being. Poverty meant the lack of these amenities and an uncomfortable closeness to the rough environment. Success meant fulfillment of the desire for more and better material goods that kept the environment at a distance.

Prosperity in the Age of Wood

Wood was America's first universal substance, as steel and concrete would become in the late nineteenth century and petrochemicals in the second half of the twentieth century. This led historian Brooke Hindle to describe American history from the first settlements until the Civil War as the Age of Wood. It persisted far longer into the modern era for the United States than in Europe or Britain. Hindle writes, "The social meaning of wood—the manner in which it determined or influenced man's life in this country—may be its greatest significance." The first sightings by Europeans of the vast, apparently untouched forests must have created a sense of wonder because Old England was already deforested, a process that had begun in the thirteenth century. On the Continent, Europeans had for centuries protected their scarce forests so zealously that wood rustlers faced death. In contrast, 95 percent of New England had been tree covered for the 13,500 years since the last ice age. New arrivees off immigrant ships to Massachusetts reported the wonderful fragrance of cedar, maple, fir, and spruce trees that could supply ship timber, pitch, tar, and turpentine. These were northern trees from the White and Green mountains and the Berkshires that sometimes marched down to the shoreline. White pine was used for construction and hemlock for tanning leather. The sight of oaks (white, red, black, chestnut, and scarlet) that stood directly on the coasts of Cape Cod, Rhode Island, and Connecticut was no doubt a heavenly one to immigrants who needed thousands of barrel staves.

Yet a great deal of the time and energy of colonial life was spent cutting down trees and consuming the wood. The time and labor required for clearing was an economic deficit. Historian Charles Carroll wrote, "Until the axmen felled trees most craftsmen could not follow their callings; crops could be neither sown nor harvested; houses could be neither built nor furnished; clothes could not be made; bodies could not be warmed; ships could not sail; rivers could not be crossed; the fires of industry could not burn; wars could not be fought; and the sick could not be healed." In early Virginia and Plymouth, lumbering preceded even agriculture. The earliest New Hampshire and Maine settlements were logging communities.

Most farm families owned and used handsaws, a whipsaw, and a crosscut saw, but depended heavily on the local sawmill. Sawmills, virtually unknown in tree-short England, dotted the American landscape. They were family operations first mechanized by water power and later by a stationary steam engine. A farmer hauled his timber to a sawmill and brought home boards and finished timbers. A shed housed a single saw that cut about 1,000 feet of lumber a day into planks, boards, timbers, and clapboards. A mill could do the work of 20 hand sawyers, although hardwoods were still sawed by hand. During a single decade, the 1840s, sawmill technology progressed through the original sash saw through the gang saw and the muley saw. The sawmill was burdened by idleness during summer drought or winter freezing and it would be abandoned after the local forest had been cleared down to a landscape of stumps and scrap. There was little sense of forest management for long-term conservation. Technological efficiency accelerated logging with the high-quality steel axes of the Collins brothers in South Canton, Ohio, later also steam donkey engines for sawmills and spur railroads for transport, and eventually the modern age of immense logging trucks and lethal chain saws.

Americans, short on both labor and capital, astonished Europeans in their extravagant and carefree use of wood. Although a log cabin used up many more trees than a frame house, it was far quicker and easier to erect, and no one worried where the material would come from. Americans probably learned their universally wasteful habits beginning with wood. Trees were treated as waste products and were usually destroyed to clear the land for agriculture. Settlers would pile up and burn large and solid trunks and long branches of trees from newly cleared land. Sawmills were necessarily wasteful of wood as they poured out beams, planks, and shingles in the rush toward better housing and fencing. In all cases, sawmill blades cut a ⅛-inch swath through the wood to make planks, leaving 312 feet of every 1,000 feet of boards as useless sawdust. European visitors found the amount of sawdust and scrap incredible and unacceptable in their eyes. Overall, one-fifth of America's timber lay waste in this way. Americans continued to consume their trees mindlessly even after national forests were set aside as precious reserves 150 years ago. By the early nineteenth century, expansive use, and waste, began to make wood scarce near eastern cities. Without realizing their culpability, owners of fuel-intensive industries like brick kilns and iron furnaces around Philadelphia began to complain about serious shortages of wood. They began to burn dirty polluting coal.

Prodigious consumption of wood helped Americans jump-start the nation into a strong economy. The first major colonial industry, excluding ocean fishing, was high-quality shipbuilding that quickly received international praise. In the first 200 years of settlement, entire forests of the ancient trees were honorably transformed into splendid ships' masts, yards, spars, bowsprits, decks, and hulls. The connection with sailing ships was first made by the famous trees marked by the broad arrow to be set aside for straight, tall, and strong Royal Navy masts. By the Revolution, fully one-third of all British shipping floated on American wood bottoms. By 1855 the American merchant marine floated more tonnage than any other nation. America's great fleet of innovative wooden clipper ships and whaling ships lasted well into the era of steel steamships. The apparent glut of wood made it the primary material used in most structures and many devices. Wood was for a long time the primary material in public buildings, sidewalks, signs, wharves, even water pumps and underground water pipes (some still function, barely, in Boston and Pittsburgh). Most containers—barrels, tubs, buckets, and baskets—were wooden. The village cooper (barrelmaker) was valued as much as the indispensable blacksmith. Every American, in town and country as well as on the frontier, had some training and minimum skill in working wood with simple tools. Skilled American cabinetmakers began to receive international attention. Wild cherry and walnut were turned into furniture and gun stocks, red maple made into spinning wheels, plates, bowls, and furniture, and sweet gum and softer woods like fir and white cedar made into inexpensive furniture. Laurel was used for pulley axles and weavers' shuttles.

Because of universally available wood structures and furniture, "men of common means" attained a higher standard of living. They could own homes, home furnishings, barns, and outbuildings that only belonged to men of status in England. Access to wood shaped technological innovation. America's early development depended on the technologies—woodworking machinery—that transformed wood into useful products. Lacking other materials, Americans turned wood into a substitute for metal in household hinges and farm hooks. American hand tools, including the improved axe (three times faster for chopping trees than the clumsy English and European models), were the best in the world. Planing machines, veneering machines, and mortising machines went through similar transformations. One of the most successful machines was Thomas Blanchard's lathe for the consistent and speedy shaping of irregular forms like gun stocks. A skilled man could turn out only one or two gun stocks in a day in 1818; now Blanchard's lathe could turn two dozen. It seemed as if Americans were tempted to try anything with wood, including clocks and technical measuring instruments. Wooden surveying equipment was commonplace and there were lathes made entirely of wood, including moving parts except for iron or steel cutting blades. When properly designed, wooden cogs and gears were serviceable moving parts for waterwheels and windmills. Americans continued to use obsolete and inefficient pitchback waterwheels because they were very cheap to construct of wood.

Wood remained the primary fuel in vast amounts for domestic cooking and fireplace heating of virtually all buildings. In a colonial New England iron furnace, a single ton of finished iron consumed 250 bushels of charcoal that used up a pile of wood $4 \times 4 \times 48$ feet. Wood was the first fuel for steam power. By midcentury the railroads alone burned 3 million cords of wood and thousands of steamboats threw 4 million cords into their fireboxes. Americans had no problem employing more efficient high-pressure steam engines that consumed many more cords of wood than low-pressure steam engines favored by the English. Not the least, wood was widely processed into chemical substances by burning or soaking. The hardwoods of the north were reduced to potash, and resinous woods in the South were turned into tar. Most of the tar made in America was produced from dead trees: A pile of pitch pine knots would be burned in kilns with inclined floors to drain the tar into wooden troughs to a barrel. Potash, potassium carbonate, was an alkali used in the manufacture of glass and soap. Wood ashes from open-air fires were collected and leached in barrels or tubs, then the lye sent to a battery of open kettles to make a black syrup. More valuable pearl ash could be made using a very hot fire in an oven until carbon burned out. Different trees also provided an abundance of pitch, turpentine, and wood alcohol; the bark became tannin for tanning leather, and maple trees were a renewable resource for maple sugar.

There were limits. Wood could not solve the problem of bad roads, since corduroy roads—rows of rough logs—remained bumpy and unstable, and costly plank roads demanded excessive tolls and wore out rapidly. The pioneering Philadelphia engineer, Benjamin H. Latrobe, fabricated some of the first steam engines out of wood, held together by metal straps. They leaked terribly, held pressure poorly, worked for a time before they "quickly decomposed," said Latrobe, "and steam leaks appeared at every bolt hole." But they were easy to fabricate without using costly machine tools from England. Even in railroad building, Americans placed their rails on wooden ties instead of England's stone blocks. Fragile-looking wood railroad bridges spanned many chasms. Locomotive frames and passenger and freight cars stayed in wood.

A distinctive forest society had been shaped by clearings of a great forest, wooden fences, shingled clapboard houses, endless fireplace conflagrations, great barns, river rafts, and canoes. By the middle of the nineteenth century iron machines and brick factory buildings became more commonplace. Coal replaced wood as a primary fuel for heating and iron production. The Age of Wood gave way to the Iron Age.

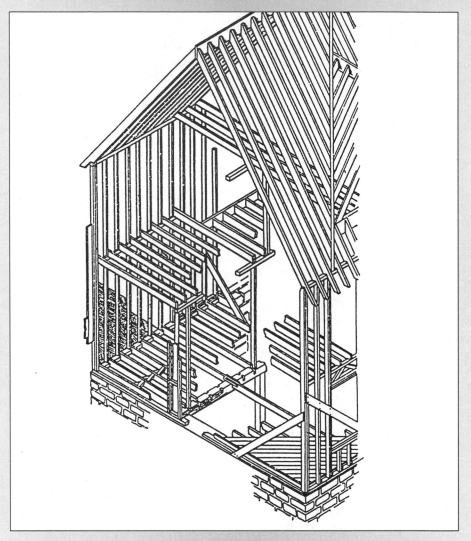

Balloon Frame for a Two-Story House. The light framework could be easily erected by one man working with hammer, nails, and saw.

THE SINGLE MOST significant American innovation in wood was the standardized balloon frame house that first appeared in Chicago in 1833. It saved wood because thin lengths of presawed and precut lumber (the memorable 2 × 4, 1 × 6, 2 × 12, 4 × 4, and so on) were nailed together as a frame instead of heavy timbers with mortised and tenoned joints. This also reduced the need for highly skilled carpenters and eliminated the lifting of timbers into place. The balloon technology allowed fast and economic construction for houses and smaller commercial and industrial buildings. This balloon framing made excellent use of America's large timber resources. It also encouraged something as mundane as the production of large numbers of nails. The unique balloon-framed wood house is still the major mode of house construction today.

America's New Mission:
The Rush Toward Industrialization

The Demand for Labor-Saving Devices,
Goods, and National Security

"Craft technology" in colonial America involved the work of a single person or a few "mechanicks" in the home or a small shop using hand tools, simple machines, and individual skills. Such workers gained a reputation for inventiveness out of necessity. There were early nineteenth-century inventions to which no one person's name has ever been attached: the Conestoga wagon, the Durham boat, the Pennsylvania rifle, and the American felling axe. One person, or several, reshaped and weighted the axe head to make it carry more leverage when it was swung, and curved the axe handle to better fit the hands. The combination of such successful improvements, the passion for material goods, and the harsh life on the wild frontier primed Americans to rush toward mechanization. The military needs of the Revolution had demonstrated the strategic role of manufacturing and the importance of national self-sufficiency. During wars or embargoes, Americans were compelled to build their own textile industry, increase domestic iron production, create small-arms manufacturing, and expand flour milling. When Rhode Island nail makers put new machinery into operation in 1791, they proudly announced they could furnish the whole country. This would become a common refrain. Manufacturers of paper, sailcloth, buttons, and soap filled national needs and even began foreign export. By the early nineteenth century, a million farmers looked to better tools to save time and reduce heavy muscle-wearying labor. Thus, in several ways, the tide began to turn toward industrialization. It was said to make the world more interesting, opened more options for personal wealth, and improved the quality of life. Sometimes there were long-term environmental effects from primitive industry. The pro-American French observer Crèvecoeur described a New Jersey site where a supply of local iron ore transformed a marshy bog into a fertile meadow. An earthen dam was thrown across the bog's outlet to supply a water wheel that blew a furnace or operated a forge hammer. The backwater of the mill pond killed the trees that covered the swamp. In a few years the local ores were exhausted, the timber consumed for fuel, and the partial drying of the bog caused the water flow to fail. Eventually the dam was opened, the pond drained, and the former swampy bog was converted into pasture or plowed fields.

Historian Walter Licht describes not a single pathway to successful industrialization, but four identifiably different tracks, depending on regional geography and social objectives. The New England mill village, free standing in the countryside, and based on families laboring together, was the foundation for later industrial communities as well as notorious company towns. They produced textiles, chemicals, machine tools, and rural iron. The one-industry city, such as Lowell, Massachusetts, has been accepted as the primary model of American industrialization, but it was just one approach. Textiles in Lowell and shoes in Lynn set a precedent with corporate-owned, highly capitalized, large-scale, fully integrated mechanized works using a cheap labor source. Licht also sees an important forerunner in the diversified manufacturing in major urban centers like New York City and Philadelphia. These were family businesses where a great diversity of production flowed everywhere: "in cellars and attics, tenement flats, artisan shops, the proliferation of indistinguishable small and medium-sized manufactories." Finally, he treats the southern slave-based plantation as cotton industrialization that anticipated modern agribusiness.

The First Revolution in Mechanization: Textiles

During the upheavals in Europe in the late eighteenth century, the high cost or disappearance of British goods forced Americans to manufacture for themselves. England had become the leader in manufacturing decades earlier because it had the extraordinary good fortune of an array of new inventions—Arkwright's spinning jenny, Crompton's mule, and Cartwright's power loom—that became the technological core of the Industrial Revolution. Americans started by pirating from England the know-how for textile manufacturing, which the English zealously guarded. In 1790 Samuel Slater, a young apprentice to an Arkwright-equipped textile mill in England, memorized the secret design for a water-powered textile frame for spinning yarn. He settled in Rhode Island and, financed by clothing merchants, established a spinning mill powered by water from the Blackstone River. At first he only employed nine children, but his success led to the appearance of other small mills, with eight soon in profitable operation. The mill village, one of several forms of industrialization, began to take shape. By 1800 Slater's mill employed over 100 low-salary children with a few adult overseers. The yarn they produced was then sold to the children's mothers and sisters, who wove it into cloth at home. Slater's move was an early version of technology transfer, in this case by stealth. The result was a classic example of imitation and innovation that characterized successful mechanization: the acquisition of an innovative device and its adaptation to local conditions, resulting in broad environmental, economic, and social change.

Thomas Jefferson's 1808–09 embargo against trade with England (in the midst of its life and death struggle with Napoleon) favored mechanization as the only way to future prosperity and national security. Congress aided the process when it legislated tariffs to protect infant industry like textiles until they reached a competitive level. Compared to 15 textile mills before its trade embargo, by 1810, 65 mills were turning out goods, with 22 more under construction. By 1815, in Connecticut alone there were 25 textile factories employing nearly 12,000 workers. Even Jefferson reluctantly admitted that Hamilton was right in urging government support of domestic industry. Senator Henry Clay coined this combination of tariffs, industrialization, and internal improvements the "American System." Looking back from the vantage point of 1816, Jefferson wrote, "We have experienced what we did not then believe, that to be independent for the comforts of life we must fabricate them ourselves. We must now place the manufacturer by the side of the agriculturalist."

Despite these advances, at the end of the War of 1812 Americans seemed to be losing ground to the English success story. As late as 1815 only 4 percent of America's labor force worked in any form of "industry." It was not clear, despite the obvious need, that Alexander Hamilton's grand plan of modernization could be put into practice. But it was clear that the struggling new nation could not succeed without industrialization. Most manufacturing still resided in the countryside and could tap only a scarce labor force. Lack of transportation prevented distribution of raw materials and finished products and access to commercial information about prices and demand outside the immediate neighborhood. All these factors kept many industries isolated, stagnant, and frozen on a small scale of operation. Americans were so short of machinery that when Robert Fulton sought to build the steam engine for the *Cler-mont* in 1807, he had to contact England. A betting man might still take odds against the future success of the United States.

In 1815 the enterprising Massachusetts merchant Francis Cabot Lowell visited another English textile plant and copied from memory its power loom, which in turn became the heartbeat of a cheap and efficient weaving operation in Waltham. Lowell's Boston Manufacturing Company was the nation's first successful large-scale integrated factory operation. It combined 200 power looms with carding, spinning, and drawing equipment, mostly powered by water and later by stationary steam engines. The plant employed boys and girls, men and women, but was most famous for its use of young farm women it housed in carefully monitored dormitories. By the 1830s textile production had moved out of the home. The new textile factories made household spinning and weaving, especially of flax, disappear. When the young farm women became wives and mothers, they could purchase the finished cloth instead of spending long hours in home production.

New England enjoyed a critical regional advantage for textile mills: They could be powered by the naturally flowing water of New England's rivers. Such facts of geography continued to encourage Americans to use natural rather than artificial forms of energy for an extended time. For example, it cost $500 to $1,000—the equivalent of a farmhouse—to build a dam and spillway, a canal to direct flow to the mill, buy the millstones and wooden gears, and construct the building for a mechanized sawmill. As late as 1840 the alternative energy source—steam power—was twice as expensive in New England as in Great Britain. The mill at Lowell put annual cost per horsepower for water at $12 and for steam at $90. Overall, numerous rushing rivers and tumbling streams in the eastern United States allowed entrepreneurs to harness abundant waterpower to ease hard labor. Wilmington, Delaware, for example, became a concentration of 12 mills grinding 400,000 bushels of wheat because it had ample and reliable waterpower, a major grain-growing district, and excellent connections to river and ocean for direct export. In all such places, clattering and bobbing machinery ground wheat into flour for bread, spun rough cotton shirts, made iron, and cut timber for houses and bridges. With New England's example in textiles and shoes, efficient factory production spread into other areas. Connecticut became the center for manufacturing pistols and clocks. Rifles came from Lancaster, Pennsylvania, and Harper's Ferry, Virginia; gunpowder came from the Du Pont de Nemours plant in Delaware.

The Limits to Industrialization

According to one critic, modernization "is not a simple, sanitary process of investing capital or introducing new technologies into a country. It is a messy, conflict-ridden business of social change." The very structure of American society began to change. Small local communities had centered on family connections and highly personal business activities. In contrast, in a factory town, this structure and cohesion was replaced by the operation of a large-scale economy that played down human relations, created a self-sustaining industrial bureaucracy, and developed an ideology centered on profit making. The well-being of the local working class might be improved, but it was not the primary interest. By the 1840s and 1850s the use of a multitude of machines driven by water or steam in large operations did bring a large leap in productivity. By 1840 real wages were also rising, but health and nutrition began to deteriorate. These contradictions were difficult to reconcile. Industrialization seems to have unleashed a lethal combination of new forces on the American scene—factory working conditions and city slum living conditions. Admittedly, housing and health in the new cities were better than rough frontier life, but only for a time. Working conditions had certainly declined for many. On the frontier farm, although farmers worked sunrise to sunset planting, cultivating, and harvesting their crops, they also had the release of idle hours during bad weather and in the winter. The urban industrial setting, in contrast, depended on long hours of repetitive tasks under dangerous conditions all year round. This put more physical stress on workers, who thus required a better diet and the emotional release of leisure time. Instead, the work week of 10 hours a day, 6 days a week (only Sunday off) remained standard until well into the twentieth century. Women and children were even more seriously overworked. As we shall see in Chapter 7, critics like Ralph Waldo Emerson feared an industrial determinism: "Things are in the saddle, and ride mankind."

What other factors made conditions worse? By the 1850s real wages started slipping because of waves of immigrants who competed for jobs. Even though the factories needed more workers than ever, the number of new immigrants made it a buyers' market for employers. American laborers began to realize that one terrible aspect of industrialization was their own insecurity. Industrial workers encountered a new phenomenon: the gross instability of the modern world when most values depended on fluctuations of the marketplace. Their jobs, and their wages, were beyond their control no matter how good their work was. Work was tied to economic fluctuations as the economy had its ups and downs. Immigrants and ex-farmers lost the stability of traditional society. True, city life was dynamic, complex, and cosmopolitan, more exciting than on the farm. But the promise of individual autonomy and free initiative was quickly lost on the factory floor. Unlike the farmer, industrial workers could not cushion bad times by growing their own food to stay healthy. Workers and their families were particularly helpless in the face of rent gouging, exorbitant prices for coal for fuel or cooking, and low-quality food with no alternatives. If Adam Smith was right in his classic 1776 manifesto *Wealth of Nations,* the marketplace had become the controlling force of society as never before. Americans enthusiastically adopted the assumption that the individual who worked profitably within the marketplace would at the same time benefit society. This invisible hand of the marketplace was said to control most human relations in an industrial society: a labor force, urban concentration, manufacturing cities, environmental exploitation. However, the decline in health and well-being among large numbers of Americans by 1840 raised serious questions about the conventional tests for the success of modernization. So-called modern economic growth through industrialization (at least 1.5 percent increase in real per capita income per year) may in fact tell us very little about the true level of a standard of living. Higher incomes might not offset the human costs of industrialization (see more details in Chapter 9).

Conclusion: America by 1840

The self-conscious choice to industrialize would have long-term human and environmental effects for the rest of American history, as we shall see in the rest of this book. It also meant that alternative modes of standard of living and quality of life were rejected, and soon were no longer possible. The unusual feature of industrial modernization is that it eliminates alternatives as it recasts human institutions, national economies, technological change, and the environment. (There would be a point of no return from industrialization in American history at some time between 1840 and 1880.) In historian Mark Weiser's words, "The most profound technologies are those that disappear. They weave themselves into the fabric of everyday life until they are indistinguishable from it." In 1790 economic activity in the new nation was remarkably diverse and depended on a variety of environmental resources:

> hunting and gathering
> subsistence farming
> market agriculture
> fishing, lumbering, mineral extraction
> artisan work
> simple manufacture
> commerce

By 1840 most economic activity defined itself in terms of the market. The variety of activities was extensive, but contained the following within a relatively small band:

> mechanization
> the factory system
> occupation change
> spread of wage labor
> separation of male and female activities
> rise of large-scale corporation
> urbanization
> social divisions within communities
> emergence of a distinctive middle class
> massive migration of people into and through the country

Between 1790 and 1840 Americans not only created a surprisingly durable political structure but also a vigorous economy. Industrialization began to create material demands that forced the American environment into a very specific mold. Industrialization was neither the only way nor was it inevitable, but it was one of the most self-conscious creations in human history. Industrialization took hold not only because of capital, workers, and innovation, but also because of dramatic improvements in transportation, by a new determination to exploit the fertility of western farmland, by foreign dependence on America's export crops (due to war and poor harvests, especially the Irish potato famine), and by backbreaking work done by slave labor on southern plantations. The momentum looked to be wonderfully self-sustaining as long as the costs in human beings and natural resources were not included in the balance sheet.

How can a nation develop itself? History now tells us, through industrialization. The economic philosopher Robert Heilbroner called industrial capitalism America's overriding adventure: "We watch the unfolding of material life as it constantly expands the limits of the possible." The innovative French historian Fernand Braudel spoke of capitalism's "great maneuvers" as it came to dominate European and American history. Nevertheless, America's success was not all private capitalization. Like most developing nations, American modernization was a mixed economics that combined government stimulation, market forces, and private initiative. The American experience suggested that certain basic rules should be followed. One was to create large supplies of staple crops like wheat or cotton and prime industries such as steel or railroads. Since most nations have a scarcity of skilled labor, the nation should develop full mechanization and fully integrated production, which the United States accomplished first in guns, machine tools (lathes and drills), and clocks. Add to this an infrastructure of transportation and communications to allow and encourage market activity. Here a strong central government is essential because of the scale and cost of such public works. Finally, an emerging nation should build schools and increase literacy, not only to create a base of skilled workers, but, in Walter Licht's words, to "inculcate modern attitudes" of a work ethic (intensive work for long hours) and consumerism (e.g., upward mobility into a middle class). This included the highly conservative defense of private property. Yet the social change labeled "modernization" is not the direct outcome of industrialization. It is the result of secondary forces shaped by industrialization, such as unbridled market activity, the shift of work from family life to the wage labor system, and industry-based urbanization. Also, as the workplace lost its dependence on local environments, a new mobility restructured cities into worker slums and upper-class suburbs.

The concept of preconditions for "takeoff" of a promising but undeveloped country were first identified by the economic theorist Walter Rostow in the 1950s. He concluded that by the early 1840s the United States met the conditions by the enlargement of uncommitted capital (e.g., high rate of national savings) and technological opportunity (e.g., the railroads). Between 1815, after the United States gained postwar stability, and 1840, the population grew dramatically at about 3 percent a year, creating more demand for textiles, shoes, and other goods. This growth was reinforced by a growth in per capita income that added another 1 percent a year. Another 1 percent a year growth came with cheaper freight transportation costs following the introduction of the steamboat and the completion of the Erie Canal. Mechanization raised the value of output per worker in flour milling four times higher and nearly three times higher in cotton textiles. (By 1860 national income was 12 times greater than it had been in 1800. By 1890 more wealth would come from industrial production than from farmland. Perhaps this can be measured in the 1890s by the fact that the United States produced more steel than its own model nation, Britain.) By any measure of the day, Americans became relatively prosperous in the 50 years between 1790 and 1840, and in truth had developed the best overall standard of living in the world. In 1804 one booster from Rhode Island noted that in the previous 20 years the nation's population had doubled from 3 to 6 million, and spread westward across four new states:

> Turn your eyes wheresoever you will, and you behold our riches in the multiplied flocks and herds, and luxuriant crops of independent landholders; in the navies and store-houses of our mercantile community; in the opulent capitals of our numerous banks and insurance companies; in the vast sums annually and profitably expended in turnpike roads, public bridges, and productive canals; in the diminution of our public debt, and in the prolific revenues arising from a lucrative commerce.

It was, he said, all of a spontaneous whole, one people and one nation that was destined to stretch from Maine to the Gulf of Mexico, and westward across mountains and prairies to Oregon on the Pacific Ocean.

Industrialization created a unique layer of material culture nationwide—the physical infrastructure—on America's geography. Critics complained that the shifts trivialized human worth; the shifts certainly reduced nature into commodity. The road Americans took to achieve material prosperity forced an increased separation from nature. Nature became an expendable commodity instead of a unique place to which the individual, tribe, or community was personally connected, as in traditional societies. Nature, when reduced to components of crops, trees, salt, and minerals, separated people from their local ecosystems. Their real world—their virtual reality—became trade relationships that energized the human-made infrastructure. People often had more connection with distant markets than with a local landscape. They might have more investment in another people's ecosystem. It became increasingly difficult to know which ecosystem was interacting with which culture.

FARMING DID NOT disappear as a force on the American scene. As we saw in Chapter 2, technological innovation such as the steel plow and mechanized reaper became important in farming improvement. As historians Brooke Hindle and Steven Lubar wrote,

> Industrialization grew in a symbiotic relationship with agriculture. It helped to produce the cities that put great demands, and restrictions, upon farmers. Industrialization depended on increasing farming productivity in order to free labor for the farmers. Farming depended on industrialization to provide the transportation, the new and mechanized farming and food processing implements, and the markets for farm products upon which the whole pattern of change rested.

Mechanical threshing reduced costs from about 7 cents per bushel for hand threshing down to less than 4 cents per bushel. It also freed the farmer from depending on unreliable outside help. Mechanization began to change farming from a lifestyle into a balance sheet: In 1850 a farmer learned he had to have about 50 acres planted in wheat at a good price to finance a standard McCormick reaper that might last him five to ten years.

Agriculture was the foundation of expansion and prosperity on which industrialization rested. Major improvements in efficiency allowed the proportion of farmers in comparison to factory workers to decline even as farm acreage grew. This was the paradox of American farming: The better farmers did to create more output, the more they released resources for industrialization. There were fewer farm workers, more investment capital, and healthier and more varied diets for all citizens. Success on the farm, where often farmers could ship half their wheat or corn to market after filling their own needs, meant that more workers were available in nonagricultural jobs. Between 1800 and 1840 the percentage of people employed outside agriculture rose from 17 percent to 37 percent. In 1840 two-thirds of all Americans still worked on the farm. In the revolutionary era, American farmers fed themselves and 4 others, by the 1830s this rose to 10 others, and then the ratio went through the roof, reaching in the 1980s more than 90 others. The importance of the shift of expansion from agriculture to industry cannot be overemphasized. It carried the United States from an undeveloped country to a developed nation.

The American experience cannot be made a universal model for national development because of unique circumstances. Unlike developing nations in the twentieth century, the fledgling United States did not have to compete with a host of already developed and modernized countries. Nor did it employ highly controlled planning by the central government. Instead, its paths toward industrialization were multiple to the point of being disjointed and uneven. Still, government did step in to shape the all-important opening of the American West by western land purchases, the seizure of territory by war or stealth, herding of the native peoples into reservations, and the survey and sale of the public domain to individuals and corporations. Not the least, the United States from the first enjoyed agricultural abundance and low commodity prices as a solid foundation for risky capitalization of industry. Other environmental factors that set apart American development were rapid population growth together with a bounty of natural resources that Licht concluded, "ushered in an open, pluralist, unadministered politics and economics by default and happenstance."

For Further Reading

Early American living conditions are vividly described by Henry Adams in the first six chapters in Volume 1 of his *History of the United States of America During the First Administration of Thomas Jefferson,* first published in 1889 and reprinted separately in 1955 as *The United States in 1800.* The standard work on daily life is Jack Larkin, *The Reshaping of Everyday Life, 1790–1840* (1988). For descriptions of an emerging material standard of living, see Henry Steele Commager, *The Empire of Reason: How Europe Imagined and America Realized the Enlightenment* (1977), and William B. Scott, *In Pursuit of Happiness: American Conceptions of Property from the Seventeenth to the Twentieth Century* (1977). Good case studies can be found in Robert E. Gallman and J. J. Wallis, (eds.), *American Economic Growth and Standards of Living Before the Civil War* (1992). Economic history can be reviewed in Curtis P. Nettels, *The Emergence of a National Economy, 1775–1815* (1962), Douglas North, *Economic Growth of the United States, 1790–1860* (1961), and *Growth and Welfare in the American Past: A New Economic History* (1974), the latter being two of the first data-based studies in the "new economic history." The literature on early mechanization, the broader impact of industrialization, economic development, and the process of modernization is very large, including an extensive Marxist approach that is not covered here. For useful conceptualizations, see a variety of books beginning with Walter Licht, *Industrializing America: The Nineteenth Century* (1995), Fernand Braudel, *Afterthoughts on Material Civilization and Capitalism* (1977), Richard D. Brown, *Modernization: The Transformation of American Life, 1600–1865* (1976), Nathan Rosenberg, *Technology and American Economic Growth* (1972), and the early analysis of UDCs in Walter Rostow, *The Stages of Economic Growth* (1960). The complete story of technology in America is deftly told in Carroll Pursell, *The Machine in America: A Social History of Technology* (1995). The remarkable details of technology transfer, innovation, and adaptation can be found in Victor Clark, *History of Manufactures in the United States* (1929), a classic and basic descriptive report. H. J. Habbakuk, *American and British Technology in the 19th Century* (1962), established the argument for technological innovation to compensate for labor scarcity. See also the able survey by David Freeman Hawke, *Nuts and Bolts of the Past: A History of American Technology, 1776–1860* (1988), Brooke Hindle's persuasive study, *America's Wooden Age: Aspects of Its Early Technology* (1976), and Brooke Hindle and Steven

Lubar, *Engines of Change: The American Industrial Revolution, 1790–1860* (1986). See also Clarence Danhof, *Change in Agriculture: The Northern United States, 1820-1870* (1969), which also describes institutional changes, and the standard histories by Francis S. Philbrick, *The Rise of the West, 1754–1830 (The New American Nation Series)* (1965), and George Rogers Taylor, *The Transportation Revolution, 1815-1860* (1962), still a reliable reference on pre–Civil War transportation.

CHAPTER FIVE

UNIFYING AMERICAN SPACE

Where else in the history of man, civilized or not, do you read the story of a 2,500-mile march through hostile country, over unexplored desert and mountain? The host led by Moses and Aaron wandered for years, but only accomplished a direct journey for a few hundred miles. Xenophon in his famous retreat from the Euphrates had a less distance to go before he reached safe harbor at home. No crusade ever extended over so great a distance, and most of the way through Christian and friendly countries. Napoleon on his disastrous trip to Moscow only essayed a march of 1,500 miles. The descendants of Oregon pioneers shall yet hear their ancestors' glories sung as we now teach our children to glorify the heroes of the past.

—E. L. EASTHAM, 1885

The movement of the people of the United States into its western territories was one of the world's great migrations. The U.S. spread across the North American continent to the Pacific Ocean was a reflection of the European drive to dominate the entire globe and carve it up for its own enrichment. Belgians and Germans, British and French entered Africa's heart of darkness, the British Empire made India the jewel in its crown; European imperialists forced their way into China; the Russians took Siberia; the U.S. Navy opened Japan; Antarctica was discovered and Europeans charted the islands of the world's connected oceans. Thus Americans were not alone when they brashly applied new technologies, sought material betterment, and forged their ideology of Manifest Destiny that combined Christian millenialism with romantic imperialism. The environmental history of the American West is above all a history of the conquest, control, and transformation of a large and complex space that is 2,000 miles across and 1,500 miles wide. Americans deliberately ignored Spanish, Indian, and even Mormon alternatives for settlement in difficult environments. The West was simply seen as a storehouse of valuable raw materials, not as the homelands of native tribes and not as self-sustaining natural ecosystems. The American takeover was simple, effective, and unique: Explore and map the land, exterminate or remove the natives, give the region equal status in the nation, measure the land geometrically, sell it to private parties, introduce a large and industrious population, and draw off the wealth. The process was ingenious and widely admired. The sequence of events sometimes got muddled, with squatters fighting Indians before the soldiers and surveyors showed up. The federal government subsidized railroads for transportation connections, handed over land to private enterprise—miners, loggers, and industrial farmers—at the lowest possible cost, and then stepped aside to allow uttermost consumption at the highest possible profit. The national government did not receive significant income from the disposal of the irreplaceable public domain. Little attention, says historian William G. Robbins, was given to the ordinary land-seeking citizenry. Yet even a maverick like Henry David Thoreau joined the mainstream when he wrote, "We go westward as into the future, with a spirit and adventure."

The West's abundance was also its downfall. Large-scale interventions into regional ecosystems went wrong, although few contemporaries recognized degradation. America's new industrial muscle and capitalistic sinew could expose and exploit the West as never before. The negative impacts of settlement would not immediately appear and most often were not acknowledged. There seemed to be enough water, soil, and minerals to last forever. As a result, tree cutting and mining consumed natural riches and spoiled the land, extensive plowing on marginal semiarid land blew away the soil, and burgeoning cities immediately outgrew their local resources, especially water, because they were often established incongruously in mountain or desert regions.

From the first, most Americans saw the West through eyes almost exclusively conditioned by the juggernaut of enterprise. Nature was worthless until reshaped. The West was not to be tended as a preserve of Indians and coyotes, bison and rattlesnakes, but to be conquered. (The concept of national parks to hold out small parcels of wilderness would come later.) Geographer Donald Meinig says of the white European intervention into the West, "The very shape of the land surface has been modified in a thousand ways, by cuts and quarries, excavations and embankments, fills, dams, culverts, terraces, revetments." The undeveloped West was "obsolete"—an antique landscape—as it stood, ill suited to the needs of agriculture, commerce, and industry. Americans invented different Wests depending on their needs. In 1869, for example, businessman Samuel Bowles saw opportunity on several levels. For him, movement into the West was "the unrolling of a new map, a revelation of new empire, the creation of a new civilization, the revelation of the world's haunts of pleasure and world's homes of wealth." More often than not, the U.S. takeover of the unknown region beyond the Mississippi depended on notions of what the West ought to be more than the reality of what it was. It became the passage to India, the barren wasteland of the "Great American Desert," the "Great American Garden" of an agricultural utopia, an Eldorado or Cibola bonanza of gold and silver, a beaver kingdom, the no-man's-land of imperial rivalries, the escape zone for badmen and Mormons, the last outpost for Catholic Spain and heathen Indians, a wilderness deserving protection. Early nineteenth-century Americans never thought of the western landscape as something "everlasting," a profound wilderness they might inhabit like the Indians, where the human presence had always been minuscule and ephemeral. The notion of environmental harmony between humanity and nature carried no weight despite long-standing Indian traditions.

The West was treated like an undeveloped country, short of internal capital, with a sketchy infrastructure, and distant from markets. Such a view provides a very different picture from the traditional frontier romanticizing by earlier historians, generations of textbooks, powerful novels, influential movies, popular tourism, and congressional rhetoric. The great Wisconsin historian Frederick Jackson Turner made his compelling "frontier thesis" of American history in a speech to historians meeting at the Columbian Exposition—the 1893 world's fair in Chicago. Turner spoke of waves of frontier settlement, moving continuously westward onto "empty land," a phenomenon that supposedly gave Americans their personal sense of individualism, enterprise, optimism, and especially their democratic institutions. Western expansionism was exceptional, he said, a triumphal history unique to Americans and one that set them apart from all other cultures. The reach to the Pacific was the final stage in the creation of the United States. Turner had taken to heart a report in the 1890 census that the western land of opportunity was being filled up, and the frontier had come to a close. He feared for a future United States that would be dominated by crowded industrial cities filled with foreign immigrants with undemocratic backgrounds. He became an energetic spokesman to remind Americans that their true identity came from continuously repeated settlement on the ever-receding frontier. His critics began to counter his appeal when American institutions faltered and changed during the Depression of the 1930s and when industrial technologies and urbanization seemed more relevant to American growth than empty prairies and pioneer cabins. According to this critique, the "farmer's west," the "mining west," and the "urban west" seem less connected to each other than dependent on their eastern counterparts, subject to eastern markets, and pawns of federal policies made in Washington.

Toward a Continent-Size Nation:
"A Restless, Sometimes Lawless, Landgrabbing People"

Settlers from the East and Midwest leapfrogged over undesirable environments—the Plains, the Rockies, and deserts—that were difficult or impossible to farm, to embrace lush land in California and Oregon. Only later would they hesitantly venture onto the Plains and other risky regions. Historian Dale Morgan described American emigrant advance onto the western landscape as "humanity on the loose." Americans possessed the technology—horses, wagons, railroads—to overrun all natural obstacles. They also had the psychology of greedy, callous, and perpetually dissatisfied nomads to drive off impediments like the Indians. Back in 1790 the settlers between the Appalachians and the Mississippi River already numbered an impressive 100,000. The Northwest Territory above the Ohio River became six prosperous new states. By 1830 the Midwest's population soared to 3.7 million; by 1850 it was almost 10 million. The historian Sidney E. Mead said, "Space, not time, defines American history."

Americans tended to forget that their western landgrab was not empty land they deserved by natural right. The Spanish (and their Mexican successors) had been entrenched from San Antonio to San Francisco for 200 years and looked at the encroaching Americans as if they were invading barbarians. The United States obliged them by seizing the region that stretched from Texas to California through diplomacy, war, annexation, and bluster. Ancient and proud Indian civilizations also stood in America's way. Earlier in 1811 the defeat of Tecumseh at Tippecanoe reduced the midcontinent Indian threat and demonstrated that the natives could be repeatedly driven off. Western history thus involved a clash between cultures, nations, and imperial systems that culminated in the Oregon boundary settlement of 1845, the one-sided Mexican War of 1846, and continuously ruthless Indian removal or elimination. In the short time between 1845 and 1853, the United States added Texas, Oregon, and California, engrossing another 781 million acres to its territory, one and a half times more than the earlier Louisiana Purchase. It is extraordinary that, on the basis of an indigestible geography alone, the United States did not break up into nine or ten balkanized independent nations.

To reach plush Oregon, emigrants concluded that the harsh northern plains, a 1,000-mile-wide windswept grassland, devoid of trees and other landmarks, scorched in the summer and storm-swept in the winter, had to be crossed like one would cross the Atlantic Ocean or the Sahara Desert. Stories were heard of people who ventured onto the plains and simply disappeared. Whoever still insisted on struggling westward would be, it was reported, raped, tortured, scalped and left to die at the bloody hands of roaming savages who were more horrible than the barbarian Tartars of central Asia. Cholera would carry off the remnant. The great nineteenth-century historian Herbert Howe Bancroft gave a biblical flavor to the enterprise when in 1888 he wrote this of migrants:

[They] trailed over plains and rugged hills of desolation, often with a miserable road, or with no road at all. Over the boundless prairies they straggled, up into the rarefied air that stifled men and beasts, down into waterless, sandy sinks; across sagebrush plains efflorescent with alkali, over sandy-white flats caked hard as stone, through blinding dust, and into heaps of sand-like drifted ashy earth where the animals sank to their bellies; resting by cooling springs, or thirsting beside fetid and acrid waters; winding along the banks of sluggish water-courses, fording brackish brooks, swimming ice-cold rivers. Sometimes miring in mud, sometimes choked in impalpable dust which saturated hair and clothes, filled eyes and nostrils, made these emigrant trains look like caravans emerging from an ash storm on the plains of Sodom.

Having crossed the Plains, the fortune-seekers searched for gateways "excavated by the finger of God" through the Rocky Mountains such as Wyoming's famous South Pass, which took wagoners toward California or Oregon. It was a one-way passage, to be completed as rapidly as possible across the apparently worthless but difficult plains, mountains, and deserts. Most did not return, nor did they intend to do so. Even New York newspaperman Horace Greeley, who coined the phrase "Go west young man," insisted that California was best reached by an ocean voyage that skirted the continent along its east coast, followed by a fever-ridden but short trek across the Isthmus of Panama, and a final stage by ship along the west coast of the continent to San Francisco.

The image of a one-sided movement across the continent is compelling. Western historian David Lavender concluded, "The westward surge was a human instinct, like the need to love or to taste spring air and believe again that life is not a dead end after all." Some nomadic migration can be contrasted with the static European landscape of manors and serfs. By comparison, the first 200 years of westward movement of white Europeans toward the Mississippi River had been gradual, even cautious, producing an almost "motionless America." Instead, the West quivered in constant motion. The Plains Indians had long been nomadic. Immense herds of migrating bison were constantly on the move. American military forces in the West were mobile cavalry, not slogging foot soldiers. The white man's civilization replaced the Indians and buffalo with herds of cattle in motion, driven by cowboys on horseback. The steers moved first on hoof across the grasslands and then were transported by rail in cattle cars to the stockyards of Chicago, Minneapolis, and Kansas City. The development of the West is primarily a story told in terms of movement: exploration, hunting, surveying, migration, transportation, travel, and, today, tourism.

Swallowing Up the Wild West

Every migrant had a compelling personal interest that encouraged him or her to take a chance by pulling up stakes and, in the words of Mark Twain's Huckleberry Finn, "light out for the territory ahead of everyone else." We can identify at least four different encounters that essentially determined the future of the American West. Some of these now look destructive, and even perverse. The West's geography became in time an environmental disaster, said Donald Meinig, "of eroded hills, flooding rivers, shattered woodlands, dying trees, dilapidated farms, industrial pollution, urban sprawl, neon strips; garbage and grit, smog and sewage, congestion and clutter, and amidst it all, people impoverished in body or spirit."

The Trapper's "Original West"

Settlers first entered the West seeking beaver pelts and a narrow selection of other animal skins because fashionable people in Europe were willing to pay premier prices for felt hats and fur clothing. The three or four large fur companies who monopolized this relatively trivial trade were seasonal visitors who traveled river valleys of the Rocky Mountains. Their goal was to collect as many skins as possible, instead of only those needed for subsistence, an approach less sophisticated and more simplistic than the natives. In this sense, the settler's first appearance was a step backward. It ignored how the Indians integrated hunting and trapping into a broader local culture. It also ignored environmental connections that it could easily have learned by experience and from the Indians. Not surprisingly, the resource was depleted because it was treated as infinitely renewable. Demand far outreached sustainable supply. The fur companies or individual fur trappers never took steps to create "beaver farms" because they had no concept of improved yields of beavers by creating beaver-friendly habitats. One side effect would nevertheless change the history of the New World: The European fashions that demanded large numbers of animal skins fatally distorted Indian cultures by introducing them to metal tools and guns, blankets and clothes, whiskey and trinkets, in exchange for thousands of pelts at a time. Once drawn into the marketplace, the natives never escaped its clutches.

   The white mountain men who supplied the fur companies have been portrayed as courageous and reckless outcasts who despised civilization and loved to roam the isolated wilderness, a combination of Shakespeare's Caliban and a Jacksonian capitalist. They pressed into mountain country that is still remote today, where they disappeared for months or years with only minimum clothing, food, or weapons. Eight of every ten trappers died from outraged Indians or infuriated grizzlies, their own diseases and alcohol, injury and starvation, freezing winters and waterless deserts. It was not an occupation for the timid. As early as 1809 such mountain men reached 2,000 miles up the Missouri River into the lands of the Blackfeet, whose hatred of whites had intensified since a deadly encounter with the Lewis and Clark expedition. Manuel Lisa and John Coulter gained keen geographical knowledge as they trapped every probable beaver stream from the Front Range (east slope) of the Rocky Mountains to streams that ran directly into the Pacific coast. Coulter and Jim Bridger got only ridicule when they made wide-eyed reports of the spouting geysers and hot springs ("Coulter's Hell") at Yellowstone. The most famous trapper, and rightly so, was Jedediah Smith. He got his start in 1822 when he joined up with a venture capitalist in skins, William H. Ashley, and survived a surprisingly long time until he was killed by Comanches in 1831. Smith rediscovered Wyoming's South Pass in 1823 and promoted it as the main route across the continental divide to Oregon. He became the first in 1826 to make an overland connection between the newly discovered Great Salt Lake and California. On his return he was the first to cross the Sierras from the west. Smith thus pieced together the earliest continuous cross-mountain and cross-desert trails between the Front Range of the Rockies and the Pacific coast. In historian Richard Bartlett's words, such mountain men "solved most of the mysteries of the great West." That is, they learned the pathways for successful movement across difficult and life-threatening terrain. They also taught Americans that the West contained hidden wealth that was worth the effort of conquest.

   The trappers worked for some of America's most outrageous early entrepreneurs—John Jacob Astor and William Henry Ashley—who looked on the West as a source of untapped wealth, ready and waiting for single-minded businessmen. Unlike later discoverers, they were not interested in settlement or development. Even Astoria at the mouth of the Columbia River was only a trading post that Astor surrendered without a fight to the British in 1812, and eventually sold to a Canadian competitor. Ashley instituted the annual "rendezvous" between Indians, trappers, and traders in Jackson Hole in northwestern Wyoming. It acted as a combined trade fair, noisy market, and an instant "tenderloin" of easy women. Trappers came down from the mountains to sell skins and get resupplied. Pelt buyers brought in knives, guns, clothing blankets, hardware, coffee, tobacco, and whiskey, and returned with a wealth of beaver. The trappers are often romanticized as white men who "went native." The opposite is true. As single-minded opportunists, these men were the unruly but representative outriders of Western civilization. Their outlandish activities anticipated the overwhelming flood of Europeans to come. From a European point of view, they were like spies who had gone behind the enemy's lines and returned with a wealth of information about conditions in unknown territory. Lewis and Clark, for example, thought of themselves as the first true explorers across the continent. But when they worked their way up the wide Missouri River in the summer and fall of 1804, they crossed paths with trappers and traders whose boats and rafts were loaded down with furs. Indeed, only after the trapper George Drouillard and his Indian wife Sacajawea joined the expedition would Lewis and Clark find their way across the mountains, locate the Columbia River, and build Fort Clatsop on the Pacific shore.

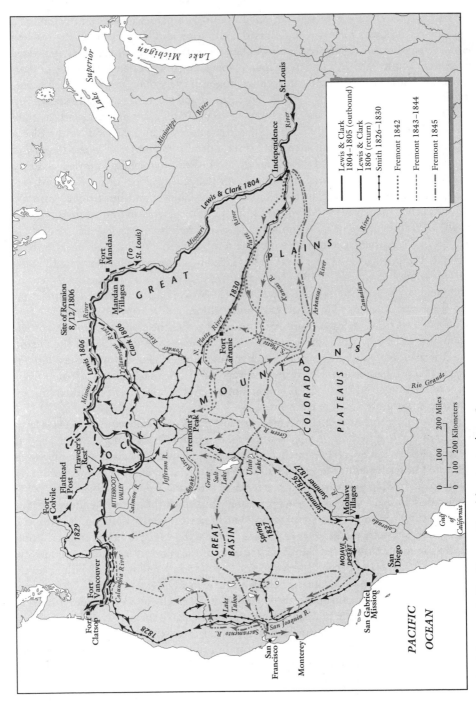

Explorer's Routes into the West. "Space, not time, defines American history."

The Explorer's West—Scientific, Military, and Commercial

How does a complex technological civilization investigate and invade an unknown territory? In the case of the West beyond the Mississippi, European-style scientific method—mapping, surveying, and inventorying—became the means for discovery and eventual control.

Thomas Jefferson initiated America's "great reconnaissance" of unknown regions, in which explorers, accompanied by mapmakers, geologists, botanists, and zoologists, were to "scientifically" fill in basic information. From the optimistic perspective of Enlightenment rationalism, he believed that the western wilderness only appeared confusing and chaotic. Underneath stood the fundamental logic of natural law. Scientific inquiry would restore order to the wild West and identify its useful resources. The latest technologies would unleash its minerals and capture its wealth. As we have seen, Jefferson had already written a comprehensive natural history in 1785, *Notes on the State of Virginia.* It inventoried terrain, climate, vegetation, animals, the material culture of natives and settlers, all in terms of economic benefits and future potential for development. Now he applied the same wide-ranging questions to the 1803 Louisiana Purchase. Later the same year, Jefferson's marching instructions to Lieutenant Meriweather Lewis and Captain William Clark was to find an American route from the Mississippi River to the Pacific Ocean. In addition, the expedition established the comprehensive field survey method that Americans used to explore regions "off the map" for the rest of American history. The objective continues today as part of modern space exploration. Lewis and Clark were to lead a well-organized and supplied military expedition that had multifold scientific assignments to be kept in voluminous records. The expedition was deliberately waterborne to "explore the Missouri River [and find] the most direct and practicable water communication across this continent for the purposes of commerce." The company was to map the region scientifically by fixing geographical positions through astronomical observations. Their duties included the survey of the "soil and face of the country," including inventory of plants, animals, minerals, metals, limestone, coal, salts, mineral waters, and saltpeter (today we might look instead for petroleum, chromium, and uranium). They were to report on the weather and climate, study the Indian inhabitants, discover possible commerce in the lucrative fur business, and spy on British, French, Spanish, and Russian activities. Jefferson had no scruples about looking beyond America's borders into Spanish, British, and Indian territory. He had learned that information about the Southwest was limited to sketchy Spanish statistics and fuzzy maps. Maps based on fantasy more than firsthand reports were the only information about the "Stony [i.e., Rocky] Mountains." The far Northwest had been reported only from the highly selective points of view of beaver trappers or ship captains along the coast. As president, Jefferson was delighted to send off expeditions that combined scientific inquiry and military force.

The 30 "good hunters, stout, healthy, unmarried men, accustomed to the woods, and capable of bearing bodily fatigue in a pretty considerable degree," made up the Corps of Volunteers for Northwestern Discovery. They began to move upstream on the Missouri River on May 14, 1804, from the small trading town of St. Charles near St. Louis. Besides living off game, birds, and fish, and receiving generous aid from the Indians, they providentially carried their own rations "into the desert": 50 kegs of meat, 14 barrels of parched cornmeal, 20 kegs of flour, 100 gallons of whiskey, together with sugar, salt, coffee, dried apples, and biscuits. Although some of the men were sent home after the first winter in South Dakota, the expedition was remarkable because not a single member died while on route. After a strenuous crossing of the northern Rocky Mountains, unintentionally in midwinter, they reached the Pacific at the mouth of the Columbia River. Their round trip covering 7,698 miles took over two years, four months, and ten days before they returned to St. Louis on September 20, 1806, after having been given up for lost.

This Jeffersonian expedition was the vanguard, in historian William Goetzmann's words, of "the gatherer of knowledge, 'programmed' consciously or unconsciously by his civilization." Once this scientific/commercial viewpoint took hold, it would become virtually impossible for Americans to see the West from any other perspective. In 1819, for example, when five crude steamboats of an army expedition began to move up the Missouri, they were seen as carrying not only soldiers and guides, but also boatloads of scientific modernity. One excited observer proclaimed,

> See those vessels, with the agency of steam advancing against the powerful currents of the Mississippi and the Missouri! Their course is marked by volumes of smoke and fire, which the civilized man observes with admiration, and the savage with astonishment. Botanists, mineralogists, chemists, artisans, cultivators, scholars, soldiers; the love of peace, the capacity for war; philosophical apparatus and military supplies; telescopes and cannon, garden seeds and gunpowder; the arts of civil life and the force to defend them—all are seen aboard. The banner of freedom which waves over the whole proclaims the character and protective power of the United States.

These explorers moved westward with the zeal of missionaries.

Invasion Routes to Americanize the West

The third phase of invasion opened new pathways across the intervening plains, mountains, and deserts. Early trails were followed by military roads, wagon trails, express carriage roads, and eventually the all-important railroads that sped Americans on their way to California and Oregon. Americans always assumed they would gobble up the golden land of California and the green valleys of the Oregon country. Zenas Leonard, one of a crew of mountain men sent by American officials in the 1830s to find a route into California, sat at his desk at San Francisco Bay in Mexican territory and wrote, "The Spaniards are making inroads on the south— the Russians are encroaching with impunity along the seashore to the north, and further northeast the British are pushing their stations into the very heart of our territory. Our government should be vigilant. She should assert her claim by taking possession of the whole territory as soon as possible—for we have good reason to suppose that the territory west of the mountain will some day be equally as important to a nation as that on the east." The government responded with daring reconnaissances to find passes through the western mountains. It sent military expeditionary forces to create an American "presence" in disputed regions. A line of 140 military forts established American control along the Missouri, Platte, Arkansas, Snake, and Columbia rivers.

The most important presence along the western side of the mountains was the federal government. Sometimes the only organized institution other than Indian societies, it was nevertheless often inadequate for the needs of the migrants. There were reports in the 1850s of destitute overlanders dying daily at the Dalles on the Columbia River, nearly at their destination but out of supplies, with dead oxen and broken wagons. Or stories of suffering and death by freezing in the California Sierras due to a late season crossing because of unavoidable delays. The most notorious was the Donner Party that resorted to cannibalism during the winter of 1846–47. Such crises were not unusual. Local citizens would send out rescue parties that risked more lives. A California newspaper urged government rescue of stranded overlanders: they were the future "producers"—farmers and mechanics who would settle permanently—whereas those who came by sea were "consumers" such as lawyers and speculators. Most people believed that the federal government, once it had opened the roads west, had become responsible for safe if not comfortable overland travel to the Pacific. Travelers demanded more government services: "guidebooks based upon exhaustive route surveys, government workshops along the trail for wagon repairs, supply stations for provisions, governmental trains to pick up straggling and forsaken emigrants and transport them safely to their destination," together with medical assistance, protection from epidemics of cholera, legal aid, and, as always, better protection from the Indians. Pressure in Congress did lead to improved assistance. The government surveyed and built the Lander Cutoff at South Pass that by 1859 saved five days of precious travel time to the West. An improved route between Salt Lake City and California's Sacramento River saved an astounding 288 miles, and cut a full two weeks from the difficult desert crossing. Overlanders began to speak of "that good Uncle Sam."

The Southwest Takeover

Trails stretched out across the plains and deserts like routes for sailing ships marked on an ocean map. The distances were indeed ocean sized, like the 780 miles between Independence in Missouri and Santa Fe, the most important city in Mexico's northern territories. On early maps the venerable Santa Fe Trail was labeled a "caravan route" similar to the pathways across central Asia. Rumors of enormous hidden wealth in gold and silver attracted aggressive, often unprincipled American adventurers. U.S. government officials looked the other way when General James Wilkinson and Aaron Burr shared a half-baked dream of building a private feudal empire that would intrude onto Spanish soil. Such schemes took advantage of the loosely guarded and uncertain boundary between the Louisiana Purchase and Spanish territory. The Spanish retaliated by lowering "an iron curtain of Spanish chain mail" that claimed for Spain all the watersheds of the rivers flowing into the Mississippi on the west side, including much of Jefferson's Louisiana Purchase. After Mexican independence in 1821, the region endured the confused state of a virtual undeclared war. American traders began to clamor for military protection from Mexican demands and Mexicans grew suspicious about American intentions. These were the circumstances when, in 1822, the first American-run trading caravan carried $15,000 worth of goods to Santa Fe. It was so profitable that the Mexican government uncovered Americans fanning out in all directions over the Southwest. In 1827 the U.S. government provocatively financed a wagon road through Mexican territory to Santa Fe. In 1846 alone, a total of 363 wagons, 50 carriages, and 750 men traveled to Santa Fe, bearing nearly 10,000 bales of goods worth $1 million. It might require 40 days to struggle from Independence to Santa Fe, but the profit could reach 40 percent. From Santa Fe, American traders looked westward, and by 1829 trails to the Pacific coast had become commercial roads to new riches. It was no small coincidence that along California's coast, tens of thousands of sea-otter skins were being harvested by New England ships. Americans noted that California produced tough hides for New England shoes and fat tallow for candles that lit Peru's deep silver mines. Americans believed Mexican territorial claims could not hold up against their commercial momentum. They claimed to be carrying freedom into a decaying medieval culture when California became U.S. territory in 1848 after the Mexican War. More to the point, they concluded that it was their duty to remove Spanish-style mismanagement of the wealth of the Southwest.

Americans thus began pushing aside a Spanish culture and institutions far older than the United States or even the original English colonies. Mexico's northern provinces had taken the shape of a well-established but loose geography of Spanish ranches and mission stations, Indian pueblos and imperial presidios, modeled after Spanish institutions. The process began in 1519 when Cortés toppled the Aztec empire. Built on feudalism, Catholicism, and serfdom for the Indians, the Spanish and Mexican way to approach the land was not the American "Anglo" way. Wealthy individuals, powerful families, and the Catholic Church received large ranches from government authorities. They took the best land around San Francisco, Sacramento, Monterey Bay, Santa Barbara, Los Angeles, and San Diego. With so much land available, primarily used to raise cattle, sheep, and horses, it made little difference that title to land was casual and boundaries indefinite. San Gabriel, for example, was a rich mission that in 1834 supported over 100,000 head of cattle, 40,000 sheep, and 20,000 horses. Oranges, wine grapes, and olives grew in abundance. More than 3,000 Indians worked like slaves, although they were described as an "ancient, industrious, happy, and contented population." The San Fernando mission grew olives, lemons, and oranges; around Fresno, raisin grapes grew from "a combination of climate, water resources, and soil occurring in but few places in the world." Under Spanish development, the Los Angeles Basin became one of the finest agricultural regions in the Southwest. In 1850 its vineyards produced almost 60,000 gallons of wine. Nowhere else in the West did Americans encounter anything similar to this long-established and productive mission society. When California became a part of the United States in 1848, titles and boundaries were so uncertain that the General Land Office Survey was not published until 1860. It was as if the U.S. Land Office had been set up in medieval Spain and tried to impose the rectangular survey. New American settlers, even squatters, trickled in slowly, wary about their claims and titles. The American method of settlement first appeared in the Mormon community of San Bernadino in the early 1850s. These American families did not build mission compounds, but followed the Jeffersonian yeoman farmer tradition of individual homesites. Instead of simple but elegant Spanish mission buildings, the farmers built rude shelters of log and adobe. At San Bernadino, the first community building was not a mission church, but a large flour mill.

The Americans did not accept existing environmental conditions as the Mexicans did. Instead they inflexibly introduced into arid regions the water-intensive farming they knew from the American humid East. Demand for scarce water for eastern-style farming became a distinctively American obsession. Intensive irrigated farmland in the San Joaquin Valley distinguished the newly arrived Americans from Spanish and Mexican predecessors. Reclamation of the Sacramento River Valley after the Civil War would become one of America's early unheralded public works projects. Irrigation turned the desertlike Great Valley into an artificial produce garden. The change was particularly dramatic in the Kern Basin at the southern end of the valley, which had once been, according to one source, "so barren as scarcely to afford subsistence for our animals, and can never be made of much value for agricultural purposes." Instead, an "irrigation empire" of aqueducts and canals soon dominated the landscape. The famous California geological survey of the 1860s served similar speculative interests by devoting itself to locate resources for would-be investors, a prominent example of "the resource West." American-style settlement and get-rich-quick exploitation would shape the rest of California's problematic environmental history. Whereas the Spanish and Mexicans were satisfied if the land produced only a few hides and a little tallow to be traded to the outside world, the Americans grew large crops for nationwide markets. Especially after the railroads arrived, the settlers of the San Fernando Valley readily abandoned cattle grazing for orchards of olives, fig, pear, peach, walnut, almond, and even pomegranate trees and vineyards. By connecting local commerce with national trade, the railroads concluded the Americanization of California.

Invasion Route to the Pacific Northwest

During the first half of the nineteenth century, the northwestern geography of the United States was murky at best, informed by dim sightings of impenetrable snow-covered mountains and sun-baked deserts, and threatened by hostile Blackfeet Indians and by counterclaims by Spain, England, and czarist Russia. In 1811 and 1812 two employees of fur baron John Jacob Astor roughly followed the future track of the Oregon Trail. By crossing the Rocky Mountains at South Pass in today's southwestern Wyoming, they proved that the overland trek to the Pacific was long and difficult, but possible. South Pass was then forgotten until rediscovered by Jedediah Smith and the Sublette expedition in 1824. Smith, who had a "natural genius for geographic detail," wrote a long and eloquent report in 1830 about the potential for settlement, farming, and trade in the Pacific Northwest. He claimed that even loaded wagons and livestock could cross South Pass. The Bonneville military expedition of the 1830s into Oregon reported that the Willamette Valley was "one of the most beautiful, fertile and extensive valleys in the world, wheat, corn and tobacco country. If our government ever intends on taking possession of Oregon the sooner it shall be done the better." By 1840 a traveler counted 120 American farms in the Willamette Valley, populated by 500 settlers, pasturing 3,000 cattle, 2,500 horses, and "an infinite number of hogs." Reports of Oregon's agricultural paradise in 1843 brought 1,000 eastern migrants embarking on the Oregon Trail from Independence, Missouri, and 3,000 more in 1845. About the same time, Missouri senator Thomas Hart Benton forged an expansionist vision of an imperial United States that would extend from coast to coast. In 1843 Benton gave his enthusiastic son-in-law Captain John C. Frémont instructions to connect his earlier reconnaissance of 1842 with the surveys of Commander Wilkes on the coast of the Pacific Ocean, "so as to give a connected survey of the interior of our continent." Frémont's mission was to survey, map, and lay out the Oregon Trail, to identify campsites with water, grass, and wood, report on Indians, and list possible locations for forts. South Pass deserves to be as famous as the Cumberland Gap for Americans, the Brenner Pass for Europeans, and the romantic Khyber pass for Asians. The United States would win the prize by the force of sheer numbers; by 1845, 6,000 Americans faced only 750 British inhabitants. British fortunes also collapsed with the fickle failure of beaver hat popularity and collapsing pelt prices. It might be justifiably said that a shift in European fashions transformed the Oregon country from a hunting wilderness to a domesticated rural farmland. From the viewpoint of the Hudson Bay Company, the region was no longer worth fighting over. The British foreign secretary, Lord Aberdeen, called it from London a "pine swamp," gave in to American demands, and the region south of "54-40" became the Oregon

Western Gold and Human Greed

One object of western desire knew no geographical constraints—the quest for gold. Gold attracted European appetites everywhere. The possibilities of Aztec and Inca gold accelerated the Spanish conquest of the Americas. In the 1520s Coronado ranged far into the trackless central plains of North America in search of fabled golden cities. The discovery of gold in 1848 at Sutter's sawmill near Sacramento in California's Central Valley led thousands of Americans to throw off geographical constraints—searing plains, virtually waterless deserts, and seemingly impassable mountains—to reach the gold fields. The attraction of gold in the American West helped enlarge trails into roads, turn mountain passes into railroad lines, and build instant metropolises. In a single year, 1849, 80,000 new arrivals—Europeans, Mexicans, Australians, Chinese, Americans—joined California's 20,000 inhabitants (annexed to the United States only the year before), a population that mushroomed to 250,000 by 1852, enough for statehood. Most came by ship, either the 17,000 miles around stormy Cape Horn or across the feverish Isthmus of Panama. Some fewer came overland, sometimes walking after their oxen perished and wagons broke. In 1849 a cholera epidemic wiped out 5,000 overland gold seekers as they traveled overland to California. The craze for gold encouraged Americans to think of the West primarily as a place for quick riches. Historian John Unruh wrote, "The forty-niners influenced national and world population movements, economies, finance, politics, transportation, and settlement patterns." Gold accelerated the pace by which the West became federal territories and subsequently formed into the states of California, Colorado, and Nevada. Unlike the steady continuous labor in farm fields that shaped the lives and dreams of most settlers, gold seekers believed in the single sudden strike for a lifetime of riches. Sailing ships, abandoned by their crews, rode at anchor at California docks. California farm towns were emptied of male adults. Army troops disappeared into the goldfields. One soldier wrote in his diary, "The struggle between *right* and six dollars a month, and *wrong* and seventy-five dollars a day is rather a severe one."

California gold was Everyman's dream. General Sherman wrote in his memoirs, "As the spring and summer of 1848 advanced, the reports came faster and faster from

Territory in 1848. The Far West had become a place to move into—to occupy and settle and develop—a geography of place that now required a process.

The Great Migration

The geography of the West required changes in transportation. The settlers of the late eighteenth and early nineteenth centuries had entered the Midwest by floating on rafts and boats on the Ohio and Mississippi rivers. But no great flowing rivers crossed the High Plains or penetrated the Rocky Mountains. The only major rivers of the vast grasslands were the Missouri, which ran too far north, and the westward-flowing Platte, whose braided streams were

the gold-mines at Sutter's saw-mill. Stories reached us of fabulous discoveries [including an 839-pound gold nugget], and spread throughout the land. Everybody was talking of 'Gold! gold!' until it assumed the character of a fever." California's mother lode was a 120-mile-long string of quartz pockets on the western slope of the Sierra Nevada mountains that sometimes ran 2 miles wide. It was not a solid chain of gold, but occasional narrow veins exposed by weathering. Specks of gold and the rare nugget (specks compacted by tumbling in water) had washed into rivers where they were easily accessible. A few found thousands of dollars of gold flecks that they dug out with ordinary spoons; others wasted their lives and fortunes. More fortunes were made by ladies of easy virtue, by merchants like Sam Brannan, who sold food and tools to the miners, and by Levi Strauss, who made durable denim trousers.

Gold seeking also brought on new environmentally destructive technologies fostered by industry-size enterprises. At first, individual prospectors had panned or built crude sluices (a wooden trough through which a running stream was diverted to wash larger loads of soil, the gold itself trapped by wooden cleats). They even tunneled into hillsides without creating major havoc. The engineering feat of hydraulic mining, however, soon accelerated the process. It used high-pressure water jets, with giant pivoting metal nozzles, to eat away entire cliffsides. Enormous amounts of water were consumed in the erosion process. These operations left behind gravel debris that was miles long. Silt from hydraulic mining polluted much of the Sacramento River. Even bottomland farms were layered with gravel. Crop irrigation was impossible and the salmon industry collapsed. By 1884 the state of California reluctantly banned hydraulic mining.

California became known as the Golden State, and its future as America's many-sided El Dorado was assured. Gold seeking also involved the famous $300 million Comstock Lode near Virginia City eastward across the Sierras in Utah Territory, and streambeds along Colorado's Front Range of the Rocky Mountains and up into Wyoming and Montana. The lure of gold in the Dakota's Black Hills persuaded the army to invade an Indian sacred land and hunting ground despite ironclad treaties of sanctuary. Col. George Armstrong Custer reported, "Almost every panful of earth produced gold in small, yet paying, quantities." Such paydirt symbolized the West.

so shallow that even flatboats scraped bottom (although the course of the river remained a good line for wagon trains to follow). The canal network east of the Mississippi, now filled with slow-moving cargo-laden barges that interconnected the East and Midwest, would not extend onto the grasslands toward the mountains. Instead, beginning in the 1840s thousands of migrants left their boats at Independence, Missouri. If they did not continue by saddling up horses, or starting out on foot, they loaded their household goods and farm tools onto modified Conestoga wagons, called prairie schooners, pulled by oxen or horses or mules and sometimes an odd coupling of different animals including the family cow. Thus early western movement took place on the sore feet of a man pushing his belongings before him in a cart, another slumped wearily on horseback, or a family bouncing in an unsprung wagon behind

Missouri to Oregon, in Stages

Across the East and Midwest, young men and ambitious families pored over detailed descriptions of the newly opened Oregon Trail. Most were farmers who already owned wagons and draft animals. They found their way to Independence, Missouri, got freshly provisioned, and joined other immigrants to make up a trail party. The start was exhilarating, since their wagons and oxen could cover 20 miles a day across the open plains on the well-marked combined Oregon/Santa Fe trail. At the end of the second day a signboard directed them to the "Road to Oregon." They required three weeks to cover 350 miles across the flat, dry, windy plains until they reached Ft. Laramie and 100 miles later started climbing into mountain country. Here they lightened their loads by selling or dumping bulky and heavy goods. One report of trail debris told of "bar-iron and steel, large blacksmiths' anvils and bellows, crow-bars, drills, augers, gold-washers, chisels, axes, lead, trunks, spades, ploughs, large grind-stones, baking-ovens, cooking-stoves, kegs, barrels, harness, clothing." They might exchange overworked animals for fresh stock in anticipation of higher mountain crossings and supply themselves with extra wagon wheels, axle trees, and a spare wagon tongue. Everyone loaded up on flour, bacon, beans, and coffee. The next marker was Independence Rock in central Wyoming, 838 miles out, and a landmark pointing to South Pass. Many migrants inscribed their names on a rock called the "register of the desert." They finally reached the fabled South Pass at 947 miles, a broad high-altitude valley of gentle slopes surrounded by rugged snowy mountains that carried them over the Continental Divide at 7,500 feet. Another 123 miles got them to Ft. Bridger, where they might meet the remarkable mountain man himself. At this point, a federal presence, including cavalry patrols and military escorts, encouraged settlers toward the frightening lands west of the divide.

Strategically located forts had doctors, sutlers (provisioners), mail service, trail advice, blacksmith shops, and swift justice. Indian agents saved many a traveler's life by negotiating treaties of passage with local tribes. Many times, however, hotheaded army officers did more to bait Indian tribes than to pacify them, and migrants suffered theft, injury and death. As for private trading posts, the great Oregon leader Francis Parkman reflected common migrant opinion that the traders were "their natural enemies." "They were plundered and cheated without mercy. In one bargain, concluded in my presence, I calculated the profits at the lowest estimate exceeded eighteen hundred per cent." Migrant Henry Allyn in 1853 wrote in his diary, "Oregon emigrants are in ten times the danger from speculators, ferrymen and traders than the Indians. It is believed that nearly or quite all the thefts that are laid to the Indians are either done or instigated by them [the speculators, ferrymen, and traders]. We have proved them to be infernal liars."

River fords were taken over by local private entrepreneurs, who built ferry rafts and occasionally fabricated wooded bridges. They charged $3 to $15 for a crossing, or whatever the market could bear. By the time a family and its wagon reached Oregon, it might have shelled out 60 hard-earned dollars to cross rivers. Bottlenecks of too many wagons at a single ferry point could lead to delays of several days. A new 300-foot bridge built across the broad Platte River was a major engineering achievement that received national attention in 1852. In the 1870s the government began to improve the trails into roads by grading, widening, cutting timber, and placing markers and guideposts. Government surveyors located shorter routes that cut off days and even weeks from a passage that averaged 4 months but often stretched out to 7 and even 15 months.

A distance of 1,288 miles from Independence found migrants at the British Ft.

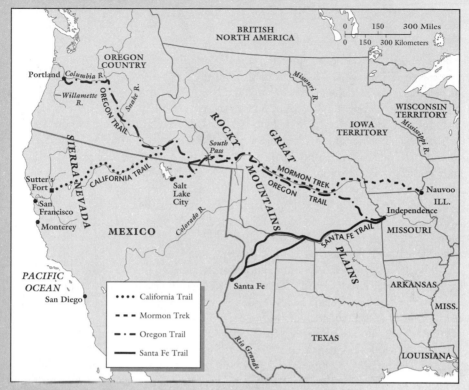

The Major Overland Trails.

Hall on Snake River. They pushed on to the Hudson Bay Company post of Ft. Boise. A difficult mountain crossing of the Blue Mountains and a hard trek across barren Oregon rewarded them with the sight of the Columbia River and arrival at Ft. Vancouver of the Hudson Bay Company. By then they were over 2,000 miles from Independence and often 3,000 miles from their starting point in New England. The company had no problems with American settlement in the gardenlike Willamette Valley south of the Columbia, but warned them not to move north of Ft. Vancouver that stood on the north shore of the river. This was still territory claimed by Britain and assigned to the company.

The entire venture was memoralized in the 1845 Congress by John Wentworth:

> Only think of it: men, women, and children, forsaking their homes, bidding farewell to all the endearments of society, setting out on a journey of over two thousand miles, upon a route where they have to make their own roads, construct their own bridges, hew out their own boats, and kill their own meat . . . where twenty miles is an average day's travel, exposed to every variety of weather, and the naked earth their only resting-place.

The trek must be counted one of the great voluntary migrations of people in all of human history. During some years, such as 1852, when 10,000 people struck out for Oregon and 50,000 for California, overlanders complained of congested trails, overcrowded and undersupplied campgrounds, and overgrazed grasses. Especially between 1848 and 1853, due to California's gold rush, it became rare for a family in a wagon to travel alone. There were stories of fathers and sons becoming separated in traffic jams of 200 wagons, not to meet again until they arrived in California.

The Mormon Experiment

One community of settlers understood the climate conditions of a western desert region and prospered. The Mormons (Church of Christ of the Latter-Day Saints) endured religious persecution and violence as they migrated from New York through Ohio, Missouri, and Illinois before 16,000 people, 3,000 wagons, and herds of cattle, horses, and sheep escaped in 1847 to the region of the Great Salt Lake at the eastern edge of the desolate Great Basin. This inhospitable desert was off the map, 1,000 miles of difficult travel and communication beyond existing settlement and outside existing political and military authority. The Mormons deliberately sought geographical isolation to establish their vision of a religious utopia. The challenge was not only to protect themselves from "gentile" scorn and attack, but also to establish a workable existence in a region that most Americans considered barren and uninhabitable. They had considered moves to Oregon, Texas, California, and Vancouver Island in Canada, but settled on a region that nobody else wanted. No one would envy those who settled alongside the shore of a lake of undrinkable saline water in an arid mountainous region. To the Mormons, however, it was Zion, the place of the world's last days described in the Bible. Although they first claimed over 200,000 square miles encompassing most of the Great Basin, the Mormons finally negotiated 85,000 square miles within the present state of Utah.

Part of their success can be attributed to community discipline imposed by a single charismatic leader, Brigham Young. Unlike the general American practice of atomized settlement and participatory government, Mormon organization was undemocratic, autocratic, with a military routine. Historically, beginning with the Egyptians and Sumerians, irrigation civilizations were such collective enterprises. So was the Mormon endeavor. Brigham Young avoided the widespread battling over water that characterized the rest of the arid West because he proclaimed, "There shall be no private ownership of the streams that come out of the canyons, nor the timber that grows on the hills. These belong to the people; all of the people." Such rigid discipline helped the Mormons to cope with a hostile environment. In this mountain and desert region, the rainfall varied from 3 to 15 inches a year and small streams emptied into the Great Salt Lake or disappeared into sinks. But along the western slope of the Wasatch Mountains stood a large natural bowl of about 30 square miles that, although treeless, was well watered by creeks flowing out of the mountains and provided several excellent mill sites. It also had strategic advantage: It was 1,200 miles west of trading posts in the Missouri Valley and bounded on the west by one of the most immense deserts in the world. The Mormon environmental response was twofold: to examine the conditions of their region thoroughly, and to get advice from the Bible. On the one hand they immediately admitted that they had "to search for land that can be irrigated" and learn dryland farming. They did not delude themselves like most settlers who tried to duplicate their eastern experience. They began to experiment, often by trial and error, with grains and seeds that would give them crops with minimum moisture. On the other hand, the Old Testament prophet Isaiah gave them comforting words: "The wilderness and the dry land shall be glad, the desert shall rejoice and blossom; like the crocus it shall blossom abundantly, and rejoice with joy and singing."

The first Mormon settlers in 1846 simultaneously plowed land and built irrigation dams, reservoirs, and ditches. "This afternoon commenced planting out potatoes," wrote one settler, "after which we turned the water on them and gave the ground a good soaking." Within months, the disciplined workers had planted irrigated fields with corn, potatoes, beans, and turnips. They laid out a large metropolis called "Great Salt Lake City, Great Basin, North America," that by 1847 contained 29 buildings, including a public sawmill, a gristmill, a community storehouse, a blacksmith shop, a stockade, and corrals. Instead of private farms, each with its own house, barn, outbuildings, fields, and fences, the Mormons lived as a community on single-family town lots that supported a vegetable garden and fruit orchard. On the city outskirts were irrigated fields of up to 20 acres. Ditches and canals dug by hand and specially designed wooden plows that each used a dozen horses converted the hard, dry soil into cropland. Later the ditches were served by high-line canals that ran along mountainsides and traversed deep ravines. The Mormons endured constant reconstruction after seasonal spring runoffs and loss by seepage. One of the key figures in the enterprise was the watermaster, who saw to it that the dams, headgates, canals, and lateral ditches were kept in good order, and who kept scarce water equitably divided.

By 1849 Salt Lake City took on a permanent look, with public meeting buildings, a tannery, a glass and leather factory, an armory, and hundreds of log and adobe homes. The Mormons were further secured when in 1849 and 1850 Salt Lake City became a way station for more than 20,000 adventurers bound for the California Gold Rush. When Utah became a U.S. territory in 1849, Mormon religious customs came under critical scrutiny, but the new civil government continued its community-based irrigation practices and distribution of land. Even territorial legislation protected community interest from private intervention. Brigham Young attempted to protect Mormon uniqueness by proposing a new semiautonomous state, Deseret, that would cover all of present-day Utah and Arizona, most of Nevada, all of southern California, and large parts of Wyoming, Colorado, and Idaho. If Young had been successful, the Southwest might have been transformed into small irrigation-based agricultural communities that promoted local self-sufficiency instead of overpopulated and overconsuming cities.

Tiny self-sufficient Mormon communities appeared at every likely place in the region. Great Basin historian W. Eugene Hollon writes,

> A glance at a Utah map shows a familiar and rather consistent pattern of ecological factors determining new Mormon settlements. Each was located at the base of a mountain front, at an altitude conducive to raising farm crops, or in a valley plain of rich soil. The nearby mountains provided a perpetual flow of life-giving water, timber for building, wood for fuel, and forage for summer grazing. Most villages likewise supported various industries, in keeping with Young's determination for self-sufficiency.

Community-based irrigation using a common water supply system with reservoirs was a highly efficient means to support a growing population in a region lacking major rivers and with insignificant rainfall. Not all communities survived, in part because of difficult transportation and communications; others were abandoned in the abortive Mormon War of 1857–58 against the military force of the gentile governor sent to replace Brigham Young. The Mormon success can be measured by the size and permanence of their settlements; the Mormon settlements totaled 150,000 people, only slightly less than all the Spanish settlements in 400 years.

plodding oxen. Overland travel was limited by the mud and floods of wet seasons, the dust and thirst of dry seasons, as well as winter wind, snow, and cold. Migrants on the Oregon Trail were still far closer to travel during Europe's Middle Ages than they were to the railroads just two decades later.

J. W. Powell, USGS, and Order on the Land

The U.S. Geological Survey (USGS) of the Department of the Interior was created by the Sundry Civil Expenses Bill that passed Congress on March 3, 1879. Henry Adams called it America's "first modern act of legislation" because it was based on the use of scientific data and encouraged economic enterprise. The USGS, according to the bill, was to be an "informational bureau" to map the great western American unknown through "the classification of the public lands, and examination of the geological structure, mineral resources, and products of the national domain." The well-known explorer, geologist, and land reformer John Wesley Powell became director of USGS in 1881. Powell quickly learned that he was not surveying a completely empty public domain, but, in biographer Wallace Stegner's terms, "planning for a public domain already planlessly, wastefully, and competitively filling up." Described as a "one-armed little man with a bristly beard and a homemade education," Powell came from Wisconsin, lost his right arm to a Civil War cannonball, and wrote a popular account of the first-ever boat trip on the Colorado River through the Grand Canyon. Powell earnestly believed that the mission of USGS went beyond the discovery of commercial resources for private development to scientific knowledge for human good, covering, says Stegner, "all earth history, earth sculpture, the laws of orographic change, the dawn and development of life, the discovery and mapping of the nation's resources of land, water, soil, timber, minerals, coal, oil."

Powell took the best of European mapping science and made certain that USGS surveys reflected highly professional topographical, hydrographic, and geological science. He organized USGS into divisions of geology, topography, paleontology, and chemical and physical studies. Powell also believed that as a federal agency, the USGS had to be involved actively in identifying and protecting the national domain for the general welfare. From his first budget of $156,000 he cajoled Congress by 1885–86 into more than half a million dollars, most of it to be spent at his discretion. By 1894 he reported 619,572 square miles, approximately one-fifth of the United States, had been scientifically surveyed and mapped on useful quadrangle maps. Powell was driven from office by angry legislators that same year for condemning western settlement policies that put farmers at risk on small acreage in poorly watered grasslands. Earlier, in 1878, he had written the landmark government conservation paper, *Report on the Arid Region of the United States,* which concluded that less than 3 percent of the West could be irrigated, and only the bravest farmers should try dryland agriculture on at least four sections, or 2,540 acres. Powell told a national irrigation convention, "I tell you gentlemen, you are piling up a heritage of conflict and litigation over water rights for there is not sufficient water to supply the land." The response was a shout of boos.

Yet the American migrants were also definitely unlike the great ancient migrations that took centuries. They did not move and settle and spend a generation or more in one place before moving on again. Instead, the Americans crossed two-thirds of a continent in a single long odyssey that took several months. Overland emigrants made physically punishing, death-defying ventures across impossible empty spaces to reach oases containing "the emigrant's trinity of good things"—water, animal forage, and firewood. A remarkably large number of people—about 350,000—trekked across the continent between 1841 and 1866. When these migrants were thwarted by geography, the government stepped in to build wagon roads and bridges, forts, and stage stations. Most important, in the 1870s government joined forces with new technology and new entrepreneurs to build the railroads, Western civilization's most phenomenal transportation system. The effect of the railroad was more dramatic and universal than the interstate highway system of the 1950s or modern air travel. Quite simply, it conquered the West.

Railroads and the Engineered West

The trails also became highways for fast travel. The famous Butterfield Overland Mail began in 1858 to run oversized mail-and-passenger stagecoaches reinforced with iron bands. They covered 2,812 miles from Tipton, Missouri, where the railroad tracks ended, on a southern "oxbow" route to San Francisco. The first run took 24 days westward and 21 days eastward, for which President Buchanan wired the company, "It is a glorious triumph for civilization and the Union." The movement of commercial goods began to pick up. A central route to California run by the firm of Russell, Majors, and Waddell was soon a major enterprise, operating with 3,500 covered wagons, employing 4,000 tough men using 40,000 draft oxen. Oxen could pull a heavily loaded wagon 15 miles each day and were less likely to be stolen by Indians. The famous Pony Express promised to carry mail between Missouri and California in an incredulous ten days, cutting the fastest previous time in half. It had the misfortune to began its runs in April 1860 and declined quickly after October 1861 when the nation was joined together by the electric telegraph wires of the Pacific Telegraph Company and the Overland Telegraph Company. The time for news and information between the coasts was instantly reduced to seconds.

An aggressive engineering culture now began to shape the West. The profession of civil engineering emerged in the nineteenth century, first among the British, Prussians, Dutch, and French. It was originally an offshoot of military engineering that built fortifications and military roadways. It is no coincidence that the U.S. Army Corps of Engineers is one of the oldest American government agencies and was given responsibility for major public works such as dams, reservoirs, irrigation systems, and other water projects. These large-scale, geography-gobbling construction projects overwhelmed seemingly unconquerable geographical spaces and molded them to serve commerce and growing population. Soon Americans could not see the West in any way other than a challenge to engineering. Historian David Emmons identifies an invasion force of "land and immigration agents, army personnel, dam builders, mining engineers, managerial elites, territorial administrators, credit managers, and bureaucrats," all connected with a familiar East and indifferent to the health of the ecosystems and peoples they encountered in the West. These were the personnel of the "engineered West."

Surveying and Inventorying the West

Surveying technologies, the "eyes" through which the land was seen, began to change. Up craggy mountainside and down icy slope pushed surveying technology beyond the old Gunther's chain of 66 feet that had served so well on flat or gently rolling country. The old army method of gauging distance by pulling a one-wheeled odometer no longer worked. The magnetic compass, which had kept the surveyors' lines roughly straight from Ohio to the Plains, began to veer off course in mineral-rich geologically tilted western terrain. In California's Sierra Mountains, Josiah D. Whitney compensated for some of these problems when he put to use an 1850s triangulation grid based on ordinary surveyor's fixes, together with barometers to measure air pressure and thus altitude. Mountain peak triangulation involved nighttime signal fires. Clarence King added the sextant and zenith telescope to confirm his base line and triangulation work. King coordinated difficult longitude lines by means of the telegraph rather than uncertain chronometers. These new technologies, and the more sophisticated methods they allowed, now required teams of professional surveyors. Civil engineers replaced the army artillerists, topographers, and fortification engineers who did the earlier mappings. After its formation in 1869, the U.S. Geological Survey of the Territories soon replaced the Land Office as the primary land survey and inventory agency. Survey maps became works of art when cartographers applied hacure (shading) to represent mountain elevations, a technique still used in European mapping today. George M. Wheeler's mapping began to use more precise contour maps for topography instead of the generalized hacuring drawing.

The American public yearned for information about western opportunities. It demanded that scientific exploration be staffed by "practical" scientists and engineers. Purely scientific classification by western expeditions was soon overtaken by reports intended to encourage mining development and boomtowns. The shift was dramatic—from a census of the West's physical features to a census of resource opportunities. Travelers began to use Frémont's or Kemble Warren's detailed trail maps on terrain, water holes, animal feeding grounds, and weather to find their way. In 1857 army civil engineer Theodore Judah wrote, "When a Boston capitalist is invited to invest in a railroad project, he does not care to be informed that there are 999 different varieties of plants and herbs. He wishes to know the length of your road. He says, let me see your map and profile, that I may judge of its alignment and grades. Have you any tunnels, and what are their circumstances." The best known government surveyor, Ferdinand Vandiveer Hayden, called himself "the businessman's geologist." When Hayden explored the great geyser basin of Yellowstone, the steam from hundreds of vents in the morning reminded him of a factory village. This was quite different from the Indian view that the spewing geysers, bubbling hot springs, and hot mud pots were a region that the creator had not yet finished or the gateway to the burning depths of hell.

Clarence King, in charge of the 40th parallel survey from California across the desolate Great Basin to Salt Lake City, also represented the new engineering view. King's marching orders were to explore all potential for economic development along the line of the railroad, particularly those opportunities having to do with mining, and

> to examine and describe the geological structure, geographical condition and natural resource of a belt of country extending from the 120th meridian eastward to the 105th meridian, along the 40th parallel of latitude, to include the line of the 'Central' and 'Union Pacific' railroads. It

should examine all rock formations, mountain ranges, detrital plains, coal deposits, soils, minerals, ores, saline and alkaline deposits, material for a topographical map, barometric and thermometric observations, make collections in botany and zoology.

Once valuable resources had been identified and mapped, particularly silver and coal, the underlying strategy involved pushing the Indians aside with General Sherman's veteran troops, building the most profitable railroad possible, and guaranteeing the future with a front-line population of settlers. One of the most revealing set of instructions went to Capt. George M. Wheeler in 1871 when he explored one of the last unknown regions, the Great Basin south of the Central Pacific tracks in eastern Nevada and Arizona. Besides the standard topographical information and accurate mapping, he was to "ascertain as far as practicable everything related to the physical features of the country, the numbers, habits, and disposition of the Indians, the selection of such sites as may be of use for future military operations or occupation, and the facilities offered for making rail or common roads, to meet the wants of those who at some future period may occupy or traverse this part of our territory." He was also to identify mineral resources, label geological formations, list the vegetation, determine the suitability of the land for agriculture, note opportunities for irrigation and reclamation, and document the weather. Wheeler became famous for his completion of all these tasks under difficult conditions, including a side trip to make the first detailed survey of Death Valley.

Railroads

The network of railroads that came to cover America was a manifestation of this engineering vision. Railroad building itself was a major feat of civil engineering. As one construction boss boasted, "Where a mule can go, I can make a locomotive go." The improvisational efforts of the individual trapper or isolated settler were replaced by collaborative efforts of trained surveyors and engineers, well-heeled financiers, and imported gangs of workmen by the thousands. The goal was astonishing—to make geographical obstacles irrelevant. Physical geography and environmental systems became the bystanders, and victims, of the technological juggernaut. Everyone marveled at the engineering miracles: cuts and grades, tunnels blasted with dynamite, track laying, and river crossings. The first transcontinental line could not have been completed without a victory over deep snow in California's Sierras that included 39 miles of snowsheds built with 40 million board feet of lumber.

Railroads became the dominant physical, economic, and social configuration that nineteenth century Americans imposed on the West. They had crisscrossed the East by the 1850s and began to bridge the West in the 1870s. They bound together an otherwise impossibly expansive nation. As late as the 1840s, the United States had existed as a nation of "island communities" loosely strung across America's wide landscape. By moving goods, wealth, and people, the grid of rails bound together the communities and became the dominant infrastructure of the nation. The railroads were the first stage of a long-term process by which America's new industrialization successfully compressed time and space. The entire nation had been compacted.

This conquest of America's space by the railroads was not inevitable. In the 1830s, the first few miles of the little Baltimore and Ohio Railroad, with its toylike leaking steam engines that covered passengers in open cars with soot, ran on flimsy ironclad wooden rails. The concept of running an engine that pulled cars on tracks seemed a curious and untested plan. Certainly the plan required very high initial investment for equipment and maintenance. It seemed overly complex and very costly to acquire a right of way, construct a level roadbed with easy curves, carefully lay parallel track, and acquire reliable locomotives and rolling stock. Could such an investment be recovered, compared to the mature steamboat industry? However, the virtues of the railroad soon became apparent. The rails need not follow the meanders of rivers, but go directly "as the crow flies." The speed of the trains was triple that of the finest horses and wagons. And the aptly named "iron horse" never tired. It was dependable in all seasons and weather. In contrast, all water traffic depended on the seasons. Not only did winter freezes idle many industries, but commerce could be thrown awry by floods and droughts. The steam locomotive could plow its way through snowdrifts and blizzards. Trains on sturdy rails and well-engineered beds were not trapped in muddy quagmires in the spring, the long-standing bane of travel by roads. Railroads had enormous flexibility for cargoes and passengers, since cars could be added or subtracted with ease. They had load capacity and efficiency still unsurpassed today. Industrial historian Victor S. Clark concluded, "railroads brought to transportation the three gifts of directness, speed, and continuity" that quickly redefined undeveloped regions of the West into directly available resource zones. By means of railroads, Europeans spread into virtually every desirable nook and cranny of the continent. "This revolution," writes Clark, "was accomplished within less than the compass of a generation. Schoolboys who saw the first train ever moved by steam in America might ride by rail from the Atlantic to the Mississippi before they were 30. . . ." to cross the continent before they were 50. As one contemporary watched the rails cross the High Plains grassland, he reported, "Everything needed had to be brought into that barren country: ties from the forests of Minnesota, stone from the quarries of Wisconsin, rails from the steel mills of Pennsylvania." The head of the Union Pacific survey, General Grenville M. Dodge, remembered, "When you look back to the beginning at the Missouri River, with no railway communication from the East, and 500 miles of the country in advance without timber, fuel, or any material whatever from which to build or maintain a road, except the sand for the bare roadbed itself, with everything to be transported, and that by teams or at best by steamboats, for hundreds and thousands of miles; everything to be created, with labor scarce and high, you ask, under such circumstances could we have done more or better?" Banking and exchange, information and technologies, moved along with goods and people. Because industrial and agricultural power could be located in New York City, Chicago, New Orleans, and San Francisco, the entire nation could be centrally managed.

Railroads accelerated the move toward an engineered America. They created new demands for iron, steel, coal, and manufacturing of locomotives, railcars, and steel rails. Between 1840 and 1860 Americans laid an unprecedented network of 26,000 miles of track. Railroads consumed so much iron, over 800,000 tons in 1860, that the nation, despite the rapid growth of production, remained an iron-importing nation. Soon larger and heavier locomotives began to wear out less durable iron rails, sometimes in less than two years. Steel, a much harder metal, began to pour from Bessemer converters in Pittsburgh and Gary, soon reaching almost 500,000 tons annually, mostly for steel rails. The iron and steel industry leaped ahead to become the fourth largest in the nation, led only by lumber and woodworking, grain processing, and textiles. The second half of the nineteenth century saw a rush of technological innovations—larger and safer locomotives, the Westinghouse air brake, the

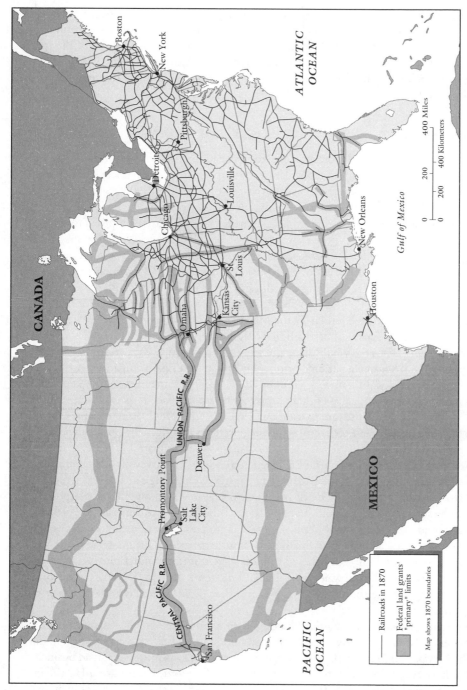

The Major Railroad Lines That Penetrated the West. Railroads had been called "the circulatory system of the middle class." They were the means by which the nation's natural resources in the West flowed to the new high-production industrial mills in the East. They moved ambitious people who sought new riches in the West. This "engineered West" was never seen in its own terms, but as the completion of an East-inspired Manifest Destiny.

universal signal system, the refrigerator car, and the Pullman car. These all made the trains attractive to a wide public and wider commerce. One important provision of the government contracts was that the gauge was to be uniform—4 feet 8.5 inches. (For decades in Europe, different gauges caused problems. Well into the twentieth century, when trains passed over the Polish-Russian border, they laboriously had to change trucks, ostensibly to prevent armed invasion by train.)

The Transcontinental Link

Now the push westward seemed more than ever to have a kind of inevitability. Americans had been incredulous in 1820 when Robert Mills, a visionary construction engineer, claimed that Americans would someday ride a train coast to coast in 60 days (by 1890 passengers crossed in seven days). As early as 1844, in only the second decade of rivet-popping boilers that drove unreliable locomotives on wooden and iron rails, financier Asa Whitney proposed to build a northern corridor from Duluth at the western edge of Lake Superior to Washington's Puget Sound's gateway to the Pacific. To counter Senate plans to support Whitney's northern route, the aggressive senator Thomas Hart Benton of Missouri rushed in 1848 to support a privately financed survey for a central route along the 38th parallel from St. Louis, with his skilled explorer son-in-law, John C. Frémont, in charge. A southern route along the 32nd parallel would cover geography made familiar by the Mexican War of 1843–46. Along what route would the first line run? The ideal destination would be San Francisco, that was clear. Whoever controlled this terminus would have the riches of the entire West in his grasp. The transcontinental link became a national priority and the public's preoccupation. A Colonel Abert of the Topographical Engineers wrote in 1849: "Unless some easy, cheap, and rapid means of communicating with these distant provinces be accomplished, there is danger, great danger, that they will not constitute parts of our Union." The combination of large profits, technology, management, and government privilege offered an unusually powerful force to make "gigantic thrusts into and across the heretofore unsettled domain." In 1853 Congress gave the Army Corps of Topographical Engineers ten months to survey all likely routes between the Mississippi Valley and the Pacific. This can-do engineering attitude was typical of the day. Army surveys by Ives and Powell swept across unknown regions and blank spots on the maps. The surveys identified four practical routes, one from Lake Superior to Portland, Oregon, a second through the well-known South Pass to San Francisco, another along the Red River to southern California, and finally across southern Texas and through the Gila Valley. One transcontinental line was believed to be sufficient into the indefinite future. Yet it seemed that the West might still wait a long time. Of the more than 35,000 miles of railroads in the United States at the end of the Civil War, less than 3,300 miles lay anywhere west of the Mississippi River.

Some entrepreneurs took matters into their own hands. It is astonishing that the U.S. railroad system was started by private enterprise and not by a public agency, as elsewhere in the world. The transportation infrastructure brought venture capitalists into the railroad business, names that have ever since stood for wealth and power—Stanford, Huntington, Harriman, Gould. Never before had an entire transportation system been created on such a stupendous scale—not the eastern canal network nor the fabled roads of the Roman Empire. Within 20 years of the first B&O run, Americans had constructed the railroad link between the Atlantic Ocean and the Mississippi River. The 1,000 miles between was soon crisscrossed with the nation's great trunkline systems. The mayor of St. Louis exclaimed, "Look at the great enterprises: the New York and Erie, the Central Pennsylvania, and the Baltimore and Ohio Railroads. What country on the face of the earth can boast of such enterprises?" By 1865 the ambitiously named Pacific Railroad connected St. Louis with the Independence, Missouri, embarkation point for the Oregon and California wagon trails. Another speculative operation constructed tracks that reached 122 miles west from Omaha. A builder ran tracks 214 miles east from San Francisco. The rivalry between St. Louis and Chicago for the eastern terminus was bitterly fought over high stakes. No city played a more important role in the transformation of the West than Chicago, strategically placed at the southwestern corner of Lake Michigan, a connecting link that used the Great Lakes to receive boatloads of goods that arrived from Buffalo, itself at the western end of the strategic Erie Canal, or from Europe by way of Canada's St. Lawrence River. Chicago became the nation's greatest transportation center, which funneled the wonderful midwestern bounty of wheat and corn and meaty animals to feed the nation and the world. As historian William Cronon has adroitly shown, Chicago in turn created a "second nature" when it sped trainloads of Wisconsin and Michigan wood to lay railroad ties and bridge streams, build farmers' fences, houses, barns, and tools of the farm family on the treeless grasslands.

Legal as well as geographical pathways had to be cleared to ensure the success of America's rail system. Chief Justice Isaac F. Redfield of Vermont set the tone in his pathfinding 1867 tract, *The Laws of Railways,* when he stated that railroad companies held "prerogative franchises" that gave them the right to eminent domain—the governmental right to appropriate private property for public use (usually with compensation to the owner). The railroads could virtually steamroll anyone standing in their way. Financial briars also had to be cleared to secure major private capitalization for roadbuilding and equipment. Merchants who made their fortunes in the ports of Boston, New York, and Philadelphia risked venture capital in railroads because they understood the power of transportation to create and control markets. Nevertheless, it quickly became clear that private investment capital, even with infusions from British and German investors, would not be enough. Government aid—through land grants, favorable loans, and direct outlays of cash—remained the key to success. Already, precedents existed by government actions to turn trails into roads, keep migrants supplied on the roads, and provide military protection against Indians. The government empowered the Union Pacific Railroad to construct a westward railroad beginning at Council Bluffs, Iowa, and it authorized the Central Pacific Railroad to build eastward from Sacramento. That these acts were passed by Congress in 1862 and 1864, in the heat of a deadly Civil War with an uncertain outcome, reveals the commitment to the maturing technology and industry. Above all, the federal government made the transcontinental railroad possible when it granted a 400-foot right of way together with ten alternate sections of land, equivalent to 10 square miles of public domain, for each mile of track laid. The railroad companies could sell off this valuable land at a handsome profit, often at twice the price of public domain in the same region because it was adjacent to the railroad. The 20 years between 1850 and 1871 marked the Great American Land Grant Giveaway. Eventually, all transcontinental rail companies together received 181 million acres of land in their alternate sections that followed the wide right of way. These grants can still be seen on western topographic maps. Federal authorities also agreed to loan the companies $16,000 for each mile built on level land, $32,000 a mile in foothills, and $48,000 for each mile in the mountains. President Lincoln, a former attorney for railroads, sweetened the pot when he played God and extended the Sierra Nevada

HORSE-DRAWN WAGONS would bring up rails, ties, and other equipment from flatcars at the end of the previous day's newly set line. The new roadbed, already graded, would be scraped smooth and leveled off. The work had to be synchronized; usually an ex-army officer (Union Army) was chief of each unit. Gangs of about 10 to 12 men worked at different parts of the job. One gang would set the wooden ties and metal plates, another heaved rails. An experienced gang set the ties in position, another laid the rails, and spike drivers and bolters completed the process: four rails to the minute, three strokes to the spike, 10 spikes to the rail, 400 rails to the mile. One newspaperman wrote,

> A light car, drawn by a single horse, gallops up to the front with its load of rails. Two men seize the end of a rail and start forward, the rest of the gang taking hold by twos until it is clear of the car. They come forward at a run. At the word of command, the rail is dropped in its place, right side up, with care, while the same process goes on the other side of the car. Less than thirty seconds to a rail for each gang, and so four rails go down to the minute. The moment the car is empty it is tipped over on the side of the track to let the next loaded car pass it, and then it is tipped back again; it is a sight to see it go flying back for another load, propelled by a horse at full gallop at the end of sixty or eighty feet of rope, ridden by a young Jehu, who drives furiously. Close behind the first gang come the gaugers, spikers and bolters, and a lively time they make of it.

It all went from dawn to dusk by commands of "Halt!" "Down!" and "On with another!" Another 6 or 7 miles of track might be laid, especially on the level Union Pacific side. Wages were $2.50 to $4 a day. Meals were large portions of buffalo meat,

Laying New Railroad Track.

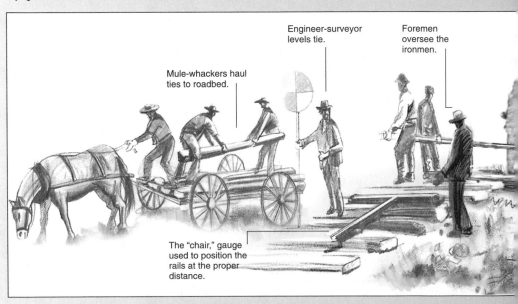

Engineer-surveyor levels tie.

Foremen oversee the ironmen.

Mule-whackers haul ties to roadbed.

The "chair," gauge used to position the rails at the proper distance.

bacon, hardtack, beans, and coffee set at long tables with tin plates nailed to them so they could be swabbed out with a bucket of water and a mop after each sitting. Men lived and slept in portable camps, usually a string of boxcars with layers of bunks. A cavalry unit protected them from angry Indians, and they were well armed themselves. Camp followers were tolerated and even encouraged to set up tents and portable shacks for food, clothing, liquor, sex, and gambling. As many as 3,000 people may have populated a track-laying operation.

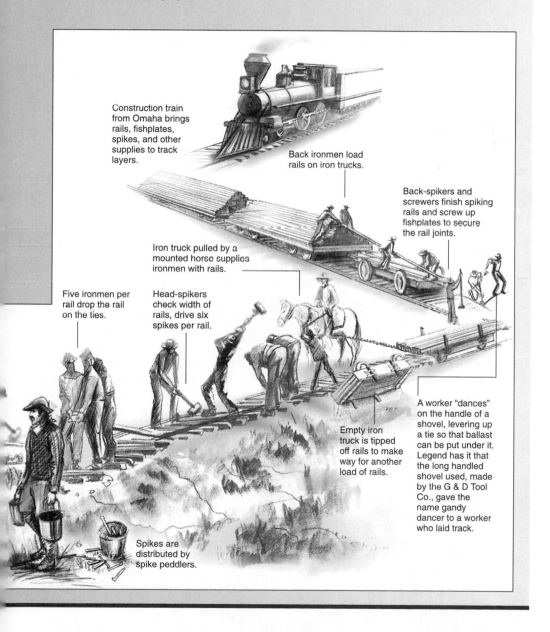

Construction train from Omaha brings rails, fishplates, spikes, and other supplies to track layers.

Back ironmen load rails on iron trucks.

Back-spikers and screwers finish spiking rails and screw up fishplates to secure the rail joints.

Iron truck pulled by a mounted horse supplies ironmen with rails.

Five ironmen per rail drop the rail on the ties.

Head-spikers check width of rails, drive six spikes per rail.

Empty iron truck is tipped off rails to make way for another load of rails.

A worker "dances" on the handle of a shovel, levering up a tie so that ballast can be put under it. Legend has it that the long handled shovel used, made by the G & D Tool Co., gave the name gandy dancer to a worker who laid track.

Spikes are distributed by spike peddlers.

mountains westward into the flat Sacramento Valley to assure the Central Pacific a better deal. Most of the route through the plains of Utah suddenly grew mountains. Congress provided an outright cash loan of more than $50 million to the Union Pacific and Central Pacific to establish the transcontinental connection.

The way was cleared for the Union Pacific and Central Pacific companies to rush toward each other. The project was the first nationwide public works project. Despite the preoccupations with the Civil War, laying the transcontinental track began in earnest in January 1863, by the Central Pacific from Sacramento. It faced the greater challenge of the California Sierra Mountains. Construction required new technologies, including the first use of volatile nitroglycerine, new engineering solutions, such as long wooden snowsheds on avalanche-prone slopes, and blasting and chiseling procedures for the ten tunnels blasted through the Sierras to obtain the desired grade on the 7,000-foot ascent to the Donner Pass. It took 13 months alone to cut the 1,650-foot summit tunnel. The Central Pacific built 360 miles of road in 1868 using Chinese labor, all its steel and rolling stock arriving by sea at San Francisco and by riverboat to Sacramento. In the same year Irish crews, supplemented by industrious Mormons, built 425 miles for the Union Pacific. The Central Pacific won a $10,000 bet by laying 10.6 miles of track from sunup to sunset with an hour off for lunch. This still stands as the alltime world record in track laying. At its peak the entire transcontinental project employed about 10,000 laborers, including Chinese, Indians, blacks, and whites. Goetzmann writes, "A whole new population moved into the West over the iron rails, and city after city sprang up along its path—each at first usually and appropriately named 'Hell on Wheels': Cheyenne, Rawlings, Ogden, Corinne, Elko, and Reno." One of the most notorious was Julesburg, Colorado, near the Nebraska border on the Union Pacific line. It got nicknamed "Sodom of the Wild West." "Thieves, gamblers, cutthroats, prostitutes, stalked brazen-faced in broad day through the streets." Records one 1869 account, "The roughs congregated there, and a day seldom passed but what they 'had a man for breakfast.'" When in 1869 the two track-laying parties of the transcontinental railroad met (and even ran past each other because they were getting paid by the mile) at Promontory Point north of the Great Salt Lake, the whole nation stopped to celebrate. Even though Union Pacific president Leland Stanford missed his first sledgehammer swing at the golden spike, Americans looked on the connection as another giant engineering feat that stepped beyond the completion of the Erie Canal and the laying of the Atlantic cable. The whole nation profited coast to coast. In Chicago, for example, boosters claimed that the value of property promptly went up 50 percent. In 1869 the Sacramento *Bee* had the insight to proclaim, "The contest is between two great Corporations," the Union Pacific and Central Pacific. The battle was not between geography and human endeavor, the result a foregone conclusion, but between two giant capitalist operations over ownership of western wealth. America's physical terrain disappeared beneath a papering of money, technology, and privilege.

The western railroad system of the United States may have been the greatest ever technological conquest over geographical space, particularly considering what had existed only a few years earlier. The nation mastered its environment by making railroad building a national agenda. The railroad was the first comprehensive circulatory system of the middle-class world (later reinforced by automobile roads and airline routes). The middle class had fabricated its own environment that swept away thousands of years of native society. American Indians were astonished when they saw armed surveyors followed by gangs of workmen who invaded their grassland—digging, building, bridging rivers, constructing the lines of the great railroad fever of the nineteenth century. Between 1865 and 1873, 35,000 miles of track were added in the United States, mostly in the West. By 1890 there were 72,473 miles of track west of the Mississippi. Even the desolate plains were crisscrossed by a map of rail lines that looked like the work of a neurotic spider. In the words of a booster in 1900, the railroads were "the absorbing passion of our people." By then, transcontinental lines, north, south, and middle, established the great western train systems, the Santa Fe, Southern Pacific, Central Pacific, Union Pacific, and Northern Pacific. The year 1887 set a record for new tracklaying that covered nearly 13,000 miles. What had been a novelty in the 1840s became an accomplishment in the 1870s and an indispensable and omnipresent necessity for national growth and cohesion by 1900. By that year railroad mileage reached 193,000, to peak in 1916 at 254,000 miles of track.

Yet it must also be said that the railroads failed to serve the nation's backbone of local farmers. Instead, the private railroad system gouged farmers with uncontrolled freight rate fluctuations that depended more on the marketplace than the needs of towns and farmsteads that had no other access to the outside world. Their sense of helplessness and frustration led to the farmer-led reform movements of the late nineteenth century. The railroad system allowed, and even encouraged, the concentration of power and control of resources. This is vividly told in Frank Norris's 1901 novel *The Octopus,* which depicts the vertical integration of wheat production in California that accelerated soil depletion and created thousands of tenant farmers, dominated by decisions that came down from distant corporate board rooms. With the advent of the railroads, the forests and prairie and coal mines and iron pits, which once seemed limitless, now moved toward depletion in a generation.

The United States in a few short years transformed itself from a nation that was spread out on an incomprehensibly large scale into a closely interconnected nation that was linked better than feudal England, France, Spain, or the Holy Roman Empire. It took less than a week to travel from coast to coast, compared to long months by horse or wagon. (A week is only twice as long as it took astronauts to reach the moon in 1969.) A 1876 special centennial train run of 3,317 miles between New York City and San Francisco astonished celebrants with a record 83 hours and 27 minutes at an average speed of 40 miles per hour. Through the combination of laying the networks of track, building locomotives and bridges, setting reliable timetables and inventing the nation's time zones, the railroad became the king of transportation from 1830 to 1950, when the interstate highway system and the airline network once more transformed America's geography.

Conclusion: What the West Might Have Been, and What It Became

Historian Susan Rhoades Neel described the presettlement West as "a dizzying swirl corresponding largely to the region's radically different topography." It contained desert, mountain, and grassland ecosystems, each self-sufficient, that offered alternatives to the eastern and midwestern experiences. Depending on what suited the environment, Native Americans were nomads on the Plains, agriculturists in the Southwest, root gatherers in northern California, and fishermen in the Pacific Northwest. Some parts of the West were inhospitable. Drought helped drive a flourishing Anasazi society out of the Four Corners region, and there were empty places in the high parks of the upper Rockies that were crossed only by hardy travelers. Among Europeans, we saw that Spanish-based settlers in the arid Southwest restricted themselves to animal grazing. But the new Americans, delighted and seduced by the combined power of technology, capital, and large populations, drove to transform virtually any region regardless of its geography into profitable mining towns and familiar agricultural landscapes. Neel adds that the High Plains, the Front Range of the Rockies, and the Southwest Desert were "environmental eccentricities" that gradually lost their uniqueness to modern development. By the twentieth century, nature was largely absent as a concrete reality that shaped the lives of people in the West. (Is this why the Dust Bowl failure stands out so dramatically? Was it the exception to the rule?) North Carolina hog factories appear in the Oklahoma Panhandle. Shopping malls and housing developments overwhelm the windswept plains lying before the Front Range. Millions of people crowd desert metropolises (Phoenix and Tucson) that demand multibillion-dollar water conduits from the distant Colorado River. Today a visitor can descend into the downtowns of western cities such as Denver, find familiar names and appearances of hotels, fast-food establishments, and shopping emporia, and not know whether it is Houston, Kansas City, or Indianapolis. The western environments were once "extreme places" now overlaid by a society not substantially different from that found in other places. A consumer society has a tremendous capacity to simplify and reduce all differences into a common denominator. There is no longer any such thing as a West, nor a South or East or Midwest, but instead a generically unified United States.

This loss is not a new discovery. In 1928 William Christie LacLeod wrote, "Europeans and later white Americans cheat, steal, and slaughter their way across the continent in one long, bloody, imperial misadventure," a process that destroyed all human (and natural) options. Anthropologist Ruth Benedict in 1934 concluded that personal self-interest based on property ownership allowed capitalism, greed, and imperial aggrandizement run out of control. Local cultures were incorporated into global capitalism. (This was equally true of Appalachia in the East, a process described in Chapter 11.) Instead of learning from the fresh experience of new environments, Americans chose to bury them in the name of economic development. With unexpected fervor, they sought to make the West interchangeable with the newly industrial, urban, and consumer-based East. Most alternatives disappeared before the industrial juggernaut. Historian David Emmons writes, "These corporations confronted no countervailing social power [in the West], no entrenched preindustrial society; no landed aristocracy . . . ; no independent commercial, mercantile or profession classes of ancient and respectable lineage; no clerical, political, or intellectual elites to challenge their own status." No significant competition stood up to the hunger for material wealth. This was aided by the federal government that owned the public domain, and gladly sold it into private corporate hands.

However, the West was never "empty land" without shape of form. Western history describes more nearly a "reconstructed" than a "constructed" region. An ecosystem, such as the Plains, is a combination of climate, topography, flora, and fauna to which nature assigns no values. But the West was also delimited by the expectations that eastern industrialists and farmers laid on it. An "arid" climate acquires meaning only in comparison to the "normal" East, where in Susan Neel's words, "the landscape is verdant, the wide rivers traversable, and all the 'customary' ways of making a life from the land are possible," versus the dry, the barren, the lifeless, and the dull. The West was thus a real, physical place that could be located on a map, but the different ecological regions were as historically conditioned as its people. William Cronon writes that each such region was itself "caught up in the flow of time and is no less a historical construction than human cultures are." This spatial construct, insists Cronon, is more real than abstractions like distant commodity markets and eastern power elites. American space was unified when the last western spaces were integrated into an industrialized America. From a region's own perspective, its ecosystems and local people did quite well prior to meddling by eastern corporations or federal bureaucrats.

David Emmons describes the West as a prize to the winners of the Civil War, who were not individual farmers, but corporate railroad, land, mining, and timber entrepreneurs. He finds that the pace of expansion and development changed as it crossed the Mississippi; it was more rapid, ferocious, and unbending in its profit seeking. This recalls the story of a midwestern farmer who, upon being congratulated for a bumper crop, said, "Yes, but look what it did to the soil," a response that the entrepreneurs or bureaucrats could not make nor would have understood. The special features of a local environment were trashed, as were the local people. In Gloria Anzaldúa's words, they were demeaned as "the squint-eyed, the perverse, the queer, the troublesome, the mongrel, the mulatto, the half-breed, the half-dead; in short those who cross over, pass over, or go through the confines of the 'normal,'" which is defined as eastern, industrial, and white. A presettlement region was thus treated not only as obsolete, but also as an environmental no-man's-land lacking internal meaning or environmental integrity. Options to eastern ways were lost by a refusal to see alternatives as anything but incoherent, inchoate, prone to savagery, and inherently unable to seek out "opportunities for development."

For Further Reading

Literature on the West remains a growth industry. For a detailed overview, Ray Allen Billington's *Westward Expansion: A History of the American Frontier* (1949) and Ralph H. Brown's *Historical Geography of the United States* (1948) are still unmatched, although both tend to accept the Turner thesis uncritically. Equally voluminous, but much more sophisticated is Donald W. Meinig's *Continental America, 1800–1867* (1993; Vol. 2 of *The Shaping of America: A Geographical Perspective on 500 Years of History*). For a classic on geographical determinism, see Ellen Churchill Semple, *American History and Its Geographic Conditions* (1903). For the geographical challenge of the West, see W. Eugene Hollon, *The Great American Desert, Then and Now* (New York: Oxford University Press, 1966). A solid and comprehensive review of the evolution of historical viewpoints toward the West can be found in Gerald D. Nash's *Creating the West: Historical Interpretations 1890–1990* (Albuquerque: University of New Mexico Press, 1991). The important theme of surveying the West and the western migrations of white Europeans are particularly well developed in William H. Goetzmann, *Exploration and Empire: The Explorer and Scientist in the Winning of the West* (1966), and John D. Unruh, *The Plains Across: The Overland Emigrants and the Trans-Mississippi West, 1840–1860* (1979), as well as the older study by Oscar Osburn Winther, *The Transportation Frontier: Trans-Mississippi West, 1865–1890* (1964). The power of industrialization and capitalism to reshape the west for private profit is the compelling theme in William G. Robbins, *Colony and Empire: The Capitalist Transformation of the American West* (Lawrence: University Press of Kansas, 1994), and given a broader context in Richard White, *"It's Your Misfortune and None of My Own." A New History of the American West* (1991). Victor S. Clark's *History of Manufactures in the United States, Vol. 1, 1607–1860* (1929; reprinted 1949) remains a masterpiece of fascinating detail despite its dated optimism. William Cronon's *Nature's Metropolis: Chicago and the Great West* (1991) should not be missed for the connections it makes between city, countryside, and region.

CHAPTER SIX

ROMANTIC AMERICA
AND UTOPIANISM:
LAYING CLAIM TO PARADISE

Americans had of necessity confronted nature as a physical world to be mastered. Nature represented treacherous seas and mountain barriers to cross or the raw materials with which to build a community. But the time had now come [during the 1830s] when Indians no longer lurked in the woods on the way to Walden Pond; when hayfields, pasture, and woodlot, separated by neat stone walls, had acquired the air of permanence that certified their right to a place in the landscape. Now nature seemed thoroughly domesticated.

— STOW PERSONS, 1958

Americans have repeatedly struggled with the meaning of their geography. The wilderness that surrounded European settlers during the earliest days was a frightening, confusing "place of wild beasts and uncontrolled lusts, of disorder and disharmony." New England Puritans concluded it was controlled by the devil. The native inhabitants were evil incarnate. A contrary version saw the wilderness as a paradise where the Puritans' duty was to construct, once and for all, the heavenly kingdom on earth set forth in the New Testament. However, they concluded they had failed, since God was punishing them with earthquakes, violent storms, destructive fires, blighted crops, sick animals, diseased and dying people, and especially "plagues of witches." This tension between human actions and the natural world would be a recurrent theme in American history, and it reached a climatic point in today's environmental crisis. Virtually no one anticipated the modern ecological view that the natural world is a complex of self-sustaining systems to be valued in their own right. On the contrary, most Americans assumed that it was right and proper to reap the highest possible rewards from their geography. When it came to nature, most Americans were developers. However, during the 1830s, a small minority of American Transcendentalists began to give the nonhuman world around them new philosophical, scientific, religious, and ethical values. This, however, did not make them instant ecologists.

The Changing Face of Nature

For most of European history the ordinary physical world was thought to be alive and animate, a frightening domain filled with lurking invisible powers that had to be appeased. The majority of Europeans lived in isolated agricultural villages where they paid careful attention to fertility rituals, which included spreading cow blood, ashes from special bonfires, and handfuls of salt on infertile places. Rain could be directed onto freshly planted crops by sprinkling water on stepping stones and decorating wells with flowers. Nature could also help humans in distress. Since the Greeks and Romans, botany had been a branch of pharmacology, with plants and herbs providing cures for headaches, stomach problems, pregnancy, flatulence, impotency, and most other human ills. The juniper berry, for example, helped cure "convulsions, ruptures, and strangled wombs," and the mandrake root was thought to be a useful anesthetic. Surrounded by all these mysterious forces, most Europeans found comfort in the belief that their earthly life was temporary. They believed they lived in a three-storied universe—heaven, earth, hell—where earth was a battleground between God and the devil. Their immortal souls belonged to the spiritual realm—"the world of unseen things"—whereas their physical lives briefly existed in a transitory natural world. Ultimately, nature was not terribly important.

Such views, which made nature paradoxically both frightening and meaningless, were rejected by intellectuals of the eighteenth-century Enlightenment. Building on Renaissance Humanism of the fifteenth century and the Scientific Revolution of the sixteenth century, they argued that nature was the principal abode of humanity. The duty of humanity was to improve on its immediate environment and let the next world worry about itself. As far as mysterious natural forces, new scientific discoveries and technological innovations were a breakthrough that reversed the balance in favor of human advancement. This new humanism quickly spread across the Atlantic, where in the new United States it created an intellectual climate that supported the rights of man, natural law, scientific method, and belief in the ultimate power of human reason. American intellectuals like Franklin and Jefferson believed the Enlightenment introduced a new modern age that stripped away the blinders of superstition, prejudice, and tyranny. In this view, the age of environmental fatalism—humans helplessly in the grasp of nature—was past history. New knowledge, fresh scientific discoveries, and new inventions were to be directed toward a better standard of living and quality of life for all humanity. This fresh interest in the natural world also began to trivialize it. Enlightenment rationalism treated nature as "other." In this dualistic separation between humans and nature, nature became a mindless entity to which the world of human rationality was infinitely superior. Franklin, Jefferson, and other rationalists looked on American history as an optimistic process that would bring the gradual conquest of the American wilderness, demonstrate control over natural resources, and build a utopia that celebrated its independence from nature.

The Ambitious Goal of Natural History: Total Knowledge of the New World

As we saw in Chapter 1, America from the first was subject to an encyclopedic examination. Captain John Smith, who combined solid reporting with his military talents, detailed the climate, the soil, the terrain, the vegetation, and the animals of Virginia. The New World might be like another planet, but it could be known through the mother of all sciences, natural history, which flourished from the Renaissance through the Enlightenment. Its method was omnivorous—to catalog all the phenomena of living nature. It was a descriptive science that pioneered on-site observation. Advocates of Enlightenment science concluded that such fieldwork was far superior to the traditional habit of knowing nature through books—"herbals" and "bestiaries," Aristotle and Galen. Yet, many early naturalists did little more than list their plants and animals in alphabetical order. Whereas today's study of nature is carved up into zoology, botany, geology, mineralogy, paleontology, meteorology, and hydrology, natural history attempted to encompass the biological and physical surroundings of all animals, including humans. It was a worthy forerunner to the equally omnivorous science of ecology because natural historians were among the first to describe systematically the impact of environment on plants, animals, and, especially, humans. This made natural history particularly apt at describing the diverse and strange wonders of the New World; it could find a pattern in the seemingly chaotic wilderness. What are the fundamental units of nature? The resulting taxonomy and nomenclature of genus and species, learned from the Swedish scientist Carolus Linnaeus, provided an organizational framework for nature that had been a fluttering chaos. A systematic worldwide survey could uncover an interconnected rational order in the world of animals, plants, water, soil, rocks, and climate. (This reassuring worldview would in time give way to Darwin's evolutionary dynamics that undermined fixity and uniformity of species.)

The Strange New World Must Conform with the Old World

Despite America's novelty, the fieldwork did not force any changes on Enlightenment science. Linnaeus's system convinced Europeans that New World strangeness could be brought into harmony with the rest of the world. Natural historians embarked on a prodigious naming and organizing campaign. In 1749 Linnaeus added the concept of the balance of nature, which he called "the economy of nature." This concept offered a means to understand environmental change or disruption. In the New World, for example, when European arrivals embarked on indiscriminate hunting, cleared the land, and established heavily populated settlements, they upset an earlier self-sustaining balance that might otherwise have continued indefinitely. The great French naturalist Georges Louis Leclerc, Comte de Buffon, reported in 1756 that the trapping of beaver in the West reduced their numbers and forced mountain men to go deeper into the wilderness. Buffon warned, "If the human species, as is reasonable to suppose, shall, in the progress of time, people equally the whole surface of the earth, the history of the beaver, in a few ages, will be regarded as a ridiculous fable." Although Buffon worried about the finality of such human interventions, he acknowledged that humans would soon gain the power to change nature into whatever image they desired. Indeed, the "new nature come forth from his hands" was superior to the original after it was "made, cultivated, fertilized." Human invention was thus not opposed to nature; it was instead the means by which nature could realize its full potential. Buffon emerged as the premier natural historian when he published 36 volumes of *Histoire Naturelle* between 1749 and 1785. He anticipated modern environmental ecosystem analysis that located plants and animals into an interactive context of soil, terrain, and climate. He said "true method" was simply "the complete description and exact history of each thing in particular . . . their procreation, gestation period, the time of birth, number of offspring, the care given by the mother and father, their education, their instincts, their habitats, their diet, the manner in which they procure food, their habits, their wiles, their hunting methods." Buffon warned however, that Linnaean classification was like playing a mental game with nature; he worried that such a taxonomy was merely a human construct which oversimplified the complexities of nature. Did human reason force its own pattern on nature?

Everything in Its Place:
The Enlightenment Catalogs the New World

Natural History, a Utilitarian Science

Peter Kalm, after his preparation under Linnaeus, was sent in the 1740s to America by the Royal Swedish Academy of Sciences. His practical instructions were to find useful plants that could grow in Scandinavia. Kalm did pioneering work that linked the distribution of plants to differences in their habitats in Pennsylvania and New Jersey. He also compared these plant populations to similar plants in the Hudson and Mohawk valleys and French-speaking Canada. Natural historian and Pennsylvanian farmer John Bartram applied his agricultural know-how to integrate soil quality, moisture, and terrain in his accounts. He marveled at the diversity of plants, the remarkable soil, and the "clear and sweet water" of Pennsylvania and the Carolinas. A primeval Carolina site included "a run of clear and sweet water along thick woody but loamy ground, looking rich on the surface by reason of the continual falling leaves, and by the constant evergreen shade rotting to soil." John Bartram's son, William, turned his 1791 travel book through the Carolinas, Georgia, and Florida less into a scientific report than a romantic adventure story about a wide-eyed wanderer through a Garden of Eden. He dazzled his readers and influenced the great English Romantic poets Samuel Taylor Coleridge and William Wordsworth. Speaking of clay soil on an island off the Georgia coast, Bartram writes that it is "little more than a mixture of fine white sand and dissolved vegetables, serving as a nursery bed to hatch, or bring into existence, the infant plant, and to supply it with aliment and food, suitable to its delicacy and tender frame, until the roots, acquiring sufficient extent and solidity to lay hold of the clay, soon attain a magnitude and stability sufficient to maintain its station." Bartram tended to focus on the natural drama before him more than report how nature functions. He also tended to anthropomorphize: "The bald eagle is a large, strong, and very active bird, but an execrable tyrant: he supports his assumed dignity and grandeur by rapine and violence, extorting unreasonable tribute and subsidy from all the feathered nations." Natural history was not an abstract activity, but utilitarian. Bartram wrote,

> Next day we passed over part of the great and beautiful Alachua Savanna, whose exuberant green meadows, with the fertile hills which immediately encircle it, would if peoples and cultivated after the manner of the civilized countries of Europe, without crowding or incommoding families, at a moderate estimation, accommodate in the happiest manner above one hundred thousand human inhabitants beside millions of domestic animals; and I make no doubt this place will at some future day be one of the most populous and delightful seats on earth.

Historian William Cronon concluded that this naturalist's view of landscape turned it into commodities—isolated and extractable units—instead of ecosystems. Bartram looked on the banks of savannas and imagined suburbs.

As early as 1769 Benjamin Franklin founded in Philadelphia the American Philosophical Society "for promoting useful knowledge" by species collections and their classifications. In its 1743 prospectus, Franklin announced that "the first drudgery of settling new colonies . . . is now pretty well over," thus allowing attention to "all philosophical experiments that let light into the nature of things, tend to increase the power of man over matter, and multiply the conveniences or pleasure of life." The mission of science was not only to reflect the world, but to improve it. Philadelphia also benefited when Charles Willson Peale's natural history museum opened its doors in 1786. A sign welcomed visitors to "the great school of nature" at the front door; the south door invited them to "the book of Nature open. Explore the wondrous world. A solemn Institute of laws eternal." Peale's plan was simple, ingenious, and economical. Keep a live menagerie next to the museum, and when an animal died, preserve and mount it. Soon Peale had the best American collection of animals, birds, and even insects from throughout the world. He also acquired mastodon bones that he associated with his stuffed modern bison. Visitors were expected to rejoice in the grandeur of the continent and wonder at the powers of nature that Americans enjoyed.

Yet the human assignment in the new enlightened era was to convert the howling wilderness into a domesticated agricultural landscape. Hector St. John de Crèvecoeur, a French intellectual who briefly enjoyed himself as a gentleman farmer in New York, wrote in 1785 the brilliant *Letters from an American Farmer* about the process. European Enlightenment philosophers made the difficult ocean crossing to eighteenth-century America because they believed it was the arena for the happy future they all contemplated. In his enthusiasm, Crèvecoeur was joined by the nobleman Chastellux, the naturalist Michaux, the great chemist Joseph Priestly, and even, in 1806, the last reputed universal man, Alexander Humboldt. Priestly reflected the new confidence in human progress by following the laws of nature: "I view the glorious face of nature, and I admire its wonderful constitution, the laws of which are daily unfolding themselves to our view." Such visitors saw the New World as a wonderful natural laboratory not yet overlaid by farming, industry, cities, and civilization. How did nature function without human intervention? Such study was not possible in long-settled Europe.

Even at the height of the Revolutionary War and in the midst of his creation of the new federal nation, Thomas Jefferson could not set aside his fascination with the natural forces that emerged from the wilderness, and the potential for human improvement. He seemed as passionately involved in natural history as in revolutionary politics. His classic natural history,

Notes on the State of Virginia (1786), reported on flora, fauna, mountains, rivers, population, laws, manufacturing, and future potential. Indians and blacks were treated as additional natural phenomena. In an 1814 letter, Jefferson wrote, "Botany I rank with the most valuable sciences, whether we consider its subjects as furnishing the principal subsistence of life to man and beast, delicious varieties for our tables, refreshments from our orchards, the adornments of our flower-borders, shade and perfume of our groves, materials for our buildings, or medicament for our bodies." Both Jefferson and Crèvecoeur described in their journals the impacts of environment on plants, animals, and, especially, humans. However, they looked to a day when humans were no longer helpless, but on the verge of taking charge over the natural world.

Natural history often featured an environmental determinism: Fevers, disease, debilitations depended on climate conditions. Had climate forces created such a hostile environment that long-term European settlement was ill advised in regions like the Chesapeake miasma country? Swampy southern lowland climate weakened the body. Such weakening increased liability to "consumption, rheumatic pains, pleurisy, cholera morbus, scorbutical dropsies, gripes, or the like." Medical opinion held that people became disease prone when they encountered excessive decaying organic matter, heavy moisture in the air, and oppressive heat. America's best known doctor, Benjamin Rush, attributed Philadelphia's yellow fever outbreak in the 1790s to exhalations from putrefied coffee on a wharf near Arch Street. The visiting Swedish naturalist Peter Kalm also believed Americans consumed too much tea, coffee, chocolate, sugar, strong liquor, and watermelons for good health and long life. He was on the right track when he complained of mosquito larvae in swamps, but he did not make the connection with malaria. On the other hand, humanity could have the upper hand over climate. A 1688 report in Virginia noted that, "thirty or forty years ago, when the country was not so open, the thunder was more fierce." Land cleared for cultivation, it was said, released more heat into the air and made winters warmer. The French philosopher Raynal concluded in 1783; "Man appeared, and immediately changed the face of North America. He introduced symmetry by the assistance of all the instruments of art. The impenetrable woods were instantly cleared, the wild beasts were driven away, while thorns and briars made way for rich harvests. Thus the New World, like the Old, became subject to Man." European agricultural improvements could make conditions bearable, such as draining swamps to eliminate "pernicious exhalations rising from stagnating filthy water" or clearing forests to reduce "the noxiousness of the effluvia from putrefying substances." Kalm and others believed that dense vegetation was the immediate cause of poor climate. Most Americans and their foreign visitors agreed that the American climate was becoming milder as the land was brought into cultivation from forests and swamps.

Natural History Applied to the Unknown Western Wilderness

Environmental reporting depended on the remarkable descriptive powers of natural history well into the nineteenth century. Jefferson's instructions to Lewis and Clark pushed this encyclopedic and omnivorous quest into the West. Together with mapping and Indians,

Other objects worthy of notice will be, the soil and face of the country, its growth and vegetable productions, especially those not of the United States, the animals of the country generally, and

IN 1817, JOSEPH Meigs, commissioner of the General Land Office of the public lands survey, put natural history principles into practice when he sent out forms to 20 land offices that requested comprehensive information:

1. The time of the unfolding of the leaves of plants.
2. The time of flowering.
3. The migration of birds, whether from the north or south, particularly swallows.
4. The migration of fishes, whether from or to the ocean.
5. The hibernation of other animals, the time of their going into winter quarters, etc.
6. The phenomenon of unusual rains and inundations.
7. The phenomenon of unusually severe droughts. This history of locusts and other insects in unusual numbers.
8. Remarkable effects of lightning.
9. Snowstorms, hailstorms, hurricanes, and tornadoes; their course, extent, and duration.
10. All facts concerning earthquakes and other subterranean changes.
11. Concerning epidemic and epizootic distempers.
12. The fall of stones or other bodies from the atmosphere; meteors, their apparent velocity, etc.
13. Discoveries relative to the antiquity of the country.
14. Memorable facts relative to the topography of the country.

The land office agents were also to record the temperature, wind, and weather three times a day. Meigs received a number of these field reports, but he made no comprehensive analysis before he died in 1822.

especially those not known in the United States; the remains and accounts of any which may be deemed rare or extinct; the mineral productions of every kind, but particularly metals, limestone, pit-coal and saltpeter; salines and mineral waters, noting the temperature of the last, and such circumstances as may indicate their character; volcanic appearances, climate, as characterized by the thermometer, by the proportion of rainy, cloudy, and clear days, by lightning, hail, snow, ice, by the access and recess of frost, by the winds prevailing at difference seasons, the dates at which particular plants put forth or lose their flower or leave, times of appearance of particular birds, reptiles or insects.

Lewis and Clark, and others such as John James Audubon, captured a wild America that amazes us today—the skies darkened with perpetual flocks of birds, the land crowded with grazing deer and elk, the waters thick with fish, rock formations that pointed to the earth's creation, in a landscape where humans, native or European, were scarce and unimpressive. Most American exploratory expeditions, even though they were military adventures, carried naturalists and artists. Travelers like the Swiss naturalist Louis Agassiz excitedly told of new wonders around every river bend or over every mountaintop. Agassiz emigrated to America in 1846 and led a pathfinding expedition to Lake Superior in the summer of 1848. His natural history survey examined in detail a single natural phenomenon, in this case a large freshwater lake. He and his team catalogued shells, birds, vegetation, fishes, reptiles, and fossils, all in the context of geology and the lake basin. Although this account falls short of being an ecological survey, Agassiz did look at environmental influences. The great military surveys by Clarence King, F. V. Hayden, and many others employed mapmakers, geologists, botanists, zoologists, and representatives of such new human sciences as archeology, anthropology, and ethnology. Their mission was to construct a total geographical inventory, "the great reconnaissance" of America's unknown territories. They believed natural history could bring Linnaean order to wilderness chaos and position the entire public domain in a scientific framework. Historian William H. Goetzmann writes, "The West began to be related to a larger totality of cultural knowledge. Though it was replete with marvels and wonders, it could be comprehended in civilization's centers of learning. Their [the surveyors'] work was still philosophical and metaphysical rather than scientific in its emphasis. The search was for unity, totality, oneness with the whole 'Kosmos.'" The scientists "appreciated the sublime, endless, empty immensity" of the West. They rarely separated what was reportorial and what was visionary. Goetzmann reminds us that natural history nevertheless stands on the other side of the "great scientific fault line" from the modern world of Darwin, Kelvin, Mendel, Einstein, Heisenberg, and James D. Watson. Yet, because of natural history, America lost its frightfulness to Europeans. With proper study, they were convinced, it could become familiar and orderly.

Everything a Divine Correspondence: The Romantic Revolt

Reason and Science Alone Cannot Explain Nature: The Transcendentalist Vision

A small number of Americans began to wonder whether nature had a deeper meaning than displayed by the catalog of natural history or when it was treated as raw material for farming and manufacturing. Did its economic development involve a loss as well as a gain? The popular essayist Oliver Wendell Holmes complained in 1839, "The mountains and cataracts, which were to have made poets and painters, have been [instead] mined for anthracite and dammed for water power." Were Americans selling their natural birthright for short-term profits when it also offered long-term personal renewal and a national identity? By the 1830s Americans had conceived of three different ways of apprehending nature: through supernatural revelation in scripture, based on divine authority; through Enlightenment empiricism, involving sense data as organized by scientific reason; and through direct personal inspiration, depending on existential experience. The new Transcendentalism of Emerson and Thoreau protested against both Christian literalism and Enlightenment empiricism and sought to replace it with the flow of a divine spirit out of nature. It meant a break with the long-standing distinctions of a three-storied universe of heaven, earth, and hell. Emerson wanted nature and nature's God to enfold him in a mystical union. Thoreau's message from Walden Pond is still attractive in its rebellious call to escape mechanical and commercial civilization in order to be immersed in nature, if only for a few months. The American Transcendentalists (similar to Romantics in England and Europe) were writers, poets, and lecturers who took a fresh look at nature in America. Transcendentalism was mostly an upper-class phenomenon from the Boston area, a liberal spinoff from Puritanism. It thought itself to possess superior sensibilities toward nature compared to a grubbing and materialistic middle class. According to the Transcendentalists, scientific rationalism did not sufficiently plumb the depths and powers of non-human nature. Enlightenment science's Linnaean taxonomy and nomenclature was a means for the consumption of nature for material profit, with humans as technological conquerors of dumb nature. Instead, Transcendentalists claimed they looked at the world "with new eyes" and discovered that "behind nature, throughout nature, spirit is present."

The Transcendentalists countered the frontier settler's aversion to the wilderness and the business leaders' desire to profit from nature. Instead, human values sprung primarily from wild nature. The Transcendentalists thus wrote an American minority report, arguing that industrial progress was not all good and its destruction of wilderness ought to be rethought. Their vision was of an America different from the industrial model. It had been inhabited by a savage, not vicious but noble savage, and now by virtuous farmers peaceably laboring in a pastoral landscape, with distant wilderness as a source of perpetual refreshment. They insisted that unimproved nature, or wilderness, was neither obsolete nor useless. America should be nature's nation. Thoreau coined the still popular phrase, "In wildness is the preservation of the world." This different America contained its own intrinsic ideas of beauty, truth, and goodness. This embrace of the wilderness, and doubts about the direction of industrialization, did much to shape the later environmental movement in America. American Transcendentalism can be described as a movement that anticipated modern environmentalism because it emphasized a holistic and organic natural world, a fundamental human need to remain in contact with nature, and a naturalistic ethic. Transcendentalists raised serious and valid questions about blind trust in science, the narrow-minded profiteering of capitalism, and the historic separation of humanity from nature fostered by Christianity and Western philosophy. Emerson and Thoreau anticipated the 1,000-mile walk of John Muir and the land ethic of Aldo Leopold. Modern environmentalists are often embarrassed by Transcendental fuzziness, but the modern movement is an outcome of this historical movement. The difference today is a substantial scientific foundation in the biological sciences.

A Hothouse Movement?

The Transcendentalists depended on a philosophical idealism that flowed from Wordsworth's England and Goethe's Germany. They learned to cultivate Romantic sentiments (later trivialized into Victorian sentimentalism) and unabashedly turned scenery into the source for moods and passions. Many of their contemporaries concluded that the Transcendentalists were naive, even silly, intellectuals in fancy clothes, who "returned" to nature by hoeing vegetables in sandy soil at Brook Farm outside Boston. Transcendentalism took shape in literature and the arts: James Fenimore Cooper's popular Leatherstocking frontier stories, Francis Parkman's dramatic histories of the struggle for control of America's wilderness between the French and the British (he called it a "history of the American forest"), the unsettling mystery stories of Edgar Allen Poe, and the man against nature drama in Melville's *Moby Dick*. Artists in New England and a group called the Hudson River School exhibited spectacular American landscapes that received wide public approval. Although the Transcendentalists became famous for their diversity, some generalizations can be made about their attachment to wild nature. Most were followers of two primary writers, Ralph Waldo Emerson and Henry David Thoreau, who labored in the 1830s and 1840s. Literary Transcendentalism may have reached fulfillment 50 years later in the richness and diversity of Walt Whitman's *Leaves of Grass,* in John Muir's life and writings out of California's Yosemite Valley, and in historian Frederick Jackson Turner's monumental "frontier thesis" that located America's genius in the receding western wilderness. Transcendentalism created few explorers, Indian fighters, trappers, farmers, business leaders, politicians, and railroad men; instead it was loaded with poets, essayists, and languid dreamers who made an impression on America far greater than their numbers.

Ralph Waldo Emerson (1803–82) was the leading essayist and lecturer who shaped Transcendentalism. A Boston intellectual troubled by poor health, he rebelled against his mainstream religious (Congregational-Unitarian) and educational (Harvard) background, and was drawn to Romanticism during a trip to Europe in 1832 where he met Carlyle, Coleridge, and Wordsworth. His published essays, "Nature" in 1836, and "The American Scholar" in 1837, gave him a reputation as one of America's most independent and influential thinkers. Emerson effectively used lyceum lectures, one of the most popular modes of public communication in the nineteenth century, to publicize his views. He told Americans that they were different from European decadence because of their intense connection with a unique and fresh natural world. In his gentle jeremiad, "The American Scholar," orated in 1837 before the Phi Beta Kappa Society in Cambridge, Emerson proposed that the American wilderness—nature still in its harmonious totality—could be the source of a new humanity unique to America. Human society was flawed; the source of renewal was nature. Nature is the seamless web of God, without beginning or end, the infinite mirror for an infinite humanity, which goes far beyond the capabilities of science. Emerson believed the new Americans could break their chains. He spoke of his "intercourse with heaven" while rooted in the earth: "Standing on the bare ground—my head bathed by the blithe air, and uplifted into infinite space,—all mean egotism vanishes. I become a transparent eyeball. I am nothing. I see all. The currents of the Universal Being circulate through me: I am part or particle of God." Such statements reflect the strong streak of nature religion, nature mysticism, and pantheism (God is everything and everywhere) in Transcendentalism. Nature was considered a sacramental force, a pathway to personal renewal—"an emblem of divine things that in some way actually contained the divinity to which it pointed," according to religious historian Cathy Albanese. "Nature might therefore have a quality of absoluteness about it," and thus, "Harmony with nature became the broad highway to virtuous living, and, more, to union with divinity."

When Emerson became one of the publishers of the Transcendentalist *Dial* magazine in 1840, one of his first contributors was Henry David Thoreau (1817–62), who also lived in the Emerson household from 1841 to 1843. Thoreau was equally unconventional and found himself drawn to Emerson's writings while a student at Harvard. He sought an independent life in Concord, Massachusetts, supporting himself as an innovative pencil maker, a schoolteacher, and local handyman. In 1845 Thoreau began to have doubts about the middle-class materialism that surrounded him. He settled into a 10 by 15-foot cabin at Walden Pond, to "move away from public opinion, from government, from religion, from education, from society," although he could still stroll to town for conversation and dinner. At the cabin he grew vegetables, did surveying and odd jobs for neighbors, and kept a detailed journal of his observations of nature, his survival activities, and personal ruminations. He believed he abandoned society in the nick of time, before the remaining primeval qualities in him had been erased. The idea was to escape further damage from civilization and enter a truly new world in nature. Already Emerson had complained, "Things are in the saddle, and ride mankind." The cure involved total renunciation of traditional habits, conventional actions, socially acceptable mores, and the well-worn paths of conduct, in order to achieve total immersion in nature. The result was the publication in 1854 of a singular American literary and environmental classic, *Walden.* "I do not propose to write an ode to dejection," Thoreau wrote, "but to brag as lustily as chanticleer in the morning, standing on his roost, if only to wake my neighbors up." It is one of the most widely read and quoted books in American letters. Thoreau's other nature writings include *A Week on the Concord and Merrimack Rivers* (1849) and the posthumously published *Excursions* (1863), *The Maine Woods* (1864), and *Cape Cod* (1865), all considered masterpieces in natural history. Thoreau's independence was also demonstrated in his remarkable 1849 essay "Civil Disobedience," a report of an overnight stay in prison because of his refusal to support the Mexican War. Thoreau was virtually unknown in his own day, but became a counterculture hero to later generations.

New Ways of Sensing, Perceiving, and Knowing: Nature Becomes Spirit

Transcendentalists believed humans could achieve, writes Albanese, "perfect correspondence between the inner nature of man and the structure of external reality, between the soul and the world." This idea opened a philosophical debate over epistemology (ways of knowing) that questioned the authority of scientific method. Was the world better seen through objective detachment or personal involvement, through the universal language of mathematics, or by a noble savage or natural man? The stakes were enormous, since empirical science tended toward the devaluation of nature, whereas Transcendentalism's approach tended to absorb humanity into nature's larger organic whole. Emerson preached against mere rationality: "A foolish consistency is the hobgoblin of little minds." Thoreau did not mince words: "We do not learn by inference and deduction, and the application of mathematics to philosophy, but by direct intercourse and sympathy." He found it essential, even when doing fieldwork observations in the Maine woods, to "let science slide" for the sake of personal communion with nature.

There was also an unresolved tension in Transcendentalism whether nature was the final source of wisdom or an intermediate tool to a higher spiritual realm. Sometimes Emerson could not hold to the tension. He tended to resolve it by surrendering the physical world to higher spiritual ends. In his 1836 essay "Nature," Emerson proclaimed that "nature is the symbol of the spirit," that "the world is emblematic." He was embarrassed by this surrender: "I have no hostility to nature, but a child's love to it. I expand and live in a warm day like corn and melons. Let us speak her fair. I do not wish to fling stones at my beautiful mother, nor soil my gentle nest." Thoreau was much more committed to the gritty materiality of nature. He knew scientific method and classification, and practiced it on his travels in New England. Thoreau could also write, "When I would recreate myself, I seek the darkest wood, the thickest and most interminable, and, to the citizen, most dismal swamp. I enter a swamp as a sacred place,—a *sanctum sanctorum.* There is the strength, the marrow of Nature. The wildwood covers the virgin mould,—and the same soil is good for men and for trees. A man's health requires as many acres of meadow to his prospect as his farm does loads of muck." Thoreau did not believe in the hobgoblin of consistency any more than Emerson. Instead, the highest human activity was contemplation of "many acres of meadow" to attain a mystical vision. "For all the material details," says the literary critic Wright Morris, "the counting of nails and beans, Walden Pond is a mythic, personal vision, the poet's imagination processing the raw-material facts." Thoreau discovered that "a mystic, spiritual life" depended on "a primitive savage life." "I reverence them both. I love the wild not less than the good." Man has a physical existence that roots him in the material world; but his soul or spirit also separates him from materiality because he can participate in transcendence or divinity. Wild nature, so pure in its wildness, was not the pathway to hell, as the Puritans feared, but the pathway to God.

According to the Transcendentalists, a clean break with civilized values and direct connection with raw nature stripped life down to its essentials. Civilization was a mere superficial web that distracted humans from the essential reality of life that unfolded in nature. Art historian Angela Miller noted, "Thoreau reminds us that only an identity rooted in the soil of place, particularized memories, and personal associations can keep us true to ourselves and our communities, allowing us to judge national objectives with greater clarity and skepticism." Thoreau worried that nature in eastern Massachusetts was on the verge of becoming a domesticated landscape in which the artifacts of civilization were fatally superimposed on the original geography. Of that view, Wright Morris concluded, "Here is the first contour map of what we might call our *natural* state of mind" in America. Thoreau's 1846 travel into the wild heart of Maine pushed him to write, "Think of our life in nature,—daily to be shown matter, to come in contact with it,—rocks, trees, wind on our cheeks! The *solid* earth! The *actual* world! The *common sense! Contact! Contact!*" Emerson's voice was more genteel: "Embosomed for a season in nature, whose floods of life stream around and through us, and invite us by the powers they supply, to action proportioned to nature, why should we grope among the dry bones of the past?" It was not civilization but nature that offered reality and regeneration. The Transcendentalists were fascinated with the savage forces that rationality and industrialization sought to subdue. They created the first truly *American* look at nature. Their ambition was to liberate, not throttle, its primeval mysteries. Poe, Hawthorne, and Melville depicted the mysterious, horrifying, and exotic aspects of nature. Our true nature was not so much in reason but in intuition, imagination, and cultivation of the senses.

Henry David Thoreau as an Environmentalist

When the young Henry David Thoreau went on his famous day hikes and long travels in New England, he strove to look at his natural surroundings directly, without cultural filters. "I had no idea that there was so much going on in [neighbor] Heywood's meadow." Environmental historian Donald Worster called him an early "field ecologist." To Thoreau, nature everywhere was wildly fecund, filled with "vegetative force." It was never thin and static, but turbulent and chaotic with a purpose. Thoreau repudiated Enlightenment and scientific descriptions of the natural world as mechanical and clocklike. Instead he saw the earth as one enormous organism pulsing with such explosive power that human understanding was constantly challenged.

Thoreau was a naive forerunner of modern ecological science because of his emphasis on the dynamic process of life and the interdependence of living things. At one point, he sought to reconstruct the original condition of nature around him at Concord, to identify "the actual condition of the place where we dwell, three centuries ago." To his astonishment he failed because he realized so much had already been wiped out by European settlement. What was left was "a maimed and imperfect nature." He was alarmed that three centuries of change could have been so devastating. He concluded that a self-perpetuating wilderness had disappeared long ago. Only a thin and dying geography was left. Less than half of the forest remained, the few remaining lynx in eastern Massachusetts were being ruthlessly killed, and New England's difficult farmland was becoming even harder to work. People instead practiced commerce, which Thoreau was convinced thinned their souls and distracted them from exploration of their real lives.

Thoreau anticipated environmental radicals when he concluded, "Either nature may be changed or man. Does [nature] require to be improved by the hands of man, or is man to live more naturally and so more safely?" Today's organic farmers, who refuse to douse their fields with chemicals, would agree with Thoreau's plea, "Would it not be well to consult with Nature in the outset? For she is the most extensive and experienced planter of us all." In a single step he anticipated modern timber conservation, ecosystem science, and environmental education when he suggested that each New England town preserve a primitive forest of no less than 500 acres "where a stick should never be cut for fuel, a common possession, for instruction and recreation."

Yet both Emerson and Thoreau were smitten with America's development. Emerson became an enthusiastic advocate of the growing network of railroads; technology could guarantee the fulfillment of America's promise as the new Garden. Thoreau, despite his antimaterialism, believed that the best of the American came out when he "redeems the wild meadow" into profitable farmland. He wrote, "The weapons with which we have gained our most important victories are not the sword and the lance, but the bushwack, the turf-cutter, the spade, and the boghoe."

The Artist Takes Charge: Thomas Cole and the National Landscape

Romantic Landscape Painting as the Medium to Know Nature

The American public was usually suspicious of effete poets like the Transcendentalists; such intellectuals inhabited a closeted indoors instead of America's great expansive outdoors. But the public was enthralled by landscape artists. When Thomas Cole, Asher Brown Durand, Albert Bierstadt, or Thomas Moran exhibited a new canvas in an eastern gallery, it was a major public event that drew large crowds and was covered by the newspapers. Such paintings were widely copied. Steel engravings based on landscape canvases were printed by the thousands and hung framed on parlor walls across middle-class American homes. The first large coffee table books were filled with text and pictures about romantic or picturesque American scenery.

The public believed the landscape artists gave them truthful details of a vast American panorama, felicitously combined with "beautiful sentiment."

The landscape had not always been the subject of art; historically, painting had focused on religious subjects and the human form. Scenery rarely appeared on a canvas before the sixteenth century except in the background as a secondary feature. However, as we have seen, Europeans began to pay more attention to the natural world during the Renaissance, the Scientific Revolution, and the Enlightenment. Landscape became a significant subject on artists' canvases. In "Nature," Emerson spoke of four "uses" of nature, and the landscape artist fulfilled three of the four. The artist left to the businessman Emerson's *commodity,* meaning material benefits and the practical arts. The artist's large landscape canvases, however, expressed Emerson's other uses: *beauty,* one of humanity's "nobler wants," served to satisfy the American soul. Painters gave Americans a visual *language* about the material land and the human spirit, and described a natural American *discipline*—the moral imperative that flowed from nature.

A landscape painting, of course, was not identical with the physical land itself. But such works provided another step in the all-important "mental mapping" that has continuously shaped American environmental history. Wherever there were not cornfields or tobacco plantations, the land was assumed to be empty and underutilized, regardless of the prior existence of successful natural ecosystems and hundreds of years of Indian civilization. When the English novelist Charles Dickens visited the United States in 1842 and took a train ride from New York City to Baltimore, he complained that instead of "scenery" all he saw was "fallen trees mouldering away in stagnant water and decaying vegetable matter, and heaps of timber in every aspect of decay and utter ruin." He wrote a friend that the reality of America failed to measure up to the mental map he brought with him: "This is not the Republic I came to see. This is not the Republic of my imagination." Similarly the English archcritic of the 1830s, Frances Trollope, said that beyond the Mississippi River lay nonsense. Dickens, Trollope, and other English writers found the Mississippi River itself beyond verbal comprehension. Modern landscape historians John Brinkerhoff Jackson and John R. Stilgoe have both argued that "landscape" is not a natural feature of the environment, but a synthetic or fabricated space, "a man-made system of spaces superimposed on the fact of the land." American landscape painting was heavily laden with messages. In 1835 the transplanted English artist Thomas Cole wrote that landscape painting contained a patriotic message: "Nature is the national past, the basis of the national identity, an infinite source of moral regeneration, and guarantee of the democratic constitution." The meaning of America came to be embodied in landscape images. We can add "landscape" to a short list of definitions of America's geography that includes commodity, empire, and wilderness.

By midcentury beautiful scenery was accessible to most middle- and upper-middle-class New Yorkers, who could travel by train along the scenic Hudson River and take a stagecoach to resorts in the Catskills and the White Mountains (see the discussion of early tourism in Chapter 12). However, many middle-class patrons of landscape art felt uneasy when they encountered the actual messy nature of real trees, rocks, mud, rain, and steep paths. Americans did not want nature on its own terms. Even though Thomas Jefferson owned Virginia's Natural Bridge as his private property, on the rare occasions when he ventured to the top of the arch he was frightened enough to get down on his hands and knees and not look over the edge. Henry David Thoreau wrote of his own dread when alone in the wilderness: The nighttime terrain is "made out of Chaos and Old Night. Man was not to be associated with it. It was matter, vast, terrific—not his Mother Earth that we have heard of." There was an awful

"Across the Continent" (1868). This was one of the most popular Currier and Ives color lithographs that Americans hung on their living room walls. Such illustrations became a "window" through which eastern Americans learned to imagine the West.

indifference in wild nature. Direct contact with nature seemed to pull a person into chaos. Art historian Angela Miller writes, "Americans' vaunted love of nature proved to be better served by images than by the thing itself."

Landscape paintings offered the viewer the safety of distance while still evoking a personal response and displaying a patriotic nationalism. Most Americans decided it was better to do their aesthetic fieldwork in the local museum or gallery. They wanted to believe that the canvases realistically reported on nature "out there." In the safety of the middle-class parlor, they looked out windows that framed a domestic scene perhaps with a vegetable garden and apple tree enclosed by a picket fence, and beyond fields bordered by a woodlot. This was the creation of the ideal "middle landscape," midway between an overcivilized Europe and the savagery of the western frontier. On the same parlor wall would be another image in a frame, a lithograph of craggy mountains, deep woods, and pristine lakes. This was a "window" too—through which one could glimpse the meaning of America. The great American wilderness, safely framed, was seen as the climactic location for sublime majesty, infinity, and transcendence. The artist sought to made the viewer proud of the American wilderness, or at least its image. It was a scene of holy power, a display of nature's force, and the acknowledgment of human frailty. The painters created a visual scripture that told of sacred places which actually existed in the public domain: Niagara Falls, Yellowstone, Yosemite Valley, Glacier Park, and the Grand Canyon. There were even groves of sacred trees like those of the ancient world; in America's case they were enormous redwoods or sequoias.

American geography was mute; landscape painting gave it a voice. Even Charles Dickens said during his visit in 1842 that the nullity of the American prairie left him stripped of words. The American landscape is a visual rather than a verbal experience. Painting had a social function; it created "the iconography of nationalism." Art historian Barbara Novak writes that landscape artists "were among the spiritual leaders of America's flock. The idea of community through nature runs clearly through all aspects of American social life in the first half of the nineteenth century." Angela Miller described the artists' "bid to become the voice of moral opposition to America's materially driven democracy." They made it their social responsibility to demonstrate the ultimate significance of the environment to Americans. As a result, Emerson's "transparent eyeball" could "go out to walk with a painter . . . [to] see for the first time groups, colors, clouds, and keepings, and shall have the pleasure of discovering resources in a hitherto barren ground."

How the Artists Conveyed Their Message: The Sublime

The landscape artists devised four filters, or mental screens, by which to turn wild nature into national scenery: the picturesque, the garden park, the Claude glass, and especially the sublime. Englishman William Gilpin's "picturesque" landscape paintings contained the requisite broken trunk and branches in the foreground—it was called a "blasted tree"—together with rustic bridges, lowing cattle, and a herdsman in English scenes, but for Americans more likely a solitary Indian in the Catskills. (The picturesque would also collapse into the trivial prettiness of a Victorian sentimentalism.) To this we can add the English landscape planner Capability Brown's "garden park" scenery that portrayed a grassy open field with a meandering stream or path in the requisite S shape, dotted with separate clumps of trees or bushes. The image became the model for American city parks as well as the lawns of middle-class homes, and its familiarity made high meadows in the Rockies attractive to tourists, such as Estes Park or Winter Park. A third convention was French artist George Claude's sepia-toned looking glass, the "Claude glass," through which a traveler looked to enhance the natural scene. The Claude glass brought on a plethora of pink, red, and rust wilderness sunset canvases. The viewer literally looked at a pleasant scene "through a rose-colored glass."

The "sublime" became the most important and powerful filter. It was popularized in the mid-eighteenth century by the English philosopher Edmund Burke, who argued that in nature there are profound elements that arouse the strongest human emotions, such as astonishment and passion. The merely "beautiful" may arouse admiration, reverence, and respect, but nature's sublime induces awe and a sense of the holy. Americans quickly attached the sublime to the American landscape, particularly its qualities of vastness, infinity, and magnificence. In this view, America's national geography was more than the merely beautiful (e.g., a pastoral landscape, rounded, discrete, orderly, full of pastels) of an Enlightenment sensibility. Jefferson in 1786 described the dramatic view from the heights of Monticello to his bosom friend, the landscape artist Maria Cosway, "Where has nature spread so rich a mantle under the eye? mountains, forests, rocks, rivers. With what majesty do we there ride above the storms! how sublime to look down into the workhouse of nature, to see her clouds, hail, snow, rain, thunder, all fabricated at our feet! And the glorious sun, when rising as if out of a distant water, just gilding the tops of the mountains, and giving life to all nature!" When a great artist created a sublime landscape canvas, it was supposed to evoke the highest human feelings out of its monumental craggy peaks, jagged precipices, mysterious dark valleys, with noble clouds and a darting consuming light, or everything obscured by a powerful storm. Water never simply flowed, it crashed and rushed and roared on the canvases. Trees and plants never were just brown sticks and green balloons; they were always primal, "animated by the breath of life," and heavily fecund. The colors were always blacks, browns, dark greens, and hazy yellows; bright pretty reds, whites, and blues did not commonly appear. The observer would not find landscape paintings of the sublime restful; they were designed to be exhilarating, cleansing, and redeeming, sending thrilling sensations of awe and dread, and sometimes joy and gladness.

The Rocky Mountains, craggy, monumental, snow covered, distant, became America's archetypal sublime. An ascent of a mountain has no practical side to it; it is devoted to the sheer act of conquest for the sake of a vantage point. The sight from this vantage point, according to a climber in 1852, "inspires the imagination more frequently than it satisfies the eye." Sometimes the experience of the sublime was literal, direct, and immediate. The government surveyor Clarence King climbed Mount Tyndall in 1871, there to encounter, he said, terrible desolation and intense self-awareness. No Jeffersonian Natural Bridge squeamishness here. The physical confrontation morphed into a spiritual encounter. On the mountain, which was a sublime expression of nature, exclaimed King, he was able to define his personal place in the vast scheme of creation. "Rising on the other side, cliff above cliff, precipice piled upon precipice, rock over rock, up against the sky towered the most gigantic mountain wall in America. I looked at it as one contemplating the purpose of his life." Instead of the Christian self or the rational self of the Enlightenment, King believed he had merged himself with a national self set in the American land.

The Social Message of Landscape Painting: Thomas Cole

In the picture on the parlor wall, the landscape painter Thomas Cole made certain that the observer saw that human beings were dwarfed by the primordial environment. Cole confessed, "I was alone and a stranger in the wilderness. Men in the midst of society and the tumult of cities do not experience those vicissitudes of feeling that result from the mutation of natural objects. But a lone man in the wild is affected by every change." One visitor to a gallery that exhibited a new landscape painting said, "How poor the boasted power of man, when the fall of a single cliff from those mountains [in the painting] would with ease destroy thousands of his race assembled on the plains below." Thomas Cole (1801–48) was born in Lancashire, England, and emigrated with his family in 1818 to settle in the upper Ohio Valley. Fellow artists and the public soon described him as America's most influential landscape artist. Cole believed the nation was abandoning its rich and powerfully evocative land to the spoils of profiteering. This exploitive path, he said, led to peril, a cycle of conquest and collapse already exposed in ancient empires such as the Persians and Romans. Indeed, Cole could not understand why Jacksonian Democrats, in power in the 1830s, admired the Roman Empire, which had been so obviously bent on self-destruction. If America instead followed its course as nature's nation, the collapse need not come. America could be humanity's first permanent civilization if it was properly footed in its particularly rich geography. Cole was nevertheless pessimistic about civilization, as shown in his five moralizing canvases of 1836, *The Course of Empire.* These were massive canvases depicting, according to a contemporary report,

Thomas Cole, *View from Mount Holyoke, Northampton, Massachusetts (The Oxbow)*, 1836. The Oxbow was a real location on the Connecticut River. On the left side, Cole depicted a rugged and tangled wilderness and, on the right side, a calm agricultural scene. Oil on canvas; 51½" x 76".

"the rise, decadence and final extinction of a nation, from the first stage of savage rudeness through all the stages of civilization to the very summit of human polish and human greatness, to its ultimate downfall." Cole's message was that civilization was a futile revolt against nature. He ambitiously endeavored to combine nature, history, and national identity in his art. The first canvas, *The Savage State*, shows a primitive humanity integrated into a rocky, cloudy, tumultuous, and sublime landscape. The second, *The Arcadian or Pastoral State*, reveals the same site now tamed, more pretty than sublime, humanity nurtured by a northern Italian city-state landscape. The third, *The Consummation of Empire*, is the American image of a Greek city-state (or Tower of Babel) that later would be embodied in the 1893 Chicago Columbian Exposition. Nature has mostly disappeared behind clusters of elaborate classical buildings crowded with people. Canvas four is *Destruction*, with smoke replacing clouds over the same site, civilization's order disintegrating into ruthless slaughter by barbarian invaders. Finally, we have *Desolation*, in which the ruins of the city are gradually overgrown by an encroaching nature. The people have disappeared from the picture, but nature serenely continues. Cole complained that the public adored the landscapes and refused to understand their message. In all five canvases, the same physical landscape stands as mute testimony to the rise and inevitable fall of human aspirations and "the final nothingness of man." Subduing the land was inevitable, but what had been lost in the futile attempt to domesticate nature?

Cole worked hard to create an iconography—archetypal scenes on the land—appropriate to American freedom and opportunity. He worried that there was still "a great defect in

American scenery." It could not find the ancient history of European landscapes, full of classical temples, great castle ruins, and Gothic cathedral towers. Americans were delighted to learn that the great English art critic John Ruskin said that mountains were scenic even if they were not dotted with romantic villages and glowering castles. Uninhabited mountains in Yosemite or Yellowstone could be scenic art. Cole insisted that he and his fellow artists could depict in the American historyless landscape, "the sublimity of a shoreless ocean un-islanded by the recorded deeds of man." Look at the paintings, Cole said, and see in them all a borderland. This line between wilderness and the pastoral can be seen in his 1836 canvas, *The Oxbow* of the Connecticut River, which reveals a landscape beyond the border, "off the map." Cole wrote, "We stand on the border of a civilized plain and look into the heart of nature."

The objective of the landscape art of Cole and his contemporaries was to bring Americans back to nature as the central source of a personal and national identity. Nature is permanent, whereas human affairs simply swing through constant historical cycles. If society was disengaged from close contact with nature, it would lose its organic balance and unleash humanity's worst impulses. Nature, Emerson had said, is a spiritualizing and moral force, without which humankind becomes a destroyer, a tyrant, and self-destructive. Americans are their best, in this view, when they are connected to the American land, a national landscape characterized by "greatness of scale, openness of prospect" that evokes in its lucky inhabitants a higher sensibility of liberty. This was a dramatic reversal from the prevailing capitalism and love of private property: Rather than owning the land, the Romantic painters rejoiced that nature owned them.

The intent of Transcendentalist landscape art was to root nationalism in the physical reality of the republic—purple mountain majesty, amber waves of grain, the fruited plain. Art historian Angela Miller writes, "Romantic nationalists located the substance of American nationalism—*the thing itself*—in the context or scene, the natural backdrop, of American society." Landscape artists saw in American scenery the textbook of a national character. The artist's duty was to create a set of common experiences and offer a set of reference points to be shared by otherwise unconnected people. One contemporary observer wrote that landscape painting combined "telescope, microscope, and kaleidoscope all in one." With a telescope one scanned the distant landscape to find a national identity; the microscope zeroed in on the bond between self and wilderness; turning the kaleidoscope gave the viewer the dazzling array of the natural environment. The Transcendentalist movement thus created an atmosphere where wilderness stood as a desirable, even utopian state, not a hostile forest to be cleared and planted as quickly as possible in domestic crops. The scenery could still be solitary, vast, mysterious, and chaotic, but it also was divine and sublime instead of demonic and life threatening. Happiness and well-being stood in reverse proportion to the degree of civilization. Yet there remained a conflict, shown early when Crèvecoeur invented the pastoral middle landscape, whether primitive wilderness or a pastoral utopia was archetypal America. Utopia was well fenced, cultivated, inhabited by happy yeoman, with a savage chaos held at bay outside.

Nature's Nation: America's Environmental Advantage

To the Transcendentalists, America was uniquely nature's nation. America had a distinct moral advantage over Europe because of its undefiled nature. Europe's environment was now overlaid by centuries of civilization; nature's voice was muffled in the Old World, but in America its song was loud and clear. The United States had the advantage that it still enjoyed an unspoiled geography where wild nature could be experienced and personally absorbed as sublime. New York's governor, De Witt Clinton, wrote, "Can there be a country in the world better calculated than ours to exercise and to exalt the imagination? Here nature has conducted her operations on a magnificent scale, this wild, romantic and awful scenery." This statement of the natural sublime invoked the newness and strangeness of America as anti-Europe. It was so decidedly different from Europe that it challenged all the old presuppositions about nature and thus also about humanity. Americans could rightly revel in their natural wonders: Jefferson's scary precipice atop Virginia's Natural Bridge, the thundering power of Niagara Falls, and later Yellowstone, Yosemite, and particularly the vista of the Grand Canyon. The Grand Canyon had a scale beyond credibility. The modern sojourner into the canyon, Colin Fletcher, wrote, "In that first moment of shock, with my mind already exploding beyond old boundaries, I knew that something had happened to the way I looked at things." Historian David E. Nye described such wonders (and wonderment) as part of a patriotic language of exceptionalism. These were signs, he said, of "a special relationship, or a covenant, between America and the Almighty . . . [they were] emblems of divinity comparable to the wonders of the ancient world and the greatest architectural achievements of modern times." Nye concluded, "Lacking the usual rallying points" of royal family, a national church, or a long history with its ruins, "Americans turned to the landscape as the source of national character." By the 1830s, they were making tourist pilgrimages to the natural wonders.

Nature's nation thus offered a fresh start in a spectacularly new Garden of Eden. Humankind's long-deformed soul would become unbent in the new landscape and be without guile, evil, or ugliness. Nature in America, where it was still untainted by civilization, projects "a roughhewn innocence and simplicity," in the words of historian Cathy Albanese, "the plain country virtue of those who dwelt in the free air of nature." America offered "the purity and wholesomeness of clean country living on the edge of an empowering wilderness." Thus Americans lived cheek to jowl with an unconquerable geography that they could unconditionally trust.

The Geography of Hope:
Utopian Communities in the Wilderness

In 1828 Thomas Cole completed a landscape canvas labeled *Garden of Eden*. He told his patron, "There are in it lofty distant mountains, a calm expansive lake, undulating grounds, a meandering river, cascades, gentle lawns, banks of beauteous flowers, harmless and graceful animals." One newspaper review said the canvas was "a landscape of gorgeous luxuriance, embued with the very spirit of repose, beauty, and happiness, and awakening the mind to a thousand delightful associations." Americans looked at Cole's painting, saw an American landscape, and imagined themselves in it. A recurrent theme in American history is that the New World environment offers humanity a second chance at Paradise. Americans believed they had the right geography for an earthly paradise if they could learn to live righteously in it.

"Utopia in Our Time": Its Inevitability

Many people in nineteenth-century America believed utopia was imminent, about to spring spontaneously from the nation's geography. The 1830s and 1840s in American history was an era, in philosopher Alfred North Whitehead's words, "when even wise men hoped." The features of the Second Eden were beginning to surface, many Americans felt, in upstate New York, where a combination of people of goodwill in a democratic society and the commercial benefits of the newly opened Erie Canal in 1836 resulted in a pastoral landscape that combined the benefits of blooming farms and light industry. A variety of utopian sects, millennial communities, and advocates for pure living began to dot the landscape. The people of the Oneida Community, who lived by manufacture of a patented animal trap and silverware, were practicing "free love" as innocently, they believed, as Adam and Eve. The Mormons got their start with Joseph Smith's discovery of sacred tablets in a cave near Palmyra, New York. The tablets were said to reveal a new scripture for the new age. The Millerites dared to set a date in 1843 (and once again in 1844) for the Second Coming. When Charles Grandison Finney's impassioned revivals brought in hundreds of instant converts, they believed they had already entered the spiritual kingdom of God despite worldly conditions around them. Sylvester Graham promoted his dietary cracker and joined other vegetarians who claimed the virtuous life started with a cleansed body. Later, in the 1860s and 1870s, Mary Baker Eddy, who founded the Church of Christ Scientist, said that when all people realized that the practice of physical health was a matter of faith, they would realize paradise. Admittedly, each group had its own ideas and practices, but most believed the differences would be sorted out in God's good time. It seemed to local folk that these were forerunners who would inevitably spread, merge, and locate the heavenly kingdom between Albany and Buffalo.

This flurry of activity led observers to call upstate New York the "Burnt-Over District." The spreading enthusiasm made it seem that utopia in America was no longer an impractical, impossible dream. Emerson wrote the English historian Thomas Carlyle in 1840, "We are all a little wild here with numberless projects for social reform. Not a reading man but has a draft for a new community in his waistcoat pocket." Public figures like newspapermen Horace Greeley and Charles A. Dana and optimistic churchmen like William E. Channing gave authority to the popular notion that the entire nation seemed on the verge of coalescing into utopia. The ideal life that was emerging in the preferred region along the Erie Canal in upper New York State would soon extend west as far as the deep prairie soils of Illinois and Iowa. The slave-holding South and the industrial slums of the East were excluded from the picture. People noted that outside the Burnt-Over District there were already several communities of clean-living celibate Shakers. In the Midwest, towns appeared with names like New Harmony and Old Economy. The peace-loving cooperative Amana Community had surfaced in distant Iowa. More than 100 experimental communities had begun to expand across wild forest and broad farmland.

Even secular developments in the 1830s and 1840s seemed to undergird the possibility of utopia in one's own lifetime. These included America's continued territorial expansion, which created fresh land to the Pacific Coast, the broader voting franchise of Jacksonian democracy, new space-conquering technologies such as the telegraph and the railroads, innovations in public schools, mental health institutions, and medical procedures, reformers who urged liberation for black slaves and for white women, and prohibitionists against alcohol, tobacco, and coffee. Ordinary life got better when Walter Hunt invented a reliable safety pin,

Elias Howe designed the sewing machine, Goodyear learned to vulcanize rubber, and others discovered how to preserve food in cans, make cheap clocks, plate glass, and safety matches, and manufacture better plows and stoves. The gradual emergence of the Promised Land, admittedly piecemeal across the American landscape, seemed to many Americans to reveal their land's designated role in God's overall plan for humanity. It was no surprise to them that America was showing the way for the rest of the world by its example of a rich and benevolent geography coupled with wise use through farming and light industry. It was a very pleasant form of environmental determinism.

Utopia Uniquely Set on America's Land

Utopian logic went something like this: The old feudal villages of Europe enjoyed close human relations, but their living conditions were terrible because basic material necessities were always scarce. It was too easy to freeze or starve to death, be killed in warfare, or simply die from bad diet and overwork. At the other extreme, modern industrial society pulled people away from family ties and face-to-face relationships and made them cogs in impersonal factories run for crass material gain only. In contrast, the idea of utopia meant provision for a combination of human needs that included material security, community participation, and personal self-fulfillment. It seemed self-evident to many Americans that utopia would not appear in a feudal or industrial environment, but could find its natural setting in the American pastoral landscape. Among the fistfuls of utopian plans that Emerson reported to Carlyle, many looked to the American environment as the place to fulfill existing plans, mostly derived from European concepts. Models from the past included not only the Garden of Eden, but the New Jerusalem of the millennium, Greek city-states, Renaissance cities of northern Italy, Thomas More's *Utopia*, Voltaire's *Candide*, Rousseau's noble savage, and even Captain Cook's report on the idyllic Tahiti in the South Pacific. Americans especially got caught up with the views of contemporary European reformers, notably Robert Owen, Etienne Cabet, and Charles Fourier. These three looked to the "empty" and "pristine" American landscape, mostly in the Midwest, as the last place left on earth to establish pilot communities (Cabet called them "villages of holiness"). Only in American space could their beliefs be practiced by relatively uncorrupted people in an unspoiled setting. Europeans projected on America their own hopes and aspirations, stereotypes of the ideal society. The details were much fuzzier about practical matters like equality, private property, physical labor, sex roles, and resolution of conflict. More than a dozen communities with European origins were established in the 1820s and 1830s, but they soon failed because they seemed to be the gathering places for uncooperative self-righteous cranks, and because no one believed it was their destiny to empty slop buckets and spread manure instead of writing poetry.

Another concept of utopia involved grassroots idealism instead of a preconceived social agenda. Americans looked to the empty wilderness as the one place the ideal society could be established unmolested. In a primitive landscape, it was claimed people could be disarmingly simple. (Americans seemed to have short memories about frontier hardships.) One could relive the excitement of "beginnings," recover a primordial humanity, and return to innocence. Romantic motifs of "escape" *from* civilization's evil and corruption, and of the path of "discovery" *into* wild nature, became the latest popular fad. Whatever their internal rationale, when Americans rushed toward ideal communities in the 1830s and 1840s, they invariably beat a path into newly opened regions that offered fertile land and was simultaneously inexpensive and readily available. Large parcels of land away from other settlements provided seclusion, a space to act out their plans without intervention.

The Environment of the Human Body

Most utopian groups thought that perfection also extended to the human body. The Shakers, who believed sexual relations had been the root of all sin since Adam and Eve, successfully practiced celibacy, but to unsuccessful ends. Religious historian Sydney Ahlstrom wrote, "In a simple Yankee way these Shaker villages were, in fact, idyllic: the wants of life were fully, even abundantly supplied; the clean-lined functional buildings, spotless interiors, gracefully practical furniture, wonderful cattle herds, fine herb gardens, and perfectly tended fields all witnessed to organizational, social, and economic success." By 1794, 12 Shaker communities had taken hold in New York, Massachusetts, New Hampshire, Connecticut, and Maine. More soon appeared in Kentucky, Ohio, and Indiana, reaching a peak between 1830 and 1850, when some 6,000 Shakers lived in 19 communities. At the other extreme, in the 1830s John Humphrey Noyes preached "plural marriage," with free choice of sexual partners to avoid the conflict of jealousy. Charges of "free love" drove his community from New Hampshire in 1848 to the more tolerant atmosphere at Oneida in New York's Burnt-Over District.

A victory over physical weakness and disease was presumed to be the wellspring for spiritual recovery as well. (Although people who were permanently maimed or crippled rarely fit into anyone's utopian picture.) Disease was considered some form of lapse from moral perfection, although faith healing was often backed up with secular medical knowledge. Popular belief in personal cleansing and well-being through diet made Sylvester Graham the high priest of vegetarianism in the 1840s and 1850s. A passage in the book of Genesis seemed to him to urge the eating of herbs, seeds, fruit, and nuts instead of meat. He concluded that bread made from whole wheat flour, chewed well, would supply nearly all basic dietary needs. Such a diet would also reduce dangerous sexual drive, together with denial of the use of salt. Graham devised a special universal cracker using coarsely ground wheat. One 1843 testimonial said, "I subsisted on a quantity of coarse bread, so small that it was barely sufficient to sustain life. I at the same time paid particular attention to bathing, exercise, &c. I had not proceeded far, before I became as 'a little child.' My mind underwent a most surprising change, and a flood of light was poured in upon it. It appeared to me that I could see into almost everything. I was a new creature, physically, morally, and spiritually." Graham's road to happiness also included abstaining from alcohol, wearing light clothes instead of the weighty wool garments of the day, sleeping on a hard mattress, and the extraordinary step of bathing three times weekly instead of once a week. The utopian groups almost universally denounced alcohol, coffee, and other stimulants. Humans were said to be like machines. Ill health was described as the disorder of malfunctioning parts that led to mechanical degeneration and physical breakdown. One benefit of these popular health nostrums was that they turned many Americans away from the "heroic" medical practices of the day, such as bleeding, blistering, physic, and ingestion of mercury.

American utopianism also included mind cure. The Burnt-Over District was home to the hypnotism movement and Mesmerist utopias. Mesmerism involved "animal magnetism," by which human beings could influence each other by means of an invisible fluid that permeates and connects all living things. When the fluid was in a balanced ebb and flow, people were healthy. Interruptions were illness. A "magnetic doctor" had the power to alter the flow in the invisible fluid to unblock obstructions. One popular practitioner, Phileas Parkhurst Quimby, explained, "I know that a belief in any disease will create a chemical change in the mind, and that a person will create a phenomenon corresponding to the symptoms." In other words, sickness was in the mind. A bad mental attitude was like sin; a good mental attitude brought healing grace. Different mind-cure philosophies argued that mental powers could create balance or imbalance in the physical body, and thus health or illness.

Many Americans believed that by changing the environment—external, internal, or both—humanity could realize its potential. Violation of nature's immutable laws resulted in the stern and debilitating judgment of disease. (This was an extension of Puritan divine judgment from nature's plagues.) A return to health came from a return to harmony with nature's laws. According to one homeopathy journal in 1851, a sick person "through ignorance has violated some law of nature, and pain and sickness is the inevitable result. Pain is but the result of violated Nature." Homeopathy, osteopathy (muscular manipulation), and chiropractic (spinal adjustment) all believed healing was restoration to a natural harmony. Hydropathy involved drinking prodigious quantities of fresh cold water daily, combined with head baths, leg baths, pelvic baths, washtub baths, and long cold showers. By the late nineteenth century, there were widely advertised cures from electrical current devices. The Sears, Roebuck and Company catalog offered for sale X-ray machines and electrical stimulation devices for the home.

Later in the nineteenth century, the picture got urbanized. Both Edward Bellamy's popular 1888 novel *Looking Backward* and the 1893 Columbian Exposition in Chicago looked forward to highly industrialized and urbanized utopias. In fact, many visions of the future saw a vast and appealing city spread across a pastoral landscape. Robert Owen's utopia in the wilderness was still a city plan. World's fairs displayed the latest improvements and promised the public that humanity's ills and conflicts would be overcome by new inventions. Recent utopian plans produced the "garden city" idea in New York, the planned community at Columbia, Maryland, gigantic enclosed shopping centers such as those in Minnesota and Edmonton, Alberta, Canada, and the obvious fabrications of Epcot Center. However, beginning with Oswald Spengler's *The Decline of the West*, published in 1919 following World War I, Americans would pay more attention to dystopia than utopia. Utopia in the American wilderness came to be treated as an unachievable myth. The concept of the free individual liberated by a seemingly utopian frontier lifestyle persists today primarily in our movie and television mythologies about fiercely autonomous cowboys, proud wise Indians, and self-sufficient farmers. None are very factual. For a time in the 1960s and 1970s, counterculture or alternative-society communes attempted a return to the simple outdoor life, mostly in mild climates.

In sum, we can speak of four patterns of environment-centered utopianism in America. First were the regional attempts, as in New York's Burnt-Over District. This utopianism espoused a special geographical location for the millennium to appear. Second claimed that the perfect society was a type of environment, the pastoral, the combination of a benign landscape shaped by honest labor. A third escaped "beyond the border" into the wilderness, away from civilization, where humans could find harmony by close existence with primordial nature. The fourth flirted with cities and technology, both cleansed of their flaws as depicted by a series of world's fairs. In all four cases, the environment plays a critical role as a renewing and cleansing force. In none of the four cases is the environment the center of evil.

The Technological Sublime: Romancing the Machine

As early as the 1820s the image of America as a romantic paradise included technology. Even Thomas Jefferson, by then the nation's elder statesman (he died on July 4, 1826), believed that his revered yeoman farmer could only be benefited by a myriad of labor-saving field and barnyard machines. Americans had come to believe hopefully that mechanical improvements would be harmonious with nature. The Erie Canal and steamboats (soon also the railroads) joined Virginia's Natural Bridge and Niagara Falls (soon also the Grand Canyon and Yellowstone) as American icons. The agrarian landscape, industrial development, western expansion, democratic institutions, and Manifest Destiny together formed one seamless national vision. Historian David E. Nye describes a "technological sublime" that complemented the landscape sublime and for some Americans surpassed it. Nye finds that Americans have long paid homage to steam locomotives, great sailing ships, bridges, skyscrapers, factories, dams, space vehicles, sports stadiums, airports, and other spectacular technological achievements. Just as the experience of the sublime in nature established a connection with "reality," so the technological sublime also unveiled the transcendent significance of a nation moving toward industrial modernity. (The concept is not really new: The so-called Seven Wonders of the Ancient World, such as the pyramids, were all man made. The Romans celebrated roads, aqueducts, and other public works.) Although Americans still romanticized about the rural landscape, they cheered its transformation into a constructed infrastructure. Andrew Jackson told Americans in his second annual message to Congress that the technological sublime was the wave of the future: "What good man would prefer a country covered with forests and ranged by a few thousand savages to our extensive Republic, studded with cities, towns and prosperous farms, embellished with all the improvements which art can devise or industry execute?" Nye described most Americans of the Jacksonian period as people who "were swallowing the world through direct action: assaulting the natural world with axes, shovels, plows, and railroads, literally reworking the landscape." They had no doubts over "usurping the place of natural things with man-made objects [and] vigorously projecting themselves into the world, mixing their labor with it, and building internal improvements." They believed in a seamless connection between landscape and technology as a single force that defined Americanism. There were very few machine-smashing Luddites in America.

The America—Nouveau Europe—of Man-Made Monuments

America's most dramatic technological sublime was the steam locomotive and the embracing network of railroads. The rail network knit together the nation's people across their large geography; virtually everyone adored the railroad, from Thoreau to Walt Whitman. The locomotive's speed and power was a triumph over both space and time. It assured Americans who feared that the nation was already too large and too heterogeneous, and might not endure. Instead, the nation learned of its own new closeness as the railroads constructed their "bands of iron." The popular orator Edward Everett spoke for most Americans when he described the railway locomotive as "a miracle of science, art, and capital, a magic power . . . by which the forest is thrown open, the lakes and rivers are bridged, and all Nature yields to man." Nye

WHEN THE ERIE Canal opened in October 1825 it became the model for all future technological sublime experiences. Americans celebrated it as a thrilling moment in the nation's history. Canal historian Ronald E. Shaw described the 300-mile-long acclamation of the victory over nature's obstacles:

> Crowds gathered everywhere. Visitors in holiday spirit flocked to the canal from miles around. Horses and carriages filled the roads. People covered the towpath, crowded the bridges, and pressed forward to hear speeches of welcome, speeches of responses, and speeches of farewell. Arches garlanded with evergreens and flowers spanned the canal at nearly every village and supported banners praising [New York governor] Clinton, republicanism, or internal improvements. Bands played and cannon thundered in salute.

In an oration as the flotilla from Albany sailed into New York harbor, Clinton told his cheering audience that the canal was comparable to an overland connection between the Mediterranean Sea and the Atlantic Ocean. It had become the nation's first technological pilgrimage site where excited tourists found proof of America's superior engineering skill. The pilgrims turned several sites into famous landmarks because locks and aqueducts and cuts through solid rock demonstrated control over natural forces. Most famous were the 802-foot stone aqueduct that carried the canal over the Genesee River at Rochester and the ladder of five locks in the aptly named Lockport that carried boats up a giant staircase over the rocky Niagara escarpment.

quotes an 1840s essayist on the permanent impact of the railroads: Americans had "dug through plains, hills, and solid rocks, in our long lines of canals and railroads, works that have stamped upon the soil a lasting impression, which, if the republic were swept away, and all records of its extense blotted out forever, would be viewed by posterity with the same wonder with which we now gaze upon the mouldering ruins of Rome, the marble temples of the Acropolis, the pyramids of Egypt, and the track of the Appian Way." The transcontinental railroad link put the vastness of the West into perspective; technology consumed America's geography. It became a yet grander object of adoration. The modern historian Susan Danly described the new technological sublime that overshadowed the natural sublime: True, humankind was dwarfed by the monuments of nature, but technology "stands triumphant" over the wilderness. Soon, she suggested, "the geometry of the new cities" would stand larger than "the panoramic vista of mountains." The technological sublime featured a new dimension: There were no limits to its powers. It permitted continuous growth, experienced continuous innovation, and would transform the world.

The newly professionalized civil engineers strode across the American landscape like conquering supermen endowed with godlike powers. In the 1830s they received public accolades for widely admired public waterworks in New York City, Philadelphia, and Boston. By midcentury they were America's new heroes. These engineers, Nye noted, were not only rational technicians, but belonged to a moral crusade to bring progress to society and "embraced transcendental ideas." The monumentally sublime objects they created were "gateways to the imagination." Dams, railroad bridges, tunnels, great harbor wharves, and hydraulic systems appeared to be triumphs over the physical powers of nature. Emerson admitted, "A scientific engineer, with instruments and steam, is worth many hundred men, many thousands." When steam engineer George H. Corliss watched while President Grant and the emperor of Brazil turned cranks to start his great central engine that powered the Philadelphia Centennial Exposition of 1876, the *Scientific American* reported that "perhaps for the first time in the history of mankind, two of the greatest rulers in the world obeyed the order of an inventor citizen." Beginning in 1876, Americans flocked to a series of technology-celebrating world's fairs, notably in Chicago in 1893 and 1933. The 1939 New York World's Fair was the leading display of a technology-based future as Americans crowded to see dioramas of a futuristic United States in 1960.

The technological sublime continued to expand into the twentieth century. The railroad network put every small town onto its schedule. Americans had celebrated the Brooklyn Bridge as a "trophy of triumph over an obstacle of Nature." Skyscrapers seemed to fulfill the literal meaning of their name in Chicago and New York. The urban skyline seemed more dramatic than the Front Range of the Rockies or the Tetons. Industrial "parks" competed with national parks. Automobile, trucking, and airplane networks replicated and intensified the railroad original. Modernity seemed to hum in the white, bright, efficient, sterile, uninhabited electric power stations, where dynamos served, as *Colliers* magazine said in the late 1920s, to bring the equivalent services of "23 slaves for every citizen." When the Empire State Building rose to completion in eleven months and Hoover Dam in less than three years in the 1930s, Americans believed even the Depression was surmountable.

Some stupendous events were momentary but nevertheless equally sublime. Americans were truly shocked when the ultimate technology, nuclear energy, was first used to blast 300,000 humans at Hiroshima and Nagasaki in August 1945. Writer Spencer Weart concluded that the bombings "seemed less like a military action than a rupture of the very order of things." The volcanic eruption of Mount St. Helens on May 18, 1980, was as monumental and affecting as the 1981 Challenger space shuttle disaster, one natural, the other technological. Other American apocalypses that crossed the line between human made and natural were the Chicago fire of 1871, the Johnstown flood of 1889, and the San Francisco earthquake and fire of 1906. Today these are matched by jumbo jet disasters, hurricanes that roar inland from the Atlantic Ocean and Gulf of Mexico, and torrential rains that turn the Mississippi and Missouri rivers into tumultuous mile-wide floods. Americans were comforted by the truly sublime experience of the Apollo space program when it put astronauts on the moon in 1969. But Americans have also deliberately stumbled into the bizarre sublime of Las Vegas.

Conclusion: The Transcendentalist Failure of Nerve

Perceptive modern observers, like the novelist and critic D. H. Lawrence, believed that Transcendentalism experienced a failure of nerve as Americans wrestled with industrial urban modernity. Fellow critic Wright Morris agreed, "Nature—even Nature tooth and claw—is child's play when confronted with *human* nature." The Transcendentalist movement, despite its apparent rebellion against religion and rationalism, was riddled through and through with civilized respectability. It was largely an intellectual movement without a social, economic, or political program. Cultural historian Perry Miller wrote that an America closely allied with nature could not face other questions. "How then it can cope with New York, Detroit, Gary . . .?" The Transcendentalist tendency to see God in all of nature—a pantheism that also encompassed humanity—seemed out of place and irrelevant as Americans entered a scientific and industrial age after the Civil War. The natural sublime required a dialogue between the individual and the object, but among Transcendentalists the observer's interior space became more central than physical place. Nye called this a slip into the "egotistical sublime" as the mind projected its interior state onto the external world. Most Americans were fascinated by the Transcendentalist view of nature, but they simply didn't believe it. They could "feel" this view of nature, but they couldn't "use" it, and therefore gave up on it. They said a resounding "No!" to Emerson when he moved toward pure spirit and away from "disagreeable appearances, swine, spiders, snakes, pests, madhouses, prisons, enemies," which he hoped would vanish. Later in the century, in Mark Twain's *Life on the Mississippi*, the tourist on the riverboat saw a sublime landscape, but the river pilot pragmatically watched the river for sandbars, snags, floating trees, perverse currents, and other dangers.

For Further Reading

Readers should start with Roderick Nash, *Wilderness and the America Mind* (3rd ed., 1982), a bona fide classic in American environmental history. In Chapters 3–5 Nash describes American romanticism and its position in both American intellectual history and the history of environmental literature. Still indispensable is Stow Persons, *American Minds: A History of Ideas* (1958). Among Persons's insightful and comprehensive essays in intellectual history see "Natural History," "Facets of Romanticism," and "Transcendentalism." The third essential classic is Donald Worster, *Nature's Economy: The Roots of Ecology* (1977, and a new expanded edition in 1994). This is still the best researched and most thoughtful analysis of the historical origins of the modern environmental movement. "Part Two. The Subversive Science: Thoreau's Romantic Ecology" remains the best study of transcendentalism, especially as it identifies how it anticipated certain aspects of modern environmentalism. See also Albert Furtwangler, *Acts of Discovery: Visions of America in the Lewis and Clark Journals* (1993). For a new analysis of the connections among nature, literature, and nationalism, see Lawrence Buell's subtle and complex study, *The Environmental Imagination: Thoreau, Nature Writing, and the Formation of American Culture* (1995). Nor should the perceptive essays by Perry Miller on Emerson and Thoreau be forgotten: *Errand into the Wilderness* (1956) and *Nature's Nation* (1967). Readers will find the original sources a real treat. There are several good editions of key writings, such as Jefferson's *Notes on the State of Virginia* (widely available in the Viking Portable Library), Crèvecoeur's *Letters from an American Farmer,* Emerson's essays (Viking Portable Library), and Henry David Thoreau, *Walden* and *Civil Disobedience* (Owen Thomas, ed., 1966), in the extremely useful Norton Critical Edition, containing full texts, background materials, and a broad spectrum of analytical reviews and essays. For the all-important landscape artists, start with Barbara Novak, *Nature and Culture: American Landscape and Painting, 1825–1875* (1980), which begins with an innovative analysis of America as a "garden." Novak identifies America's "iconological roots"—rocks, clouds, and plants—and how humans' traces—axe, train, figure—took over. See also Angela Miller, *The Empire of the Eye: Landscape Representation and American Cultural Politics, 1825–1875* (1993), which is a comprehensive study of the ambivalence of American landscape painters toward American nationalism and sectionalism. Recent views are also collected in Mick Gidley and Robert Lawson-Peebles (eds.), *Views of American Landscapes* (1989). Utopia and the wilderness are covered in Persons (earlier) and in the creative study by Catherine L. Albanese, *Nature Religion in America: From the Algonkian Indians to the New Age* (1990). The broader cultural and historical context of this minority report that valued wilderness and nature can be found in Nash (earlier), Hans Huth, *Nature and the American: Three Centuries of Changing Attitudes* (1957, 1990), and especially Max Oelschlaeger, *The Idea of Wilderness, from Prehistory to the Age of Ecology* (1991). David Nye's *American Technological Sublime* (1994) was anticipated by Perry Miller's posthumous fragments, *The Life of the Mind in America* (1965), Leo Marx's *The Machine in the Garden: Technology and the Pastoral Ideal in America* (1964), and John Kasson's *Civilizing the Machine: Technology and Republic Values in America, 1776–1900* (1976).

PART THREE

CREATING THE INDUSTRIAL INFRASTRUCTURE

CHAPTER SEVEN

DETERMINING AMERICA'S ENVIRONMENTAL FUTURE: THE RUSH TO INDUSTRIALIZE

I look upon the invention of Mr. Bessemer as almost the greatest invention of the ages. I do not mean measured by its chemical or mechanical attributes. I mean by virtue of its great results upon the structure of society and government. It is the great enemy of privilege. It is the great destroyer of monopoly. It will be the great equalizer of wealth. Those who have studied its effects on transportation, the cheapening of food, the lowering of rents, the obliteration of aristocratic privilege will readily comprehend what I mean.

—INDUSTRIALIST ABRAM HEWITT ON THE
BESSEMER BLAST FURNACE FOR STEEL PRODUCTION, 1892

The man who builds a factory builds a temple, the man who works there worships there.

— CALVIN COOLIDGE, 1926

The Attractions of Industrialization

Why Work in a Factory?

There is a story that in Afghanistan in the 1950s, after the Russians built a cement factory, local tribesmen refused to work in it because the labor was too inhuman and demanding. The Afghans, a proud, rugged, and fiercely independent people, said they would not become like slaves. In the last half of the nineteenth century in the United States, when iron foundries, coal mines, and manufacturing plants began to dominate the landscape, tens of thousands of men, women, and children did voluntarily leave their rural farms or village shops to take on killing, dirty, wretched, physical work in the factories. They were joined by millions of immigrants from the Old World.

Over history, most people sought to avoid such horrible labor. Fear over physical contact with coal and metal ores reaches far back in time. When the Romans wanted to dig coal or make iron, they had to use foreign prisoners or Christian slaves because no self-respecting citizen was willing to do the work. Underground coal mining not only required hard labor to acquire a filthy product but also it was said to waken demonic powers because it intruded on the realm of Hades. Above ground, the heat, fumes, and labor of the big vats of molten ore meant that the iron puddler rarely lived into middle age. His work, because it metamorphosed raw materials from an ore with the texture of dirt or stone into the hardness of iron, seemed close to the mysteries of alchemy and witchcraft, like a compact with the devil. Mining and smelting remained limited, although useful, occupations that were considered outside the powers of ordinary people.

By the time of England's Industrial Revolution in the eighteenth century, French visitors wondered how villagers and farmers near the new iron forges could abide the filthy smoke and soot, horrible smells and pounding noises, as well as the intense, constant, and life-threatening work. The French, who had not yet undergone the Industrial Revolution, produced small quantities of wrought-iron grillwork for the rich. This did not change daily life for ordinary people. In contrast, the efficiently productive English factories poured out an endless stream of pots and pans, iron hearths, and the latest farm tools that were available to all classes of society. The greatest ambition of ordinary laborers was to buy what they made. Despite the unpleasant grime, uncomfortable and intense labor, and immense investment that might have gone elsewhere, tireless mechanization did produce a staggering abundance of cheap, desirable goods. What had formerly been luxury items became commonplace. Across the newly industrialized regions, ordinary people living on bread and cheese nevertheless ate off real plates, used a knife and fork, drank from a cup or mug, had a four-poster bed, glass in their windows, and washed their meals down with wine in France, beer in Germany, gin in England, and whiskey in America. As a result, one writer said in astonishment, "Never have so many wills been coordinated so closely by voluntary mutual consent as in the western metropolis, and for such material splendor!" The eighteenth-century French philosopher Jean-Jacques Rousseau called it the willingness to "bear with docility the yoke of public happiness." Almost 200 years later, the optimistic slogan over the entrance to the 1933 Chicago World's Fair told respectful visitors, "Science Finds—Industry Applies—Man Conforms." Industrialization seemed to be a rational decision about a rational process of production. Revelation of its human costs and environmental devastation lay mostly in the future.

In truth, factory work is not a natural human activity, whether for Afghan tribesmen or American steelworkers. The question of work is a global human question. Factory work requires extremely rigid, repetitive, and mechanical activity. Human nature works best at a variable rate, in fits and starts, with bursts of creative energy and periods of rest and contemplation. No one anticipated the severe demands from the steady unbroken output of the new factory discipline in the early textile mills or shoe or clock factories (described in Chapter 4). Everything began, paused and stopped, and restarted in unison, according to the needs of the steady whirring, clanking, or click clack of the spinning machines, steam engines, lathes, and presses of the nineteenth century. Workers had to be literally broken into the unremitting demands set by machine and clock. Clock time has always been out of phase with human time. Factory workers were reduced to "hands" while "skill" was built into the machines so workers needed little themselves. The continuous mechanical activity of the factory floor seemed to be precisely the kind of work that minimized humanity's unique superiority to brute creatures. There seemed to be no need for education, mental sensitivity, or initiative. The less they had of these, the more workers would be docile servants to the machines. Workers were expected to be mindless cogs in the industrial process, similar to the equipment and raw materials.

The factory system found its most favorable climate in America. On American soil, economic advancement was understood to be a personal duty, part of a work ethic that goes back to Puritan rigorousness. A middle-class dogma stated that the virtues of hard work and self-discipline in a factory system would reap enormous rewards. Americans made the consumption of goods one of their life's goals. At the turn of the century, the philosopher John Dewey complained, "We have harnessed this power [of industrialization] to the dollar rather than to liberation and enrichment of human life." American commitment to work and to the "job" often went deeper than personal roots, family connections, and geographical location. The controlling feature of most people's lives was the factory, its machines, hours on the job, and the wages received in compensation.

Mechanization Takes Command

By the late nineteenth century, the Industrial Revolution had altered the physical structure of America more swiftly, steadily, and radically than anything else. America had slipped comfortably within the memory of a single generation from thousands of self-contained communities in rural isolation to an interconnected industrial society. The drama of the change cannot be overstated. The earlier rural and agricultural world had become obsolete. The local artisan who once served farmstead and town, and who had been intimate with nature, was superseded by the blue-collar worker, professional engineer, and middle-class manager, now serving the new industrial technology together with corporate capitalist organization. The steam railroad and electrified streetcars offered cheap and convenient transportation for workers and travelers as they linked cities, towns, and rural villages. The telegraph and telephone sped information across the country in split-second time. Middle-class city dwellers enjoyed the advantages of technology-based networks, including electric power distributed to homes, stores, and factories, and fresh water supplies and sewer systems to wash away society's wastes. Machines took over the hard labor of hammering, cutting, shaping, grinding, and drilling iron, stone, and steel. Successful factories that hummed in the cities seemed the necessary condition for a democratic, individualistic, and opportunistic society. It assumed that an accelerated flow of goods would be cumulative and self-sustaining—a perpetual-motion growth machine. Those among the poor in the slums dreamed that such prosperity would be theirs in the near future. Whereas in 1850, 8 out of 10 Americans lived on the farm, by 1900 farmers made up 5 out of 10 Americans. By 1950 only 4 out of 100 Americans were still on the farm, which apparently leveled off at a mere 2 out of 100 in 1970.

Whatever price would be exacted by the harsh laws of economic competition was tempered by faith in abundant opportunity. Americans fervently believed that anyone could open a store, a mill, a machine shop, even a railroad. Such entrepreneurs faced no feudal constraints to reduce their opportunities or take their wealth. They could even fail without recrimination and start again, confident they would eventually succeed. Generous bankruptcy laws assured a second and even third chance. There were other favorable factors: American society experienced a chronic shortage of skilled labor that encouraged labor-saving devices. It enjoyed an ever-growing market based on a large middle class with disposable income. Not the least, Americans also were privileged inhabitants of a highly supportive physical environment. They had the material advantages of a benign climate, seemingly infinite supplies of soil and water, and, it appeared, mountains of iron, copper, lead, and other industrial raw materials. Americans also enjoyed an unusual level of political unity and public order across an extensive geography.

Most Americans believed that a technological triumphalism had overwhelmed nature and removed its burdens from their backs. Nature ceased to be life's master. The newly mechanized workplace itself depended less on the daily rounds of sunrise and sunset, the changes of the seasons, and the mercy of shifting winds and fickle weather. Electric lighting turned night into day. Factories know no seasons. Despite the Transcendentalist's appreciation of nature's intrinsic value, most Americans believed they owned an infinitely rich and expanding territory that in its raw state was useless. And by midcentury, they were convinced that industry, technology, and the spirit of enterprise were the tools to capture and enjoy the wealth previously entrapped within nature. Nature would soon be theirs to be used for personal enrichment. One economist, David A. Wells, looked back over the previous 30 years from the vantage point of 1889: "Man in general has attained to such a greater control over the forces of Nature, that he has been able to do far more work in a given time, produce far more product, measured by quantity in ratio to a given amount of labor, and reduce the effort necessary to insure a comfortable subsistence in a far greater measure [than had ever before been possible]."

What in fact became of the preindustrial "nature's nation"? Americans wanted both—a society linked to the land as its birthright, but also pushing aggressively toward industrial wealth. Cultural historian John Kasson wrote in the 1970s, "For the bulk of Americans, to be both Nature's nation and a rapidly developing industrial power was not a contradiction, but the fulfillment of America's destiny." Historian of technology Howard P. Segal added that Americans believed that "America's special nature would somehow allow the nation to preserve its pre-industrial character while absorbing the latest technological developments." Historian Walter Licht suggests that Americans had for a time enjoyed several options before they fell under the hegemony of industrial capitalism. They might have continued their evolution as a "self-regulating society of self-sufficient yeoman producers" resulting in a "nation of ordered, ethical communities." They might have enlarged on the emergence of "Republican Virtue"—"modern-minded, inventive producers who sought not personal gain but simple well-being and rights for all," or, third, an "enterprising, commercialized, individualist order where merit and not privilege or favor reigned." Instead, Licht joins other historians such as Carroll Pursell to find the emergence of a "modernized nation-state administered and advanced by civil and corporate elites" that swept alternatives aside. Despite a new class of predatory "robber barons," technological triumphalism was taken to be so beneficial that it did not require the checks and balances which keep the political process from spinning into chaos.

Admittedly, some Americans did not participate in the new material abundance. Distant dryland farmers on the Plains or mountaineer families in Appalachian hollows envied city dwellers. Rural electrification and paved roads did not reach them until the New Deal rushed these improvements to them in the 1930s. Millions of the poor in city slums only dreamed of middle-class material wealth. Americans were slow in coming to recognize the difficulties of city life for workers and their families. They had long been committed to the unregulated use of private property, adoration of the aggressive entrepreneur, and a self-help ethic even for those in the poverty-stricken ghettos. Not until the 1830s did a Jacksonian reformer, Theodore Swdgwick II, determine that the problem of cities was not moral but material: "Do something about people sleeping in cellars and garrets and living in holes and dens, clean up the filthy streets, provide the means of cleanliness and health [and] then the city would assume its place as the site of opportunity and no longer be a social problem." According to this view, the city may house evil but it has the potential for humane community. It is easy today to condemn the negative results of industrialization—the terrible pollution, waste, and ugliness of America's old rust-belt heartland. Even those cities that have recovered in the best of ways, like Pittsburgh, Cleveland, and Cincinnati, or those still characterized by obsolete mills and factories, like Youngstown or Gary or Newark, were indelibly scarred by their industrialization. It is equally easy to damn nineteenth-century Americans who accepted the human and environmental degradation of the factory system. But they were not stupid or foolish people, and they had hopes and dreams and expectations much like ours. Everywhere they turned, it seemed that industrialization created new wonders. One was the steel industry.

The Dramatic Example of Steel

After the Civil War, by 1870, iron and steel production became the fourth largest American industry, surpassed only by lumber and woodworking, flour and gristmilling, and textiles. In the 1870s and 1880s steel magnate Andrew Carnegie (1835–1919) was among the first to create a vertically integrated industrial operation. An immigrant from Scotland, he soon controlled the process of making steel from digging the iron ore to selling finished steel rails to the railroads. Even he said he was amazed at the industrial miracle that allowed him to become a very rich man by selling steel for two-thirds of a cent a pound. Into this pound of steel went 2 pounds of iron ore that had been dug by enormous steam shovels out of Minnesota's open-pit Mesabi mines ("the biggest hole ever made by man"), then transported 1,000 miles to Pittsburgh first by large ore ships to be reloaded onto long ore trains. One pound of steel also consumed 1.3 pounds of coal mined in West Virginia and shipped 50 miles to Pittsburgh to be roasted into coke. To the coke was added one-third of a pound of limestone, quarried in Ohio and carried 150 miles to Pittsburgh. There the materials were combined in one of many Bessemer blast furnaces at the Carnegie Steel Works along the Monogahela River on Pittsburgh's south side. A blast furnace is one of the most massive structures of the industrial world. The red-hot new steel was then rolled, drawn, and shaped into rails. The steel rails went to the industry at two-thirds of a cent a pound.

Americans moved faster to use the Bessemer furnace than other industrial nations because they were less encumbered by traditional steel-making processes. They quickly learned how to make one American converter do the work of five British or European units. By 1900 the United States surpassed Britain's formidable steel industry of a million tons a year. In that year, dozens of American companies shipped out 10 million tons of steel for railroads and locomotives, bridges and buildings, machine tools and household appliances. Among other demands, Americans desperately needed steel rails, which were seven times more durable than iron rails, for the expanding railways that would bind together the nation. Americans everywhere stood in awe of the promise of widespread steel production; its use became the physical manifestation of American political democracy and economic opportunity. In 1892 the industrialist Abram Hewitt praised the Bessemer converter as a great technological feat that would bring enormous benefits to the outermost reaches of society. Hewitt's view reinforced the common belief that technical solutions abounded to correct social problems. Steel became the universal substance of American development for the century between 1850 and 1950. Before that, as we have seen, it had been wood. Later it would become petroleum (e.g., fuels, plastics, and textiles).

Extractive Industries and Nonrenewable Resources

The paradox of mass production that so astounded Andrew Carnegie was that industrial products which cost mere pennies poured out of far-flung networks of mines and miners, factories and factory workers, and a transportation system, all costing hundreds of millions of dollars. Despite this amazing infrastructure, the entire process would have ground to a halt without the discovery and consumption of physical resources lying underground. Americans believed they had a genius, reflected in the rise of the professions of civil engineering and mining engineering, to transform a bounty of minerals and oil into steel and fuel. Historian William Cronon revived the phrase "second nature" to describe this transformation: "The industrial revolution had redefined the environment; it was now a vast 'natural resource.'" Americans enjoyed successive environmental windfalls of gold and silver, coal and iron, lead and copper, and petroleum and other sources of industrial wealth.

A Nation of Natural Resources

Before industrialization made its prodigious cuts into seams of coal and iron ore, Americans primarily consumed local soil, water, and woodlots. Early extraction of mineral ores was limited. Highly local use may have been a temporarily regressive step that typified an undeveloped nation. At first colonial and revolutionary Americans imported iron, copper, and lead. Local demand encouraged on-site iron making, nail factories, rope walks, shoe factories, and the fabrication of farm tools. Limestone quarries in Pennsylvania and Rhode Island

STEEL IS EVEN tougher and stronger than iron. It was for centuries used only in expensive tools and swords because it was difficult to make in large amounts. The major difference between iron and steel is its carbon content. Pig iron contains about 3.8 percent carbon; steel contains only about 0.4 percent. Carbon was long known to have a strong affinity for oxygen, but all known methods to make steel by removing more carbon from iron by intense heat took up to six weeks. In 1850 the British metallurgist Henry Bessemer thought to blow a blast of air through a cauldron of molten pig iron. The result was excellent steel. It was a simple and elegant solution, as a stroke of genius often is.

The pyrotechnic "Bessemer blow" created a violent explosion (combustion) that drove off carbon and created hot malleable steel. It is one of the most impressive moments in industrial manufacturing anywhere and became a widely used metaphor for American industry. A modern computer chip factory cannot compare with the thrilling scene of raw power in a steel mill at full blast. Alexander Lyman Holley, who in the 1860s started up the Pennsylvania Steel Company in Harrisburg, celebrated the process:

> A million balls of melted iron tore away from the liquid mass, surged from side to side and plunged down again, only to be blown out more hot and angry than before. Column upon column of air, piercing and shattering the iron at every point only to be itself decomposed and hurled out into the night in a roaring blaze. And the discharge from its mouth changes from sparks and streaks of red and yellow gas to thick full white dazzling flame. Then all is quiet, and the product is steel, [white hot], smooth, shiny, and almost transparent.

When the steel-making process became more refined by Robert Mushet's recarburization, 2.5 tons of steel could be produced in 20 minutes. It could then be poured into any desired shape. Shortly the similar open-hearth method, first developed in 1859 by William Siemens, took hold because it efficiently used hot waste gases, leaving the furnace to heat incoming air for the blast.

supported tanning, masonry, and glassmaking. Glassmakers found sandstone in Pennsylvania and western Virginia and white sand in New Jersey. Good supplies of clay across the new nation supported thriving brickyards and potteries. The forests yielded to production of potash and pearl ash. In America seams of coal had shown up when householders dug cellars and wells across Pennsylvania, western Virginia, and eastern Ohio. Even with a cheap, ready supply of coal, people disliked handling the dirty dusty mineral. It burned hot, but produced filthy soot and black smoke. Wood remained the preferred fuel.

In the early decades of the nineteenth century, Americans did begin to move into a few selected industrial niches where they did better than the English: cheap cotton goods, flour milling, small-arms manufacturing, and production of hand tools like axes. Nevertheless, as long as they continued to depend on so-called process industries that directly used raw materials—making pitch, tar, turpentine, potash, brewing and distilling, dyeing, tanning, salt making, sawing lumber, and grinding flour—that used untrained labor, they were not adding value from machinery. Even the earliest uses of power machinery in the United States were not to

John Ferguson Weir, "The Gun Foundry" (detail). Most Americans quickly became enthralled by such powerful images of their new industrial might.

mass-produce finished goods, but to prepare raw materials for further manufacturing—to saw lumber, forge iron, grind grain, break hemp at the mill, the furnace, and the tannery. The earliest value-added manufacturing came with glassworks or iron making.

Extracted Minerals

Unlike its role in the Industrial Revolution in England, iron in America was not at the cutting edge of change. Early American ironsmiths resisted innovation because readily available water power made it easy to run antiquated and clumsy machines. In addition, the limitations of individual water wheels kept existing iron works small. Mining the rocks of iron ore and then pulverizing them before mixing the ore with charcoal was dirty, hard, and dangerous work. At the time of the American Revolution, the wealth of metal ores was virtually untouched. The limited iron deposits in bogs and rocks of the iron belt from Rutland County, Vermont, through the Berkshires of Massachusetts, through Orange County in New York and Morris

County, New Jersey, temporarily supplied the nation's needs. Iron ore was often fished with an oyster rake from the bottom of a pond or dug from open trenches. There were also iron mines in valleys south of Pittsburgh, in western Maryland, and from the southern Piedmont to the Appalachian slopes. Charcoal remained the common fuel, limestone or seashells the flux. America's fragmented iron industry supplied the nation with the array of articles from nails and spikes to shovels and hammers; edged tools like axes, knives, saws, and scythes; heavy items like anvils, anchors, and cannons; household kettles and skillets; and casings for machinery in mills as well as parts for wagons and plows. Demand began to grow for barrel hoops, wagon tires, and sheet iron. A few local forges and bloomeries made wire, nails, farm tools, and weapons. Most country blacksmiths could set up a temporary bloomery as needed. This was a large blacksmith's forge in which local iron ore would be processed using a power-driven bellows over an open charcoal fire to produce a semimolten mass—the bloom—of wrought iron, which was hammered into shape on an anvil. Iron ore in early America was simply treated as another natural resource, like clay for bricks and silicon for glass, that did not yet offer sufficient incentive to attract capital and labor.

Ore furnaces did not change much from colonial times up to the Civil War. By the end of the War of 1812, however, new technologies based on steam power began to raise production. As farmers poured into the midwestern prairie heartland, the first great demand for iron came from agriculture, not only for John Deere's innovative steel-tipped plows, but also for iron and steel seed drills, and reapers and harvesters by Hussey and McCormick. Nail factories put heavy demands on iron supplies following the invention of a successful nail-making machine that could turn out 100 nails a minute at one-third the cost of hand-wrought nails. In 1810 America had to import 11,000 tons of iron from Russia, Sweden, and England, compared to production of only 918 tons domestically. As late as 1830 the United States produced iron overwhelmingly by traditional methods of charcoal and water power. After 1830 the cheap widespread use of hard hot-burning anthracite coal in eastern Pennsylvania began the long process of weaning Americans from wood. Soft smoky bituminous coal from western Pennsylvania was soon commonly consumed in Philadelphia and Richmond and shipped as far as Boston. Demand for coal rose because of a multiplying population, improvements in grates and furnaces, better industrial techniques, and especially the appearance of railroad steam locomotives by the 1820s. In 1820 less than 50,000 tons of coal had been mined; by 1860 this soared to over 14 million tons as coal became a primary extractive resource.

Mining the West

Early colonial French fur traders know of lead from Indian-dug pits in southwestern Wisconsin. The nearby Illinois town of Galena is named after lead-sulfide "galena" ore of the region. Demand came from plumbing, paints, weights, and bullets. Vertical shafts went down about 40 feet where the ore could be dug out with ordinary tools. The ore was burned on a log fire in which the melted lead filtered to the bottom for collection. Later a Scotch-invented hearth furnace took over. It was a tall chimney with an oven beneath, in which a blast of air directed by a bellows produced convenient 70-pound pigs, or "plats." Lead mining and smelting spread across southern Wisconsin with the influx of experienced miners from England's Cornwall, where the mines had reached exhaustion. In the peak year of 1845 the region produced 25,000 tons of lead. Fantastic rumors of mountains of pure copper, backed by the appearance of Indian copper ornaments, drew government interest to the wild and distant Lake Superior region. In 1820 territorial governor Lewis Cass looked for, and failed to find, any pure copper mountain. Two decades later, nevertheless, a more realistic survey revealed rich copper ore from which "Kewennaw copper" was mined in Michigan's Upper Peninsula. It produced 80 percent of the nation's copper until 1887, when the famous Anaconda mine outside Butte, Montana, began operation in earnest. The Lake Superior iron ore region became famous for its Marquette open pits from the 1840s through the 1880s. Ice blockage in the severe winter months remained a serious drawback even with larger and stronger steamships. Nevertheless, during the Civil War the North depended on these mines and nearby the newly opened Minnesota Mesabi open-pit holes to supply eastern steel centers.

Further west, in the Rocky Mountains, reports of useful minerals attracted hardy adventurers into the western wilderness well before the arrival of more cautious farmers and townspeople. Historians speak of the "mining frontier," which in reality was an extension of the process of industrialization. The federal government gave generous terms, some still available today, to aid in the search for mineral ores. The 1872 mining law established that mineral development hold preference over all other uses of the land because it represented the highest economic use. The discovery of large ore supplies would, it was believed, assure Americans a long future. The costs of pollution of streams and wasteful consumption were ignored. The federal government had effectively abandoned any long-term management of strategic natural resources. The terms for resource exploitation were so generous, set for long or indefinite terms, and under lax review, that the nation's bounty of copper, iron, coal, and lead were virtually given away. Later, the same turnover of resources for private benefit was applied to bauxite for aluminum, and petroleum and natural gas for energy demands. The American West was also the storehouse for other mineral ores used in industrial alloys, such as tungsten, molybdenum, vanadium, manganese, zinc, and mercury. Some westerners complained that they were being treated like a colony by eastern capitalists; resources were removed with no local benefits. For example, by 1914 the Bingham Copper mine just outside Salt Lake City, "the richest hole on earth," had produced a billion dollars worth of copper for easterners like the Guggenheim family and the Kennecott Copper Company.

Mining created its own social phenomena. Wherever miners appeared at a wilderness site they were carriers of a rough-hewn exploitive brand of civilization. It was a world of short-lived boomtowns and dug-up landscape. East of the Mississippi they were the grim coal towns of Appalachia and central Illinois. In the West, miners often were the first white men after the roaming trappers in the distant reaches of Wyoming, Colorado, and Montana. Towns on the edge of society, like Rock Springs in southwestern Wyoming, Leadville in central Colorado, Virginia City in northern Nevada, and Coeur d'Alene in Idaho transplanted the worst aspects of industrial wastelands and slum dwellings directly onto the wilderness. This was not even the thin veneer of civilization, but instead the underside of industrial capitalism. The boomtowns were single-purpose mining communities, isolated and distant from civilization and intentionally focused on short-term profits that ignored human well-being and environmental stability. These unpleasant and vicious places were tolerated, and even encouraged, because they provided the raw materials for industrial civilization.

The Energy Revolution: Petroleum

For centuries, human and animal muscle power were aided by windmills and water wheels. Americans had harnessed abundant water power in New England's rushing rivers to power the region's textile mills. When steam engines powered riverboats and railroads to link Americans across their broad landscape, they consumed enormous amounts of wood and coal.

As late as 1860 there was no such thing as a petroleum industry. Petroleum was, like coal, originally a largely undesirable substance that polluted wells and fouled croplands. Since early human history, oil from surface pools had been used in small amounts to coat walls and seal boat hulls, and even as a fire weapon for defensive warfare. Pioneers learned from the Indians to use petroleum as a medicinal salve and take it internally. Before the Civil War, early commercial demand for better lighting for a growing population and its new workshops had overtaken limited supplies of natural substances such as whale oil, beeswax, and tallow candles. Human-made illuminating oils were camphene (alcohol and turpentine) and kerosene (at first made from coal). The invention of a workable oil lamp soon required supplies beyond the few dozen local surface oil "springs."

Western Pennsylvania was the home of the simple beginnings of the underground oil industry. In 1859 oil pioneer E. L. Drake drilled the first of many oil wells. When this crude oil was refined into kerosene for lighting, one waste product was a clear fluid called gasoline. Another residue was a black tarry substance called asphalt that was used in "macadam" road construction and as a roofing material. Drake's wells turned Titusville, Pennsylvania, into the first of America's raucous, hard-drinking, and often short-lived boomtowns linked to oil production. Titusville was nicknamed "Sodden Gomorrah." By the end of the century, the Pennsylvania oil pools were overshadowed by many new finds in California (even under Los Angeles), Texas (the famous Spindletop oil field), and Oklahoma (which brought instant statehood in 1907 to what had been set aside "forever" as Indian Territory). Americans unleashed so much oil that the first Spindletop gusher near Beaumont, Texas, burned 3,300 barrels an hour for days before it was capped. Natural gas was simply released into the atmosphere or burnt off. Exploration kept up with demand as new fields opened around Bakersfield, the San Joaquin Valley, and southern California. Oil refining became California's largest manufacturing industry as its production soared from 5 million barrels in 1900 to 15 million barrels in 1914.

As the oil industry took off, by 1900 more than a billion gallons of kerosene were refined to burn for lighting; 300 million gallons of oil fueled factories and homes; and 170 million gallons reached industry as lubricating oil. This was before the gasoline internal combustion engine created the true petroleum revolution. The burgeoning automobile industry—450,000 "gas buggies" by 1910—produced entirely new markets for gasoline and lubricating oil. During the 1920s petroleum emerged as "the most glamorous mineral of the West," on which great fortunes were made or lost. Wealth from oil was so tantalizing it stood at the center of the infamous Teapot Dome political scandal involving oil magnates and the federal secretary of the treasury. Western historian Gerald D. Nash wrote, "What gold was to the West in 1849, petroleum was in 1929." Vast new fields came under production in Oklahoma, Texas, and soon Louisiana, including some of the richest in the world. By 1929 California alone was producing 250 million barrels of oil annually. Heavy less refined oil was consumed by the new diesel locomotives that gradually replaced coal-burning steam engines. Efficient new oil-fueled motorships began to replace coal-burning steamships.

By the early 1920s pessimists began to warn of the impending exhaustion of the world's supplies of crude oil. In 1909 President Taft's executive order had withdrawn many government-owned oil fields from immediate production and set them aside as strategic "naval reserves." Then chemist William Burton of Standard Oil of Indiana invented "thermal

THROUGH MOST OF their history, Americans accepted technological hazards for the sake of the benefits. One example is connected to the rapid impact of the automobile in the 1920s, after Henry Ford began to mass produce his Model T. Charles Kettering and Thomas Midgley of General Motors searched for a gasoline additive to reduce engine knocking and bring higher compression engines for faster, quieter, and more efficient driving. Their hunt ended with the use of tetraethyl lead, leaded gasoline, and the creation of the Ethyl Gasoline Corporation. The new leaded gasoline, for all its virtues, caused unexpected problems. In 1924, 45 people working at a pilot tetraethyl lead plant had fallen ill and 4 died from lead poisoning. Public health pioneer Alice Hamilton wrote in 1925, "I am not one of those who believe that the use of this leaded gasoline can ever be made safe. No lead industry has ever, under the strictest control, lost all its dangers. Where there is lead, some case of lead poisoning sooner or later develops." At a 1928 conference that focused on the problems of tetraethyl lead poisoning, a physiologist found, "In this room [there are] two diametrically opposed conceptions. The men engaged in industry, chemists and engineers, take it as a matter of course that a little thing like industrial poisoning should not be allowed to stand in the way of a great industrial advance. On the other hand, the sanitary experts take it as a matter of course that the first consideration is the health of the people." Workplace safeguards kept leaded gasoline on the market. However, new information on lead as a toxic substance in the 1960s brought the additive under attack as a widespread environmental hazard. Unleaded gasoline is now universally available at the pump and leaded gasoline difficult to find.

cracking." It doubled the yield of gasoline and made $150 million of additional profits for Standard Oil of Indiana. Burton's convenient batch process refining, which held petroleum in tanks as it was processed, was soon accompanied by a continuous cracking operation developed at the Universal Oil Products Company by the aptly named engineer, Carbon Petroleum Dubbs. Production rose so uncontrollably that in 1927 gasoline sold at 10 cents a gallon. The Depression years brought industry-enforced production curbs, including the 1935 Interstate Oil Compact, ostensibly to protect oil reserves. Despite claims to the contrary, these curbs were based more on protecting prices than on conservation of a nonrenewable resource. The needs of World War II again spurred unlimited production, particularly as the Allies were cut off from supplies in the Dutch East Indies, Romania in the Balkans, and the Caucuses in Russia.

Postwar gasoline prices remained low at 20 to 30 cents a gallon, which encouraged the further expansion of the American automobile industry. Oil became widely used for household heating instead of coal. It became the fuel for the nation's new fleets of diesel trains and ships. The new plastics industry was petroleum based. The United States had become oil dependent, notably on Middle Eastern fields. Americans were shocked by the artificial "oil crisis" of 1973 when oil prices skyrocketed from less than $3 a 55-gallon barrel to $30 a barrel, and drove gasoline to $1 to $1.50 a gallon. To complete the story, natural gas, which had earlier been a waste product like gasoline, came into its own as a clean transportable source of energy. Its production rose from 4 trillion cubic feet in 1945 to over 12 trillion cubic feet in

1960, mostly for domestic use. One of the major energy consumers—coal, oil, hydroelectric—was the electric power industry. It provided electric generation for both light and power that had first become a practical reality in the 1880s. Before the First World War, industry alone used more than 11 million kilowatt hours. The total horsepower for doing basic industrial work from all sources rose from 2.5 million in 1860 to over 46 million in 1900, nearly an 18-fold increase applied to industrial production in one lifetime.

Another Raw Material for the Factories: 40 Million Immigrants

Most of the people reading this book are not Native Americans. They are the descendants of migrating individuals and families, mostly from Europe. (One out of 10 Americans today, the African Americans, do not have forebears who came by choice, and their story is different.) Generations of European immigrants abandoned their homes and risked everything in America not only for liberty, but also because of the promise that a better standard of life was accessible to ordinary people, not merely to an entrenched upper class. The United States received a large immigrant class willing to work in factories and ready to accept inequality (temporarily, they believed) as a necessary ingredient for industrial growth. In 1860 Abraham Lincoln spoke of the "prudent, penniless beginner" who labored to learn a skill and then became self-employed who himself employed others. "If any continue in the condition of a hired laborer for life, it is because of a dependent nature which prefers it, or singular folly or improvidence or misfortune." One reason that a classic Marxist proletariat revolution did not take place in America was the blue-collar workers believed, through hard work and pluck, they would attain middle-class prosperity.

Between 1840 and 1900 more than 16 million immigrants landed on America's shores, almost as many as the total population of the United States in 1840. They willingly bent their bodies, minds, and spirits to hasten the industrial transformation. Beginning in the 1880s America's industrial boom swallowed up these increasing numbers of cheap laborers who now settled in cities rather than on farmland. This was an important switch from the earlier fears that the immigrant who saved a little cash would rush off to buy his own land and "quit the loom for farming." A congressional commission reported that in 1910 nearly 60 percent of all employees in 21 industries were foreign born. Between 1900 and 1930 an additional 18.5 million immigrants entered the country (including both of the author's parents, one from Ukraine and one from Bohemia). By 1930 over 36 million Americans described themselves as wage earners, 8.5 million of these working in factories and 56 percent living in urban settings.

The impact of immigration was serendipitous: New immigrants needed to find work quickly and American industry needed an inexpensive labor force. As social historian Loren Baritz has noted, "However onerous and unrewarding the work, this was a bargain that satisfied both parties." The bargain brought a total of 40 million people to the United States by 1923, the largest movement of people anywhere in history. But Baritz also sees a paradox: Even while America moved toward its technology-based future, the work force of millions of immigrants from rural Europe had arrived only with medieval farming skills designed to work in the now obsolete rural environment. With this disability, "Most were unequipped for industrial life, [and] fell neatly into their unskilled slots in the new economic order, which depended on their muscle to operate the nation's industrial plant." They were treated as a resource as raw as iron ore. Immigrants quickly discovered, in Baritz's words, "that big businessmen ruled the golden land as kings, wielding more influence over public opinion than even the czars back home." As one immigrant sagely wrote, "It is business that can be called the god of this country."

What the immigrants felt above all was poor, but they were not the "wretched refuse" invited by the Statue of Liberty. Senator Daniel Patrick Moynihan said, "They were an extraordinary, enterprising, and self-sufficient folk who knew exactly what they were doing, and doing it quite on their own," which was to improve their material well-being—homes, furniture, healthy food, leisure time. Baritz concludes that the immigrants "were trading their cultures, often more religious and idealistic, for economic opportunity. Whether the trade was worth it depended on how much money could be made how soon." The tradeoff also included a shift from a familiar geography to an alien environment. Stefano Miele, who came from near Naples, admitted, "If I am to be frank, then I shall say that I left Italy and came to America for the sole purpose of making money. America was the land of opportunity." Many immigrants nevertheless clung to their own cultural traditions and looked on Americans as a cold money-grubbing breed that lived unsatisfying lives. Americans did not know how to laugh and enjoy life. Many immigrants long sensed they were living in someone else's country. They were openly grateful, nevertheless, for the better economic opportunity of industrialization. Most never looked nostalgically to farming. They could make money that would be a fortune in the old country. Moynihan added, "But some believed there were limits, that if their new country could not order its priorities better it would deform its people" (see Chapter 9 on the ills of industrialization).

The American Corporation: Making Industrialization Permanent

Factory production alone is not an irresistible force that can sweep everything else away. Nor is American history a story of technological determinism. More to the point, a new technology must turn a profit for investors who put their hard-won resources into its development. One leading example, as we have seen, was the tentative appearance of the early railroad lines in the 1830s and subsequently the triumph of a national but privately owned railroad network by the 1880s (and its decline and virtual collapse by 1950). This was not a natural "organic" process of rise and fall, but based on deliberate choices. A technology is always "socially constructed" because its success or failure depends on decisions made in a corporate board room, in a government bureaucracy, and by a public debate. (The best recent example is the failure of nuclear power.) By the end of the nineteenth century, some Americans began to conclude that the nation went through a transition from a nation of independent property holders to a troubling dependence on a few big private corporations. According to this view, the first proprietor of a new factory may have often been motivated by an idealistic concern for the working man or woman as well as his own profitability. In time, however, the proprietor, because his factory operated in a fiercely competitive system, paid less attention to the well-being of the work force. Workers who had once taken pride in their mechanical skills, had their own well-maintained tools, and been paid for a quality finished product, now became "wage slaves" who only performed repetitive operations in a mass production process for a fixed daily wage. Personal on-the-job satisfaction of the mass of workers did not seem to be one of the attributes of mature corporate industrialization.

By the late nineteenth century, the industrial superstructure of new transportation and communications technologies, interlocked with financial and management institutions, was in place—vertical integration combined with horizontal expansion. The American economy was soon controlled by a handful of wealthy entrepreneurs: Vanderbilt, Hill, and Harriman in railroads, Rockefeller in oil, Carnegie in steel, McCormick in farm machines, Armour in meats, Morgan in investment banking, and Jay Gould in anything that would make money. Gould's Western Union Telegraph Company, for example, controlled communications nationwide. In the American Southwest, he also told Americans what trains to ride, and how to ship their goods, and what shipping rates to pay. These entrepreneurs were nicknamed "robber barons" who were "hard, ruthless, narrow, and uncivilized." In historian Bernard Weisberger's words, "When they made a mistake, every business establishment in the country was likely to rock because of it." Weisberger added, "The nation could not afford to lose many really big players, since they took too many investors and employees down with them." Hence, to some extent, the game had to be "rigged" in favor of the big players. They broke up labor unions, bribed and controlled local politicians, and forced competing companies out of business. Secret pacts carved up market territories and set floors on prices. The barons were goaded and reviled in a free press, and often responded by buying the newspapers and magazines to shut down criticism and unpleasant revelations. Above all, they enjoyed an extraordinary freedom from government intervention to pursue their predatory and acquisitive habits. New York Central Railroad mogul Cornelius Vanderbilt said, "Law? What do I care about the law. Hain't I got the power?"

Despite this exercise of raw power, or because of it, many Americans looked favorably on the robber barons as the captains of industries that poured out an incredible swell of goods and transformed human lives and natural landscapes. Robber baron greed was widely accepted as a natural extension of the boundless American right of private enterprise, and not its violent perversion. Such business magnates replaced steely war heroes and eloquent politicians as the new heroes of American society. The captains of industry were idealized as more than rich men. They powered the wheels of the American economy and steered its course.

Critical to business success was the monopolization of a profitable technology. Early inventors like Eli Whitney (cotton gin) and Oliver Evans (grain milling) rarely succeeded in protecting their devices from copying when they had to secure patents from each of the states individually. The Constitution in 1787 empowered Congress to secure "to Authors and Inventors the exclusive Right to their respective Writings and Discoveries." Following several flawed laws in 1790, 1793, and 1800, Congress established the modern patent system in 1836. Previously only 9,957 patents had been issued in 46 years. The creation of a patent commissioner and a bureau with quasi-judicial powers determined absolute ownership based on originality and usefulness. By the late twentieth century, more than 5 million patents had been issued. Patents reinforced private ownership and the right to profit from private property, in this case "intellectual property." In corporate circles, this provided proprietary protection for an array of patents, copyrights, trademarks, and the clouded area of "trade secrets."

It can be argued that industrialism took off because of a natural extension of private enterprise—the business corporation. Corporations are large-sized nongovernment business enterprises with an enormous amount of freedom from government or public regulation or interference. They raise capital by selling shares of stock that represent ownership and are transferable. Since decisions by English courts in the fifteenth century, their officers and shareholders enjoyed the tremendous leverage of "limited liability"—the most an individual can lose due to a firm's misdeeds or failure would be the actual amount he had originally paid for his shares. As large enterprises, corporations function better than the individual small businessowner because they can better amass great sums of capital to spend over long periods of time that modern industrial operations require. One of the most important features of corporate structure is that it allowed major companies like Westinghouse Electric, Bell Telephone, Carnegie's U.S. Steel, Insull's Consolidated Gas, and Rockefeller's Standard Oil to long outlive their founders, financial wizards, and inventive geniuses. Directors might come and go, shareholders might die and sell out, but the corporation could go on raising millions of dollars in capital, building new factories and shutting down obsolete operations, hiring and firing generations of workers. The corporation became the enduring foundation for industrialization, a force stronger than natural resources or a labor force, with the capacity to survive the swings of business cycles, changing presidential terms, and even warfare. The corporation became an institutional version of perpetual motion that spun the wheels of the technological superstructure.

Did corporations receive privileged status in the United States? Probably. Was the Constitution a "capitalist tool"? Probably not. Article 1, Section 10, reads, "No state shall . . . pass any . . . Law impairing the Obligation of Contracts," which was a late addition for unknown reasons because of the secrecy of the Constitutional Convention. Yet the Constitutional Convention did not create a document that aggressively supported economic expansion. It urged "internal improvements" but did not create federal "think tanks" or grant rewards or immunities for advancement in manufacturing, agriculture, or commerce. Nor did it build a banking and credit structure. But it did directly stimulate market activity by a somewhat piecemeal economic order: Congress received the right to coin money and regulate its value, to establish uniform bankruptcy laws, and to create a national postal system with national post roads. Indirectly, it sought to establish a peaceful climate for economic development by the authority to assemble militias to suppress insurrectionists. A militia could be raised for forceful protection of private property and interests and to quell labor unrest. Most importantly, the Constitution offered easy access to incorporation and its privileges by leaving the powers to the states. Since colonial times, the building of wharves and bridges, turnpikes and canals, as well as public water supplies, banks, insurance, and sometimes manufacturing, had been put in private rather than public hands. The accumulation of wealth by private chartered companies, and later corporations, was justified on the grounds that they benefited the community and contributed to the welfare of the public. Investors subscribed cash to a company's capital stock, which spread the risk of failure beyond individuals, partners, or a government agency. This capital was then applied to a major infrastructure project that also performed a useful public service. Between 1775 and 1801 the states of the struggling new nation issued 326 charters (compared to only 20 in highly commercial Great Britain) to corporations, mostly organized to build bridges, turnpikes, and canals. Between the 1790s and the 1820s, private corporations gained even more autonomy. They briefly gained the power to issue private tradable currency notes, engage in their own banking, and became virtually untouchable autonomous enterprises. The nation's infrastructure of roads, canals, and bridges began with private hands and public blessing. Incorporation also allowed for large-scale capital ventures that could cross state borders. The silence of the Constitution did allow courts to favor business. Judges provided sympathetic protection of creditors through bankruptcy laws. Favorable decisions reinforced the principle of limited liability, which meant investors confined their risks even for shoddy goods and workplace risks. The 1819 case of *Dartmouth College* v. *Woodward* upheld the inviolability of contracts, which provided a high level of business security. The antimonopoly Charles River Bridge case of 1837 disallowing exclusive privileges to corporations encouraged their proliferation.

This probusiness stance became deeply imbedded in the body politic by a flurry of legislation during the Civil War as part of the northern Republican political agenda. The Morrill Tariff of 1861 was highly protective to American industry. The Morrill Land Grant College Act of 1862 encouraged think tanks in "agriculture and the mechanic arts" that would incubate new technologies for industry. Congress established the Department of Agriculture to modernize agriculture. The Homestead Act of 1862 opened western lands to more than individual farmers. Several bills were passed by Congress and signed by President Lincoln to tie the nation together by heavily subsidized regional and transcontinental private railroad systems. A National Banking Act established a banking and currency system in 1863. And Congress created the National Academy of Science to foster technical learning. But after the war the federal government receded again into the background. This decentralization of politics to state and local levels allowed virtually uncontrolled corporate expansion—it was said that Jay Gould ruled New Jersey, Thomas Scott of the Pennsylvania Railroad had his way in the state, and that John D. Rockefeller was prince of Ohio.

Corporations had become so important to industrial growth that the courts gave them extraordinary safety for their wealth by treating them as individuals under the Fourteenth Amendment that protected against the invasion of private property—"nor shall any State deprive any person of life, liberty, or property, without due process of law." The Fourteenth Amendment had originally been adopted in 1866 to protect the nation's black citizens. A Supreme Court decision in 1886, *Santa Clara County* v. *Southern Pacific Railroad,* made it the Magna Carta of big business and corporate America virtually immune from government regulation. The court ruled for the first time that a corporation should be construed as a "person" and thus entitled to Fourteenth Amendment protection. After a state granted a corporate charter, it virtually abdicated control over corporate operations. Not surprisingly, the major corporations exercised this unusual independence to establish monopolies of basic railroad, steel, petroleum, and coal industries through pools, trusts, and holding companies. Even sugar, biscuits, and whiskey came under monopolistic corporate control. For example, by 1898 John D. Rockefeller's Standard Oil of Ohio refined 84 percent of the oil in the United States as he bought up or undersold the competition. Standard Oil may have supplied plentiful, regular, and cheap quantities of petroleum products, but it ruthlessly cut down any competitors. Financier J. P. Morgan insisted competition was wasteful.

For decades the 500 largest corporations accounted for three-quarters of business profits in the United States. By 1904, 7 out of every 10 production workers in the United States were employed by corporate enterprise. Most land use and natural resource consumption came from corporations: lumbering, coal mining, mineral development, agribusiness, recreation and resorts. By 1929, 80 percent of all the profits of manufacturing went to fewer than 1,350 corporations. By adroit exploitation, a mere 200 industrial companies owned nearly half of all the nation's corporate wealth and 22 percent of the total national wealth. Using their enormous wealth as leverage, such corporations hired brigades of lawyers, accountants, and congressional lobbyists to keep them free from public scrutiny and governmental restraints. "Big business" manipulated whatever markets and institutions it could not control. Critics and labor leaders complained that the corporation had neither a soul to be damned nor a body to be kicked. These vast businesses not only dominated the American economy, but also wielded great social, political, and cultural influence. They monopolized local communities known as "company towns" and determined the lives of ordinary individuals who were virtual "wage slaves."

In reality, the situation was a contrivance out of a mix of government support, the power of great wealth, the existence of monopolies, and the manipulation of markets. Government was not benevolently neutral; it had always practiced "corporate welfare." In 1880, for example, Congress raised tariffs (not for the first or last time) so that English factories, which were selling steel rails at $36 a ton, paid an additional $28 a ton duty to import them into the United States. Labor laws kept unions under wraps, and banking acts gave easy access to borrowed capital. These actions were hardly "natural," and certainly not according to spontaneous market forces. In fact, the corporate objective was to avoid a constant Darwinian struggle of existence. Historian Henry Bamford Parkes went so far to say that the autonomy of late nineteenth-century American capitalism "had, in fact, been deliberately and carefully planned." More likely, a combination of "free" natural resources, cheap labor, and a benevolent political climate offered irresistible opportunities for limitless profits that made America a capitalist utopia. Social philosopher Karl Polanyi observed, "There was nothing natural about laissez-faire. The road to the free market was opened and kept open by an enormous increase in continuous, centrally organized and controlled interventionism."

Although corporate America has been stereotyped as inherently conservative and even reactionary, in reality it has been a revolutionary development. It is historically unusual in that the natural resources and economic enterprise of a large nation are directed by private interests. The United States, for example, has been the only major nation to allow its all-important railroad network to originate in private hands. (In contrast, even the postal system is government run.) Parkes called the picture essentially Hamiltonian, with an emphasis on the right of a rich and powerful oligarchy to control the nation. According to this view, the long-standing traditions of private property, free enterprise, and individual liberty apply, above all, to protect personal wealth. Parkes concluded that the mood of the nation in the late nineteenth century allowed that "If able and energetic individuals were encouraged to develop the country's resources and were permitted to enrich themselves in the process, then the whole of society would benefit. The unchecked drive of the will of ruthless men toward wealth and power was presented as a civilizing force." The robber barons were "doing God's work and promoting civilization." The public came to believe that laissez-faire ("hands off") capitalism acted in accord with nature. Although it has long been clear that corporate activities have major public consequences, their public accountability has remained unclear. Some marginal restraints on corporate abuse did begin to appear in the 1880s after Rockefeller's Standard Oil Trust monopolized the industry and exceeded public sentiment. Americans finally reacted against trade associations and holding companies that were blatant conspiracies for personal or corporate dominion over large pieces of the nation's economy. Yet the federal Sherman Anti-Trust Act of 1890 has been exercised only rarely to break up giant firms when they dominate markets and diminish competition. In reality, between 1894 and 1904, 131 mergers consolidated more than 1,800 companies. Government regulation of industrial corporations began to build up in the twentieth century, but when compared to business operations in other industrialized nations, corporate freedom remains essentially untouched.

Through most of American history no human, social, ethical, or environmental needs seemed capable of overriding corporate self-interest and profit making. When environmental regulations took hold in the 1970s, they were an abrupt turnaround away from the historic premise that corporate profitability was the primary means to serve the public good.

The Second Industrial Revolution: The Progressives and Social Efficiency through the Technological "System"

Between 1890 and 1920, during the era of the new "Progressive" ideology, most Americans confidently believed that industrialization had led them to the promised land. England's Industrial Revolution had already been compared to classic golden ages in history: Greece's Age of Pericles, the Italian Renaissance, Elizabethan England, and France's Age of Reason. By 1890 Americans joined the list. The contemporary social commentator James K. Paulding said, "Machinery and steam engines have had more influence on the Christian world than Locke's metaphysics, Napoleon's code, or Jeremy Bentham's codifications." The appearance of large-scale industrial systems was hailed as "the second creation of the world" and "the second discovery of America." Curious foreign tourists may still have visited Philadelphia to see Independence Hall, but many rushed to see the real foundation of American power at Pittsburgh's Carnegie Works. It was the steel capital of the world. Later, in the 1920s, foreign visitors arrived to wonder at Henry Ford's River Rouge plant in Detroit because more automobiles came off the assembly lines there than anywhere else. By the 1940s tourists made special trips to enjoy the technological sublime at grandiose electrification projects at Hoover Dam on the Colorado River, Grand Coulee Dam on the Columbia River, and the Tennessee Valley Authority (TVA).

Working in the midst of these currents was a highly ideological but diffuse group of reformers, the American Progressives, whose key word was "efficiency." They believed they could improve on England's Industrial Revolution. Industrialization, they admitted, produced great wealth and brought material improvements, but it grievously wasted labor and squandered natural resources. The invisible hand of the market, which the captains of industry had praised so effusively, in fact functioned poorly as a control mechanism. The Progressives honestly believed that humans had a deep psychological need to order, centralize, control, and expand human activities that was even greater than the lust for power and money. The new systems of electric power generation were their models: supremely clean, quiet, and powerful. The chaos of the first Industrial Revolution—smokestacks that indiscriminately dumped soot, monstrous clanging machines, crowded tenements—could now give way to perfect cleanliness, continuous efficiency, quiet factories and neighborhoods, and social harmony. By the 1930s the massive TVA system of dams and reservoirs and power plants fulfilled "a faith," scholars said, "that electricity will exorcise social disorder and environmental disruption, eliminate political conflict and personal alienation, and restore ecological balance and a communication of man with nature."

The Progressives concluded that a technological environment was much trickier to work with than the state of nature. The new world of industrialization demanded highly centralized management, effective government intervention, and expert planning. The industrial system acted as an invented network overlaid on existing ecological systems. This layer of industrialization, said the Progressives, generated its own "natural laws," embedded in machines, devices, processes, and systems, that acted independently of natural forces. Having won the battle with nature, all-knowing "technical experts" could take the next step in human progress by applying technological tools to social renewal: Technological "fixes" would solve human problems. The Progressives valued expert knowledge—historian Carroll Pursell called it "wise-man's burden"—from an elite class of specialists more than broad-based public opinion. The social sciences, such as sociology, psychology, anthropology, economics, and political science, came into their own during the Progressive Era. Important decisions about public welfare could be made, it was believed, based on masses of data and scientific impartiality of expert testimony. Social scientists joined engineers as a technocratic priesthood. Much later, in the 1970s and 1980s, such dependence upon expertise as the final word was questioned because it failed to recognize the "social construction" of science and that technical evaluation was a political instrument to be trotted out when it served a specific political agenda.

Conservationist Gifford Pinchot and President Theodore Roosevelt also believed they could apply the Progressive gospel of efficiency directly to the natural world. Disinterested scientific fact would displace political prejudice and economic greed (see also the discussion in Chapter 11). They did not see technology and environment as opposites. Unlike most environmental advocacy movements in American history, the conservation movement led by Pinchot and Roosevelt was part of the mainstream of the day in its optimistic commitment to science and technology. For example, the great federal dam-building agency, the Reclamation Service, was established in 1902 as a conservation agency. Natural resources, such as primeval forests, empty plains, and free-running rivers, could be efficiently managed toward high productivity by technical experts in the fields of forestry, soil science, hydrology, and geology. Efficiency required that natural places be defined in terms of "multiple use" and not lay unknown and undeveloped, obsolete and useless. Forestry, for example, meant "tree farming"—careful cultivation, the improvement of trees for better timber, and proper harvesting. In management terms, trees became "virgin feedstocks" for the manufacturing process, a viewpoint that rejected an ecological perspective. Technical efficiency would overcome environmental waste, which in Pinchot and Roosevelt's view was immoral and did not serve the public good. Technical prowess also laid an ethical framework on an otherwise brutal and amoral nature because it could serve a higher good. The Progressives repudiated the Transcendentalists: Society should not emulate nature but instead become a finely balanced, well-oiled, and efficiently humming machine.

Progressives emphasized a systems approach to the new industrial society. They were delighted, for example, when inventor Elmer Sperry adapted a child's toy, the gyroscope, for automatic controls on ships and airplanes. This feedback control engineering (which anticipated mathematician Norbert Weiner's cybernetics of the 1940s) "proved" that an efficient self-regulating mechanical system could work. When enlarged to include a total industry, a systems approach encompassed machines and workers. Large systems, such as those in the business of energy, manufacturing, communication, and transportation, were at the heart of the Progressive vision. This was heady stuff that suggested a planner's utopia. Historian Thomas Hughes notes that inventions such as incandescent light, the radio, the airplane, and the gasoline-driven automobile symbolized the modern era because they were embedded within large-scale technological systems, such as the electric power grid or the interstate highway system. Just as Andrew Carnegie had done with steel in the 1880s, Henry Ford in the early twentieth century pushed forward a vertically integrated automobile manufacturing system that included mines, railroads, and blast furnaces to make steel for his cars. Essential to the system were financial, managerial, labor, and sales organization. Less well known but equally important was Chicagoan Samuel Insull's web of integrated private utilities—the Commonwealth Edison Company, People's Gas, and Public Service of Northern Illinois—that included hydroelectric dams and reached out to encompass investment banks, brokerage houses, and state regulatory agencies, as well as the usual dynamos, transmission lines, and incandescent lamps. The entire goal was to make way for the easy and inexpensive transmission of electricity traveling at the speed of light (at the highest possible profit). Most controversial was the human systems engineering devised by Frederick Winslow Taylor ("Taylorism"), who treated workers as if they were components of machines and nothing else. Taylor believed his approach was objective and scientific. He not only used a stopwatch to time the way employees worked, he broke down complex work motions into simple actions and used the most efficient workers as models for the rest. He was naive in denying to workers individual freedom of action. Taylor disciple Harrington Emerson believed that no one could argue against the proposition, "If man's progress is slow, it is because of wastes—wastes of everything that is precious." Taylor himself believed that Americans were so enthralled by the benefits of efficiency that the work force would rush toward regimentation. "In the past, the man has been first; in the future the system must be first." A 1932 *Fortune* magazine article concluded, "from the purely productive point of view, a part of the human race [that cannot be fitted into the system] is already obsolete."

Industrialization in the Twentieth Century

In the twentieth century the momentum of industrialization continued to reshape American society. Technological infrastructures thickened and took on new layers. The age of iron and steel of the late nineteenth century matured and became the foundation in the twentieth century for innovations in other fields, such as energy and chemicals, transportation and communications, and information processing. An enlarged superstructure of chemicals and electronics involved a shift from mechanical means to a world of flow and change. It seemed that Americans could use each new technological system to continuously recreate their worlds. (In the case of computerization, "virtual reality" invented an immaterial world lost in hyperspace.) Success was still measured by the distance gained from the raw forces of nature. A publicist from the chemical industry, Edwin P. Slossen, wrote an article in 1920 titled, "Back to Nature? Never! Forward to the Machine!" He announced, "The conquest of nature, not the imitation of nature, is the whole duty of man."

Humanity could still stumble on the way to utopia. World War I was seen as a temporary but frightening setback for the advance of material well-being. Military demands produced a series of dismaying technological surprises: the machine gun, poison gas, the tank, the submarine, and the destructive use of the airplane. Mass destruction instead of better living through technology disillusioned Americans—the "lost generation" of the 1920s—who became cynical about humanity's so-called progress. Some practical lessons were learned that suited the Progressives and corporate thinking. The wartime mobilization of the business community under government management was a large-scale experiment in social coordination. The war also created new sources of capital through exorbitant profits and brought more venture capital into the marketplace than ever before. This accelerated the pace of corporate hegemony that would characterize the twentieth century.

After World War I the industrial bloom seemed to expand continuously. Between 1923 and 1929, a higher standard of living, despite inequity of wealth, spread as never before. Already between 1914 and 1926 wages had risen by almost 30 percent. While prices of consumer goods were falling because of increased productivity (which rose 40 percent in the period), the purchasing power of the ordinary worker grew by 50 percent. This combination meant that most Americans enjoyed, or believed they would shortly find, an end to economic insecurity. Ford's Model T automobile symbolized a "democracy of consumption" when it sold in the millions instead of the thousands. Its price that started in 1909 at $950 fell to $290 by 1924. Consumer goods replaced land (property) as the most conspicuous statement of each American's stake in society. The world of plastics and synthetics came into its own. By the 1920s Americans delighted in new applications of chemistry to daily life: Bakelite, cellophane, rayon, paints, and cosmetics. The chemical industrial revolution also produced herbicides, pesticides, fungicides, and chlorofluorocarbons (CFCs) that would not be questioned until the 1960s. The United States maintained its ascendancy in electric power generation, the spread of electric lighting, and electrified factory machinery. Household appliances included electric irons, vacuum cleaners, washing machines, and the refrigerator, which was gradually replacing the icebox. Conveniences and labor-saving devices brought more Americans into modernity than any other peoples. They enjoyed indoor plumbing instead of fetching water by the bucket and tramping out at night or midwinter to the privy. The "good old days" of the isolated rural community at the turn of the century were happily abandoned, when women remembered that they "just spent the summer canning" or at the soap vat and butter churn. Food became widely available in packages and cans, with fresh fruits and vegetables in the stores year-round, and ready-made clothes replaced home-sewn garments. The United States dominated the all-powerful electric mass media of commercial radio, talking movies, electric signs, and later television and computers.

Coming Full Circle: Industrializing the Farm

We will see in Chapter 11 how the fabled Jeffersonian farmers took their environmental licks on the High Plains, but American agriculture also tumbled happily into industrialization. Farmers enthusiastically mortgaged the farm for the sake of labor-saving machinery to overcome heavy physical drudgery. Over several decades in the late nineteenth and early twentieth centuries, American agriculture enjoyed a dramatic shift from its underequipped condition in an undeveloped United States to heavily mechanized and highly productive operations that became models for the rest of the world. Machine-based farming mimicked machine-based manufacturing. One vivid impact of the change was in man-hours per acre to harvest a crop of wheat, from 40 man-hours in 1800 to 12 in 1880 to only 8 in 1900. In 1800 one farmer's production fed less than 3 others; in 1900 this doubled to 6 others. By 1990 one American farmer could feed, incredibly, 96 others because of genetic plant breed-

ing and industrial-type farm management, as well as liberal applications of chemical fertilizers, pesticides, and herbicides.

Some early changes were as simple as harrows with steel teeth on iron frames instead of
all wood. As pioneers edged warily onto the treeless open country of the midwestern prairie
and the midcontinent High Plains, they found that success (or even survival) required technological innovation and new farming practices. Back in the eastern forest, 20 or 40 or even
80 acres could be worked with hand tools, a plow, and horses, but not 160 acres in Illinois or
320 acres in a half-section in Iowa or 640 acres in the full section required to prosper on the
Plains. The new dryland farming required far bigger farms to field a decent crop, and machinery to cultivate the bigger farm. The potential for success seemed better with the appearance of John Deere's iron-moldboard steel-tipped plow in the 1840s. Word spread that it "cut
through the sod like a hot knife through butter"; Deere sold more than 10,000 in 1857. The
midland farmer learned to use a variety of technologies to figure out how to get along without
trees. The invention of ready-made wood frame "balloon" houses gave him a needed boost
after years in dusty, muddy sod houses. Joseph F. Glidden's invention in 1874 of easily manufactured barbed wire for fencing, boundary lines, and animal control may have been a truly
revolutionary step. Careful to establish a monopoly by patent in 1876 to eliminate competition, he developed automatic barbed-wire fabrication machinery. By aggressive marketing,
Glidden sold 10,000 pounds of barbed wire in 1874 and six years later shipped 80.5 *million*
pounds. In 1874 he offered his barbed wire at $20 for 100 pounds, which went down to $10
in 1880, $3.45 in 1890, and reached a low of $1.80 in 1897. Glidden, a classic case of smart
entrepreneurialism, was as amazed at his accomplishment as Andrew Carnegie had been (see
earlier) about the price of steel.

Farmers joyously embraced other technologies as they found new regions to conquer.
The native people had been subdued and pushed westward. The 1862 Homestead Act offered
free prime farmland to settlers committed to five years of toil and survival to "prove up" their
property. The network of railroads expanded farmers' opportunities when it connected them
with eastern markets. A rush of new inventions offered them prosperity, including windmills
to get along without surface water, and may have made them overconfident. Legend has it
that as early as 1854, an old midwestern "pump doctor," John Burnham, weary of constant
repairs, suggested to a young Connecticut mechanic, Daniel Halladay, that if a windmill
could be made self-governing, it might well transform western farming. Halladay devised a
windmill that turned itself into the wind and controlled its speed, all by the centrifugal force
of a weight. The response was astonishing. Halladay moved to Chicago to be closer to potential dryland markets. Quantity orders from railroads allowed the United States Wind Engine
and Pump Company to dominate the big new industry by 1862. By 1879, as the railroads
spread across the Plains and independent Plains farmers became a significant market, 69 manufacturers sold more than $1 million of windmills. Competitive shakeouts reduced the num-
ber of manufacturers to 31 by 1919 and sales reached nearly $10 million. Important
refinements in that period included reduction in size from 30-foot diameters to a range from
4 to 16 feet, with 8- or 10-foot windmills becoming standard. The introduction of curved
steel blades led to higher efficiency, reductions in size, and lower cost. And the wonder of the
self-oiling mechanism delighted farmers who otherwise had to climb up in the midst of a
blizzard or dust storm to lubricate the linkages. Manufacturing guidelines established by Fairbanks, Morse & Company included many features of new industrial products that defined
modernity to contemporaries on and off the farm. It could be shipped knocked down and yet
readily erected with simple tools by ordinary mechanics; parts were interchangeable and re-

placeable; lubrication and maintenance were simple. By 1895 farms around Garden City in western Kansas sported about 150 "wind-reservoir irrigation" operations. They typically included one or two windmills, a reservoir, and up to 5 acres under irrigation, planted in vegetables and fruits for human consumption or alfalfa for animals. One Kansas official revived a popular claim that a farm family could live well on 5 irrigated acres and become rich on 20 acres. But a windmill could only pump from 30 feet down to supply only the household, its vegetable patch, and a few animals. The technological combination of deep drilling to groundwater, electric, or gas turbine pumps and center-pivot irrigation did not rescue Plains farm families until the 1960s, after they had suffered mightily during the Dust Bowl of the 1930s.

Cyrus McCormick, who combined invention and showmanship, began selling a workmanlike mechanical reaper (14,000 in 1876 alone), and his International Harvester Company soon offered the combine that cut, threshed, and bundled wheat on one machine. The reaper alone multiplied eightfold the land a farmer could harvest and seemed destined to guarantee success for prairie and plains farming. Back east, the new roller process for milling wheat for bread encouraged larger plantings on more land. In time, fields of wheat and corn covered hundreds of acres instead of tens of acres. The new mechanized equipment that seemed designed for flat open country also included massive and unwieldy steam tractors (weighing as much as 25 tons!). Small gasoline-powered tractors from Ford (the Fordson for only $750 in 1917, but it tended to rear up like a bucking horse and turn over under a load), International Harvester (Farmall), and John Deere (Poppin' Johnny) were far more practical and economical and sold in the tens of thousands even during the Depression. Tractors were soon recognized as being more than mechanical horses because they could work faster, longer, and did not require rest. The Farmall seemed most modern with a self-designated systems approach that offered a power takeoff and a line of easily attachable machinery for plowing, tilling, and harvesting. Most tractors soon standardized into two large rear steel wheels, a four-cylinder engine, electric starter, automobile-type transmission, two small front steering wheels, dirt proofing, and universal applications for row crops. Later advances included rubber tires, full-power takeoffs, mufflers, and enclosed cabs with air conditioning. In one generation between 1920 and 1950, most American farms went through the profound change from dependence on draft animals (which freed one-quarter of grain production from animal feed) to dependence on mechanical power (which created new dependencies on cash flow and external inputs for retooling and fuel). Farmers were soon told, "If the tractor doesn't fit in with your system of farming, try changing your farming."

In the decades following World War II, farmers became as much small business owners as they were people whose boots were covered with clods of gummy sod. Excellent farmland began to move toward $1,000 an acre on the rich prairie; the entrepreneurial farmer might own and work 2,000 acres of varying quality. Equipment costs might have started in 1950 at under $25,000 for tractor and machinery to plant the seed, fertilize and cultivate the burgeoning plants, and harvest the crop, but by the 1980s a profitable farm might require $500,000 in large, complex machinery. A million dollars sunk into land and equipment was not unusual. The deep pockets to stake such operations fell increasingly not to traditional family farmers, but to true industrial operations first described in 1955 as "agribusiness." Such corporate farming paid more attention to the fiscal bottom line than to the husbanding of the land and a stable family life. The change was dramatized in the 1930s when farm families, whose overworked soil was blowing away in the Dust Bowl, were "tractored out" by large-scale corporate enterprise. This was poignantly described in John Steinbeck's best-selling 1938 novel, *The*

Grapes of Wrath. Single-crop, or monoculture farming had always been typical of European farming in the New World, but in the twentieth century it made intensive consumption of the soil that required infusion of artificial nutrients provided by the chemical industry.

Conclusion

The historian of the frontier, Frederick Jackson Turner, complained in 1893 that the wilderness experience, which had so demonstrably determined American democratic institutions, had come to an end. He feared the new industrial America had no connections with the western geographical expansion that had shaped the nation's original powerful ideals and values. Factory America was a different country, he said, from frontier America. As early as the 1890s, most Americans realized that industrialization created a distinctive society that now had a life of its own. In 1929 the social critic Joseph Wood Krutch looked at the previous 50 years in his book *The Modern Temper* and wondered whether industrialization is "helping us very rapidly along the road we wish to travel." He admitted he could not forecast the future path of industrialization or whether it conformed to the best future path for American democratic society. It was clear to Krutch and other social commentators that the nation had reached a point in its historical development from which it could not return. At its worst, industrialism, with its single-minded focus on profits, seemed only to feed mindless indifference to human suffering, to ferocious class and racial violence, and the squandering of innumerable lives and talents. Social commentator Lewis Mumford called this a "psychological absenteeism" that characterized industrial societies. Since industrialization encouraged single-minded attention to material gain, it left no room for personal involvement with "the ultimate realities of life—birth and death, sex and love, family devotion and mutual aid, sacrifice and transcendence, human pride and cosmic awe." Such critics believed, for the first time in history, that industrialization was a new economic solvent which dissolved the traditional bonds of society, including religion, family cohesiveness, and community loyalty. As wealth continued to pour out of the factory system, these earlier values lost their priority. Mumford likened the single-mindedness of industrial capitalism to a military siege of a city during wartime. He concluded that the entire structure of a once attractive urban life—churches, public baths, taverns, family life—were dismantled or subordinated, not for patriotic defense of a city against enemy attack, but for impersonal money and abstract profits. When in 1934 the Depression dragged Americans down to their lowest point, Mumford, in *Technics and Civilization,* concluded that the machine age degraded humans. By its materialism it forced "a throwback to lower levels of thought and emotion."

By the mid-twentieth century, social critics described an era of alienation, violence, disorientation, and "future shock." In the late 1950s, at the height of America's post–World War II economic boom, the social critic David T. Bazelon said, "The industrial system is a wonderful wealth-machine; and especially here in the United States, in its advanced state. But I want to be clear and very firm about what it is *not;* it is *not* a human society." Fiercely loyal advocates of industrial society pointed out that the lowliest worker did acquire middle class comforts like a refrigerator, television, and an automobile, and the middle class enjoyed extravagances, like a second or third car or multiple television sets, that might have previously belonged only to the very rich. In 1995 historian of technology Carroll Pursell wrote, "Whether one looks at industrial production, biological reproduction, domestic workplaces, the mechanism of war, or the machinery of government, the same restructuring of meaning through modernist technology can be seen and increasingly appear problematic."

A century and a half before, in 1851, the novelist Herman Melville had Captain Ahab, a leading character in his novel *Moby Dick,* say of the technologies of his day, "All my means are sane, my motive and my object mad." Industrialization seemed to feed a narrow and mean-spirited view of the human condition. Said a critic in the 1980s, "No one identified the thousand dollars he made yesterday with the misery of the homeless person he encountered today." Nor did Americans yet consider that their industrial prowess and personal materialism were consuming their natural resources at an alarming rate and throwing the natural environmental systems around them into disarray, collapse, and extinction.

For Further Reading
Hardly anyone is neutral about industrialization. An enthusiastic stance is taken by Nathan Rosenberg, *Technology and American Economic Growth* (1972), together with a broader perspective in Nathan Rosenberg and L. E. Birdzell, Jr., *How the West Grew Rich: The Economic Transformation of the Industrial World* (1986). The classic study, still unsurpassed, remains Siegfried Giedion, *Mechanization Takes Command* (1948). The most thoughtful overviews are by Walter Licht, *Industrializing America: The Nineteenth Century* (1995), and Carroll Pursell's *The Machine in America: A Social History of Technology* (1995). Other broad historical perspectives are Bernard A. Weisberger, *The New Industrial Society* (1969), John F. Kasson, *Civilizing the Machine: Technology and Republican Values in America, 1776–1900* (1976), Howard Mumford Jones, *The Age of Energy: Varieties of American Experience, 1865–1915* (1971), Gilman M. Ostrander, *American Civilization in the First Machine Age, 1890–1940* (1970), Howard P. Segal, *Technological Utopianism in American Culture* (1985), and Thomas P. Hughes, *American Genesis: A Century of Invention and Technological Enthusiasm* (1989). Corporate America is unveiled in Alan Trachtenberg, *The Incorporation of America: Culture and Society in the Gilded Age* (1982), Alfred Chandler, *The Visible Hand: The Managerial Revolution in American Business* (1977) and *Scale and Scope: The Dynamics of Industrial Capitalism* (1990), David Noble, *American by Design: Science, Technology, and the Rise of Corporate Capitalism* (1977), and Martin Sklar, *The Corporate Reconstruction of American Capitalism, 1890–1916* (1988). See also Harry Braverman, *Labor and Monopoly Capital: The Degradation of Work in the Twentieth Century* (1974). Resource exploitation in the American West is examined in detail by Duane A. Smith, *Mining America: The Industry and the Environment, 1800–1980* (1987), Alan Derickson, *Workers' Health, Workers' Democracy: The Western Miners' Struggle, 1891–1925* (1988), and in a larger context by Gerald D. Nash, *The American West in the Twentieth Century* (1973). To learn more about standard of living, quality of life, and the power of middle-class expectations in American society, see Loren Baritz, *The Good Life: The Meaning of Success for the American Middle Class* (1982), and the continuing Harper "The Everyday Life in America Series," notably Thomas J. Schlereth, *Victorian Life: Transformations in Everyday Life, 1876–1915* (1991), and Harvey Green, *The Uncertainty of Everyday Life, 1915–1945* (1992). On the Progressives, see the unequaled analysis by Samuel P. Hays, *Conservation and the Gospel of Efficiency* (1968). On the celebration of industrialization, see Robert W. Rydell, *All the World's a Fair* (1984), and the perceptive essays by John B. Jackson in *American Space: The Centennial Years: 1865–1876* (1972).

CHAPTER EIGHT

RESHAPING THE NATION: THE BUILT ENVIRONMENT AND PUBLIC WORKS

Where she [Nature] denied us rivers, Mechanism has supplied them. Where she left our planet uncomfortably rough, Mechanism has applied the roller. Where her mountains have been found in the way, mechanism has boldly leveled or cut through them. Even the ocean, by which she thought to have parted her quarrelsome children, Mechanism has encouraged them to step across. As if her earth were not good enough for wheels, Mechanism travels it upon iron pathways.

— Industry Spokesman Timothy Walker, 1831

I think that I have never knowed, a sight as lovely as a road. A road upon whose concrete tops, the flow of traffic never stops; A road that costs a lot to build, just as the City Council willed; A road the planners saw we need, to get the cars to greater speed; We've let the contracts so dig in, and let the chopping now begin; Somebody else can make a tree, but roads are made by guys like me.

— Newspaper Columnist Mike Royko, 1993

The Way Americans Saw It: From Geographical Determinism to Technological Liberation

By 1880 many Americans were convinced they had won the war against raw nature. They were no longer merely nature's nation; instead, they had grabbed the initiative from the natural world. This was a major shift that cannot be overemphasized. Earlier in the century, their preindustrial society could not cope with cold and dampness, distance and terrain, heat and aridity, deeply buried minerals, predatory animals, viruses and bacteria, and other nonhuman obstacles. Settler life in the wilderness was accepted as a difficult but temporary step backward from the benefits of civilization. With industrialization, however, the American people could pry apart their obsolete nature-bound way of life to build a new life founded on technology-based "unnatural" connections. In the first half of the nineteenth century, they had already watched with excitement as gangs of men, horses, mules, and machines dug a 300-mile-long ditch across New York State called the Erie Canal. Industrious teams of men cut down forests and bridged hundreds of rivers and streams to push the National Road across the Allegheny Mountains and into the midwestern heartland. After the Civil War, great public works were compared with the total mobilization of war because each project marshaled so many skills and consumed so much money and materials. The first major postwar achievement was the successful transcontinental railroad line that bridged empty plains, rugged mountains, and barren deserts.

A Network of Cities Captures the Inland Landscape

Contrary to the traditional belief espoused in Frederick Jackson Turner's "frontier thesis" that the frontier slowly moved westward primarily through trappers and intrepid pioneer farm families, cities immediately appeared and in some cases stepped out beyond the frontier line. Pittsburgh, Cincinnati, Louisville, and St. Louis, "planted before the surrounding soil was broken for cultivation," were commercial outposts from which settlement spread; each city created its own hinterland into which explorers, fur traders, and farmers could fan out, not vice versa. American towns were different from their European counterparts, which appeared late on the largely rural landscape in conflict with the social edifice of serfs, manors, and noble estates. Pittsburgh called itself "the gateway to the West" (also claimed by Cincinnati and St. Louis), the strategic frontier outlet for travelers and goods and its merchants the source of supplies for travel. As early as 1794 over 13,000 easterners passed through the city heading westward. In 1803 it was the outfitting center for the Lewis and Clark expedition. By the early years of the nineteenth century, the city boasted 23 general stores. In the Midwest, cities in the wilderness did not evolve into a new form, but repeated eastern patterns. The Philadelphia gridiron was forced on Cincinnati's hills, even the same street widths and similar alleys. The gridiron plan prevented a new city from taking advantage of local woodland, waterways, lakes, and ancient paths. One critic of Louisville regretted that it had "turned its back upon the varied and interesting prospect presented by the Ohio and its Falls." San Francisco endured "an inebriated gridiron staggering up colossal inclines and hurtling down precipitous declines." Inhabitants and visitors complained about the dull monotony of the gridiron plan of most western cities, although it made the land easy to sell and build on.

By the third decade of the nineteenth century Americans devised an industrial geography that captured the vast rural landscape which had once been the nation's dominant feature. This urban web enlarged from a few local pinpoints of commercial cities to an extensive industrial network that stretched through New England, the mid-Atlantic states, and soon made connections across the Midwest. The old core cities of Boston, New York, Newark, and Philadelphia remained diversified industrial and commercial centers. New factory towns included Worcester (machinery) in central Massachusetts, the transformed port of Providence (tools, woolens, jewelry) in Rhode Island, Bridgeport (machine tools and rifles) and Waterbury (brass manufacturing) in Connecticut, Passaic (woolen mills), Paterson (silk textiles), and Trenton (iron manufacturing) in New Jersey, and Wilmington (leather goods) in Delaware. A string of industrial enterprises took hold along the Erie Canal, including Albany (iron manufacturing), Cohoes (cotton textiles), Troy (iron manufacturing), Schenectady (steam locomotives), Utica (textiles and garments), Rome (copper wire), Rochester (diversified industries), and Buffalo (iron and steel production). The American ambition was not merely to defeat nature's purposes, but to redirect it and reshape it. True, much of America's landscape, particularly in the West, still lay as unaltered wilderness barely scratched by settlements. Yet advances in science and engineering persuaded Americans that it was just a matter of time until they would collapse the nation's vast spaces and physical barriers into manageable pieces.

Older midwestern trading centers were entirely reshaped and enlarged by large factory zones: Pittsburgh (steel), Cleveland (iron, steel, and oil production), and Cincinnati (specialized machinery). Small Ohio villages became factory towns: Canton known for watches, Springfield for agricultural machinery, Youngstown for steel, Dayton for railroad cars and office machinery, Akron for rubber, East Liverpool for pottery. In Michigan the old Fort Detroit became submerged under factories producing railroad cars, machinery, pharmaceuticals, shoes, and myriad other goods. Grand Rapids became the leading furniture maker in the nation. Across Lake Michigan in Wisconsin, Milwaukee enjoyed a reputation for beer production, but stood in the shadow of nearby Chicago, 90 miles to the south. Moline in Illinois and Davenport in Iowa and soon Minneapolis, Omaha, and Kansas City became urban centers intimately connected with the great agricultural heartland of the Midwest, for which they stored and processed grain, slaughtered its animals into meat products, and manufactured machinery for farmers. The neighboring rural countryside and regional natural resources rarely withstood the demands from a prospering city. The surrounding geography, as William Cronon has noted, became a "second nature," a support system for burgeoning urban growth of the juggernaut factory city. By 1900 half of all Americans lived in cities and their factories churned out 40 percent of all of America's industrial goods.

The Building of an Infrastructure System

Cities epitomized the *built environment,* made up of streets, gutters, and curbs, sidewalks, street lights, and the walls and windows of concrete, steel, brick, and wooden buildings. Below the surface was the "underground city" (Lewis Mumford's term), a hydraulic, pneumatic, and electrical maze of subway and service tunnels, tracks, platforms, storage rooms, and shops, as well as water mains, sewers, gas mains, and ganglia of power lines. When seen from the point of view of their connections, the built environment is made up of a variety of *systems*. The parts in turn can be subdivided into a variety of subsystems, and the system itself may be part of another larger system. For example, the plumbing for drinking water in a house is itself part of an interior household system, which in turn is part of a citywide water system, itself served by a system of reservoirs and filtration plants. A major metropolitan region such as New York City depends on distant water supplies in upstate environmental reserves that use dams, reservoirs, and aqueducts to deliver water through underground mains, supply lines, storage tanks, hydrants, and water heaters, pipes, drains, and faucets in private homes. Wastewater travels through a sewer system including toilets and sinks, household plumbing, sewer pipes, and treatment plants. Electrical power grids require networks of steam turbines and electric generators to make electricity, transformers to raise or lower voltage, and transmission lines to connect with industrial, commercial, and residential customers. To Lewis Mumford, this electric grid that serves telephone, radio, television, and computer communications existed as "the invisible city." Urban historian Martin V. Melosi added, "The buildings and bridges standing as concrete forests above the streets are not merely the products of obscure mundane technologies or a backdrop for human action, but integral components in a dynamic environmental system." Melosi reminds us, "Cities are not static backdrops for human action, nor are they organic metaphors, but ever-mutating open systems." The different pieces of a system are interactive and interdependent, and participate in diverse activities that are structural, functional, and dynamic. Thus the natural terrain of a city would recede into the background. The combination of these systems can be labeled an *infrastructure*, which broadly describes the physical apparatus of a city and how it functions to serve its population.

Each individual urban landscape was itself connected by a busy network—an *infrastructure system*—that transported people, goods, and information between America's cities and effectively removed humanity's historic constraints of distance and physical obstacles. This wider network involved bridges, roads, railroads, tunnels, harbors, and eventually airports. Dams, reservoirs, aqueducts, tunnels, and canals reshaped and dominated large geographical regions such as California's interior farmland (see Chapter 10). On a regional, even national basis, an entire geography would be conquered and bypassed by a totality of physical grids, industrial systems, and urban infrastructures. In its short history, the United States had engineered a remarkable, widely admired, and widely imitated infrastructure, a technological layer upon the environment "to improve the standard of living and to diminish toil." Overall, Americans began to live and work and play in fabricated networks more than they inhabited the natural world.

By the early twentieth century the Industrial Revolution had transformed the American landscape from vast distances requiring months of travel to a closely knit network of industrial cities. Steam-powered trains of the New York Central, Pennsylvania, Baltimore and Ohio, Union Pacific, Santa Fe, and innumerable other railroad corporations carried Americans between cities and across the continent. Electric streetcars whisked them across town, and they began to tinker with the internal combustion engine of the "horseless carriage." Messages crossed the nation in a few seconds by Western Union telegraph. Americans talked with each other over extensive Bell Telephone networks. Much of this infrastructure depended on complexes of capital industries that fabricated steel, produced oil, and manufactured household goods.

The South Finds Its Own Well-Worn Path

Despite the travail of the Civil War and the dislocations from the end of slavery, the South remained a region that produced raw materials—cotton, rice, livestock, lumber, and other agricultural staples—for outside consumption, and in turn consumed manufactured goods from the outside. It was a limited economic program—each crop entirely dependent on markets beyond its control—that fostered continuous consumption of a depleted landscape. Even banking and shipping services came from the North, to which the South was attached virtually as a colony. It was at the mercy of northern investment and marketing strategies. Wealth rushed outside, and little returned to protect a naturally rich environment. It is surprising how little was changed by the Civil War despite most battles fought on southern territory, or by Reconstruction, whose northern controls were temporary. Some states, like the Carolinas, Alabama, and Mississippi, did not have metropolitan regions, not even large port cities, until well into the twentieth century. The postwar transportation infrastructure of the South, already fallen behind the Northeast before the Civil War with limited railroad development and few canals, would not for decades receive capital infusion that the Midwest and West earlier enjoyed. With a surplus of low-paid workers, the South was not pushed into capital development of labor-saving industrial mechanization that definitively reshaped the Northeast. The only exceptions to this endemic stagnation were in the 1870s and 1880s a string of textile mill villages powered by mountain streams in the backcountry Piedmont of the Carolinas, Georgia, and Alabama, and steel production centered on Birmingham, Alabama, that used regional coal and iron ore. Although forest cutting became a major cash product after the Civil War, one lumber mill operator described the lack of an expansionist mood in the late nineteenth century: "Instead of installing machinery to do the work, we always undertook to do it putting in another cheap negro." As late as 1900 no more than 10 percent of the South's work force was in manufacturing. Nor was the work force infused by millions of self-sacrificing immigrants; mobility after World War I instead meant the departure of ambitious blacks and whites for the beckoning industrial cities of Cleveland, Detroit, and Chicago.

Southern geography remained a rural landscape of farms and small towns, in which blacks and poor whites remained an impoverished underclass that formed the majority population in many regions. In many cases this already abused rural geography was deliberately perpetuated by local authorities and business interests who created an underclass in perpetual "debt peonage." Well into the 1940s poor white southern sharecroppers or tenant farmers in isolated regions like northeastern Alabama lived at the end of dirt paths, rarely owned a mule, traveled by foot, and were treated as contemptible outsiders by townspeople only 4 or 5 miles away. For the majority of southerners, daily life was intensely local, concentrated within a few hundred yards of a tired "dog-trot" house. Lacking mechanical devices that were commonplace elsewhere, and using tools that would have been familiar to a medieval serf, poor whites and blacks tended their farm plots lightly with low yields, and contradictorily, with environmentally poor methods that accelerated land depletion and heavy erosion. Deep debt meant virtually no geographical mobility, which so profoundly aided personal prosperity elsewhere in the nation. Not the least, racial hostility divided an already weakened society. Economic weakness—per capita income in 1900 was half of the rest of the nation—drove inhabitants into environmental overuse and waste. There was no urban, industrial "new South" until well after World War II.

Still Painfully Close to Nature:
Three "Poor-White" Families in
Northeast Alabama

They were the Ricketts, nine in all, the Woods, an extended family of eight, and the six Gudgers, the first two tenant farmers, the latter a half-cropper. They were visited during July and August in 1936 by the novelist and screenwriter James Agee and the photographer Walker Evans on assignment to do an article for *Fortune* magazine: Instead the two produced an American classic, *Let Us Now Praise Famous Men*. Their book depicted the daily living and immediate environments of poor white families during the depths of the Depression, a marginal existence in a difficult geography that had probably changed little in the 80 years since the Civil War. In detailed, almost voyeurlike descriptions of rooms and furniture in houses, personal belongings and trash piles, immediate scrub forest environments, and cotton picking in unfriendly clay fields, Agee uncovers the bone-deep fatigue, sense of abandonment, and hopelessness of the three families. They are beaten down by the unyielding features of their environment on which they depend for life and crops, and sunk under an economic servitude that is fatal to them. All are in debt to their landlord, and none can escape to better jobs or lives elsewhere. George Gudger rents house, land, and farm implements from his landlord Chester Boles, and pays back half his corn, cotton, and cottonseed to Boles before he can sell the rest at depressed prices. Gudger and his entire family do manual labor on 11 acres in corn, 9 in cotton, and 1 acre in home produce. Agee writes, "These fields are workrooms, or fragrant but mainly sterile workfloors without walls and with a roof of uncontrollable chance, fear, rumination, and propitiative prayer." At home, their water supply is a difficult 150-yard descent and climb to a spring, "not a short distance to walk for every drop of water that is needed." There they store their "small crocks of butter, cream, and milk [that] stand sunken to their eyes, tied over with pieces of saturated floursack." The spring does not bubble with fresh water: "It is about the temper of faucet water, and tastes slack and faintly sad, and as if just short of stale. It is not quite tepid, however, and it does not seem to taste of sweat and sickness, as the water does which the Woods family have to use." The house of unpainted pine is wood "with a texture and look like that of weathered bone," an attempted home that is "a human shelter, a strangely lined nest, a creature of killed pine, stitched together with nails into about as rude a garment against the hostilities of heaven as a human family may wear . . . a skin of one thickness alone against the earth and air." Around it "the dirt is blond and bare, except a little fledging of grass-leaves at the roots of structures" and lacks trees or bushes. Agee compares the Gudgers' place to "a frontier house in 1800 in newly cleared country." The Woods' and Ricketts' places are only slightly better. "The land that was under us lay down all around us and its continuance was enormous as if we were chips or matches floated, holding their own by their very minuteness, at a great distance out upon the surface of a tenderly laboring sea. The sky was even larger. . . . The sphere of power of a single human family and a mule is small; and within the limits of each of these small spheres [resides] the essential human frailty."

The Profession of Engineering

A class of highly trained experts—civil engineers—emerged in the nineteenth century as a respected profession dedicated to the design and construction of the built environment. The technological devices and skills of these professionals was so essential that it is appropriate to describe the transformation as the "engineered environment." Engineering is, according to one encyclopedia, "the art of directing the great sources of materials and power in nature for the use and the convenience of humans. It is the useful applications of natural phenomena." According to this definition, engineers have a built-in bias that favors "improvement." They are always dissatisfied with present methods and equipment. When civil engineers send an entire superhighway through an urban neighborhood, the project involves the building of the roadbed, revetments, ramps, and bridges, new placement of water, sewer, and power utility lines, and the removal of entire neighborhoods of homes and stores. The result is a public work. Private civil engineering is similar, including the construction of pipelines, shopping malls, housing tracts, and other large construction for industrial, commercial, or residential use.

Civil engineering spun off from military engineering. Back in the Revolutionary War era of the 1770s and 1780s, newly independent Americans, cut off from British services, found that their desperate need for fortification experts and wharf and bridge builders was hardly satisfied by a few French military engineers. When in 1802 West Point was established on the Hudson River as a military academy, its primary agenda was to produce military engineers, many of whom retired to serve civilian projects. (The U.S. Army Corps of Engineers, also created in 1802, is described in Chapter 10.) Americans soon learned that their famous reputation for self-taught, jack-of-all-trades skills did not serve well for the complexities of public structures, especially the enormous demand for canal, road, bridge, and railroad construction during the nation's rapid expansion across its raw landscape. Yet during the early decades of western expansion, most engineering skills were still learned by the ancient system of several years of apprenticeship to a master builder, a practice that was highly idiosyncratic and without standards in mathematical instruction, basic science, materials know-how, and construction techniques. The obvious needs for professionals in numbers that West Point could not produce led to the founding of nearby Rensselaer Polytechnic Institute in 1829, and the formation of practical engineering training at otherwise haughty institutions like Harvard in 1842 and Yale in 1847. The turning point came when President Lincoln signed the all-important Morrill Act of 1862, which deliberately required applied education in "mechanics" and agriculture in land-grant colleges at central locations in every state and territory.

Civil engineers, both military and civilian, were in time joined by other like-minded professionals. The first mining engineers were graduated from Columbia in the early 1870s, the same time that Yale and the Massachusetts Institute of Technology sent off their first mechanical engineering graduates. Cornell and MIT were in the vanguard of the newfangled electrical engineering field in the 1880s. Nevertheless, as was true across much of American higher education, many Americans believed the best training was available in Germany. As late as 1889 at least 150 Americans were studying in German engineering schools. Not until 1900 were there enough engineers in the field to become a professional class between the traditional "mechanick" and the entrepreneur. Soon engineers emerged as the quintessential American heroes who built the national infrastructure, more lauded than the traditional professional clergyman, doctor, or lawyer. They seemed everywhere in large-scale projects that re-worked the American landscape. Geotechnical engineers asked mundane but essential questions of rock and soil mechanics. Is the terrain stable and can it bear the weight of the project? Structural engineers dealt with foundations and the steel, concrete, and masonry needs of new buildings. Transportation engineers asked what kind of facilities are needed to ease the traffic burden of the completed project on local roads, subways, highways and airports. Only in more recent years, since the early 1970s, have environmental engineers (earlier they were sanitary engineers) entered the picture to solve problems of sewage treatment, water pollution, refuse disposal, hazardous waste disposal, air pollution control, potable management (drinking water), protection of local animal and plant life, status of historic sites, noise, and physical appearance, all to meet government requirements aimed at protecting the public and the environment. In sum, the numbers of all engineers numbered in the hundreds in 1870, leaped to 230,000 by 1930, and soared upward of 800,000 by 1990.

Better water systems, building construction, electrification, and transportation required engineering skill; growing populations needed the technical advances to keep America's cities habitable. Consulting engineers who traveled from one large project to another often became resident or city engineers with their own staffs or departments. The best known was Rudolph Hering, who finished his bridge building training in Dresden in Prussia in 1868 and began his career as a surveying assistant for the new Prospect Park in the city of Brooklyn. His surveying work continued on the new Fairmount Park in Philadelphia, included an excursion to faraway Yellowstone National Park to set its boundaries, and he finally became engineer in charge of construction of Philadelphia's Girard Street Bridge. Hering exemplified the image of the engineer as social hero who practiced civic virtue when he took charge of Philadelphia's massive reconstruction of its main sewers and bridges, including breaking the hold of corrupt contractors. Engineers who followed in Hering's footsteps experienced a crisis of conscience: Was their primary professional obligation to employers, to the highest standards of their professional expertise, or to a broader public interest? In 1896 Stevens Institute of Technology students were told, "The financial side of engineering is always the most important. [You] must always be subservient to those who represent the money invested in the enterprise." The high point of engineering participation in the centers of power took place during the Progressive era of the first decades of the twentieth century, when they were idealized as archetypal "experts" to lead the nation into a heavily planned industrial utopia. Progressive leaders like President Theodore Roosevelt earnestly believed that primarily through engineering "objective" science could replace political "prejudice." Engineers were prominent spokesmen at presidential conferences on waterways and ambitious planning convocations by state governors. Roosevelt and colleagues like Gifford Pinchot added that the nation's natural resources, notably its vast forests and waterways, could be efficiently controlled, used, and conserved, through engineering know-how. For a time in the first half of the twentieth century, the engineer embodied the widely held conviction that he (rarely she) was the most ethically responsible person in the nation: Technological solutions could solve social needs and ills. Historians like Lynn White, Jr., wrote, "Engineers are the chief revolutionaries of our time. Their implicit ideology is a compound of compassion for those suffering from physical want, combined with a Promethean rebellion against all bonds, even bonds to this planet. Engineers are arch-enemies of all who resist the surge of the mass of mankind toward a new order of plenty, of mobility, and of personal freedom." Industrialization, said White, who was not an engineer, is a "prime spiritual achievement."

Public Works for Private Cities

The objectives of the industrial city were not different from the earlier wharf port or market-place town or railroad city. All were physically constructed to provide the greatest profit to the industries who settled in them, almost regardless of human consequences. When large integrated steel production entered Pittsburgh in the last third of the nineteenth century, it took over the best riverfront sites along the Monongahela. The steel-making factory was the sole justification for the existence of brand-new cities carved out of the established rural country-side, such as Hammond and Gary to the south of Chicago, and Birmingham in Alabama. Railroad sleeper cars led to the construction of Pullman south of Chicago, and the American Bridge Company was served by Ambridge west of Pittsburgh. Later, the same was true with aircraft fabrication by Boeing near Seattle and Douglas in southern California. But the industrial cities faced enormous crowding and expansion problems. By the middle of the nineteenth century, city populations were doubling and tripling every decade. There were 136 New Yorkers per acre, nearly 83 per acre in Boston, over 80 in Philadelphia, and over 68 in Pittsburgh. Together with geographical expansion away from the old central city, urban "reclamation" drained marshes, filled in a bay or cove, or leveled a hill.

Infrastructure in the City: Public Utilities

A new institution, the city utility, served both private interests and public needs. The first utility anywhere covered the building and maintenance of London's ferryboats, docks, and warehouses. Despite a bad experience with the private Manhattan Company in New York (see Chapter 10), other private ventures supplied water to Boston until 1848 and to Baltimore until 1854. As late as 1860 more than half of the urban waterworks in the United States were privately owned. Private utilities moved into urban mass transit, electricity, natural gas, and sewage treatment. But private investors were often unwilling to invest enough capital to serve everyone and devoted themselves to the wealthy section of the city. Some had also skimped in fire hydrants, public fountains, and street washing. Soon most cities turned to municipal ownership. Urban needs had reached a scale that required taxpayer payment for the construction of large-scale public works. One answer was the creation of some of the nation's largest private monopolies "in the public interest." In the United States, the first such public-private hybrid industry—private profit "affected with a public interest"—involved water management in Philadelphia. It was usually impossible to offer duplicate services for water, natural gas, and electricity; one supplier created a "natural monopoly." In the late nineteenth century, Chicagoan Samuel Insull took advantage of the nature of utilities to create a large monopoly of integrated private utilities (Commonwealth Edison Company, People's Gas, and Public Service of Northern Illinois) that included the usual dynamos, transmission lines, and incandescent lamps, as well as hydroelectric dams, and reached out to investment banks, brokerage houses, and state regulatory agencies. The entire goal was to make the way for the easy and inexpensive transmission of electricity traveling at high speed (at the highest possible profit). Such utilities often received the privileges of low tax rates on their property and revenues, and the use of public land for private profits. For example, it is impossible to store electricity;

nevertheless, generating capacity must be as high as needed for peak periods. The output must be generated at the instant of its use. This results in wide variations in the loads imposed on an electrical utility. The largest possible capacity, measured in kilowatts or horsepower, must be available for occasional total demand. Much of the capacity may be idle during extended periods when there is no demand for output. Hence a utility might claim a monopoly was necessary because of its high initial investment.

The Industrial City Spreads across the Landscape

The Transformation of America by the Railroads

As we saw in Chapter 5, astute business leaders in Baltimore dared to apply an untested English technology—the railroad—to connect the city to the westward-flowing Ohio River, 400 miles away and across the Appalachian Mountains. Although the Baltimore and Ohio Railroad, chartered in 1827, did not reach Wheeling, downstream from Pittsburgh on the Ohio River, until 1853, the railroad quickly became the technology of choice. The railroad could "climb tall mountains, leap yawning chasms, and ford raging rivers," a conquest of both space and time that carried Americans far beyond what steamboats and canals had done for them. The Mississippi River remained the nation's great north-south avenue of commerce, but the railroads redirected America's spatial momentum toward the West. What began with a few hundred miles of track in 1840 became a nationwide network by 1870 and would continue to dominate transportation for the first four decades of the twentieth century. It seemed that Americans could ignore nature's natural paths.

Successful urban centers could seemingly be created anywhere along the reach of rail roads, such as inauspicious places like Columbus, Ohio, or Indianapolis, Indiana. Rail lines connected dots of trade scattered across the vast nation. Western boosters and promoters almost invariably pictured great cities. Typically across the Midwest, a real estate speculator backed by eastern funds bought several hundred acres of wilderness (at $1.25–$2.50 an acre) where a railroad might run a new line. The tract would be surveyed and staked into a grid of lots and streets. An optimistic map—"the nation's greatest fictional resource"—would show a train on a nonexistent line surrounded by nonexistent houses. Americans went on a land-buying boom to get in cheaply and knew they might be swindled; lots were sold sight unseen, often in towns that would never exist. Speculators failed at Michigan City, Indiana, which they believed was a better railroad-water link than Chicago. Competition in western Kansas for county seats and railroad centers led to violence and gunfire. For every successful town, there were tens of failures. Between 1860 and 1910 the connective railroad network did turn regional trading posts into boomtowns. The list is impressive: Albuquerque, Atlanta, Birmingham, Butte, Cheyenne, Dallas, El Paso, Fort Worth, Kansas City, Los Angeles, Memphis, Minneapolis, Nashville, Oklahoma City, Omaha, Portland, Reno, St. Paul, Salt Lake City, San Antonio, San Diego, San Francisco, Santa Fe, Seattle, Spokane, and Tacoma. The "blank spaces" between the dots came to be regarded merely as geographical impediments. Rail lines shot across or bypassed regions that lacked an identifiable urban focal point, such as

The Continuing Power of Private Ownership: Restrictive Zoning

The industrial cities remained in private hands. A new feature that strengthened the hand of property owners was restrictive zoning. It originated in San Francisco in the 1880s by applying nuisance laws to legally discriminate against "undesirables," the Chinese who settled in after they were imported to build railroads and work in gold mines. Zoning declared Chinese laundries, which were also social centers, as nuisances and fire hazards. Similar nuisance-zone statutes spread down the Pacific coast to be applied not only against minorities, but also against undesirable activities, including livery stables, saloons, dance halls, pool halls, and slaughterhouses. Los Angeles soon was zoned into residential, industrial, and mixed districts. The first cities to use zoning in positive ways to regulate fire safety, building heights, and types of construction were Washington, D.C., Baltimore, and Indianapolis. New York City passed the earliest comprehensive zoning ordinance in 1916 to prevent skyscrapers and multistory commercial lofts from intruding on the more fashionable businesses of Fifth Avenue. The skyscraper challenged the centuries-old relationship between street width and building height. Masonry construction limited buildings to a maximum height of 8 stories; steel-frame construction allowed skyscrapers to rise as high as 16 stories. This greatly affected land values, utilities, and crowding. Small older buildings were torn down for profitable high-rise construction. In New York City, after public hearings in which the Fifth Avenue merchants told their fears of the loss of well-to-do customers to crowding and congestion, zoning maps were drawn "to preserve the character of the district" and the right to "protect health, safety, morals, and general welfare of citizens."

The New York zoning law was so successful that by 1926 it was copied by 591 other cities. Zoning was strengthened in 1926 by a U.S. Supreme Court decision, *Village of Euclid, Ohio* v. *Ambler Realty Company*, which prevented a developer from entering residentially zoned land to capture property for industrial purposes. Zoning became a common action for community planning and social control. Local governments have used zoning to abate a "nuisance," which was defined as "noise, traffic, fire hazard, or any other danger to the safety, health, morals, and general welfare of a residential area." Zoning, for example, prevents the construction of a gas station on a residential corner lot. City neighborhoods and suburban communities also applied zoning to keep out "undesirable" blacks, Jews, Asians, Catholics, and other ethnic groups. Such "restrictive covenants" were not declared illegal by the courts until 1948. Zoning has also been used to ensure "light settlement" of large single houses on substantial lots as large as 2 or 4 acres. This was de facto segregation that prevented lower income families from settling in such a zoned neighborhood. At best, zoning allowed the common good to override individual or corporate property rights. This was nevertheless criticized as a "taking" of the rights of private property. Today environmental regulatory constraints on the uses of private property are hotly debated as takings that reduce or restrict property dollar value. Zoning has been extremely useful in land use planning to control traffic, health, lighting, utilities, and housing, but it has done little to overcome slums and urban blight because it tends to ratify the status quo.

Appalachia or the High Plains. Each urban center was more likely to be influenced by other urban centers—even hundreds of miles away—more than by its parenting region. Boston, for example, came to have more in common with Philadelphia or Chicago than with western Massachusetts. Here began what Richard C. Wade has described as an "urban imperialism" that shaped the rest of American history. The great transformation that came with railroads lasted for approximately a century before the highway system took over.

America's Love Affair with Mobility

Freedom of movement was the third leg of the stool on which America's built environment sits, together with private property and profit making. From their beginnings, Americans have cherished freedom of movement as a personal right. A European visitor in 1847 wrote, "If God were suddenly to call the world to judgment, He would surprise two-thirds of the American population on the road like ants." Geographical mobility enlarged the opportunities Americans had for social, occupational, and economic improvement. Horizontal mobility enhanced vertical mobility across social and income classes. The greatest migration in world history—the movement of 40 million people from greater Europe to the United States— went mostly to crowded American cities between the Civil War and the 1920s. Southern blacks began their remarkable influx into the northeastern industrial cities—Pittsburgh, Detroit, Cleveland, Chicago—in the 1920s. American farm boys and girls continued to seek their fortunes in the city to the extent that today only 2 percent of Americans are still on the farm, compared to 30 percent in the 1930s. Until recently, 1 out of 5 American families moved each year to seek a better job, a nicer climate, and other benefits. In most cases the migration is from one metropolitan region to another: New York to Atlanta, Chicago to Denver, Los Angeles to Seattle.

Mobility in the Industrial City

If we lived in an American city before 1850, we would walk to work, no matter whether we worked on the factory floor or managed the plant. We would also walk to school, places of worship, and stores. Walking determined the size and shape of the city. People were willing to travel on foot for 30 to 40 minutes, a range of perhaps 2 miles, to work or to shop or to visit. (Today's rule of thumb for maximum acceptable commuting by car or train is 75 minutes.) If we were upper middle class we would have our stableman harness the horses (from the small backyard barn) to a light carriage in order to be off to the park or see friends. Wagons, carriages, horses, mules, and pedestrians jammed the central streets, which, aside from a few miles paved with cobblestones or gravel, raised dust or drowned in mud. The omnibus—a large two-horse-drawn coach carrying 12 to 15 people—marked the beginning of public transportation over fixed routes for fixed rates. At 6 to 12½ cents a ride, the omnibus was still too costly for laborers and kept them living in crowded housing near the factories. Streetcars and commuter railroads would long remain out of their reach. For the factory worker and his family, a ride on the trolley at 5 cents was a luxury reserved only for a rare weekend excursion for a picnic or to an amusement park.

Downtown crowding brought on a bottleneck in transportation. Congestion on city streets, even before the appearance of automobiles, had led people to look for transportation

The Power of the Railroads to Bring Change: Chicago versus St. Louis

Geographic determinism encouraged people to predict the success of a city like St. Louis because of its location at the center of the country's great natural waterways: It had long been a primary port for trade from the east from Pittsburgh by way of the Ohio River. It had forged a historic link to the great port city of New Orleans on the Gulf of Mexico via the Mississippi River. It was newly connected to the wealth of Denver and the Rockies by the old established migrant trails and the new transcontinental railroad. Its long-standing success as a center of commerce and travel was, therefore, its citizens believed, virtually guaranteed.

The leaders of St. Louis, in their overconfidence, did not recognize the capability of the new railroad technology to divert trade and migration from established routes that followed natural terrain and waterways. The struggling city of Chicago was beset by a river whose entry was repeatedly blocked by a sandbar. Its plans to make a long-sought link between Lake Michigan and the Mississippi River involved a canal connection that required the river. Without other alternatives, such as the river traffic that lulled St. Louis into complacency, Chicago's leaders recognized that their future instead depended on the railroad. Their business activities centered on the new railroad terminal that spawned adjacent warehouses and a manufacturing district. Nearby, Chicago's "Loop" covered only a few square blocks, but it was at the strategic center of the city's activities. The railroads came from north and south, east and west, connected at several terminals (Union Station, Northwestern Station, Randolph Street Station). Retailers (Marshall Field and Company, Carson Pirie Scott and Company) established themselves nearby all these operations. Chicago became the hub for eastern railroads that began to stretch westward in its direction and extend their own railroads westward into the rich prairie and plains farmland. In such a way Chicago captured trade from all di-

alternatives above and below the streets. Cities had been reticent to build elevated railways because they were powered by dirty and dangerous steam power. Once they had been converted to run on electricity, however, the famous "El" systems became fixtures as alternative people-moving networks in American cities such as New York, Chicago, Boston, Philadelphia, Brooklyn, and Kansas City. By 1902 there were almost 22,000 miles of electric "trolley" and "El" lines in urban areas. American cities also hesitated to build subways, first built in London in the 1860s, because they were also originally steam-engine powered. Boston ventured to build America's first subway in 1897. Although tunneling costs soared to more than $4.3 million for less than 2 miles, the system successfully carried more than 50 million passengers and ran up to 400 cars each way during peak hours in its first year of operation. New York City followed Boston's lead in 1904; Philadelphia followed shortly, and Chicago built its smaller system in the 1930s. Americans were unusual among industrial nations because they looked on mass transportation as a private business, not a government service. Transportation systems were usually monopolistic franchises and treated like utilities. Whether the system used streetcars, elevated railways, subways, or commuter trains, it required a heavy outlay of capital, which was sometimes possible only with a taxpayer-based public bond issue. As monopolies,

rections as Americans realized the potential of railroad technology. As a result, during the 1860s Chicago tripled its population while St. Louis failed even to double its inhabitants. New Orleans fared worse, losing its role as the major outlet for midwestern goods to become a regional cotton-dependent port. The message was clear: Railroad lines could, and would, be built almost anywhere regardless of "natural" geographic paths.

A fan of waterways and railroads that linked Chicago with its regional agricultural and forestry surrounding overcame its swampy location. On a national level, its strategic location as the southwestern terminus of Great Lakes shipping and its successful promotion of itself turned it into the nation's largest boomtown (until Los Angeles in the twentieth century) based on massive transfers of goods and frenzied real estate and commercial development. With its unequaled connections with the rest of the nation, Chicago also emerged as the center for the processing of raw materials—meatpacking, flour and lumber milling, and a burgeoning iron and steel and agricultural machinery industry. These industries were supported by mercantile exchanges, banking, insurance companies, and other essential services for business. Names connected with Chicago are Armour and Wilson in meatpacking, McCormick in agricultural machinery, and both Sears, Roebuck and Montgomery Ward in mail-order merchandising. Chicago demonstrated that city and country were not separate places; they were more connected than autonomous, with country inevitably outstripped. This reordering of natural resources formed a new order that "modernized" the original first nature. First nature was judged of little value until it was absorbed into second nature. Construction of the built environment has also been called "the great transformation" by the philosopher Michael Polyani because it locked modern civilization into a specific technological pathway from which civilization cannot now leave or extricate itself except with great difficulty.

the mass transit businesses were extremely profitable even at the long-sacred fare of 5 cents. These private profit-making operations to serve the public were also so often chaotic and uncontrolled that cities began to regulate public transportation by licensing operators, locating omnibus routes, inspecting vehicles, and setting speed limits.

Flight to the Suburbs: Streetcar and Commuter Train

City life, once freed from the limits of walking to jobs on harbor wharves or inside factories, began to move on a vastly expanded stage. Middle- or upper-class families escaped the congestion, pollution, and crime of the center city for the sake of peaceful, green and homogeneous outer-belt neighborhoods. Metropolitan problems, it seemed, found technological solutions. New York City became a metropolis by 1830 when steam ferries allowed settlement of the Jersey shore across the Hudson River from Manhattan, and Brooklyn across the East River. Bridges opened suburbs of South Boston, Roxbury, Cambridge, and Charlestown near Boston and allowed settlement across the Schuylkill River at Philadelphia, across the Allegheny and Monogahela at Pittsburgh, the Cuyahoga at Cleveland, and New Buffalo Creek

Moving Goods and People in an Ever-Expanding Metropolis: New York City, the Blizzard of 1888, and the Building of a Subway System

The infamous Blizzard of 1888, with walls of snow that reached the second-story windows of West Side brownstones, shut down every public transport in the city—omnibuses, horse railways, and elevated lines. Pedestrians were trapped and some froze to death in the streets. The city stopped commuting and working, and necessities like bread, milk, and eggs disappeared from the stores. Coal deliveries failed and homes went without heat. It was a turning point that drove New Yorkers to experiment with subways as a safe and speedy public transit.

It is easy to forget New York City's complex geography and geology that has now largely disappeared under its densely populated complex of buildings, streets, bridges, and highways, all also linked by tunnels and subways. In fact, the city, in historian Clifton Hood's words, is an urban archipelago sprawling over several big islands and the adjacent mainland to the north. It is similar in this way especially to Hong Kong. The five separate boroughs—Manhattan and Staten Islands (islands in themselves), Brooklyn and Queens on the western edge of Long Island, and the Bronx on the mainland, formidably divided by the Upper Bay, the Hudson River, and the East River—were brought together in 1898 to form modern New York City. The other participants in this complex are cities in New Jersey—Newark, Hoboken, Jersey City, and others—on the west shore of the Hudson River. New York's continual challenge was how to keep its different boroughs conveniently connected to support its enormous population and commercial growth. In 1800 the city's population was under 80,000, smaller than Philadelphia; by 1900 it contained almost 3.5 million people. In 1910 Manhattan's population alone was over 2.3 million people, with more inhabiting the 23-square-mile island than in 33 of the 46 states. A sixth of these were crowded in the small patch below 14th Street, at the scale of 700 poverty-stricken immigrants per acre on the Lower East Side. New York has remained one of the most congested urban places in the world. Even as late as 1994 an independent planning commission provoked doubts about the city's future unless it embarked on a massive transportation reconstruction to make the city functional.

The first widely used modes of public transportation were horse-drawn stagecoach wagons called omnibuses that carried 12 to 15 persons, but they rattled passengers' bones on lumpy, muddy unpaved or cobblestone streets, nor could they cope with increased crowding. The first horse railway that instead rolled on smooth iron rails opened in 1832. Each car carried up to 45 people at 8 miles per hour (instead of a pokey 3 miles per hour on an omnibus) from Prince Street to 14th Street. These convenient and comfortable "streetcars" allowed a massive construction boom including middle-class brownstone housing in the open countryside as far north as the future Central Park neighborhood. By 1860 Manhattan alone enjoyed 14 horse railway companies that scheduled an average of 10 trips daily uptown and downtown. They also increased congestion on the streets, together with commercial traffic, that regularly broke down into gridlock at key intersections.

By 1860 the northern boundary of concentrated settlement had moved dramatically from Houston Street to 42nd Street, increasing demands to improve city transport. Newfangled elevated trains on iron roadways mounted above key streets offered the city's first rapid transit system, defined as having its own right of way that did not compete for space with other vehicles. Later subways would fit the same definition. By 1880 three popular "El" lines snaked northward to reach the Harlem River at the top of Manhattan and even connected by bridge to the mainland, a trip that took only 45 minutes compared to more than 2 hours by omnibus. The northward construction boom filled the Upper East Side by 1890, but the West Side and Harlem remained largely open other than for rough shantytowns of squatting "Irish villages" and "goat towns" in the west 60s and 70s. In addition, neighbors to an El line complained bitterly about bulky iron superstructures that blocked out the sun and the coal-burning light steam locomotives that dumped ashes, cinders, and sparks on them as the clattering trains raced past their homes.

But the innovative elevated trains whetted public demands for far better carrying capacity and higher speeds to serve the city's rapid population growth and its challenging archipelago geography. In 1888, when the blizzard enveloped the city, New Yorkers depended on the largest urban transport system in the world, its jewel being the 94 miles of elevated railways that transported people above the congested streets from one end of Manhattan Island to the other. There were also 265 miles of horse-drawn railways, and old-fashioned horse-drawn omnibuses still clogged the streets over 237 miles of scheduled routes. Manhattan's population was wildly uneven, with pitiful crowding of Irish, Italian and black working families in the notorious Five Points district several blocks north of City Hall compared to the acres of open space in the Upper West Side, Harlem, and Washington Heights, as well as empty land in Brooklyn and the Bronx, and open meadows and wetlands in Queens where hunters shot wild ducks. It was not that New York was running out of space to house its residents: The city needed high-speed, high-capacity transport to open outlying, literally unsettled neighborhoods for development.

The answer was a dedicated subway system, but the problem was its high cost that required an alliance of public and private interests. The technology, even electric traction from distant steam-driven power plants, was already tested and reliable. New Yorkers struggled against their long-held belief in small, passive government that let laissez-faire business run the city's utilities. Not until 1891 did the state legislature pass the Rapid Transit Act that allowed a city commission to lay out routes for an underground railway system and then assign the franchise to a private company for construction and operation. This became a highly profitable monopoly, which held until the entire system was forcibly unified under city control in 1940 under the New York City Transit System.

The long overdue construction of the IRT (Independent Rapid Transit) line began in 1900 using 7,700 Irish and Italian workers who, in Clifton Hood's words, "literally gouged the subway out of the raw earth" in hand and shovel labor largely without mechanized equipment. Dozens died from rockfalls and dynamite explosions. Their "cut and cover" method dug a trench the width of each designated street in which they erected a steel and concrete elongated box the length of the line. To keep almost half of the subway relatively level, they also laboriously dug tunnels through granite rock (with dangerous veins of gravel and sand) as well as above-ground steel viaducts. The IRT line opened in 1904 as the most important public transit connection from Brooklyn, across Manhattan, and into the Bronx. The next year it carried 3.6 million people per mile of track, twice as many as the elevated trains. (By 1914, 9.5 million traveled per mile, far more than in Paris, Berlin, or London.) It gave Times Square its modern identity as a theater district and populated the Upper West Side and the Bronx in a gigantic construction boom. The system was doubled by new construction between 1913 and 1920 that included the BMT lines. By the early 1920s city dwellers proudly reported that "a New Yorker could spend the morning swimming or riding the roller coaster at Coney Island, travel to Yankee Stadium for a baseball game that afternoon, and then head to Times Square for a movie that evening." In 1940 the IND (Independent) line added 7 major new routes on some 190 miles of track, the last major construction that totaled 722 miles across the five boroughs. New Yorkers were close to the truth when they said, between 1905 and the deterioration that began in the 1960s, that their high-speed subway—including separate express service—was the best run and most reliable transit system in the world.

The subway was far more than a well-engineered, privately run unit of New York City's physical infrastructure; it became a tool for city planning and civic improvement. The Progressives early in the twentieth century found in rapid transit the means to clear out inner-city slums as hotbeds of crime and disease and political radicalism, particularly to disburse the 550,000 poverty-stricken immigrants densely crowded into a square mile on the Lower East Side to Manhattan's uptown and into Brooklyn, Queens, and the Bronx. The Progressive goal was idealistic but sincere—"to replace the squalid nineteenth-century metropolis with an efficient city that would be attractive, prosperous, healthy, and orderly." Already some of the pressure had been released when between 1903 and 1909 the Williamsburg Bridge, the Manhattan Bridge, and the Queensboro Bridge joined the Brooklyn Bridge, which had opened in 1883, as connections between downtown workplaces and tenements and apartments outside Manhattan. Rail and auto tunnels under the Hudson River to New Jersey would follow. The idealism was less clear when city planner Robert Moses was given a free hand to create a web of auto parkways that reached pleasant outlying neighborhoods, but had low overpasses which precluded public buses that would have carried blue-collar workers between jobs and home.

As a densely populated commercial and industrial city, New York has always been unusually dependent on mass transit to move its workers and dwellers rapidly, cheaply, and safely. Even in 1990, 46 percent of all New York workers depended on the subway to commute to their jobs, far more than any other U.S. city. Yet any vision to serve an increasingly crowded and growing city was severely undermined by a new technological innovation that demanded a new infrastructure—the wildly popular private automobile, together with highways and parking to serve it. America's romance with the automobile encouraged many urban planners in the 1920s to see mass transit as old-fashioned and not the primary mode of transportation. American cities went through a fateful turning point that put them awash in vehicles and demanded unexpected attention to traffic patterns, parking regulations, and highway construction.

The parkways of the New York metropolitan area were the first in the U.S. to provide the modern high-volume, high-speed, limited-access highway, restricted to passenger cars. Their physical layout made them like multilane aqueducts for cars, with no interruptions for intersections and gentle curves for high-speed travel. Median strips separated traffic moving in opposite directions for safety, and gave long, uninterrupted lines of sight. With 200- or 300-foot right-of-ways, the highways began to consume enormous amounts of valuable land both in the suburbs and in the downtown. First was the 15-mile Bronx River Parkway, completed in 1925. It was bordered on both

sides by broad bands of green parkland that also controlled access from side roads. The Merritt and Westchester parkways ran between New York City and Connecticut.

A 1931 New York transit plan did allow for subway improvements but emphasized a vast interlocked metropolitan highway system that allowed automobiles to pour into the city from bridges and tunnels from New Jersey as well as parkways from Long Island and counties north of Manhattan. The popular and proactive Mayor Fiorello LaGuardia and his single-minded planner, Robert Moses, saw the automobile, not rapid transit, as New York City's future, resulting in the construction after World War II of more than 200 miles of highways and bridges. Yet, without the subways, which were deteriorating badly in the 1960s and 1970s but revived in the 1980s and 1990s, New York City could not have come into existence. Today the cost of replacement is estimated at $55 billion.

at Buffalo. In an accessible flatland city like Chicago, by 1873 over 50,000 people lived in nearly 100 suburbs. Suburbs grew less rapidly in a city like Pittsburgh, where rivers had to be crossed and then mountains crossed or tunneled through.

The railroad passenger train expanded the acceptable distance to work to 50 miles, compared to a maximum 2-mile walking distance. Americans loved to travel on wheels. Steam-powered commuter trains rumbled along city streets, to make stops several times 5, 10, or 15 miles from the downtown at new suburbs: Evanston north of Chicago, Germantown outside Philadelphia. New horse-drawn passenger streetcars that ran over fixed rails created networks of mass transit. By 1890 the nation's street railways included 5,700 miles of track for cars operated by animal power, 500 miles of track for cable cars, and 1,260 miles of electrified track. One revolutionary technology was the electric trolley, using a four-wheeled electric "troller" pulled along an overhead wire for its power, first tested by engineer Frank Sprague in Richmond, Virginia, in 1888. Only 14 years later, by 1902, 22,000 miles of streetcar lines were electrified, and horse railways were down to 250 miles. Streetcars became the common link between downtown, workplaces, and city homes and suburbs. Their convenience, relative simplicity, and cleanliness encouraged electrified lines between cities. Tales were told of young men who on a dare traveled without a break on this interurban system, starting outside Boston and not running out of electric streetcar lines until they stepped out on the prairie west of St. Louis, as long as the rider did not mind dozens of changes. The rise of the automobile—Americans became passionate about personal freedom of travel—proved the death knell for the streetcar as a convenient and effective mode of transportation; few trolley systems lasted beyond 1950.

America's vaunted mobility was, in reality, a middle-class entitlement. The flight to suburbia may have been an escape from the city; it was also movement to a world that the middle class believed urban life should be—exciting but not threatening, a combination of "the country's natural surroundings, the city's social surroundings." The late nineteenth-century futurist, Edward Bellamy, described the idealized American city when he wrote of "miles of broad streets, shaded by trees and lined with fine buildings, and for the most part not in continuous blocks but set in larger or smaller enclosures, stretched in every direction. Every quarter contained large open squares filled with trees, among which statues glistened and fountains flashed in the late afternoon sun." The transportation networks encouraged real estate subdividers and builders to repeat the gridiron pattern of the city ever further outward, based on convenience and cost. The homeowner was reassured by rows of similar detached wooden or brick houses on identical lots in identical blocks: "There was comfort in knowing that your neighbors were neither better nor worse than you." Racial exclusion ran strong. Yet movement to the suburbs was relatively democratic, open to recent immigrants as well as ancestral families, to a mix of ethnic and religious groups, as long as they had reached middle-class status. Speculators created a mania for suburban living in new boomtowns like Oak Park and Wilmette around Chicago, Grosse Point and Ferndale near Detroit, Beverly Hills and Inglewood near Los Angeles, and Cleveland Heights and Shaker Heights near Cleveland.

Roads and Highway Improvement

Because of the success of steam-powered railroads in connecting distant cities and electric streetcars in moving people in expanded metropolitan regions, America's roads had received indifferent attention. Of 154,000 miles of rural roads in the early twentieth century, less than 20,000 were paved. Most were simply dirt tracks. Graded roads with a crown in the middle for drainage were a major improvement, as were those spread with gravel or paved with macadam (compacted stones bound with asphalt). In older settled places, uneven cobblestone roads collected animal wastes, garbage, and other sources of disease on their uneven surfaces. Wood blocks absorbed water and grew fungi and deteriorated within five years. Brick pavements, granite blocks, and iron plates were expensive and noisy. The first public crusade for smoother, quieter, and economical concrete-paved roads came during the bicycle fad late in the nineteenth century. About the same time a national Good Roads Movement lobbied for an expanded system of national roads to join together major population centers. Massachusetts and New Jersey were the first states to improve and expand their roads in the 1890s. Wisconsin was the first state to identify its roads with letters and numbers. In 1916 the Federal Roads Aid Act created a nationwide plan for highway connections between states. Its goal was twofold: to pave farm-to-market "trunk," or connecting routes that had remained dirt tracks, and to forge yet another set of arteries between cities. The act appropriated a total of $5 million nationwide, but left the actual improvements to the states, which did not devise any collaborative planning among themselves. Demand for improved roads grew between 1916 and 1921 when the number of motor vehicles rose from 1.5 million to 3.6 million. The Federal Highway Act of 1921 sought to use major state roads to devise an interstate highway system. When the Bureau of Public Roads was created in 1923, its mission was to connect all cities of 50,000 or more. Road building became one of the main forms of civic improvement during the 1920s and took funds from other forms of rapid transit. By 1926 American drivers in their cars and trucks were able to find their way between major cities on uniformly numbered "U.S." highway routes. Even during the Depression, the number of vehicles rose from 25.3 million in 1934 to 31 million by 1939.

The newly paved highways poured vehicles into urban downtowns. Two-thirds of the land area of some central cities was soon taken up by freeways, existing streets, and new parking lots. Automobiles, and the places to drive and park them, became the dominant features of most metropolitan districts, more than the wharf, market, factory, or railroad had ever been. Without the least attempt at planning, people, commerce, and industry moved chaotically outward toward the cheaper, uncrowded, and safer outskirts. This included a greater number of workers who could afford mass-produced automobiles that made outer areas of cities more accessible. As auto prices declined by 1930 to $300 for a basic Ford, 1 out of 5 Americans owned their own automobile. Their drivers demanded free movement on uncluttered roadways. Most roads were unplanned, such as U.S. 1 that stretched along the Atlantic coast, which was a four-lane highway without a center divider in order to assuage local merchants whose businesses were strung adjacent to the road. Such a road design risked accidents with left turns across traffic and tolerated thousands of entryways that ran directly onto the main lanes. Americans looked enviously at the efficient, high-speed, multilane networks of Europe—the Italian autostrada system of the 1920s and the German autobahns of the 1930s. A 1939 federal study had called for a national system of turnpikes, and the public imagination had been impressed by the widely publicized General Motors Futurama exhibit at the New York World's Fair, which depicted a typical future countryside crisscrossed with smooth highways dotted with private cars. Planning for the Pennsylvania Turnpike took advantage of an abandoned railroad right-of-way that offered superior grades and existing tunnels. Americans felt they had entered the modern automobile age when the turnpike opened in the early

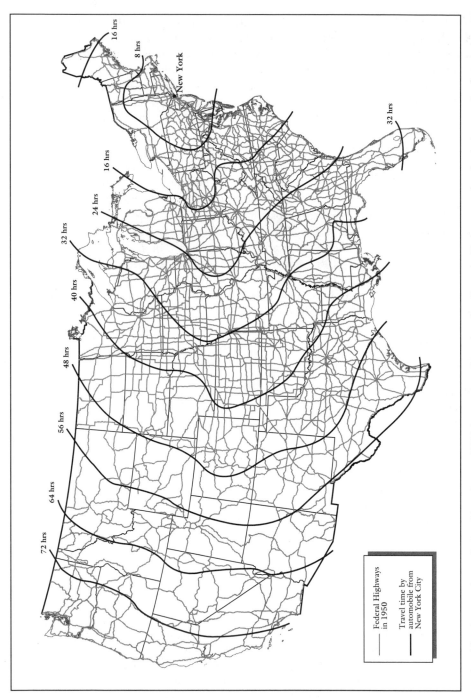

How long did it take to travel across the United States by car in 1950? Compare this to the weeks and months required by horse or wagon a hundred years earlier. However, the time-distance equation is a little different from what the railroads achieved in the late nineteenth century.

1940s. Superhighway construction across Ohio and Indiana took the shortest route directly across prime farmland and occasionally split towns like South Bend into pieces.

After World War II, highways took over the American countryside. With pent-up demand because auto production was halted during the war, automobile ownership rose from 25 million in 1945 to over 40 million in 1950, and neared 65 million by 1956. In 1947 Congress had authorized a 37,000-mile national highway network primarily to improve auto and truck links between cities and to tie the countryside more firmly to 182 metropolitan areas. Within two years the federal government was spending $2 billion a year on highways (up to $6 billion by 1956). In 1956 the Interstate Highway Act promised a limited access city-connecting highway system of 42,500 miles at the cost of $60 billion. Its features, based on the experience on eastern parkways and turnpikes, included the cloverleaf interchange, a separating median or greensward between opposing directions of traffic, and limited access. As one of the largest engineering structures in the world, its cost was rationalized by President Eisenhower as essential to the movement of resources for national defense. By 1970 it became possible to drive from New York City to San Francisco without encountering a stoplight. The interstate system was mostly completed by 1980 but at much higher cost. One of its most striking features was that it rarely followed the roadbeds of existing highways because the federal government determined that upgrading existing routes would be more costly than acquiring additional land for access. Across Indiana, for example, today the interstate parallels the perfectly serviceable U.S. 12 and U.S. 20 a few miles to the north and the equally usable U.S. 6 and U.S. 30 a few miles to the south.

The result was a separate highway network overlaid on existing transportation systems, with every major city a hub. Today we can speak of large metropolitan corridors—from Boston to Washington ("BosWash"), Pittsburgh to Chicago ("ChiPitt"), and San Francisco to San Diego ("SanSan"). Others run southwest from Atlanta, between Dallas and Houston, along the Front Range of the Rockies in Colorado (Fort Collins through Denver to Colorado Springs) and from Portland, Oregon, through Seattle, Washington, to Vancouver, British Columbia. Within these corridors, federal and state funding encouraged the use of the private automobile instead of mass transit by streetcar, bus, or train. By the 1950s Americans added to their transportation problems when passenger use of railroads and rapid transit began to fall away to the convenience of private transportation using artificially cheap gasoline. The size of typical automobiles began to reach 2 tons, usually carrying one person. (The oil crisis of 1973 tripled gasoline prices and began to reverse this giantism.)

The highways, particularly in and near cities, spread the problems of air pollution, noise, and ugliness. Most urban centers were so ill prepared that the federal highway act was amended in 1962 to coordinate highway planning to integrate auto parkways and truck routes with rapid transit, railroad commuting, and air connections. Despite this effort, modern transportation inside and outside the cities had not been rationally developed, and much new construction was haphazard and destructive. Commercial strip districts (sometimes ironically called "the miracle mile") grew up between interstate highways and city lines, chaotically surrounded by tract housing developments. A city like Hartford, Connecticut, would be severed in two by an interstate highway, the neighborhoods of Los Angeles ("the city without a center") were made meaningless by crisscrossing highways, and Brooklyn was profoundly changed by the construction of overhead parkways for commuters from Long Island suburbs. Road construction in rural areas such as Appalachia shattered the isolation of the mountaineer, and not incidentally gave outside industries greater access to timber and coal. Highway construction, particularly in the 1950s and 1960s, seemed almost a sacred trust. Yet it ran into objections raised when it consumed land dedicated to parks, golf courses, other green areas, and recreation areas. In this radical making over of the existing environment, complaints arose about the destruction of historic buildings and landmarks. One halfhearted response to the objections was the federal Highway Beautification Act of 1965. It sought to control billboards and junkyards. It was less successful in its attempts to fit the roadway to the terrain and to retain native trees and shrubs and landscaping. The 1960s and 1970s also saw attempts, mostly flawed, to devise mass transit systems as alternatives to private auto use, such as San Francisco's BART (Bay Area Rapid Transit System).

The Collapse of the Cities

Urban Decay and Failed Renewal

Unbridled speculation in banking and markets together with industrial overproduction brought on the Depression of the 1930s. City dwellers, who were thought to be in the vanguard of American success because they lived in the new built environment, were particularly hard hit. By 1933 unemployment scaled to 40 percent in Chicago and 30 percent in New York City. Property tax delinquency shook city budgets that had been overextended to build the urban infrastructure. In the largest 145 cities, nonpayment hit 11 percent in 1930 and over 25 percent by 1933. The large bond issues of the 1920s defaulted in the 1930s. The urban network now seemed excessive and exaggerated; had the nation overcommitted itself to a flawed built environment with no alternatives? President Franklin Delano Roosevelt's New Deal became the center of a vigorous ideological debate over the future of the built environment. It sought to attack America's problems wholesale during the 1930s and has been called "the third American Revolution" because a new concept—government protection—was put into action and soon blanketed many areas of American society. A liberal or left-wing viewpoint urged that it was the government's responsibility to be proactive in removing slums and providing decent housing. Conservative landowners and businesspeople were equally concerned with blight because it created falling property values, but they repudiated so-called socialist government intervention. These differences also reflected the tension between the traditions of thrift, self-help, and rugged individualism and traditions of mutual benefit and public responsibility.

Roosevelt's New Deal created a juggernaut of relief operations, not all of which passed the scrutiny of the courts. Relief operations effectively made the federal government the primary force in modernizing metropolitan environments. By the spring of 1933 federal intervention became a permanent feature of urban recovery. New jobs—"work-relief projects"— were created by government-paid metropolitan public works projects. Within a year after the stock market crash, by the end of 1930, 75 of the nation's largest cities were spending $420 million, mostly federal funds, on public works projects. The Public Works Administration built a new water supply system in Denver, a municipal auditorium in Kansas City, and generally cleared slums and built new schools and hospitals across the nation. By late 1933 the Civil Works Administration (CWA) put the unemployed to work on road and school repair, park and playground maintenance. Workers for the CWA built 500 airports, developed city parks, dug city swimming pools, and laid city sewer lines. By 1935 the WPA (Works

Progress Administration) employed almost a fifth of the nation's work force. By 1941 it had spent $10 billion of federal funds to build almost 600 airports, 500,000 miles of roads and streets, 100,000 bridges and viaducts, 500,000 sewerage connections, and 110,000 libraries, schools, auditoriums, stadiums, and other public structures. Although some were "make work" ("We dig ditches and fill them up again"), most made long-lasting improvements on the built environment. Pittsburgh's Schenley Park still has paths and footbridges with "WPA" emblazoned in concrete. Similar plaques can be seen throughout the nation. Housing relief became a national agenda in 1934 through the Federal Housing Authority (FHA). The FHA was to build low-cost housing, but many urban renewal projects were in fact designed to attract more desirable middle-class occupants. They merely pushed the poor into other slums. The U.S. Housing Authority in 1937 built units for $2,720, but this was still too costly for the poorest families most in need of housing. Despite federal interventions, the cities were not solving the problems of crowding, slums, alienation, and social disintegration. World War II intervened to prevent further action.

After the war, Americans looked forward to enjoying the benefits of a middle-class, consumer-oriented, and suburban nation. They continued to live in highly urbanized metropolitan regions centered on industrial and commercial operations. Low-cost federal loans to veterans created an enormous suburban housing boom. In 1950 alone almost a million single-family houses were built, mostly in bedroom suburbs like Levittown on New York's Long Island and Park Forest outside of Chicago. Mobility was everyone's experience: The average Levittowner moved once every 2.5 years. In Park Forest a third of the apartments and a fifth of the houses changed occupants yearly in the 1950s. Cultural historian Daniel Boorstin wrote that this perpetual motion was changing American society: "A small town was a place where a man settled. A suburb was a place to or from which a person moved. Suburbanites expected their children to live elsewhere." Urban historian Howard P. Chudacoff was particularly severe in his criticism: Even while Americans yearned in the 1950s and 1960s for their bilevel, ranch-style dream house with a two-car garage, a backyard grill, and good schools, the real outcome was a terrible trivialization of the metropolitan landscape. According to Chudacoff, "In the race for profits after World War II, developers bulldozed away natural beauty, created tacky houses, and reserved prime land along feeder highways for motels, gas stations, and fast-food franchises." A Princeton architect discovered that the sprawling shopping malls were like autonomous feudal kingdoms, with their own rules, bureaucracies, police power, and tax privileges, scarcely responsible to the local town and county. Chudacoff saw a tragic failure in America's 250-year-old unplanned urban explosion. Without social planning to build humane cities, private profit-making interests continued to accelerate urban collapse and suburban expansion.

Back in the inner city, postwar despair reinforced the disillusionment that had begun during the Depression. Americans continued to abandon the decaying physical plants and the collapsing revenue bases of the inner city. All the failures of modern American society seemed to collect in the cities—crime, poverty, racism, housing congestion, traffic congestion, unemployment, ugliness, waste, and pollution. Government programs had not attempted to overrule the power of private landholding. Congress's housing act of 1949 sought slum clearance and public housing, but more often enhanced private businesses, middle-class shopping, and costly apartments that would boost property values. These were supposed to encourage the return of private investment and raise property taxes. Entire lower-class neighborhoods were leveled to serve this purpose; the black population was simply sent elsewhere into another ghetto. In this "Negro removal," the nation lost 200,000 housing units each year between

1950 and 1956, and 475,000 a year between 1957 and 1959. Federal support seemed locked into seemingly destructive urban renewal in which, said Chudacoff, "Programs that targeted a decent home for every American destroyed twice as many dwellings as they built." The 1949 act was to create 810,000 new public housing units within 4 years; diversion of funds to private enterprise instead delayed it for 20 years. In recognition of the continuing collapse of the inner city, the Johnson administration in 1966 launched the Model Cities program, which offered federal assistance only to carefully planned urban renewal. President Ford's Community Development Act of 1974 also emphasized local decisions and autonomy. Neither program brought dramatic improvements. America's cities languished during later administrations while the built environment crumbled. In the 1980s and 1990s federal urban policy remained committed to the belief that answers lay with the private sector. Chudacoff found two long-term obstacles to urban revival: "One is the notion of land as a civil right of private exploitation; the other is the tradition of local autonomy." He concluded that a more positive future depended on a national policy that "carries two prerequisites foreign to the past: land as a public resource, not as a private right; and the metropolis as a forum for confederates, not as an arena for combatants."

Flaws in the Infrastructure System

If the nineteenth-century Transcendentalists were right when they called cities "unnatural," then the United States is well on its way to being largely unnatural. By the late nineteenth century, Americans had already reshaped their environment in a highly specific way, centered on the profitability of urban trade, commerce, and industrial operations. There are major differences when a landscape is seen from the point of view of cash value or human habitat, industrial artifact or functional ecosystem (see Chapter 9 for the impacts of industrialization). Where a homeowner might see an ugly abandoned gas station next door to his house, a businessperson might envision the site rebuilt as a potential income-producing convenience store, a planner might wish for a children's playground, but the pollution officer might see a dangerous chemical waste dump, the tax officer a declining tax property, and the civic association another urban eyesore. Thus infrastructure is not just bridges and highways, but includes essential economic interests, political institutions, community public interest, and social values. Geographer Isaiah Bowman observed that Americans had the technological agility to build "a comfortable well-lighted city and provide education, opera, and games at the South Pole," but continued to struggle with human degradation in the cities. A century and a half of industrialization could rework the natural world, but had more difficulty reworking itself. After building cities that failed to serve human well-being, Americans were burdened with "many defective layouts it would cost too much to alter." Modern critics such as Lewis Mumford complained that the physical features of the new metropolitan network were neither spontaneous nor "natural" nor inevitable, but simply reflected the greed of the builders. Cultural geographer Peirce F. Lewis wrote, "Our human landscape is our unwitting autobiography, reflecting our tastes, our values, our aspirations, and even our fears, in tangible, visible form." There are no secrets in the landscape. Lewis continued: "All our cultural warts and blemishes are there, and our glories too; but above all, our ordinary day-to-day qualities are exhibited for anybody who wants to find them and knows how to look for them."

Historical geographer Donald Meinig wrote about the environmental impact of urban development, "You cannot find a scrap of pristine nature. The very shape of the land surface has been modified in a thousand ways, by cuts and quarries, excavations and embankments, fills, dams, culverts, terraces, revetments." It was a rare instance, he concluded, that the natural ecosystem that once stood where the built environment now stands is still functional. Hawks, trout, and deer were replaced by humans' urban coinhabitants—rats, cockroaches, and pigeons. At best, urban historian Martin V. Melosi reminded us, cities usually exaggerate and distort some important natural processes. Some natural features are virtually eliminated, such as a local stream or pond or hill. Hills are leveled and valleys filled. When the small stream becomes a city culvert, flooding increases dramatically because the hydraulic cycle loses the filtering capacity of soil and water control of streams. The natural hydrological system is replaced by concrete sewers; the soil is replaced by streets and basements; chemical factories replace biological exchanges; electric power systems substitute for solar energy chlorophyll transformation in vegetation. Factories and other buildings create "heat islands" in which urban temperatures (as the TV weatherperson reports) are significantly higher than in the countryside. The atmosphere is filled with airborne pollutants creating smog that can kill; hence there are urban pollution health alerts in cities as different as New York City, Denver, and Los Angeles. Urban life produces huge concentrated volumes of waste materials that require complex and costly disposal procedures. One outcome is that the built landscape is not as self-sustaining as the previous ecosystem once was. A workable city requires continuous human intervention. Once trees are removed, the hills erode and the rivers flood. Industry is not self-cleansing of its pollution. Urban slums and sprawl are not self-correcting. These become design problems that challenge the best know-how by engineers, civic leaders, and an aroused public.

Conclusion

The city, prime example of the built environment, was the vehicle for environmental conquest. Chicago was America's "shock city" toward the midwestern environments, like Manchester toward England's Midlands earlier and Los Angeles later toward the West. Such cities recast the nation's geography, but often grew chaotically where people were, in Peirce Lewis's words, "impoverished by garbage and grit, smog and sewage, congestion and clutter," and their citizens complained about urban failure. Cities continued to mutate, infrastructures continued to be modified, and results continued to be unpredictable too often, throwing city inhabitants into harm's way. Technological innovation could bring major benefits, but could also uproot people and take a toll on the stability of families, neighborhoods, and even entire cities. Pittsburgh lost its way in the late nineteenth century and became an industrial slum pocketed by diseased ghettos. The classic modern case was the contrast between an enhanced personal autonomy enjoyed with the private automobile, but which also resulted in a metropolitan scene dominated by roadways, parking lots, and pollution on an ever-expanding scale.

The geography of the countryside *between* the cities lost its identity and became a mere resource to be exploited by the new urban imperialism. Cleveland and Pittsburgh compete with distant Atlanta, Kansas City, and Denver. Miami and Los Angeles are more alike in terms of multiculturalism than their warm ocean-bred climates. Chudacoff added that America's major cities—New York, Boston, Philadelphia, Detroit, Chicago, and Los Angeles—rose "above the screen of state government, which had formerly intervened between municipalities and Washington." In the second half of the twentieth century there was often more exchange between cities and the federal government than between cities and state governments. This national urban network emerged as the dominant environmental feature of the nation.

Urban historians Joel Taar and Gabriel Dupuy add, "Technological infrastructure makes possible the existence of the modern city and provides the means for its continuing operation, but it also increases the city's vulnerability to catastrophic events such as war or natural disaster [and technological failure, such as a blackout]. While technology may enhance the urban quality of life, it may also be a force for deterioration and destruction of neighborhoods, as well as a hindrance to humane and rationale planning." A built place was mostly measured as a form of capital, by the dollar value of square footage or front feet on the street or air rights, with special attention to its long-term depreciation, and development potential, at the loss of alternative values. Sam Bass Warner reminded his readers that the modern inhabitants of the industrial infrastructure were not helpless pawns: Democratic citizen-participation urban planning provides opportunities to address the inevitable conflicts that do occur. The complaint was the built landscape may have generated a great deal of wealth, but it was not the livable society that had been promised. Warner reported that Americans squandered the opportunity provided by the "great once-only experiment" of technological innovation and "endlessly failed" to build and maintain humane cities. The failure arose, he said, from inherent flaws built into American industrial capitalism that promoted private profit-making competition and innovative change without regard to community: "a safe, healthy, decent environment for everyone, regardless of personal wealth or poverty, success or failure."

For Further Reading

Several introductory histories of urban America provide contrasting viewpoints. There is no better place to begin than Howard P. Chudacoff's *The Evolution of American Urban Society* (1975). This should be followed by a look at Sam Bass Warner, Jr., *The Urban Wilderness: A History of the American City* (1972), and Charles N. Glaab and A. Theodore Brown, *A History of Urban America* (1967). Constance McLaughlin Green, *American Cities in the Growth of the Nation* (1957), provides excellent mini-histories of selected cities ranging from Boston to Chicago to Denver. Unsurpassed for their analysis of the built environment are several important essays in D. W. Meinig (ed.), *The Interpretation of Ordinary Landscapes* (1979). For construction of the physical city, see Carl W. Condit, *American Building: Materials and Techniques from the Beginning of the Colonial Settlements to the Present* (1968). The best place to comprehend the New York subway system, and mass transit infrastructures generally, is in the semipopular and well-researched analysis by Clifton Hood, *722 Miles: The Building of the Subways and How They Transformed New York* (1993). For the profession of engineering and its impacts, see Terry S. Reynolds (ed.), *The Engineer in America* (1991), and, particularly, Edwin T. Layton, Jr., *The Revolt of the Engineers: Social Responsibility and the American Engineering Profession* (1971). Other essential reading must include the fresh approach to urban regionalism by William Cronon, *Nature's Metropolis: Chicago and the Great West* (1991). The problem of city planning is addressed in David R. Goldfield and Blaine A. Brownell, *Urban America: From Downtown to No Town* (1979), John W. Reps, *The Making of Urban America: A History of City Planning in the United States* (1965), and Christopher Tunnard and Boris Pushkarev, *Man-Made America. Chaos or Control* (1963). These should be compared with Jane Jacobs's two classic critiques, *The Death and Life of Great American Cities* (1961) and *The Economy of Cities* (1969).

CHAPTER NINE

THE ENVIRONMENTAL COSTS OF INDUSTRIAL AMERICA: CITIES AND LANDSCAPES IN TROUBLE

Sluggish clouds of thick smoke hung over the roofs and the air was full of soot and fine dust. Noise pressed in from every quarter—from the roaring mill, from the trolley cars clattering and clanging through the narrow street, and from the [railroad] sidings which were in constant use for the hauling of freight to and from the mills. I saw men who had been working on the night shift lying like fallen logs, huddled together in small, dark, stuffy rooms, sleeping the sleep of exhaustion that follows in the wake of heavy physical labor. Dirt and noise are inseparable adjuncts to life in a mill district, but workers in the mills need not necessarily be deprived of sufficient light and air, such as it is, and water, and the common decencies of life. [This is the story of an industry that] could overhaul an old plant and make it pay, but [which] had not brought water a few paces up the hill, or dropped a sewer a few paces down to the river below, so that men and women and children might live as human beings should live.

—Social Worker F. Elisabeth Crowell's Report in 1908 on Painter's Row,
U.S. Steel–Owned Workingmen's Housing in Pittsburgh

Daily Life and Work in the Factory Cities

There is a bitter irony that all the buildings at the 1893 Chicago World's Fair were painted with white lead paint, long recognized as a poison. Public health historian Christopher Sellers writes, "The fair's emblematic whiteness thus bore an extensive history of human damage, as this metal had been wrested from the earth, melted and separated out from other elements, transformed into a pigment, and spread over the fair buildings themselves. A vast amount of paint, some 60 tons on the Hall of Manufactures alone, coated this and the fair's other four hundred buildings through the work of hands whose nerves and muscles had failed them and brains that had gone awry." Sellers continues, "Fin-de-siècle American capitalism, in pouring forth the varied bounty of White City, pushed innumerable workers' bodies past their limits, with near impunity and little regret."

Pollution, Waste, and Human Degradation Undermine the Industrial Revolution: The Negative Infrastructure

The factories that built capital goods like electric generators and steam locomotives, or turned out consumer goods like telephones and victrolas, also pumped tons of black particles and noxious gases out of their smokestacks onto worker neighborhoods, threw scrap metal onto the empty lot next door, and dumped waste chemicals into the rivers. Industry has historically dumped its effluents onto the "commons" of rivers, ponds, open fields, streets, and sewers wherever there was a space in a city that no one owned or cared about—a hillside, streambed, backlot, curbside. The problems of pollution, even when demonstrated by long historical experience or scientifically known, were largely ignored, repudiated, and denied by those in power. Pollution, most Americans believed, was the price of progress. Healthy working and living conditions deteriorated so much that army recruiters rejected city boys for military service. Men who worked in the factories ran dangerous machines that could cut human flesh or break human bones as well as shape iron and steel. Factory workers breathed poisoned air in crowded, dirty, and badly lit buildings. By 1900 social workers like Elisabeth Crowell or Chicago's Jane Addams campaigned for workmen who endured these life-threatening conditions for 12 hours a day, 6 or 7 days a week, to earn an average of $48 a month (workwomen made much less in shirtwaist sweatshops).

The American factory system, despite its spectacular productivity, was dysfunctional in human services. We can say that a negative infrastructure had taken over the factory cities. Pollution, waste, and crowding made living conditions far worse than they had been. These problems, difficult enough to solve individually, were compounded by their own terrible interconnected network. America's crowded worker housing, for example, ran into a ganglia of problems: bad drinking water and human waste seeping through deficient sewers, ineffective garbage disposal, polluted air and "smoke nuisance," endemic disease like typhoid fever and tuberculosis, unsafe, ugly and dilapidated tenements, and nonexistent health care. These were the components of the negative infrastructure. Overcrowding—a family of six might share two rooms with two itinerant boarders—meant the spread of disease, not to mention the destruction of privacy. In single homes where three or four families were crowded, and in tenements, two dozen people would share a single kitchen sink and its disease germs. Industrial slums intensified physiological problems: rickets in children deprived of sunlight and malformed bones by a bad diet. Dysentery was a fact of life in the city and cholera a regular occurrence. The backyard privy might adjoin a neighbor's private well, and a newly arrived immigrant family might be living in a basement amid foul seepage from the walls and muck on the floor.

Looking back with hindsight, we can now see that the environmental and human costs of industrialization should not have been ignored because they undid much of what the large-scale industrial systems promised to do. The counterproductive damage was not supposed to happen but it did, and it gravely compromised industrialization. There was thus a darker side to the industrial transformation. Side effects of the factory system should have induced a negative cost accounting because of harm done to the commons and public health. In Pittsburgh, for example, an unnecessary typhoid epidemic in 1906–07 cost the city $540,000 in expenses and lost wages. Overall, typhoid cost Pittsburgh $9 million between 1883 and 1908, when a water filtration plant was finally completed. A balance sheet that included environmental and human costs would have significantly lowered America's annual Gross National Product (GNP) and reduced to realistic levels the benefits of material progress and industrial growth. However, harmful impacts were not usually taken into account. Overall, perhaps because of no negative cost accounting, America's historic record in solving the problems created by industrialization has been fair to abysmal.

After the Factory, Everything Else Was an Afterthought

Thomas Jefferson's worst fears about the evils of cities came true when festering slums appeared, grew, and surrounded America's noisy and dirty factories. Had Americans made a bad bargain between industrial productivity and corruption of the environment? In older established cities like Pittsburgh and Philadelphia, their shops, parks, and individual homes were once pleasant livable neighborhoods. The natural organic wastes of a crowded city were bad enough, such as the putrid smells and leftovers from tanneries. Beginning in the 1850s a troublesome new list of wastes appeared: sulfur, cyanide, and ammonia gases of industrial operations, kerosene smoke from lanterns, acid fumes from metal plating shops, everywhere cinders and coal dust, and the heavy particulates of black industrial smoke. Smoke was equated with progress; Pittsburghers took pride in listing 14,000 smokestacks in their region. The early debate over public health did not examine industrial wastes because they were not seen as carriers of disease. Many medical authorities believed chemicals, salts, and poisons from the factories actually killed disease-bearing germs in rivers and streams. Not until after World War II did many municipalities interfere with the rights of business to dump their wastes on open land or into convenient ponds and rivers.

The physical needs of a garment factory or steel mill or slaughterhouse dominated the new industrial town. A ganglia of rail lines to import raw materials and export manufactured products ignored earlier footpaths and community roads. Everything apart from the factory was an afterthought. The gridiron layout of streets, blocks, and housing paid little attention to landscape or human use. Individual building lots were valued according to "front feet," which encouraged narrow frontage, a deep lot, and airless and lightless tenement apartments. This was advantageous to the land surveyor, real estate speculator, commercial builder, and the lawyer, but rarely to the dweller. The city had been transformed from a vital living center into a warehouse for the factory's labor force. This storage of people in layers of five or six levels of tenement floors guaranteed a work force no matter whether the market was good or bad, and provided an underlayer of extra workers, unemployed except at peak manufacturing periods. Full production capacity in the mills or factories was rare enough that the surplus workers kept wages low and conditions poor for those who were working. This exploitation of people, constriction of daily life, dilapidation of the environment, and trivialization of meaning repudiated the notion of civilized existence. Very rarely did public interest or civic need—schools, recreation, arts, and health care—receive priority in city life.

A Public Debate:
Was Industrialization Inherently Flawed?

The influential English historian Thomas Carlyle had lamented back in 1829 that truly human values disappeared when "men are grown mechanical in head and heart, as well as in hand." Factory machines and industrial structures had overrun all other human institutions. Yet Carlyle believed industrialization need not be destructive; properly developed, it could be the source of spiritual uplift as well as material improvement. A Cincinnati lawyer, Timothy Walker, responded to Carlyle's critique in an 1863 essay, "The Paradise within the Reach of

ENVIRONMENTAL HISTORIAN JOSEPH M. Petulla described the impact of the horse on urban health in the nineteenth century: "Although responsible for most of the transportation, hauling and much of the heavy labor of the era, horses represented a special environmental problem. There were 3.5 million of them in American cities at the turn of the century and they generated a monumental smell before and after evacuating their wastes. Every city had large horse populations: 83,000 in Chicago, 12,000 each in Milwaukee and Detroit." Urban historian Joel A. Tarr added, "The faithful, friendly horse was charged with creating the very problems today attributed to the automobile: air contaminants harmful to health, noxious odors, and noise." New York City had 120,000 horses in 1908. Petulla continued, "Experts at the time asserted that the normal city horse dropped 15 to 30 pounds of manure a day." It was said in Rochester, New York, that the city's 15,000 horses produced enough manure every year to make a pile 175 feet high over a full acre of ground, "enough to breed 16 billion flies and spread life-threatening sickness and disease." No wonder, says Petulla, that there was a strong demand for a convenient "horseless carriage" in America's cities.

All Men." Walker told Carlyle, "In plain words, we deny the evil tendencies of mechanism." He admitted that industrialization would bring fundamental changes to civilization and diminish the power of nature, a profound shift from Carlyle's favored "organic" social order to a "mechanical" social order. The function of machines and structures was to redesign or replace an increasingly obsolete natural environment in order to foster a world of considerable freedom from hard labor, which in turn would bring intellectual, social, and spiritual progress. "There would be nothing to hinder all mankind from becoming philosophers, poets, and votaries of art," since "the whole time and thought of the whole human race could be given to inward culture, to spiritual advancement." In spite of the growth of monopolistic corporations, Americans remained committed to economic progress, laissez-faire competition, the rights of private property, and free opportunity.

However, by the 1890s many Americans began to doubt whether industrial capitalism was the logical fulfillment of American ideals. The more the nation was industrialized, the less it seemed to retain its unique dedication to liberty and opportunity, and the more it began to slip into class warfare and extreme contrasts between wealth and poverty like that of Europe. Reformers like Jacob Riis in New York City and Jane Addams in Chicago drew public attention to tenement squalor that contradicted the American dream. In response, Pittsburgh's Andrew Carnegie went to great lengths to justify trickle-down economics in his "Gospel of Wealth." He shaped public sentiment that said victims of the economic system required only individual moral uplift to change their fortunes. Churchman Russell Conwell was widely quoted when he said, "Let us remember there is not a poor person in the United States who was not made poor by his own shortcomings." Conwell also insisted, "If you can honestly attain unto riches, it is your Christian and godly duty to do so." American industrial society has never resolved these contradictions between private rights and public welfare. The industrial infrastructure, which had spread its web across the nation, also created great and unexpected disjunctures that were reaching crisis level in the late nineteenth century. Ironically, this internal festering, like a hidden cancer, took place simultaneously with the emergence of the United States as the richest and most dominant industrial nation in the world.

Social Darwinism: An Intellectual Debate

The late nineteenth-century movement called Social Darwinism offered a "scientific" explanation of the new corporate industrial society. Social Darwinism looked on human affairs as the continuation of the evolutionary process of natural selection in which organisms compete for the "survival of the fittest." Psychologist and philosopher William James concluded that only by struggling against the forces of nature did the human spirit have "a fighting chance of safety" against an indifferent physical world. It was a cosmic struggle between human self-worth and the "essential vulgarity" of the environment (a view that would be reversed by the modern environmental movement). When the winners in the struggles of industrialization took all the wealth and stomped on the losers, it was natural and just. Social Darwinism spokesman William Graham Sumner minced no words: "Liberty, inequality, survival of the fittest; not liberty, equality, survival of the unfittest. The former carries society forward, the latter carries society downwards and favors all its worst members." Monopolies and corporate interlocking trusts thus fulfilled "natural selection" because they drove out weaker

HISTORIAN HENRY BAMFORD Parkes's description of the novelist Mark Twain, author of the classic *Huckleberry Finn,* applied to most Americans in the late nineteenth century:

> Twain can be cited as a case study of how the agrarian American submitted to capitalism. He had all the characteristic virtues of his agrarian background; a natural democrat, with the fundamental American respect for the rights of all human beings, he despised pretense and sham, and hated injustice and exploitation. At the same time, he had no coherent social philosophy; his political affirmations were instinctual rather than reasoned. He had no capacity for abstract thought and little respect for intellectual speculation, and his opinions, in spite of his homely and realistic common sense, were often remarkably naive. Moreover, he was personally as eager as most other Americans to achieve material success and to discover some easy way of making money. Transplanted from the frontier to the East, he could neither accept nor repudiate this new environment. He saw the dishonesty and the exploitation that accompanied the rise of capitalism; but he had no alternative social doctrine to propound, and he was too honest merely to condemn the robber barons without recognizing that they were doing what other Americans would have like to do if they had the opportunity.

Parkes concluded that Mark Twain, who in his later years succumbed to financial failure and deep melancholia, "was, in a sense, broken by capitalist America."

competitors. Individuals might suffer in the short run, but that was part of the price of progress. Few people asked whether the suffering individuals willingly sacrificed their well-being for the greater evolutionary good. Yet Americans found it very difficult to accept the images of wealthy industrialists wearing diamond stickpins and top hats contrasted with broken-down workers and diseased women and children.

Social Darwinism suggested an updated environmental determinism in which individuals had little choice but to conform to their newly industrialized surroundings, now technology based (mechanistic) rather than nature based (organic). Theologian Walter Rauschenbusch attempted to soften the edges of the harsh subordination of workers through an ethically responsible "Social Gospel" that emerged in the late nineteenth century. Rauschenbusch believed that the source of evil rested in the now-dominant economic system that exploited both humans and the environment. One of his strongest examples anticipated modern environmental protection. He asked for a Christian ethic "so large and intelligent that it will persuade an ignorant people to build a system of waterworks up in the hills, that will get after the thoughtless farmers who contaminate the brooks with typhoid bacilli, and after the lumber concern that is denuding the watershed of its forests." He concluded that the polluted brook and the denuded mountain were not the inevitable products of a materialistic culture, but were the results of ignorance and thoughtlessness that could be readily corrected.

Thorstein Veblen, one of the most perceptive analysts of the baffled society, applied Darwinian struggle and natural selection to explain adaptation to the new human and nonhuman circumstances. In ways that anticipated modern environmentalism, Veblen strove for a holistic approach to avoid separating humanity from larger environmental forces. Veblen admitted that humans will always be pugnacious, but in the new business era they had switched from a struggle to master the natural world into an disastrous and self-defeating struggle of man against man. When humans are encouraged to be predatory toward nature or toward other humans, "ferocity, self-seeking, clannishness, and disingenuousness—a free resort to force and fraud" take hold everywhere and bring inordinate suffering. He acknowledged that Americans enjoyed industrial efficiency, productivity, and technological improvements, but it was at the enlargement of contention, distrust, and chicanery. Human nature took a turn for the worst. The new rich monopolized the wealth of the nation while the new poor (craftsworkers without their own tools as machines took over) rose up in rage against their failure to enjoy their share of the nation's wealth. In a vivid anticipation of ecosystems analysis, Veblen concluded that because humanity, technology, and the environment inescapably form an organic whole, a change at any given point initiates changes everywhere else. Nevertheless, the voice of Veblen and other critics did little to distract most Americans from their joyous embrace of industrialization.

The People Rebel: Disillusionment about Industrialization

Charles Flint, the crusty founder of the powerful U.S. Rubber Company, was not alone among the robber barons to be convinced that corporate capital and equipment contributed more to renowned American mass production than did the thousands of workers he favored with jobs when they filed into his factories. Worker anger and frustration also took hold because of seemingly random "boom-and-bust" swings in the economy in 1873 to 1878, 1884 to 1886, and 1893 to 1897. These were induced largely by rash speculation by a few financiers on the financial markets, but kept wages low for most workers and unemployment for as much as 30 percent of the work force. Most factory workers in the 1890s earned between $400 and $500 a year, which gave them and their families subsistence in crowded tenements, and usually required child labor while ignoring worker and family health and education. This factory hand could also expect to be laid off for months at a time when business was slow, shut down like a factory machine with no compensation and little public charity. In a society of enormous disparities, the top 1 percent of the population owned 51 percent of the property, which averaged $264,000 compared to the worker's net worth of $150.

The American worker, having committed himself (most strikers were men except for garment workers) to the industrial infrastructure, demanded his share of the promised benefits. It was a battle deep within the infrastructure interior. Workers attacked the mainline industries of the new industrial web: railroads, coal mining, steel manufacturing, construction, and the clothing industry. In the workplace itself, strikers believed they deserved the benefits of industrial productivity by receiving a shorter working day, safer and healthier working conditions, and the right to participate in decisions about factory floor operations. Strikers walked off their jobs to fight for wage increases and against wage reductions because their earning power was the entry gate to the promised land of the new consumer society. Samuel Gompers of the new American Federation of Labor called strikes for "bread and butter issues" to improve the workplace and assure decent family life. The disillusionment with corporate factories often became communitywide: Striking workers got credit from local shopkeepers, soldiers fraternized with strikers, journalists uncovered corporate skullduggery, even farmers organized into granges against railroad shipping prices and extreme fluctuations on the commodity markets.

In July 1877 after their wages were cut by 10 percent, railroad workers struck against the Baltimore and Ohio Railroad and destroyed buildings and equipment in West Virginia, Baltimore, Pittsburgh, and Chicago. Railroad officials, with easy access to government forces, used police and soldiers to club down the strikers. In 1886 factory workers struck the McCormick Reaper Works in Chicago to push for an 8-hour workday instead of the prevailing 12 hours. A rally at Haymarket Square led to a violent clash between strikers and police in which 16 were killed, more than 50 wounded, and 4 workers hung as "conspirators." In 1892 the Homestead Steel Strike near Pittsburgh was a bitterly violent encounter between angry strikers and company men. The Carnegie Steel Company, which sought to break the workers' union, fortified the steel mill grounds and locked union workers out. A fierce battle between workers and the private army of Pinkerton guards left 16 dead before government troops restored order. In 1894 at the company town and factory of the Pullman Railway Car Company south of Chicago, a reduction of wages, a worker strike, and the factory shutdown led to clashes between workers and federal troops with 25 killed and 60 seriously wounded. Overall, the early 1880s saw nearly 500 strikes a year involving 125,000 workers in 12,000 businesses; the early 1890s experienced 1,300 work stoppages a year involving 250,000 workers in 30,000 businesses. The employees involved represented only 2 or 3 percent of the nation's work force, but the events were highly visible and most people feared they were only the tip of the iceberg of frustration.

Pittsburgh, Unfortunately, Had It All

In the United States, fortunately, public dismay could at times be heard. Public attention came with Jacob Riis's shocking photographs of New York City's sweatshops and slums. Upton Sinclair's novel *The Jungle* revealed conditions in Chicago's meatpacking industry, Frank Norris's *The Octopus* told of exploitation in California's new industrial farms, and later John Steinbeck's *The Grapes of Wrath* described degradation and rebellion in an uncontrolled capitalist environment. The dramatic and influential 1914 report on Pittsburgh's degradation by the Russell Sage Foundation told of the depth and permanence of industry's fouling of the human and natural environment.

One journalist wrote in 1884 that Pittsburgh once had the makings for a beautiful city: "Its narrow river valley is surrounded by hills rising to the height of four or five hundred feet. These hills once possessed rounded outlines, with sufficient exceptional abruptness to lend them variety and picturesqueness." By this time, Pittsburgh was "not a beautiful city, with the heavy pall of smoke which constantly overhangs her." The surrounding hills had "been leveled down, cut into, sliced off, and ruthlessly marred and mutilated, until not a trace of their original outlines remain. [Now] great black coal cars crawl up and down their sides, and plunge into unexpected and mysterious openings. Railroad tracks gridiron the ground everywhere, debris of all sorts lies in heaps, and is scattered over the earth, and huts and hovels are perched here and there, in every available spot." Pittsburgh was once famous for its "boscage"—lush green forested hills and valleys. Another account in 1909 compared Pittsburgh's natural site favorably with Edinburgh, Scotland, or Florence, Italy, but "a wonderful natural picturesqueness is contrasted with the utmost industrial defilement, smoke and grime and refuse pervading one of the finest city sites in the world."

The Russell Sage Foundation Report of 1914:
"The Pittsburgh Survey"

The reformist report by the Russell Sage Foundation in 1914 set precedents as a rigorous critique of the negative infrastructure. It proposed direct political action to bring economic and social change. The executive director of the study, Paul U. Kellogg, called the project "a demonstration in social economy made graphic against the background of a single city—a city set as it were on the hill of our material improvement." The report concluded that Pittsburgh's central city might be a great industrial enterprise, but it was hardly a human metropolis. Instead it contained "great central commercial activities, the railroad terminals, several large industrial plants and numerous smaller ones, together with the homes of some thousands of unskilled (immigrant) work-people" who eat and sleep in the shadows of the factories. "The congestion of machinery and work space within industrial plants . . . is particularly conducive to trade diseases and trade accidents."

A year before its staff came to Pittsburgh, the Russell Sage Foundation completed a muckraking reform study of Washington, D.C. There Congress had defeated child labor restrictions, voted down the first mandatory public schooling in the District of Columbia, refused health programs to reduce excessive infant mortality, and ignored alley shacks next to the Capitol "not fit for cow stables." The foundation found precedents for its "modest undertaking" in the public health work in Paris by the French doctor Louis Pasteur, in London's East End renewal led by Arnold Toynbee's "Oxford men," and the pioneering work of Jane Addams at Hull House on Chicago's South Side. Paul U. Kellogg admitted that the study of Pittsburgh started as a muckraking journalistic project in 1905. The invitation to pursue a detailed analysis came first from Pittsburgh's chief juvenile probation officer, Alice B. Montgomery, and belatedly from the mayor, the president of the chamber of commerce, and a local federal judge. Funding started with $7,000 from the Russell Sage Foundation and $1,350 from Pittsburgh citizens, coupled with $19,500 more from the foundation for a full year's work. Research personnel were detached from national organizations like the YMCA and the National Consumer's League.

"We injected into Pittsburgh in September, 1907, what might be called a flying wedge of investigators who were on the ground for from six weeks to two months," said Kellogg. He led a staff of "trained investigators—housing inspectors, sanitarians, lawyers, engineers, labor experts, and the like." "Our field work," he said, "was done in railroad yards and mill towns, sweatshops, and great manufacturing plants; in courts, hospitals and settlements. The investigators talked with priests and labor leaders, [school] superintendents, claim agents and labor bosses, landlords, housewives, butchers and bakers,—the workers themselves and those who live close to them." The final study covered worker wages and housing, tax structures, alderman government, typhoid and sanitation, public and parochial schools, playgrounds and parks, and social services like libraries. The investigation into housing, for example, was directed by Lawrence Veiller, a commissioner of the New York Tenement House Department and a founder of the National Housing Association. The Survey's study of the economic impact of 500 cases of fatal workplace accidents in Allegheny County in one year was the first in the nation. So was the analysis of the economic impact (dollar costs) of typhoid fever in six representative wards.

The Russell Sage Foundation made certain that the Pittsburgh Survey, with its harsh critique and specific recommendations for reform, would not be buried by the city fathers. Its findings were published in 35 articles in national magazines and reported to the annual meetings of the National Municipal League, the American Civic Association, the American Economic Association, the American Sociological Society, and the American Association for Labor Legislation. Kellogg summed up Pittsburgh's problems as the result of two factors especially: the 12-hour workday and social neglect by industry and the city fathers. The Survey tried to avoid blacklisting Pittsburgh by describing comparable conditions—"similar overcrowding, similar sanitary horrors, similar disease and squalor"—in Cincinnati, Cleveland, and St. Louis; New York City "exceeded them all in mass and in misery." Nevertheless, "the extent of the evil was no excuse for tolerating such conditions in Pittsburgh or anywhere else in America; it was a warning to head them off." Pittsburgh, Kellogg said, was unique only because its industrial development had already reached such a high level and had already revealed, in its slums and degradation, the "real character" of industrial activity and its "inevitable goal."

Pittsburgh's Plague of Typhoid: Human Costs

Between 1883 and 1908 almost 55,000 Pittsburghers caught the "plague" of typhoid and almost 7,500 men, women, and children died of it. "Those who could not afford to buy bottled water continued to drink filth." Pittsburgh's death rate was 130 per 100,000 people, or 30 times worse than Germany's Berlin, over 10 times worse than London (hardly a model city for sanitation), 6 times worse than New York City, and more than twice as bad as the notoriously unhealthy swampy city, Washington, D.C. A civic reform group described the 7,422 people dead from typhoid as unnecessarily "sacrificed" to the indifference of politicians and industrial leaders. One report noted that as late as 1904 Pittsburgh still experienced 503 deaths from typhoid out of a population of slightly more than 350,000; cities with relatively pure water did not have over 25 deaths annually per 100,000 people, which would have been 88 deaths in Pittsburgh. One report attached a dollar value to the deaths. It said that a single death from typhoid can be valued at $6,000, which meant that between 1883 and 1908 Pittsburgh lost $9 million, enough to pay for the $5.7 million filtration plant and needed services. To highlight the tragedy, one group said that the fatalities would have formed a line 5.6 miles long, enough to extend from the courthouse to the newly opened water filtration plant. The plant opened in the summer of 1908, after 12 years of political infighting.

Pittsburgh's public drinking water was drawn from the Allegheny or Monongahela rivers several miles upstream of the city. Unfortunately, the upstream industries along the river shores dumped soluble chemical products—"organic and inorganic, acid and alkali; oils, and other carbon compounds." Further upstream the human sewage of 350,000 people of 75 towns flowed untreated into the rivers. The Russell Sage Foundation reported "flesh-disintegrated and putrescent" dead animals and the "off-scourings of iron and steel mills, tanneries, slaughter houses" floating on the rivers. The report told of a family of five with a 16-year-old daughter who caught typhoid and tuberculosis. "Not being strong enough to return to her former employment, she secured work in a bakery where she was subsequently seen coughing as she wrapped up bread for customers."

The Russell Sage Foundation kept returning to dollar costs because it was the most effective means of reaching the industrialists and politicians it sought to influence. In one study of 338 families of 2,045 individuals, 448 (or 22 percent) caught typhoid in 1906–07, and 187 wage earners lost 1,901.5 weeks of work, which came to 10 weeks lost per wage-earning patient. (In 1910 the average factory worker earned $491 a year.) The actual loss in wages was $223,573, or an average of $126 per patient. This included the costs of a doctor, nurse, or servant, of drugs, ice, and milk if the patient stayed home, of hospital expenses and funeral expenses, and of loss of wages by patient and family members who stopped working to care for the ill. Those caring for the sick lost a total of 322 weeks of work, $3,327 in wages, for a total of $26,900 in lost wages. Of the 448 who caught typhoid, 20 percent, or 90 people, could afford to go to a hospital, which cost $4,167; 357 stayed home at an aggregate cost of $22,000. For others, sick care would have been much higher except for charitable aid. The total funeral expenses of the 26 who died was $3,186. In sum, for the years 1906–07 alone, these typhoid cases cost the city $540,000 in expenses and loss of wages, "setting no value at all on the [future] earning power of lives snuffed out." The foundation report concluded that the dollar losses would have paid the interest, depreciation, and sinking fund charges for the new filtration plant for an entire year.

Contrasts: The Tenement and the City Park

As late as 1896, Pittsburgh had no planned parks. It benefited from open places that totaled hundreds of acres and were named Highland Park, Schenley Park, and Riverview Park, but they were mostly barren and treeless places, or tangled ravines in the hilly city. Once again, the Russell Sage Foundation report took the city leaders to task: "No town of its size in the country had so neglected to provide for public parks. What suggestion of play could parents or children find in a city of iron whose monster machinery rested neither day nor night?" In one of the mill and tenement districts there was only "a little 30-foot-wide strip of grass on Second Avenue near the courthouse, and upon this the adjoining property holders were looking with covetous eyes." As a result, recreation, if it could be called that, took place "in a steaming kitchen or a home workshop, narrow sidewalks, and the space between the curbs, filled with a constantly increasing traffic." Critics reported the rise of "degeneracy" among tenement children, that the boys were already sneak thieves and the girls had a "pathological condition, their feverish, unchildlike desire for work."

A newly formed Civic Club forced the city in the 1890s to open local schoolyards to the public and add swings and slides. After five years of open playgrounds, reformers claimed the children had improved and their parents benefited. Early in the twentieth century the Civic Club and its successor, the Park Association, fostered the creation of five well-developed parks that were accessible to the poor. The start was shaky in 1904, when a polluted pond called Bedford Basin was filled in and renamed Washington Park, but it really was a rough and uneven field of about 5 acres, bounded by a broken wall in sight of a cinder dump. Lawrence Park in the middle of the city included a brick field house, swimming pool, and ball fields. Nearby Arsenal Park contained gardens and playing fields. Washington Park eventually got a field house that included a basketball gymnasium. The two larger and older open spaces toward the outskirts of the city, Highland Park and Schenley Park, were landscaped into strolling walks, open fields, ball fields, and picnic grounds. In 1910 a $1 million bond issue passed for park enlargement and improvement. This largess encouraged the city council to take the parks out of the hands of the private association and place them under the dubious control of the city's bureau of parks.

These public parks were called "the playgrounds of Pittsburgh." Elsewhere in the United States the name given them was often "pleasure ground." In some cities, like Cincinnati, Brooklyn, and Cambridge, even cemeteries were designed for public strolling as antidotes to the ills of the city: fresh air, open space, tranquillity, and accessibility. The park visitor was to have the illusion of being in the open country. Urban reformers and far-sighted politicians in Cincinnati, New York, Brooklyn, Boston, and Chicago reshaped empty inner-city land or outskirts farmland, before it was enveloped by urban growth, into a specific mental picture of gently sloping lawns, with clusters of trees, a pond or winding stream, and rambling walkways that led to picnic grounds and ball fields. When Frederick Law Olmstead in the 1850s planned Central Park in New York City, he even sought to exclude competitive sports and parades that would mirror the busy life of the city; strollers should instead enjoy self-renewal in "sacred space" by contemplating beautiful scenery.

Although workingmen's families occasionally escaped to a city park, it was always the tenement to which they returned. The parks movement stands in sharp contrast to the spread of tenement housing for factory workers and their families. As industrialization overran the older commercial cities like New York City or Pittsburgh, urban landlords rented private houses in older neighborhoods. Landlords would offer rooms to two, three, or four families without subdividing the house. The families shared a single kitchen, bath, and toilet. Older apartment buildings were partitioned into smaller and smaller units. New construction was almost invariably a walk-up tenement apartment of three to six stories, with one or two long parallel apartments on a floor. The "tenement" usually followed the "dumbbell" shape with connected rooms that allowed the most efficient use of space (on a 25 by 100-foot lot) while barely meeting city regulations concerning windows, doors, and exits. The largest rooms measured 10½ by 11 feet. The dumbbell shape involved a narrow and dangerous air shaft that was supposed to offer ventilation but often became a garbage chute or gave draft for a fire to follow. The Pittsburgh report concluded, "The fire danger seemed to overshadow every other evil. A few puffs of smoke would have choked the narrow passageways, a single tongue of flame would have destroyed the ropes by which the lanterns were hanging and plunged the place into darkness. The confusion and the loss of human life that would have ensued can easily be imagined." The city regulations for a basement apartment did not require a ceiling more than a foot above street level. New York City was the most notorious tenement city. In 1900 it had 42,700 tenements housing 1.5 million people, with sometimes as many as 12 families living on one floor.

The Pennsylvania tenement house law of 1903 followed New York City's regulatory reform. Each room must contain a minimum of 400 cubic feet of air space for each adult and 200 for each child. If the building was three or more stories tall, an outside fire escape route was required, but its location was not specified. There must be a water supply on every floor accessible to all tenants "without the necessity for their passing through any apartment but their own." In existing tenements, one toilet was required for two apartments. The toilet could be an outdoor water "vault" in the backyard. The minimum standards of a single sink and water closet on every floor, regardless of the number of people, were not often observed.

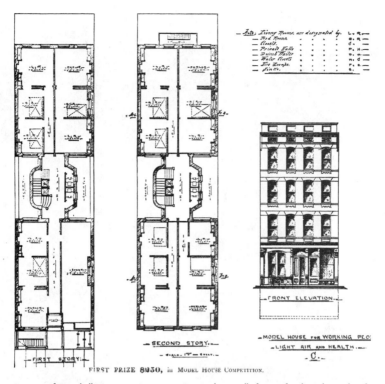

FIRST PRIZE 8950, in MODEL HOUSE COMPETITION.

Diagram of "Dumbell" Tenement Apartment. Designed originally for one family and to make efficient use of property frontage, the tenement apartments that spread across most metropolitan regions became symbols of the worst of urban slums. Often several families and "guests" crowded into each apartment under squalid sanitary conditions.

Overall, Pittsburgh's tenement law was indifferently enforced. Ironically, tenement regulations were considered so rigorous that they accelerated the subdividing of existing apartments and the conversion of private houses into uncontrolled multiple units.

A "Double Standard of Civil Morality"

The Russell Sage Foundation report about Pittsburgh as a typical industrial city caused civic embarrassment and national outrage. The report accused the city of Carnegie, Mellon, Jones, and Laughlin of a "double standard of civic morality." On the one hand, the rules for business operation were treated as sacred, particularly rigid adherence to a 12-hour workday, often 7 days a week. On the other hand, the workers who had to commit themselves to the rules of business found that the same industries paid low wages, ignored the destruction of family life in terrible slums, and paid no attention to civic improvement.

Business interests tried to gloss over the health and welfare problems they created. They told the public that heavy smoke from the mills actually prevented the spread of airborne disease. (The same self-serving argument was used for copper-rich smelting operations in Butte, Montana.) The foundation report fumed that the industrialists who created the problems

Photo from the Famous 1914 Russell Sage Foundation Report on Industrial Pittsburgh.

were callous toward their employees and indifferent about the future. "Big men of a generation ago said, 'After us the deluge.' They cut the forests off the Alleghenies, and Pittsburgh
suffers the curse literally in destructive floods. The way of life about many of the great steel
plants is inevitably preparing for the near future a worse form of deluge in a mass of unfit,
undervitalized, unproductive citizens." The contrasts were overwhelming and unacceptable.
On the one hand, said the report, Pittsburgh was one "of the most prosperous of all the communities of our western civilization, with its vast natural resources, the human energy, the
technical development, the gigantic tonnage of the minds and mills, the enormous capital of
which the bank balances afford an indication." On the other hand, business operations fostered "the neglect of life, of health, of physical vigor, even of the industrial efficiency of the
individual."

"We Are Manufacturers, Not Real Estate Dealers"

Very often Pittsburgh's civic and industry leaders (and corporate landlords) blamed the sorry
living conditions on "primitive" habits brought by immigrants from southern and eastern
Europe, but this was consistently disproved. A director of a social service center reported
in 1907,

It is no wonder that they are stooped and broken in health. The conditions under which they must live mean constant hardship, sickness, and bitter struggle. Pick your way through the narrow alleys between the houses, look into the [privy] closets and shacks, go up the narrow, black stairways, note the ceilings patched with papers where the leaking roof has sent the plaster to the floor, feel the wintry wind as it drives its way through rattling windows and flimsily constructed doors, look at the worn, tired bodies and faces of the mothers, at the little children huddled about the stove.

The director wondered whether Pittsburgh had any future when its people lived under such conditions: "Go out on the street and scan closely the faces of the boys and girls who are growing into manhood and womanhood and see what kind of men and women these environments are producing." He angrily concluded: "These people are not asking for charity. They are asking for living conditions under which their children may grow up into clean, decent, respectable manhood and womanhood. The wonder to me has been, not that so many were sick, but rather that any at all could be well." In Ewing Street in Skunk Hollow, "No visitor can tell whether the shacks are for cows, horses, or human beings."

The president of a major steel company retorted, "We are manufacturers, not real estate dealers. In an old, settled community let the laboring man take care of himself. We don't believe in paternalism." One of the Russell Sage Foundation workers wrote of housing owned by a steel company:

> When the Carnegie Steel Company took over Painter's Mill, it renovated the plant so as to turn out the sort and quantity of output which the Carnegie name stands for. When it took over [the adjacent company-owned housing] Painter's Row, it did nothing. The company had not recognized it to be worth while as a business consideration to house its human machinery with a view of maintaining such machinery at its highest state of efficiency. Its mills, with their equipment, were repaired and improved in order to increase the quality and quantity of their output. But common laborers were too easily replaced for an effort to be made to conserve their health or well-being by repairing or improving these houses in which they lived. If 10 men fell out, 10 more were ready to step in and fill their places.

Pittsburgh's real estate property taxes, which paid for city services and schools, were notoriously unequal; inner-city poor people lucky enough to own their wooden row houses on unlighted unpaved streets next to the mills paid the full city rate of $1.60 on each $100 of valuation; the brick and stone mansions of the upper middle class on spacious avenues, still conveniently in the city, paid far lower "rural" rates of $1.05 per $100, and land held for speculation on the outskirts of the city was taxed at minimal "farm" rates of 83½ cents per $100. Thus the city workman paid 50 percent more than his middle-class neighbor and nearly 100 percent more than the wealthy speculator. The foundation data and analysis was so scandalous that real estate tax reform in 1914 began to wipe out the differences.

Pittsburgh: "Public Moral Adolescence"

The Russell Sage Foundation report was proactive. It called for a one-third decrease in the workday, from 12 to 8 hours, with Sundays off. This was to be coupled with "the increase of wages, the sparing of lives, the prevention of accidents, and raising the standards of domestic life." Pittsburgh's terrible conditions were the result of its "public moral adolescence." This crass indifference was matched by the city's "overwrought materialism" in which its energies were "absorbed in the subduing of nature and the achieving of a great material destiny." Denial of ordinary human well-being was a "very costly process thought necessary to industrial prosperity." As late as 1914, for workers in the mills and railroad yards, "there was no seventh day save as it was stolen from sleep." The report condemned the middle class and the wealthy, who carried the most responsibility for Pittsburgh's terrible condition and had moved across the rivers and over the surrounding hills into the suburbs, protected by toll bridges and 10 cent fares on the electrified trains. The report concluded that Pittsburgh's leaders were simply morally "backward." The city's terrible condition was no little matter, since the census of 1910 showed that it had a metropolitan population over a million, fifth in rank in the nation after New York City, Philadelphia, Chicago, and Boston.

The Struggle for Urban Reform: An Uphill Battle

The Pittsburgh Survey concluded,

> Hundreds of industrial towns, a score of great industrial centers, are growing up in this country. Of their technical and commercial success we have evidence in plenty. What of their human prosperity? In so far as work-accidents are the crudest exponents of human waste in industry, the Pittsburgh District had been spendthrift of its own life blood. . . . We did not turn to Pittsburgh as a scapegoat city. Yet at bottom the District exhibits national tendencies. The present volume reveals a community struggling for the things which primitive men have ready to hand—clear air, clean water, pure foods, shelter, and a foothold of earth.

The problems were national. To be a little more fair to Pittsburgh's attempts at reform, in 1909 the Pittsburgh Civic Commission made strong proposals to improve drinking water and sewerage, smoke and dust abatement, building codes, public utilities, funding for public works, interurban steam, electric, and water transportation, paved streets, city lighting, recreation on public lands, and regulations to prevent future abuses. The 1914 Russell Sage Foundation report acknowledged that, "while the biggest men of the community made steel, other men built water companies, threw bridges across the rivers, erected inclines, and laid sectional car lines." After World War II, Pittsburgh went through dramatic urban redevelopment, the first phase in the 1940s called the Pittsburgh Renaissance and the second in the 1960s called Renaissance Two. In the first phase the city's basic industries were modernized, urban renewal initiated, and pollution significantly reduced; the second phase brought on the dismantling of the major steel plants and employment redirected toward hospitals and higher education, which became the city's two largest employers. As a result, by the 1970s Pittsburgh became, according to a popular national survey, the nation's "most livable city." Nevertheless, the old industrial rancor had not entirely disappeared. In the late 1960s the president of U.S. Steel took out a full-page ad in the city's newspapers in which he threatened to pull the company out of the city unless it received relief from costly correction of air pollution from its mills and smokestacks.

The Beginnings of Urban Cleanup

Workers and their families in industrial slums were prime candidates for pellagra and goiter, diseases with a chemical or mineral diet deficiency rather than an infectious origin. Lead poisoning from laboring in smelting and paint factories had long been known. Other hazards involved the dust disease silicosis among coal miners, called "miner's asthma" or "miner's consumption." "Nail-maker's consumption" in 1870s came from the dust from nail grinding. New chemicals and processes posed new uncertainties and potential dangers. For decades, however, reformers usually paid more attention to traumatic accidents and alcoholism than to industrial disease. Part of the reason was the lack of standardized data and the ambiguity of symptoms of cardiovascular illnesses and infectious lung diseases. Public health historian Christopher Sellers writes, "Even the mental disturbances of lead encephalopathy could be impossible to distinguish from alcohol intoxication." Long-term exposures involving small doses and gradual poisoning were impossible to assess accurately. Whatever the reason, for individual workers the sacrifice was terrible, from loss of a job to permanent disablement and death.

One success story was the creation of controls over exposure to phosphorus. White phosphorus was widely used in manufacturing matches. But heavy exposure caused a unique disease known as phosphorus necrosis, or "phossy jaw," in which a victim's jaw became inflamed and pus ridden as the jawbone gradually disintegrated and had to be removed. Victims were gruesomely disfigured and stirred public sympathy. Britain had banned manufacture of poisonous phosphorus matches in 1908. Most of Europe followed shortly. In the United States, health officials identified 16 phosphorus match factories that put workers at risk, and documented cases in 1909. Congress acted indirectly but effectively when it passed a law in 1912 that taxed white phosphorus out of existence.

George Waring, Water Flushing, and Sanitary Engineering

As early as the 1770s, English medical men promoted the idea of using running water in "water closets" to carry off human wastes and garbage. Control of typhoid by sanitation had been widely known since the 1840s. Typhoid was the result of drinking water polluted by human and animal waste. Epidemics of crisis proportions during the early nineteenth century in both England and America drew attention to the need for metropolitan water systems to provide fresh drinking water and to carry off wastes. By the mid-nineteenth century water as a flushing agent became the most favored mode of cleaning the cities. The doctors deferred to a new professional, the sanitary engineer, who used the methods of dilution of waste material in flowing water, as well as assimilation, meaning the discharge into a stream up to its capacity to carry away the wastes "harmlessly" downstream. Between 1848 and 1890 Chicago had developed its exemplary Sanitary District system of canals that disposed of the city's sewage in the Illinois River, which emptied into the Mississippi. A medical problem had fostered an engineering solution. The federal Public Health Service Act at the turn of the century supported the belief that rivers and streams could purify themselves of the chemicals and wastes they received as they passed through the nation's industrial cities.

Insufficient water supply made household cleanliness and sanitation almost impossible. One survey worker in Pittsburgh wrote,

> The marvel was not that some of the homes were dirty, but that any of them were clean. I talked with one mother whose two rooms on the top floor were spotless, and whose children were well looked after. Day after day, and many times a day, she carried the water up and down that her home and her children might be kept decent and clean. I looked at her bent shoulders, gaunt arms, and knotted hands. Those shoulders and hands had to strain laboriously over unnecessary work. "God! Miss, but them stairs is bad," she said.

A plague spot like the back alley called Saw Mill Run had double- and triple-decker rear privies that simply discharged onto the banks of an intermittent stream that flushed away the wastes of 35,000 people living in Saw Mill Run only after a rain. Even then the sight was "deplorable and disgusting." A city inspector reported, "One unsewered vault represented the sole closet [toilet] accommodations for the 19 families living in this group of houses (including the boarders, a total of 151 persons). The privy was reached by crossing a rickety platform so full of holes that its use was dangerous after nightfall. One especially large hole near the center of the platform was evidently used as a garbage dump."

Engineer George E. Waring was asked to review sanitary conditions in Memphis after more than 5,000 of its inhabitants died from a yellow fever epidemic, and he persuaded the city to build his dual system, one for rainwater and the second for raw sewage, despite the higher cost. Waring's approach lost out to the combined-pipe system because his pipes still flushed into a river without treatment, and he believed on the miasma theory of disease (influence of sewer gas) that was soon discredited. Nevertheless, by offering technical answers to health problems, George Waring became the national symbol of the new, highly respected profession of sanitary engineer. In the 1890s he was appointed street-cleaning commissioner in New York City. Waring became public spokesman for the virtues of cleanliness, appearing at every problem area in a spotless uniform, pith helmet, and shining riding boots. He rode a prancing steed in city parades, leading his "White Wings" sanitary employees. His crusade as "the apostle of cleanliness" touched on factory wastes, manure from horses, garbage, human waste, snow removal, and even the recycling of ashes into fireproof building blocks. Elsewhere, sanitary engineers took the lead as most American cities built and owned their own water systems. By 1910, 7 out of 10 cities with 30,000 or more people had built water supply and wastewater disposal infrastructures. Americans at the turn of the century believed that most urban problems could be solved by good engineering and modern technology.

Alice Hamilton, Occupational Disease, and Early Environmentalism

Dr. Alice Hamilton risked a promising medical career by dedicating herself to the unknown problems of occupational diseases. Her innovative work put her at the head of a pioneering Illinois commission to study occupational disease. In 1910 she became the first physician-investigator for the U.S. Bureau of Labor, where she innovated on-site factory inspections. This "shoeleather epidemiology" (historian Robert Gottlieb's words) utilized factory interviews, home visits, discussions with physicians and apothecaries, information from charity workers and visiting nurses, and even contact with undertakers. During an inspection at the

Wetherill white lead factory in Philadelphia, Hamilton found heaps of white lead stretched from wall to wall where immigrant workers packed the dried compound for shipment. The factory floor foreman and his immigrant workers showed no concern about stirring or breathing the omnipresent dry lead dust. Hamilton documented 27 cases of lead poisoning in the previous 16 months at the Wetherill, which astonished the owner and management and shamed them into a cleanup. When Hamilton gathered information for her 1908 Illinois Commission on Occupational Diseases, she began to note that "the foremen deny everything and the men will not talk."

Hamilton's sweeping innovations identified the connection between disease, environment, and politics. She called public and medical attention to the "dangerous trades" that caused poisoning in chemical factories, consumption in the clothing industry, rheumatism in glass works, and lead poisoning in metal processing. Although other materials such as phosphorus had substitutes, lead was less susceptible to phaseout and was used across a broad spectrum of industry, including the painting and pottery trades, lead smelting and refining, and the manufacture of storage batteries. Too much exposure to lead had long been recognized as a source of convulsions, abdominal pain, paralysis, temporary blindness, extreme pallor, loss of weight and appetite, indigestion, and constipation. Once the poison took hold, remedies were limited. Hamilton urged coveralls to cover workers, a cap to cover the hair, and some form of respirator, as well as washing facilities and regular physical examinations. She crusaded for plant cleanliness, "so clean that one could quite literally eat one's dinner off the floor." Following studies in a Harvard laboratory, the clinician Joseph Aub recommended a specific treatment of calcium-rich foods that would drive lead into harmless deposits in the bones. Some white lead companies had for many years provided milk "to allay colic." In her early public health work in Illinois, Hamilton uncovered 578 cases of lead poisoning among 77 industries using lead. As a result Illinois passed new stricter laws in 1911 for the lead, arsenic, brass, and related industries. As a federal official, she documented 358 cases of lead poisoning among the 1,600 workers in the white lead factories she inspected, 1,769 cases among 7,400 workers in lead smelting and refining operations, and 164 cases among 915 workers in storage battery factories. These were much higher rates than in Britain or Germany where health codes were in effect. Hamilton recognized that better occupational health would not come primarily from the cleanup of old industrial processes, but better working conditions in new industries, such as storage battery and rubber production. She reflected the probusiness views of her era when she made little or no effort to hang a price tag on workplace disease or risk, nor for her recommended cleanups. Hamilton instead worked energetically to change corporate behavior. She assumed that employers would do their duty once they were informed of disease among their workers. She laid most blame on "ignorance and an indolent acceptance of things as they are." Most company owners of the 25 white lead paint factories in the United States believed that they had lead poisoning under control. The editor of a mining business journal reflected industry opinion when he wrote that there was "a tendency among workmen to attribute all of the ills to their vocation." By 1914 Hamilton began to admit the limits to moral persuasion. As late as 1946 a "virtual epidemic" of lead poisoning hit 19 workers out of 120 at a foundry run by the National Lead Company.

Hamilton had transformed medical scrutiny of the workplace into an accepted function of the federal government. Such a fusion of medical and state authority was already in effect in Britain and Germany. She laid the groundwork for expansion of federal agencies into environmental management from its small beginnings in PHS (Public Health Service) to the modern OSHA (Occupational Safety and Health Administration). She opened the way to a scientific and medical foundation for occupational disease by applying pathological, clinical, chemical, and experimental approaches to lead poisoning.

Conquering Industrial Diseases

Following Alice Hamilton's lead, a growing number of doctors, chemists, and engineers were early "whistleblowers" on industrial risks. Who was responsible for worker welfare: industrial hygienist and sanitary engineers, company doctors, government regulators, corporate owners and managers, or the workers themselves? Such professionals began to urge measurable national standards, including threshold concentration levels for disease. They also began to make the distinction between the normal and abnormal levels that underlie today's environmental law, policy, and science.

Employers were increasingly held responsible for employee health. Several major corporations began to employ doctors paid by the company, including Sears and Roebuck, Youngstown Sheet and Tube, Goodrich Tire, Cincinnati Milling, the Norton Company, and National Lead. Overall, however, company doctors remained rare: Of 1,521 factories in Cleveland in the early 1900s, only 72 employed a physician in any capacity. One beneficial result was that doctors were not just treating but were preventing accidents. Their work also reduced claims. But as an employee, a doctor came under suspicion for serving the company's interest more than worker health. Samuel Gompers, leader of the aggressive American Federation of Labor, suspected that medical examinations were tools to get rid of activist workers and an invasion of "worker privacy." Because of this conflict the new Public Health Service claimed its own examining physicians were neutral and unbiased, and it acquired a solid reputation for objectivity. PHS health inspectors found resistance from firms such as the Moline Plow Company, Peoples' Gas, Light and Coke Company, and Carnegie Steel Company because of fears of discovery of costly illness.

Christopher Sellers also described the "masculine ethic of toughing it out." Most everyone recognized that "impure air, dust, and fumes" were serious dangers but saw these as normal risks. Skilled craft workers saw pollution and machinery hazards as a test of personal fortitude. They played down risky symptoms and prided themselves on their courage and endurance. In Wheeling, West Virginia, nail factories rented out nail-making machines on their premises and paid nailers by the piece, leaving working methods in the hands of the nailers themselves. Sellers writes, "Many Wheeling nailers chose not to wet down their cutting machines, which would have reduced the volume of dust to which they were exposed, since dry nail-cutting went faster and was more lucrative—at least over the short term." Coal miners simply learned to tolerate breathlessness. Those who made white lead paint bravely suffered the pain of colic and even muscle weakness. When unskilled workers, often recent immigrants, showed disease symptoms, they were often replaced by new unaware immigrants. This constant turnover was cheaper for a company than to help heal the incapacitated workers. Workers were fatalistic. They saw disease as ubiquitous, capricious, and ultimately unavoidable. Many used home remedies and patent medicines. Medical care was too costly or simply unavailable. When they fell ill, workers were told, and believed, that they simply had not taken sufficient precautions or were especially susceptible to the workplace poison.

Yet doctors like Alice Hamilton and muckraking journalists like Lincoln Steffens helped to create a changing public sense of responsibility that joined new science with governmental power. What health protection did Americans feel entitled by law? As early as 1885 New Jersey anticipated many states when it passed legislation that prohibited harmful dust and impurities in the workplace, but the law was difficult to apply to specific cases. There was no federal regulatory agency. In most cases it was said that if a health hazard was present, "a man may change his occupation." A Utah court decision in 1896, upheld in 1899 in the U.S. Supreme Court, *Holden* v. *Hardy*, supported a law limiting the workday of smelter employees to

THE U.S. PUBLIC Health Service (PHS) was established in 1912. It soon took over health management of the garment industry where tuberculosis and anemia came to be recognized as occupational diseases related to carbon monoxide poisoning from gas-powered pressing irons in garment shops. Other symptoms, such as tremors, heart palpitations, gastric discomfort, headaches, and "general weakness," were more difficult to separate from other diseases because they were the result of low-level, long-term exposure. In 1914 the Public Health Service opened a well-organized program of physical examinations for garment industry workers on New York's Lower East Side. Christopher Sellers writes,

> Pressers or finishers sought out the office at 131 Union Square West and found themselves headed toward special rooms set aside for the medical examinations. There, they encountered men and women with stethoscopes and dark military-style uniforms. In the rooms for men patients, a male physician, after asking a man to remove his clothes, spent forty to fifty minutes questioning him and carefully scrutinizing, measuring, testing and palating his body; female physicians did the same to the women workers. The workers told of their past and present jobs, their family life, and their habits of alcohol, tea, coffee and tobacco use. One or another of the physicians weighed them, measured their height and girth, punctured their skin to draw blood, and requested that they urinate into a special container. A doctor pressed on their stomachs, applied a stethoscope to their chests, hammered their knees, encircled their arms with expanding cuffs, and had them squeeze a grip as hard as they could. These physicians in their trim identical uniforms probably provided garment workers with the most thorough and inquisitive physical examination they ever received.

In 1915 Joseph Schereschewsky of PHS began to work toward a common set of public health standards by which to establish public health goals. He argued that standard setting belonged to the federal government. The result was an early combination of science and "command and control" regulation that anticipated the dominant mode of operation of environmental protection in the 1970s and 1980s. But Schereschewsky also concluded in a 1915 report that "personal hygiene" and "disadvantageous economic conditions" of workers remained more influential than any aspect of the workplace in cases of tuberculosis and related diseases.

eight hours, since the noxious gases of the smelters unduly endangered the health of workers. But in 1905 the U.S. Supreme Court, in *Lochner* v. *State of New York,* struck down a state law limiting bakery work to 10 hours a day and 60 hours a week: "There is no reasonable ground, on the score of health, for interfering with the liberty of the person or the right of free contract, by determining the hours of labor, in the occupation of a baker." This "freedom of contract" between employer and worker showed the continuing power of free enterprise capitalism in the United States and the perceived autonomy of workers. Nevertheless, public awareness and medical authority forged the beginning of the no-fault workers' compensation system, a shift that switched most decisions about legal awards to injured workers out of the courts and into new administrative agencies. A series of state-based compensation programs were established between 1910 and 1914.

Winds of change began to reach from medical experts and reformers down to the workplace. During World War I, for example, when a Massachusetts shoe factory installed a new process for making the toes of shoes, its employees soon walked out, complaining that the new chemicals had a bad odor and caused headaches and stomachaches. They stayed off the job until owners promised to put in a blower system. During the 1920s food poisoning from insecticides on apples and other produce aroused public protests that led to product bans and stronger regulatory actions by the Food and Drug Administration. One of the best-selling books of the 1930s was Arthur Kallet and F.J. Schlink's *100,000,000 Guinea Pigs,* which focused on the hazards of consumer and industrial products and called for a ban on lead arsenate. Worker health and safety actions succeeded during prosperity, but regressed during bad times such as the Depression. In the early 1930s, one of the most publicized examples of employer indifference felled over 100 tunnel workers, mostly black, from heavy doses of silica dust during the building at Gauley Bridge in West Virginia.

Chicago: "Hog Butcher to the World"

Pittsburgh had its steel mills; Chicago had a meatpacking industry. By the late nineteenth century, the journalist Lincoln Steffens wrote of Chicago: "first in violence, deepest in dirt, loud, lawless, unlovely, ill-smelling, new; an overgrown gawk of a village, the teeming tough among cities." Chicago would have even been worse except that its 1871 fire cleansed the city of a large part of its original dilapidated wooden housing.

Preindustrial Meat Processing

The old word for slaughterhouse was *abattoir.* It was usually a long shed of individual stalls in a remote place away from other human activities, often by a riverside in which to dump offal. A single ox or calf or pig was penned inside each of the stalls, where it was wrestled down and slammed on the head with a hammer or its throat pierced with a sharp knife. Frederick Law Olmstead described the meat-processing scene before mechanization had been put into place: "We found there a sort of human chopping machine where the [just slaughtered] hogs were converted into commercial pork. . . . By a skilled sleight-of-hand, hams, shoulders, clear, mess, and prime fly off, each squarely cut to its own place, where attendants, aided by trucks and dumbwaiters, dispatch each to its separate destiny—the ham for Mexico, its loin for Bordeaux. We took out our watches and counted thirty-five seconds, from the moment when one hog touched the table until the next occupied its place." Olmstead could not bear to visit the actual slaughter room with its "river of blood." It was bad enough to see in the cutting room the strange commingling of rows of living human workmen and rows of "dead swine upon their backs, their paws stretching mutely towards heaven." Such an operation cried out for mechanization.

The biggest packinghouse problem was not diseased animals, but, before mechanical refrigeration, rapid spoilage into rotten meat. Before the Civil War, slaughtering was concentrated at Cincinnati because it was convenient to riverborne shipping. Waste was still enormous. An oversupply of hogs meant that the prime portions—hams, shoulders, and sides—were shipped out by boat; the heads, spareribs, neck pieces, backbones, and internal organs were dumped as waste into the Ohio River. The river was thus the conduit for all parts of the disassembled creatures. Only with the appearance of industrial management would the saying become true, that of the hog everything was turned into soap, lard, glue, brushes, buttons, and candles, "except for the squeal." When railroad transportation became more efficient after the war, meat processing moved to Chicago.

Railroads, Chicago's Stockyards, and Refrigerator Cars

The first railroad reached Chicago from the east in 1856. Railroads quickly spread their net across the prairie and plains, from which pigs and cattle would be shipped to the hub of the industry in Chicago. Chicago's Union Stock Yards was built in six months in 1865, capitalized at a million dollars on a half square mile at the southern edge of the city. These would soon be an enormous grid of 2,300 open wooden pens, each for dozens of animals, crisscrossed with narrow streets and alleys. A mix of 21,000 head of cattle, 75,000 hogs, and 22,000 sheep could be held at the same time. Amid the yards were the wooden slaughterhouses, "a true labyrinth of sheds and enormous halls that communicate in various ways by passages, staircases, and suspension bridges," over which pass the workmen, animals, and railroads. Polluted water and offal continuously emptied into two great sewers that reached the Chicago River, which now became a stinking moving cesspool.

One critical new ingredient that improved the system was the new refrigerator car, conceived by George Henry Hammond and perfected by Gustavus F. Swift, both soon famous names in the Midwest. Decay was still the great enemy of the meatpacker because beef or pork would quickly change, if it was not properly cooled—first into something unpalatable, then inedible, and finally dangerously toxic. But direct contact with ice discolored the meat badly. Swift filled boxes at both ends of the car with ice and brine, venting them so a current of chilled air constantly flowed past the packed, suspended carcasses. Eastern consumers were still dubious about eating beef a week old, but vigorous promotion and 2 cents less a pound helped persuade them. By the late 1880s Chicago packers controlled most of America's meat supply, driving out local suppliers, especially in the East. Philip D. Armour, a born speculator, turned meatpacking into big business by manipulating the commodity markets on the Chicago Board of Trade. J. A. Wilson replaced processed meat packed in traditional barrels with his invention of the still famous truncated steel can of corned beef: "The meat would come forth in a solid cake, in a natural and palatable condition, cooked, ready to be sliced and eaten." (The author's engineer father patented a mechanical press that shoved the meat into the cans pneumatically.)

Mechanization in the Meatpacking Factory: The Disassembly Line

One of the great challenges of industrialization would be how to create metal machines that could continuously adjust to the organic variations of animal bodies. Unprocessed animal bodies on hooks and conveyors are moved past rows of men with long sharp knives. For some processes, such as skinning the body, mechanization has never replaced hand work with a knife because of the irregularities of a once living animal and its vulnerability to bruises and blows. Siegfried Giedion writes, "The head skinner, who skins the head and severs it from the body, handles his knife with so much skill that he can skin the head of the animal and sever it exactly at the junction of the skull and vertebra in the fraction of a minute." Nevertheless increased mechanization created distance from the animals and reinforced the modern indifference toward nature. The famous British novelist Rudyard Kipling, who said he had encountered everything around the world, wrote that the most frightening thing he saw during a Chicago stockyards visit was one young woman visitor who was not instantly appalled. She stood "the red blood under her shoes, the vivid carcasses tacked round her, a bullock bleeding its life away not six feet away from her, and the death factory roaring all round her. She looked curiously, with hard, bold eyes, and was not ashamed." The public was separating itself from the messy reality of slaughter, bloody cutting, and smelly wastes. It was another disengagement from the natural world. In a 1948 book, *Mechanization Takes Command,* Siegfried Giedion described the dismantling of once living animals, in this case pigs. The first step was slaughter as the animals hung by one leg attached to an overhead moving chain:

> The death cries of the animals whose jugular veins have been opened are confused with the rumbling of the great [conveyor] drum, the whirring gears, and the shrilling sound of steam. Death cries and mechanical noises are almost impossible to disentangle. Neither can the eye quite take in what it sees. On one side of the sticker are the living; on the other side, the slaughtered. In twenty seconds, on the average, a hog is supposed to have bled to death. It happens so quickly, and is so smooth a part of the production process, that emotion is barely stirred. What is truly startling in this mass transition from life to death is the complete neutrality of the act. One does not experience, one does not feel; one merely observes.

Giedion reflected on assembly-line slaughter: "Has this neutrality toward death had any further effect upon us? It may be lodged deep in the roots of our time. It did not bare itself on a large scale until [World War I], when whole populations, as defenseless as the animals hooked downwards on the traveling chain, were obliterated with trained neutrality."

In addition, the perishability of meat demanded an uninterrupted production line that translated a living organic animal into consumable parts. The killing-floor operation moved the warm body into the eviscerating, cleaning, and cutting areas. Giedion continues,

> Now the endless chain takes over, imposing a uniform speed on its part of the process. Hanging on the conveyor, the carcass is opened at the chest and neck; the head is all but severed; the lymph

glands are inspected by a veterinary; condemned animals are switched onto a separate line for non-human consumption. The stomach is opened; intestines are removed, the entrails inspected, the liver and heart cut out, the spine is split in twain; the internal and external surfaces are again cleansed; the meat is inspected a second time, and stamped; finally the carcass is slowly conveyed into the cooler [because it is still warm from its own body heat].

Upton Sinclair, the famous muckraking novelist, wrote about Chicago's meatpacking industry in *The Jungle* (1906). He described the integration of the workmen into the mechanized process: "The carcass hog was then against strung up by machinery and sent upon another trolley ride; this time passing between two lines of men upon a raised platform, each doing a certain single thing to the carcass as it came to him. . . . Looking down this room one saw creeping slowly a line of dangling hogs, and for every yard there was a man working as if a demon were after him." This happened 500 times an hour. Sinclair added, "One could not stand and watch very long without becoming philosophical, without beginning to deal in symbols and similes, and to hear the hog-squeal of the universe."

AUTHOR'S NOTE: I remember visiting the killing floor of the nation's leading wiener maker with my father, who manufactured meatpacking machinery. It was the mid-1950s; I was a teenager working in Dad's plant on the South Side of Chicago during the summers. The killing floor was in an old brick multistory factory next to the Union Stock Yards. I almost slipped on the layers of grease and blood that impregnated a floor made up of vertically set blocks of wood. I can still hear the squeals of large pigs hung by one hindleg on hooks and chains that moved slowly along an overhead conveyor which ran along the left wall and then turned in front of me. There a very large black man stood on a platform, grabbed the head of each pig as it passed in front of him, and slit its gurgling throat. The conveyor carried the dying animal past me, turned right into the middle of the room, and lowered the pig into a scalding vat to remove the bristles. The carcasses then rose up still hooked to the conveyor, and other men slit open the bodies to remove the guts. My father's job was to build new stainless steel inspection pans for the offal; we made measurements with a folding ruler. I was to put to practice my newly acquired draftsman's skills to draw up the plans for the pans and the conveyor on which they were to run, which I did.

The Chicago Union Stock Yards were a mile or so north of Dad's plant. When I wasn't at the drafting table I drove a small truck to make deliveries of stockyard equipment to Wilson, Armour, Swift, and Oscar Mayer. Sometimes I would drive behind an open truck loaded—overloaded and overhanging—with stinking cattle bones, ribs, hooves and torn-up hides, all blood red and bone white, mixed with unidentifiable black and brown and tan objects—on the way to a nearby rendering plant to melt down the stuff into soap and other good things. When my father carried his job estimate to the company offices, however, I put on some better clothes and we arrived at white-collared business offices (not yet air conditioned in the 1950s) unlike the killing floor and away from the bone truck. We met with friendly vice presidents who liked my father and kidded with me.

"ANDY" ANDERSON OF IBP (Iowa Beef Processors) captured a quarter of the nation's beef business when in the 1970s he created the meatpacking revolution called "boxed beef." The IBP plant in Holcomb, Kansas, built in 1981 and 8 miles west of Garden City, is called the largest and most efficient beef processing operation in the world under one roof. The new plant immediately doubled the largest earlier capacity, with an "annual kill capacity" of over 1.5 million head. Production consumes 400 gallons of water to process one head of beef. The plant slaughters over 5,000 head per day, requiring 600 million gallons of water pumped annually from the underground Ogallala aquifer.

At the Holcomb plant, streams of cattle are crowded up a long ramp. One reporter made the rounds in the plant:

> I enjoy eating meat, and I know that the cows must be killed. A laborer clamps a chain around the hind leg of each steer and heifer. Another places a foot-long cylinder against each of their heads, and fires a steel rod into the skull. A huge chain sweeps down from an overhead trolley line. It swings the cattle upside down, and sends them clanging a couple of feet apart down a long chute. And the disassembly process begins. Man and machine merge to separate the various parts in stages. The workers use electric knives. No chaps or spurs necessary, just ear plugs, rubber boots, belly guards, and chain-mesh gloves. Within fifteen minutes, 1,200 pounds of corn-fed steer have been reduced to tenderloins and ribeyes.

The Interconnected Meat Industry

By 1883 Chicago's Union Stock Yards annually processed 1.9 million cattle and over 5.6 million pigs for America's butcher shops and family stoves and frying pans. Foreign visitors made special excursions to see the stockyards and the meatpacking industry as one of the modern wonders of the world. By 1933, when Chicago held its centennial world's fair, meatpacking was arguably America's largest industry. It produced 50 million pounds a day, with a turnover of $3.3 billion annually. The vertically integrated system included mass production of raw material (grain into cattle, corn into pigs). As historian William Cronon has deftly shown in his 1991 book on Chicago as "nature's metropolis," the meatpacking industry drew a net over a vast geography (1,500 miles east to west, 1,000 miles north to south) that ranged from cornfields just west of the Alleghenies to cowboys on the Plains facing the Rocky Mountains, down into the old cattle kingdom of Texas drylands and up toward the vast plains extending into Canada. It was wherever corn could be converted into more convenient and more valuable pigs, and otherwise useless plains grasses translated into money-making cattle who could be moved on the hoof or in railcars. "What is a hog but fifteen or twenty bushels of corn on four legs?" The mass production of meat transformed the great heartland of the nation from a natural grassland into a servant to the stockyards and the production of meat.

The mechanization of processing through the disassembly lines took animals apart faster than Ford put cars together in his Detroit assembly lines. To this infrastructure, we can add transportation and storage (railroads with refrigerator cars and refrigerated storehouses) to local butchers (and later supermarkets). The great Chicago commodity markets

When IBP opened Holcomb's doors, the company admitted that 6 out of 7 workers who applied for work at the plant would find the work too hard and distasteful and would quit. In several of its plants, IBP has been cited by OSHA for "shocking and dismaying working conditions." A study by the Kansas Rural Center concluded,

> Meat packing is the second most dangerous industry after underground mining. Most workers stand on a production line and cut the same piece of meat with a knife all day long. The most common physical complaint among workers is sore and cramped hands, due to gripping a knife all day in a 30–50 degree Fahrenheit environment. Workers often develop tendonitus, bursitus, arthritis, muscle strain, or back strain, besides constant fatigue.

IBP's Holcomb plant never delivers the carcass to the supermarket butcher's door, as had always been done when Swift and Armour were big. Instead, chilled meat arrives, mostly bone out, in manageable boxes. Not the least, when beef carcasses were hung up to cure before delivery to retailers, a considerable amount of water weight was lost. With boxed beef, the water remains and each cut of meat weighs more. The Holcomb disassembly line does the heavy and difficult work before the boxes go out the door. Old-line meat packers—Swift, Wilson, Armour, Hormel, and Oscar Mayer—quickly lost their lead to boxed beef newcomers—IBP, Excel, and Conagra.

in wheat futures and hog bellies were also part of the enterprise. Where animal slaughtering had once been an activity of a local farmer during a fall season, now it was continuous and year-round. Cronon called the appearance of the livestock industry, "another manifestation of second nature . . . a new animal landscape governed as much by economics as by ecology." It made "meat seem less a product of first nature and more a product of human artifice. . . . Fewer of those who ate meat could say that they had ever seen the living creature whose flesh they were chewing; fewer still could say that they had actually killed the animal themselves."

Hammond, Swift, Armour, and Wilson had all made the important discovery that they were not simply killing animals: They were selling chilled or safely preserved meat (just as IBM became a giant in its industry only after it realized it was not simply selling calculators, but processing information). Slaughter became only one step among many in a continuous mechanized process that included cleaning the animal of slime, blood, and dirt, removing its bristles and hide (a mammal's largest single organ is its skin), and preparing the carcass for the cooler. An entire network flourished that connected corn farmers, ranchers, railroad magnates, commodity brokers, the meatpackers themselves, local butchers, and consumers, all intent on growing animals, moving and killing them, and preparing animal flesh for human consumption. Chicago's great meatpacking industry was compared with other great systems, like railroad networks, automobile assembly lines, or electric power grids. By the 1960s the stockyards that made Chicago famous were torn down and the great meat companies disappeared or were absorbed into conglomerates. Meatpacking became decentralized out of Chicago to regional centers such as Kansas City and Minneapolis.

Cityscapes and Landscapes in Trouble

For most of America's industrial history, workers simply accepted the health risks of toxic fumes and corrosive substances as part of their employment. It was the price of progress. Undesired substances are almost always left over from chemical production. Sometimes an entire batch went wrong because it overheated or was not mixed correctly. These residues from chemical production may have been solids, liquids, gummy, or sludge mixtures that are always messy to handle. They were usually more deadly and toxic than the industry or the public realized. Such waste materials were often mixed with ordinary commercial garbage and emptied onto the town dump, or into a local pond or river. One age-old mode of disposal was to fill 55-gallon steel drums and store or dump them somewhere. The drums were called "the garbage cans of the chemical industry." The dumping became more serious after World War II when American industry and consumers developed a chemical dependency, with more than 80,000 synthetic and organic compounds in daily use by the hundreds of millions of tons. Modern chemicals were essential to food additives, plastic consumer goods, and almost every manufacturing process in the nation. Concern over the dumping and accumulation of hazardous wastes is a recent phenomenon, dating from the early 1970s, although industrial discards affected human well-being and local environmental systems for more than a century before that. Under new regulatory constraints, most factory operations recycle wastes or dump them into their own landfills. Or they leave waste management to the local community, but hazardous wastes cannot be handled by conventional municipal wastewater treatment.

Three Case Studies

The Classic Western Boomtown: Butte, Montana

"Butte may not be Yellowstone, but it speaks just as vividly of the American encounter with wilderness. Welcome to a town perched on the edge of an abyss," said a journalist in 1996.

AUTHOR'S NOTE: WHEN I worked summers in the 1950s at my father's metal fabricating plant on the South Side of Chicago, no one worried over the dumping of barrels of old lead paint, used lubricating and motor oil, and sheets of asbestos insulation on the back lot by the railroad siding. I spent several summers on a plant reconstruction job, ripping out old asbestos insulation, tarpaper walls, and asphalt roofs, piling them in an open lot, and burning them in a huge fire that poured out a stifling black smoke and left a sticky residue. Inside the plant, few workmen bothered with face masks in the painting shed, although most of the welders and machinists wore goggles to avoid metal splinters in their eyes. The only other standard safety item was steel-toed shoes in case something heavy got dropped carelessly. Safety helmets were unknown. Once every two or three years one of the men who worked the 300-ton presses that cut and bent 12-foot-long sheets of half-inch-thick steel would have a couple of fingers sheared off. The workers saw such accidents as terrible risks, but all part of their jobs.

The town of Butte, Montana, during the height of mining the "richest hill on earth" of copper sulfate in the late nineteenth century, was not a pretty place despite its spectacular Rocky Mountain setting. The cave-ins, slag dumps, settling ponds, and noxious smelting operations kept moving closer to the heart of town as the best ore was uncovered. Soon the streets, buildings, privies, and stalls of the company town of 30,000 in 1900 sat on land honeycombed in 3,000 miles of tunnels that went down as far as 4,000 feet. Miners were blasting copper ore 1,900 feet under the Butte post office. Above ground, slag heaps grew to cover 5 square miles. The overall landscape became sterile for miles around, colored obnoxious yellow and dull gray, with virtually all trees (four remained), shrubs, and grass killed off by sulfur, copper, and arsenic fumes from the world's largest smelter. Its smokestack, the world's tallest, was a futile attempt to reduce air pollution that kept sick miners, and therefore useless miners, off the job. Underground, miners sweated out their lives in the tunnels, risked permanent maiming, and feared an early death from silicosis in their lungs. Mining historian Rodman W. Paul writes,

> The air deep underground was all too often a foul combination of fumes left by the last blast of black powder or dynamite, the smell of rotting timbers, and the stench of human excrement (no toilet facilities provided). Many mines became exceedingly hot as greater depth was reached, and underground water kept getting into the working areas despite continuous pumping. The arrival of electricity was a boon unless a miner with a steel tool carelessly touched the bare, high-voltage copper wires. The power drills spun off sharp-edged granitic dust that settled in men's lungs and caused the growth of an enveloping tissue that ultimately made breathing impossible.

Mining at Butte was a boomtown phenomenon at its most extreme. Butte's condition was the result of heavy demand for copper with the dawning of the electrical age that needed hundreds of tons of the highly conductive metal for wiring, coils, and connectors. Edison's Pearl Street Power Station, the first in the nation, alone required 65 tons of copper to light a few square blocks in Lower Manhattan. The industry grew exponentially after George Westinghouse set a standard of alternating current for long-distance electric power transmission. Historian Richard A. Bartlett wrote that Butte "reeked of the worst of nineteenth-century despoilment; and people put up with it without ever asking why." The local newspaper *Butte Miner* bragged in the 1890s, "The thicker the fumes the greater our financial vitality, and Butteites feel best when the fumes are the thickest." Anaconda Copper Mining Company became the world's largest producer of copper, with about three-quarters of Montana's workers on its payrolls. Butte's population ballooned toward 100,000 during World War I, by then "a mile high and a mile deep." Names attached to the wealth produced by the copper ore that came out from underneath Butte were not only the lesser known founders William Andrews Clark and Marcus Daly, but also major American figures like Rockefeller and Guggenheim, organizations like the Industrial Workers of the World ("Wobblies"), and numberless American, Cornish, and Irish miners.

Copper prices swung with world conditions during the rest of the century, mostly on the low side. By 1977 the Anaconda Copper Mining Company, now part of a Chilean mining conglomerate, was absorbed at a fire sale price by the oil giant ARCO. ARCO, with its interests primarily in energy, shut down operations in 1983, sought to leave town, but was saddled with several Superfund cleanup sites with probably the world's worst concentrations of toxic metals, including copper, cadmium, zinc, nickel, and lead, all interlaced with arsenic.

Inhabitants of Butte, sometimes cruelly nicknamed "Butants," still have extraordinarily high rates of cancer, kidney disease, cardiovascular disease, and learning disabilities, no matter whether they descended underground or not. When ARCO stopped mining, it turned off the pumps that removed water from underground mines at the rate of 5,000 gallons a minute. The abandoned mine works were soon submerged, and in the great Berkeley open pit ("We moved as much as 300,000 tons in a 24-hour period") appeared so-called Lake Berkeley, which in 1995 was a 26-billion-gallon toxic stew, 850 feet deep, and growing by 5 to 7 million gallons each day of scarce fresh Montana water. One scientific study reported that the lake "contains metals and sulfate concentrations thousands of times those found in unconta-minated water," with a pH level around 2.5, equivalent to battery acid. Keeping watch over Lake Berkeley is the Environmental Protection Agency (EPA), with a policy of perpetual containment. Its plan is to allow the water to rise, but before a spillover can take place, to pump off further inflow as often as needed. A state legislator fears that there are no known means for cleanup, which requires perpetual vigilance in a active seismic region with residential neighborhoods. In 1995 a flock of rare migrating snow geese made the mistake of landing in the lake, and 171 died an acute death of external lesions and internal corrosion. Lake Berkeley has also become a tourist site, claiming 100,000 visitors each year.

The Industrialization of the Indiana Dunes

By 1900 it seemed no place in the American landscape would be left untouched by industrialization. The Indiana Dunes at the south end of Lake Michigan had been a primitive vacation escape for Chicagoans since the 1880s. The original 1821 land survey reported they had no significant economic value. If anything, their shifting sands were viewed as an obstacle to the economic growth and progress of Chicago and the southern Lake Michigan region. The lakeshore region is the product, either directly or indirectly, of the last great ice age. Lake Michigan, which evolved from glacial Lake Chicago, and its accompanying sand dunes, is the result of 12,000 years of the combined energies of glaciers, wind, and water. Where the shore is unaffected by industrial development, it demonstrates how wave and currents along the shore continually build and destroy portions of the expansive sand beaches.

Around 1910 the U.S. Steel Corporation quietly acquired large tracts of duneland near its major mills at its company town, Gary. As the steel company's actions became known, they were enthusiastically supported by most Hoosiers as signs of the state's continued economic expansion. But in nearby Chicago, a public interest citizen's coalition in the Progressive-Conservation mold called attention to the value of the Dunes for recreation. A small state park was established in the 1920s, but a probusiness viewpoint prevailed well through the 1950s.

After World War II, the nation's steel mills, including the biggest, U.S. Steel, operated at full capacity to serve the postwar economic boom. The Dunes came under intensive development pressure to expand production. This momentum might have won the day, except that it was countered by sophisticated and experienced conservationists who formed the Save the Dunes Council. They reminded the public that the Dunes was a rare example of a multi-directional ecological zone where biological ecosystems from north and south, east and west, converged and overlapped. (Other similar zones are the Niobrara River valley in northern Nebraska and the classic merged forest in southern Appalachia.) A national park would protect bogs, swamps, lakes, and dense forests of tall oak, pine, and maple trees, all features of distinctive dune plant successions of grasses, shrubs, and trees. The Dunes, they noted, was also the site of the famous Cowles Bog, where the pioneering ecologist Henry Cowles did fundamental research on his important dynamic ecosystem secession theory, which stated that environmental systems continuously change instead of reaching a static or climax condition. To industrialize the Dunes, said these defenders, would be to tear apart forever one of the nation's rarest natural places.

Nevertheless, with considerable secrecy, Bethlehem Steel Corporation began development of its large-scale Burns Harbor plant in the midst of the most important remaining Dunes region. The turning point of the story was reached when prime duneland was leveled in 1962 and the sand sold to Northwestern University for its own lakeside expansion north of Chicago. Despite this major loss, the changing political and environmental climate of the 1960s protected the remaining duneland with the creation in 1963 of the Indiana Dunes National Lakeshore, administered by the National Park Service. If the National Environmental Protection Act (NEPA) had been passed by Congress in 1960 instead of 1970, it would have required a comprehensive Environmental Impact Statement (EIS), which would have prevented the steel industry from enlarging on the Dunes. As a result of this checkered history of the last 100 years, the Indiana Dunes contain a major industrial zone. The Dunes also offer Chicagoans recreation, fulfilling the Progressive-Conservation ideology of multiple use. Whether the unique Dunes ecology exists in sufficient size, and is adequately protected, is less assured.

The Chemical Poisons Never Go Away: The Case of Love Canal

One industrial operation near Niagara Falls in New York filled waste chemicals into thousands of 55-gallon steel drums that it dumped into a nearby ditch. This went on for ten years. The ditch was Love Canal near Niagara Falls in New York, named after William T. Love, who began digging a canal in the 1880s to run around the falls. The canal was never completed, its partial ditch filled with stagnant water, and it was gradually filled in as the region grew, except for a small remnant about three blocks long. In 1942, when Americans gave most of their attention to full-bore industrial production to win World War II, the neighboring Hooker Chemical Company got the right from the canal's owner, the Niagara Power and Development Company, to dump war work wastes there. In 1946, after the war, Hooker bought the site and dumped over 20,000 metric tons of recognized highly toxic wastes there, including the deadly poison dioxin and carcinogenic PCBs (polychlorinated biphenyls). This was not an unusual procedure nationwide.

Then, in 1952, the growing city of Niagara Falls acquired the land to construct an elementary school for families in the newly built homes in the neighborhood. Hooker sold the land as a public service for $1 in exchange for a release from any further liability. The company did not attempt to hide its dumping. The deed of sale noted that the site was filled with "waste products resulting from the manufacturing of chemicals." The company took the extra precaution to seal the dump with a clay cap covered with topsoil. This precaution was thought to be very effective protection. Workmen removed part of the clay cap in January 1954 during construction of the school. By this time the steel drums, exposed to moisture from the outside and strong chemical agents from the inside, had begun to rust and corrode and leak.

Between the late 1950s and the late 1970s, the rusting and leaking barrels of toxic waste buried in Love Canal began to surface. Children played near them, suffered chemical burns, and some became ill and died. Medical reports on inhabitants of Love Canal began to include unusually high levels of epilepsy, liver disease, rectal bleeding, miscarriages, and birth defects. Hooker warned the school board not to let children play in the contaminated areas, but neither parents nor city officials received the warning. By now chemical fumes took the bark off trees, destroyed lawns, and wiped out vegetable gardens. After heavy rains, when the water table rose, basements in new homes built adjacent to the school began to flood with a thick black sludge of toxic chemicals. In the spring of 1977 particularly heavy rains turned the schoolyard and neighboring lots into a muddy poisonous swamp.

State investigators came on the scene to find that nearly 1 of every 3 pregnant women in the area had miscarried, an unusually high rate. Over half of the children born between 1974 and 1978 had birth defects, more than twice the national rate at the time. A public out-cry led by Love Canal resident Lois Gibbs gained national proportions. The media and public officials became aware overnight that Love Canal had serious environmental problems. Some experts argued that the case was overblown, since it was impossible to prove that the health conditions were directly caused by chemical poisoning. Others made direct connections and worried about greater disasters at Love Canal and elsewhere where chemicals had long been spilled or dumped. Love Canal was seen as the tip of the toxic waste iceberg, particularly since it was commonplace to top off and seal old industrial landfills and use them for housing de-velopments, schools, and shopping malls.

The school was soon closed, the canal fenced off, and a number of homes evacuated. By 1987 Love Canal had already cost the state of New York and the federal government about $200 million for cleanup, study, and relocation of residents. The EPA dredged the sewers and creeks to remove about 35,000 cubic yards of the toxic sediments, which were incinerated and then reburied in a safe landfill. EPA concluded that further migration of remaining toxic chemicals, virtually impossible to remove, was unlikely, and declared the Love Canal site "habitable." But Lois Gibbs argues that the site is still contaminated and resettling Love Canal would put more people at risk. In December 1995 a settlement was reached totaling $129 million.

A few years after Love Canal, 164 additional chemical waste dumps were identified within 3 miles of the Niagara River, with toxic contaminants leaking directly into the river. Love Canal and other similar cases such as Times Beach, Missouri, in 1983, helped bring pas-sage by Congress in December 1980 of the $1.6 billion Comprehensive Environmental Re-sponse, Compensation, and Liability Act (CERCLA), commonly known as Superfund, and amended several times to almost $9 billion. It established stringent identification, responsibil-ity, and cleanup procedures for over 30,000 potentially hazardous waste sites in the United States. But action has been extremely slow and thrown a cloud of doubt over the effectiveness of Superfund (more on environmental legislation and regulation in Chapter 14). Estimates put cleanup costs nationwide at more than $100 billion. In the meantime, the impact of im-proper waste disposal continues to spread. It contaminates groundwater, closes water wells, destroys habitat for wild creatures, increases human disease like cancer, contaminates soil, kills fish in streams, increases livestock diseases, damages sewage treatment plants, shuts down homes, offices, schools, and businesses at identified sites, and forces difficult, costly, and often impossible cleanup.

It is cheaper and faster to relocate people than to detoxify a contaminated site. By 1988 federal cleanup funds out of Superfund legislation were used to relocate almost 1,400 families in over 40 communities nationwide. Together with Love Canal, the towns of Times Beach,

Missouri; Globe, Arizona; and Centralia, Pennsylvania, have received the most attention. Candidates in the near future are long-standing petroleum industry regions in Louisiana and Texas. Cleanup of a toxic waste site is often gravely compromised because the wastes are complex chemical substances that change over time. The chemicals that were dumped may not be identifiable because records were never kept or have been lost. Since the basic materials (literally their atoms) cannot be destroyed, cleanup is actually carried out by either isolating the wastes to avoid further contamination or by converting the wastes to nonhazardous materials. Another problem is whether to do the remediation at the waste site or transport the wastes elsewhere, each of which causes additional problems. Current experiments include recycling and reuse, detoxification, incineration, low-temperature decomposition, secured landfills, and perpetual storage/encapsulation, all of which carry high costs.

Conclusion

The modern environmental movement is usually described as having its origins in the efforts of John Muir to preserve the wilderness and Gifford Pinchot to manage natural resources (see Chapter 12). This involved the protection of "unspoiled nature" outside the network of industrial metropolises. A strong case can also be made that environmental awareness got its start with the recognition of workplace diseases, polluted urban slums, and the rise of the public health movement. Another roster of names must include less-known reformers like Alice Hamilton and Joseph Schereschewsky. The city-country connection should not be surprising, since a good deal of the mining frontier, for example, took place because of industrial demands, and struggling frontier farmers would eventually prosper because they sent their bounty to the burgeoning factory cities. The factory cities became the geography most thoroughly transformed by human activity. It is essential to see the origins of the modern environmental movement not only out of wilderness protection, but also at the core of industrialized America where capitalism functioned as a form of "creative destruction."

The environmental advocate Murray Bookchin went even further to insist that most serious environmental issues are largely urban: pollution, energy, clean air, transportation, and social justice. The city's continuing growth "spreads over the countryside like a rampant cancer and destroys waterways and masses of land." The land use planner Ian McHarg wrote in the 1970s:

> Epidemiologists speak of urban epidemics—heart and arterial disease, cancer, neuroses, psychoses. All of us record stress from sensory overload and negative hallucinations responding to urban anarchy. When you consider that New York may grow by fifteen hundred square miles of "low-grade urban tissue"—[social critic] Lewis Mumford's phrase—in the next twenty years, you may recall [anthropologist] Loren Eiseley's image of our cities as gray, black, and brown blemishes on the green earth. These blemishes have dynamic tentacles extending from them. They may be evidence of a planetary disease—man.

McHarg compares the process of industrialization to a dangerous fungus or metastasizing cancer. It is a negative infrastructure. Recovery will be difficult and costly, if possible at all.

Anticipated by the Pittsburgh, Chicago, and New York reformers, the fractious social reformer Ralph Nader and his teams of young activists—Nader's Raiders of the 1970s—proposed that many of America's social ills could be traced to raw corporate power that went largely unchecked in a highly individualistic American society. Citizen action, whether in terms of consumer protest, the labor movement, or environmental activism, was the best means, he said, to counteract the callous profiteering of industry. The engaged citizen was America's best instrument for change. In this sense, environmentalism was part of a broader, anticorporate movement. Environmentalism can thus be seen as closely linked to a complex of social reform movements that first appeared in reaction to the negative effects of industrialization.

For Further Reading

To understand human and environmental collapse resulting from industrialization, readers will find a wealth of information and a strong viewpoint in Siegfried Giedion's pre-environmental classic *Mechanization Takes Command* (1948). The Russell Sage Foundation study of Pittsburgh, Paul Underwood Kellogg (ed.), *The Pittsburgh District* (1914; reprinted 1974), is part of the important Arno Press reprint series, *Metropolitan America.* For working conditions, see Robert Blauner, *Alienation and Freedom: The Factory Worker and His Industry* (1964), and Warren G. Bennis and Philip E. Slater, *The Temporary Society* (1968). Earlier views are summed up in an influential book, Thomas Oliver (ed.), *Dangerous Trades: The Historical, Social, and Legal Aspects of Industrial Occupations as Affecting Health* (1902), which is worth the search. Good brief overviews of urban problems can be found in Marcia D. Lowe, *Shaping Cities: The Environmental and Human Dimensions* (Worldwatch Paper 105, 1991), Jodi L. Jacobson, *Environmental Refugees: A Yardstick of Habitability* (Worldwatch Paper 86, 1988), as well as Harrison Brown's "Technological Denudation," in William L. Thomas, Jr. (ed.), *Man's Role in Changing the Face of the Earth* (1956). Martin V. Melosi's *Garbage in the Cities* (1981) is a fine review of increasing waste and public health problems, and attempts to solve them. The best new study is Joel A. Tarr, *The Search for the Ultimate Sink: Urban Pollution in Historical Perspective* (1996). On industrial intrusions on the Indiana Dunes, see Kay Franklin and Norma Schaeffer, *Duel for the Dunes: Land Use Conflict on the Shores of Lake Michigan* (1983). William Cronon's *Nature's Metropolis: Chicago and the Great West* (1991) offers a fresh and stimulating statement on Chicago's constantly expanding infrastructure. Christopher Sellers, *Toxic Order: Workplace Disease and the Birth of Modern Environmental Health Science* (1996), persuasively argues for the centrality of emergent urban public health as a primary source of modern environmentalism. Alice Hamilton's autobiography, *Exploring the Dangerous Trades,* was published in 1943 and reprinted in 1985. See also Barbara Sicherman, *Alice Hamilton: A Life in Letters* (1984), as well as Paul Starr, *The Social Transformation of American Medicine* (1982), Diana Chapman Walsh, *Corporate Physicians: Between Medicine and Management* (1987), William Brock, *Investigation and Responsibility: Public Responsibility in the United States* (1984), and John Duffy, *The Sanitarians: A History of American Public Health* (1990). There is no major history of the Public Health Service, but see its official history by Bess Furman and Ralph C. Williams, *A Profile of the United States Public Health Service, 1798–1948* (1973). For the pervasiveness of lead poisoning, see Richard Wedeen, *Poison in the Pot: The Legacy of Lead* (1984), and Richard Landsdown and William Yule (eds.), *Lead Toxicity: History and Environmental Impact* (1986). Silicosis is covered in David Rosner and Gerald Markowitz, *Deadly Dust: Silicosis and the Politics of Occupa-*

tional Disease in the United States (1991). Overviews are available in Judith Walzer Leavitt and Ronald Numbers, *Sickness and Health in America* (1985), and David Rosner and Gerald Markowitz, *Dying for Work: Workers' Safety and Health in Twentieth-Century America* (1987). One of the best critiques of industrial cities, in a broad historical context, is still Lewis Mumford's *The City in History* (1961), notably Chapter 14, "Commercial Expansion and Urban Dissolution," and Chapter 15, "Paleotechnic Paradise: Coketown." For a more recent attack, see James Howard Kunstler, *The Geography of Nowhere: The Rise and Decline of America's Man-Made Landscape* (1992).

FROM NATURE'S WATER TO PUBLIC WORKS WATER: AMERICA BECOMES A HYDRAULIC CIVILIZATION

Water runs uphill to money.

—WESTERN IRRIGATION SAYING

Introduction: The Water Network Is Another Infrastructure

As we saw in Chapter 8, nature disappeared under a physical network of roads, canals, railroads, and bridges that spanned the continent and connected the great sprawling metropolises. This built environment now functions as the dominant space in which most Americans live and work. The built environment is itself tied up with systems of economic, political, and social power that are often little related to natural boundaries such as watersheds or ecosystems. This chapter looks at another network of concrete and steel that conveys a single commodity: fresh water to serve human needs. This water infrastructure is composed of dams and reservoirs, canals and aqueducts, tunnels, pipes, pumps and turbines, penstocks and spillways, flumes and ditches, mains, hydrants, and storage tanks, toilets, tubs, sinks, faucets, and garden hoses. Over the last 100 years, especially, Americans have devised a geography of public works to move water across hundreds of miles, regardless of mountains and deserts. The goal was to move fresh water from where it was abundant but inconvenient, and carry it to where it was scarce but needed. The Colorado River became less a naturally flowing stream than a flowing reservoir out of which water could be assigned to irrigate crops and serve thirsty cities. The Columbia River, jewel of the Pacific Northwest, is virtually no river at all above the Bonneville Dam but a 600-mile-long succession of reservoirs to the Canadian border, "backed flush up against one another."

The building of eastern waterworks and western dams became epic contests between technology and nature, but not necessarily the elimination of the natural power of water. Historian Richard White recently described the Columbia River as an "organic machine." It can be modified by human intervention such as dams, spillways, channels, and reservoirs, but like all powerful rivers, it has unyielding natural or "unmade" qualities. The challenge was immense. Water is a powerful fluid. When frozen it cracks granite boulders and heaves roadways. Its flow is irresistible; it seeks out every tiny crevice in a rock wall and carves gushing fountains. Rain or snow are fickle and unpredictable sources of fresh water. Too much brings destructive floods and mudslides. Too little water defeats the farmer and rations the cities. It evaporates at a maddening rate, more than 50 percent a year in exposed aqueducts, ponds, and fields. It becomes useless by turning silty, saline, or brackish. White noted that rivers rearrange the world over millennia by cutting, draining, and flooding, by which they channel their gravity flow. In this sense, he said, they are "historical products of their own past history." White's description of the Columbia is applicable to many American rivers such as the Colorado, the Sacramento, and major segments of the Ohio, Missouri, Mississippi, and Rio Grande. Segments of rivers with little or no human manipulation, like on the New or Snake, have become so rare and valuable they receive federal protection as wild rivers.

A bountiful supply of water has long been recognized as one of America's great natural assets. Back in 1910, for example, a comprehensive report on the need for efficient water development took up a quarter of the classic Progressive era study, *The Conservation of Natural Resources in the United States,* by Charles R. Van Hise, a scientist at the University of Wisconsin. Van Hise described water as "by far the most important of all the non-organic products of the world,—more important even than coal or iron," because it was the basis of life. A bushel of corn demanded 10 to 20 tons of water, including 2.5 tons lost by transpiration and even more by evaporation. A single pound of beef, he said in amazement, soaked up 15 to 30 tons of water, when all direct and indirect requirements, such as the growth of feed, are accounted for. Later estimates found that while a city dweller in the early nineteenth century used 20 gallons a day, in the 1970s the average consumption in many cities for all services was about 200 gallons per person per day.

Most Americans, said Van Hise, paid little attention to water supplies because they lived in the humid eastern parts of the United States. Unlike most other industrial nations, he noted, America did no national or regional water management until the twentieth century, and then only when politically expedient. Without planning in the East, "injudicious farming and deforestation" had lowered local water tables as much as 40 feet and dried up three-quarters of shallow wells, as well as springs and small brooks. Van Hise was not an environmentalist who promoted free-running water; instead he urged the highest possible efficient use. He complained of the waste and inefficiency because one-third of the annual runoff of the entire United States "escapes to the sea through the Mississippi River." Overall, he noted, more than 75 percent of the nation's runoff was not used for any purpose. He urged Americans to apply water, before it "escaped," for electrical energy, agriculture, industrial uses, pollution dilution, navigation, and domestic purposes.

Van Hise reminded Americans, as John Wesley Powell had observed 40 years earlier, that about two-fifths of the United States, mostly west of the 103rd meridian, was arid land, with an average rainfall of less than 12 inches a year. In the dry and sunny climate about half of the precipitation soon evaporated, a sixth went into plants or the ground, and the remaining third was "wasted" runoff into rivers and the sea. Van Hise proudly described the efficiency of Los Angeles, which would soon capture 258 million gallons a day using a new 225-mile-long aqueduct from the Owens River. San Francisco, too, would soon use an aqueduct 182 miles long to capture water from a 450-square-mile watershed. New York City was constructing a water system that would take 500 million gallons a day from a drainage area of over 900 square miles. He compared these modern wonders to the primitive Zuni Indians, who "must climb down hundreds of feet into a cañon, and there place a jar under an opening from which slowly trickles the water, sometimes drop by drop." Van Hise especially urged the building of a nationwide network of dams and reservoirs for water storage, so that water might be more efficiently allocated for power generation, irrigation, and flood control. True to his Progressive heritage, Van Hise insisted that such water systems must not be run for private profit, but be publicly owned for the common good, for adequate development, and for safety (remembering almost 2,200 people killed by the force of Pennsylvania's Johnstown Flood from the broken dam and reservoir of the Little Conemaugh River in May 1889).

Engineering Urban Water Systems in the East

Demand for city water that exceeded local capacity was already a serious problem along the eastern seaboard by the late eighteenth century. The first national census in 1790 showed that Philadelphia, with 43,000 inhabitants, and New York City, with 33,000, created demands for fresh water that could not be satisfied from public wells at intersections, or from local ponds, rivers, or springs. Citizens also began to complain about the bad taste and smell from these local sources, which were contaminated from privies and street waste. The greatest problems were epidemics of cholera, typhoid, and dysentery that killed thousands of people in the 1790s. In Philadelphia, after yellow fever in 1798 killed 5,000 people and frightened 30,000 inhabitants out of the city, the city fathers rushed to accept a bold plan by engineer Benjamin Latrobe to introduce new supplies of fresh water by using newfangled and untested steam engines. One pumped river water into a tunnel to the central square. There a second steam engine lifted it up into two wooden tanks, from where it was distributed by gravity under the streets through bored wooden logs. Latrobe's trust in his innovative wooden, iron-banded engines was premature: They leaked, broke down, lost pressure, and could not keep up with the rapidly growing city. Philadelphia's city fathers took an alternative path by building new reservoirs on a high rocky hill, replacing the old wooden pipes with iron mains and ordering better engines and pumps. In 1822 a new waterworks included a dam across the Schuylkill River. Its water was lifted by pumps powered by giant water wheels into high reservoirs that held 22 million gallons.

Not until a cholera epidemic in 1832 killed 3,500 people and drove 100,000 from the city was New York City's government jolted into action. City engineers boldly went 40 miles north to the Croton River for a water supply, but not soon enough to prevent a December 1835 fire that destroyed over 500 stores in 20 blocks in the business district. A $5 million bond issue was quickly approved, and water from the Croton reached the city in 1842. The

Chicago Innovates to Solve Its Water Problems

In the Midwest, Chicago's water supply struggled to keep up with its rapid population growth. In 1854, 21 years after its incorporation in 1833, Chicago's water mains totaled 30 miles; by 1900 the city had 1,847 miles of mains, and daily pumping rose from 591,000 gallons to 322 million gallons. After six summers of cholera between 1849 and 1855 and several failed private attempts to construct a workable water system, the city's municipal government took over construction of a comprehensive public water system. A most dramatic step was to raise the entire city's level, since Chicago was notorious for bad drainage, with its land level so close to Lake Michigan's water table. Sewers had no place to empty, with terrible results in swampy and stinking streets and city lots. Starting in 1849, the city council passed ordinances that required the grade levels of streets to be raised as much as 14 feet. Over the next two decades, large buildings were raised by manual jacks so that new foundations could be built underneath. "It became common to see large frame and masonry structures rolling through city traffic" as owners decided on new sites. Over the long term the city's altitude rose a dozen or more feet out of the muck. The publicly owned Chicago City Hydraulic Company, managed by three elected commissioners, was established in 1851, and within ten years, water pipes had been laid across the districts most vulnerable to fire and disease. Water supplied directly to a home was considered a personal luxury; most people went to a public hydrant. By 1856 a majority of houses were connected to city water, and the public hydrants were phased out by the end of the Civil War. In 1889 different municipal operations were reorganized into the Sanitary District of Chicago, creating a unified network of water pipes and pumping stations drawing from Lake Michigan, which was being polluted from the Chicago River. The city answered its pollution problem in 1900 by building the Sanitary and Ship Canal, which took the dramatic step to reverse the flow of the Chicago River from Lake Michigan into the Illinois and Mississippi rivers, where the dangers were diluted. By 1902 the city of Chicago had hundreds of miles of water pipes and sewer mains that extended into annexed communities. By midcentury the district served an area of over 850 square miles of the city and over 100 suburban communities. It had 536 miles of intercepting sewers and mains ranging in size from 1 to 27 feet in diameter. Pollution and flood control works included almost 50 miles of tunnels up to 39 feet in diameter, some of them 300 feet underground, together with one of the world's largest water reclamation plants and 23 pumping stations.

engineers, using 3,000 Irish laborers, built a masonry dam across the Croton River, creating a lake 5 miles long. To deliver the water to the city, they constructed a masonry aqueduct that crossed valleys, tunneled through hills, and moved the water through iron mains across the Harlem River. On Manhattan Island the aqueduct carried water to a receiving reservoir in what is now Central Park. Three large iron mains carried the water down to a distributing reservoir, a great masonry waterworks on the site of today's Public Library on 42nd Street and Broadway. "The crowds particularly enjoyed the great fountain near City Hall shooting the Croton water fifty feet in the air."

When in the 1880s and 1890s it became clear that typhoid fever was transmitted through human wastes and many water supplies were contaminated with such sewage, Philadelphia and other cities also began to filter their drinking water, following the lead of Scottish and English cities. Chlorination of water became commonplace after 1910. Urban population growth continued to put increased demands on water systems. Philadelphia still used the Schuylkill River, but New York found it necessary to bring water from the Catskill Mountains and the upper Delaware Valley through deep underground tunnels. Boston also outgrew local sources and began drawing water from the Cochituate Reservoir 14 miles west in 1848, added another reservoir 19 miles further west in 1909, and the large Quabbin Reservoir 60 miles west in 1946. But there was a public uproar about unfair displacement when the Quabbin Reservoir began to fill, since four towns disappeared under the water, 2,500 people were forcibly resettled, and 7,500 cemetery plots had to be moved.

The Army Corps of Engineers in Charge of Waterways

The best and the worst of public works to "improve" nature or eliminate environmental impediments have historically belonged to the U.S. Army Corps of Engineers. The idea of an engineer corps first arose in eighteenth-century France where modernization was to be achieved through engineered highways, waterways, aqueducts, and other grandiose projects to "harness rivers, control flooding, irrigate, reclaim swamps, beautify the kingdom, and cleanse its population." This approach to remodel nature rather than adapt to it was quickly incorporated as a tenet of the American faith in progress. According to historian Todd Shallat, the federal government, as it strived for a more perfect union, was expected to perfect nature as well. The Corps of Engineers was created in 1802 as a war academy and fortbuilding agency. Early in the nineteenth century its mission included the maintenance of navigable rivers by dredging and channelizing and the promotion of water commerce by building jetties and piers. By 1824 its activities also included the construction of locks, dams, and other river structures. In the words of public works historian Michael C. Robinson, "Rivers were regarded primarily as avenues of commerce and the Corps mandate was to conduct surveys, remove obstacles, build structures, and dredge channels so that waterway traffic would flow safely and expeditiously." After 1879 the Corps of Engineers became responsible for flood control projects. Corps-constructed breakwaters, piers, and canals soon covered 26,000 miles of navigable waterways, "turning North America into one of the world's most extensive hydrological systems." By 1900 the Corps dredged and channeled long stretches of the Mississippi-Missouri river system. In 1928 alone, the Corps was actively engaged in the improvement of 200 harbors, 292 rivers, and 49 canals and other waterways. Americans began to think of rivers as technological systems.

The continued success of the Corps's monumental construction projects (at high costs to taxpayers) reflected a widespread faith in problem solving through technology. Corps projects in the twentieth century were reputed to be the best examples of the new social engineering advocated by the Progressives at the turn of the century. The Corps itself has always maintained that good engineering is neutral: It only executes the will of the people when expressed in legislative form. A long-term Corps project in Louisiana, for example, has been to prevent the Mississippi River from breaking into the Atchafalaya Basin far upstream from New Orleans, stranding the city and its important docks. In Florida, after devastating flooding from a hurricane in the 1920s, the Corps reshaped the 103-mile meandering Kissimmee River, into a 50-mile canal, intended to protect local populations and ensure economic development. But like a growing number of Corps projects in Florida and elsewhere, the environmental results were devastating, in this case depleting the rich and unique biodiversity of the Everglades region. By the 1980s, after decades of debate between conflicting development and environmental interests, the Corps is now committed to undo its work and restore the original flow patterns of the Kissimmee and surrounding wetlands.

The Problem of the West: Not Enough Water

In the western half of the United States, agriculture today still consumes up to 90 percent of available water, with little reduction in sight because of the unyielding needs of growing plants. Water abounds in the far West, but it is concentrated in several regions. For example, in northern California, western Oregon, and western Washington, large amounts of rain and snow roar inland from the Pacific Ocean and soon bump into the exposed backbone of the Sierra Nevada and Cascades mountains. The simple undeniable fact is that mountains block the advance of weather fronts. Rain or snow piles up on the near side while the far side stays parched. East of the mountains, in eastern Washington and Oregon, and down into Nevada and Arizona, only 4 to 12 inches of rain reaches the ground in an entire year. The weather systems again race eastward, picking up atmospheric moisture that becomes rain or winter snowfall 800 miles east, high in the Rocky Mountains. There each spring it melts to rush into valleys in Idaho, Montana, Wyoming, Colorado, and New Mexico. In turn, the Rockies effectively block further eastward movement of moisture onto the parched High Plains, as we will see in Chapter 11. Thus farming in most of the West is inherently more challenging than in the East or Midwest. Constant winds dry up the landscape faster. Sandy soil does not hold moisture, and poisonous alkaline soils continue to spread. These problems were exacerbated because westward-moving settlers and speculators believed that 30 inches of rain needed for corn was "normal." In addition, the East and Midwest received year-round rainfall, particularly important during the spring and early-summer growing seasons. Droughts were rare. In the West, drought was the rule. Wheat, which needs 20 inches of rain, could be grown in Oregon's Willamette Valley but not under the semiarid conditions of California's Central Valley. But the Willamette Valley is the exception. On the semiarid High Plains, under the rain shadow of the Rockies, farmers endured a series of "dust bowls" each longer than seasons of nourishing rainfall. Farmers failed as independent landholders, and only persisted after they became clients of long-standing government patronage and after they turned to short-term irrigation (1960–2010) from the heavily pumped groundwater of the Ogallala aquifer.

The Federal Land System Worsens the Situation

Congress had passed the Homestead Act of 1862, the Timber Culture Act of 1873, the Desert Land Act of 1877, and the Carey Act of 1894 to fulfill the long-standing dream that the West would become a great natural paradise of virtuous yeoman farmers. Instead, from the first farmers were, in the words of a folk song, "starvin' to death on their gov't claims" because the Homestead Act limited a farmer to ownership of a 160-acre quarter section long after it became clear that western low-rainfall farming required at least a full 640-acre section and that two or three sections were even better. Congress tinkered with settlement alternatives that simply extended widespread failure and terrible hardship. For example, the Timber Culture Act of 1873 offered free land to farmers if they successfully planted trees on one-quarter of new land. Congress's intent was to get trees planted in places they had not previously grown. They wrongly believed that this would force the eastern forest westward, induce rainfall, and change the West's climate. Although a few groves of trees did take hold in western Nebraska, in most of the West the plan was doomed to failure. Four out of five farmers who held land under the Timber Culture Act did not make their final entries for full title, and by 1892 farmers avoided seeking land under the act. The Desert Land Act of 1877 allowed parcels as large as 640 acres to be sold at fire-sale prices. All a buyer had to do was find water, bring it to the land, and irrigate a certain percentage. But to bring water from a distant stream was far beyond the economic reach of the individual settler. Some farmers took a stick or plow and smartly ran "irrigation" furrows up and down hills to prove up their claims. By 1888 the federal government feared that such land might never be settled, and in fact only a third of the entries ever received final title. However, the Desert Land Act was not repealed until 1976. The Carey Act of 1894 promised six semiarid states up to a million acres each to promote irrigation where possible. The arrangement was an experiment both in expanding irrigation and in federal-state government relations. Van Hise in 1910 was optimistic: "The Carey Act is likely to result in a large increase in the irrigated land of the West." States found the requirements too risky. They lacked the engineering skills and financial resources to make the improvements.

Agricultural survival on private property in an arid landscape was the great American experiment in the West. Value did not lie with a tract of fertile land. Value lay with water, which was a fickle asset, constantly on the move and impossible to own, often described as a "fugitive" resource. To protect access to all-important water supplies, Americans had long depended on the English common-law doctrine of *riparian rights:* Whoever owned the land along a riverbank had a right to use the water flowing past their lands as long as they did not change its course, contaminate it, or appreciably diminish it. But riparian rights did not suit westerners well: They needed to redirect scarce water. Westerners instead invented the legal concept of *prior appropriation;* based on the realization that there was not enough water for every potential user, so "the one first in time is the first in right." Not only did the first users have the right to take as much as they needed, but they could do it every year. Later users had to wait their turn in line, even if it meant they received little or no water. Prior appropriation helped guarantee investment in an irrigation system. At the same time, however, water was often needlessly wasted under this concept, since it involved the notion of "use it or lose it." States like Colorado, with insufficient rain but with fairly predictable spring runoff from the mountains, established prior appropriation as their exclusive water law. States like California, where some regions along the northern coast had plenty of rainfall, but others like the Central Valley were often arid, established a mix of both riparian rights and prior appropriation. Wyoming followed a third method, by which the state took title to all the water, and state officials controlled its delivery to consumers. The American West thus forced a fundamental shift in attitudes toward water. In the East, to "waste" water was to consume it needlessly or excessively. In the West, to waste water was not to consume it—to let it flow unimpeded and undiverted in rivers. To easterners, "conservation" of water usually means protecting rivers from development. In the West, conservation means building dams. This difference would shape public works development for most of American history.

Roads Not Taken: Alternative Settlement Patterns

Americans who entered the arid West remained firmly committed to the concept of the individual family farm on its own privately owned land. When farming depended on irrigation of dry but fertile land for its survival, this seemed instead to require a broader community to create political and social structures that could direct stream flow and build the ditches. Entire civilizations, like the ancient Sumerians in the Middle East, depended on collective engineering skill and large work forces to build and manage irrigation networks.

Anasazi Indians

The fortunes of the Anasazi Indians of Chaco Canyon in the desert of northwestern New Mexico displayed the necessity of cooperation and the risky nature of settlement in the arid Southwest. A flourishing culture of up to 10,000 people existed after A.D. 600. Tightly packed in multiple-story structures in more than 50 small towns and villages, it was one of the most densely populated early societies. The Anasazi society depended entirely on a complex water distribution system using springs and drips from side canyons supplied by an intermittent stream that supplied water from nearby mountains. Their irrigation system was even more remarkable, since they had no large domestic animals and had not invented the wheel. Gradually, however, the climate wore them down because it was primarily droughty with intermittent seasons of light rain. Nor did the Anasazi help themselves by stripping the region of its pine forests for pueblo construction, which changed their watershed into a desert while also eroding their soil, since trees help store water and hold soil in place. Not the least, Anasazi intensive irrigation brought an accumulation of salts into the farmland that reduced crop production. Nevertheless, despite the apparent inevitability of their failure, the Anasazi persisted for 600 years; Americans invaded the Southwest less than 150 years ago.

The Spanish Alternative

The older Spanish settlements of the Southwest accepted the land as semiarid and ran a few cattle and horses on thousands of scruffy acres. The Spanish had extensive experience with

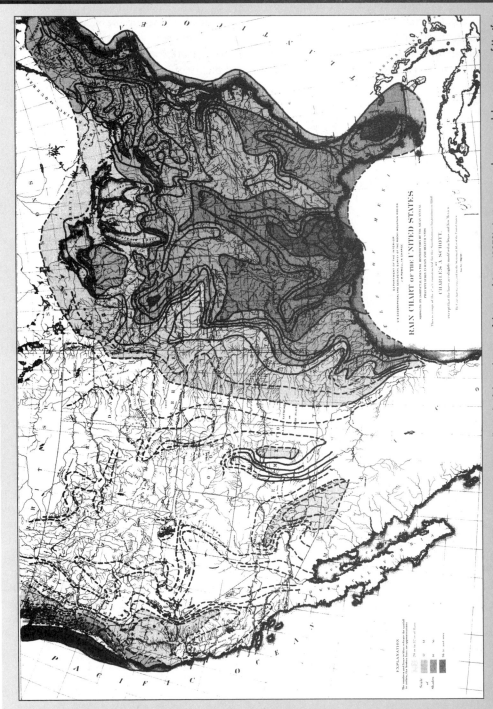

The Innovative "Rain Chart of the United States," in John Wesley Powell, *Lands of the Arid Region of the United States* (1879). Against western boosters and the momentum of Manifest Destiny, Powell argued against settlement of the West "in eastern terms" because most of the region had far too little rain, and frontier farm families would suffer severe hardships.

John Wesley Powell, the Threat of Catastrophe, and a Watershed Geography

A few recognized the semiarid West for what it was. John Wesley Powell was a respected government scientist, ethnographer, and leader of the U.S. Geological Survey. Despite the loss of his right arm in the Civil War, he became a public hero when in 1869 he led the first boatloads of explorers through the canyons of the Colorado River, America's last large unknown region. In his famous 1878 *Report on the Lands of the Arid Region of the United States,* Powell urged an alternative to the 160-acre homesteading limit. He tried to warn away settlers who plowed up the dry land and expected eastern-style rainfall. They might survive for two or three years but they would invariably fail and be driven off the land at great personal cost. He predicted that the western two-fifths of the United States had less than 3 percent of the land that could be farmed in any ordinary way. The rest could only be farmed with artificial watering. Hence, in the first real attempt at land reform since Jefferson's Land Survey Act of 1785, Powell urged a moratorium on future western settlement until a new institutional system had been put into effect that saw water rather than land as the primary natural resource. Whoever controlled a local water source and its distribution, concluded Powell, would determine the usefulness of nearby land. Powell believed that a responsible government (and ordinary human decency) should not allow settlements anywhere in the arid West except on ir regularly shaped watersheds. The advantage of a natural watershed was that it had its own water supply, timber, pasture, and zone of irrigable land, without competition or confusion because each district was part of a natural geography. Powell recommended that the arid West be remapped into 150 irrigation districts that conformed to natural drainage basins. Settlement along rivers and streams in watersheds could use irrigation, which meant more efficient farming on smaller tracts. In the many regions where farmers could not irrigate, Powell urged that the government should sell farmers parcels of land no less than 2- to 4-square-mile sections totaling 1,280 to 2,560 acres.

Powell did not agree that America's Manifest Destiny predetermined that prosperous farms would fill every corner of America's territory. He concluded that sooner or later the federal government would have to intervene to save starving farmers. But few critics could successfully challenge the myth of the happy and prosperous homestead on a 160-acre quarter section. Powell unfortunately made his courageous proposal for land (and water) reform in direct contradiction to the popular Irrigation Crusade of William E. Smythe that was uncritically supported by western congressional boosters (see later). He lost and later resigned from the Geological Survey that he helped establish. Powell anticipated the realities of farm settlement in the West but not the scale of modern urban water needs and its water rights controversies. Much later, in the 1930s, a new federal agency, the Soil Conservation Service, would successfully map its water conservation districts along watersheds, regardless of the grid.

water-shy geographies, beginning on the parched central highlands of Spain and continuing in the desolate badlands of northern Mexico. They realistically concluded that supplies of water in the Southwest were too limited for individual management and belonged to the community for the common good. The Hispanic culture also avoided independent and isolated farmsteads and instead emphasized the importance of cooperation in an agricultural village. A local river was diverted into the communitywide "mother ditch," which branched off to feed crop rows. The community as a whole repaired breaks in the floodgates, removed weeds from the ditches, and planted crops and tended orchards. Regulations going back to 1681 emphasized community efforts that centered on collective prosperity rather than personal profit. Water historian Donald J. Pisani has observed, "The main purpose of irrigation [in a Spanish settlement] was to create a permanent community, not to encourage individual enterprise." Americans who settled in the Southwest, however, looked on the Hispanic experience as an outmoded feudal relic, which used gangs of Indians in forced labor to build the aqueducts and dig the channels. Americans followed the path of private property and individual self-interest. One irrigation booster said in 1889, "We believe the Anglo-Saxon needs no example from Mexico or Spain, but will find in itself the intelligence, virtue, and grit to conquer this land as it has every country where it has ever set its foot." The California gold rush was a sorry exaggeration of American rapacious appetite for personal profit that overran the Spanish-Mexican heritage. There was nothing wrong, gold speculators believed, with capturing the water of others regardless of law, equity, or justice. When gold seekers turned to the high-powered hoses of hydraulic mining, they fought over the vast amounts of water and ignored the riverbeds they blasted into ugly rubble. Men became wealthy by overwhelming a local landscape with dams, reservoirs, flumes, ditches, and pipes to feed their hoses. The mud and silt flows were so bad downstream that they killed fish, polluted water for people and animals, filled and obliterated river channels, and flooded farm fields tens of miles downstream. This compelled the California courts reluctantly to ban hydraulic mining in 1884. The destruction can be compared with strip mining for coal that continues to wrack the Appalachian landscape today.

Cooperative Irrigation Communities

Two Irrigation Colonies: Greeley, Colorado, and Cody, Wyoming

One of the most ambitious alternative irrigation experiments depended on the philosophy of the Frenchman Charles Fourier. Early in the nineteenth century he gained the attention of American utopians with his belief that humankind's passions can be properly channeled into social harmony if allowed to develop naturally outside the constraints of civilization. The influential newspapermen Horace Greeley and Nathan Cook Meeker sponsored an isolated townsite of 12,000 acres in the Cache la Poudre River Valley in north central Colorado, about 50 miles east of the Rocky Mountains. The first 50 families arrived in May 1870, each to settle on a town lot and 160 acres of nearby farmland. The colony was committed to a cooperative irrigation canal system to water 120,000 acres. The total cost was estimated to be $20,000, but the first ditch cost over $50,000 and served less than 3,000 acres. Many of the problems came from Greeley and Meeker's naiveté about the West and ignorance about the basic principles of irrigation. The first ditch was far too small. The town of Greeley eventually prospered but without any of its social idealism and little of its irrigation.

Such colonization rarely worked elsewhere. It went against the grain of individual homesteading, was too authoritarian, too regimented, and too expensive. One of the most notorious failures was headed by the flamboyant William F. "Buffalo Bill" Cody in Wyoming's northwestern Big Horn Basin. The Shosone Land and Irrigation Company contemplated irrigating 28,000 acres from ditches that would cost $100,000, but found in 1896 alone it had spent $80,000 on only 15 miles of ditch, and attracted a mere dozen farmers who watered only about 400 acres. The company nevertheless grandly promised a 150-mile-long aqueduct system costing $1.75 million, but ended up selling distress bonds at a discount, and Cody poured good money after bad from profits of his Wild West Show. As would often become true, the new Reclamation Service stepped in and in 1910 built the 328-foot-high Buffalo Bill Dam and ultimately spend near $26 million to provide water to less than 100,000 acres. Of Cody's original venture, only the small town of Cody remains, outside Yellowstone Park.

The Mormon Venture
Mormons laid the foundation for America's most ambitious desert civilization. They confidently attacked the indifferent desert and flooded it into a Sumeria in America. Although their primary objective was to establish a spiritual utopia in the West, they were also worldly wise enough to build a successful material society. In order to follow freely their own communitarian instincts, they established themselves by the Great Salt Lake, hundreds of miles away from abuse for their unique beliefs and far from the temptations of individualism and capitalism. They put the central authority of the Church above personal interest. As environmental historian Donald Worster put it, "The common people learned that the war against nature required them to become an army of obedient soldiers who would unquestioningly march out again and again to rebuild dams, making them bigger and stronger each time in defense of the Church and its righteous cause." The speed of successful Mormon irrigation in Utah was astonishing to contemporaries. By 1850 there were over 16,000 irrigated acres growing a bounty of potatoes, wheat, hay, corn, oats, and rye at five times the rate of unirrigated land. By 1890 irrigated acreage rose to more than 263,000 acres that supported more than 200,000 people. By 1902 they had 6 million acres under full or partial irrigation over several states. The federal Bureau of Reclamation (see later) used the Mormon experience (the agency was run mostly by Mormons) to launch its own irrigation program.

There were economic advantages in using a system of farming in which wealth did not accrue to individuals, but to the community. A hydraulic technology of dams and reservoirs, ditches and canals, had to distribute water fairly to all. The Church limited farms larger than 20 acres and prohibited any farmer from owning more than one such farm. Ownership of scarce natural resources like water belonged to no individuals and remained in public control. The near-dictatorial Mormon leader Brigham Young said, "There shall be no private ownership of the streams that come out of the canyons. These belong to the people: all the people." In the twentieth century the Mormons would enter the American middle-class mainstream, but in the nineteenth century they saw themselves in a world outside American expansionism. Water historian Donald Pisani wrote, "Utah was exceptional: it was the only state or territory to use water law to *discourage* the inflow of outside capital and to *limit* settlement." In this sense the Mormons fulfilled John Wesley Powell's hope for the arid West by limiting speculation and controlling settlement. They were unlike their homesteading neighbors who created a rural society of towns and isolated ranches and were instead an outpost that followed the pattern of integrated communities in New England or even Europe. Ironically, with their emphasis on family life as well as communitywide cooperation, the Mormons also came to personify the best example of the Jeffersonian yeoman farmer transplanted from the lush, humid East to the harsh realities of an arid climate.

The American Answer to the Problem of the West: Reclamation and Irrigation

Americans decided that the only way to make over semiarid regions was to irrigate them by constructing a massive plumbing system. Irrigation for farming was a very attractive and even comforting technology that overlaid a seemingly worthless landscape. Despite its structures and technologies, irrigation was not a step away from dependency on nature, but intertwined western farmers even more with nature as they consumed far larger amounts of fresh water than had the original trappers or ranchers. In some cases along the Colorado River, irrigation began with dams and reservoirs, or on the High Plains and in California's Central Valley, with wells and pumps. The water arrived at the fields through aqueducts, canals, pipelines, ditches, and laterals. The goal was a dependable living and a measure of prosperity that were otherwise impossible in arid or semiarid country. Yet irrigation was a type of agriculture that was thoroughly alien to eastern farmers, despite its ancient origins. They enjoyed flat, equally watered land with a forgiving climate, but in the West low rainfall, high altitudes, relentless winds, sandy soil, and alkaline lands took their breath away.

Reclamation is irrigation on a larger scale. The word *reclamation* is a misnomer because it suggests recovery of something lost. Instead it means economic development, often against great odds. By bringing billions of gallons of water to parched landscapes, reclamation had the flavor of a messianic effort toward greening the desert and building the West. The environmental impact of large reclamation projects serving hundreds of square miles made the earlier domestication of the eastern wilderness seem like child's play. Water, a heavy and gravity-directed fluid, is expensive to move. In addition, very often half of it evaporates in reservoirs or open canals. When farmers finally got water, they tended to overwater their crops. They let their irrigation systems silt up. Despite heroic efforts and many billions of dollars, the pieces of western landscape made green together equal only the size of Arkansas.

The Irrigation Crusade

Yet wherever irrigation was successful, it seemed to transform desert into garden. It became a vehicle for Progressive social reform to redistribute the nation's opportunity and wealth. Charles R. Van Hise wrote in 1910, "The importance of irrigation cannot be overestimated, since it transforms lands which are semi-arid or arid and almost worthless to a more highly productive condition." Quoting one of his sources, he reported, "Under irrigation one hundred heads of grain replace the blade of grass, and one hundred head of kine [cattle] graze where an antelope or two wandered before." Twentieth-century irrigation technology, in combination with virginal soils, constant sunshine, and warm climate, allowed two or three profitable crops a year, even five crops of alfalfa. Because water was free, Van Hise also warned about waste of water through careless use, such as overflooded fields. Prior appropriation demanded consumption even when it was not needed, overapplication could turn soil alkaline, and poorly built and maintained systems leaked and evaporated water. As soon as water was placed on an acre of previously arid land, it skyrocketed in value from $1.25 to $2.50 up to $100 to $150 an acre (in 1910 dollars), and on an acre of fruit trees in Colorado or California, a common price could soar from $1,000 to $4,000 an acre. Van Hise reported that at the end of 1908 more than 13 million acres of western land were under irrigation, and more than 45 million acres of western land had irrigation potential, which could support 9 million people at 5 acres of irrigated land per person. Van Hise also concluded that irrigation could be expanded across the arid western landscape by means of four interlocking programs—the establishment of farmer cooperatives and small corporations, the creation of irrigation districts, the policies of the Carey Act, and through the new Reclamation Service.

Progressive idealism forged a concept of the ethical "duty of water" that reached a high point in the "Irrigation Crusade" from approximately 1890 to 1910. Its charismatic prophet was William E. Smythe, its voice was his journal, *The Irrigation Age,* and its bible, Smythe's 1899 book, appropriately titled *The Conquest of Arid America.* His message was that irrigation was the technological master of the arid West, the indispensable means for achieving a more humane order of life. He also declared, "The essence of the industrial life which springs from irrigation is its democracy." Smythe's Irrigation Crusade organized several nationwide irrigation congresses, the first held at Salt Lake City in 1891, then in 1893 in Los Angeles (with the theme, "Irrigation: Science, Not Chance"), in 1894 in Denver, and in 1896 in Phoenix. At each congress, state officials, land developers, and civil engineers were joined by representatives from equipment companies, water cooperatives, private water companies, and irrigation districts with common agendas to shape public opinion in favor of funding and development by the federal government of large-scale irrigation projects. Smythe led the agitation for federal grants to the western states of a million acres each of land from the public domain dedicated to reclamation. This effort led directly to the Carey Act of 1894, which is still operative (but never applied after 1902).

Smythe's Irrigation Crusade promised that the American dream of universal prosperity would be fulfilled when struggling farmers turned to irrigation. They could match a factory worker's wages ($490.95 a year) on a single acre of well-watered land and yet retain agrarian values. This was the long-awaited "parity" for the nation's farmers whose earning power had always been less than city factory workers. Intensive farming meant raising onions, cabbage, sweet potatoes, tomatoes, grapes, cherries, and apples—plenty of work for a farmer on 20 acres. People were told that $25,000 invested in orange groves on irrigated land in California would double in five years and then continue to generate a yearly income of $70,000. They heard the story of William Turner of Wenatchee, Washington, who in 1901 planted 32 acres of apple trees and while he waited for the trees to bear, he profited nicely by growing strawberries in the rows between the trees. After six years his apples earned him $585 an acre. Some of his neighbors began to earn as much as $2,500 an acre from 7- or 8-year-old trees. When irrigated land was treated strictly as a business venture, as Timothy Paige did when in the 1870s he bought almost 9,000 acres of unimproved land in the San Joaquin Valley, the results could be spectacular. Paige paid only 60 cents an acre, but when water reached the land within ten years, he sold 1,500 acres for $86.66 an acre.

Nationwide, irrigation was treated as a farmer panacea almost beyond credibility, although few farmers in reality prospered if they limited themselves to only 40 acres of irrigated land. Smythe continued to moralize about the independent family on its irrigated tract: "It hurts me to ride through Western Kansas and see the desolate houses that serve as homes. We will change all this with irrigation. We will have little homes of pleasing architecture. We will surround them with pretty lawns, we will fringe them with trees and hedges, we will drape them with vines and deck them with roses, in a new Kansas dedicated to industrial independence." Smythe condemned the bonanza wheat farmers along the Red River of the North for "skimming the fertility" from hundreds of square miles. In contrast, said Smythe, the virtuous irrigator "farms a few acres and farms them well." "Forty Million Forty-Acre Farms" became a national slogan. The 1890 census reported 3.5 million acres under irrigation, with 52,500 people working on farms averaging 68 acres, producing $14.89 of products per acre.

Smythe was joined by public officials. Richard J. Hinton's report to the U.S. Department of Agriculture, "Irrigation in the United States," was the first systematic survey of American irrigation as an appropriate farming practice. He estimated that 245 million acres could be made fruitful through irrigation, but later he admitted that known water resources could serve only 121 million acres. Hinton also acknowledged that average cost to irrigate an acre would be $7, totaling more than a billion dollars. But the benefit would be enormous: The average per acre value of the irrigated land would be $30, a dramatic increase from the $1.25 or $2.50 a farmer paid the government. The results would build up national wealth and end poverty by attracting lower classes to the land. It was worthy public aid to increase private property. Hinton's data compelled John Wesley Powell to take another look at his original prediction that only 3 million acres had irrigation potential in the West; now Powell saw 100 million acres irrigated at $10 an acre, or a total of a billion dollars, "including all the construction work involved in building dams, reservoirs, canals and irrigation ditches." By the late twentieth century, 9 million acres had been irrigated by the Reclamation Service at the cost of $10 billion. If private projects are included, the total reached almost 26 million acres, a small fraction of Hinton's "authoritative" estimates.

The Government Takes Charge:
Federal Reclamation Reinvents the West

Private irrigation projects, such as the Mormon settlements in Utah, Colorado's famous Greeley Colony, California's "colonies" in Ontario, San Bernadino, Pasadena, and Anaheim, and the industrial farmers of Kern County, were often highly successful but on a local scale. By 1900 most of the West's dryland that could be irrigated from nearby rivers had been taken. Only major capital investment could bring water to large outlying areas of arid land from rivers like the Sacramento, Colorado, and Columbia. Many early private irrigation projects were risky enterprises, poorly engineered by underskilled and profiteering builders, as in the cases of Greeley and Cody. Matters of proper drainage, adequate water supply, and modern dam construction were unknown or ignored. By 1902, 90 percent of private irrigation companies were in or near bankruptcy. Western water historian Marc Reisner observed, "For the first time in their history, Americans had come up against a problem they could not begin to master with traditional American solutions—private capital, individual initiative, hard work—and yet the region confronting the problem happened to believe most fervently in such solutions."

Government water management projects began to replace private enterprise, but they revived long-standing complaints that such projects devoured everyone's taxes to benefit a few local people. Decades earlier, Henry Clay's "American System" stated otherwise that it was the duty, even the moral responsibility, of government to promote a strong national economy through public works. Smythe had preached, "When Uncle Sam waves his hand toward the desert and says, 'Let there be water!' we know that the stream will obey his command" and bring moral regeneration to the nation. But it was a tall order. The first publicly financed dams and levees were intended to limit the destruction caused by flooding from rivers swollen by midwestern rainstorms or snowmelt in western mountains. The U.S. Army Corps of Engineers became responsible for flood control over the often rampaging Mississippi and Missouri rivers. Flooding by California's Sacramento River regularly turned the upper Central Valley into an inland sea; private and public ventures built high levees to keep the river in its channel and off rich farmland. The resulting landscape was bizarre; the river ran in channels 20 feet above neighboring farmland.

The Newlands Act: Reclamation Act of 1902

In large part the Newlands, or Reclamation Act of 1902, was a rescue operation for settlers already in the West, including private irrigation operations. A severe western drought in the 1890s that came on top of the nation's worst economic depression brought public pressure for federal intervention. In his state of the union message in December 1901, new president Theodore Roosevelt announced he was giving high priority in his administration to "water for the arid states." Following up on his commitment to conservation, and his long-standing love for the West, Roosevelt told Congress they must pass legislation for a full-bore campaign to change dry worthless land into irrigated land for the West's hard-pressed farmers. He proposed a new government-managed series of expertly engineered and federally funded water storage works, dams, canals, and irrigation projects. This encouraged Nevada congressman Francis G. Newlands to push federal reclamation for arid lands states. In its debate over the Newlands reclamation bill, Congress made pious pronouncements about America's moral duty to safeguard struggling western farmers. Western congressmen also saw pork-barrel opportunities for their states and districts.

Passage of the Newlands, or Reclamation Act of 1902, was also a long overdue admission that independent family farmers were near collapse when they tried to settle west of 20 inches of rain, the 98th meridian. John Wesley Powell was vindicated but not mentioned. The "excess lands" provision of the act, which limited federal water dollars to owners of 160 acres or less (a married couple could double this to 320 acres), attempted to exclude large developers and speculators. As soon as it appeared that a locality would benefit from a new reclamation project, Americans, great and small, rushed to practice their favorite new pastime, speculation that a piece of dry land costing $10 an acre would immediately mount in value to $100 or $250 an acre because it could be irrigated. The act recognized that everything in the West depended on the manipulation of water. It must be captured behind dams, stored in reservoirs, and rerouted in concrete rivers over distances of hundreds of miles. Not the least, the act required expert scientific and engineering attention to rainfall, stream flow, soil and rock conditions for dams and reservoirs, construction techniques, and soil quality on potential irrigated farms. Funding for reclamation was to come from the sale of public lands in 16 western states and small payments by the irrigation farmers who directly received cheap water from a Reclamation project. It was a terrific deal, since farmers could receive water at a tenth of the real cost to bring it to their land. Their payments on the construction costs of the project were interest free over the original ten-year payment period. This was a hidden subsidy that amounted to about 90 cents on the dollar. Not the least, farmers quickly learned that the government would repeatedly extend their payment periods, discount the payments, or forgive them entirely. Reclamation projects cost taxpayers hundreds of millions of dollars. Although the use of Reclamation dams for hydroelectric power was not a stated part of the 1902 act, the sale of electricity became an important new source of income that sometimes covered almost 80 percent of the costs. Private utilities complained bitterly about the unfair competition and low prices. But most often project costs were never paid back, directly or indirectly. Thus the federal government became the dominant planner, funder, and developer of water projects for the benefit of private landowners.

The Reclamation Service

The first director of the Reclamation Service was Frederick Newell, an MIT graduate and John Wesley Powell's senior irrigation survey assistant. To his credit, Newell set a high technical standard that innovated the design and construction of massive high-level dams, and the application of structural and hydraulic engineering to major irrigation works. In 1910 the service built the world's then highest dam at 328 feet, Shoshone in northwestern Wyoming, and 1911 saw the completion of what is still the world's largest stone masonry dam, Roosevelt Dam. It was 220 feet high, 723 feet long, and impounded 1.4 million acre-feet (an acre-foot is a foot of water across one square acre, or 325,851 gallons) of water in a reservoir on the Salt River near Phoenix in Arizona. This was the service's first noteworthy project, and it replaced a defective private dam. Newell oversaw the shift from masonry to concrete (block pouring and cooling of concrete castings) construction and the transition from hand-dug channels, horse-drawn scrapers, and wagons to steam engines, gasoline-powered tractors, trucks, and oversized earth-moving machinery. Another technological advance offered by the service was economical long-distance electrical power transmission, which made possible Hoover, Grand Coulee, and Powell dams. The service set world-class standards for systemwide planning that integrated flood control, irrigation demands, and hydroelectric power generation. It was not surprising that the Reclamation Service (renamed the Bureau of Reclamation in 1923, to revert briefly back to a Service in the 1980s) attracted the best engineering talent in the country. It is also not surprising, as reclamation historian Michael Robinson told, "There was a tendency for some engineers to view public works as ends in themselves. Despite official declarations from more sensitive administrations that 'Reclamation is measured not in engineering units but in homes and agricultural values' the Service regarded itself as an 'engineering outfit.'" It also operated at "Tiffany" costs.

Within four years after its 1902 establishment, the new Reclamation Service spent $39 million to irrigate nearly 2.5 million acres—"land for the landless"—across the West. In 1907 Newell reaffirmed that "the object of the reclamation law is primarily to put the public domain into the hands of small land owners—men who live upon the land, support themselves, make prosperous homes, and become purchasers of the goods manufactured in the East and the cotton raised in the South." On the Malheur plateau in eastern Oregon, the Reclamation Service created a speculator's windfall when it charged landowners $42 an acre for land that was instantly worth $100 an acre. At the Salt River Project in Arizona, where a dry acre cost $5 and then under reclamation soared to $250, speculators outmaneuvered honest settlers. But few complained, since in America everyone has the right to make a quick buck. According to the original 1902 act, a typical irrigation project was to be funded for $5 to $15 an acre. In reality, construction costs immediately soared as high as $160 an acre and averaged nearly $85 an acre. The projects were intended to pay their own way. Heavily subsidized projects, in which the government was to make up the difference, were not part of 1902 policy, but soon become the most common action. The irony was that because projects usually took more than a decade to complete at double or triple the anticipated cost, the hundreds of farm families who rushed to settle the region in anticipation of the benefits of irrigation were living in poverty, hunger, debt, and disillusionment. Not that a completed project put them on easy street. A reclamation project in Nevada, on the Truckee-Carson rivers, cost so much that the government tried to recoup by means of a "building charge" of $22 to $30 an acre for water rights. This, together with maintenance charges, was too costly, and many settlers failed.

By 1910 the Reclamation program needed help and corrections. It became clear that government water had to be cheap for farmers, but this would not be true for taxpayers. Whether costs were high or not, it seemed that farmers in an irrigation project often could not meet payments of constructions costs even when spread over a 50-year period. Farmers were also captives to crop prices, which fell through the floor after World War I. Even while Reclamation lands expanded, the value of all crops grown on them fell from $152 million in 1919 to $83.6 million in 1922. Only 10 percent of the money farmers owed had been repaid, and 60 percent of the irrigators were defaulting entirely on their interest-free payments. The 1920s was thus a time of troubles for the Bureau of Reclamation. By 1923, $143 million had been invested in irrigation projects, and only $16 million recovered. Yet federal reclamation acreage was at 1.25 million acres, only a fraction of the 19 million acres of irrigated farmland in the West. Problems of settler hardships, project debt, and low occupancy had not been solved. Reclamation gained a reputation for superb engineering achievements but got brickbats for its failure in administration that sent costs soaring while feeding speculators and industrial farmers. The bureau began to ignore its original mission to fabricate a watered landscape for the private small farmer, and it soon became notorious for its cozy relationships with agribusiness and thirsty western cities. This was particularly embarrassing because of the proud moralizing about saving family homesteading and homemaking. The Hoover administration began to direct hundreds of millions of additional dollars to accelerate the building of irrigation projects.

The post–World War I agricultural depression continued through the 1920s and 1930s and prevented recovery of costs. Reclamation rarely turned off the water and even devised a system of water pricing based on the farmer's "ability to pay." Congress repeatedly had to shift other funds into Reclamation to keep it going. During the Depression of the 1930s, as national unemployment soared toward 30 percent, the newly inaugurated president, Franklin Delano Roosevelt, made western reclamation a cornerstone of the New Deal administration. Roosevelt said he wanted to be remembered as the greatest conservationist and greatest developer of all time. In the Bureau of Reclamation he recognized that he had a vast job-creating engine, and when its projects remade the western landscape, he had a place where the dispossessed could go. He treated public works funds as emergency relief appropriations. Federal monies poured into the Central Valley Project in California, which used water from the

Sacramento River to irrigate the upper San Joaquin Valley, into the Columbia River and Snake River dams that irrigated over a million acres in the Northwest, and into the Colorado-Big Thompson Project to carry water from the Colorado River through a tunnel under the Rocky Mountains to serve Denver and to irrigate farms on the High Plains. Yet, as recently as 1969, despite the scale and distribution of federal reclamation, its projects covered only about a fifth of total irrigated land in the 17 western states.

Reclamation in the Late Twentieth Century: Rethinking Dams

Floyd Dominy, leader of the Bureau of Reclamation, testified at Senate hearings in 1958 about the changing contribution of irrigation to the West: "You take 160 acres that has to provide automobiles, modern school facilities, taxes for school buses, for good roads, to provide deep freezers, electric stoves, electric refrigerators, the modern conveniences that the farm housewife ought to have and deserves, it puts a much greater demand on the income of that land than was necessary to support us at a subsistence level prevailing for my father or grandfather." Thus the federal reclamation program, despite its enormous costs that were not being recovered, continued to be seen as the salvation of the West. Dominy continued, "Did one prefer a wild and feckless Colorado River to one that measures out steady water and power to ten million people? Should we *not* have built Hoover Dam?" By the 1970s reclamation was seen as primarily the servant of big business and big government. The actual shift from agricultural irrigation to multipurpose projects that served urban centers was never fully recognized in reclamation policy. Its original client, the homestead settler, had been forgotten. This was a turnaround from the historic reclamation mission.

The story of public reclamation in America began with a broken private dam and reservoir that wiped out the city of Johnstown, Pennsylvania, in 1889. The Bureau of Reclamation's dominion over the West nearly ended with another collapse, Idaho's Teton Dam in 1976. The bureau had earlier in 1965 dodged the bullet when the new Fontenelle Dam on the Green River in southwestern Wyoming began leaking, but the reservoir was emptied before the dam broke. The Fontenelle Dam was built where the rock contained so much sodium carbonate that it accelerated the setting of concrete, which then developed invisible fissures. Teton Dam was 300 feet high and 1,700 feet wide at the base in an admittedly terrible site where constructors discovered caverns in the rock. A local university geologist observed, "It was such an obviously lousy site to a trained geologist. It makes you wonder what happens to human judgment inside a bureaucracy." The yawning gaps were filled with 503,000 cubic feet of concrete grout, more than twice the project estimates. In May 1975, because of heavy snow meltoff, the reservoir behind the newly completed dam began filling at three times the acceptable rate, pressure built up on the dam site itself, and the surrounding rock began leaking. Then a dark spot showed up on the dam face itself, which quickly opened to break out a full third of the dam. A 20-foot-high wall of water rushed down on the towns of Wilford and Teton, which disappeared in a tumult of houses, trees, topsoil, stores, animals, and 11 dead people. Teton Dam was Reclamation's version of the *Challenger* space shuttle disaster in 1987. The agency, like NASA, never quite recovered its authority or reputation.

Only in the late 1980s would the Bureau of Reclamation begin to rethink, and eventually abandon, its mission to build costly and controversial large-scale irrigation and power projects. Local Colorado attorney Glenn Saunders was not alone when in 1984 he lambasted the bureau at a public meeting:

> The people who support these boondoggle projects are always talking about the vision and principles that made this country great. "Our forefathers would have built these projects!" they say. "They had vision!" That's pure nonsense. It wasn't the vision and principles of our forefathers that made this country great. It was the huge unused bonanza they found here. One wave of immigrants after another could occupy new land. There was topsoil, water—there was gold, silver, and iron ore lying right on top of the earth. We picked our way through a ripe orchard and made it bare. We've been so busy spending money and reaping the fruits that we're blind to the fact that there are no more fruits. By trying to make things better [by building dams], we're making them worse and worse.

One of the bureau's most severe critics, Marc Reisner, concluded, "What had begun as an emergency program to put the country back to work, to restore its sense of self-worth, to settle the refugees of the Dust Bowl, grew into a nature-wrenching, money-eating monster that our leaders lacked the courage or ability to stop." In 75 years Reclamation spent $9.4 billion on projects that created 9 million acres of highly productive farmland yielding crops worth nearly $5 billion and household water for 17 million people, but with subsidies that could never be recovered. Public outcry brought a national moratorium on high dam construction. By then Reclamation was a major institution that over its history had operated 333 reservoirs, 345 diversion dams, 50 power plants, 188 pumping plants, 14,590 miles of canals, 990 miles of pipelines, 230 miles of tunnels, and 35,160 miles of smaller laterals. In 1979 its name was changed to the Water and Power Resources Service. In 1977 President Jimmy Carter had taken a public stand against 80 western irrigation projects that were consuming $5 billion a year, particularly in an era of soaring deficits and soaring interest rates. Marc Reisner noted, however, that Carter faced more opposition from Congress than he bargained for: "Water projects are the grease gun that lubricates the nation's legislative machinery. Congress without water projects would be like an engine without oil; it would simply seize up."

By the 1960s and 1970s environmental quality entered the public's vision of quality of life. The Bureau of Reclamation was reviled as the enemy of a better life instead of its advocate. Dams built in the 1960s at spectacularly scenic places like Flaming Gorge in southwestern Wyoming and Glen Canyon in southern Utah seemed to demonstrate the power of congressional pork-barrel legislation against public outcry, wilderness values, and environmental common sense. The Bureau of Reclamation gained a reputation for indifference to the environment in its construction projects. It ran into an environmentalist buzzsaw that included full-page ads in newspapers across the country by organizations like the Wilderness Society and the Sierra Club. The virtual freedom of action that the Bureau of Reclamation had enjoyed for most of its history was severely restricted by controls set on western waterways by the Wilderness Act of 1964 and Wild and Scenic Rivers Act of 1968. Water resource projects now came under unprecedented scrutiny on the basis of water shortages, pollution, and environmental deterioration. Passage of the National Environmental Policy Act in 1970 required environmental impact statements (EIS) for all major public projects. This changed the climate for reclamation. The massive California Water Project and Central Arizona Project came under severe attack for their ecological consequences. As we shall see in Chapter

12, environmental lobbying saved Dinosaur National Monument from a reclamation project at Echo Park in the heart of the monument to enlarge water storage capacity in the upper Colorado River basin. Public opinion and its impact on Congress forced the Bureau of Reclamation to abandon plans for a series of dams through the Grand Canyon and in Hell's Canyon on the Snake River.

As early as 1968 the National Water Commission recommended that the bureau move away from big dams and other water development projects and confine itself to water management in arid regions, a shift that the bureau reluctantly accepted in 1990 as reclamation policy. Environmental troubles that affect reclamation and irrigation began to arrive in bunches in the 1960s and 1970s. Reclamation irrigation projects accelerated salt poisoning of the soil and groundwater mining. Critics complained that many of the bureau's reservoirs will silt up within three or four generations from their completion (an astonishingly short time) and produce attractive waterfalls but store little water. Hoover Dam's storage capacity had already declined from 32.4 million acre-feet in 1936 to 30.7 million acre-feet in 1970; many other dams had more extreme losses. Since most of America's big dams were built between 1915 and 1975, they would be silting up at roughly the same time. The era of the big dams was over.

Hydrological Giantism in California

If modern California were an independent nation (some say this is not a bad idea), its economic boom would make it the number-four economic power in the world. As it is, the state has for some years enjoyed number-one ranking among the United States in population, agriculture, and industry. California gained this status largely because of environmental opportunities—its own benign climate, rich soils, precious metals, and petroleum. But little of this prosperity could have been put in place without the manipulation of water since the early twentieth century. Californians took water from its north to build its south. To feed its appetite, it captured Colorado River water that belonged to several other western states. The state's environment is dominated by 1,200 major dams, the two biggest irrigation projects on earth, and more irrigated acreage than any other state. Not that this exploitation was built on self-sufficiency; the state continues to receive 40 percent more federal assistance than any other state. California novelist Joan Didion wrote, "The apparent ease of California life is an illusion, and those who believe the illusion really live here in only the most temporary way."

Historically, eastern immigrants refused to accept the environmental reality of the arid Central Valley and most of southern California. The notion that they might stay with cattle ranches and small towns did not cross their minds. That was the Spanish and Mexican way. They lobbied for water at federal cost. When a network of irrigation projects began to spread water from isolated mountains, lakes, and rivers to the fertile but dry inner valleys of the state, California emerged as the fruit and vegetable capital of the nation. Legions of civil engineers, project managers, and politicians bearing bushels of money moved in to plan, finance, and construct dams, reservoirs, canals, and ditches. The state pioneered new technologies in hydraulic mining, flood control, and irrigation systems. It innovated the irrigation district and the mutual water company. More than any other state, California influenced water law throughout the American West. Environmental by-products included waste, pollution, land and water salinity, and land subsidence. Direct competition for the same scarce water pitted arid southern California against water-rich northern California. Los Angeles still drinks from the Owens Valley-Mono Lake Basin and battles with the water needs of cities of the San Fernando Valley. San Francisco has never fully owned up to its destruction of the remarkable Hetch Hetchy Valley, a twin to Yosemite Valley. California has also been the arena of battles between the Army Corps of Engineers against the Bureau of Reclamation, which itself ran up against the California Water Resources Control Board. The Los Angeles Metropolitan Water District stood against the Imperial Valley for Colorado River water. The powerful utility Pacific Gas & Electric took on the U.S. Department of the Interior. The California Farm Bureau Federation is fighting a losing battle with the California Department of Water Resources to protect irrigation against urban needs.

California Water Wars: The Problem with Los Angeles

Nowhere was urban imperialism more evident than in Los Angeles. In 1860 Los Angeles barely existed as a small agricultural community of 4,300 people. The small Los Angeles River that ran through town supplied a network of canals and irrigation ditches that fed water to local farms. These farms, canals, and ditches began to disappear under the spread of businesses and homes. City water was first delivered from the river using giant wooden lifting wheels and leaky wooden pipes. But fires, epidemics, and perpetual low water pressure drove the citizens around the turn of the century to a workmanlike distribution system of pumps, iron pipes, gate valves, and fire hydrants. By the 1870s it irrigated about 4,500 acres for a mixed produce of fruits, grapes, and grains. Real city lights belonged to exciting San Francisco far to the north. Instead, Los Angeles gained notoriety for harboring lawless renegades. Anticipating the "water wars" of the future, in the 1870s Los Angelenos were already fighting upstream farmers by using secret buyouts, destruction of irrigation works, and blackmail.

Los Angeles enjoyed its first considerable growth spurt when it luckily became the western terminus for transcontinental railroads, the Southern Pacific in 1876 and the Santa Fe in 1885. Its population ballooned to 50,000 by 1890. It responded to its growth by reviving the so-called pueblo water right that in 1895 gave the city exclusive rights to the 500-square-mile Los Angeles River watershed, including a 900,000 acre-feet reservoir. By 1900 the city had grown to over 200,000 people and far overreached its own watershed. It could not continue this heady expansion unless it pumped water from 250 miles away over the mountainous horizon to the north in the fertile Owens Valley and nearby Mono Lake. The city never wavered from its belief that its population growth was more important than growing distant crops. In a daring move, its new Board of Water Commissioners, which employed the legendary self-taught engineer William Mulholland (memorialized in the movie *Chinatown*), used every subterfuge and every legal ploy to buy up local water rights to the Owens River, 235 miles north over the Sierra Nevada Mountains, and with a perpetual flow guaranteed by snowmelt from 14,495-foot Mount Whitney. Mulholland's claims were supported by the newly created federal Reclamation Service, which looked at the river valley as underdeveloped, abandoned the valley farmers, and moved aside to let Los Angeles have its way. The city benefited enormously from the enthusiastic support of President Teddy Roosevelt, who shouted, "It is a hundred or thousandfold more important to the State and more valuable to the people as a whole if [this

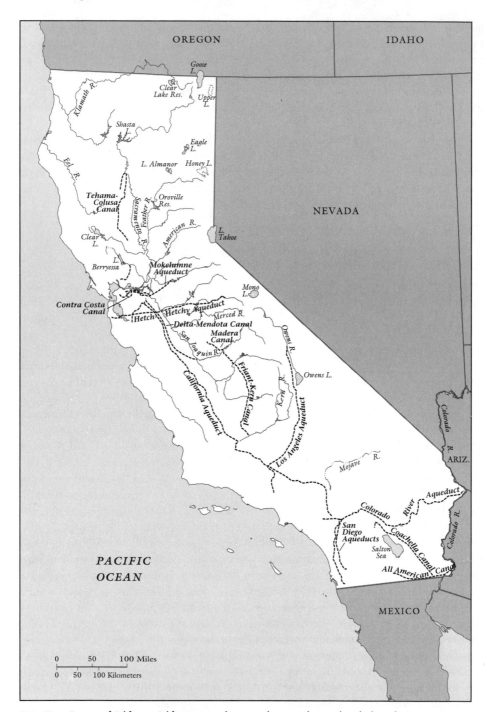

Major Water Projects of California. California, more than any other state, became largely dependent upon enormous "hydraulic" projects for its agricultural, population, and industrial growth, especially since the early 1900s. Most of the water was moved toward San Francisco, the Central Valley, and Los Angeles and San Diego.

water is] used by the city than if used by the [farming] people of the Owens Valley." At the same time, dubious interlocking shenanigans by J.B. Lippincott of the Reclamation Service, Fred Eaton, a former Los Angeles mayor, and Thomas Rickey, a local land-rich farmer, assured a Los Angeles victory, and coincidentally, made their fortunes. The people of Owens Valley retaliated by regularly dynamiting the aqueduct and waterworks, but to little avail.

Mulholland moved aggressively to build the first great urban aqueduct in the West. (New York City simultaneously constructed its own remarkable aqueduct system to supply water from the Catskills.) For six years between 1907 and 1913, through bitter winters and deadly summers, 2,000 to 6,000 men worked on Mulholland's project, which, like Boulder Dam 30 years later, was finished underbudget and ahead of schedule. The result was a natural geography transformed into mechanical hydraulics. When finished, the aqueduct ran 223 miles from Owens Valley across the scorching Mohave Desert and through some of the most mountainous fault-ridden topography in the West. Fifty-three miles ran through tunnels using the latest engineering technologies. Where the geological structures were too porous or crumbly to hold water, siphons in huge metal tubes carried large volumes of water preposterously up ridges and down valleys. In addition the project was serviced by 120 miles of railroad track, 500 miles of roads and trains, 240 miles of telephone line, and 170 miles of power transmission line. Two new hydroelectric plants on Owens River provided power to the pumps.

The Owens Valley project assured the future growth and expansion of Los Angeles, which boosters predicted could reach 2 million people. Only later was it also learned that three-quarters of the water had secretly been designated to water the desertlike San Fernando Valley, where most of the land was owned through a mysterious syndicate of wealthy men, among them real estate magnate Henry Huntington, Union Pacific president E.H. Harriman, water commissioner and trolley company owner Moses Sherman, and newspaper owners Harry Chandler and Harrison Gray Otis. Historian Marc Reisner called it "a monopolist's version of affirmative action." Irrigated acreage in the valley rose from 3,000 acres in 1913 to 75,000 acres in 1918. William Mulholland, who proudly masterminded the entire Owens River caper, however, received few financial rewards. Ironically his career was destroyed after he oversaw the construction of the Saint Francis Dam, 40 miles north of Los Angeles, only to have it immediately collapse on March 12, 1928. It sent a 100-foot wall of water into the Santa Clara Valley, where it wiped out towns, farms, fields and orchards, roads, bridges, railroads, and killed thousands of livestock and more than 400 people. Whatever the dubious machinations and deadly results, Los Angeles got its water, which helped it to become the preeminent city of California and the West. In 1850 Los Angeles stood far behind San Francisco with 1,601 people on 28 square miles. By 1910 it had 319,000 people on 101 square miles acquired by incorporation of neighboring towns. In 1920 the city gained major national status with 577,000 people on 364 square miles. By 1930 it mushroomed to 1.2 million people on 442 square miles and in 1990 passed Chicago to become the nation's second largest city at 3.5 million people on 469 square miles. If it had stayed within the bounds of its own water supply, its population could not have risen much above 100,000 people. Now it is the second largest desert city in the world, topped only slightly by Cairo in Egypt.

Los Angeles began to experience setbacks to its urban imperialism with the rise of public environmental awareness in the 1960s and 1970s. Environmental activists challenged city water entitlements to streams that supplied the ancient saline Mono Lake in the northern Owens Valley. The lake had been declining at the rate of about a foot a year after Los Angeles started tapping northern valley water in 1941. As the 500,000-year-old remains of a primeval inland sea, the lake was the only habitat for a rare brine shrimp and a brine fly that also supported the second largest breeding ground for California gulls in the United States. It also served as a stop-off along a major flyway for migratory birds like grebes and phalaropes. When in 1970 Los Angeles completed its second aqueduct up to the Mono Basin, the water started declining at 1.5 feet annually because of 90,000 acre-feet diverted annually to the city. In 1979 a coalition of environmental organizations filed suit against Los Angeles, using a new legal argument that the city's diversions violated the legal doctrine of "public trust." By 1980 the lake had fallen by 45 feet to half its volume, and its salinity doubled to threaten the shrimp, flies, and food chain for the birds. The suit argued that adverse changes diminished public benefit from unique ecological and scenic values of the lake. In 1983 after the state supreme court, in *National Audubon Society* v. *Superior Court of Alpine County,* validated the concept of public trust, no longer could a water developer merely argue that a use was reasonable and beneficial. The state was obligated to assess possible impacts on the environment and prevent harmful changes. The court, however, muddied its decision by allowing that water diversions from the lake might continue as a "practical necessity."

Agriculture, Cities, and Environmental Impact: California Water Projects

The Central Valley Project

California's Central Valley Project tapped the Sacramento River in the north to irrigate the San Joaquin Valley in the south. Where once there had been cattle ranchers and wheat barons,

HOW TO BECOME rich on Bureau of Reclamation water in California? With your spouse, buy your legal maximum of 320 acres. Avoid high altitudes and cold climates so you can raise two cash crops a year. The best money is in oranges, where you could make more money than a lawyer. Excellent income comes also from peaches, grapes and raisins, and figs. Low-value crops like cotton or alfalfa are for your less greedy cousin. Stay with bureau water, since it is by far the cheapest in the West, sold at a fraction of its free-market value, probably a penny for 4 tons of water. If you are willing to wink at the rules, you might rule a small kingdom of thousands of acres through lease-out, lease-back arrangements, dummy corporations, and compliant relatives. The bureau tends to ignore your little subterfuges. You might scout around a little to find Corps of Engineers land and work out some better deals yet. Get some insider knowledge, and you can buy land in a new project area and sell it later for 50 times as much, but the competition is heavy and vicious. Check out the operations of the Irvine Ranch as your model; it is one of the largest private landholders in the entire world that dips widely into taxpayer-subsidized Reclamation water. When you look into retirement and sell off your land, you can make your children and relatives rich.

now irrigation farmers claimed high profits in fields of vegetables, groves of nut trees, and orchards growing grapes, apricots, cherries, oranges, and lemons. As early as 1900 irrigation from groundwater covered a million acres. But farmers began to notice in the 1930s that the underground water levels were declining. Still, they continued to expand their operations. The project got its start when President Franklin Roosevelt released "emergency funds" to the Bureau of Reclamation in 1935 as a jobs effort that built canals from Shasta Lake in northern California to send water to the Central Valley and as far south as hot and dry Bakersfield at the edge of the Mohave Desert. By 1940 irrigation covered 3 million acres, with 35,000 wells pumping 6 million acre-feet each year, "far in excess of replenishment." In Tulare County in the San Joaquin Valley, the valley's groundwater table dropped 60 feet between 1920 and 1960, and another 33 feet in the next three years. Soon the valley farmers looked in astonishment when the very surface of the land sank down as much as 30 feet. In Kern County pumps had to reach for water from 275 feet in 1945 down to 460 feet by 1965. The Bureau of Reclamation's Central Valley Project was intended to guarantee water to these profitable but water-intensive farms. Life was more entangled with water than ever before. By 1951 the project had already consumed federal funds of a half-billion dollars, far more than the $170 million estimated by the state of California. From the project, Bureau of Reclamation water irrigated 109,000 acres belonging to the Southern Pacific Railroad, 80,000 acres owned by Standard Oil Company, 66,000 acres owned by three other oil companies, and 67,000 acres possessed by corporate farmers. By the mid-1980s, water was delivered to this Westlands Water District at $97 per acre-foot but local farmers, whose main crop was surplus cotton, were charged between $7.50 and $11.80. As complaints about unrecoverable costs built up, a 1978 review of reclamation costs discovered that only 3.3 percent of the total $3.62 billion spent by the Bureau of Reclamation had been recovered from irrigators. By 1980 government irrigation subsidies averaged $500 per acre per year and rose as high as $1,787 for each acre, often far higher than the market price of the land.

The State Water Project

Historian Norris Hundley, Jr., estimated that water flowed through a state-funded project from northern into southern California on such a scale that it could fill the Rose Bowl in Pasadena every hour and a half. The early centerpiece of the State Water Project was the Oroville Dam, built in 1959 in the hills north of Sacramento. Wide enough to span San Francisco's Golden Gate with a solid wedge that would have overshadowed the city's Transamerica Building, its reservoir could hold a trillion gallons. The dam's spillway, which roared at 70,000 cubic feet per second, was compared to a storm-filled Hudson River transplanted to northern California. The released reservoir water headed through a strange hydrological contraption to pass through the Delta, including reclaimed marshland where the Sacramento River meets San Francisco Bay. Then it entered the new California Aqueduct, which delivered 1.35 million acre-feet for Kern County at the southern end of the Central Valley and 2.5 million acre-feet destined for southern California cities and farms. This latter water barreled to a battery of pumps (each of 10,000 horsepower) that lifted it a total of 3,400 feet over the Tehachapi Mountains into southern California. Traveling 444 miles from its source, the project created the longest single stream in California, in this case encased in steel and concrete. Marc Reisner wrote, "To some engineers, the Edmonston pumps [raising the water over the Tehachapis] are the ultimate triumph, the most splendid snub nature has ever received; a sizable river of water running uphill," with a peak annual energy requirement of 6 billion kilowatt hours. The entire system of water removal infuriated the people of northern California to the extent that in 1982 they voted to deny the construction of the Peripheral Canal that in part paralleled the California Aqueduct as still another freshwater channel.

The Projects Fall Apart: Costs, Environment, Conservation

California's hydraulic empires unexpectedly began to fall apart in the 1960s and 1970s. They were vulnerable to glutted vegetable markets that led to unacceptably low prices. Some farmers had always defaulted on their payments for the water systems, and now, saddled with expensive equipment and rising water costs, too many went bankrupt. The nation's taxpayers, angered and frustrated over federal deficits and the spiraling costs of ever-larger pork-barrel projects, told their congressmen to turn against their old heroes, the farmers, and repudiate the exorbitant subsidies that had kept agricultural operators on the irrigated land. It became widely known that most of the funds had been skimmed off by wealthy farm corporations. A raised social conscience, awakened by labor leaders such as Cesar Chavez, questioned spending billions of dollars spent on reclamation that had not improved wretched working conditions for California field workers.

Beginning in the 1970s, environmental pollution hit the Central Valley. Decades of uncontrolled agricultural fertilizer and pesticide runoff accumulated unnaturally high concentrations of toxic chemicals, such as selenium and the manufactured toxic compounds aldicarb and dibromochloropropane (DBCP), in the still productive soils. Reports in 1988 showed a high incidence of stillbirths, children born with birth defects, sterility, and cancer. This was particularly evident on 400,000 acres of farmland along the western side of the San Joaquin Valley that lacked natural drainage. Simultaneously, the San Joaquin farmers were warned that continued high levels of irrigation from groundwater would so empty the freshwater aquifer that a saltwater aquifer down below would start percolating upward. When salt water invades an aquifer, it can never be restored. Farmers also received scathing criticism from a mix of environmentalists, agricultural economists, government policy makers, and the public for inefficient and wasteful water practices such as continuous flood irrigation instead of controlled management. In 1990 agriculture took 83 percent of California's water, but only contributing about 2.5 percent to the state's $735 billion economy. Farmers were told they could easily cut water consumption by 10 percent and reduce flood irrigation by 50 percent. Imperial Valley irrigators were told they could conserve about 250,000 acre-feet if they lined their earthen canals with concrete and accomplished better water management.

California cities were also urged to conserve water. In 1977 during a major drought, Los Angeles learned it was able to cut its water use by 13 percent. In three urban water districts, mandatory water conservation, well publicized and strictly enforced, led to reductions of 53 percent, 38 percent, and 47 percent. Immediate water savings via all these strategies were estimated at up to 1.6 million acre-feet, or about a third of the shortfall during the 1990 drought. In a shortage marketplace, a single acre-foot might rise to $300 to $400. This was not a major problem for cities that could afford several thousand dollars an acre-foot. But farmers had set $70 per acre-foot as the most they could afford to pay. Alternatives such as desalination were too costly, about $1,600 an acre-foot. Even simple wastewater reclamation could run more than $500 an acre-foot.

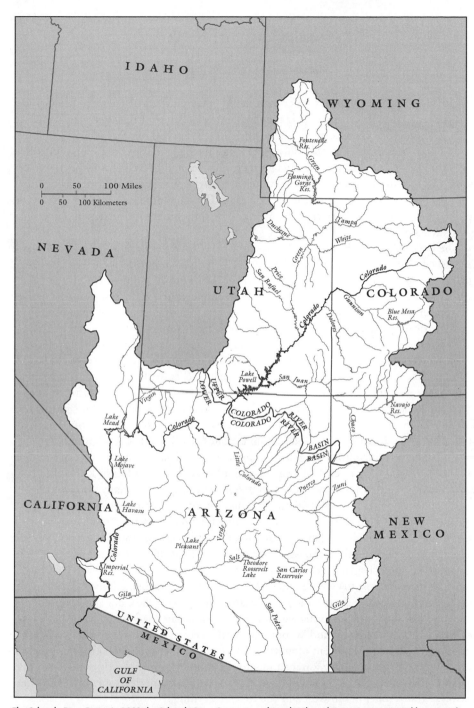

The Colorado River Basin. In 1922 the Colorado River Compact sought to distribute the river's water equitably among the surrounding states, but turned the river into a "deficit resource" because the announced total distribution of 17.5 million acre-feet actually has averaged 13 million acre-feet.

Reclamation Takes Over the West

Harnessing the Colorado River

The Colorado River moves far less water than the Mississippi, the Missouri, the Rio Grande, or even the Columbia, but it is arguably the most important river of the American West. Fed by historic streams like the Green, San Juan, and Gila, it descends a precipitous 13,000 feet from the Rocky Mountains in Colorado, cuts through the highlands of the Colorado Plateau, and into the Baja in Mexico, a 1,400-mile journey. The Colorado River runs through some of the most arid regions of the United States, which are nevertheless populated by growing numbers of people and increased agricultural production. They are more vulnerable to its natural whims than any comparable river in the world. The only other similar dependency is on Egypt's Nile River.

The Colorado River Basin—500 miles long and 200 miles broad—was a great blank space marked "unexplored" on maps as late as 1857; permanent human settlement had been limited to Anasazi and Hohokum Indians hundreds of years earlier and their Navaho and Zuni successors, white Mormon settlements in the nineteenth century, and a few nomadic natives and European trading posts. Its watershed includes 244,000 square miles of seven American and two Mexican states, and, when its waters flow in the All American Canal, an additional 600,000 acres of the Imperial Valley in California. Seventeen major dams and reservoirs have changed the river into a row of holding tanks. It is also one of the siltiest rivers in the world, which helped it carve the Grand Canyon. By the time it reaches the Baja today, it is also one of the most saline and unusable. The United States was compelled in the 1980s by international treaty to build one of the world's largest desalination plants to refresh the river for Mexico's use. The basin remains largely a region hostile to human existence, much less prosperity, except for narrow strips along the rivers. Even today, uninhabited public land covers 350 million acres of the landscape, on which livestock graze 250 million acres. This grazing land feeds 5 million head, only 8 percent of the beef cattle in the nation. River historian Philip L. Fradkin concluded, "Probably never in history has so much money been spent, so many waterworks constructed, so many political battles fought, and so many lawsuits filed to succor a rather sluggish four-legged beast. . . . No other activity uses so much land area in the West as cows eating grass." He added, "Through hay [alfalfa] water has flowed to cows" because at least 85 percent of Colorado water does not flow into Mexico but is spread annually over a patchwork of 2 million acres of irrigated farmland, mostly planted in low-value alfalfa and sorghums for cattle. (Another 10 percent is lost to evaporation, and 5 percent for municipal, mining, and industrial use.) There are almost three times more people than cows. Today, if the Colorado River stopped running, most of southern California would have to be evacuated, and large parts of Nevada, Utah, New Mexico, Colorado, and Wyoming would revert to frontier conditions. The Colorado River, which gets 70 percent of its water supply from snowmelt along the Continental Divide, has become the primary water supply for 21 million people mostly concentrated in four major urban regions—Las Vegas, Tucson, Phoenix, and Los Angeles. Journalist John Gunther wrote, "Touch water in the West and you touch everything."

What has happened to the Colorado River is a litmus test for everything that was done right (says the Bureau of Reclamation) or wrong (say environmentalists) with the western environment. For example, the river has continuously been a "deficit river" (more water allocated for irrigation and cities than it actually contains) since the Colorado River Compact was signed in 1922. The Compact—"a western equivalent to the Constitution"—was an attempt to distribute the river's water fairly among the surrounding states. Before the Compact went into effect, California, which contributed nary a drop to the river, was beginning to take the lion's share without admitting responsibility to other states' needs. By capturing the single largest amount of Colorado River water through the All American Canal, California's Imperial Valley could grow crops 12 months of the year, despite natural rainfall of 2.4 inches a year. Los Angeles, "growing like a gourd in the night," feared its population would outrun Owens Valley water and looked to Colorado River water as its next distant victim. Other states, particularly Arizona, feared that California might claim a prior-use right to more than its share. The Compact divided the river arbitrarily into two geographical basins at Lee's Ferry in Arizona just below the Utah border. The upper basin included Wyoming, Colorado, Utah, and some of New Mexico; the lower basin included southern California, Nevada, Arizona, and a slice of New Mexico. Each basin was entitled to 7.5 million acre-feet of the river's flow a year, another 1.5 million acre-feet was designated for Mexico, and to sweeten the settlement, the lower basin got an additional million acre-feet. The problem was that the agreement was based on a period of time when the average annual flow of the Colorado River was, it was learned later, at its highest peak ever at 17.5 million acre-feet. The actual typical flow was approximately 13 million feet, making it a river with a significant deficit. Not that the river felt the loss, but that western development asked more than it could deliver.

Planners and developers found it hard to admit the reality of the deficit and sought to bypass nature's problem with technological solutions. In 1946 the federal Department of the Interior set the foundation for all future assessment in a "blue book" (significantly subtitled, "A Natural Menace Becomes a National Resource") that identified 134 potential projects. It admitted that not even existing projects could be supplied with enough water. Yet the only answer seemed not to be restricted development defined by the arid geography, but more construction defined by faith in unlimited water. In 1956 the Colorado River Storage Project Act authorized more than 40 new projects. A series of dams and reservoirs included massive construction planned for Flaming Gorge at the Wyoming-Colorado border, Echo Park in Dinosaur National Monument, Glen Canyon just above Grand Canyon National Park, and two dams within the park itself. Only the sites at Flaming Gorge and Glen Canyon were dammed and filled following a vigorous national campaign by environmental groups. In 1958 Congressman Wayne Aspinall ("Mr. Colorado Development") desperately called for higher efficiency and in vain to increase water supply "by some means or other." Ten years later, in 1968, the National Academy of Sciences, the prestigious think tank, concluded, "The Colorado basin is closer than most other basins in the United States to utilizing the last drop of available water for man's needs." About 1978 a lawsuit from three environmental organizations, using the 1970 National Environmental Protection Act, demanded a comprehensive environmental impact statement for the entire Colorado River Basin. The suit argued that the system must be understood as a whole and not by project-by-project, state-by-state wish lists that revealed more about political compromise than environmental realities. Congressmen from the region, seeing their favorite pork-barrel projects threatened by a basinwide rationality, made certain the lawsuit got nowhere. The Colorado River Basin remained primarily a political entity of two overlapping power triangles: the "Iron Triangle" of congressmen, a federal bureaucracy, and water users, and local triangles of the state water engineer, water boards or commissions, and congressmen.

Boulder Dam in the 1930s

By the time of the Depression in the 1930s, the Bureau of Reclamation had planned ever-larger projects. This was encouraged by the interest of Franklin D. Roosevelt's New Deal in using federal funds to create jobs. One prime example was Boulder (Hoover) Dam. The storm-swollen Colorado River had devastated southern California in 1905 to 1907, when the river overwhelmed dikes and swept before it the grain, cattle, fruit, vegetables, hogs, barns, fences, houses, and structures of the new Imperial Valley irrigation system. The river threatened a repeat in 1909 that was barely staved off by herculean levee-building efforts. Arthur Powell Davis, the director of the Bureau of Reclamation, took a broad look at the entire Colorado River region and conceived of a comprehensive system of dams, aqueducts, and canals to exercise human control over the entire river. The grandiose project would be paid for by hydroelectric plants selling almost 4 billion kilowatt-hours power to the burgeoning cities of the Southwest. Boulder Dam was to be the system's centerpiece.

The construction of the dam required heroic organization, logistics, and technological know-how so unprecedented in scale and complexity that of 40 large state-of-the-art public works construction companies in the United States, only 3 chose to provide bona fide bids. The winning bid of $49 million came from a consortium called the Six Companies, who trusted their future to the skill and bravado of a single experienced civil engineer, Frank Crowe. (Several major American construction engineers came into their own with the dam project, including names like Kaiser, Bechtel, and Morrison-Knudsen.) Construction of Boulder Dam could be said to be the first modern public works project, since horses and mules were entirely replaced by trucks, bulldozers, power shovels, and draglines. A unique engineering innovation was the specially designed motor-driven rig, the "Williams Jumbo," equipped with thirty 144-pound man-operated rock drills to highball four 56-foot-wide diversion tunnels. All earth-moving and construction equipment, 80,000 volt power lines, and townloads of work-

Taming the Columbia Basin: The Hydroelectric Infrastructure

The Columbia Basin Project in the Pacific Northwest, notably its mobilization of electric power and water, was celebrated as essential to the industrial transformation of the Pacific Northwest. Popular radio folksinger Woody Guthrie was hired to publicize the project ("Grand Coulee Dam," "Roll on Columbia," "This Land Is Your Land") whose giant dams were to reclaim over a million acres of arid lands in the Northwest. The Columbia River Basin encompassed 258,200 square miles in Canada and the United States as the river flowed 1,214 miles to the Pacific Ocean. Its supporting rivers included the Kootenay, Salmon, Willamette, and especially the Snake. But unlike the Colorado, the Columbia River was not the irrigator of arid land, since it flowed through some of the wettest regions of North America. Instead, the first human value attached to the waters of the Columbia was food, its huners had to be imported. All supplies to build the dam were also imported, except local gravel and sand. The proposed concrete arched-gravity dam depended on the principle that concrete stands up best in compression. It was to be a wedge of 66 million tons of concrete, 45 feet thin and 1,282 feet wide at the top, reaching down 726 feet (60 stories) to become 660 feet thick at the bottom that would transmit the river's force into abutments (the rock walls of the canyon) and press its weight down into the canyon floor. Spillways 650 feet long and 170 feet deep prevented flooding over the top of the dam. Twin intake towers 395 feet high delivered water to the power plant at the downstream base of the dam. The four concrete-lined diversion tunnels required digging, drilling, blasting, and removing material for 56-foot-wide tubes averaging 4,000 feet long. These tunnels, designed to move the flowing water around the dam site, were themselves mighty engineering and construction feats.

Visitors yesterday and today say the sight of the dam matched its grand and dramatic setting in a deep red rock canyon. It was built in the forbidding Black Canyon of the Colorado abutting both Nevada and Arizona, surrounded by a sun-baked desert. Workers had been carried off prostrate (and died) when summer temperatures reached 120° or 130° F. The renowned English writer J. B. Priestly came to see and wrote in awe, "It is like the beginning of a new world, a world of giant machines and titanic communal enterprises. When you look down and you see the men who have made it all moving far below like ants or swinging perilously in midair as they were little spiders, and you note the majestic order and rhythm of the work, you are visited by emotions that are hard to describe, if only because some of them are as new as the great Dam itself." Boulder Dam was finished under schedule and below cost in 1937. It would not keep its title as the largest engineering project in the world, but it remains America's most memorable monument to public works that put an entire geographical region under control. Behind the dam, the reservoir called Lake Mead extends 108 miles upstream. With the Boulder Dam project, the Bureau of Reclamation gained new life and began to dominate water resource development in the West. It turned the lower Colorado, in Philip L. Fradkin's words, into "a set of liquid steps, a slow, drawn-out descent into the dry sandbox of the delta."

dreds of tons of salmon fish. Before the arrival of Europeans, the Chinook and other Indian tribes included the salmon in an elaborate web of social meaning that closely connected natural forces and the human world. When the troop of men led by Lewis and Clark in 1804 was succeeded by hordes of European traders and settlers, a unique connection between human and salmon was replaced by turning fish into a commodity. Technologies, such as steamships and salmon factories (canneries), forged a new interface that placed the new Americans as superiors rather than equals with the salmon and the Columbia River. The fish and the river became defined as mere elements in networks of economic power that stretched to the mines of Idaho, the wheat fields of Washington, the financial centers of New York City, and the policies and bureaucracies of Washington, D.C. In this way the federal Army Corps of Engineers was brought in to dredge the now obstructive sandbar at the mouth of the Columbia River and build jetties to hold the river in place. Similarly, the transcontinental railroad connection that terminated at Tacoma on Puget Sound allowed Americans to ignore the transportation value of the river. The transformation was complete in Richard White's quote from a dismayed participant: "What did it matter if a great good producing industry was destroyed solely for private gain, so long as few made fortunes and the fisherman and laborer starved amidst plenty? Capital, you know, must be protected."

Modern industrialization came to the Pacific Northwest with electrification. As we saw the Progressives exhort in Chapter 8, electric power meant a new kind of civilization. It was no longer centered on gritty, polluting, and heavy-labor factories that lived off coal and iron, but energy that, in White's words, had "no material expression." Electrification was its own combination of systems and networks: Edison's electric power, Westinghouse's alternating current that could send power over longer distances, and Parson's hydraulic turbines that claimed 94 percent efficiency. The result seemed to contemporaries a miraculous mix of nature (water), technology (electric power), and a benign version of industrialization (power utilities) to transform "a poor hardscrabble place." The resulting infrastructure, said White, "seemed more real than the physical river which almost disappeared among the kilowatts."

The change came through the plans laid out in 1938 by a large new federal agency, the Pacific Northwest Regional Planning Commission (PNWRPC). Its goal was to light great cities, power large factories, and revive an exhausted land by irrigation and chemical fertilizers. President Franklin D. Roosevelt justified the benchmark dam at Grand Coulee more as the source of thousands of new jobs (and a way to rebuild America's morale during the Depression) than any need for electric power or irrigation for the handful of settlers in the region before the dam was built. Its original $270 million cost would rise to $3.24 billion. The result in 1941 was the largest and longest concrete dam in the world, totaling 10.5 million cubic yards of concrete along four-fifths of a mile; 127 miles of steel pilings went into the west cofferdam alone; 22 million cubic yards of earth were moved; 130 million board feet of lumber were consumed in its construction; and 77 workers died. The dam became the classic example of the nation's enthusiastic funding of pork-barrel projects and its belief in the latest engineering technologies regardless of need. The Grand Coulee Dam offered the biggest single source of electricity in the world at over 2.1 million kilowatts. One benefit was so much electricity that it was the cheapest in the nation; homeowners did not bother to insulate their houses because the insulation cost more than electricity. What seemed to be superfluous power would, however, be consumed first to produce energy-intensive aluminum for tens of thousands of military aircraft for World War II, and second to supply the prodigious electricity needs to create plutonium for nuclear weapons at Hanford, Washington. In 1933 the main course of the Columbia River had no dams on it; by 1968, 11 major dams had tamed it. Not to dam the river was likened to washing the energy of 15,000 oil wells into the Pacific ocean. The cost was particularly severe for fisheries and led to the collapse of one of the great salmon populations in the world, directly related to dams on the Columbia River.

The Central Arizona Project

The Central Arizona Project (CAP) to channel and lift Colorado River water to the desert metropolises of Phoenix and Tucson has been completed at a cost of over $3 billion. CAP built an open canal of 333 miles with evaporation that can tap 50 percent of the water before it reaches its destination. It uses pumps and energy to lift the water 1,249 feet. The project stands in sharp contrast to Arizona's earlier underuse of the river water it was allocated under the 1922 Colorado River Company. The state of Arizona realized that southern California would not be satisfied with its river allotment of 4.4 million acre-feet while Arizona's share was 2.8 million acre-feet, but not directly available because most of its people and farmland were in the central part of the state nearly 200 miles from the river. Hence Arizona developed the Central Arizona Project to connect river and people, to take advantage of its rightful share of the water.

But with the new national mood of environmental awareness and reaction against pork-barrel projects, CAP has been criticized as wasteful of water and money to bring water to large air-conditioned cities, suburbs with swimming pools, and water-intensive golf courses, all set in the wrong geography and climate. Modern Phoenix, for example, sits in a huge natural bowl that holds heat and pollution. Its average summer temperature is 94° F, its average annual rainfall, little more than 7 inches. Both Phoenix and Tucson boomed after World War II with retirees and others seeking escape from the wintry Northeast. Air conditioning, which had been unusual in the prewar sun belt, became virtually universal to insulate tens of

The Problem of Salinity

Increased salinity turns fresh water into unusable salt water because of repeated irrigation applications. One 1981 report estimated that of the 120 million acre-feet Americans applied to irrigation, 90 million were lost to evaporation and transpiration use by plants, with the remaining 30 million acre-feet carrying virtually all of the salts from the originally 120 million plus residues in the soil. Critics with a historical or global background remembered the decline of ancient Near Eastern civilizations like the Sumerians as their farmland turned salty, and today Egypt and Iraq struggle with large-scale soil salinity. As water runs through an irrigation project, it picks up soil salts (plants capture the fresh water but leave the salts) that it carries downstream to the next irrigation project, where more salts are received, then to the next project, and so on. Evaporation of the large water masses held in reservoirs also increases the concentration of salts. In a typical example of the results, just before the Colorado River crossed the border into Utah, it held around 200 parts mineral salts per million. After it ran through irrigation canals of the local Grand Valley it reentered the river with 6,500 parts per million. Further downstream, on the lower Colorado River, farmers needed to irrigate with more water to compensate for the heavy salt content, or they made the difficult switch to more salt-tolerant crops that were less marketable. Further downstream yet, the United States built a costly desalination plant where the Colorado River crossed the border, following Mexico's vigorous protests about uselessly saline water. In Los Angeles and other cities, higher concentrations of salts meant higher costs as heaters and pipes corroded, water treatment became more intensive, more soap was consumed, water-softening bills rose, and trees and shrubs were damaged. By 1980 fully a third of the homes in southern California used bottled water for drinking and cooking, compared to 1 in 17 in the rest of the nation.

thousands of new immigrants from the blistering summers. No one worried about enough water for the growing population, until after the local aquifers became so depleted—at the rate of 2.2 million acre-feet a year—that the surface subsided and developed long earthquake-like open fissures. The millions of people, and millions of acres of irrigated farmland in Arizona, had nowhere else left to turn but the Colorado River. However, Arizona farmers soon felt betrayed because they could not afford the delivery costs, whereas the people of Tucson and Phoenix could pay thousands of dollars. The state of Arizona, which once gave priority to water for farming, did a turnaround in the early 1990s, allocating scarce water from CAP first to the growing cities.

Reconstructing Appalachia

The Tennessee Valley Authority

The grandest public works project intended to transform a region's geography and people was the Tennessee Valley Authority (TVA). Appalachia had been particularly devastated by the Depression. The problems in the 41,000-square-mile Tennessee River basin were daunting

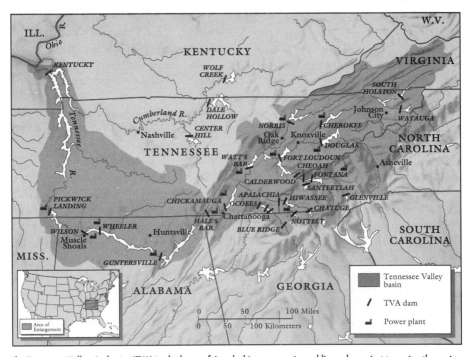

The Tennessee Valley Authority (TVA) in the heart of Appalachia was a major public works project to revive the region through flood control and electric power for industrialization.

because they seemed chronic: a combination of devastating floods, badly eroded lands, a deficient economy, and wealth removed by outsiders had created a steady outmigration. The 1933 TVA Act launched one of the world's most ambitious plans of regional development. TVA, governed by a three-person board of directors, enjoyed enormous autonomy with little government oversight. For the first time, a single federal agency was directed to address boldly all environmental and human development in a large region. The answer provided by TVA was a controversial public experiment that used a massive infusion of capital for planned economic development, particularly flood control and inexpensive power, to revive the people and reshape the environment into a supportive and habitable region. Advocates claimed that TVA would "control nature, not by defying her, as in the wasteful past, but by understanding her, and harnessing her in the service of humanity" through electrical energy by means of engineering know-how. Appalachia's geography would be transformed into a garden by means of managerial enterprise.

TVA's public works were the jewels in its crown—a system of 42 multipurpose dams and reservoirs for flood management. According to public works thinking, a free-flowing river went to waste unless a series of dams and reservoirs created safe electric power and large quantities of irrigation water at low cost. A free-flowing river was also an enemy if it was prone to destructive flooding, such as the Tennessee River, and a dam was a form of flood management. Hence the dams were intended to provide the answer to poverty in Appalachia by removing natural and social obstacles. TVA's foremost spokesman, David E. Lillienthal, wrote in 1944, "When [builders and technicians] have imagination and faith, they can move mountains; out of their skills they can create new jobs, relieve human drudgery, give new life and fruitfulness to worn-out lands, put yokes upon streams, and transmute the minerals of the earth and plants of the field into machines of wizardry to spin out the stuff of a way of life new to this world." By the 1960s TVA-based industrial development brought a rise in personal per capita income and halted the rapid outmigration. Local observer Harry Caudill called the TVA region "a new Ruhr," comparing it with Europe's largest and most concentrated industrial complex. Its advocates looked on TVA as the model public works project for the nation and for the world. TVA did devise a planned socioeconomic program of cheap power, fertilizer, reforestation, soil conservation and flood control. TVA also set up social programs in public health planning, adult education, and recreation that covered large parts of Tennessee, Kentucky, Georgia, Alabama, Mississippi, North Carolina, and Virginia.

TVA especially had a passion to produce cheap electricity as the leading answer to most of Appalachia's ills. Access to eight hydroelectric plants brought in energy-intensive aluminum, steel, and uranium enrichment plants. Between 1940 and 1970 TVA shifted its building policies beyond its system of dams to build coal-burning electric power plants. Over 80 percent of TVA power would come from these plants. TVA began buying its own strip mines in the 1960s, apparently heedless of the destruction that surface mining operations wrought on the lands of the people it claimed to serve. The rush to electrification also encouraged TVA to add nuclear power plants at Browns Ferry and Sequoyah in the early 1970s, but accidents, cost overruns, and design flaws often shut the plants down and halted construction at a Watts Bar nuclear facility in 1985. Despite the protests of environmental groups, TVA reopened its Sequoyah nuclear power plant in 1988 and the Browns Ferry plant in 1991.

The structure of TVA gave it enormous autonomy, which it exercised to avoid environmental controls that began to appear in the 1960s and 1970s. Critics complained that TVA was not accountable to the public and barely accountable to Congress. TVA was already the biggest strip miner and the single biggest polluter in the United States (aside from such behemoths as the U.S. Army and the U.S. Department of Energy). In 1961, for example, it contracted for 16.5 million tons of Kentucky and Tennessee coal at the lowest possible cost, which gave new life to declining regional strip mining. It continued to buy immense quantities of strip-mined coal to fuel its fossil fuel power plants that in turn became notorious air polluters. To compensate for its high levels of air pollution, in 1992 the TVA purchased pollution credits from the Wisconsin Power and Light Company. In one case, Tennessee's Tellico Dam project came under attack from environmentalists because it produced no power and only assured water levels for another hydroelectric dam. The dam's end seemed sealed with the discovery of a rare fish, the snail darter, that existed only in Tellico's domain. Construction was halted according to the regulations of the Endangered Species Act. Congress retaliated by exempting Tellico Dam from all laws, and the $100 million project was resumed. TVA had repeatedly claimed to be exempt from the environmental impact statements required by the 1970 National Environmental Protection Act (NEPA) for any major federal project.

TVA remains America's preeminent experiment at the "rationalization" of nature, the gathering of technological forces under a central control that seeks to make the most efficient use of resources. The environment, and its people, become absorbed into a larger public works infrastructure. Critics said TVA began as a benevolent paternalism and grew into a bureaucratic monster. TVA remains America's leading example of comprehensive planning for an entire region. It has not been duplicated anywhere else since.

The Corps of Engineers and the Tennessee-Tombigbee Connection

The Tennessee-Tombigbee Project was built to provide an alternative commercial waterway to an overloaded Mississippi, as well as to revive an economically depressed region. Talk about the value of a shortcut from mid-America to the Gulf of Mexico had been going on since the eighteenth century but began to receive serious attention after the Civil War, with feasibility studies in 1875 and 1913. The New Deal's TVA just to the north revived interest until World War II intervened. First authorization came in 1946 after the war, planning progressed in the 1940s and 1950s, federal funding got the project started in the 1970s, and it was completed in the mid-1980s.

Nicknamed the "Tenn-Tom," the waterway is 234 miles long, a combination of a straightened, deepened, and widened river, a canal that parallels a river, and the biggest earthmoving cut (27 miles through hilly terrain to connect the watersheds of the Tennessee and Tombigbee rivers) since the Panama Canal. Ten locks and five dams accommodate commercial barge traffic, but it is restricted to less than a third (105 by 585 feet) of the barge unit size allowed for Mississippi River traffic. The project's costs ran out of control, even accounting for inflation and engineering changes, from an original estimate in the 1950s of under $200 million to a total cost of over $2 billion. And $2 billion did not account for major cleanup and maintenance costs that were deliberately stretched over the cost horizon and discounted into the future. Brent Blackwelder of the Environmental Policy Center said of the costs, "You could build both an expressway and a railroad from Mobile to Corinth, Miss., for less than the cost of building Tenn-Tom." The project became the Corps' largest endeavor, with possibly the lowest economic reward (the barge traffic never met minimal expectations) and extreme environmental threat (by joining the different ecosystems of two large river valleys). Advocates of Appalachia and of local minority groups were deeply disappointed when contractors brought in their own skilled labor from Oklahoma and elsewhere. The depressed region found itself largely bypassed and ignored by the project, which was called "a cruel hoax" played on Appalachia. Blackwelder added, "A basic question of social justice arises over the expenditure of more than a billion dollars to put a barge canal through a very poor area of the country, an area which certainly has much more compelling needs than a barge canal." Even Tenn-Tom's biggest boosters now admit that the project will never be commercially successful and certainly not pay for itself. In its first two years barge traffic was less than a tenth (4.8 million tons) of the commercial activity predicted by the Corps (27 million tons a year), and it has not risen substantially. There is more pleasure boat activity than barge traffic.

Tenn-Tom was also the scene of the first major confrontation between the Corps and the newly established (1970) EPA. The confrontation became a microcosm for the larger public reassessment of the relationship between nature and technology and between economic growth and intangible public values. The more important environmental changes included the transformation of flowing water systems of rivers into still water systems of impounded lakes, drastically changing the environment for large and varied fish and wildlife populations. The Tenn-Tom project invaded over 100,000 acres of forest and farmland, including about 40,000 acres flooded by the project, and 51,000 acres of valuable hardwood forest and some of the richest wildlife habitat in the Southeast were sacrificed. Local universities complained about the permanent loss of historic, archeological, and unique geological sites. One of the prime environmental worries that the Corps usually did not concern itself about was the removal and dumping of 260 million cubic yards of excavated material. The project would take the biblical injunction literally: to level mountains and fill valleys. Environmentalists also became concerned about the low organic content of the excavated material that precluded farming or replanting. The greatest remaining unknown is still the ecological consequences of mixing the waters of the Tennessee and Tombigbee, and what permanent losses might occur with the intermingling of fishes, exotic plants, and different water qualities.

In the words of the Tenn-Tom historian Jeffrey K. Stein, the story of the waterway is "not only a history of what engineers can do, but also of how environmental politics came to influence what they may do." The Corps treated the construction of the waterway as "a foregone conclusion," which made its critics conclude that the agency was unlikely to make a complete and honest evaluation using the new guidelines of the EPA. The Corps took EPA-mandated environmental impact statements lightly until pressure was applied from private environmental organizations, the media, Congress, and EPA itself. EPA saw the project as its first major opportunity to establish environmental protection as a national agenda. The turning points that eventually favored the old-guard approach of the Corps was tepid approval by the President's Council on Environmental Quality in 1971, President Nixon's refusal to intervene in 1971, and two federal court decisions in 1972 and in 1980 that largely accepted Corps data and arguments that the economic benefits outweighed environmental costs.

The impact of the controversy on the Corps went further than environmental issues alone. For the first time, Corps planning, which had usually been hidden from public view, received great citizen scrutiny. The Corps was embarrassed by doubtful benefit-cost analysis, wildly optimistic predictions of barge traffic, its stonewalling on environmental impacts, and cost overruns. Tenn-Tom may be the Corps' last large civil engineering project, in large part because of negative environmental impacts that invariably result when public works reshape a region's soil, water, plants and animals.

Conclusion

Conquering nature's water supplies only entangled Americans more with their environment. In the humid East, battles over the last remaining pieces of forested land came down to whether watersheds for New York City or Boston can also suffer higher value residential development. In the West, Americans planted cities like Los Angeles, Las Vegas, Phoenix, and Tucson in outrageous places that could not support their growth and then captured water from hundreds of distant miles away in complex delivery structures. By the end of the twentieth century the scramble was on for the last trickles from rivers and lakes. Equally outrageous was the planting of crops, often water-hungry vegetables, onto thousands of acres of land characterized by rainfall—12 inches or less—that defined a desert. At least 80 percent of the West's water is still flooded or sprinkled or dripped onto farmland.

But putting water to work where it had not previously existed was a technological and management marvel, a new access to nature that seemed to double and triple what opportunities Americans could find in the West. Historian Richard White described this achievement as "nature and machines in proper combination [that] provided the opportunity for immense wealth and power." But building a dam does not guarantee a better world. "Humans had to be better than the machine [that was] dumb, servile, abject." He added that the outcome of the West's hydraulic civilization was in large part misused, distorted, and otherwise wasted by a consumption-centered society. The utopia that was expected in southern California or the Pacific Northwest did not emerge. "The [Columbia] river is not gone; it is our hopes for it that have vanished." The western geography will continue; a recognizable human society may not. White identified a failed relation with nature. This happened in large part because water systems, both natural and artificial, were not seen as integrated wholes across both space and time. Instead they were "conceptually disassembled" into parts that served farmers, factories, cities, power utilities, fishermen, barge owners, tourists, and environmentalists. The result, White concluded, was also an incomprehensible "babel of discourses: law, religion, nature talk, economics, science, and more." The blame lays not with the lack of water but with human actions.

The water infrastructure is at the center of western politics, economics, lifestyles, and social institutions. The basic pattern for the West has been to bypass its essential aridity by building dams, reservoirs, pipelines, and ditches to assure a dependable lifestyle, a satisfying measure of prosperity, and the promise of guaranteed future growth. The water infrastructure is more than a physical system that snakes across mountains and desert. It also involves the long arm of political muscle from state capitals and federal might in Washington, D.C. Its economic pipelines funnel cash and credit from New York, London, Tokyo, and Berlin as well as Washington. The costs have run into tens of billions of taxpayer dollars, with massive subsidies for the region and minimal payback. Direct benefits are hard to measure and assess, but the cities continue to mushroom, vegetables are delivered nationwide year round, and the lifestyle remains seductively attractive. The seemingly limitless frontier of the West is inevitably defined and limited by nature's water, which is running dry.

For Further Reading

The best place to begin on the western water infrastructure is still Marc Reisner's incisive and opinionated *Cadillac Desert: The American West and Its Disappearing Water* (1986), followed by the lucid and scholarly analysis by Donald J. Pisani, *To Reclaim a Divided West: Water, Law, and Public Policy, 1848–1902* (1992), and the powerful argument about hydrological civilization in Donald Worster's *Rivers of Empire: Water, Aridity, and the Growth of the American West* (1985). Because the principal issues and problems center on California, see the excellent comprehensive studies by Norris Hundley, jr., *Water and the West: The Colorado River Compact and the Politics of Water in the American West* (1975), and *The Great Thirst. Californians and Water, 1770s–1990s* (1992). In more specific terms, the long-suppressed critical analysis by Abraham Hoffman, *Vision or Villainy: Origins of the Owens Valley-Los Angeles Water Controversy* (1981), is indispensable reading. The reclamation movement has yet to receive a full treatment, but a good brief analysis is in Paul W. Gates, *History of Public Land Law Development* (1968), especially Chapter 22, "Reclamation of the Arid Lands," pp. 635–698, and see also Doris Ostrander Dawdy, *Congress in Its Wisdom: The Bureau of Reclamation and the Public Interest* (1989), and Dorothy Lampen, *Economic and Social Aspects of Federal Reclamation* (1930). Joseph E. Stevens's *Hoover Dam: An American Experience* (1988) provides a comprehensive and largely upbeat history. James R. Kluger's *Turning on Water with a Shovel: The Career of Elwood Mead* (1992) covers the history of reclamation from its earliest days to the halcyon dam-building 1930s in terms of one of the movement's major figures. The Colorado River story is well told by Philip L. Fredkin, *A River No More: The Colorado River and the West* (1981). Richard White's *The Organic Machine: The Remaking of the Columbia River* (1995) provokes rethinking of the water infrastructure as a "second nature" that does not liberate humanity from nature but creates more complex entanglements. Progressive science and ideology is best told in Samuel P. Hays's classic, *Conservation and the Gospel of Efficiency: The Progressive Conservation Movement, 1890–1920* (1959). The first hundred years of the U.S. Army Corps of Engineers is succinctly and critically told by Todd Shallat in *Structures in the Stream: Water, Science, and the Rise of the U.S. Army Corps of Engineers* (1994), which should be compared with Forest G. Hill, *Road, Rails, and Waterways: The Army Engineers and Early Transportation*, (1957), and Arthur Maass, *Muddy Waters: The Army Engineers and the Nation's Rivers* (1951). A provocative update of Corps policies and controversies can be found in Jeffrey K. Stein's *Mixing the Waters: Environment, Politics, and the Building of the Tennessee-Tombigbee Waterway* (1993). Much of western water infrastucture is tied to law and litigation, so special attention should be given to Robert G. Dunbar's near-classic, *Forging New Rights in Western Waters* (1983), with a vivid update by Charles F. Wilkinson's *Crossing the Next Meridian: Land, Water, and the Future of the West* (1992).

CHAPTER ELEVEN

HITTING THE WALL: ENVIRONMENTAL LIMITS IN APPALACHIA AND ON THE HIGH PLAINS

Look, you're all riding high out here on the midcontinent Plains. We all like to pretend that great things are going to last. But no [Ogallala] aquifer can sustain this rate of pumping. There goes your whole economy. This corner of the world is going to be an Appalachia without trees unless you get off your fannies and try to save it. I don't know if you can save it; I frankly don't know if it makes any sense for the nation to invest billions of dollars in a rescue project to keep a few million acres irrigated and a few hundred thousand people employed out here.

—Jim Casey, Deputy Chief of Planning for the Federal Bureau of Reclamation

Introduction: Environmental Challenges, Human Mistakes, and Industrial Misuse

Two large regions of the United States, Appalachia of the eastern mountains and the High Plains of the continental heartland, became major environmental challenges to successful human habitation. Native Americans had left large parts of both regions as either transitory hunting grounds or no-man's-lands between tribes. European invaders brought waves of severe environmental misuse. The impact covered a sixth of the contiguous United States across two geographical regions, involving significant areas of 19 states. Both regions remained chronically vulnerable. In Appalachia, the rugged terrain kept a rural society divided in isolated pockets. On the High Plains, the semiarid climate, with its lack of a reliable supply of water, kept traditional European farming on the edge of failure. These natural difficulties were compounded by human mistakes.

In Appalachia, first primitive farming destroyed thin soil, afterward the primeval forest was logged out, and later large seams of coal were stripped off, with the remains left to erode and poison watersheds. On the High Plains, the soil blew away in several cycles of dust storms of which the 1930s Dust Bowl was only one example. In addition, the incredibly large Ogallala groundwater aquifer (equivalent in volume to Lake Ontario) under the High Plains was reached in the 1960s by new pumping and irrigation technologies, to be rapidly depleted as a temporary means to irrigate crops. Overall, both the High Plains and Appalachia enjoyed so-called industrial golden ages that consumed the best of their respective soil and water, trees and coal. These eras of prosperity were temporary and cannot be repeated in either case because the natural resources are gone or fast disappearing. Both Appalachia and the High Plains were from the beginning environmentally misconceived, treated as simple economic resources rather than distinctive natural ecosystems. Very little of the profits were returned to sustain either environments or human populations. Both regions were like colonies exploited for the benefit of the rest of the nation; they might as well have been as distant and strange as Chad or Nepal.

As a result, both Appalachia and the High Plains persist with frontierlike conditions that cannot be self-sustaining. Despite decades of incredibly difficult and costly human effort, the farms and towns of both regions remained artificially constructed entities that are perpetually vulnerable to collapse. In Appalachia and on the Plains, poverty had taken on a grim persistence for decades and generations. Federal plans in the 1930s for resettlement outside each region were too suspiciously similar to Soviet farm collectivization during the same years for widespread acceptance by American society. Both "mountaineers" and "Okies" were forgotten and seemingly superfluous people. They were sometimes romanticized as people who accepted poverty—the lack of cash—because they would not risk the loss of personal integrity and family kinship. In reality, the mountains and the plains at different times were vast ghettos of unemployables. Attempts at rescue, however, has never been internal sustainability, but an attempt to integrate the regions into the consumer mainstream.

This willingness by the federal government time and again to shore up Appalachia and the Plains from total human collapse suggests an extraordinary public sense of responsibility (or guilt) toward the two vulnerable regions. In Appalachia, the dam building by the Tennessee

Valley Authority for electric power and flood control during the 1930s and 1940s committed hundreds of millions of dollars, gathered by the federal government from the nation at large, to revive a regional society. On the High Plains, new federal agencies, like the Soil Conservation Service of the U.S. Department of Agriculture, were given the idealistic mission of changing the treatment of soil in the Dust Bowl region from severe erosion to soil conservation. Here the final objective was similar, to create a working habitat that would protect the existing social pattern, local family farming, at almost any cost. Allen Batteau's words about guilt toward Appalachia can also be applied to the Plains: "From the wispy substance of these symbols—nature, folklife, and poverty—tens of thousands of high-minded citizens have been galvanized into action, millions of words have poured forth from journalists and novelists, and billions of dollars in federal programs have been spent."

The Demolition of Appalachia

Appalachia, Like the Plains, Was First a Barrier

Appalachia is a landlocked mountain massif covering 100,000 square miles. Many millennia ago Appalachia was as snow peaked and glacier filled as the Alps Mountains in Europe or the American and Canadian Rocky Mountains, all of which in some future eon will also be worn down to forest-covered peaks. Appalachia today encompasses several rugged regions defined by steep ridges and narrow valleys—the Blue Ridge Mountains, the Allegheny Mountains, and the Cumberland Plateau and Mountains. As late as 1850 one gazetteer characterized Logan County, in what was then western Virginia, as uninhabitable. In southeast Kentucky the terrain was so rough that railways did not reach county seats of Hazard, Harlan, and Whiteburg until the 1920s. Appalachia's assets are largely environmental—its varied and abundant forests, wild beauty, abundant water, thick veins of coal, and relatively uncongested land space. Appalachia's environment also shapes its liabilities—a maze of hills and valleys, a landlocked geography, no major river thoroughfare, and a forest so dense as to seem impenetrable. The activist lawyer Harry Caudill, native voice for justice and reform, wrote that Appalachia still "is a baffling profusion of hills and mountains with ridges and spurs running off them at close intervals. Between these great and small mountains lie narrow valleys, some no more than a dozen yards across and, even at the widest, seldom more than a few hundred yards. The entire region was [once] matted with an immense primeval forest, so dank and so dense as to amount almost to a jungle." To frontier Americans, mountainous Appalachia stood as an uninhabitable barrier to the fertile and desirable lands of the Ohio River Valley. Beginning in the 1780s it was left behind in the nation's westward expansion (see Chapter 3). When several of the original 13 states claimed western territory they looked beyond Appalachia. America's major experiment in orderly land reform, the Land Survey Ordinance of 1785, did not apply to Appalachia but to regions further west. The Northwest Ordinance of 1787, which helped forge national unity, also looked beyond Appalachia into the fertile and desirable Midwest.

A Prolonged Frontier History: The Appalachian "Mountaineer"

The first serious settlers into the Appalachian mountain country were unpaid Revolutionary War veterans who got land rights from the cash-poor Congress. Before them, since the 1730s, a thin scattering of English, Scottish, and Irish poor people had filtered into the region. They had been hardscrabble farmers in Ireland's northern counties who may also have endured near slavery as indentured servants in Virginia, North Carolina, and South Carolina. Most families simply carried with them an axe, hoe, rifle, cooking pot, a few clothes, and bedcovers strapped on the back of a horse or mule. They walked along hidden streams and clambered up densely wooded hills until they found a barely workable hollow. The land was no bargain. They were joined at the end of the century by a steady migration of veterans that continued for about 25 years until another war broke out in 1812, although people still showed up sporadically until about 1830. Appalachia's European history has been a prolonged frontier of seemingly perpetual subsistence farming. While the rest of the nation rushed westward, bound for Ohio and Illinois, Iowa and Kansas, and eventually California and Oregon, Appalachia turned inward to become its own "frozen frontier" with people scratching out a living in an inhospitable geography. On the eve of industrialization the region was a zone of scattered communities separated like islands from each other by a maze of inaccessible ridges.

The "mountaineers" who settled Appalachia's Cumberland Plateau in eastern Tennessee, says Harry Caudill, found themselves clearing and plowing slopes that should never have been disturbed. To them, a kingly farm life meant a small plot cleared out of a narrow bottoms or along a hillside, where they created a life based on Indian corn, squash, potatoes, beans, pork from near-feral hogs running and eating in the woods, perhaps milk from a cow, and home-grown tobacco and whiskey. Patches of corn yielded 40 to 90 bushels an acre, wheat, 30 to 60 bushels. An orchard first produced peaches, and later apples and plums. Their geography shaped them into family isolation, limited their access to transportation, kept them from enjoying modern housing and material goods provided by the Industrial Revolution, and cut them off from information (newspapers, travelers) about the outside world. Railroads moved in—the Lexington and Eastern, Louisville and Nashville, and Baltimore and Ohio—and tied the region closely to the great Pittsburgh steel mills. This powerful link broke Appalachia's isolation and connected it to the modern resource-hungry world. Mountaineers were said to intensely protect their separation from an industrial consumer society. Their lifestyle can also be described as an alternative to modern consumerism rather than an early stage in economic development. They placed a higher value on kinship ties, family household communities, and maintaining the family farm. But this lifestyle should not be romanticized, since it eroded the land and forced poverty on the people. Nor can bad health and poor education be explained away. Not much had changed in the 100 years since the Civil War. The inhabitants were forgotten and ignored, liked it that way, and have bitterly resented outside exploitation. Rural electrification and the radio, post offices and rural free delivery of mail, improved roads and the Model T Ford, and the mail-order catalog marked a great transition that began in the 1920s and 1930s. After the economic boom following World War II, "Mountain people could order the same clothes, hear the same news, and watch the same TV programs as do city dwellers." Yet in 1960 Harrison E. Salisbury of The *New York Times* linked mountain geography, the coal extraction industry, and human poverty as forces that had created a "depressed area" in West Virginia. Even Harry Caudill in

1963 urged resettlement in regional urban centers. A Berea (Kentucky) College professor concluded that what the Appalachian mountaineer saw as assets, others would see as liabilities—attachment to local community, hostility to outside "do-gooders," indifference to material things, and personal freedom rather than conformity to the expectations of outside society. This also showed up in the popular *Foxfire* books in which the students of North Carolina schoolteacher Elliot Wigginton wrote proudly about the "plain living" of their parents and grandparents.

Wasting the Birthright: Bad Farming

In the Appalachians, primitive agriculture exhausted and eroded the land, with no fertilizer, rotation, or cover crops. Caudill observed, "The precious humus accumulations of millennia vanished leaving semi-sterile, yellow sub-soil whose fertility was low and which annually declined in productivity. Sometimes the second year did not produce more than ten or fifteen bushes of corn per acre." By the late nineteenth century hillside mountaineers, stuck with sterile and eroding soil (of their own making), became sharecroppers or tenants. By World War I, perhaps a third of Appalachian farmers were living on and working the lands belonging to others. It provided a bare living that effectively pauperized the tenants, since they could grow only enough corn and pork for a year and never enough to make a surplus to get them back on their feet. During the New Deal mountaineers became dependent on new federal food relief programs. Husband and wife and brood of children lived on bags of dried rice, dried beans, meal and flour, and slabs of salt pork. Caudill and others described the mountaineer's condition as a "pathology of poverty," resistant to new ideas, fatalistic, suspicious, and distrustful.

Selling the Birthright: The Great Appalachian Forest

Inside Appalachia stands one of the most dense variety forests in the world—the Great Smoky Mountains complex that straddles eastern Kentucky and Tennessee, western North Carolina, and Virginia. It is a rare ecological treasure. It alone contains 130 different species of deciduous trees; all of Europe lists only 85. Nowhere else in America and the world, except perhaps in central China, can one see so many different kinds of trees so densely packed together. Northern hemlock and spruce join temperate beech, walnut, and elm trees, as well as southern tulip trees, linden, and sassafras, separated only by altitude, exposure, or soil. All of West Virginia was once, when white people first saw it, a 15-million-acre stand of trees, 90 percent deciduous hardwoods, the rest pines, spruce, hemlock, and cedar. Poplars ran 175 feet tall with trunks 7 or 8 feet in diameter. Over the last 130 years, in the blink of an eye, almost all of Appalachia has been razed to the ground, at first turned into noble ship hulls and later into mundane wooden supports in coal mines.

The Industrial Invasion Begins with Lumber

The first settlers had only interrupted Appalachia's great primeval forests with clusters of 5- or 10-acre clearings. The trees were cut for buildings, fuel, and fences, but were mostly burned as trash. The mountaineers' first commercial sale of trees was limited to a few trees cut and floated downstream to a mill. Their great poplars and white oaks, lesser oaks and chestnuts, were simply an enduring part of their landscape. After the Civil War a second European invasion by modern tree-cutting operations was far more intrusive. Outsiders introduced portable sawmills that followed the lumbering. Railroads began snaking into the region after the Civil War to bring out timber (and later coal). The lumber was not used locally, but became the raw material in the East and Midwest for house frames and siding, commercial buildings, fences, and railroad ties. A woodland that had been part of a local family livelihood for generations was drawn into the wide and perilous net of a capitalist economy. It transformed a "homeplace" into a commodity. This transformation became an unequal clash between two cultures, the self-sufficient largely cashless mountain farm life and the dollar-driven, profit-oriented commercial society. To the mountaineers $100 was a great fortune; they were ripe for the picking, and the timber hunters knew it. In 1875 huge forests were selling "dirt cheap" for as little as 26½ cents an acre. An outside lumberman once said, "All we want here is to get the most we can out of this country, as quick as we can, and then get out." The timber hunters set highest priority on the straight tall poplars, then sought out the white oaks and lesser oaks, and afterward the hickories and maples. Huge timbers, some 36 inches on the side and over 40 feet long, were used in the building of wooden ships. This process by which Appalachia lost its forest heritage continued until the Depression. There were a few brave attempts to preserve primeval forests, but the last disappeared during World War II. (The forests of Appalachia's two national parks and several national forests are not virgin forest.) A second lumber boom came after World War II. By the 1940s the region had produced enormous second-growth forests of oaks, walnuts, beeches, hemlocks, and poplars, but the forests were now largely owned by timber and coal companies. Leslie County on Kentucky's Cumberland Plateau "was a huge forest ruled by agents of Fordson and other coal and timber corporations." Mammoth logging operations clear-cut the forests and left behind eroding hillsides and abandoned hauling roads as well as enormous wastage and high fire risk from piles of logs and residue. Most of the wood went for jack props and collar poles in coal mines. Farmers were left with a treeless, scarred landscape that started eroding into their streams. An ecological legacy was forever lost to Appalachia. Enormous profits disappeared into the outside world while the ecological and human costs—waste, danger, and ugliness—remained inside. A "pitiful remnant of cull and second-growth timber cloaks the plateau today." Not the least, many mountaineers, hired by timber companies to cut and ship the trees, were maimed and killed.

The Birthright Denied: Coal Mining and Stripping the Land

The Grab for Mineral Rights: The Coal Mining Infrastructure Overwhelms the Land

Early in the twentieth century a coal mining infrastructure took over Appalachia's landscape like a great net made tighter and tighter. It was the era of great cash-rich corporations: Inland Steel, Consolidation Coal, Elkhorn Coal, United States Coal and Coke. They spread over Appalachia, building mines and tipples surrounded by grimy company towns called "coal camps." Coal barons manipulated state and local politics to keep their industry largely unregulated in a workplace extremely prone to accidents leading to injury and death. The first great coal boom invaded Appalachia in the 1880s and 1890s, to be repeated between 1912 and

1927. In 1887, for example, West Virginia produced almost 5 million tons of coal. By 1897 this rose to over 14 million tons, and by 1912 almost 67 million tons. The "Pittsburgh" coal seam of the northern Appalachian basin (West Virginia, western Pennsylvania, and eastern Ohio) has been called "the world's most valuable mineral deposit." It is 6 to 8 feet thick over thousands of square miles in "benches" of alternating coal and shale. Nearby, "Kentucky Bituminous High-Volatile A Coal" has the highest heating value (BTU/lb.) of any of America's common coals, at least a third higher than coal from the American West in Wyoming, Colorado, or North Dakota. This Appalachian coal went to make steel in Pittsburgh, to fuel the nation's steam locomotives, stoke fleets of steamships, feed household furnaces, and produce steam in electric power plants. Coal was the single most important energy source for the first major phases of America's industrialization. Even when coal consumption by the railroads, the steel industry, and home heating virtually ended by the 1960s, coal remained the source for dyes, explosives, plastics, antiseptics, drugs, and antioxidants and solvents.

Mountaineers rarely understood the mineral wealth under their land, which sometimes contained several thick seams of high-grade bituminous coal. Often the coal mining companies were pleasantly surprised when, on a single acre, several coal seams yielded 15,000 or 20,000 tons of coal for which they had paid 50 cents. When mountaineers sold their mineral rights, they still had the illusion of property ownership because they believed the agreement did not touch their houses and animal sheds, patches of soil, scattering of trees, or wells and streams. Most agreements, however, were "broad-form" deeds, which passed to the coal companies rights to excavate for the minerals, to build roads and structures on the land, and to use the surface for any purpose "convenient or necessary" for company business. Broad-form deeds included the right to take timber for mining props, to divert and pollute the water, and to cover the landscape with toxic mining refuse. When local people first complained about the above-ground impacts of underground mining, the courts decided against them: The landowner rights were perpetually "servient" to superior or "dominant" rights of the owner of the minerals. Caudill reported that Kentucky's highest court held that "a majority of the people had 'dedicated' the region to the mining industry." The value and meaning of property changed. For generations the land had been measured by crops produced by plow and hoe; now it became a commodity priced by distant markets. By 1910, 85 percent of the coal lands had been locked up in absentee corporate hands, together with 75 percent of the remaining salable timber. In the space of 20 years, a primitive but independent agricultural region was transformed into an industrial servant.

The Momentum of Strip Mining and Its Great Machines

Surface or strip mining so destroyed the landscape that it ended any hope for Appalachian recovery. After World War II, enormous dragline or stripping power shovels, some of which were the world's largest machines, began stripping away overburden (trees, soil, and layers of rock above the coal seam) and coal in single truckload-sized swipes. The great bucket of Consolidation Coal Company's "Gem of Egypt" can remove 200 tons in one pass in the Egypt Valley of southern Ohio on the northwestern edge of Appalachia. "Gem" had a double meaning, since it also stands for Giant Earth Mover. To produce 1 ton of coal it was sometimes necessary to strip off as much as 30 tons of overburden. The advantage was that productivity of open pit mines is very high, at perhaps only one-quarter the costs of underground mining. Conventional contour strip mining started with an initial cut along the outcrop line on the

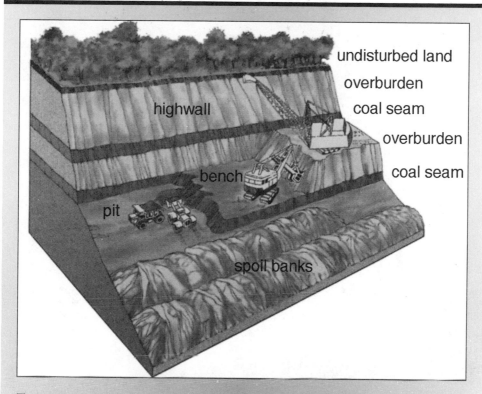

undisturbed land
overburden
coal seam
overburden
coal seam
highwall
bench
pit
spoil banks

THE COAL AUGER was a gigantic horizontal power drill 6 feet in diameter. It looked strikingly like the front end of one of the sand creatures in the movie *Dune*. The coal auger drilled directly into the coal seam, "spewing out huge quantities of the mineral with each revolution of the screw." The coal auger came into demand because it recovered coal from the highwall side of the contour strip mine that might otherwise be lost. Not the least, it was relatively cheap and used few workers. One triple-head auger in West Virginia averaged 225 tons of coal production per shift. But it was an environmental horror. Wherever the auger went, it severely undermined a coal-bearing hill. Even so, it reached only so far underground. Even if a large amount of valuable coal remained, it could no longer be reached. An auger operation was considered highly successful if 20 percent of the coal had been removed.

mountainside. The overburden was indiscriminately dumped over the side of the hill and the underlying coal extracted. The resulting excavation left a high collar of spoil around the mountain. When this contour mining became illegal in the 1960s, it was replaced by the so-called haulback method that eliminated the dumping downhill of the spoil and included reclamation as part of the continuous process. This restoration involved reshaping the broken terrain from strip mining into a gentle, rolling contour. A layer of limestone and topsoil was laid on the surface. It was finally planted in grasses and trees to prevent erosion. When strip mining included reclamation as part of the whole operation, it was supposed to control the

THE D-9 BULLDOZER is the largest built by the Caterpillar Tractor Corporation. It weighs some forty-eight tons and is priced at $108,000 [1972 dollars]. With a blade that weighs five thousand pounds, rising five feet and curved like some monstrous scimitar, it shears away not only soil and trees but a thousand other things—grapevines, briars, ferns, toadstools, wild garlic, plantain, dandelions, moss, a colony of pink ladyslippers, fragmented slate, an ancient plow point, a nest of squeaking field mice—and sends them hurtling down the slope, an avalanche of the organic and the inorganic, the living and the dead.— Harry Caudill, 1972

all-too-common overflow of poisoned water and prevent spill of waste material into hollows or low areas where people might live. Restoration was supposed to prevent disturbance to the landscape and contamination of more distant streams. More to the point for industry, the haulback method also used much less equipment, mostly wheel loaders, trucks, dozers, and scrapers. As one textbook description blandly put it, "The result of mountaintop removal is the transformation of a rugged topography into more level land, but in the process total coal recovery is obtained." Even with the most careful reclamation, strip mining destroyed the land and usually eliminated the ability of mountaineers to stay in their old home place. A court case in 1949 of local citizens in Pike County, Kentucky, complained that the Russell Fork Coal Company had cut off the top of a mountain, leaving unstable rubble that descended on communities in August 1945 in a cloudburst and flash flood. The court determined the river of debris was an act of God. Strip mining often removed a piece of mountain land from the tax rolls entirely, and thus brought a negative ripple effect that took away resources from schools, public health, roads, sewers, and other services.

People at Risk: A Matter of Public Health

Local mountaineers were ill prepared for industrialization, since their lives were previously tied to small patches of land. They forsook the land for the apparent safety of regular wages in coal mines. Mountaineers found themselves put at extreme levels of industrial risk that would have even shaken the nervy steel mill workers of Pittsburgh. Coal mining was historically notorious for accidents that maimed and killed. Miners also risked explosions from finely powdered coal, loss of consciousness or death from methane, nerve degeneration (convulsions and facial distortion) from gaseous hydrocarbons, and the hacking debilitation and early death from black lung disease. The result was gangs of cripples that looked like gassed survivors from World War I trench warfare. The mountaineer families moved into company-sponsored housing. Company towns were miserable habitations with rickety stinking schoolhouses, little doctoring, no sewage disposal other than into a downhill "swamp," and no work alternatives. The coal companies were very paternalistic, even creating their own town currencies called "script," which was used to pay ever-mounting debts at the company store. Workers' compensation for mine-injury cripples was marginal; if a miner could not work any longer, he and his family received a rent-free month in the company house before being thrown out. Caudill tells of "rat rows" in nearby hollows and neighboring towns where these discards tried to live on meager insurance checks and a vegetable garden.

When mountaineers realized their homes might be torn down in a strip-mining operation and their health frittered away as they toiled deep underground, they fought back. But they had no heart for politics or community action; even newly arrived union organizers in the 1920s found them uncooperative. By 1919 labor leader Samuel Gompers called the region an industrial feudal society. Disputes erupted into mob violence, by police as well as strikers, at Matewan in 1920 and Blair Mountain in 1921. The Depression intensified the Harlan County, Kentucky, mine wars of 1931. An important turnaround only came after disaster, when on the day after Christmas in 1945, 24 men died in an explosion and fire in Bell County, Kentucky, followed four months later by the enormous mine explosion that killed 111 men at Centralia, Illinois. This led to an unusually competent and pathfinding federal review of health conditions in the bituminous coal industry chaired by navy admiral Joel T. Boone. The "Boone Report," published in 1947, shattered the industry-led silence about mine conditions. The new United Mine Workers' Welfare and Retirement Fund levied 5 cents per ton mined by the participating mine operators. The fund provided small but acceptable retirement pensions, disability pensions, and a broad health-care program. World War II did bring a boom time that temporarily raised hopes. Post–World War II abundance nationwide did not reach Appalachia. Disinterested county and state governments, dominated by coal companies, and lacking a sufficient tax base, meant that the inhabitants of Appalachia endured shoddily built highways, rickety stinking schoolhouses, crumbling courthouses, no county libraries, and rusting steel bridges. Between 1950 and 1960, 25 percent of the people left for jobs in the northern industrial cities, "one of the most drastic population shifts in the nation's history."

Attempts at Recovery and Restitution

Public interest in Appalachia heightened in periods of national reform, such as the Progressive Era around 1900, the Depression of the 1930s, and the Great Society of the 1960s. The Progressive conservation movement spearheaded by President Theodore Roosevelt and his forest service head, Gifford Pinchot, concluded that the self-destructive and headstrong individualism of the mountaineer wasted human and natural resources. Blame for the chronic agricultural depression, said L. C. Gray of the U.S. Department of Agriculture, must be laid on too many farmers working too much marginal land, and not markets or price conditions. Eventually public responsibility toward the poverty stricken and unemployed became a national agenda during the 1930s Depression. A miner in Morgantown, West Virginia, told a journalist, "These folks in the city are yapping a lot about the depression. We had the depression in the camps years before they ever heard of it." The New Deal embarked on the Tennessee Valley Authority (TVA) and the generation of clean electric power to save Appalachia. TVA's production of nitrates for fertilizers, flood control, and rural development would create a brave new world, in Allen W. Batteau's words, populated by "heroic engineers, grateful citizens, progressive farmers, and [a few] suspicious hillbillies." The cycle of public guilt and taxpayer money funneled into Appalachia revived during President Lyndon Johnson's welfare projects of the Great Society. In 1960 the Appalachian Governor's Conference used the word "Appalachia" as a synonym for poverty. The "three weird sisters of poverty, crime, and decay" were blamed on short-sighted business greed, venal and corrupt politics, the collapse of public infrastructure, education, and medical services, and a suspicious and delinquent population. Federal officials and the *New York Times* compared Appalachia to depressed Third World nations. A national magazine concluded, "People in this backward land are oppressed by overpopulation and underemployment, by sheer neglect, ignorance, and despair. No less than Latin Americans or Africans, they can use more American aid. They are entitled to it because they are our own people." Books by Harry Caudill (*Night Comes to the Cumberlands* in 1963) and Jack Weller (*Yesterday's People* in 1965) brought to the public eye the industrial exploitation of the environment and debt peonage of the people in the coal camps. President Johnson rushed a bill through Congress in March 1965 that created the Appalachian Regional Commission and the Appalachian Development Corporation to bring the region into the American economic mainstream. It appropriated $1.2 billion for road building, hospitals, schools, sewage treatment, and land rehabilitation, but a pork-barrel 80 percent was earmarked for roads instead of environmental protection and locally appropriate jobs. Disasters continued into the 1960s and 1970s. A Consol mine at Farmington used illegal equipment that killed 78 men. The collapse of a Pittston company's slag dam at Buffalo Creek in 1972 killed 125 residents and threw thousands out of their homes. Thousands of miners still went through the slow death from pneumoconiosis caused by coal dust.

America's 130-Year Mistake: Appalachia's Environmental Lesson

Appalachia can be called America's 130-year environmental mistake. In that time, Appalachia had its own natural wealth —timber and coal—wrested violently from the land at immeasurably higher environmental and human costs, estimated into the hundreds of billions of dollars with very little returned. Caudill wrote that the nation "cannot afford to leave huge islands of its own population behind, stranded and ignored." Appalachia had been treated as a mere colonial appendage to the industrial East and Midwest rather than an integral part of the nation. One community worker wrote, "We were strangers in our own country, among people who did not seem to understand us, and whom we did not seem to understand."

Appalachia embodied "anticivilization," a people whose values contrasted with the American mainstream. The tightly knit bonds of family and kinship meant that a simple lack of cash—poverty—was not the decisive fact about a people's condition. Appalachian subsistence questioned the mainstream American fetish about commodities and consumption. Appalachians (and the Plains farmer, as we see later) had for a brief time offered the possibility that their isolated society might represent a different response to the environment and human needs rather than be stigmatized as lower and more primitive stages of economic progress. The problem of Appalachia was not its "underdevelopment," but instead its domination by an uncontrolled and extremely invasive coal extraction industry (almost a caricature of capitalism). Harry Caudill's message in 1963 was that environmental destruction also leads to the destruction of human resources: "In all America there is no worker who occupies a position more exposed and helpless than the men who dig coal in these little pits." Caudill wondered, "If there had been a decent regard for the land in eastern Kentucky, its mountaineers might have thrived like the Swiss." He compared strip mining of the American landscape to what Roman plows did to Carthage or chemical defoliants did to Vietnam. Appalachia's human tragedy is compounded by environmental collapse—abandoned strip mines, industrial waste, and ugliness beyond comprehension. Today, in an ironic twist, states like West Virginia, in order to generate revenues, energetically seek out toxic chemical waste dumping from other states. There is also a bittersweet irony because Appalachian farmers try to sell their cattle, hogs, and other produce on the market in competition "with the tremendous avalanche of meat and grain which annually pours out of the Great [High] Plains."

The High Plains

Semiarid Climate: The Environmental Challenge of the High Plains

Does climate still matter? One of the major objectives of human toolmaking has been better protection for humanity against too much cold and heat, rain and snow. In the long run, however, climate, because it is extremely fluid and fickle, is the part of the environment that humans find the most difficult to control. Climate still influences construction, transportation, communications, fisheries, forestry, and tourism. Above everything else, agriculture is climate dependent to the extreme. Agricultural plants and domesticated animals need the right proportions of rain and sun and temperature to prosper. Aside from Alaska, nowhere in the United States was this agricultural vulnerability to a climate more formidable than on the High Plains (also known as the Great Plains). The High Plains extend north-south entirely across the United States in an approximately 300-mile-wide swath whose eastern border is roughly at the 98th meridian (which neatly bisects the nation into eastern and western halves). The western border is at the foothills of the Rocky Mountains, where the Plains altitude can run as high as 5,000 feet above sea level. It is a region of startling climate extremes, buffeted in the summer by a hot sun, dry heat, a perpetual wind, and limited rainfall. The winters are severely cold, with blizzards of wind and snow. The region is labeled semiarid because rainfall averages 12 to 20 inches a year. "Semiarid" is a relative term because most American farming had taken place where rain was 30 to 40 inches a year. Corn, which was the frontier settler's primary crop, demanded 30 or more inches.

Not that the High Plains did not have plants. The original Plains grew a variety of grasses that lived in a symbiotic balance with each other. The balance involved poorly understood natural forces such as enormous grass fires, climate fluctuations, animal grazing, together with low-level Native American interference. Such grasslands would have continued indefinitely for millennia. Today over 90 percent of the Plains is sodbusted—the plow-up of the grassland resulting in wind-erodible soil—and planted in so-called foreigners, with wheat the dominant crop. Bare soil exposed by plowing was also invaded by useless weedy annuals from the Old World such as cheat grass, Russian thistle, and halogeton. Cultivation of the High Plains grasslands increased ecosystem damage by soil profile disturbance due to tillage, soil erosion, and accumulation of toxic materials. After heavy machinery became commonplace early in the twentieth century, half of the cultivated land of the Plains was affected by "tillage pan," an impervious, compacted subsoil layer. This disrupts water percolation, root growth, and the effectiveness of fertilizers. The chemistry of Plains soil under cultivation for the last century changed, including the loss of half the nitrogen, up to 40 percent of the sulfur, and up to 30 percent of the potassium. Crop yields began to decline until about the mid-1950s, when chemical fertilizers were widely introduced. Yields suddenly surged upward, but natural fertility has collapsed with the "mining" of natural soil chemical compounds. Botanist John T. Curtis added, "Man's actions in this [grassland] community almost entirely result in a decrease in its organization and complexity and an increase in the local entropy of the system. . . . Man, as judged by his record to date, seems bent on asserting the universal validity of the second law of thermodynamics, on abetting the running-down of his portion of the universe." The natural diversity that would have saved an ecosystem under stress from drought had been lost through monoculture crops. Until the Dust Bowl, most Americans believed the optimistic but mistaken credo that nature was strong enough to resist destruction by human agency.

From a global environmental perspective, the Plains is another zone of "frontier cultivation" that goes back to the earliest archeological records of civilization in Europe, Africa, and Asia. Frontier cultivation describes the boundary land between land plowed and used for growing crops and land used for grazing and hunting. The question for the Plains, according to geographer William Riebsame, and reinforced from the earlier views of A. H. Clark and Paul Sears, is whether the region could support "the human creation of socially nurturing landscapes," or was it a grassland too fragile for European settlers to build a society? Plains farmers worked closer than other pioneers on the edge of survival and were less likely to sustain themselves. Lured by generous homesteading laws, and patriotically moved by Manifest Destiny that American settlement could not fail, several generations of farmers attempted to force changes in the vegetation, soil, topography, and hydrography of the Plains. The small farmer was beaten down and often driven out by the combination of drought and economic depression. He was replaced by consolidated capital-intensive industrial farms that by 1980 were three times larger than the typical settler's farm. Riebsame concludes, "After a century of settlement and transformation, the Great Plains still spark controversy over the proper human use of semiarid grasslands."

Early History of the Plains

The "Great American Desert"

Lt. Zebulon Pike in 1810 first shaped American opinion about the High Plains when he reported that "a barren soil, parched and dried up for eight months in the year, presents neither moisture nor nutrition sufficient to nourish the timber. These vast plains of the western hemisphere may become in time equally celebrated as the sandy deserts of Africa." For most of the first half of the nineteenth century, the High Plains was described by explorers and travelers as the "Great American Desert," a label first applied by Major Stephen H. Long in 1821. Edwin James, a botanist with Major Long, wondered how local animals survived in the region. As late as 1856 Joseph Henry, the influential secretary of the new Smithsonian Institution, concluded, "The whole space to the west, between the 98th meridian and the Rocky Mountains, denominated the Great American Plains, is a barren waste . . . a country of comparatively little value to the agriculturalist." After the Civil War the military commander of the Plains region, Gen. William Tecumseh Sherman, reported that western settlement reached its workable limits at the 99th meridian, "fit only for nomadic tribes of Indians, Tartars, or buffaloes." The actual visible scene across the American heartland was, and is, daunting—a minimalist landscape of a sea of grasses that seemed to flow like waves, bounded only by the flat surrounding horizon and the infinite sky. Any human presence shrank into nothingness. Today for most Americans, the great grassy flatness seems interminable and a mediocre place, with few scenic or picturesque stops, as they rush across the 1,000 miles between Chicago and Denver on parallel cross-country routes, interstate highways 70 and 80, and U.S. highways 6, 12, 20, and 30.

Settlement on the High Plains: America's 70-Year Mistake

When settlers in the East labored to cut down trees, pull stumps, dig out boulders, and urge a mule up a steep slope to pull a plow, they dreamed fitfully of treeless, rockless, and flat fertile soil. They began to peer from the edge of the familiar forest to try their hand at farming the unfamiliar tall-grass prairie of 30 to 40 inches of rain a year that began at the Indiana-Illinois border. Much to their delight, settlers discovered that prairie land in Illinois and Iowa was the best farmland yet—flat, treeless, and covered with prime soil as much as 6 feet deep. It is still America's extraordinarily productive corn belt. The conquest of the midwestern tallgrass prairie encouraged settlers to move further west onto the dryer short-grass High Plains. The Plains were the last frontier of the lower 48 states. In it homesteading began in the 1870s and continued into the 1910s and 1920s. To the nineteenth-century American, settlement of the High Plains was the final chapter that would complete the nation's Manifest Destiny to domesticate the continent. Back in 1831 Joshua Pilcher told Congress that anyone who saw the open grasslands as an impossible obstacle "must know little of the American people, who supposes they can be stopped by any thing in the shape of deserts." Thus the High Plains was first populated under a boomer psychology that often denied geographical realities and would lead to extraordinary hardships and wholesale failures. Like troops sacrificing themselves on the battlefield, fresh waves of farmers seemed always ready to step forward. When they lost their crops under a rainless bleaching sun, and began to starve, newly settled farmers felt betrayed. Paradoxically, they also believed they had betrayed the

American dream by their failure. They believed it was unpatriotic (and possibly even sinful) to desert their homesteads.

Newly arrived settlers learned painfully that less corn or wheat grew on 160 acres in western Kansas than sprang forth on 40 acres in Illinois or Iowa, despite more difficult labor and higher financial risk. New waves of settlers endured the invasion of millions of grass-hoppers in the summer of 1874 and escaped death during the desperate winter of 1874–75. They reluctantly shifted from corn, the symbol of American prosperity, and turned to wheat, strange new winter wheat—hard Turkey Red wheat brought by newly arrived Russian-German Mennonite communities—instead of spring wheat. Russian tillage methods, unlike those from the humid eastern United States, worked better in the unfamiliar Plains soil and climate. Despite these innovations, settlers were still forced back by the lack of rain or ground-water. Water became the Plains' obsession. Congress tried to legislate an environmental fix by imposing an eastern landscape of trees and meadows on the short-grass Plains. The Timber Culture Act of 1873 promised to give free title for 160 acres to each farmer who planted trees on one-quarter of his claim. He had to keep them growing on 40 acres for ten years, in which time it was believed that the trees would eventually spread and improve the climate. Both trees and climate change failed. In 1877 Congress tried again with the aptly named Desert Land Act, which discounted a full section of 640 acres to settlers who would water their land. The resulting irrigation "ditches" were often no more than plowed furrows that ran uphill and downhill. Both acts produced more fraud and speculation than honorable results. It also became abundantly clear that the celebrated 1862 Homestead Act, which restricted settlers to an inadequate 160 acres, failed to suit conditions beyond the 98th meridian. The five years of farm residency it required before they received free title was soon labeled "the period of star-vation." The 1912 passage of the Three-Year Homestead Act admitted that the point of star-vation was far short of five years.

The Temporary Miracle on the Plains: The Desert Becomes a Garden

Then a seeming miracle happened. For a decade—approximately 1878 to 1887—extraordi-narily heavy rains fell on the High Plains country west of the 97th meridian from Texas to Canada. A rush of new farmers concluded that by plowing up the sod, they had altered the forces of nature. In 1878–79, the land office at Bloomington, which covered southwestern Kansas, entered new homesteads totaling over 307,000 acres. New arrivals in western Kansas were undeterred when they rode past deserted claim shanties abandoned during the drought of three or four years earlier. "Rain follows the plow" became the popular slogan and gained sup-port in scientific circles. This was not a strange claim in the age of Manifest Destiny; God, after all, was on America's side. In addition, farmers, scientists, and the public widely believed that the spread of the railroads and telegraph also brought rains, since the steel rails and electric wires modified natural electrical cycles in an arid place to induce the fall of moisture. Civil War veterans also remembered that artillery fire at the Battle of Gettysburg seemingly contributed to several days of heavy downpour immediately after the battle. If Sherman would use more cannon to clear the Plains of Indians it might have the added benefit of bringing rain.

Between 1885 and 1887 the population of the western third of Kansas rose 370 per-cent, from 38,000 to 139,000 people, just as the rains inexplicably halted. The boom ended more suddenly than it began, its collapse accelerated by the disastrous blizzards in early 1886 in which 80 percent of all range cattle died. Drought returned in the late summer of 1887. In the successive summers of 1889 and 1890 farmers got only 2.5 bushels of wheat an acre in western Kansas and an even less productive 8 bushels of corn. Farm families holding some of the most fertile land in the world were living, they said, on "Andersonville fare," remembering the notorious Civil War prison in the South. Between 1890 and 1900 the 24 counties of western Kansas declined from 14,300 to 8,900 farms. Across the Plains 200,000 settlers felt fortunate to escape the region, now trailing a new slogan, "In God we trusted; in Kansas we busted." (In the author's house sits a mantlepiece clock that went by wagon to Kansas in 1883 and was back in Illinois by 1891.) Few people were ready to acknowledge that dry times were the norm rather than the exception, and most settlers (and bankers and businessmen) waited expectantly for the next rainy season and a return to "normal" weather. The rains returned in 1891 and 1892, but a combination of more drought and the nationwide financial collapse, the Panic of 1893, once more created desperate conditions in western Kansas. This was followed in 1894 by one of the driest years on record (only 8 to 9 inches of rain) and a particularly heavy plague of grasshoppers. In 1901 U.S. Geological Survey official Willard D. Johnson called the rush to settle the Plains between 1870 and 1900 an "experiment in agriculture on a vast scale. It nevertheless ended in total failure, [resulting in] a class of people broken in spirit as well as in fortune."

Unlike successful earlier settlement that leaped across the Appalachians into the fertile flat Midwest, vaunted American farmers seemed unable to conquer the drought-prone High Plains. In the 1870s they lived under conditions of extremely high risk. They were undertooled, underinformed, and undercapitalized. A single incident of a broken axletree or smashed kneecap, bad seed corn or a rainless June, could put them out of business. A series of technological breakthroughs seemed to compensate for the limitations of the Plains. The arrival of ready-made wooden balloon-frame houses taught farmers how to get along without trees, as did Joseph Glidden's miraculous barbed wire. Railroads were soon to connect them with markets. Daniel Halladay's economical semiautomatic windmill could tap shallow water tables to supply house and farmyard. Word spread that John Deere's new steel shear plow "cut through the tough matted sod like a hot knife through butter." Cyrus McCormick began selling a workmanlike mechanical reaper. It alone multiplied eightfold the land farmers could harvest and seemed destined to guarantee success for dryland farming. Back East, the new roller process for milling wheat for bread encouraged larger plantings on more land. In time, large-scale farming covered hundreds of acres instead of tens of acres. The new mechanized equipment seemed designed for flat open country. And, finally, for a time between 1900 and 1920, when grain prices went high, Plains farmers prospered.

The Dust Bowl and Plains Disaster

In the 1920s grain prices fell through the floor and the Dust Bowl struck in the 1930s. Seventy years of repeatedly failed settlement now reached its climax.

In July 1931 dryland farmers in southwest Kansas harvested the biggest crop they had ever seen. Extensive fall rains and winter storms offered water-laden fields that farmers rushed to plant, cultivate, and harvest. But wheat had fallen to only 25 cents a bushel, one-tenth of its price at the end of World War I. In the middle of abundance farmers were going broke. Then they experienced the second blow: A rainless August and September was so severe it burned the season's feed crop. The dry spell continued into the winter. Reeling from this double stroke of misfortune, by the spring of 1932 many farmers abandoned fields that now went bare. March's strong winds built up into more than 20 dust storms that drifted blowing topsoil as high as fence rows. The farmers who tried to plant a spring crop averaged only 5 bushels per acre. Prices hovered between a low 30 and 36 cents a bushel. More fields were abandoned and more bare soil lay exposed. With wry humor, farmers said they now "dusted" their seed into the soil. Whatever remained of wheat, alfalfa, and milo went down to plagues of grasshoppers and rabbits, and 1934 recorded the lowest level of rainfall during the entire 1930s drought. The land drifted into desertlike dirt dunes, the topsoil gone and hardpan exposed like a flayed skin laid open. New Year's Day 1935 opened with a severe dust storm, followed by repeated blowings in February, and damaging winds of hurricane force in March. Respiratory diseases, including "dust pneumonia," received attention in newspapers across the nation. The emotional strain of months and years of wind and blowing dirt led to suicides, beatings, and murders.

Few of those who experienced it will forget the blackness and confusion of the apocalyptic dust storm of April 14, 1935, which darkened skies from Colorado to the East Coast and layered dirt on ships 300 miles into the Atlantic Ocean. It was fixed in American popular culture by folksinger Woody Guthrie's new song from Pampa, Texas: "So Long, It's Been Good to Know Ya." The federal government offered to resettle farmers elsewhere, but this seemed too similar to the harsh Soviet farm collectivization going on at the same time. Half a million people did abandon the land, symbolized by the Okies that headed for California and were described in John Steinbeck's novel *The Grapes of Wrath* and John Ford's popular movie of the same name. To compensate for the environmental damage and agricultural helplessness, federal relief arrived in the spring and summer of 1934. President Franklin D. Roosevelt's New Deal administration singled out the independent family farmer for protection, almost at any price. The New Deal offered assistance in the form of farm subsidies, credit programs, agricultural extension, and the Soil Conservation Service. The New Deal would spend more than $2 billion to keep the struggling independent Plains farmers on the land.

Nature and the market teased farmers at harvesttime in 1935. Wheat prices went from 79 cents in July to over $1 in August and to $1.21 in September, the best since 1929. But farmers who got 30 bushels in 1934 faced bare blowing fields in 1935 and 1936. In 1937 harvests doubled in Texas County, Oklahoma, and the weather generally was less severe across the region. Prices dropped from $1.09 to 88 cents per bushel between July and August, but it was enough to sustain farmers for another year. A grasshopper invasion in 1937 and 1938 seemed a final blow, to be followed by army worms; stretches of roads in the Oklahoma panhandle and eastern Colorado ran slick from dead insects. Prices again collapsed in 1938 to under 60 cents a bushel, but the worst was over in 1939. Rain and war, a strange mixture of good and evil, revived Plains life in the early 1940s. Even in places where 5 or 6 inches of topsoil had been lost, the central Plains produced in 1942 a record wheat harvest that surpassed the bumper crop of 1931. The 1942 crop record was topped in 1943 and again in 1944 as farmers patriotically set themselves to offer more food for a war-ravaged globe. Farm income rose 165 percent in the war years (1939–1945), and farm mortgage debt declined almost 20 percent. But, although grain production in the Texas panhandle country rose in value to $37.7 million between 1935 and 1942, it cost taxpayers $43.3 million in federal aid. The nation had to invest more than $5.5 million to keep a boom going.

Federal intervention continued to support farmers through the "little dust bowls" of the 1950s, 1970s, and 1990s. Twenty years after the Great Dust Bowl, the rains once again failed over southwest Kansas and the Texas-Oklahoma panhandle. At the end of March 1950 the lack of rain set new all-time records. In February 1952 winds that reached 80 miles an hour created a "dust front" up to 12,000 feet. In early 1954 several inches of topsoil had been removed from the entire old Dust Bowl region, damaging about 11.7 million acres. March 1954 was the worst month of several years of dust storms with familiar results: wheat fields blown out, choking cattle, street lights at noon, stranded travelers. "Normal" rainfall, as farmers still hopefully called it, did not return until the spring of 1957. This time $25 million of government support held farmers on the depleted dry land. By August 1954 the Farmer's Home Administration and other agencies provided emergency loans, crop insurance, government commodity price supports (forward pricing), long-term loans with variable payments, grain and feed storage, short-crop alternatives, and sophisticated livestock marketing. These efforts kept the farmers solvent and on the land. Drought returned in the 1970s. In the drought year 1974, with rain 7 inches below average, irrigators ran their pumps nearly twice as long as in the normal year 1973, and energy consumption rose 64 percent. Farmers recorded that water levels in their wells were dropping as much as 3 feet a year. These high levels continued into 1975 and 1976. "Normal" rainfall returned in 1978. But now geographer John Borchert could write that there is "a widespread belief that, though there will be future droughts, there need be no future dust bowl." Not that the climate had changed, but government and society had learned to compensate. Government policy to keep the people on the land continues today. Federal aid turned independent farmers into dependent clients. The mid-1990s saw some of the driest years on record in western Kansas and the Oklahoma-Texas panhandle, the heart of the old Dust Bowl. Dry times and black blizzards seemed to appear on a predictable two-decade cycle.

Irrigation: The Technological Answer to the Plains Climate

Irrigation from underground water supplies would be the climate beater of the High Plains, but it did not start well. Farmers for decades struggled endlessly to find water. Where there was a town well, a common sight on the open prairie was a horse-drawn wagon or even a box on skids bumping along loaded with water barrels covered with burlap. Hundreds of wells were hand dug by the homesteaders themselves so they could supply the family, but well water did not go much further than for a small garden patch and a few steers. One promising technology was the familiar windmill, its blades and vane perched on a steel skeleton over a simple pump and narrow shaft to the water. One of its most attractive new features was its rudderlike vane that automatically turned it into the wind. The best version was self-lubricating so the farmer did not have to climb up and oil it in a blizzard. Although farmers erected thousands on the Plains by 1880, the windmill was oversold as the answer to the dry Plains because its wind-driven pumping suction could only reach down about 30 feet. Windmills could flood 10 acres, but farmers needed at least 16 times that in order to prosper. What was needed was an efficient deep-pumping technology.

The Ogallala Aquifer: Water for Irrigation

By the time of the Dust Bowl and Depression in the 1930s, geologists had learned of groundwater under the High Plains. The enormous Ogallala aquifer is more than 3 billion acre-feet of groundwater trapped below 174,000 square miles of fertile but otherwise dry Plains

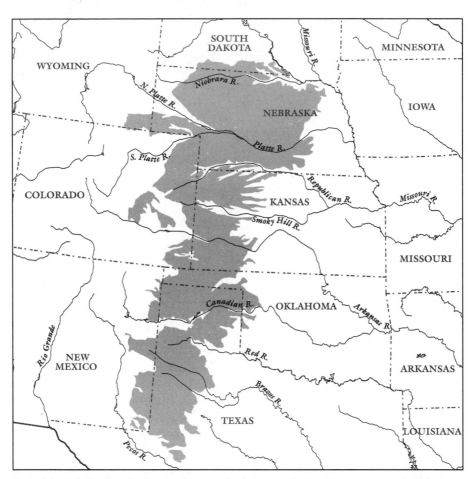

The Ogallala (High Plains) Aquifer. This groundwater aquifer, the largest in the United States, was originally 3 billion acre-feet. Already a billion acre-feet have been consumed, another billion is unreachable, leaving agriculture on the High Plains to manage the remainder as best it can for the longest possible time.

farmland. This territory covers large parts of Texas, Oklahoma, Kansas, and Nebraska, and extends into Colorado and South Dakota. It is the largest underground body of water in the United States. Unlike most of the world's underground water supplies, Ogallala groundwater is mostly irreplaceable because its sources were cut off thousands of years ago. The Ogallala is essentially "fossil water" that descended onto the Plains 10,000 to 25,000 years ago from the glacier-laden Rocky Mountains to the west, before the melting ice and snow was diverted by geological forces to the Pecos and Rio Grande rivers. Today, the Ogallala trickles very slowly southeastward through sandy gravel beds, 500 feet a year, less than 2 feet a day. These vast water-saturated gravel beds are 150 to 300 feet thick but 50 to 300 feet below the surface. It was mostly impossible for early pioneers to dig a well that deep, nor could a windmill pump that deep.

After World War II a successful irrigation system began to fall into place. Efficient turbine impeller pumps that could pull water from deep levels began to appear in the 1930s, but they lacked cheap and efficient engines. After the war, farmers turned to used automobile engines, especially the durable low-revolution Ford V-8 and six-cylinder Chevrolet L-Head. Cheap fuels for irrigation engines lasted until the energy crisis of 1973. Gasoline sold for 11 cents a gallon in 1947 and would not top 35 cents a gallon until the early 1970s. Often irrigators could also depend on free natural gas tapped from gas and oil wells on their own land. The world's second largest field of natural gas—the Guymon-Hugoton—had been known since 1904 to exist under the Dust Bowl country. Farmers also took advantage of new materials, particularly the widespread postwar use of inexpensive aluminum piping. Plains farmers, for the first time, could ignore the lack of rain by flooding their fields with pumped water. The other new technology was the center-pivot irrigator. Invented about 1950 by Colorado farmer Frank Zybach, the center pivot irrigator was called in a 1975 *Scientific American* article "the most significant mechanical innovation [worldwide] in agriculture since the replacement of draft animals by the tractor." Irrigation, which is 10,000 years old, as old as agriculture itself, had always been synonymous with hard work for long hours. Traditional "flood irrigation" required constant tending of ditches that got overgrown with weeds, water

Frank Zybach's Center-Pivot Irrigator. Central-pivot irrigation revolutionized agricultural water consumption on the High Plains because of its ease of application in scheduled, selective irrigation. Originally it was only 50 percent efficient because of evaporation, but with sprinklers low to the ground, it can reach 90 percent efficiency.

gates that got stuck, and channels that collapsed. The self-regulating mechanical center-pivot sprinkler answered the Plains farmer's dream.

A Golden Age on the Plains, 1960–2010

Beginning in the 1950s and 1960s, water was pumped from each of hundreds of wells at the rate of 1,000 cubic feet a minute to water quarter sections of wheat, alfalfa, grain sorghum, and even corn. Commitment to irrigation came earliest on the Texas High Plains where the number of irrigation wells rose from over 2,500 in 1941 to more than 42,200 wells by 1957. By 1977 farmers on the Texas High Plains had installed over 71,000 wells, each pumping furiously. Drilling and casing a basic well ran approximately $1,300, the pump and gearhead about $2,200, and $500 for a small used Ford V-8 or Chevrolet engine, for a total of $4,000. In 1950 Plains farmers had irrigated 3.5 million acres of farmland; in 1990 it was 15 million acres. Land values rose rapidly for productive irrigated land. In Lubbock, Texas, farmland was valued at over $400 an acre, compared to $20 an acre in 1935. Much of the land, like the Sandhills of southwestern Kansas, was more suited to light cattle grazing than wheat production. After center-pivot sprinklers were installed on hundreds of quarter sections, the Sandhills yielded corn, sorghum, and wheat yields that matched those of Iowa and Illinois. Irrigation on the High Plains was not merely a response to climate, but its replacement. Corn demands the most water during the season, an astonishing 900,000 gallons laid on 130 acres of a 160-acre quarter-section, wheat and sorghum half that amount. In 1990 a center-pivot sprinkler system, from drilling the well to watering the milo, would cost a farmer $70,000 to $100,000 per 160 acres, depending on well depth and field needs. Once committed to irrigation, Plains farmers discovered their work habits changed dramatically. Their physical labor was different, but not eased. The noisy motors, running day and night, changed farming from a pastoral and seasonal life into machine-dominated labor. Farmers had less direct contact with their soil and water and more with the mechanisms—pumps, gearboxes, motors, valves, and piping—of their watering systems. Sometimes they worked like unskilled factory laborers in the daily maintenance of their leaky, grinding, and noisy machinery. Most irrigators need 6 to 10 units for efficiencies of size. To pay for it, irrigators need good wheat or sorghum prices, which were in the late 1980s half of what they were ten years before. Yet, from any rational perspective, irrigation is a marvelous technology, and alternatives to irrigation are gloomy.

In some places on the High Plains today, irrigation has taken all but 5 or 10 feet of usable Ogallala groundwater. Back in 1970, farmers around Sublette, Kansas, concluded they had 300 years of water left in the aquifer, based on current pumping and known supplies. By 1980 their estimate had fallen to 70 years as pumping rose dramatically, and by 1990 their estimate dropped to less than a 30-year supply. Today, using current techniques, many local irrigators say they will be happy to hold on for another decade. About 1 billion acre-feet of Ogallala water were consumed by irrigation farmers between 1960 and 1990, mostly in southwest Kansas, the Oklahoma panhandle, and west Texas. (Western Nebraska, which is mostly cattle country, holds more than 60 percent of the remaining aquifer water.) Nothing can accelerate Ogallala flow, and artificial replacement remains unlikely.

In 1981 farm economist Willard W. Cochrane described an emerging pattern on the High Plains: The 1930s was a Dust Bowl and Depression era of uncertainty and instability.

Gradually, new irrigation technologies in the 1950s and 1960s rewarded farmers with an extraordinary 50 years of high-speed groundwater consumption. But these 50 years cannot be repeated because of the depletion of the aquifer. Cochrane sees two additional factors that make the next 50 years more difficult. One is that many farmers stayed in business only because of large government subsidies. The other is that the smaller family farmer is uncompetitive with large industrial farming ("agribusiness"). A vertically integrated agribusiness in wheat, beef, or pork needs copious water to serve its demand for high yields. The threat of the next drought (possibly intensified by global warming) would triple water consumption.

It is hard to argue against the productivity of the Plains, despite the price paid in depletion of water and soil. Industrial farming plays a major role in the ability of each American farmer today to feed a whopping eight dozen other people, compared to four others when the nation began. It is remarkable that less than 2 percent of Americans work on the farm, compared to 30 or 40 percent of a nation's population elsewhere in the world. This success story, perhaps the most important in all of modern history, does much to define American prosperity. Kenneth A. Cook, of the Center for Resource Economics, called for "a new social contract between farmers and society." He said, "For its part, society will have to recognize the enormous cost farmers already bear to conserve natural resources and protect the environment. Taxpayers will have to be willing to share more of that burden—probably a great deal more—as external costs of agricultural production becomes internalized." The contract was to sustain the family farm, which Americans esteemed as the place where patriotic virtues of rugged individualism, hard-working industriousness, and personal self-sufficiency were practiced best. Yet, instead of achieving independence, when this farming encountered the environmental limits of the Plains, the independent farmer became a long-term government client. Government aid to farmers, to compensate for low grain prices, became part of their way of life during the difficult Depression years of the 1930s and has not been denied them until the gradual letdown scheduled by the 1996 farm bill. As a result, the American family farm has persisted for more than 100 years on the Plains (and more than 200 years nationally) as a decentralized cottage industry in an increasingly industrialized world.

Alternatives

The forced abandonment of the Plains to light grazing or empty grassland first came up in the 1930s, but a federal resettlement program was resented because it pushed failed farmers into reservations like Indians. The most radical proposal was offered by land use planners Frank and Deborah Popper in late 1987. Let us finally admit, they argue, that more than a century of repeated farm abandonments, dust bowls, costly government interventions, and environmental destruction has resulted in the failure of the American experiment to live successfully on the High Plains. Despite irrigation, between 1950 and 1970 half the people left the region, and between 1980 and 2000 it is expected that half again will have departed, leaving half a million farmers across the entire High Plains compared to 2 million in 1950. The Poppers identified a county-by-county wide swath of hopeless decline in 139,000 square miles across the Plains from Texas to North Dakota. They concluded, "Over the next generation, the Plains will, as a result of the largest, longest-running agricultural and environmental miscalculation in American history, become almost totally depopulated." The Plains should be returned to their preagricultural condition. The Poppers recommended a publicly owned

"Buffalo Commons" across the entire High Plains from Canada through Texas. The Buffalo Commons would become open land and wildlife refuge, "the world's largest natural and historic preservation project."

The innovative Land Institute at Salina, Kansas, was founded by the visionary agriculturalist Wes Jackson. The institute is committed to keeping independent farmers on the High Plains by returning them to the self-sustaining grassland ecosystem prior to settlement combined with ecologically sound food production. Its primary objective is "to develop an agroecosystem that reflects more the attributes of climax prairie than do conventional agricultural systems based on annual grain crops." The Land Institute, and other alternative operations like the Kansas Rural Center, advocate a broad environmental paradigm—biocentrism. Biocentric farming follows the natural patterns of the local ecosystem. This turns on its head the historic Western view that nature is humanity's raw material. As a result of a biocentric viewpoint, farming cannot be like any other industry. North Dakota farmer Fred Kirschenmann observed, "A farm is not a factory—it is an organism made up of numerous suborganisms, each alive and interdependent, each affected in numerous, complex ways" by outside forces—money, chemicals, technology, market prices—that are invariably disruptive.

The early struggle of frontiersfolk on the semiarid High Plains had not led to comfortable settlement, but only to more struggle. One of America's premier geographers, Carl Ortwin Sauer, argued that the midcontinent grasslands was where the nation's frontier history really began. It was where Americans had to solve new environmental problems. This frontier is not yet over because the environment has not been mastered; in the long run the Plains environment, because of its climate, may never be conquered. As a result, the old Dust Bowl region has been an inadvertent "experiment station" in crisis management. Because of environmental conditions, when the High Plains was settled as an agricultural region it also went on permanent alert, experiencing crisis with no solution and no end. This is particularly true if one sees today's dependency on declining Ogallala water levels as a mere brief blip in time—1960 to 2010—compared to long-term forces at work. The joker in this poker game is global warming. The High Plains is inescapably threatened by the world's changing climate due to greater quantities of industrial and automobile carbon dioxide, methane, and other substances pumped into the upper atmosphere. According to computerized global climate modeling at Princeton, New Jersey, and Boulder, Colorado, the U.S. High Plains is one of several regions around the world that will turn into a major desert if the predicted CO_2-induced greenhouse effect takes place. Farmers will have a harder time responding to this desertification because they would need to take three times more water than today's rate to compensate for global warming. This would seriously harm most strategies for survival on the High Plains. The arid climate of the High Plains, newly intensified by global warming, may once again have the direct impact it has not had for 50 years.

Conclusion

In both Appalachia and the High Plains, Americans learned, at the price of great suffering and cost, of the risks in drastically and permanently altering ecosystems. Ideally, ecosystems are richly diverse, nonlinear, self-sustaining dynamic entities. Badly disturbed environments become erratic. It must be remembered that an ecosystem—natural or human induced—is not exclusively biological, but involves a symbiosis with local physical and chemical processes as well as climate and rainfall. When ecosystems are disrupted frequently and stressed in their fundamental features, their natural functions become chaotic and unpredictable. Species are lost, grasses and forests die away, the soil disappears in gullies, all as the result of chronic ecosystem illness. On the High Plains, the troublesome activities of sodbusting and soil erosion were joined in the 1960s by an onslaught of groundwater depletion. Both soil and water were nonrenewable resources in any human time frame. Americans found it difficult to admit that homesteading, sodbusting, and monoculture farming were mistakes. Andrew H. Clark writes that "during the sorriest 'desert' years of the thirties, an actual alteration which was more than an extra kick to the swing of the pendulum in a normally 'oscillating equilibrium' had in fact occurred." Appalachia was settled much earlier than the Plains and degraded by industrial misuse into a virtually uninhabitable zone. Most of the collapse for both regions, however, took place during the same period, approximately 1870 to 1940. Both regions were natural communities that fell into collapse through European intrusion. Their ecosystem integrity can never be reestablished, including the features that had once made them attractive to European settlers. Many Americans nostalgically support the two regions because they embody the nation's pioneering heritage and American traditions of rugged individualism, tightly knit families, and rural society. Both farmer and mountaineer offer disturbing (and tantalizing) challenges to a consumer, object-oriented, commodity-based society. Some advocates argue that they offer America environmentally based alternatives to modern consumerism, but this seems more an ideal than a reality because few Americans are rushing onto the Plains or into Appalachia.

Part of the historical problem is that American dependence on marketplace (profit-based) mechanisms that ignore environmental costs keeps such profound failures hidden until restitution became impossible. American society is at high risk because of massive environmental transformations in which Americans have been routinely engaged in their history. What is less recognized is that Americans have very limited means, even with the best scientific, technological, and political tools, to ameliorate or counteract the transformations. In most cases Americans have not monitored or understood the changes, and virtually did not even notice them. We have far to go in learning to read the environment.

For Further Reading

For Appalachia
The best place to start on Appalachia is the classic insider's appraisal by Harry M. Caudill, *Night Comes to the Cumberlands: A Biography of a Depressed Area* (1962), which should be combined with Henry D. Shapiro, *Appalachia on Our Mind: The Southern Mountains and Mountaineers in the American Consciousness, 1870–1920* (1978). Other important statements of Appalachia's troubles can be found in Jack E. Weller, *Yesterday's People: Life in Contemporary Appalachia* (1965), and Ronald Eller, *Miners, Millhands, and Mountaineers: Industrialization of the Appalachian South, 1880–1930* (1982). Basic geographical and natural history descriptions are in Karl B. Raitz and Richard Ulack, *Appalachia: A Regional Geography* (1984), and Maurice Brooks, *The Appalachians* (1965). The classic statement of the Tennessee Valley Authority as an engineering and public works answer to Appalachia's problems remains

David E. Lillienthal, *TVA: Democracy on the March* (1943; reprinted 1953). For a new appreciation of the special qualities of Appalachia and its people, without denying profound human and environmental dysfunctionalism, see two quite extraordinary far-ranging books, Rodger Cunningham, *Apples on the Flood: The Southern Mountain Experience* (1987), and Allen W. Batteau, *The Invention of Appalachia* (1990). One true American classic that should not be missed, and makes poor whites in southern Appalachia into American icons, is James Agee and Walker Evans's *Let Us Now Praise Famous Men* (1941; reprinted 1969).

For the High Plains
Readers can find no more enjoyable and profitable way of starting to learn more about the High Plains than with Walter Prescott Webb's 1931 classic, *The Great Plains,* which opened the subject. Follow this by a look at John Wesley Powell's 1878 *Lands of the Arid Region of the United States,* arguably the best-ever-written government report. Both Webb and Powell are available in paperback reprints. See the breakthrough ecology-based articles by Paul B. Sears, William A. Albrecht, John T. Curtis, Andrew H. Clark, and Carl O. Sauer in the now classic 1956 *Man's Role in Changing the Face of the Earth,* edited by William L. Thomas, Jr. A solid overview of mid-America farming can be found in Gilbert C. Fite, *The Farmer's Frontier, 1986–1900* (1966), and more details are in the articles collected by James W. Whittaker in *Farming in the Midwest, 1840–1900* (1974) and Thomas R. Wessel in *Agriculture in the Great Plains, 1876–1936* (1977), both publications of the Agricultural History Society. There are also important and provocative essays on the Plains in *The Great Plains: Environment and Culture,* edited in 1977 by Brian W. Blouet and Frederick C. Luebke, and *The Great Plains: Perspectives and Prospects,* edited in 1981 by Merlin P. Lawson and Maurice E. Baker. The journal *The Great Plains Quarterly* helps update analysis and interpretation of the Plains. The environmental study of the Plains has also been greatly enriched by several highly suggestive and controversial interpretations. Readers should not miss the writings of the irascible James C. Malin as collected in 1984 by Robert P. Swierenga, *History and Ecology: Studies of the Grasslands.* Several relevant essays by the pathfinding geographer Carl Ortwin Sauer are in the collection edited by John Leighly in 1963, *Land and Life.* Study of Plains environmental history has also been shaped by Paul B. Sear's *Deserts on the March,* first published in 1935, and W. Eugene Hollon's *The Great American Desert, Then and Now* (1966). No reader should leave the subject of the High Plains, however, without a full reading of Donald Worster's 1979 classic, *Dust Bowl: The Southern Plains in the 1930s,* which reshaped the modern study of the High Plains. One hopes that Frank and Deborah Popper will produce a book out of their provocative articles on the future of large parts of the High Plains as a "Buffalo Commons." For a recent analysis, see John Opie's 1993 book, *Ogallala: Water for a Dry Land,* which, despite its title, is a broader environmental and historical analysis of the High Plains.

PART FOUR

RETHINKING AMERICA:
THE MAKING OF
ENVIRONMENTALISM

CHAPTER TWELVE

RECOVERING "ORIGINAL AMERICA": THE WILDERNESS MOVEMENT

Oh, beautiful for spacious skies, for amber waves of grain, for purple mountain majesty, above the fruited plain. America, America, God shed His light on thee . . . from sea to shining sea!

George Catlin and the Idea of National Parks

In May 1832 New York artist George Catlin arrived at Fort Pierre on the Missouri River in the Dakota country. He paused in astonishment to see a mound of 1,400 fresh buffalo tongues that Sioux Indians had traded for a few gallons of whiskey. The Indians "lay drunk" in their villages where he "saw also the curling smokes of a thousand stills." Catlin publicized the scene in a New York newspaper and in his famous book on the North American Indians. He also told of "Hundreds and thousands [of dead, stinking, reddened buffalo carcasses] strewed upon the plains, [left to] bands of wolves and dogs and buzzards. The skins were dragged and dressed for white man's luxury!" Catlin sadly concluded that the advance of white man's so-called civilization was quickly and inevitably degrading the nobility of the native peoples and wiping out immense herds of millions of buffalo. As a counterforce, Catlin proposed that Americans create a magnificent wilderness sanctuary on the High Plains where the "great protecting policy of government preserved [buffalo and Indian] in their pristine beauty and wildness. . . . A nation's park, containing man and beast, in all the wild and freshness of their nature's beauty!" The Indian, of course, could not be corralled in a national park, but Catlin's vision helped launch Americans on a patriotic crusade to set aside a part of their disappearing wilderness in publicly owned parks.

The United States was the first country to create national parks. In 1872, 40 years after Catlin's dream, President Grant carved 1,600 square miles out of the Wyoming Territory to create Yellowstone National Park. California's Yosemite region became a national park after 40 years of transition—1864 to 1906—from federal land to state park and finally back to federal property. In 1888 New York State set aside over 800,000 acres of its northeastern wilds in the Adirondacks as the nation's largest state park. Since the 1860s the citizens of New York City have strolled, picnicked, and played in Central Park. By the early twentieth century, Americans proudly pointed to an unprecedented array of city parks, state parks, and national parks. They were America's crown jewels. They also acted as an escape for the masses from the pressures of industrial society. No other nation had done such a thing. Americans enjoyed several major advantages to take the lead among Western nations to conserve the wilderness. America still consisted of nation-sized tracts of "empty" wilderness in an enormous public domain of hundreds of millions of acres. Not the least, national prosperity made preservation acceptable; Americans were rich enough to set aside land. Ironically, this wealth had come out of intensive exploitation of much of the eastern and midwestern environments.

Nineteenth-century Americans had several motives for setting aside natural places. To some, national parks have always been a string of unique monumental wonders held in perpetuity on otherwise worthless land. They were America's answer to the great castles, fortresses, temples, churches, ancient squares, and arenas of the Old World. To others, national parks were like the great European spas and resorts, set in even more dramatic surroundings, designed for recovery of health and light recreation. Railroad companies that held exclusive rights of entry to isolated places like Yosemite, Yellowstone, Glacier, and the Grand Canyon promoted national parks as extremely profitable way stations on their stretched-out lines. For several decades, approximately 1880 to 1960, a conservationist viewpoint dominated park policy; it emphasized public access to the parks for "the greatest good for the greatest number," often at the price of wilderness preservation. Since the 1960s, increased demands for recreation have competed with biological management and ecological integrity. A new environmental viewpoint came to decry the limits, smallness, and scarcity of the nation's parks and monuments.

"Preserve the Wilderness!"
The Disappearance of Original America

Catlin returned to the urbanized eastern United States with a remarkable collection of drawings and paintings of disappearing noble Indians. There, a few sportsmen, travelers, vacationers, urban planners, and social reformers were having new thoughts about the disappearing wilderness.

During most of the nineteenth century, Americans were understandably enthusiastic about their westward conquest of vast regions of open land. In this light, the United States seemed to be an unlikely place for any appreciation and protection of "undeveloped" primitive regions. Since the days when the Puritans battled demons in the primeval forest, pioneers had looked on raw wilderness as a fearful and hostile place that was frustrating and meaningless. In a modern historian's words, "Telling a westerner to be kind to trees was like urging a southerner to save the mosquitos." Most Americans enthusiastically cut, plowed, dug, blasted, and bridged the wilderness. A few other voices can be added to the Transcendentalist minority described in Chapter 5. The great bird man John James Audubon heard "the din of hammers and machinery, the woods fast disappearing under the axe." Francis Parkman, influential mid-nineteenth-century historian of the colonial forests, worried that "civilization has a destroying as well as a creating power." James Fenimore Cooper decried the massive slaughter of millions of passenger pigeons that had once darkened entire skies with their flight (the last died in captivity in 1911). Bayard Taylor, who traveled worldwide, worried over the loss: "Nature here [in America] reminds one of a princess fallen into the hands of robbers, who cut off her fingers for the sake of the jewels she wears." Washington Irving worried that Ameri-

George Perkins Marsh: Environmental Prophet

One early wilderness advocate was the remarkable American renaissance man, George Perkins Marsh (1801–82)—congressman, scientist, ambassador, writer, proto-ecologist—proficient in 20 languages. Born on the Vermont frontier, an eye affliction deprived him of reading in childhood, forced a prodigious memory, and drove him outdoors where "the bubbling brook, the trees, the flowers, the wild animals were to me persons, not things." As an adult, he failed at law and business, and entered politics to serve in the Vermont legislature and Congress. A turning point came when he was appointed in 1849 as ambassador to Turkey. His diplomatic career meant extensive travel and leisure to study and write. Marsh's wide-ranging scholarship earned him a solid reputation in fine arts, Scandinavian studies, history, and linguistics. The English poet and critic Matthew Arnold praised him as "that *rara avis,* a really well-bred and trained American." His diplomatic visits to Greece and Palestine made him sensitive to the human destruction of once lush environments and the inevitable decline of civilization in such depleted regions. He continued his diplomatic career to the new Kingdom of Italy, where he lived in Turin, Florence, and Rome until his death in 1882, a tenure unmatched by any American diplomat before or since.

In 1864, while overseas, Marsh produced the first true environmental classic *Man and Nature,* subtitled *Physical Geography as Modified by Human Action.* His often quoted line is "Man has too long forgotten that the earth was given to him for usufruct alone, not for consumption, still less for profligate waste." *Man and Nature* was a cautionary world history that described how Middle Eastern and Mediterranean civilizations had wasted and thrown into imbalance their entire ecosystems, lost their natural foundations, and inevitably declined and disappeared. His comparative assessment of environmental conditions in the United States convinced him that Americans were rushing toward their own predetermined fall. Both the natural world and civilizations

cans would repeat their habit of abandoning worn-out farmland and depleted plantations in the East and South, move on to tear down the fertile lands of the Midwest, and exterminate the western Indians and exhaust the land to the Pacific shore. Irving insisted that large western regions should remain forever beyond settlement. Among the nature-loving Transcendentalists, Thoreau retreated to his Walden Pond cabin for solitary enlightenment, Emerson lost himself in nature's divine embrace, and Thomas Cole's great landscape canvases invited Americans to treasure their wilderness bounty. (A modern art historian noted that "no object is so frequently found in America's landscape art as the tree stump.") After newspaper editor Horace Greeley returned from a European tour, he "never before prized so highly" America's "glorious, still unscathed forests." According to this small but influential group of writers, Americans were trivializing their environment. By midcentury Washington Irving worried that America was turning into "a transient state of things fast passing into oblivion," a nation not fundamentally secured to its natural geography. In 1871 the popular utopian writer Henry George declared, "A generation hence, our children will look with astonishment at the

depended on a stable geography. *Man and Nature* was the first book to question seriously the myth of America's inexhaustible resources. It warned that Americans, regardless of their confident expansionism and trust in technology, could destroy themselves by misusing their geography. He observed that Europeans protected their forests with strict regulations and controlled harvesting, whereas Americans were rapidly losing their wilderness forests. America's collapse still could be averted by "careful control and intelligent planning" by the national government, the only agent with the skill, resources, and authority to "restore the garden we have wasted."

Marsh's book was not simply a lament; he provided specific remedies for the damage humans had done, including reforestation of barren land, erosion control, restored water supplies through irrigation and dams, and even biological controls. Marsh was among the first to realize that modern civilization had acquired the power to transform nature permanently. Although humans have applied their power in selfish and shortsighted ways, they could change their ways once they were better informed. Geographer David Lowenthal, in his introduction to the 1965 reprint of Marsh's classic, concluded, "The great lesson of *Man and Nature* was that nature did not heal herself; land, once dominated and then abandoned by man, did not revert to its primitive condition but became impoverished." The first printing run of 1,000 copies of *Man and Nature* sold out before the end of 1864; the book remained in print in many editions through 1908. Reviewers judged that the book was provocative in its new emphasis on respect for nature but too pessimistic about the outcomes of human impact. Marsh was praised for his "investigation of a subject so abstruse, so vast, and so complex, that he had no rival in the work." *Man and Nature* was one of those rare books (like *Uncle Tom's Cabin* and *Silent Spring*) that directly influenced U.S. government policies, notably in the formation of federal forest reserves. Gifford Pinchot called *Man and Nature* "epoch-making." It was also published abroad in England and Italy, and influenced French, Italian, and Indian policies to reduce forest destruction and implement forest renewal.

recklessness with which the public domain has been squandered. It will seem to them that we must have been mad." Fifty years after Thoreau, as we see later, Scots-born, Wisconsin-bred John Muir retreated from San Francisco into the high Sierras, rode the heights of trees during electric thunderstorms, and put in motion the modern wilderness movement. In the 1920s and 1930s the wilderness guru Robert Marshall would tap into Freud to argue that industrial urban civilization is so narrow and repressive that it is responsible for human conflict and discontent; in contrast, he insisted, the human spirit needs the wilderness for purification and enlightenment.

Nature in the Cities: The Parks Movement

Nineteenth-century city dwellers described their public parks as "nature museums," although little was left natural in the green lawns, curving paths, decorative ponds, and carefully located clusters of shrubs and trees. According to this view, the landscaped parks were primarily antidotes to the inner city, where nature has disappeared under belching pollution, concrete surfaces, sewage pipes, and unwelcome alien co-dwellers such as street pigeons and rats. The result, it was widely believed, was needless stress, heart disease, lung disease, and mental disorders. City dwellers needed solitary walks and playing fields in open green space, in the words of one advocate, to "enjoy, with convenience, the exercise that is necessary for health and amusement."

New York City neared a million people in the 1850s. Far-sighted New Yorkers looked to protect Manhattan's remaining woodland when dense building began to move onto the farms of the upper half of the island. Through the efforts of planners Frederick Law Olmstead and Calvert Vaux, Central Park covered a mile-square tract of land extending from 59th to 106th streets between 5th and 8th avenues. As the city quickly grew around it, it was soon called the "lungs" of the city. Other large green parks designed by Olmstead and Vaux appeared in the midst of Brooklyn, Philadelphia, Boston, Pittsburgh, and Cincinnati. In a curious step, new cemeteries were designed into parklike campuses for strolling and contemplation—Mount Auburn in Cambridge in 1831, Laurel Hill in Philadelphia in 1836, Greenwood in Brooklyn in 1837, and Cincinnati's Spring Grove Cemetery in 1855. Mount Auburn even had a circuit route called the Tour. The guidebook to Laurel Hill described "its expansive lawns, its rugged ascents, its flowering dells, its rocky ravines." When a cemetery became a park, it was said that the landscape of hope replaced the fear of death. Much later zoos in Chicago, St. Louis, and the Bronx would mix parklike pathways with exotic caged animals, like an outdoor Noah's Ark or a safe Garden of Eden. In the 1880s Olmstead brought the park to the home in his development of a new model suburb, Riverside, Illinois (the author's hometown), 12 miles west along the CB&Q tracks from downtown Chicago. Here the residential streets curved around little parklets and village shops abutted playing fields and strolling paths in the verdant floodplain along the Desplaines River. Olmstead also laid out the parklike grounds of the monumental 1893 Columbian Exposition, and Chicago itself followed suit by building its lakefront parks and its Park District greenbelt. Simultaneously, several Garden City communities sprang up like hopeful little Utopias in the East. One contemporary pondered, "If our American men could be drawn from their offices to forest and field, they would be benefited, physically, morally, and mentally, and come to enjoy a larger existence."

The Fragmented Wilderness: Natural Wonders and Curiosities

Outside the cities, and beyond the rural countryside, Americans looked with wonder and pride at spectacular natural "freaks," "decorations," and "curiosities," such as the geysers, hot mud pots, and boiling springs of Wyoming's Yellowstone. The first natural wonders were in the East, since western sites were not yet discovered or early reports disbelieved, and most were inaccessible. Thomas Jefferson was so overwhelmed by the unusual rock formation known as Virginia's Natural Bridge—"the most sublime of nature's works"—that he bought it. On the top of the arch, "You involuntarily fall on your hands and feet, creep to the parapet, and peek over it" to see the rushing stream far below. Seen from below, "So beautiful an arch, so elevated, so light, and springing as it were up to heaven! The rapture of the spectator is really indescribable!" (He would have been shocked in the 1930s when a highway ran across the bridge and billboards blocked the view. Entry was through a souvenir shop and a hidden organ played inspirational music, which most tourists applauded.) Jefferson also called attention to the gap where the Potomac River cuts through the Blue Mountains and the then distant Niagara Falls.

The first nationwide debate over America's natural wonders took place over the extensive commercialization of Niagara Falls that followed the opening of the Erie Canal in 1825. Private developers quickly bought up the best overlooks, fenced them off, built gaudy shelters, and charged high admission prices. Commercial tourism sought to draw visitors to souvenir shops, tacky restaurants, unrelated amusement parks, tightrope stunts across the river, the man-in-the-barrel-over-the-falls craze, and other so-called attractions more profitable than the falls. The falls, which had no equal in Europe, became less a sublime natural phenomenon and more another commodity to be consumed. When Alexis de Tocqueville, author of the classic 1831 work *Democracy in America*, visited the falls, he took special note to say, "I don't give the Americans ten years to establish a saw or flour mill at the base of the cataract." Later, private hydroelectric operations nearly turned off the water. By 1885 the state of New York, to its credit, purchased and condemned property around Niagara Falls, and at the cost of $1.4 million it created Niagara Falls State Reservation. However, because of prior development, difficulties of restoration, and remaining commercialization, the cataract would never be restored to the natural wonder it once was.

America's "Crown Jewels": The National Park System

Easterners glorified the West; it was the zone of hope, the stage for noble adventures, larger-than-life events, and national greatness. Better still to find groves of extravagant giant trees, mountain ranges that overshadowed the Alps, unique geysers, and a multitude of spectacular waterfalls that all surpassed Europe's castles, churches, and ruined temples. They were *natural*, existing since Creation. A much photographed mountain in the Rockies was emblazoned with a natural cross. One visitor said of Yosemite Falls, "Think of a cataract as high as St. Peter's in Rome, and multiply it by six." When Horace Greeley visited California's groves of giant sequoias, he wrote that the trees "were of very substantial size when David danced before the ark, when Theseus ruled in Athens, when Aeneas fled from the burning wreck of vanquished Troy." Americans thus claimed their own ancient monuments of nature's nation.

Yosemite

Yosemite Valley stands only 180 miles due east into the Sierras from San Francisco. It lay hidden like a Shangri-la, deep and enclosed in sheer granite walls that rose dramatically 3,000 feet above the valley floor. The valley floor fulfilled the dreamlike pastoral of a garden park, with the sparkling Merced River meandering through open meadows and clusters of primeval trees. Newspaperman Horace Greeley boasted in 1859 that Yosemite Valley was the world's "most unique and majestic of nature's marvels." The popular churchman Thomas Starr King enthused in 1860 that "nowhere in the Alps, in no pass of the Andes, and in no Canyon of the mighty Oregon range, is there such stupendous rock scenery." Spectacular waterfalls, "Niagara magnified" (Yosemite Falls is 2,425 feet compared to Niagara's 167 feet), completed the idyllic setting that moved visitors to paroxysms of religious ecstasy and patriotic joy. A series of overwrought large canvases by the German landscape painter Albert Bierstadt delighted the public and virtually clinched the preservation of Yosemite. Nearby, in the Mariposa Grove, stood the world's greatest trees. Americans looked on the Sierra giant sequoias (different from the coastal redwoods) as natural counterparts to the architectural monuments of the Old World. They were thought to be the world's oldest living things. In reality, the big trees were being treated like enormous souvenirs: One was cut down and its base made into a dancing floor 25 feet in diameter. Bark stripped from others was displayed like animal skins at world fairs in New York and London in the 1850s, Philadelphia in 1876, and Chicago in 1893. Fortunately, the trees could not be logged, since, unlike the coastal redwoods, they were so brittle that they shattered when toppled to the ground and were treated by loggers as nuisances that stood in the way of sugar pine harvesting.

The city park pioneer Frederick Law Olmstead chaired the state Yosemite Commission, which was responsible for the future of Yosemite Valley and the Mariposa Big Tree Grove. In 1864 Congress had withdrawn from public sale 10 square miles of the Yosemite Valley and 4 square miles of the Mariposa and transferred the sites to the state as a park "for public use, resort and recreation, inalienable for all time." The land lacked minerals worth mining, which made it "for all public purposes worthless." In 1890, when Congress went through a flurry of park creation, it established a 1,500-square-mile Yosemite National Park, although the original sites at Yosemite Valley and the Mariposa Big Tree Grove did not return to federal control until 1906. Olmstead's commission's report in 1865 admitted to a conflict between wilderness preservation and public recreation that would become the dominant battle over the role of the national parks in American society. He put wilderness first, but insisted that this did not exclude "pecuniary advantage." The Swiss, with their Alps, he said, enjoyed a major tourist industry including hotels, restaurants, inns, carriage roads, and railroads.

After a railroad was built in 1907 from San Francisco to the park's entrance, Yosemite became a fashionable resort in a spectacular setting. Tourists amused themselves at Glacier Point by pitching stones, wooden boxes, and small animals over the 3,200-foot brink. One fabricated attraction was the popular nighttime firefall over Glacier Point, in which fireworks and burning coals were pushed over the cliff until the practice ended in the 1950s. Soon visitors complained of the tawdry commercialism of cheap camps, souvenir stands, and light entertainment that covered the valley. As late as 1936 a writer for a national magazine wrote that "dance halls, movies, bear pit shows, studios, baseball, golf, swimming pools, wienie roasts, marshmallow roasts and barbecues" covered the valley, none of which had "any relation whatever to the purpose for which the national parks were established." Critics condemned the carnival atmosphere as inappropriate for a place where nature's own wonders were remarkable enough. As early as 1872 there were plans to "fix the [several Yosemite] falls" by cutting off side cascades and constructing an upstream reservoir to guarantee a steady flow of water, since often the waterfall stopped during summer months or a droughty season, and tourists complained or stayed away. Would the valley repeat the commercialization at Niagara Falls? Spokesman John Muir began to tell visitors to head into the park's high country—the Toulemene Meadows—for a true wilderness experience.

Steven Mather, in 1916 the first head of the National Park Service, saw no problem in "making a business of scenery." In the same year, people began to enter Yosemite more by automobile than by rail, and by 1928 automobiles crowded the narrow valley. In 1955 more than a million visitors visited the park, virtually all by automobile, as many as 30,000 in a single day. In 1960 the canyon floor was covered by 9 general stores, 7 gasoline stations, and rooms for 4,500 overnight guests, which did not count thousands of campers. As late as 1974 the private concessionaire, who virtually "owned" the park's facilities, proudly unveiled plans for a new hotel on Glacier Point, connected by a tramway to the valley floor. The plan announced that "the restaurant at the top would be one of the great tourist attractions of the world." Neither the hotel or tramway were built, but the idea persists as a developer's dream.

The Places No One Knew

Had commercialism already overwhelmed eastern wonders like the Catskills and the White Mountains? Regions could be lost. The dramatic Wisconsin Dells would never recover from its early commercialization. North Dakota's Black Hills disappeared under the crush of mining, commercial tourism, and Indian claims. The singular Florida Keys became a highly profitable strip of fancy hotels, elegant shops, and costly restaurants. California's dramatic Monterey Peninsula is covered by wealthy homes and golf courses that exclude the public. Kentucky's Mammoth Cave, a "dark, silent, and mysterious" place, became a festival of colored lights, romantic boat trips, and theatrical tricks, many of which remained when the cave became a national park.

Yellowstone

In its early years, the Yellowstone region had been a fabled and mysteriously distant place, crossed only by wild mountain men like John Colter and Jim Bridger. Few believed their reports of hot spouting water and boiling mud pots. The American public began to take the bizarre place more seriously following a more trustworthy Montana businessmen's expedition in 1869 that reported the unusual formations and hot fountains at the Lower Geyser Basin and told of the colorful Grand Canyon of the Yellowstone and the high-altitude Yellowstone Lake. Unlike the idyllic Yosemite Valley, Yellowstone's geyser basin represented a grotesque underworld. Even the Indians looked on the geysers and hot springs as the place left unfinished by the creator, the very entrance to infernal regions and better left alone as a spirit-filled place. It was a collection of apparitions, such as the lumpy misshapen Grotto Geyser and other formations comparable to Breugel's Hell. It seemed that Yellowstone was a unique array of America's distinctive natural wonders all in one place. Another company of businessmen, this time wealthy eastern entrepreneurs, visited the region in 1870 to inspect its economic potential. Instead, to their everlasting credit, they urged federal authorities to set it aside from private ownership as the nation's wilderness park, "a public or pleasuring ground for the benefit and enjoyment of the people." These spokesmen for a public park were not advocates of wilderness preservation in any modern sense. One, Nathaniel Pitt Langford, envisioned resorts, villas, and grand hotels on Yellowstone Lake on the model of Italy's Lake Como or the French Riviera. Another, Cornelius Hedges, looked at the Upper Falls of the Yellowstone River: "I fancied I could see in the dim distance of a few seasons an iron swing bridge." Shortly afterward, the government surveyor Ferdinand V. Hayden led a survey expedition to the Yellowstone country, which included the artist Thomas Moran and the photographer William H. Jackson. Upon their return, the three led a public campaign that advertised Yellowstone as a world-class wonder and an American birthright to be protected before it was disfigured. Already in 1871, two men were seen cutting poles along the Firehole River to fence off the geyser basin in order to charge admission. Private development would, in Hayden's words, "fence in these rare wonders so as to charge visitors a fee, as is now done at Niagara Falls, for the sight of that which ought to be as free as the air or water." Like Yosemite, the fundamental conflict was between private development and public ownership.

In 1872 President Grant and Congress carved out a national park from over 1 million acres—1,600 square miles—"dedicated and set apart as a public park or pleasuring ground for the benefit and enjoyment of the people." Yellowstone had the advantage that it appeared to be a distant and otherwise worthless part of the public domain, good only for the tourists that would eventually come. The final necessary inducement came from direct lobbying by the Northern Pacific Railroad, which had a new line nearby that gave it a monopoly for public access. The railroad saw profits surpassing vacation meccas like Saratoga Springs and Niagara Falls. The most successful promotion of the national parks came less from wilderness protectionists than from railroad companies. Jay Cooke's Northern Pacific lobbied for Washington's Mount Rainier in 1899. The Great Northern advocated Montana's Glacier National Park in the same year, the Union Pacific controlled entry to the south rim of Arizona's Grand Canyon, and Harriman's Southern Pacific and Central Pacific encouraged Yosemite as a national park.

The new Yellowstone National Park was put "under the exclusive control of the Secretary of the Interior," who was responsible to "provide for the preservation, from injury or spoliation, of all timber, mineral deposits, natural curiosities, or wonders within said park, and their retention in their natural condition." Congress then ignored Yellowstone, leaving it with no funding for the next five years. It was first policed haphazardly by a nearby U.S. cavalry unit to control poaching of park animals, prevent vandalism of rare formations (tourists would chip off souvenirs), and keep speculators from illegal fencing and fee collection. Within a few years, however, the Northern Pacific Railroad aggressively advertised its tourist lodges and the wonders of Yellowstone. Visitors sought to fill their curiosity about the "freaks of nature" while enjoying soft beds and fine food in stylish resorts that featured safe strolls and light recreation.

Other National Parks and the National Park Service

Despite the popular attention Yosemite and Yellowstone had received, no national agenda to save wonders and curiosities had emerged. Not until 1890 did Congress set aside the towering snow-capped dormant volcano, Mount Rainier, in the state of Washington. In this case the boundaries of the park protected an individual natural wonder, but not its surrounding timbered environment that was even more vulnerable. John Muir warned, "The icy dome [of Mount Rainier] needs none of man's care, but unless the reserve is guarded the flower bloom will soon be killed, and nothing of the forests will be left but black stump monuments." Congress allowed resource exploration and mining to continue inside the park, following the multiple-use philosophy of Progressive conservationists. This issue of important environs around a monumental scene led in the 1920s to a protracted debate over Jackson Hole. This was a flat plain of woodlands, grasslands, and sagebrush flats south of Yellowstone that provided the setting for the new Grand Teton National Park. John D. Rockefeller, Jr. covertly bought up 35,000 acres of Jackson Hole and, against the angry objections of hunters, ranchers, and developers, persuaded President Calvin Coolidge to withdraw four times more acreage, all of which eventually went into the expanded park, but not until after a battle that lasted until 1950. The final settlement incorporated 298,000 acres into Grand Teton National Park.

Two high Sierra redwood groves, Sequoia and General Grant (later Kings Canyon), were also set aside in 1890, but as "reserved forest lands." The Forest Reserve Act of 1891 gave presidents the authority to proclaim permanent forest reserves on the public domain, but, unlike national parks to be kept in their natural condition, the new national forests would be managed for long-term harvesting under the principles of multiple-use conservation. Progressive resource management policy that deliberately excluded wilderness protection was reinforced by the creation of the Reclamation Bureau in 1902 and restated in the 1908 governor's conference chaired by President Theodore Roosevelt. It was no little matter that the new Forest Service became part of the Department of Agriculture instead of the Department of the Interior, the future home of the National Park Service. The stakes were not small: By 1916 five presidents had put an extraordinary 176 million acres of western forests into the new category. Elsewhere, local cowboys, government explorers, and ethnographers reported mysterious prehistoric cliff dwellings and romantic pueblo ruins in the southwestern deserts. The Antiquities Act of 1906 empowered the president of the United States to reserve "historic landmarks, historic and prehistoric structures, and other objects of historic or scientific interest" on public land as national monuments. Theodore Roosevelt set an important precedent when he broadly interpreted the act to give him blanket authority to set aside noteworthy public land of any type. In total, he proclaimed 18 national monuments, including 12, like

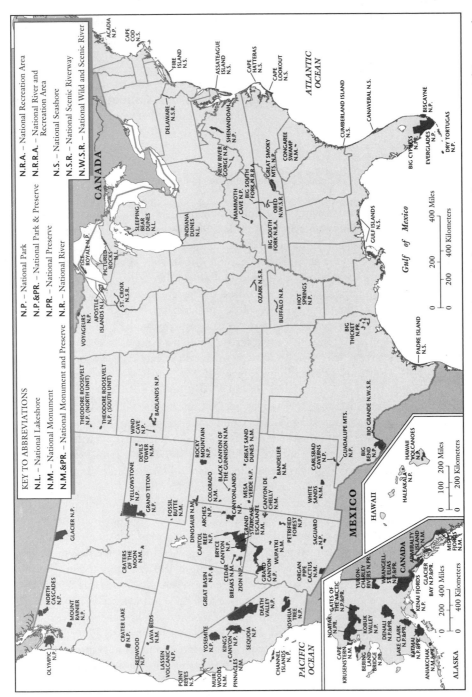

Primary Natural Units of the National Park System. While the United States was the first to set aside public "parks" for recreation and protection, new ecosystem policies suggest that most of the units are far too small to prevent harmful interventions from neighboring economic development.

Devil's Tower in northeastern Wyoming, that were primarily natural sites. President Franklin D. Roosevelt used the Antiquities Act to proclaim more than 2 million acres as natural monuments, including the desert sites of Joshua Tree in California, Organ Pipe Cactus in southern Arizona, and Capitol Reef in south-central Utah, and he added to Zion, Death Valley, Dinosaur, Glacier Bay, and Badlands. After 1978 Congress prevented presidents from using the Antiquities Act to hold out natural places except with congressional cooperation. The last major proclamation was Jimmy Carter's set-aside of 11 large monuments in Alaska. In all, presidents had used the authority of the Antiquities Act to create a total of 99 national monuments, only 38 historic or prehistoric, the remaining 61 primarily natural. Out of these emerged 25 national parks, such as Arizona's Grand Canyon, Utah's Arches, and Alaska's Glacier Bay, overall a quarter of the entire modern national park system.

Crater Lake in Oregon received national park status in 1902, Mesa Verde in Colorado in 1906, Glacier National Park ("1,400 square miles of mountains piled on top of each other") in Montana in 1910, Rocky Mountain National Park in Colorado in 1915, and California's Mount Lassen and Hawaii National Park in 1916. By then Americans had set aside 16 national parks and 18 national monuments, but with no consistent planning or coordinated management, and especially a lack of organizational continuity that made the parks dependent on the whims of each interior secretary, each Congress, and each presidential administration. They had been "improved" and managed by the Forest Service, the War Department (U.S. Cavalry and Corps of Engineers), and indifferently by the Department of the Interior. It took 44 years after Yellowstone to create a separate government agency, the National Park Service (NPS) in 1916, as a unit of the Department of the Interior. Gifford Pinchot's Forest Service vigorously resisted a separate national park agency with a preservationist philosophy. Momentum especially built up when in 1915 the Forest Service reduced the size of Washington's Mount Olympus National Monument (a national park in 1938) by more than half to allow lumbering operations. The first park after the NPS was established was Alaska's Mount McKinley in 1917, followed by Arizona's Grand Canyon and Utah's Zion in 1919, and Bryce Canyon in 1928. Wyoming's Grand Teton followed in 1929 and New Mexico's Carlsbad Caverns in 1930. Wilderness environments in the parks were also vulnerable to the prevailing philosophy of utilitarian conservation that might allow mining, forest harvesting, dams and reservoirs (see later for the Hetch Hetchy controversy), as well as expansion of roads, resorts, and services for tourists. In 1911 R. B. Marshall of the Geological Survey told a New York outdoorsman audience, "Manage the national parks on a business basis and work for good transportation facilities to and from them, so that the multitude may visit them." In the lobbying effort for a park service, conservation leader J. H. McFarland reported, "The park idea in America has come to be the idea of service and efficiency, and not an ideal of pleasure and ornamentation at all."

Changing Agendas for the National Parks

An alternative view advocating wilderness preservation did not have an official voice in the federal government. In his popular 1917 book on the parks, Colorado's Enos Mills stated the park mission succinctly: "A national park is an island of safety in this riotous world. Within national parks is room—glorious room—room in which to find ourselves, in which to think and hope, to dream and plan, to rest, and resolve." It is no accident that the first NPS park director was a businessman, Stephen T. Mather, who made his fortune in the western borax industry. He stated, "Our national parks are practically lying fallow, and only await proper development to bring them into their own." Preservationists, who had grave doubts about railroad terminals, paved roads, and resort hotels, blanched at the "civilizing" of the parks, but admitted that the threat of dams, reservoirs, power lines, water conduits, and other massive structures was worse. They admitted that the promotion of tourism would increase public affection for America's crown jewels. Mather's associate, Robert Sterling Yard, wrote in 1922 that although basic services require "roads, trails, hotels and camps sufficient to permit the people to live there awhile and contemplate the unaltered works of nature, no tree, shrub or wild flower is cut, no stream or lake shore is disturbed, no bird or animal is destroyed."

A string of eastern parks—"islands in a growing sea of civilization"—came into existence with the creation of Lafayette (Acadia) National Park in Maine in 1919, Shenandoah National Park in Virginia in 1926, Great Smoky Mountains National Park that bridged Tennessee and North Carolina in 1926, and Everglades National Park in Florida in 1934. These parks differed because, in one official's words, "they are second to the West in rugged grandeur, but they are first in beauty of woods." The Great Smoky Mountains and the Blue Ridge Mountains were promoted as botanical refuges, one of the world's great concentrations of tree and plant species. This was a shift of attitude: The eastern mountains were not set aside primarily for their scenic value as geological wonders, but as protection zones for wildlife and forests. The eastern parks were also different because they had to be acquired mostly out of privately owned land at high cost; with the help of private associations, Congress authorized 512,000 acres for Shenandoah and 704,000 acres for Great Smoky Mountain National Park. Unlike the delayed tourism in the inaccessible West, the eastern parks immediately experienced intense visitor pressure and competition from nearby metropolitan regions.

The Reorganization Act of 1933 gave the NPS an entirely new agenda, which would conflict with its wilderness mission. It was to run military battlefields such as Yorktown in Virginia and Morristown in New Jersey, memorials such as the Statue of Liberty in New York harbor and Mount Rushmore in South Dakota, and national cemeteries like Arlington in the District of Columbia. This shift was reinforced by the Historic Sites Act of 1935 that gave it responsibility for rural and urban locations as well as the wilderness. In Washington, D.C., this included Rock Creek Park, still a well-preserved natural area in an urban environment, and Potomac Park, reclaimed swampland along the Potomac River, the Washington Monument, the site of the Lincoln and Jefferson memorials, and more recently the Vietnam Veterans Memorial. Other national memorials that came under NPS aegis included, among many, Ellis Island, the Wright brothers' Kill Devil Hill in North Carolina, and battlefields like Bunker Hill, Gettysburg, Shiloh, Vicksburg, Appomattox Courthouse, and Custer/Little Big Horn. NPS wilderness priorities were also clouded by its administration of recreational areas designated primarily for public use, such as reservoirs and parkways. The 470-mile Blue Ridge Parkway in southern Appalachia, authorized in 1934, turned a local road into a restricted recreational road with scenic and historical sights. The NPS came under attack for compromising its wilderness principles when it constructed the Skyline Drive through Shenandoah National Park and Trail Ridge Road in Rocky Mountain Park, both designated U.S. highways. Equally controversial were NPS management of national recreational areas at dams built by the Reclamation Service, notably at Nevada's Boulder Dam, Colorado's Flaming Gorge, and Arizona's Lake Powell. The NPS received praise, however, for its acquisition of coastal strips at Cape Hatteras, North Carolina, Cape Cod National Seashore, Point Reyes north of San Francisco, and the Indiana Dunes National Lakeshore.

After World War II, Americans enjoyed three decades of unusual abundance that created disposable income, leisure time, and ownership of automobiles. Most visitors began to look at the wilderness framed by their windshields. From a prewar 6 million visitors, 33 million visited the parks by 1950 and 72 million by 1960. The NPS initiated Mission 66, which surveyed 600 potential new natural landmarks for inclusion in the system. Mission 66 was primarily, however, a ten-year billion-dollar development program to upgrade roads, campgrounds, hotels, sanitary facilities, visitor centers, and staff to suit the new influx of visitors. It came under severe opposition for its apparent promotion of recreation and lack of interest in wilderness protection, which helped passage of the Wilderness Act in 1964. In the 1960s a scientific committee chaired by biologist A. Starker Leopold proposed a new ecologically based management of the park system: "As a primary goal, we would recommend that the biotic associations within each park be maintained, or where necessary recreated, as nearly as possible in the condition that prevailed when the area was first visited by the white man. A national park should represent a self-contained vignette of primitive America," including the return of predators like wolves, spontaneous environment-cleansing fires, and the protection of park ecosystems that extended beyond park borders. Both the NPS and the Forest Service delayed the setting-aside of the first designated wilderness regions until 1968.

By 1964 additions were made to Grand Canyon and Hawaii national parks, and new parks created, notably North Cascades National Park in the state of Washington, which covered over 500,000 acres, and the Canyonlands National Park that included the historic confluence of the Green and Colorado rivers. Canyonlands was uniquely authorized to remain in a relatively primitive condition without paved roads or modern facilities. By the mid-1970s the NPS had difficult digesting all its additions and changes and began to apply the brakes on new acquisitions and tighten its criteria for national parklands. In 1981 President Reagan's first interior secretary, James G. Watt, refused to expand the number of regions protected by national park status despite a congressional mandate and budget appropriations. Preservation was losing out to recreation. Most NPS officials were disillusioned by the continuous erosion of remaining wilderness areas in the parks. Park Service morale sank. For more than 50 years, the National Park Service had earned an enviable reputation for a high degree of professionalism; the public gave park rangers the respect usually afforded doctors, lawyers, and the clergy. In the 1980s, however, the shift of many career positions in the NPS into political appointments was particularly troublesome. A turnaround began in 1993, when the Clinton administration, led by Interior Secretary Bruce Babbitt, began to restore the earlier professionalism. However, severe federal budget constraints hampered the future picture. It became clear that wilderness protection, even within reserved lands of designated wildernesses and the national parks, was not inviolate, but depended largely on the goodwill of each presidential administration, as well as the political climate. Visitor attendance to the parks had doubled and tripled into the hundreds of millions of annual visits. The parks were being loved to death.

Battle over National Park Concessions

The first director of the NPS, Stephen Mather, encouraged commercial concessions, such as resort hotels, tennis courts, swimming pools, and other recreational facilities to attract tourism

A Difficult Ecological Challenge: Everglades National Park

One troubled national park covered a large but ecologically incomplete part of a vast swampland, the Everglades of southern Florida. Southern Florida had been virtually empty unsettled land—the Everglades was a blank spot marked "unexplored" on maps—until the tourist boom of the 1920s. Florida then went through uncontrolled resort development that in turn created large metropolitan areas. As early as 1848, when the U.S. military chased Seminole Indians through the swamps, they reported that the land should be drained for cattle raising and for growing rice, sugar cane, fruits, and vegetables. Not until the early twentieth century did the state of Florida take a serious look at drainage for farmland, and not until after World War II did the Army Corps of Engineers plan a drainage system. The Everglades scene seemed unlikely for national park status, compared to the mountains, canyons, geological formations, waterfalls, and clean crisp air of the western parks. No one has ever called the Everglades "Grand." Instead, it was "a river of drowned grass" 40 miles wide and only a few feet deep, that descended slowly—the drop was only 17 feet overall—100 miles to the southern coast. Most local people saw it as a mosquito-ridden, monotonous swamp of snakes and alligators that only deserved to be filled, made into solid ground, and developed into real estate subdivisions, malls, and resort facilities. Its aggressive advocates Marjorie Stoneman Douglas and Ernest F. Coe argued that the new park, created in 1947, was primarily the preservation of an increasingly rare primitive landscape. Nevertheless, even after the park was established to the north two major causeway-style highways and a canal system compromised the once-pristine, free-flowing river of grass and its natural balances.

The Everglades was one of the world's great bird habitats, supporting "thousands and thousands of ibis, egrets, and herons flocking in at sunset," of spoonbills, storks, and pelicans. At last count there were also 26 species of snake (4 poisonous), 12 species of frog, 6 species of lizards, 24 species of spiders, and 43 species of mosquitoes. The act

as a "public good." Already for some decades the Curry Company had virtually controlled how tourists arrived at Yosemite, where they ate and slept, what souvenirs they purchased, what scenic sights to find at an "inspiration point," and overall access to the park. The famous Fred Harvey enterprises did the same for a number of other major parks, including the Grand Canyon. In most cases, the concessionaires had exclusive noncompetitive contracts with the NPS that were renewed with little critical review. Mather added, "As Uncle Sam is not an innkeeper nor a liveryman, private enterprise must provide the means of living in and enjoying these great national playgrounds." He concluded, "It is the duty of the government representing these millions to provide each one who comes as nearly as possible the degree of comfort, even of luxury, that he requires." An elevator should carry people to the foot of the Lower Yellowstone Falls. An aerial tramway should rise to Glacier point in Yosemite. Cable cars should cross the Grand Canyon to link the resort hotels on opposite rims. These enter-

that established the park stated that "the said area or areas shall be permanently reserved as a wilderness," and no improvements for visitor access could "interfere with the preservation intact of the unique flora and fauna and the essential primitive conditions." This was more revolutionary than the creators realized, and equally difficult to sustain. Only gradually did it become clear that the Everglades depended upon a massive water ecosystem that covered most of the southern half of the state. Even though 2,000 square miles (today 1.4 million acres) had been set aside, making the Everglades at the time the nation's third largest national park, its biological integrity depended upon more than 90 percent of Everglades still outside in private hands. The Everglades was actually the overflow of the large Lake Okeechobee in south central Florida. The lake flooded its banks during the June to October rainy season and regularly drowned farmland between the lake and park. To help farmers, the Army Corps of Engineers built levees and channels for flood control. As a result, water levels fell in the park and threatened the survival of unique plant and animal populations. Chemical pollution from agriculture and development had already affected birdlife and alligators since early in the century. By 1947, the flow to the Everglades had dropped enough to threaten the future of its uniqueness. The nature writer Peter Farb reported in 1961 that "I found no Eden but rather a waterless hell under a blazing sun. Everywhere I saw Everglades drying up, the last drops of water evaporating from water holes, creeks and sloughs." As water levels dropped the numbers of wading birds alone declined by 93 percent since 1930. By 1962 engineering projects on the lake and upstream could shut off drainage into the park completely, in order not to flood farmlands in between. A compromise in 1966 among the conflicting interests allowed scheduled releases of limited amounts of water for minimal maintenance, but not nearly enough for "preservation of the primitive." Not until the 1980s and 1990s, with a better understanding of ecosystem science, did the Corps of Engineers and other agencies begin to undo some of their drainage and canalization, in order to revive the entire Everglades system, inside and outside the national park.

prises were defeated, but skiing facilities, including lifts, were built in Mount Rainier, Rocky Mountain, Sequoia, Yosemite, Lassen, and Olympic national parks. Mather also proudly reported, "Splendid cooperation developed among chambers of commerce, tourist bureaus, and automobile-highway associations for the purpose of spreading information about our parks and facilitating their use and enjoyment."

By midcentury, however, the NPS publicly voiced concern about the overcrowding of the park system, the deterioration of facilities, and intrusions into the wilder areas of the parks. Nevertheless, it encouraged the concessionaires toward further commercial development. For example, in 1974, when Music Corporation of America (MCA) acquired the concession in Yosemite National Park, it sought to expand facilities in the already overused valley. Old cabins were to be replaced with modern motel units, the aerial tramway would finally reach Glacier Point for "viewing, eating and sundry sales," backcountry camps would be run

THE PURPOSE OF reserving natural areas is not to keep people in their cars, but to lure them out; to encourage a close look at the infinite detail and variety that the natural scene provides; to expose, rather than to insulate, so that the peculiar character of the desert, or the alpine forest, can be distinctively felt. The novice, the elderly, and the infirm, as well as the experienced backcountry user, can all be embraced within the same policy. Those who have little vigor or impaired capacity may be limited to a smaller area or to less grueling terrain, but there is an abundance of experience to be had within easy reach in any complex natural ecosystem for those who are willing to trade intensiveness for extensiveness of experience. Indeed, the more immediately nature is met, the less total land that is required. Places become much bigger when we are on foot, and a slower pace enlarges the material on which to expend our leisure.

—Environmental law professor Joseph L. Sax, 1980

by the concessionaire, park streams stocked with non-native trout, and more winter recreation and convention business would be vigorously promoted. Public protest led to sharply negative congressional hearings that forced a reluctant NPS to redo its management plans. Similar pressures continued at Great Smoky Mountain, Grand Teton, Glacier, and other popular national parks. For a time during the Reagan-Bush presidential administrations (1980–1992), under the policy of the privatization of public services, park concessionaires enjoyed the upper hand over a demoralized NPS. Private tourist-related operations seemed to advance regardless of a compromised wilderness. This included expansion of tourist facilities, a move toward mineral exploration, and refusal to enlarge the overcrowded parks system. Grandiose proposals for the Grand Canyon included flooding for easier viewing from tourist boats. But recent NPS policy has instead emphasized rigorous monitoring of park concessions and competitive awards of contracts.

John Muir, Yosemite, and the Sierra Club

John Muir (1838–1914) is the father of American wilderness preservation. He founded the Sierra Club in 1892, helped set up six major national parks, popularized wilderness tourism, and wrote books and articles that created a national audience favoring wilderness protection. Probably more than anyone else in American history, he developed the wilderness philosophy that wild nature was a healing escape from the urban industrial society which America had become. He could without affectation join Thoreau and Emerson to say, "Idle sentimental transcendental dreaming is the only sensible and substantial business that one can engage in." But Muir separated himself from Emerson and Thoreau when he recognized that they were more comfortable with a tamed nature than a true wilderness. A half century later, wildlife manager Aldo Leopold added scientific rigor to Muir's philosophy.

In his late twenties, Muir himself experienced wilderness as a religious epiphany. He was born in 1838 to a dour Highland Scottish grocery family. His dominating father believed in a vindictive God, Bible memorization, childhood beatings, and punishingly hard work. In 1849 the Muir family moved to the harsh frontier of southeastern Wisconsin. Even as a boy, he found escape from the tedious routines of farm life in the vitality of the wild trees, plants, birds, and animals of the Wisconsin countryside. A skilled inventor and natural teacher, he attended the University of Wisconsin for two years. Then in 1864 he took off to Canada to avoid military conscription. Although a conversion experience can easily be overdramatized, it is true that he went through a personal change when, on a hike above the Great Lakes, he collapsed into tears at the sudden sight of a rare exquisite wild orchid (*Calypso borealis*) in forlorn country. Muir discovered a seamless intermingling between the human self and the cosmos: "Presently you lose consciousness of your own separate existence: you blend with the landscape, and become part and parcel of nature." Never quite escaping his biblical background, Muir also saw God blended into nature in a kind of pantheism. Upon his return to the United States, Muir worked in a wagon parts factory in Indianapolis, where he was nearly blinded in an accident. After recovery of his sight, he embarked in 1867 on a 1,000-mile walk to the Gulf of Mexico that was also a spiritual pilgrimage through nature's nation. This walk produced the first of a series of popular books that promoted the wilderness. Walking through virgin forests in the Cumberland Mountains or the steamy Florida swamps, he saw nature as a community in which all living creatures served their own purposes and humans had no special privileges.

Inspired with a sense of mission by the time he turned 30, John Muir abandoned conventional Christianity, found traditional scientific knowledge too restrictive, and abhorred conventional consumer society. Muir concluded that human separateness from wild nature only inspired arrogance, materialistic greed, and spoliation of humanity's own nest—"the gross heathenism of civilization." Despite his antipathy toward traditional orthodoxies, Muir had a religious fervor that still flavors the environmental movement. "I am lost—absorbed captivated with the divine and unfathomable loveliness and grandeur of Nature." In contrast, civilized society was a necessary evil, barely to be tolerated. "Somehow I feel separated from the mass of mankind, and I do not know whether I can return to the ordinary modes of feeling and thinking." Muir was equally critical of modern science when it merely saw nature as Newtonian matter in motion; such science turned wilderness into a resource to be cut and sawed, eroded and paved. Among the first generation after Darwin, Muir struggled with the meaning of nature's dynamic evolution instead of a fixed creation. But he seldom did research in books; instead, he worked energetically in the field. He was the first to describe the origins of Yosemite Valley on a colossal time scale that allowed for glaciers to scoop it out, instead of one sudden catastrophic accident claimed by most scientists of his day. All in all, Muir believed wild nature was the first place to find beauty, glory, spirituality, sacredness, and ultimate truth: "Going to the woods is going home; for I suppose we came from the woods originally."

By 1868 John Muir showed up in the California Sierra mountains and spent one unfortunate season alone in a squalid hut in charge of 1,800 domestic sheep that he called stupid and harmful "hoofed locusts," totally different from noble wild mountain sheep. He moved to Yosemite Valley where he built a simple cabin near the base of the Lower Yosemite Falls and barely supported himself at a sawmill. He wrote, "Now I am no longer a shepherd with a few bruised beans and crackers in my stomach and wrapped in a woolen blanket but a free bit of everything." Like Thoreau, Muir left society behind, to "learn to live like the wild animals, gleaning nourishment here and there from seeds, berries, etc., sauntering and climbing in joyful independence of money or baggage." This was only a slight exaggeration, for his fellow climbers were astonished when he loped across the county for days carrying only a bit of tea, oatmeal, crackers or bread in a sack, wearing ordinary work clothes and hobnailed low-cut shoes, to sleep wrapped in a blanket on a bed of spruce branches. His first summer in the Yosemite Valley included a second epiphany induced by brilliant "waves of the sun" that spotlighted a field of alpine flowers. At the Vernal and Nevada waterfalls "water does not seem to be under the dominion of ordinary [Newton's] laws, but rather as if it were a living creature, full of the strength of the mountains and their huge wild joy." Another time he intercepted a violent windstorm by climbing near the top of a wildly swaying 100-foot Douglas spruce.

Muir began to write elegant and pithy articles on wilderness appreciation for eastern magazines, which entranced a growing national audience. He pleased readers with books and articles of travel accounts, adventure stories, and nature descriptions, such as his tale of the unusual water-diving bird, the ouzel. The public adored his personal accounts. Once, marooned in a darkening snowstorm on the Taylor glacier in Alaska with the dog Stickeen, Muir called on his "other self" to cross a thin ice bridge to safety. "At such times one's whole body is eye," remembering Emerson's "transparent eyeball." "Common skill and fortitude are replaced by power beyond our call or knowledge." Stickeen "showed neither caution nor curiosity, wonder nor fear, but bravely trotted on as if glaciers were playgrounds. His stout, muffled body seemed all one skipping muscle." Muir's fame grew. Eastern luminaries came to visit him at his Yosemite cabin. He hosted aging transcendentalist Ralph Waldo Emerson and the nature writer John Burroughs at Yosemite, but he discovered that they were too citified to spend nights with him high in the Tuolumne Valley. When the outdoors-minded President Theodore Roosevelt made a pilgrimage to see Muir and the Yosemite, the two had a bully good time high in the mountains. Muir urged his contemporaries to duplicate his liberation in the wilderness. "Thousands of tired, nerve-shaken, over-civilized people are beginning to find out that going to the mountains is going home; that wildness is a necessity; and that mountain parks and reservations are useful not only as fountains of timber and irrigating rivers, but as fountains of life." He also recognized the irony of this appeal, since he would have to work hard to save the wilderness from roving bands of enthusiastic Muirians. By 1915, 335,000 visitors enjoyed the growing national park system, compared to only 69,000 in 1908 and only handfuls in the late nineteenth century.

During the time when Muir made Yosemite his home, local business leaders formed the Yosemite Stage and Turnpike Company to carry tourists from railroad heads and serve them with hotels, camps, restaurants, and shops in the formerly pristine valley. In response, John Muir and New York publisher Robert Underwood Johnson began a public campaign to make Yosemite into a federal reserve. This was the first of a series of historic confrontations between private development versus public protection. Muir and Johnson also gained the support of the politically powerful Southern Pacific Railroad, whose rail line would control access to the park, to ram through Congress an 1889 bill protecting 1,500 square miles of the Sierra, including Yosemite Valley, the Mariposa Tree Grove, nearby Lake Tenaya, and the adjacent Tuolumne River watershed. Yosemite became the nation's second national park in 1890, but Muir could not hold back gaudy concessions and lax management. The victory at Yosemite encouraged a group of San Francisco Californians to start in 1892 a mountain recreation club with Muir as its first president. Modeled after the existing Appalachian Mountain Club, the new Sierra Club mirrored Muir's wilderness philosophy. For many decades it remained a small but successful California club dedicated to mountain trampings, wilderness education, and social gatherings, with the now famous John Muir as its main attraction. Much later, in the 1960s, the Sierra Club would become a national environmental force with half a million members.

From the Defeat at Hetch Hetchy
to the Victory at Echo Park

Hetch Hetchy means "grassy meadows" in local Indian language. The Hetch Hetchy Valley caught John Muir's attention as equal to neighboring Yosemite Valley. It had been set aside as a wilderness preserve within the new national park. But the city of San Francisco saw the Hetch Hetchy valley, with its spectacular high walls, as the ideal location for a water reservoir dam to help keep up with projected population growth. The city became even more insistent after the earthquake and citywide fires in 1906, which gave it widespread national sympathy. Muir and Johnson protested to President Roosevelt about the "irrefragable ignorance" of the plan, "trying to make everything dollarable." Roosevelt was sympathetic but deferred to his chief forester, Gifford Pinchot, who saw in the Hetch Hetchy dam and reservoir a prime example of Progressive conservationism. According to Pinchot's multiple-use philosophy, a dammed Hetch Hetchy would provide water for a growing city and expand public recreation (boating, fishing, floating sightseeing) in the national park.

The battle between wilderness preservation and utilitarian conservation was clearly joined. Muir found himself in a public struggle with his old wilderness compatriots, Pinchot and Roosevelt, which grieved him for the rest of his life. Hetch Hetchy became his personal moral crusade: "Dam Hetch Hetchy! As well dam for water-tanks the people's cathedrals and churches, for no holier temple has ever been consecrated by the heart of man." Pinchot put the issues succinctly. The question was whether "leaving this valley in a state of nature is greater than using it for the benefit of the city of San Francisco." During the congressional debates over Hetch Hetchy, a California representative reported that the total value of "old barren rocks" of the valley could be set at $300,000, whereas the reservoir was worth millions. A magazine editor retorted that it was a mistake "to turn every tree and waterfall into dollars and cents." An Arizona senator reflected the final prodam vote when he said that although "we all love the sound of whispering winds amid the trees, the wail of a hungry baby will make us forget it as we try to minister to its wants." Muir's Sierra Club was joined by the Izaac Walton League and the Audubon Society to coalesce into a formidable national campaign. But these amateur part-time conservationist organizations could not match a skilled campaign led by the city of San Francisco that outlasted them. A permit for the dam was granted in 1908, saying that "domestic use is the highest use," but congressional committees responded to a letter-writing campaign led by Muir by blocking the project in 1909. The new president, William Howard Taft, was impressed by Muir's impassioned pleas during a visit to Yosemite and the new interior secretary Richard A. Ballinger toured Hetch Hetchy, which earned a delay until late 1912. Anti-Muir forces effectively linked wilderness protection with sentimental effete asceticism by "short-haired women and long-haired men." They took up a refrain that would be used repeatedly in the future about Glen Canyon and even the Grand Canyon: A lake at the valley site would enhance its beauty and open the region for public recreation. The preservationists retorted, "You may as well improve upon the lily of the field by hand-painting it." President Woodrow Wilson and Congress approved the dam in 1913, and the first water flowed 150 miles west to San Francisco in 1934 from a dam that cost $100 million, or twice the original estimate. Before John Muir died of pneumonia in late 1914, he wrote Johnson, "I think you must feel, as I do, that a child of ours has been mutilated."

The same tensions between preservation and conservation shaped a wilderness debate in the 1950s and 1960s far more extensive than Hetch Hetchy. Beginning in the 1940s, the federal Bureau of Reclamation, dedicated to the development of the West by "taming" its rivers, sought to turn the entire Colorado River basin into a series of dams and reservoirs for irrigation, flood control, and electrification. It had started with the popular Boulder Dam on the lower Colorado River. The billion-dollar Colorado River Storage Project included a dam at the junction of the Green and Yampa rivers, which feed into the Colorado River at a place called Echo Park. Echo Park was a spectacular hidden canyon deep inside the 320-square-mile Dinosaur National Monument on the northern Colorado-Utah border. It was also one of a few remaining prime dam sites in the entire basin. The Bureau of Reclamation received

The Controversial Bureau of Land Management

In the 1930s several government agencies promoted commercial use of large parcels of the unsold public domain by selling to private interests the rights to timber cutting, cattle grazing, and mining for minerals and petroleum. This activity was centralized in 1946 by the U.S. Department of the Interior when the new Bureau of Land Management (BLM) replaced the controversial Grazing Service and the outmoded General Land Office. The BLM was made entirely responsible for most of the remaining public domain encompassing 270 million acres of public land, almost entirely in the West and Alaska, and mostly leased as grazing and mineral lands. BLM continued to allow private development, which earned it a long-standing reputation for truculent indifference toward resource protection. Much, but not all, of that reputation was deserved. BLM continued to sell grazing rights and grazing fees at low cost. It received the ire of preservationists in the 1960s and 1970s by allowing the Alaska pipeline to run across pristine wilderness, permitting off-road-vehicles (motorcycles, jeeps, snowmobiles, etc.) in designated wildernesses, and by fighting interagency battles with the Forest Service and National Park Service. Certain personalities stand out, including Marion Clawson's activist leadership from 1948 to 1953 and Charles H. Stoddard's quality professionalism from 1963 to 1966. Stoddard described BLM's still unresolved split personality: "BLM must remain a land management agency—in place of its real estate disposal past." Today BLM oversees more than a quarter of the nation's entire landmass. As such, it is an underrated giant. Its modern mandate comes from FLPMA—the 1976 Federal Land Policy and Management Act—which gave BLM a specific environmental protection mission, forced in large part by the necessity of environmental impact statements mandated by the 1969-70 National Environmental Protection Act (NEPA). FLPMA did bring direction and professionalism to the agency, and started it on its way to land classification, inventory, and planning operations. Controversy still rages over wilderness preservation in several western states, where ranchers and miners seek to keep their old privileges on millions of acres in BLM hands, such as California's Mohave Desert or most of southern Utah.

approval from the secretary of the interior in 1950. But an ever-growing number of conservation organizations, led by David R. Brower of the Sierra Club and Howard C. Zahniser of the
Wilderness Society, built a sophisticated public campaign that compelled both Congress and
federal agencies to back off. An unprecedented letter-writing campaign was spurred by
national newspaper advertising, articles in major magazines, and pamphlets that asked, "Will
you DAM the Scenic Wild Canyons of Our National Park System?" "Shall We Let Them
Ruin Our National Parks?" "What Is Your Stake in Dinosaur?" and "Hetch Hetchy—One Is
Too Often." Popular writer Bernard DeVoto called for protection of Echo Park as one of
America's few remaining places where "the balances of nature, the web of life, the inter-
relationships of species, [and] massive problems of ecology" can be studied and understood.
The Colorado River Storage Project, but without the controversial Echo Park Dam, was
authorized by Congress in 1956. A sentence in the bill added, "that no dam or reservoir constructed under the authorization of the Act shall be within any National Park or Monument."
The cheering by wilderness groups fell silent, however, when they realized Echo Park was
saved because it involved a bittersweet compromise that authorized the Bureau of Reclamation to build other dams, one upstream from Dinosaur to drown the spectacular Flaming
Gorge and the other to cover the little known but large wonder, Glen Canyon, upstream
from the Grand Canyon.

From Scenery to Ecosystem:
The Modern Wilderness Movement

By the 1960s, particularly after the publication of Rachel Carson's *Silent Spring* (1962), the
new science of ecology (see Chapter 13) persuaded Americans to think about wilderness not
as individual scenic "wonders" but as complete ecosystems. Environmental law professor
Joseph Sax said, "Our interest in preserving natural systems is not merely sentimental; it rests
on preservation of nothing less than an enormous knowledge base that we have no capacity to
replicate." It became clear that the borders of existing national parks such as Yellowstone
often did not include critical watersheds, wildlife ranges, buffer areas, or reflect the larger
ecosystems of which they were a part.

The Wilderness Act of 1964

The successful defense of Echo Park gave wilderness organizations momentum to continue
their crusade. They had captured public approval while federal agencies like the Bureau of
Reclamation, the Bureau of Land Management, the Forest Service, and even the National
Park Service were publicly censured for abandoning a fragile heritage for a few minerals, kilowatts, acre-feet of irrigation, powerboats, and motor homes. It had long been a dream among
wilderness leaders like Robert Marshall, Aldo Leopold, David Brower, and Howard Zahniser
to establish a federal system of wilderness preserves. The idea of designated wildernesses had

also been floated in government circles in the 1930s by Harold L. Ickes, secretary of the interior to President Franklin D. Roosevelt. A wilderness bill first sent to Congress in 1957 sought "to secure for the American people of present and future generations the benefits of an enduring reservoir of wilderness." It listed over 160 areas of untouched public land, as much as 50 million acres (2 percent of the nation's total) free of roads, public facilities, mining, drilling, grazing, or other human use. The listed areas were already publicly held lands in national forests, national parks and monuments, wildlife refuges and ranges, as well as Indian reservations. Vehement opposition to the wilderness bill came from the forest industry, oil field and mining corporations, ranchers who grazed their cattle on public lands, the commercial tourism industry, and the Forest Service, the Bureau of Land Management, and the Bureau of Reclamation. They complained that the bill would require a perpetual lockup of public land for the sake of a few elitist backpackers who might venture into such desolate areas. David Brower of the Sierra Club retorted, "The wilderness we now have is all men will ever have," a fragmented remnant of an entire continent that future generations also deserve to experience. The public was won over by a widespread campaign by the environmental lobby; letters to Congress favored designated wildernesses by more than 8 to 1.

The final Wilderness Act, passed in 1964, was a compromise that authorized 54 areas—"where man himself is a visitor who does not remain"—totaling a little over 9 million acres out of 310 million acres held by federal agencies. They were to be set aside from timber harvesting, road building, motorized vehicles, and other interventions. Even in these, mineral prospecting and mining development could continue until 1984, prior valid mining claims could be developed indefinitely, and the president could authorize dams, power plants, power lines, and roads. Three of the four largest federal land management agencies— the U.S. National Park Service, the U.S. Forest Service, and the U.S. Fish and Wildlife Service—reluctantly took on the enormous task of reviewing potential wilderness areas under their jurisdictions. Not until the 1970s were wilderness areas designated inside existing national parks and monuments, such as Petrified Forest, Lassen Volcanic, Badlands, Isle Royale, Mesa Verde, and Shenandoah. The Forest Service's Roadless Area Review and Evaluation (RARE, and later, RARE II) became a political battleground. In 1971 and 1972 the Forest Service studied almost 1,500 roadless areas covering 56 million acres, a process that included 300 public meetings and 50,000 comments. But at the end the agency refused to assess the impacts of clear-cut logging and strip mining until the Sierra Club Legal Defense Fund forced the issue with a court order. The fourth, and largest federal agency, the Bureau of Land Management, delayed until 1976 when it got its marching orders from the Federal Land Policy Management Act (FLPMA). The Omnibus Park Bill of 1978 (the National Park and Recreation Act) added 1.85 million acres of wilderness from other NPS units, such as the Everglades and Hawaii Volcanoes. RARE II in 1979 recommended only 10 million acres (excluding Alaska) for wilderness, 11 million acres for further study, and opened 36 million for logging and mining. The Wilderness Society complained that another 18 million acres of roadless land in the West had not even been included in the study, but was now opened for development. In 1980 the Reagan administration decided to help the coal industry by eliminating all BLM roadless areas of less than 5,000 acres from wilderness consideration. In the 1980s the logging industry and radical environmental groups like Earth First! literally came to blows over wilderness protection. After 25 years, the National Wilderness Preservation System had grown to encompass more than 90 million acres in 474 units.

Battling the Bureau of Reclamation

Another wilderness controversy involved the powerful Bureau of Reclamation. Since the late 1920s, during its survey of Colorado River sites that led to Boulder Dam, the Bureau of Reclamation had set its eyes on Bridge Canyon and Marble Canyon inside each end of Grand Canyon National Park. A loophole in the 1919 act establishing the park deliberately allowed reclamation projects within its borders. The Marble Canyon dam would back water upriver 53 miles, and Bridge Canyon's impoundment would be 93 miles upriver. The Marble Canyon dam project included, as an inducement for Arizona politicians to support authorization, hydroelectric power for the forthcoming Central Arizona Project to deliver water to Tucson and Phoenix. Ninety percent of Colorado River water impounded in the Marble Canyon reservoir would have run through a 40-mile tunnel under the Kaibab Plateau to a hydroelectric plant. The river below the dam would have trickled through its normal riverbed in the Grand Canyon, far too scanty a stream to continue its historic canyon-cutting erosive power. Wilderness groups and national park supporters were appalled by the audacity of the

A Case in Point: Disney and Mineral King

The continued tension between wilderness and development flamed up in the mid-1960s when Walt Disney Enterprises sought to build an alpine ski complex in California's Mineral King Valley. The test was whether a large-scale private enterprise could use national forest land, in this case just outside the southern tip of Sequoia National Park. The secluded snowy valley stood at 7,800 feet, surrounded by peaks over 12,000 feet. Yet it was close to California's burgeoning metropolitan areas. Mineral King, as its name implied, had once been mined but had reverted to a primitive if not pristine condition. The Sierra Club turned the fate of Mineral King into a national debate over the Forest Service's traditional role as midwife to recreational development versus the public's new interest in protecting high-quality natural ecosystems. If the Disney interests had kept to a minimum facility, they might not have lost when the case was taken to the U.S. Supreme Court. However, they proposed to invest $35 million to bring 8,000 people a day into a valley of 300 acres, served by 13 restaurants seating 2,350 (including a 150-seat coffee shop at the top of an 11,000-foot mountain served by a high-capacity gondola), parking for 3,600 cars, 22 ski lifts, and swimming pools, a horse corral, golf course, tennis courts, and specialty shops. As environmental law professor Joseph Sax noted, the developer was not merely meeting demand but stimulating it. Sax was not arguing to keep people out of Mineral King, but said, "If we are to draw people to the valley, it should be because the place provides a special opportunity for a distinctive kind of recreation; or it is a needed site, because of its physical characteristics, for activities that cannot reasonably be accommodated elsewhere." The proposed resort was rejected on the grounds that it had no place in a primitive valley.

Bureau of Reclamation. Stung by their recent failures at Flaming Gorge and Glen Canyon against the same federal agency, they marshaled a vigorous and expensive campaign against dams in Grand Canyon, which included photographer Eliot Porter's book, *The Place No One Knew: Glen Canyon on the Colorado,* and dramatic full-page advertisements in the *New York Times* and the *Washington Post,* with slogans, "Now Only You Can Save Grand Canyon from Being Flooded . . . For Profit" and "Should We Also Flood the Sistine Chapel So Tourists Can Get Nearer the Ceiling?" Letters began to reach Congress 80 to 1 against the dams. Howard Zahniser of the Wilderness Society said, "We are not fighting progress, we are making it." Public outrage grew when the Internal Revenue Service removed the Sierra Club's tax-free status because of its public promotion. The IRS action was taken to be a gag and intimidation. Sierra Club membership grew from 39,000 in 1966 to 67,000 in 1968. (It went as high as half a million during the Reagan-Watts years in the 1980s.) In 1967 the Central Arizona Project was authorized without either dam, with electric power to come from a still controversial coal-fired power plant at the Four Corners, whose smokestack effluents reduce visibility at the Grand Canyon and other regional parks. Two days after the defeat of the dams, President Johnson also signed the National Wild and Scenic Rivers Act, making into federal policy the popular understanding that although major American rivers can be controlled to serve reclamation purposes, others must be protected "in their free-flowing state." Within a decade more than 1,600 miles of 19 rivers came under protection.

Alaska: The Last Great Wilderness

Beginning in the 1970s the wilderness debate shifted to Alaska. Alaskan wilderness went to extremes, from Mount McKinley (natives called it Denali), the highest peak in North America, to the great calving glaciers of Glacier Bay along Alaska's southward strip, to its frozen arctic coastline, sweeping stretches of swampy inland permafrost and tundra at Yukon Flats, and the isolated mountains of the Brooks Range. In wildlife or ecological terms, Alaska's arctic environment had unique elements nowhere else experienced in the United States.

Since its opportunistic purchase from czarist Russia in 1867, the Alaska territory had been maligned as an icebound worthless "folly." A gold rush in the 1890s that spread to Alaska from the neighboring Canadian Yukon attracted adventurous speculators and settlers. It continued to be viewed as a formidable and unknown wilderness attractive only to misfits, wild adventurers, and primitive natives, a world of polar bears and igloos, with fishing the only profitable industry. More Americans became familiar with Alaska during World War II because of the Japanese invasion of its Aleutian Islands and the construction of the AlCan Highway across Canada for the first overland road link with the lower 48 states. Little changed with statehood in 1959. Its three-week summer growing season and winter temperatures of $-40°$ F in darkness put Alaska less easily under human control. Most of the population of 150,000 clustered around the rail line between Anchorage and Fairbanks. Not until the 1970s did modern technology make a dent in Alaska's challenging environment: Winters can now be endured with prefabricated heated buildings, airplanes for long-distance transportation, and more recently the snowmobile, which has replaced the husky sled team. Tourism often required an expensive float plane trip, mostly to shoot caribou or wolves. Despite the technological challenges, successful oil field exploration in 1968 led to aggressive development on Proudon Bay on the Arctic Sea. Alaskans are still wrestling with the environmental effects—oil spills and caribou migration disruptions—wrought by the above-surface heated-oil Trans-Alaska pipeline that crossed the state to the southern port of Valdez. The large oil spill in Valdez's bay in 1989 demonstrated the ongoing conflict between jobs and development on the one hand and environmental protection and wilderness values on the other.

In contrast to technological opportunism that has characterized most of Alaska's history, wilderness advocates from the earliest days saw Alaska as the nation's last chance to do things right. John Muir was enthralled by the pristine ice fields of Glacier Bay in 1879, which he sharply contrasted to the wretched shacks of the lawless mining town of Wrangell. Government geographer Henry Gannett, a member of Edward Harriman's lavish cruise along the Alaska coast in 1899, argued that tourist visits to its mountains, fjords, and glaciers were worth far more than its timber, fish, or gold. A presidential decree created Glacier Bay National Monument in 1925. Wilderness guru Robert Marshall was another outsider who found personal fulfillment deep in the isolated mountains of the Brooks Range, which he called "two hundred miles beyond the edge of the twentieth century." Marshall spoke for many lower-states visitors who saw in Alaska the opportunity to return to wilderness. Against the wishes of many Alaskans, the NPS established in 1960 the Arctic National Wildlife Range, covering 9 million acres. Alaskan opposition to this "lockup" from industrial development complained of an "armchair clientele" of environmentalists who wished to keep Alaska primitive. The Ramparts Dam proposal by the Corps of Engineers would have created the world's largest human-made lake across the Yukon Flats tundra and destroyed salmon spawning and one of the world's major bird flyway breeding grounds. Electric power from the project would have opened northern Alaska to industry, mining, and logging. But following the defeat of the Echo Park Dam in 1956 and passage of the Wilderness Act in 1964, the dam project was dropped in 1967. In 1971 the Alaska Native Claims Settlement Act (ANCSA) deeded 44 million acres of federal land to natives for self-rule and to follow native lifestyles. "From the natives' perspective the whole concept of wilderness was a curious, white myth that ignored history." They had been hunting, trapping, and fishing on the land they had called home for 10,000 years. Its mountains, valleys, and rivers already were well traveled and had names.

Five leading wilderness organizations—the Sierra Club, Friends of the Earth, the Wilderness Society, the National Parks and Conservation Association, and the National Audubon Society—formed the Alaska Coalition to support President Carter's statement in 1978 that "We have the imagination and the will as a people to both develop our last great natural frontier and also preserve its priceless beauty for our children and grandchildren." Passage in 1980 of the Alaska National Interest Lands Conservation Act set aside 104 million acres of federal land that was 28 percent of the state, an area larger than California. Historian Roderick Nash called it "the greatest single act of wilderness preservation in world history." Nearly 57 million acres became designated wildernesses, or more than three times the rest of the nation's wilderness regions, another 26 million joined the National Wild and Scenic Rivers System, and Alaska's national parks doubled in size with the remaining 21 million acres. Overall, about a third of the state ended up as designated wilderness. Supporters of the act used a new argument, based on the new environmental sciences, that its passage will help protect entire ecological systems. In the lower 48 states, they said, wilderness was so fragmented that complete ecosystems were no longer available for protection, whereas Alaska still contained enormous undeveloped regions. John Kauffmann of NPS argued that only in Alaska can

Americans still have a last chance to preserve "whole ecosystems, whole ranges, whole watersheds," places "where we can learn how to live in close harmony with the earth." The final act, however, allowed for some intrusions into ecosystems like Yukon Flats for subsistence hunting and fishing, for bush living in cabins, and for oil and mineral prospecting "in the national interest."

Advocates of wilderness no longer believe that once a wilderness preserve is established, in Alaska or anywhere, it is inviolate forever. They have learned that protection depends on the political process and economic conditions. Although Alaska was described in 1974 by Peggy Wayburn of the Sierra Club as "the greatest remaining wildlife, wilderness, and scenic resource on earth," it was also identified by industrial interests as "the nation's last major repository for timber, minerals, oil, natural gas, fresh water, and hydroelectric power." The future of wilderness in Alaska depends on a national commitment to environmental protection.

Aldo Leopold, Ecological Science, and the Land Ethic

No name is more revered in contemporary environmental circles than Aldo Leopold (1886–1948). No book has been more treasured than *A Sand County Almanac*, published in 1949 after Leopold's death. Leopold had scientific credibility as a technical forester and pioneer in wildlife management. Near the end of his life he incorporated a carefully thought out land ethic into his scientific worldview. He is still widely admired for putting both his science and ethic into practice by personally reviving a tract of worn-down farmland in central Wisconsin (30 miles west of where John Muir grew up). Leopold's essay "The Land Ethic" in the 1949 book is the undisputed sacred text of the modern environmental movement. Not the least, Leopold's eloquent writing style, in three books and more than 300 articles, attracted the attention of a wide public.

Born into a prosperous and nature-loving Iowa family in 1886, Aldo Leopold received his boyhood single-barreled shotgun with the admonition that he could shoot partridges, quail, and ducks only when they were in flight. This sense of fairness toward the natural world stayed with him for the rest of his life. College at Yale's School of Forestry, which had been endowed by Gifford Pinchot's family, and his first job in 1909 in Pinchot's new federal Forest Service, immersed him in the utilitarian conservation of the Progressive era. This meant he protected deer for hunters and urged the eradication of natural predators. In 1924 he helped establish New Mexico's Gila Wilderness Area, the nation's first, where he immediately strove to wipe out the wolf population. However, over time he came to understand that nature was not merely a stockpile of raw materials for human consumption. He would eventually move toward John Muir's wilderness preservationism, which valued wild nature for its own sake. In an essay, "Thinking Like a Mountain," he told how he once in the Gila Wilderness shot a mother wolf, and saw in its wild animal's fierce dying eyes another world of which humans knew little. Such "varmints" had as much right to exist as humans did. In 1924 Leopold was transferred, because of his superior aptitude for research, to the U.S. Forest Products Laboratory in Madison, Wisconsin. His resulting work anticipated modern ecological science when he concluded that all the parts of any environment, living or not, existed in a dynamic interrelationship. Preserving game by controlling predators was a failure, since game like deer would overpopulate a forest and die by starvation or be culled out by hunters, thus bringing more human intervention. He found laboratory work confining and left in 1928 to do pioneering game management surveys for the private Sporting Arms and Ammunitions Manufacturers' Institute. Leopold quickly realized that destruction of habitat, even more than overhunting, put animal populations at risk. In 1933 Leopold wrote his still classic textbook, *Game Management,* and received a permanent teaching position at the University of Wisconsin. At the same time he helped establish the new Wilderness Society, today a major advocacy force for wilderness protection.

In 1935 Aldo Leopold and his family began planting pine trees, as many as 6,000 a year, together with other trees, shrubs, grasses, and flowers, at an abandoned 80-acre farm. He had watched too many New Deal cleanup crews do more harm than good when they took out brush needed for wildlife food and shelter, silted trout streams, and planted rows of identical trees. He turned the farmland, with its weekend cowshed "shack," into a working laboratory in an effort to restore the worn-out land to its state of "aboriginal health." "Land, then, is not merely soil; it is a fountain of energy flowing through a circuit of soils, plants, and animals. Food chains are the living channels which conduct energy upward; death and decay return it to the soil. The circuit is not closed. It is a sustained circuit, like a slowly augmented revolving fund of life."

Leopold, using his experience as a private landowner, began building an alternative view that became the "The Land Ethic" in *A Sand County Almanac.* "The real end is a *universal symbiosis with land,* economic and esthetic, public and private." A land ethic meant that privately owned land required personal responsibility by the owner to restore property to ecological integrity. Such landowners are rewarded with a powerful sense of belonging to something greater than themselves. According to Leopold, ethical duty toward the land particularly meant restraint in its use, and thus cast doubt on the workability of development to raise its economic value. This was a radical and controversial concept. An obsession with profit, Leopold declared, leads to the destruction not only of the environment, but also trivializes the more noble aspirations of human civilization. Leopold summed up the land ethic in the often quoted dictum: "A thing is right when it tends to preserve the integrity, stability, and beauty of the biotic community. It is wrong when it tends otherwise."

Leopold brought up to date the alarm that Thoreau, Marsh, and Muir had felt about a flawed human-environment connection of a materialistic civilization. He took their holistic but vague philosophies and turned them into science. He dreaded the romantic effusions of popular "nature fakirs," the badly informed protectors of wilderness, who had "a zeal so uncritical—so devoid of discrimination—that any nostrum is likely to be gulped up with a shout." He himself integrated his widely recognized scientific work in ornithology, soil science, forestry, and game management into an ecological overview, and combined them with land ethics and wilderness aesthetics. Although most of forestry and land management science had become "narrow as a clam," Leopold went in the opposite direction to turn the new science of ecology into a more comprehensive discipline. Leopold was not without his critics. Scientists doubted his ecology, and philosophers, his ethical theories. He retorted by saying that scientific fact could do damage unless it was used responsibly, and moral sense went begging unless it could be applied to a problem scientifically. The land as an ecological community is a complex empirical fact, a highly organized structure of interlocking food chains, trophic levels, and energy circuits, all flowing toward diversity and stability. No land ethic was defensible unless it was grounded in this scientific data. The best philosophy combined a rigorous science with a strong moral sense.

Leopold also expanded on the long-standing American tradition that made scenic beauty an important measure for successful conservation and preservation. He enlarged the idea of the beautiful beyond the classic mountains, waterfalls, canyons, and lakes to include nonscenic swamps, dunes, prairies, and deserts. According to Leopold, natural beauty was not a simple mirror of human notions of the sublime or picturesque. There was a spontaneous beauty in interconnected living things and their "fit" with a natural geography that went beyond whether a landscape was worthy of painting or a color slide. The beauty of a swamp or prairie involved the historical or biological story it told in both geological time and human time. In environmental philosopher Baird Callicott's apt phrase, "We cannot love cranes and hate marshes." Without the marshes the cranes perish. Without the cranes the marshes lose a prime quality. Ecology gave substance to scenery.

In a single summary statement Leopold wrote, "The practice of conservation must spring from a conviction of what is ethically and esthetically right, as well as what is economically expedient. A thing is right only when it tends to preserve the integrity, stability, and beauty of the community, and the community includes the soil, waters, fauna, and flora, as well as people." Aldo Leopold died in the spring of 1948 while fighting a fire that was spreading on a neighbor's hay meadow.

The Impact of Tourism on Wilderness

Once upon a time it was not easy to reach America's natural wonders. The journey to Niagara Falls was an impossible land and water trek until the opening of the Erie Canal in 1825. Then the falls became overrun with visitors. The 180 miles from San Francisco to Yosemite Valley in the 1860s required a boat to Stockton, 16 hours of jostling in a stagecoach to Coulterville, and then an endurance test of 37 more hours on horseback to the valley. When Yellowstone became a national park in 1872 there was no better access than beaver trappers and the U.S. Cavalry had 50 years earlier, except that the angry Blackfeet and other Indians were gone or subdued. Most of the nation's wonderlands stood untouched, waiting for the railroads to lay track and build lodgings.

Not that everyone had much respect for pristine wilderness. When a group of travelers arrived at Sequoia National Park, for example, they brought axes to chop away at the bark to take home for souvenirs. One early report from Yellowstone reported that "visitors prowled around with shovel and ax, chopping and hacking and prying up great pieces of the most ornamental work (in the geyser basin) they could find." The scars are still visible at Mammoth Hot Springs on the northern border of the park, adjacent to the first railhead. Burro riders on the Grand Canyon's Bright Angel Trail carried colored paints, brushes, and stencils to autograph canyon walls. Despite this vandalism, many of the early tourists reported back that America's Rocky Mountain scenery far surpassed the Swiss Alps.

Travel for pleasure was not a common activity. Few of us today would willingly endure the jostling, dust, and sweaty fellow passengers for days on end. Food was indifferent at best, and usually execrable. Night lodgings often meant three strangers to a bed. At first, Americans only traveled long distances as explorers on scientific expeditions, as immigrants, businessmen, or soldiers, or perhaps a young man might seek his fortune in California's gold fields. Most travel journals during the nineteenth century were published by Europeans. A few affluent Americans took trips as sportsmen, and the rich traveled to second vacation homes. Not until after the Civil War did the American middle class invent the "summer vacation" to escape the city's heat. Most typical was the jaunt to a resort. The most fashionable American resorts of the nineteenth century were built around natural hot springs that supposedly cured a variety of aches and pains. Saratoga Springs in New York, White Sulphur Springs in West Virginia, French Lick in Indiana, and Hot Springs in Arkansas sought to replicate famous European spas like Karlsbad and Marienbad in Bohemia. A successful spa required a grand hotel connected to the spring houses and bath houses, fine dining, and genteel recreations like golf, tennis, horseback riding, and polo. A daily schedule of baths and spring water also included walks on the grounds, small talk, people watching, music concerts, and constant changing of clothes, but little attention to natural scenery. When Americans first began to visit their national parks, they demanded, and got, the same resort vacation.

Some travelers began to seek out scenic wonders. As early as the 1830s, Americans self-consciously imitated the Grand Tour of great sights taken by elegant young European gentlemen and gentlewomen. A trip up the Hudson shadowed the Rhine journey. The Catskills and White mountains imitated England's Lake Country and Europe's Alps. Lake George became Italy's Lake Como. This inability to take America on its own terms reflected a long-standing sense of cultural inferiority compared to European antiquities and culture. American tourists regretted that they did not have any equivalent to the historic ruins at Rome's Forum, Athens's Acropolis, or Egypt's pyramids, although they could point to the uniqueness of Virginia's Natural Bridge or Niagara Falls. One of the earliest justifications for national parks was to protect natural "wonders" and "curiosities" that demonstrated America's geographical distinctiveness. Americans stretched their credibility when they claimed that Niagara Falls or the Catskills were equivalent to "sacred places" for pilgrimages comparable to Lourdes, Canterbury, Rome, Jerusalem, or Mecca. In Europe the best scenes belonged to the rich and powerful. Colorado's Rocky Mountain National Park, for example, emerged in large part because the English nobleman, the Earl of Dunraven, had moved to buy Estes Park and its surrounding mountains to keep as his private hunting preserve. Such a fiefdom was commonplace in Britain or on the Continent, but outraged Americans.

In the nineteenth century, best-selling travel guides instructed tourists on the conventions of each site, what emotions to experience, and what scenic values to appreciate. Guidebook authors, in travel historian John Sears's words, "treated scenery as art and sightseeing as a cultural activity equivalent to a concert or visit to an art museum." Timothy Dwight's famous 1822 *Travels in New York and New England* described the falls of the Catskills: "This magnificent current, after dashing upon a shelf, falls over a second precipice when it vanishes into the midnight beneath. A cloud of vapour rises above the forests. On the bosom of this elegant volume of mist appears a succession of rain-bows." Tourists went into raptures twice, first by reading Dwight in anticipation of the visit, second by reading it in front of the falls. Guides took visitors through the rocky spires of the "Garden of the Gods" near Colorado Springs, where "they will do their utmost," according to one travel writer, "as guides always do, to make you imagine that you are really seeing something. They will point out inane formations—the 'kissing camels'—in the sandstone rock, and will attempt to make you see that there are 'pictures.'"

After the Civil War, reports about the little known West enticed travelers. They found powerful landscapes at Yellowstone and Yosemite on which the drama of Manifest Destiny would be played out. This was often a West of the imagination more than reality. We already saw in Chapter 6 the extraordinary influence of Romantic artists like Albert Bierstadt, Thomas Moran, and Frederick Church on an American public that wanted instruction as to how to see its wild places. A visit to a national park like Yellowstone, Glacier, the Grand Canyon, or Yosemite was soon sought as a once-in-a-lifetime adventure, not just another summer vacation trip. When numbers of tourists began to arrive at a western national park, it was after enduring days in a train and hours in a carriage that were like a rite of passage. Their reward was to eat and sleep "Grand Hotel Style." The visit had its own ritual. Most visitors lazed away the daytime on hotel porches and verandahs, perhaps strolling 100 yards from El Tovar Hotel for a canyon vista at the south rim of the Grand Canyon. One could watch Yellowstone's Old Faithful geyser's hourly spout and overlook much of the geyser basin while drinking tea and eating cakes from the porch of the large rustic pile called Yellowstone Inn. Carriages might make tours of a few miles, but only the hardiest expended the energy to ride horseback into the nearby wilderness. To take a hike of 5 or 10 miles was rare, and an overnight stay sleeping on the ground unthinkable.

Americans began to view the national parks mostly through an automobile window. The private automobile made the previously exotic wilderness parks available to a broader spectrum of the middle class. More leisure time, matched by more disposable income, brought mass tourism to America. For the blue-collar worker, nonexistent vacation time in 1900 yielded by midcentury to two or three weeks of paid vacation. Reliable automobiles on smooth highways carried entire families to the nation's garden spots. Henry Ford was serious when he said, "I will build a car for the great multitude. No man making a good salary will be unable to own one—and enjoy with his family the blessing of hours of pleasure in God's great open spaces." By the third decade of the twentieth century, tourism became a hyperactive form of consumerism. American tourists in a two-week vacation raced along to "collect" six national parks while putting 6,000 miles on the family car. In 1932 the travel writer Charles Finger reported, "We boiled an egg in the Frying Pan Hot Spring, watched artists painting the Yellowstone Canyon, rowed on Yellowstone Lake, saw Old Faithful erupt three times, admired Morning Glory Pool, and witnessed an eruption of the Lioness Geyser, which is a rare sight." A visit to Niagara Falls covered a checklist of Inspiration Point, Luna Island, Hurricane Bridge, Overlook Tower, and perhaps a ride down the inclined railway and a boat trip to enjoy the spray below the falls. One British traveler wrote, "Americans add [the sights] to their collection, as an entomologist adds a beetle." America's natural attractions provided in the 1930s an escapist counterpoint to the woes of the Depression, and American wilderness tourism continued to grow. In the same era, Kodachrome photography brought new attention to previously ignored colorful canyons, arches, and redrock country in the arid regions of southern Utah. World War II stifled tourism, but after the war it exploded into a major impact on the wilderness.

Early in the century, Teddy Roosevelt and John Muir had preached an alternative tourism: the invigorating "strenuous life" centered on backcountry tent camping. They said that a stay in a natural wilderness, with all the historical, emotional, and patriotic baggage it carried for Americans, remained an ideal vacation goal. "Thousands of tired, nerve-shaken, overcivilized people," Muir contended, "are beginning to find out that going to the mountains is going home; that wilderness is a necessity; and that mountain parks and reservations are useful not only as fountains of timber and irrigating rivers, but as fountains of life." But to move away from rail lines and highways onto hiking trails and overnight backpacking was not part of most vacationers' agendas. Most overnight hikers were considered as eccentric as Muir. When David Brower spent ten weeks on the Sierra Nevada in 1934, he rarely saw anyone and was the first to visit numerous alpine lakes and upland meadows. Wilderness historian Roderick Nash described a mid-1960s revolution in lightweight tents, stoves, sleeping bags, backpacks, and dehydrated foods. Seekers for wilderness solitude found their way into remote areas of national parks, uncrowded national forests, vast reaches of BLM land, and, after 1968, into newly designated wilderness areas. The venerable Appalachian Trail, which followed the crest of the Appalachian mountains from Georgia to Maine, enjoyed immense popularity. A comparable Pacific Crest Trail reached from the Mexican border to Canada.

The National Park Service, official guardian of tourism into the wilderness, continued to wrestle with conflicting demands on its "true" purpose. Wilderness advocates complained that opportunities for wilderness contact were getting scarce and the most popular parks were deteriorating through overuse and misuse. Tourism in the parks, especially on the bumper-to-bumper roadways of Yosemite and Yellowstone, and in the snack-bar-cum-souvenir shop facilities, became an extension of the city. Joseph Sax said that in Yosemite Valley or the South Rim of the Grand Canyon, "one finds all the artifacts of urban life: traffic jams, long lines waiting in restaurants, supermarkets, taverns, fashionable shops, night life, prepared entertainments, and the unending drone of motors." The motor home that squatted on its concrete pad (with hookups to water and electricity) at the Jackson Lake Campground in the Tetons was usually equipped with its own television. Today's debates are about snowmobiles in Yellowstone in the winter, ORVs (off-road vehicles) in the California desert, and airplanes and helicopters noisily intruding at low altitudes over the Grand Canyon. This "industrial tourism" that caters to the conventional vacationer may have changed the parks forever. The question remains whether the mission of the national parks is fulfilled when visitors use them as they use amusement parks such as Disneyland or Epcot Center for passive, managed, and sanitized entertainment.

Historian John F. Sears reminds us that tourism usually involves a pilgrimage—tourists are seeking to find something that is personally rewarding and which they hope will reach the level of religious passion. It would not be too extreme to look on American tourists like medieval pilgrims. When pilgrims reached their holy place, Sears writes, "They expected it to be fabulous. When they left home they stepped out of their usual routine. Their journey was a metaphor for their passage through life to heaven." Away from the routines of workplace and domestic life, tourists floated in time and space to learn of their real selves.

Conclusion: Deep Ecology—
Toward a Wilderness Philosophy

A definitive idea of wilderness does not exist, mostly because the idea of wilderness is in the eye of the beholder. In American history we have seen several important shifts in the nation's treatment of wilderness, beginning with open hostility to its dangers by pioneer settlers and later energetic mining and forest cutting based on the viewpoint that wilderness is meaningless, even obsolete, except as raw material for industry and civilization. In Chapter 6, we also saw a small but influential group of writers, poets, artists, and philosophers—the Transcendentalists—who looked on wild nature as the revelation of God, spirit, and universal being. This chapter has focused on preservationists like John Muir, who believed human salvation lay in the reality that the natural world is valuable in itself, and their uphill battle against conservationists, especially Gifford Pinchot and Theodore Roosevelt during the Progressive Era who emphasized that nature is meaningful only when it serves multiple human purposes. The idea and value of wilderness, said some of these preservationists, including the nineteenth-century ecological pioneer George Perkins Marsh and the twentieth-century apostle Aldo Leopold, may not be in the eye of the beholder. Nature, they contended, contains its own purposes, its own internalization of energy and matter, and its own self-validating ethics and aesthetics. According to this view, human values do not exhaust all possibilities, humanity no longer lies at the center of things, nor is it the final stage of evolution.

These defenders of wilderness devised a philosophy, a science, and a strategy. Philosophers like Arne Naess, David Rothenberg, William Duvall, and George Sessions are called "deep ecologists." In the 1970s and 1980s they began to say that even the preservationist viewpoint is still too closely connected to "value-free" science that, in fact, is a product of industrial civilization and remains committed to the control of nature. They described the modern status quo as dysfunctional and sought to point humanity toward a radical alteration of society so as to reposition humans within nature. "Once we abandon the signposts, the directions that define the conventional world, we see wild nature, and there, in wildness, lies preservation of the world," said wilderness philosopher Max Oelschlaeger, paraphrasing Thoreau's famous statement. We are trying to live monoculture lives, Oelschlaeger says, in a pluralistic world.

In its philosophy, deep ecology begins by asking what is good for the natural system itself. Humanity is neither separate from nor superior to nature; humanity is only one among many features of the natural system. Certainly, like any organism, humans must satisfy their own basic needs, but they cannot claim privilege. Second, deep ecology does have a method, holistic rather than reductionistic or utilitarian, a science that focuses on ecosystem analysis. Ecosystem analysis (also discussed in Chapter 13) finds in wild nature the unveiling of the forces that continuously and persistently surround and interact with human life. A third feature of deep ecology is its energetic prowilderness activism, ranging from the moderation of the Wilderness Society to the radicalism of Earth First! These advocates worry about the future of the nation's scattered islands of wilderness. They believe wilderness is still in jeopardy and still declining. Pristine ecosystems are particularly scarce, perhaps remaining in beleaguered form only in Alaska. They fear that the highly regarded 1964 Wilderness Act, for all its virtues, has not served whole ecosystems well. As a next step, the United States needs an Endangered Ecosystems Act.

Deep ecologists are often criticized for their religious fervor, lack of methodological rigor, and hopeless utopianism, "green bigots who ignore the legitimate needs of underprivileged human beings." For example, deep ecologists tend to argue that human population growth must be dramatically slowed, even decreased, to protect the richness and diversity of wilderness. Defenders of deep ecology say that its viewpoint is valuable because it challenges most forms of conventional wisdom, opens debate about the nature of human identity, and forces discussion of meaningful alternatives to modern postindustrial society.

For Further Reading

The best summary and overview of the emergence of an American sensitivity to wilderness remains Roderick Nash's *Wilderness and the American Mind* (3rd ed., 1982). Supplement this with Max Oelschlaeger's more penetrating historical and philosophical analysis, *The Idea of Wilderness* (1991). Hans Huth's *Nature and the American: Three Centuries of Changing Attitudes* (1972) and Arthur A. Ekirch's *Man and Nature in America* (1973) remain important and perceptive analyses. See also the unheralded classic by the botanist May Theilgaard Watts, *Reading the Landscape of America* (rev. ed., 1975), and Wallace Stegner's rewarding *Beyond the Hundredth Meridian: John Wesley Powell and the Second Opening of the West* (1954). The protection of wilderness by means of national parks and monuments, and the debate over their use for recreation, is vividly described in Alfred Runte, *National Parks: The American Experience* (1979), Joseph L. Sax, *Mountains Without Handrails: Reflections on the National Parks* (1980), Hal Rothman, *Preserving Different Pasts: The American National Monuments* (1989), Alfred Runte, *Yosemite: The Embattled Wilderness* (1990), and Mark W.T. Harvey, *A Symbol of Wilderness: Echo Park and the American Conservation Movement* (1994). See also John Ise, *Our National Park Policy: A Critical History* (1961). Tourism as an unexpectedly powerful environmental force has not yet received full attention, but see John F. Sears, *Sacred Places: American Tourist Attractions in the Nineteenth Century* (1989), Earl Pomeroy, *In Search of the Golden West: The Tourist in Western America* (1957), and John A. Jakle, *The Tourist: Travel in Twentieth-Century North America* (1985). There are several excellent biographies of landscape and wilderness advocates that include their broader historical contexts. Still definitive is Laura Wood Roper, *FLO: A Biography of Frederick Law Olmstead* (1973). For George Perkins Marsh, see David Lowenthal's 1964 biography and his introduction to the 1973 reprint edition of *Man and Nature*. John Muir has received two excellent interpretive biographies by Michael Cohen, *The Pathless Way: John Muir and His Legacy* (1985), and Steven Fox, *John Muir and His Legacy: The American Conservation Movement* (1981). Aldo Leopold is well served by Susan L. Flader's interpretation of his early years in *Thinking Like a Mountain: Aldo Leopold and the Evolution of an Ecological Attitude Toward Deer, Wolves, and Forests* (1974) and Curt Meine's complete biography, *Aldo Leopold: His Life and Work* (1989). An excellent introduction to Leopold's work and influence are the essays in J. Baird Callicott (ed.), *Companion to A Sand County Almanac* (1987). The emergence of "deep ecology" as an integrative philosophical stance on wilderness is best described in books and articles by its two leading American advocates, George Sessions and William Duvall, and in critical analyses by David Rothenberg and Eric Katz. The best reading on wilderness in America remains the books, articles, and essays by George Perkins Marsh, John Muir, and Aldo Leopold, many of which are still available in convenient editions.

CHAPTER THIRTEEN

ENVIRONMENTALISM ENTERS THE AMERICAN MAINSTREAM: ENVIRONMENTAL SCIENCE, RACHEL CARSON'S *SILENT SPRING,* AND PUBLIC AWARENESS

I know of no safe repository of the ultimate powers of the society but the people themselves; and if we think them not enlightened enough to exercise their discretion, the remedy is not to take it from them, but to inform their discretion.

— Thomas Jefferson to William Charles Jarvis,
September 28, 1820

Disputes over the "facts" about pollution merely confirm that there are no truly objective facts to be had. Measurements are made within the context of a theoretical approach to the question; change the theory and you change what counts as a relevant fact. If we accept that all science is based on theories that can be related to human values, then we can no longer use science to decide on the values we wish to adopt. . . . Whether you support the free-enterprise system, or see industry as a curse that must be removed, you should do so because that is how you feel about the

*situation in which you live, not because you think science offers
unequivocal support for your position.*

—HISTORIAN OF SCIENCE PETER J. BOWLER, 1992

New Environmental Conditions: Human Action Dominates the American Earth

By the end of the nineteenth century, conservationists of the Progressive era acknowledged modern technological society could drastically alter the American environment. But they optimistically concluded that most changes, such as eastern urban growth and western irrigation projects, were improvements on nature. In 1929 the Viennese psychologist Sigmund Freud tapped into Western society's self-image when he defined successful civilization primarily as the conquest of nature: "A country has attained a high state of civilization when we find everything in it that can be helpful in exploiting the earth for man's benefit and in protecting him against nature. In such a country the course of rivers is regulated. The soil is industriously cultivated; the mineral wealth is brought up assiduously from the depths; wild and dangerous animals have been exterminated." Fifty years after Freud, technological optimists like Herman Kahn and Julian Simon insisted that human inventiveness was, in fact, the world's "ultimate resource" to build a satisfying future. Technological "fixes" would continue, they said, to solve the world's problems.

This historic American optimism did not dispel the fears of a growing number of outspoken doubters. An army of writers began to launch salvos against continuous industrial development. The social critic Lewis Mumford lambasted the industrial city as an inhuman place. The influential journalist Bernard DeVoto decried a disappearing wilderness. Another turning point took place in 1945 as Americans began to agonize over a truly marvelous discovery—the near infinite energy released out of the core of the atom—that was first deployed as a military weapon to massacre 200,000 people in two Japanese cities. The threat of "nuclear winter" seemed to guarantee the global collapse of civilization, the likely extermination of humanity, and an end to most innocent plant and animal species. Americans learned to fear science in the nuclear age. Popular opinion was molded by eloquent environmental writing that began with William Vogt's *Road to Survival* and Fairfield Osborn's *Our Plundered Planet,* both in 1948, and Osborn's *Limits of the Earth* in 1953. Vogt, for example, believed that American free enterprise was deeply flawed. It was "divorced from biophysical understanding and social responsibility, [and] must bear a large share of the responsibility for devastating forests, vanishing wildlife, crippled ranges, a gullied continent, and roaring flood crests." Vogt and Osborn were joined by social critic Murray Bookchin, economist Barry Commoner, and the associate justice of the Supreme Court, William O. Douglas. A small number of scientists, led by René Dubos, Garrett Hardin, Paul R. Ehrlich, and Eugene Odum, were also convinced that humans were destroying the environment. Two ingredients of the future environmental perspective were still missing: scientific ecology that established the human-nature interaction (this chapter), and a belief that government must intervene as environmental regulator (the next chapter) because the private sector failed to correct abuses and provide answers.

The New Science of Ecology

Beginning in the 1970s and 1980s, newly defined environmental sciences began the arduous task of uncovering the nature and scale of worldwide pollution and ecological changes wrought by 250 years of industrialization. Half of the total transformation took place after World War II:

> continuous depletion of limited fossil fuel resources
> massive withdrawals of fresh water
> the cumulative releases of noxious sulfur, phosphorus, nitrogen, and lead
> the creation of tens of thousands of organic chemicals with unknown long-term impacts
> the increase of atmospheric carbon dioxide
> chlorofluorocarbon-induced declines in Antarctic ozone
> acid rain plant and lake destruction
> deforestation
> degraded and desertified croplands and rangelands
> irreversible losses of biodiversity

Yet little was known about planetwide natural forces, much less human-made influences. Environmental science has also warned, in B.L. Turner's words, about "the very limited means we have to ameliorate or counteract. . . the massive environmental transformations in which we are now almost routinely engaged." It is to environmental science that we now turn.

In 1961 when Stewart Udall, a congressman from Arizona, became John F. Kennedy's secretary of the interior, he recalled that "people would say, 'Udall, what are you going to do about ecology?' And I would answer, 'What's ecology?'" Later, Udall would be one of the science's most vocal advocates. In the early 1960s ecology was an unknown word to the public and most scientists; by the early 1970s it was widely used (and misused) as a universal explanation of the environment. In 1866 German biologist Ernst Haeckel coined the word *ecology* from the Greek word for the study of the home. Haeckel defined his new science as "the whole science of the relations of the organism to the environment including, in a broad sense, all the 'conditions of existence.' These are partly organic, partly inorganic." Haeckel's holistic approach had been anticipated by the great Swedish biologist Carolus Linnaeus, who in 1749 emphasized the balance and economy (efficiency) of nature, and by Charles Darwin, who in his 1859 *The Origin of Species* wrote of evolution in terms of the dynamic movement of all of nature. In its primary emphasis on organisms in their environmental context, ecology also had roots going back to Aristotle, Hippocrates, Gilbert White, Buffon, Humboldt, and the natural historians (the latter discussed in Chapter 6). The Ecological Society of America had been formed as early as 1915 by 88 plant ecologists, 86 animal ecologists, 43 foresters, 39 entomologists, 12 agriculturalists, 14 marine ecologists, 3 limnologists, and

3 parasitologists. But few formally described themselves primarily as environmental scientists. By 1925 the society had about 600 members, with little further growth until the 1950s. Amateur ecologists, who functioned like data-gathering natural historians, played an important role well into the 1950s. Ecology was also treated as a branch of biology that looked into the organism's relationship to its surroundings. Until recently, the majority of the scientific community treated ecology as an interesting point of view—an updated version of the old natural history—rather than as a verifiable science. Many scientists like oceanographers and foresters "do ecology" while retaining their primary disciplinary loyalty elsewhere. In the human sciences, geographers and anthropologists took the lead in environmental research, followed closely by sociologists, and economists and historians only later began to pay attention to the humanity-nature connection.

Emergence of Ecology

Nineteenth-century environmentalism had a literary and philosophic flavor because it had been filtered through the work of Ralph Waldo Emerson, Henry David Thoreau, George Perkins Marsh, John Muir, and John Burroughs (see Chapters 6 and 12). But many scientists would find such a connection with nonscientific literary figures highly suspect. Ecology also had to shed a negative connotation as the place for old-fashioned plant-collecting amateurs. The new science began to find its own identity only after it applied a post-Darwinian dynamic perspective that wrestled with randomness and extinction, variation and change. But these were not yet grounded in experimental results. Only gradually did field studies of animal populations and ecosystem impacts began to build scientific credibility by adopting the techniques of measurement and quantification that had proved so effective in the hard sciences.

The Balance of Nature, Biotic Community, and Human Intervention

American scientists played a major role in the modern configurations of ecology, often with little or no knowledge of Haeckel. In 1880 Illinois zoologist Stephen A. Forbes (1844–1930) found the concept of the balance of nature especially useful. He wrote, "Primeval nature, as in the uninhabited forest or the untilled plain, presents a settled harmony of interaction among organic groups." In an important step that anticipated future environmental concern, Forbes blamed humanity for its unthinking and needless disturbance of such balance. This natural stability, he said, "is in strong contrast with the many serious maladjustment of plants and animals found in countries occupied by man." After human intervention, a onetime self-contained environment such as a lake ("a little world within itself") required continuous artificial augmentation for survival. Fortunately, if human intervention was removed, such a microcosm could recover its primeval condition. Left to the balance of nature, it would return to a "healthful and just equilibrium."

Frederic Clements, Henry Cowles, and the Debate over "Climax"

By the turn of the century, Frederic Clements (1874–1926) at the University of Nebraska pioneered ecological research when he examined degrading farmland on the High Plains grasslands. Like Forbes, he emphasized that all plant communities, left alone, moved not haphazardly but developmentally toward a stable "climax" condition in which the balance of nature is achieved. Clements thought that most of America's grasslands, before white man's plow disturbed the sod, were in a climax state and stable since the last ice age. An environmental ethic emerged: A "good" species had the adaptive powers to help move a plant community toward climax. But when farmers planted their wheat and corn in a field, they denied the field's "right" to grow a natural grass to reach a climax state. Unlike Forbes, Clements concluded that a community which was destroyed might never be reestablished; other species, possibly less desirable, would invade the territory and prevent the original inhabitants from reclaiming it. Clements's environmental climax became one of the most influential and most hotly debated concepts in the modern environmental movement. Clements also provoked a long-standing debate in ecological science when he described plant communities as superorganisms. The plant community was more than a collection of species working together for mutual advantage. It obeyed laws that could only be understood at a level transcending that of the individual organisms. If the High Plains were examined as a self-sustaining superorganism, its functions would be far clearer.

Early in the twentieth century, Henry Cowles (1869–1939) of the University of Chicago attempted to understand the dynamics of ancient self-contained bogs in the sand dunes along the south rim of Lake Michigan. The historic "Cowles Bog" in the dune country helped justify the creation of the Indiana Dunes National Lakeshore in the 1960s. Contrary to Clements, Cowles emphasized not equilibrium and climax but the continuously changing dynamic of ecosystems. Change was more rapid and extreme than could be explained by climate or geography. "Succession is not a straight-line process. Its stages may be slow or rapid, direct or tortuous and often they are retrogressive." Later generations of ecologists came to believe that such chaotic disturbance was the rule. One of Cowles's students, W. S. Cooper, carried these dynamics closer to modern chaos theory when he described a forest as a stochastic "mosaic" comprising different ages and different stages of disturbance in continuous change yet having its own self-regulating equilibrium. In 1964 R. G. West also rebutted Clements with his opinion that "our present plant communities (in the American grasslands) have no long history in the Quaternary [the most recent geological period], but are merely temporary aggregations under given conditions of climate, other environmental factors, and historical factors." Without the concept of climax, which offered an orderly explanation of environmental processes, ecologists were left with a much messier world to explain.

Ecology Taken Seriously as an Applied Science

Ecology first received acceptance as a serious science through pathfinding studies of the distribution and abundance of animal populations that gave unprecedented attention to their environmental niches as critical factors for survival. Wisconsin naturalist Aldo Leopold (see also Chapter 12) is often called the founder of modern environmental science because in the 1920s and 1930s he applied ecological principles to the existing field of game management. Environmental variation—available food, cycles of disease and parasites, and shifts in climate— was "the chief cause of fluctuations in animal numbers." His 1933 book, *Game Management,* remains the primary study in the field. He also gave ecology a wider popular appeal in his classic 1949 book *A Sand County Almanac,* in which he advocated the concept of human responsibility toward nature through a "land ethic." Scientific knowledge had to be supplemented with an ethical judgment based on recognizing the right of all components in the ecological chain to exist. Yet he also stated that "the important message to extract from ecology was the complexity of the system, not a lesson about how to behave." Unlike the role given them in the 1970s and 1980s, most early ecologists were not wilderness protectors but dedicated advocates of the human use of resources. For example, C. Hart Merriam, influential head of the federal Division of Economic Ornithology and Mammology (later Division of the Biological Survey) presumed that humankind has the right and the duty to alter nature for its purposes. Science must be applied, he concluded, to eradicate "pests" such as wolves in national parks and prairie dogs on the Plains. Grassland ecologists like Frederic Clements sought to help farmers by improving their interference with natural systems. They offered the essentially optimistic message that nature was strong enough to resist destruction by human agencies—the climax could easily be restored. (This optimism would be undermined by the Dust Bowl of the 1930s, which showed that the destruction of the soil made possible by farming would have a permanent effect on the land.) Nevertheless, ecologists found themselves in the center of modern environmental protectionism when ecological concepts began to shape popular thinking and public policy in the 1970s and 1980s.

A.G. Tansley, Raymond Lindeman, and the Invention of the Ecosystem

The concept of "ecosystem" first appeared in 1935 in a technical paper, "The Use and Abuse of Vegetational Concepts and Terms," published in the scientific journal *Ecology* by the English ecologist Arthur George Tansley (1871–1955). This vital concept revolutionized ecology by identifying the ecosystem as "the functional unit of nature," the smallest workable unit in which living things can possibly be studied. Nevertheless, Tansley refused to see the ecosystem as identical with Clements's superorganism. "The organisms may claim our primary interest," but "we cannot separate them from their special environment, with which they form one physical system." An ecosystem, although self-sufficient (except for solar energy), could also connect to other ecosystems and become a feature of a larger system. The controversy over ecosystem science focused on the scientific validity of its top-down, begin-with-the-system research approach instead of traditional scientific reductionism. One college president in the 1930s criticized ecology as "the study of the sty with the pig left out." Harvard ecologist R. C. Lewontin contended, "It is not that a whole is more than the sum of its parts but that the parts themselves are re-defined and re-created in the process of their interaction." Photosynthesis and metabolism, for example, were organism functions that connected food webs, organic debris, inorganic minerals, atmospheric gases, and water.

Minnesota zoologist and botanist Raymond Lindeman (1915–1942) advanced ecosystem science in his now classic 1942 *Ecology* article, "The Trophic Dynamic Aspect of Ecology." He was the first to apply fully Tansley's original definition of ecosystem, using the small Cedar Bog Lake (depth of 1 meter, an area of 14,480 square meters, and a shoreline of 500 meters) near the University of Minnesota. In 1940 University of Wisconsin professor Chancey Juday had attempted a similar functional description of the much larger Lake Mendota in Madison: "The annual energy budget of a lake may be regarded as comprising the energy received from the sun and sky each year and the expenditures or uses which the lake makes of this annual income of radiation. In general the annual income and outgo substantially balance each other." Juday's budget covered solar radiation, melting ice, the heat produced by the water and the bottom, evaporation, and albedo (reflection). A separate biological budget covered the energy converted by photosynthesis and its use by each organism, using information on the energy uptake and loss in plankton, bottom flora and fauna, and fish. Lindeman introduced experimental fieldwork based on ecosystem methodology by focusing on biomass, environment, trophic levels, and energy or food flows. At Cedar Bog Lake, Lindeman and his wife Eleanor Hall sampled the biota of the lake with plankton nets and bottom dredges through the different seasons. They analyzed the water and bottom sediments. They observed the growth, development, and distribution of the littoral vegetation, vertebrate animals, and even the relationship of the lake to the forest. The Lindemans' goal was to sample all elements of the biota during the same period of time and to reduce the elements into a single mode—the food cycle as a representation of lake metabolism and energy flow. They learned that a short list of energy [food]-related features common to all ecosystems might include photosynthesis, respiration, nitrogen fixation, and nitrification, shaped by the carbon, oxygen, nitrogen, and water cycles.

According to ecologist and historian Frank Golley,

> Lindeman introduced most of the major questions and concepts of modern ecological energetics, including questions about the length of food chains, the efficiency of trophic transfers, the storage of energy at different levels, the rates of primary productivity, the problems of correcting energy values for losses due to respiration, predation, and decomposition, and the role of bacteria and microorganisms in cycling dead organic matter. In addition, he made clear the idea that

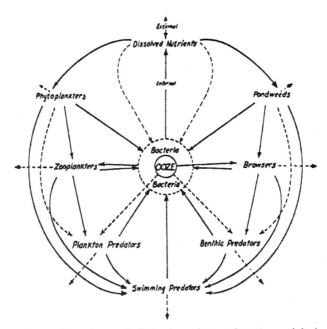

Lindeman's famous diagram of a food cycle in Cedar Bog Lake in Wisconsin helped usher in the new science of ecology and ecosystems.

ecosystems develop through ecological succession and are tied to the energy dynamics of the system and the concept that nutrient cycling, as food cycling, is linked to the wider biogeochemical cycles coupling one ecosystem with another.

Lindeman's focus on energy also allowed better quantification of complex phenomena, which helped ecology qualify as a recognizable science. Ecosystem analysis became especially rewarding in the environmental protection movement of the 1970s and 1980s because it revealed the limits of toleration by different species under less than optimum environments. These less than optimum environments usually resulted from human interventions, such as lakes with problems of eutrophication from organic dumping or forests disturbed by clear-cutting. Celebrated cases where species existence became endangered by a declining environment included the Tennessee snail darter fish in the 1970s and the spotted owl in Pacific Northwest forests in the 1990s. A debate often began over an endangered species but quickly turned into a battle over an entire ecosystem.

A Quantifiable Science

The complexity and diversity of ecosystems made them particularly "stubborn about fitting into mathematical formulae." Back in 1887 Stephen A. Forbes had already complained that the life sciences, particularly field studies of species and their surroundings, required "such a vast number of observations, for so long a period of time." Because ecology was derived from the biological sciences and looked on the world as organisms and ecosystems, it had never been comfortable in the mechanistic world of "hard" Newtonian physics that so dominated scientific thinking in the nineteenth and early twentieth centuries. Such mechanistic research, with its demand for quantification, nevertheless defined what was credible science. Science historian Peter J. Bowler concluded, "Defenders of ecology argued that it cannot be compared to physics or chemistry, and had more in common with the immeasurability and unpredictability of other natural phenomena such as earthquakes and meteorology, or even economics." In this light, Frederic Clements in Nebraska helped saved the day when he devised a method between 1898 and 1905 to quantify plant geography and grassland ecology. He marked off a tract of land and counted every individual plant within it. This became the technique of intense study of typical "quadrats" or squares that sampled vegetation. A quadrat was often only a meter square. Clements sought to test his climax hypothesis by clearing a quadrat of all plants and checking it periodically to discover the succession of plants that would lead to a mature sustainable climax vegetation.

Since the work of Clements at the turn of the century, ecologists admit that ecosystem limits or boundaries are established arbitrarily and often persist as fuzzy and imprecise. In most scientific thinking this was tantamount to an admission of failure. New technologies of data gathering and analysis became available in the second half of the twentieth century that served the complexities of ecosystems well. What was needed was the capacity to examine multiple variables. Mathematical tools and instruments to process quantitative data are still scarce. As the twentieth century closes, research tools available to the environmental sciences—a mix of computerization and highly sensitive instrumentation—can now identify and measure complex dynamic systems, energy fluxes, and biogeochemical flows. Recent developments include geographical information systems (GIS) that allow dynamic modeling of the environment and satellite imagery that monitors the global environment on a continuing basis. Ecologist Frank Golley writes that he and most ecosystem scientists "realize that their research has just begun, since data on time-space relations in ecosystems is virtually nonexistent. The problem remains to capture enough real system behavior at a given point in time and space to represent the system, and to connect this to information about earlier (baseline) analysis and future trends." Quantification for ecological science was both essential and problematic. "Organisms do not behave like gas molecules."

Ecology as a Modern Science: Eugene P. Odum's Textbook

Most environmental scientists date the modern origins of ecology with the publication of *Fundamentals of Ecology* in 1953 by Georgia scientist Eugene P. Odum. This basic textbook has gone through many editions, shaped several generations of scientists, and is still in print. Odum built on the earlier work of Forbes, Tansley, Lindeman, and others. He applied several post–World War II innovations to ecological analysis: cybernetics, operations research, information theory, and general systems theory. A systems engineering approach seemed particularly suited for the study of large-scale and complex ecosystems, and even more so when computer-based simulations came into their own in the 1970s. With these new tools, ecosystem analysis became a guiding paradigm of ecological science. Odum described the ecosystem as "any entity or natural unit that includes living and non living parts interacting to produce a stable system in which the exchange of materials between the living and non living parts follows circular paths." Following the lead of Lindeman, Odum described the usefulness of making energy transfers a primary explanation of how ecosystems worked:

> Energy is defined as the ability to do work. The behavior of energy is described by the following laws. The *first law of thermodynamics* states that energy may be transformed from one type into another but is never created or destroyed. . . . The *second law of thermodynamics* may be stated in several ways, including the following: No process involving an energy transformation will spontaneously occur unless there is a degradation of the energy from a concentrated form into a dispersed form.

The first law of thermodynamics told ecologists to expect that all the energy entering the system would equal all the energy leaving the system, plus that stored within it. The first law provided a balance sheet to check inputs, outputs, and storages. The second law told ecologists that at each transfer of energy in the food cycle, energy is lost as heat and can no longer do work. Odum's approach expanded the ecosystem concept beyond its narrow fieldwork origins and made it a comprehensive definition with vast theoretical and applied significance.

Odum did not hold back from controversial conclusions. The new science demonstrated, he said, that humans have a frightening capacity to drastically alter ecosystems beyond recovery. This power over the basic units of nature was all the more serious because new use of data had revealed the inherent vulnerability of ecosystems. For example, a typical energy transfer between levels in the food chain/pyramid rarely exceeded 10 percent efficiency. Human impacts, such as soil erosion, forest cutting, lake eutrophication, desertification, and acid rain consumed valuable energy and removed it from ecosystem well-being. The greatest challenge was how to manage the environmental stresses imposed by human activities. This caution, Odum insisted, is fundamental to ecology and to human affairs generally. Not one to pull his punches, Eugene Odum joined a small number of scientists who stated publicly that humans were destroying the environment and thus threatening their own survival.

From an Applied Science to a Visionary "Subversive" Science

Rachel Carson's *Silent Spring*

The publication of Rachel Carson's *Silent Spring* in 1962 can be described as the start of the modern environmental movement. The book enjoyed 31 weeks on the *New York Times* best-seller list, with hardcover sales of more than a million copies, unusual for a nonfiction book. Carson sounded the alarm that synthetic pesticides, particularly chlorinated hydrocarbons such as DDT, were poisoning the entire globe. DDT, first introduced in the 1940s as an effective and wide-ranging killer of insects that fed on crops and spread disease, won the 1948 Nobel Prize for its discoverer, the Swiss scientist Paul Müller. After World War II, massive pesticide applications became a kind of miracle product for agricultural production, forestry, roadways, golf courses, and suburban developments. By the late 1950s chemical pesticides had replaced most other pest control methods and programs of insect eradication. Carson wrote in dismay, "For the first time in the history of the world, every human being is now subjected to contact with dangerous chemicals, from the moment of conception until death." Using ecological principles, Carson showed how hydrocarbons become concentrated at dangerous levels as they move along the food chain in fatty tissues of plants, fish, animals, and humans. The effects included significantly higher cancer risks and genetic disorders. In historian Linda Lear's words, Carson's book "made people stop in their tracks and see the world in a new way" that introduced ecological science to an interested public. Carson acknowledged that the world's people need pesticides for better health and adequate food, but their indiscriminate spread disregards the complex balance of nature.

Rachel Carson had first encountered the negative impacts of pesticides in the 1930s as a staff member of the Fish and Wildlife Service of the Department of the Interior. FWS was the only federal agency concerned with pesticide dangers; the Department of Agriculture, the Public Health Service, and the Food and Drug Administration had repeatedly proclaimed that synthetic pesticides were harmless. Carson's dual talents as a graceful and persuasive writer and as a rigorous field researcher had already given her national recognition in her best-selling natural histories about the ocean and ocean shore: *Under the Sea Wind* (1941), *The Sea Around Us* (1951), and *The Edge of the Sea* (1954). She retired from FWS to live on the Maine seacoast. Alerted by reports of the adverse effects of DDT on the reproduction and survival of birds, she intensified her research on the aerial application of chlorinated hydrocarbon pesticides. Several incidents attracted her attention: wildlife damage from the 1957 USDA campaign to eradicate imported fire ants from the southern states by massive applications of dieldrin and heptachlor, two of the most persistent and most toxic new pesticides, complaints in newspapers about bird mortality caused by the aerial spraying of DDT mixed in fuel oil for mosquito control along the northern Massachusetts coast, and a trial on Long Island to enjoin the federal government from further aerial pesticide spraying. From the trial records, Carson acquired a flood of testimony, documentation, and expert contacts about significant damage by pesticides to fish, birds, wildlife, livestock, and possibly humans.

Five years in the research and writing, *Silent Spring* was picked up first by William Shawn and E.B. White of *The New Yorker* magazine and excerpted in three issues (June 16, 23, and 30, 1962). Carson vividly detailed the negative impact of the spread of the non-degrading insecticide DDT into the global food chain, ranging from declining songbird populations (hence the title) to the ever-growing threat of cancer in humans. The result was, in the words of an editorial in the *New York Times,* the "noisy summer" of 1962. Her report caused a ground swell of public concern about environmental decline and threats to public health. The Kennedy administration was joined by representative John Dingell (D-Mich.) and senator Abraham Ribicoff (D-Conn.) in a full-fledged government investigation of the abuse of pesticide use. Carson was attacked by Ezra Taft Benson, former agriculture secretary under Eisenhower, as "probably a communist." Benson and other critics labeled her a "hysterical female." Why was a "spinster so worried about genetics"? Many scientists recognized that the book raised serious doubts about their friendly connections with the chemical industry. Most old-line environmental organizations were slow to arouse: The National Wildlife Federation decided that Carson could cause "unneeded restrictions which would hamstring future research and progress. It might mean that we would never have another DDT, the chemical miracle that rescued millions of lives from hunger and disease," but later the NWF gave her its book prize. The chemical industry (including the Velsicol Corporation, one of the chief manufacturers of chlordane) put intense pressure on Houghton Mifflin, Carson's Boston publisher, to suppress publication, which it rejected, and published *Silent Spring* in September 1962.

Environmental protection became part of the national agenda after a CBS prime-time television special in April 1963 strongly restated Rachel Carson's evidence and conclusions. CBS went to great lengths for a balanced report, but what viewers saw was a calm and strong Carson stating her deep concern in contrast to a blustering Dr. Robert White-Stevens of American Cyanamid Corporation, who represented the chemical industry. Ravaged by cancer since 1960, Rachel Carson died on April 14, 1964, at the age of 56. Her crusade was picked up by a younger generation of environmental reformers that included Ralph Nader, Barry Commoner, David Brower, and Stewart Udall. After a decade of impassioned debate, DDT use was banned in the United States in 1972, and soon wildlife populations began to recover, represented by the bald eagle and the osprey. Using the new tools of ecological science developed by Forbes, Clement, Cowles, Tansley, Lindemann, Odum, and others, Americans could compare the positive and negative impacts of new technologies. Publication of *Silent Spring* has been compared to the impact that Harriet Beecher Stowe's *Uncle Tom's Cabin* had on slavery in America. In an extraordinary synthesis that created a revolution in environmental action, *Silent Spring* meticulously identified a technological risk, opened a rigorous scientific debate, reported on industrial indifference, created a high level of public concern, and demanded governmental responsibility. Environmentalism, with ecology as its science, moved into the American mainstream and began to steer the national agenda in government, science, and industry. Concepts of ecology provided a new language of environmental concern. Public doubts about technological progress and fears over pollution seemed to be confirmed as parts of the nation began to fall apart—the 1965 power blackout and garbage strikes in New York City, the burning of Cleveland's industrially polluted Cuyahoga River in 1969, the industrial eutrophication of Lake Erie, and the 1969 Santa Barbara oil spill on California beaches that killed sea life.

With Carson's ecological critique of chemical pesticides, Americans had their first rigorous understanding of an inherent defect in an important and useful technology. The public discovered technological "sin." Never before had doubts been cast about the core activity of a major American industry, in this case the fabled chemical industry. The petrochemical industry, although acknowledged as essential to modern life, was newly blamed for toxic dumps, air pollution, contaminated water supplies, and farm soils loaded with pesticides and herbicides. Despite vigorous attacks on Carson as an uppity female, and on her scientific credentials and research, she provided a credible analysis of the negative impact of DDT. Rachel Carson joined scientists already mentioned—Aldo Leopold and Eugene Odum—in stating that the environmental debate was also a moral debate. Near the end of her life, Carson wrote, "Through our technology we are waging war against the natural world. It is a valid question whether any civilization can do this and retain the right to be called civilized. By acquiescing in needless destruction and suffering, our stature as human beings is diminished." *Silent Spring* offered a new form of environmental advocacy that deliberately combined science and advocacy on the grounds that evidence of public danger compelled a moral duty to warn about existing and potential harm. Linda Lear concluded, "The debate between Carson and the scientific establishment was not fundamentally over scientific fact or institutional objectivity. It was a quarrel about values, and consequently, about power."

Beginning in the 1970s ecology's big-picture approach received more credibility as scientists in other fields began to explore and accept large-scale discoveries, notably the acknowledgment of plate tectonics in the earth sciences, global climate patterns (El Niño, the Antarctic ozone hole) in meteorology, and the modern synthesis of Darwinism and genetics. The International Geophysical Year (actually mid-1957 to the end of 1959) was hailed as a scientific attempt, admittedly short lived, to connect the human species with global forces. Some enterprising ecologists proposed to apply ecology to study the human condition. As early as 1940 E. C. Lindeman described ecology as the middle ground "where the physical and biological sciences leave off and the social sciences begin." In 1967 the influential geographer Clarence Glacken put a heavy burden on ecologists when he argued that their science was the best means to consider three major questions in Western civilization: Is the earth purposefully made or designed? Has the environment influenced humanity? Has humanity made major significant changes on the earth's original environmental condition? In 1969 a psychiatrist was not alone when he proposed that ecology requires a human framework, an "inter-intra confrontation of biological, social and historical factors that embrace one's family, school, neighborhood, and the many overlapping communities that teach values, defenses, and offenses, the meaning of oneself and one's existence." Some biologists, like E. O. Wilson, even claimed that human values could be grounded in objectively determinable ecological relations within nature. In his 1975 book, *Sociobiology: The New Synthesis,* Wilson stated, "Let us now consider man in the free spirit of natural history, as though we were zoologists from another planet completing a catalog of social species on Earth. In the macroscopic view the humanities and social sciences shrink to specialized branches of biology; history, biography, and fiction are the research protocols of human ethnology; and anthropology and sociology together constitute the sociobiology of a single primate species." In 1977 Eugene Odum described a human being as "not only a hierarchical system composed of organs, cells, enzyme systems, and genes as subsystems, but is also a component of supraindividual hierarchical systems such as populations, cultural systems, and ecosystems."

By the 1970s ecology was also treated as a panacea. Laypeople looked to ecologists to solve the world's environmental problems of pollution and waste where other scientists and technologists had failed. The public role of ecologists, and their credibility, became a crucial issue with the creation of the EPA in 1970. EPA's mission included the authority "to conduct investigations, studies, surveys, research and analysis relating to ecological systems and environmental quality." Most professional ecologists were uncomfortable with extreme claims made for the powers of ecology to solve environmental problems that were equally social problems. They worried about distortions that would weaken ecology's scientific credibility, particularly its coopting by nonscientists as a tool for environmental advocacy and its trivialization into a notorious "pop" science.

Ecology Becomes "Big Science"

Ecology's ability to understand problems of increasingly heavy pollution and environmental exhaustion brought it into the world of "big science"—science that shapes national economies and global decisions. This challenged the influence of multinational corporations (big business), international superpowers (big government), and the Cold War (big military). Environmental problems crossed political and economic boundaries, the classic cases being the Chernyobl nuclear accident, the ozone hole, climate warming, and above all, uncontrolled population growth. International relations were often shaped by environmental debates: The European (GATT) and North American free trade talks (NAFTA) were riddled with environmental questions, although the resulting agreements were often environmentally unfriendly. The great debates of modern society, ranging from energy to poverty to war, were often translated into environmental issues. The number of ecologists tripled between 1945 and 1960, and doubled again by 1970. Ecological science took hold in the United States like no other nation, although it also gained notable influence in Sweden and Great Britain. It was much less effective where traditional science held sway, such as in Germany, France, and Japan, and the distorted science of the old Soviet Union. The United States had built up a network of government agencies during the Depression and the war, which offered centralized funding and organization. Research universities grew rapidly after the war, and ecologists worked in enlarged biology, botany, and zoology departments. Ecological interests also benefited, ironically, from military applications of disciplines like meteorology and oceanography and specializations like seismology, acoustics, and remote sensing. Industrial opportunism in oil exploration and widespread mining supported intensive research in the earth sciences. Extensive funded support into ecosystems came first from the U.S. Atomic Energy Commission (to study the distribution of radioactive fallout in vertebrates, insects, vegetation, and soils—e.g., radiation ecology), by the International Biological Program (IBP) that ran from 1964 to 1974, and by the National Science Foundation (NSF). Ecosystem studies would be encouraged by the National Biological Survey of the U.S. Department of the Interior in the early 1990s, but this program was threatened with extinction in the mid-1990s by the probusiness, antienvironmental stance of the U.S. Congress.

After the 1970s ecology served many masters. Eugene Odum had given it scientific credibility. Aldo Leopold had insisted that ecology provided an essential ethic and aesthetic. Nonscientists turned to ecology as a model for philosophy, humanities, and social sciences. Philosophers used ecosystem analysis and balance of nature as a framework to derive ethical values. Environmental advocates used ecology as a weapon against the polluters and foot-dragging government officials.

Has Science Failed to Keep Its Promise to Discover and Solve Environmental Problems?

A widely accepted concept of science is that it presents disinterested and objective results that others can apply for public benefit and private profit. When environmental issues became intensely technical, such as auto emission levels or the toxicity of PCBs, scientists as "expert witnesses" described themselves as disinterested parties who stood above controversy. What was not expected was the extent to which different scientists could analyze the same experimental results on problems like radiation, sulfur emissions, and lead and see different "facts" from the same scientific studies. According to a recent study of the federal EPA, "The result is at best confusion about the appropriate role (and limits) of technical knowledge, and, at worst, the widespread belief that experts are mere hired guns who have nothing to contribute to the policy debate." As Donald N. Langenberg, chairman of the board of the American Association for the Advancement of Science (AAAS), wrote in 1991, it "has been a hard lesson for many scientists to learn," that politics is ruled by what the public wants to believe. He wrote, "Only in politics are facts negotiable." It is not that science is right and politics is wrong; instead, two sets of operating rules are at work in science and politics. Despite these ambiguities, Langenberg nevertheless concluded, "It is our civic duty to bring to bear the full power of science and technology in the service of society . . . to bear on the great public issues of our time." Environmental historian Samuel P. Hays also distinguished between "conventional" scientists who required absolute proof before regulation and "frontier" scientists who believed an environmental problem might be serious enough to require regulation despite limited proof. This debate over scientific uncertainty in environmental action has become a central issue as matters of toxic wastes, acid rain, causes of cancer, and global warming became public issues in the 1980s and 1990s. Because scientists cannot agree on what is happening, should policy makers wait until better information is available before acting? This is the "uncertainty principle." Yet if society fails to act, the situation may deteriorate rapidly and irreversibly. This is the "precautionary principle" or "worst case scenario." This conflict seems to be an all too common situation in environmental debates.

NGOs: The Empowerment of Nongovernmental Organizations

The American public has unfailingly advocated a proenvironment ethic throughout the 1960s, 1970s, 1980s, and 1990s. Even during the conservative years of the Reagan-Bush administrations and the open antienvironmentalism of the Republican Congress of the mid-1990s, more than 70 percent of those polled wanted better environmental protection even at taxpayer cost and personal sacrifice. The public give high marks to simpler lifestyles (even if they didn't practice simplicity) that saved resources, turned waste recycling into a status symbol, advocated renewable energy sources, and questioned the values of a consumer society. One powerful voice for environmental protection came from public interest groups called NGOs (nongovernmental organizations).

The Remarkable Role of the NGOs

Voluntary environmental organizations came into their own in the 1970s and 1980s. Environmentalism appealed to a broad spectrum of Americans (although minorities were largely left out except occasionally at the local level). Such voluntaryism, defined as citizens joined together in common interests, has long been a defining force in American society. In the past it had promoted causes like the abolition of slavery, prohibition, child labor, women's rights, and civil rights. Often these citizen action groups initiated the first steps toward public law. NGOs usually enjoyed tax-free status, comparable to religious institutions and public service foundations. American environmental NGOs were a rainbow of different interests that also shifted over time. They ranged from older sporting and mountaineering clubs to land and wildlife preservation operations to highly professional lobbying and litigation activists to local grassroots organizations—labeled PIRGs and NIMBYs. Nonenvironmental groups discovered that environmentalism was a relevant national agenda, including the Steelworkers Union, the American Civil Liberties Union (ACLU), National Taxpayers Union, AFL-CIO labor union, various consumer groups, the League of Women Voters, the American Association of Retired Persons (AARP), the National Council of Churches, social investment companies, and members of the civil rights movement. Overall, most environmental NGOs, large and small, shared a common recognition of the deteriorating state of the environment, a desire to halt such deterioration, and opposition to those who fostered it.

During the Reagan-Bush years between 1980 and 1992, the older organizations received a rush of new members (the Sierra Club mushroomed to 500,000 members) as a result of public anger over the default of the federal government. In the late 1980s they bypassed ponderous and intransigent government regulatory bureaucracies (even the EPA) by taking their case directly to the public through the media, particularly television and local newspapers. In 1989, in a controversy over the carcinogenic threat of Alar, a food additive sprayed on apples for cosmetic reasons, environmental groups raised such a public stir that Alar was taken off the market even though the environmental case was flawed. The 1980s also saw the rise of Earth First! and Greenpeace that turned to aggressive local activism to outflank federal intransigence and corporate hostility. This radicalism also reflected a growing disenchantment with lobbying, litigation, and political channels used by the more traditional organizations.

Traditional Environmental Organizations

By the 1970s and 1980s American environmental groups were the vanguard for change. Some of them were old guard, such as the Sierra Club (1892), the National Audubon Society (1905), the National Parks and Conservation Association (1919), the Wilderness Society (1935), the National Wildlife Federation (1936), and the Nature Conservancy (1951). They stayed in

America's mainstream, willing to settle for reform without changes in society's basic culture of economic growth, technological development, and material progress. They expanded their original wilderness preservation mission into a wider environmental net that includes population growth, energy efficiency, pollution control, global warming, and nuclear winter. They devised basic strategies: lobbying, lawsuits, scientific research, and electoral politics.

The Izaak Walton League

The Izaak Walton League, named after the legendary hero of anglers, was formed in Chicago in 1922 by wealthy hunters and fishermen, and came under the leadership of the unstoppable Will H. Dilg. He voiced the popular mood, "I am weary of civilization's madness, and I yearn for the harmonious gladness of the woods and the streams. I am tired of your piles of buildings and I ache from your iron streets. I feel jailed in your greatest cities and I long for the unharnessed freedom of the big outside." Although John Muir's Sierra Club was the first environmental organization to receive national attention in the 1890s, the Izaak Walton League was the first with a mass membership. By 1925 the League's journal, *Outdoor America,* reached over 100,000 members, compared to 7,000 in the Sierra Club, which had lost its charisma upon Muir's death and limited its attention to mountain outings and the national parks. The league was the first environmental organization to confront publicly both industry and government on the controversial issues of forest harvesting, power development, water pollution, and wetlands protection. The league's most famous member, Herbert Hoover, helped it lobby successfully for federal wildlife refuges in the 1920s. The league also attracted many members primarily nostalgic for lost youth, nature worship, and outdoor masculinity. This romantic tendency, together with its midwestern provincialism, meant a decline during the more realistic 1970s. The League's membership remained frozen at about 50,000 while other organizations rose into the hundreds of thousands.

The National Audubon Society

There has always been a degree of ambiguity and uncertainty about the role of the Audubon Society, which has existed under different names over the last 100 years. Ironically, the society was first proposed in 1886 to protect rare bird species from hunters, although its namesake, John James Audubon, who contributed so much to early American nature awareness, shot hundreds of birds for specimens on his outings. In 1905 several state Audubon groups formed the National Association of Audubon Societies. It became a powerful lobby under the leadership of the farsighted naturalist George Bird Grinnell, advocating laws protecting birds at the time when feathered hats were fashionable. In 1911 its objectives were clouded by "blood money" from the Winchester Repeating Arms Company that nevertheless kept it financially afloat. During the next several decades, with only about 5,000 members, it reverted to a minor bird watching organization, and most power lay with state Audubon societies. Much later in the 1970s, a newly revitalized National Audubon Society, redefined with a broad-based conservation mission, and led by Russell Peterson, grew from 45,000 members in 1966 to more than 320,000 in 1975 and 600,000 in 1990. More moderate than the Sierra Club, and deeply involved with popular media, it has been criticized for "more ecotainment than wildlife preservation," but it has also been a well-informed leader in the fight for threatened regions like the Florida Everglades.

National Parks and Conservation Association

In 1919, three years after the creation of the federal National Park Service, the National Parks Association (later the National Parks and Conservation Association) became a citizen's watch-dog over untouched wilderness regions. A series of strong leaders—Robert Sterling Yard, Devereaux Butcher, Sigurd Olsen, Anthony Wayne Smith, and Paul Pritchard—were highly visible critics of the tendency of the NPS (see Chapter 12) to emphasize recreation over preservation. Should Yellowstone bears be fed at garbage dumps as public shows? Should Mammoth Cave continue its colored light show? It urged high standards of wilderness quality for the creation of new federal parks that were criticized as "purist." It emerged as an effective defender of national parks during several government "wars against wilderness" during the development rush of the 1920s, retrenchment during the 1930s, and the proindustry climate of the 1980s. It urged the creation of more wilderness parks such as Sequoia and North Cascades and the protection of unique places such as the Everglades. It fought lumbering, grazing, private inholdings, water projects, and exploitive concessions in several western parks. It raised doubts about the primeval value of eastern parks like Shenandoah, and only reluctantly supported the NPS interest in historic sites like Gettysburg and the C&O Canal, and recreational areas such as Sandy Hook. By 1975 it began a transition, like many sister organizations, from traditional wilderness site protection to a broader environmental approach based on new ecosystem science. This was recently reflected in its defense of a larger Yellowstone ecosystem threatened by mining interests.

The Wilderness Society

In 1935, the Wilderness Society, built on New Deal conservationism, appeared out of the efforts of wilderness guru Robert Marshall, Aldo Leopold, and a small select group of like-minded wilderness advocates. Marshall preached that wilderness remained "a human need rather than a luxury or plaything," especially under the pressures of an industrialized, urban society. Robert Marshall's dominant personality (and independent wealth) made the Wilderness Society unusually influential with the National Park Service and Forest Service. Its numbers remained small, no more than 5,000 even into the 1950s, but its leadership, including Olaus J. Murie of the Fish and Wildlife Service and Howard Zahniser of the Department of Agriculture, made it among the most effective environmental organizations. They "prowled the halls of Congress and the Cosmos Club in Washington." Zahniser joined forces with David Brower of the Sierra Club to forge a juggernaut alliance against the Bureau of Reclamation's dam at Echo Park in Dinosaur National Monument. Zahniser would also become the primary figure behind passage of the Wilderness Act in 1964. Ex-senator Gaylord Nelson led the Wilderness Society's Washington-wise staff. Its membership rose to 370,000 by 1990. The organization's hard-line advocacy was tempered by corporate sponsorship, but it still lobbied successfully to expand the Everglades National Park by 110,000 acres and to protect Alaska's Tongass National Forest. In 1993 the Wilderness Society reached new heights of influence when its president George Frampton joined President Clinton's Department of the Interior and alumnus George Baca became head of the Bureau of Land Management.

The Sierra Club

The organization most widely praised, and damned, has been John Muir's Sierra Club. In the mid-1960s the soon legendary David Brower transformed the club from its marginal status as a small club of mountain hikers into the archetypal environmental advocacy organization. It became adept at raising money and power politics. *Life* magazine called Brower the "country's No. 1 working conservationist," and the *Nation* said, "even his enemies regard him with a respect tinged with awe." Historian Stephen Fox wrote, "In a *realpolitik* sense the movement came of age during Echo Park, and Brower was its Bismarck." Brower opened a legislative office in Washington, fought major highly publicized aggressive battles against federal agencies and private business to save Storm King, Mineral King, Echo Park, and Canyonlands. Sierra Club lobbying and advertising forced the Bureau of Reclamation to abandon $2 billion dam projects in the Grand Canyon. It attracted popular interest with its stunning photography-and-essay books by such luminaries as Ansel Adams, Eliot Porter, Joseph Wood Krutch, Loren Eiseley, and Edward Abbey. Membership rose to over half a million. Nicknamed the "Arch-druid" by his friends, Brower also became the most visible target of critics of the environmental movement. Doubters used the words "Sierra Club mentality" as a negative catch phrase. Brower left the Sierra Club in 1969 in a conflict over its objectives and finances to establish a similar organization, Friends of the Earth, and later the Earth Island Institute. The Sierra Club itself continues to be a dominant environmental organization, with a particularly effective lobby on the federal level—it provided lead floor lobbyists on the new Clean Air Act. Simultaneously, grassroots activism often made local Sierra Club chapters the leading environmental organizations in their regions.

Sierra Club Legal Defense Fund

A Ford Foundation grant in 1971 allowed the spin-off of the Sierra Club Legal Defense Fund as the legal arm of its parent organization. The Sierra Club, smarting from its leadership battles with David Brower and over threats to its tax-free status by the IRS, became fearful of so-called left-wing radical activism and separated its legal activism from its mainstream activities. The Legal Defense Fund moved to Washington, D.C., where it aggressively targeted energy-industry polluters, even while its San Francisco-based parent remained cozy with the nuclear and coal power industries. The Legal Defense Fund nevertheless was still beholden to Sierra Club chapters and membership while it simultaneously worked toward a higher degree of professional independence. This fundamental contradiction divided its staff into factions that weakened the organization. In the 1970s SCLDF attracted attention when it sued the government to force it to abide by its own environmental laws. It has also led the attack of the litigates on the *Exxon Valdez* oil spill case in Alaska, and it stalled logging in the Northwest by having the northern spotted owl added to the endangered species list.

The Nature Conservancy

Founded in 1951, the Nature Conservancy has been called "the pin-striped real estate broker of the environmental movement." Its primary mission is to buy environmentally significant tracts of land that it manages itself or turns over to government. A major recent achievement was the acquisition in January 1989 for $18 million of the historic large-scale (500 square miles) ecologically unique Gray Ranch in New Mexico, after the federal government could not be persuaded to buy it. The Nature Conservancy is the richest environmental NGO by far, with assets totaling more than $600 million, including what critics call large sums of guilt money from corporations like Exxon and Alcoa. The organization gained important recognition in its face-off against James Watt, Reagan's secretary of the interior, when it replied to attempts at public lands sell-offs by enlarging its acquisitions. Overall, the Nature Conservancy is one of the most successful environmental organizations in meeting its goals.

Professionalization of the NGOs

In the environmental movement, there was a discernible shift in the 1970s from dedicated amateurs to highly skilled professionals. The old-line organizations added scientists, lawyers, and lobbyists to their staffs. During the 1970s and 1980s new environmental organizations such as the Environmental Defense Fund (1967) and the Natural Resources Defense Council (1970) appeared on the scene specifically dedicated to research, lobbying, political action, and litigation. These latter applied the tools of economic analysis and public interest law to negotiate with polluting industries and government agencies to improve pollution controls, to establish more rigorous energy policies, to enlarge wilderness areas, and so on. They became a virtual shadow government. According to one report, "lawyers from the Environmental Defense Fund may draft a bill, lobbyists from the Sierra Club may help push it past Capitol Hill, and a popularizer like Greenpeace may land the issue on the evening news." They learned to respond quickly to crisis. For example, when the EPA decided to allow polluting industry to move to "clean air states" like Wyoming and Idaho in order to comply with the law by spreading (thus diluting) pollution, environmental organizations led a public outcry that added a nationwide "nondeterioration" policy to the Clean Air Act for pristine air quality regions.

The Conservation Foundation

Founded in 1948, The Conservation Foundation did not have its origins among wilderness-loving amateurs. Its credentials instead came from Fairfield Osborn, former head of the New York Zoological Society and author of the pathbreaking environmental manifesto *Our Plundered Planet*. Based in Washington as a private think tank, it emphasized the importance of expert research to address the primary issues of resource management and population control. It sought to influence government policies through conferences and publications. Instead of traditional old-line wilderness preservation, The Conservation Foundation explored the impacts of modern technology, such as the positive and negative effects of chemical insecticides. It did not condemn economic development as much as urge a shift in emphasis that would put less trust in the absolute power of technology and promote conservation strategies such as efficiency, temperate consumption, and improved management of resources. Unlike the Sierra Club and other organizations, it sought to avoid public advocacy and instead promoted collaboration among industry, government, and universities. Often labeled probusiness because it supported the free enterprise system, it sought to make government and industry practices more rational.

Resources for the Future (RFF)

Similar in its cautious expert-based approach, Resources for the Future (RFF) gained an enviable position as a major source of scientific information and policy opinion that shaped national and international environmental agendas. RFF originated out of a 1953 conference in Washington, D.C., on America's (and the world's) simultaneous need for population control, a continuously expanding economy, the guarantee of materials for military preparedness, successful technological innovation, and environmentally appropriate resource development strategies. RFF's first annual report set the organization's agenda when it confirmed that "progress toward greater control [of the environment] reflects basic discoveries in pure science and the ability to adapt new principles for the benefit of society through improved patterns of organization and cooperation." Technology, even in the hands of industry, remained the best tool for environmentally balanced development. This included, for example, productive uses of nuclear energy, a view that most other environmental organizations found unacceptable. Like The Conservation Foundation, RFF focused on a problem-solving approach to "enlarge understanding of the role of natural resources in the growth of the American economy and the welfare of the American people." RFF argued, "Start with a basic and critical problem, stated usually in economic, political or social terms, and then pursue it by means of research, fundamental or applied, as may be indicated." By the 1960s RFF began to pay attention to the environmental impacts of resource development: water pollution, solid waste, air emissions. As pollution and scarcity became public issues, RFF became a leading advocate of cost-benefit analysis as the foundation for responsible government policy.

Environmental Defense Fund (EDF)

The more aggressive Environmental Defense Fund (EDF) emerged in 1967 out of a coalition of Long Island scientists from the Brookhaven National Laboratory, faculty from the State University of New York at Stony Brook, and local citizens concerned about groundwater pollution, dump sites, wildlife habitat protection, and uncontrolled development. These groups had enjoined the government from aerial DDT spraying in the court case that attracted Rachel Carson's attention and provided her with significant information for *Silent Spring*. The coalition, after it failed to find support from the Audubon Society and other old-line NGOs, formed itself into the Environmental Defense Fund. Led by a dynamic local lawyer, Victor Yannacone, EDF first gained national attention by its move against the use of dieldrin, a chlorinated hydrocarbon far more toxic than DDT, in a program to control Japanese beetles in Berrien County, Michigan. Yannacone's trademark phrase, "Sue the bastards," came out of his understanding of the power of litigation, grounded in expert scientific testimony, to stop the use of dangerous chemicals. Environmental activists had found a new weapon—the courts—that would confound government and industry for decades to come. EDF, convinced that only implacable opposition to environmental injury could bring timely change, became a leading force in adversarial politics and legal action against "the evasions, temporarizations and data tampering of the polluters and of the cozy-with-industry regulatory agencies." When, in 1970, Yannacone's aggressiveness seemed more a liability, he lost his leading role to more cautious leadership that received support from the Ford Foundation. Nevertheless, EDF remained a successful litigator in several highly publicized debates over lead toxicity, the fight against the ozone-producing supersonic transport (SST), as well as a continuing presence in pesticide control. In recent years, EDF has promoted a so-called win-win policy of "free-market environmentalism" that seeks industry cooperation and incorporates market strategies instead of regulation and litigation.

Natural Resources Defense Council (NRDC)

The Natural Resources Defense Council (NRDC) enjoyed Ford Foundation support from its start in 1970. Several Yale Law School graduates, committed to public interest law, became involved in a highly publicized battle against the construction of a power plant and water-storage faculty at the Storm King scenic site along the palisades of the Hudson River. Gus Speth, Stephen Duggan, and Whitney North Seymour, Jr., established NRDC as a legal advocacy group that would go beyond "disorganized, one-shot, finger-in-the-dike" litigation to be a "law firm for the environment," able to respond to the rapid growth of environmental legislation and regulation. NRDC influenced the passage and implementation of the Clean Air Act, the Clean Water Act, strip-mining controls, the Alaska lands bill and drilling in the arctic refuges, as well as regulation and litigation in forestry, land use, and agriculture. It is unique among the major environmental organizations by paying attention to public health and urban decay. NRDC also became well known for watchdog monitoring of the implementation of regulations. In the 1980s it began to pay more attention to international environmental issues, including global warming. Because its role was similar to the Environmental Defense Fund, the two organizations agreed to divide responsibilities for legal action: NRDC focused more intensively on expertise in science and lobbying, and EDF gave more attention to law and economics. By the 1980s NRDC had emerged as the primary organization that used professional expertise to shape environmental policies and decisions. Criticized by probusiness conservatives for its adherence to bureaucratic "command and control" environmental policies, it did place former staffers in President Clinton's EPA, the Energy Department, the National Security Council, and the Agency for International Development. One of these said, "I fully expect to be sued by my friends in NRDC."

Local Action Organizations: PIRGs and NIMBYs

On the local level, volunteer citizens' groups forced public disclosure and government action to correct neighborhood environmental hazards such as toxic dumps, pesticide spraying, contaminated water supplies, radioactive wastes, nuclear plants, and proposals to build garbage incinerators and hazardous waste disposal facilities. They often sought to outflank delays and obfuscation from federal intransigence and corporate hostility. Acronyms such as NIMBY (not in my backyard), LULU (locally unwanted land uses), and NIABY (not in any backyard) gained public attention. They were rarely connected with either the old-line or new lobbying organizations already mentioned, but found friendly national networks in the Citizen's Clearinghouse for Hazardous Waste (CCHW, founded by Lois Gibbs of Love Canal fame in 1981) and the Boston-based National Toxic Campaign (1984). The CCHW is an environmental justice movement that provides organization, research, and media skills for rural groups in the Midwest and South to fight dumps and incinerators. Funded largely by foundations, CCHW is unique in its connection with churches. The archrival National Toxics Campaign is "a big, angry network" of 1,300 community dump site groups that has effectively applied sophisticated technical and policy tools for correction and cleanup. It fought for Superfund reauthorization in the mid-1980s and continues to press polluting companies to sign "good neighbor" agreements with local communities. After Earth Day 1970, local action often took place through state and local Public Interest Research Groups (PIRGs) that originated on campuses in Oregon and Minnesota.

Such local action groups gave priority to public health involving urban and industrial problems far more than wilderness protection. They effectively compelled major pollution-generating corporations such as 3M Corporation and DuPont to consider more closely the environmental consequences of their actions. In 1983, for example, Dow Chemical decided to withdraw the herbicide 2,4,5-T rather than face more public attacks. Such bottom-up action led to the passage of Proposition 65 in California in 1985, which set rigorous limits on toxic substances in the state's agriculture and chemical industries. In response to community groups, industry created "environmental flying squadrons" of public relations and scientific experts "to explain the truth about an environmental hazard." Historian Robert Gottlieb writes, "Without a strong basis for citizen action . . . corporate power would remain unchecked." These local citizen volunteers emphasized public participation in environmental decisions; they distrusted "expertise" from government and industry as a tool to intimidate nonexpert local citizen organizations while disguising crucial political or economic choices. In the past, local communities had regularly been told by government agencies and industrial polluters that the risks of substances like lead and mercury were insignificant. Citizen action groups sought to empower local communities against the seemingly impossible challenge of technical expertise, industrial resources, and government bureaucracies.

Citizen Access to Environmental Policy

Environmental organizations feared that they were closed out of important decisions by a growing alliance between government and industry, sometimes called the "iron triangle," the pork barrel of private industry, government agencies, and Congress. By 1980 NGOs began to doubt the commitment of EPA and other agencies to aggressive environmental advocacy. NGOs made widespread use of the 1966 Freedom of Information Act to prevent withholding by government agencies of information "primarily benefiting the public interest." This public access and right to review became an integral part of the administrative process established by the Clean Water Act, Toxic Substances Control Act, Endangered Species Act, Safe Drinking Water Act, Solid Waste Disposal Act, the Clean Air Act, and a myriad of other environmental legislation. By 1986 the Superfund Act included "community right-to-know" provisions. Mechanisms for citizen participation included litigation, public hearings, public surveys, voter initiatives, citizen review panels, advisory commissions, written comment processes, and site-specific dispute mediation. Citizen Oversight Councils assured citizen participation in the administrative process, notably in the aftermath of the 1989 *Exxon Valdez* oil spill. The councils acted to avoid any repetition of corporate, state, and federal "complacency and neglect" that, in the case of the oil spill, created "an accident waiting to happen." These citizen "outsiders" were often so successful that by the mid-1980s there were government and industry attempts to limit citizen "interference." A rider to a 1990 Department of Interior appropriations bill, for example, sought to limit the public's ability to delay timber sales in an Oregon national forest and to restrict public participation in debates concerning the northern spotted owl.

Radical Environmental NGOs

The Reagan-Bush era (1980–1992) saw the expansion of more radical and openly aggressive organizations: Greenpeace USA (1971), Sea Shepherd Conservation Society (1977), Earth First! (1980), and the Earth Island Institute (1982). Facing an antienvironmental backlash, mainstream NGOs had experienced growing confusion and began to lose faith in lobbying, litigation, and political action. More radical groups preached social change that included a stinging critique of modern industrial society. Radical environmentalism appeared first among an intellectual wing with extremely diverse positions: some called themselves deep ecologists (see Chapter 12); others were believers in the controversial Gaia principle (see Chapter 15). Deep ecologist William Duvall proposed a green social philosophy with four pillars: ecology, grassroots democracy, social responsibility, and nonviolence. So-called green consumerism was based on the pledge, "Do as little harm as possible." The activist Christopher Manes, for example, wrote that deep ecology arose out of "one simple but frightening realization, that our culture is lethal to the ecology that it depends on." Radical environmentalists refused to join forces with the lawyers and scientists of the 1970s and 1980s. They complained that the NRDC, EDF, and RFF were too narrowly focused on economics and public policy that got them into bed with corporations and government agencies, resulting in harmful and unnecessary compromises on pollution controls, energy policies, and resource protection. Outside the United States, similar environmentalists who sought a basic shift away from industrial society had often formed themselves into "green" political parties or action organizations. Within the United States, green party politics was less viable because of the historic failure of alternative political parties. The radicals believed environmental issues would not be resolved except through change in society's basic culture.

Some radicals became environmental activists who followed the principles of nonviolent civil disobedience patterned on India's Gandhi or the American civil rights leader, Martin Luther King, Jr. Like the civil rights, women's rights, and antiwar movements of the 1960s and 1970s, some used tactics such as demonstrations and sit-ins. A small but highly visible minority advocated "ecotage"—destructive violence toward road-building equipment and power transmission lines—and other types of aggressive interference in government and industry actions judged harmful to the environment. Advocates of ecotage were loosely anarchistic (almost none were so-called Reds, or communists) and found a model in the revolutionary characters of Edward Abbey's 1975 novel *The Monkey Wrench Gang,* a book that gave advice on disabling a bulldozer or wrecking electric power pylons. (Earlier, in 1968, Abbey wrote the nature classic *Desert Solitaire,* of which Susan Zakin, in her 1993 history of Earth First!, wrote, "Abbey almost single-handedly made it impossible for nature writing to lapse back into babbling brooks and heavenly birdsong.") Abbey cautioned in 1984, "'Monkeywrenchers' were saboteurs, not terrorists. Sabotage is violence against inanimate objects: machinery and property. Terrorism is violence against human beings. I am definitely opposed to terrorism, whether practiced by the military and state—as it usually is—or by what we might call unlicensed individuals."

Earth First! and Ecotage

America's most visible radical environmental group was David Foreman's Earth First! It emerged after the eloquent and energetic Foreman became disillusioned with his work as a Washington lobbyist for the Wilderness Society. Foreman and four friends, after a common desert experience in Mexico, created the loose alliance called Earth First! in 1980, dedicated to Abbey-inspired monkeywrenching. Philosophically, Earth First! called for the environmental movement to move from scenery worship to ecosystem awareness. Earth First! disavowed any centralized organizational structure. To its surprise, by the late 1980s, the self-proclaimed "nonorganization" had more than 5,000 subscribers to its newsletter. Earth First! initially received national attention on March 21, 1981, when members gained access to the controversial Glen Canyon Dam upstream on the Colorado River from the Grand Canyon and unfurled a 300-foot-long plastic "crack" on the face of the dam. Earth First! was highly sensitive to the importance of media attention to create public awareness of specific environmental problems. In 1982 Earth First! successfully blocked construction of an oil exploration and logging road into the Gros Ventre section of the Bridger-Teton National Forest in northwest Wyoming. Some members committed one of the first cases of "ecotage" damage when they disabled construction equipment. Also in 1982 Earth First! blocked the construction of logging roads in the unspectacular but ecologically important Siskiyou Mountains of northern California and southern Oregon, described as "one of the greatest concentrations of botanical diversity in the United States." Elsewhere, some Earth First! members sabotaged road-building equipment and oil-exploration rigs in wilderness regions; they toppled power transmission lines that ran across forests and wildernesses. Other activities soon included climbing and sitting on the tops of trees slated for lumbering, blocking logging roads with sit ins, and driving metal spikes in trees (with warnings) to prevent their being cut down with chain saws. One logger in Washington state in early 1990 found that someone had put sand and salt water in the fuel system, water cooling pipes, and hydraulic system of several pieces of equipment, causing damage, he said, that totaled $187,000. Radical Earth First!ers insisted that such action—"ethical sabotage"—was a last-resort attempt to protect forests under immediate threat of wrongful destruction. In 1988 David Foreman had written *Ecodefense*, a handbook for "ethical monkeywrenching," which emphasized the Earth First! principle, "Do no harm to human lives." Foreman said monkeywrenching was an honorable revolutionary sequel to the Boston Tea Party.

Middle-of-the-road environmentalists responded that monkeywrenching didn't work. They feared a negative public backlash against all activism. A Forest Service official said, "I don't know of one timber sale that has been stopped by tree spiking." An Audubon Society official in Washington concluded, "Most of the progress on the ancient forest issue has been made by the Sierra Club Legal Defense Fund." Earth First!ers retorted that their significance was not in the number of trees they saved, but in the debate they provoked. In Susan Zakin's words, "Earth First! was fast becoming a highly charged electrode stuck to the body politic— the shock it delivered was based on intensity, not size." On May 31, 1989, Foreman was arrested with several others and charged with alleged conspiracy to damage power lines and towers leading to and from several western nuclear power plants. It was true that since October 1987 a band of ecosaboteurs had taken cutting torches into the San Francisco Peaks, mountains sacred to Indians near Prescott, Arizona, and toppled ski chairlift pylons and power transmission towers leading to a coal mine neighboring the Grand Canyon. After a highly politicized trial, Foreman agreed to plead guilty to a felony conspiracy charge, but with sentencing to be delayed for five years and his charge reduced to a misdemeanor. Others received sentences from six years to one month. Then on May 24, 1990, a pipe bomb exploded under the passenger seat of a car, seriously injuring Judi Bari and Darryl Cherney, both Earth First! activists (Bari's pelvis was shattered.) By July 1990 a coalition of environmental groups, members of Congress, and the media forced an investigation of police mistreatment of Earth First! activists. Contrarily, Earth First! was also publicly excoriated as misanthropic and insensitive when writers in its newsletter called AIDS "a welcome development in the inevitable reduction of human population," when it looked on famine in East Africa as a blessing, and even cheered when a hostile public official in California contracted incurable lung cancer. Cherney reflected the Earth First! philosophy when he said at a lunch meeting, "I'm not an environmentalist. I'm an Earth warrior. I am the Earth defending itself. I trying to de-domesticize myself. I'm trying to feralize myself. Once you start thinking biocentrically, you start to see everything in a new light. This is not a napkin, it's a tree. The language becomes different. If you want to call someone something bad, call him a human."

Greenpeace

Greenpeace became a successful radical organization on the international scene. Like Earth First! Greenpeace was particularly effective in creating media events to mobilize public support for its environmental battles. Policy analyst Sean D. Cassidy described its activities as "flamboyant events," including parachuting off smokestacks, bathing in toxic wastes, and attaching protest banners to Trident submarines. He called it the "world's first made-for-and-by-TV mass movement." Greenpeace played up its image of one-David-against-many-Goliaths. Greenpeace had been formed by two expatriate Americans, Jim Bohlen and Irving Stowe, in February 1970 out of a small British Columbia chapter of the Sierra Club. The Sierra Club eventually donated $6,000 to early Greenpeace efforts, but disavowed Greenpeace confrontational tactics as "too risky." As its name suggests, Greenpeace combines environmental and antiwar objectives. It first received international attention in 1970 when it tried to sail a decrepit halibut fishing boat, renamed *Greenpeace,* into the off-limits "danger zone" of U.S. nuclear testing on Alaska's Amchitka Island. The first boat broke down far from Amchitka, and a second attempt with *Greenpeace Too,* a converted Canadian minesweeper, only got within 700 miles of the site when the blast occurred on November 6, 1971. Protests about the "ecological vandalism" of nuclear testing became an outlet for bitter Alaskans, helped focus the anger of Canadians against fallout risks, and gave Greenpeace a wide swath of attention on national television like CBS News and in major newspapers like the *New York Times.* Greenpeace continued its confrontational tactics with the highest possible media visibility. In 1972 and 1973 it sailed a ketch, *Greenpeace III*, into waters near the French atmospheric nuclear test site on Moruroa Atoll in the South Pacific. The French reacted violently to repeated Greenpeace interventions with a commando raid on board in August 1973 that injured skipper David McTaggart's kidneys, spine, and head. In a New Zealand port in 1985, the French secret service planted two bombs on the *Rainbow Warrior* that killed a photographer and sank the ship. Greenpeace also received widespread attention in its campaign in 1976 against the long-standing annual clubbing death of newborn harp seal pups off Newfoundland by the Norwegian commercial sealing fleet. It established a long-term program of whale protection, in which individuals maneuvered themselves between whales and Soviet whaling ships with high-powered harpoons. Greenpeace by the early 1980s helped bring international accords on the protection of dolphins enmeshed in Japanese fishing driftnets. It was instrumental in getting low-level radioactive waste dumping at sea outlawed (the 1983 London Dumping Convention), enforcing controls over supertankers in risky areas like the Strait of Juan de Fuca in Washington's Puget Sound, and bringing bans on mineral development in Antarctica. Greenpeace acted directly against the chemical giant DuPont, manufacturer of ozone-depleting CFCs, when in 1989 activists chained themselves inside a metal box bolted to the railroad tracks by which raw materials were delivered to DuPont's Chambersworks plant in Deepwater, New Jersey, and CFCs were shipped out. In 1992 Greenpeace was particularly critical of what it described as the prodevelopment and anti–Third World climate at the UN Environment and Development Conference (UNCED) in Rio de Janeiro, Brazil. Greenpeace especially attacked UNCED's connections with the World Bank. It said UNCED failed to deal with critical issues like global warming, the flow of Third World resources to the developed nations, transport of hazardous wastes, proliferation of nuclear wastes, destruction of ecosystems, and loss of biodiversity. It unfurled a banner on Sugarloaf Mountain overlooking Rio which declared that the world's leaders had sold out the planet. Greenpeace claimed to represent 5 million supporters in 30 countries. During the 1980s it enjoyed the most successful record of financial support of any environmental organization, but this was halved by the mid-1990s.

The Antienvironmentalist Movement

Doubts about the real threat by pollution to the environment were raised largely by the industrial polluters themselves. Nevertheless, a relatively small number of scientists, economists, and policy makers believed that (1) the evidence didn't show problems deserving the cost or effort, or (2) the public has always willingly accepted some levels of public health risk as the price for the benefits of continuous growth of an industrial consumer society. Although no one played down the harm of substances like lead or mercury, the doubters entered the mainstream of environmental debate in their critiques of the high costs of correcting global warming, ozone depletion, acid rain, nonpoint pollution, and even toxic waste dumping.

The Sagebrush Rebellion

An antienvironment backlash was part of the nation's turn to the right that included the 1980 election of Republican president Ronald Reagan. Reagan stated his disregard of environmental problems, claiming they were too costly to correct and enforce. James Watt, his secretary of the interior, openly denounced wilderness protection and environmental controls in favor of economic expansion. Western landowners and developers embarked on a "Sagebrush Rebellion" based on the West's frontier individualism and long-standing distrust of eastern government. The stakes were not small, since over 700 million acres of land and wilderness, together with coal, uranium, oil, and natural gas resources, mostly in the West, were owned and managed by the federal government. These had been treated as a public trust to be protected on ecological grounds since passage of the Wilderness Act of 1964, the Endangered Species Act of 1973, and the Federal Land Policy and Management Act and the National Forest Management Act, both in 1976. After 20 years devoted to protecting western wilderness from development, a national conservation consensus began to unravel, which put the environmental movement on the defensive. Ranchers, loggers, and land and mineral developers felt that the public lands had been locked up with unreasonable restrictions on livestock grazing, logging, and mining. The rebels sought dramatic change by transferring ownership of public lands to the state governments, and thus freeing their development by sympathetic local interests. The rebels found friendly support from state land commissioners, state legislators, and several U.S. senators. Sponsorship came from natural resource industries like Conoco, Chevron, Atlantic Richfield, U.S. Borax, Louisiana Pacific Timber, and the American Gas Association, and private associations like the National Inholders Association and the International Snowmobilers. One Sagebrush critic, Ted Trueblood, said, "You don't have to be a genius to see who's really behind the Sagebrush rip-off." The Sagebrush Rebellion burned out after two years, but it publicized a conservative alternative to a protectionist view of public land management. The rebels' strategy was to use local activists working in the field to dismantle the conservation consensus and encourage local authorities to derail federal agencies and regulations. The benefit would be more mining, more logging, more energy exploration, and more grazing as the federal hand was lifted. Their tools, which "copied the success of the old Left," included intensive media coverage and litigation in the courts. They directed carefully planned attacks on the Bureau of Land Management (BLM) and the Forest Service, the two agencies that held most of the disputed land. BLM personnel privately confirmed that the Sagebrush Rebellion "is already putting federal land managers on the defensive, undermining their ability to make and enforce professional management decisions." Under rebel pressure, western legislatures, already inherently suspicious of federal actions, shifted further from proenvironment agendas. Economic arguments began successfully to counter ecological and public interest positions. One result unanticipated by the Sagebrush Rebellion, however, was the rapid increase in western membership of proenvironment organizations.

The Wise Use Movement

Wise use is a venerable term coined in 1907 by U.S. Forester Gifford Pinchot, and espoused by Theodore Roosevelt. It reflected a Progressive era focus on scientific and efficient (e.g., "rational") use of the national forests that would both serve economic growth and protect resources for the future. In the 1990s wise use has become the slogan of a right-wing plan to discredit environmental organizations, roll back environmental regulations, and assert unlimited rights for property owners. It built on the Sagebrush Rebellion, but with much more sophistication, and took advantage of a proindustry and antienvironmental mood that elected the 1994 Republican Congress. Wise use has been described as a "professional grassroots" movement that seeks to appeal to rural communities and individualistic values, claiming to speak for average working people and small property owners. The Wise Use Movement can be dated from a 1988 "multiple use strategy" conference held in Reno, Nevada, by about 200 organizations that set the stage for a campaign "to destroy environmentalism." Represented were the American Petroleum Institute, the American Mining Congress, the National Rifle Association, and the Council of Forest Industries. Corporate interests were from Exxon, DuPont, Louisiana-Pacific, Georgia-Pacific, and Weyerhauser. James Watt's old employer, The Mountain States Legal Foundation, was in attendance, as well as the Center for the Defense of Free Enterprise (CDFE). Recreation interests were represented by motorcycle clubs and off-road vehicle groups.

Like the Sagebrush Rebellion, Wise Use focused its activities against government regulatory policies in mountain and western states involving land and resources. It chose specific issues: Increase petroleum and timber extraction from protected lands in Alaska, raise timber harvest quotas in national forests including old-growth forests in the Northwest, and increase resource development in and adjacent to western national parks such as Yellowstone. It proposed economic or community impact statements to counter the environmental impact statements required for development. Ron Arnold of CDFE told a journalist, "In an activist society like ours, the only way to defeat a social movement is with another social movement." The complaint against Wise Use was that it became the voice for corporate interests and property speculators. Wise Use projects provoked media attention in their attacks on "eco-freaks" who, according to Ron Arnold, are "the new pagans who worship trees and sacrifice people." Wise Use rhetoric is highly ideological and draws on private militia, conservative Christian, and right-wing doctrines: "Like it or not, we are involved in a war with the preservationists and the animal rights radicals. To win this war, we must gain control of the hearts and minds of the public." Like its archenemy, Earth First!, the Wise Use Movement threatens possible violence. James Watt said in 1993, "If the troubles from environmentalists cannot be solved in the jury box or at the ballot box, perhaps the cartridge box should be used." The Sahara Club, dirt bike enthusiasts in California, said, "You can't reason with eco-freaks, but you sure can scare them." Environmental activist homes have been burned, cars vandalized, government offices attacked, and in one highly publicized case in northern California, two Earth First! campaigners were gravely injured when a bomb exploded under the front seat of their car.

Despite its tendency toward extreme activism, the Wise Use Movement finds support from a broad spectrum of citizenry that is disaffected by a perception of cynical government bureaucracy, a maze of confusing and contradictory environmental regulation, a sense of political disenfranchisement, and a long-term economic depression in many rural communities and regions. It indicates that the conflict is not over between the historic ethic of taming the West and Leopold's restorative land ethic. Above all, it reflects the ambiguities of a national debate on private property ownership. Wise Use is a classic backlash movement.

Conclusion: Environmental Science, Public Activism, and Earth Day 1970

Historians Peter Rowley and Samuel Hays concluded that contemporary science is not yet up to the task of true environmental analysis. Ecology still did not fit readily into the familiar modes of modern science, partly because it was holistic and synthetic rather than reductionistic, inclusive rather than specialized, in one writer's words, "at best a polymorphic science." Eugene Odum, in a 1977 article in *Science*, nevertheless saw ecology as a new integrative discipline: "It is in the properties of the large-scale, integrated systems that hold solutions to most of the long-term problems of society." To this quandary, Hays added, "Environmental issues had pushed science far beyond conventional knowledge on many questions about which the evidence was either limited or mixed. This was especially the case on the long-term, chronic effects of low-level exposure [to pollution], which required more sensitive measurements than had yet been perfected and which often were so complex that the myriad relationships they entailed were subject to various interpretations." The public was disappointed and frustrated. It saw the need to act, but felt thwarted by insufficient scientific knowledge as well as inadequate technologies. A basic disjunction appeared between the substantiation of scientific evidence and public insistence on swift action. This often created a paralysis for protective action. Nor was the marketplace out of the picture. Economists asked how much individual citizens would be willing to pay for cleaner air and better scenery.

As we have seen the modern environmental movement opened through a series of events beginning with the publication of Rachel Carson's *Silent Spring* in 1962. It culminated with the demanding regulations to clean up toxic chemical sites through Superfund (CERCLA) in 1976 (see Chapter 14). One turning point was the highly publicized Earth Day on April 22, 1970. Between 10 and 20 million Americans joined in protest against environmental degradation in rallys, marches, and teach-ins in hundreds of college campuses and tens of cities. Earth Day was also a celebratory event that crossed social, economic, and political lines to include industry, conservationists, and minorities, government and the middle class, and also radicals who sought to revolutionize society and also put scrubbers in smokestacks. Earth Day was more a result than a cause. Since the 1960s Americans had been troubled by the disappearance of wilderness, the ugliness of billboards and junkyards, and pollution of the nation's air and water. The National Environmental Protection Act (NEPA) was signed by President Nixon on January 1, 1970, about five months before Earth Day.

Earth Day was itself the product of the activism of the 1960s, a sense of crisis that had already produced an effective civil rights movement and the powerful anti–Vietnam War demonstrations. In September 1969, in a speech in Seattle, Wisconsin senator Gaylord Nelson proposed a "National Teach-in on the Crisis of the Environment." Nelson declared that environmental collapse was among the "most critical issues facing mankind," making "Vietnam, nuclear war, hunger, decaying cities, and all the other major problems one could name . . . relatively insignificant by comparison." Nelson recruited 25-year-old Harvard law student Denis Hayes, who took the position that environmental action meant radical criticism of existing government and industrial policies: "Ecology is concerned with the total system— not just the way it disposes of its garbage." President Nixon's state of the union message in January 1970 described environmentalism as the great public issue of the decade, partly to counteract a leading Democratic presidential challenger Maine senator Edmund Muskie. Muskie connected Earth Day with the contemporary race and antiwar issues: "Those who believe that we are talking about the Grand Canyon and the Catskills, but not Harlem and Watts, are wrong." Hayes added that the Vietnam War was "an ecological catastrophe." Direct participation in Earth Day activities also came from Monsanto Chemical, Dow Chemical, the Ford Motor Company, and two of the nation's most powerful utilities: Commonwealth Edison in Chicago and Consolidated Edison in New York City. A significant part of industry was very suspicious and saw the marshaling of public opinion in Earth Day as a left-wing attack on capitalist society. April 22, 1970, was peaceful, even festive, with major rallies in New York City and Washington, D.C., as well as hundreds of college campuses.

The popular appeal of Earth Day indicated that Americans no longer accepted the disappearance of wilderness or industrial pollution as inevitable costs of progress. Instead, environmental quality became an essential feature of the quality of life and standard of living that they demanded as a national birthright. The celebration did usher in environmental politics that forged a national environmental policy for the next 25 years, and perhaps longer. Most participants did not seek social and economic revolution that would transform American industry and metropolis, which disappointed a radical faction. Nevertheless, the combination of NEPA and Earth Day created a climate for a comprehensive legislative agenda that took two specific directions. It sought to use technological tools to clean up environmental problems but did little to remove the sources of environmental messes. And it emphasized "command and control" regulations that forced environmental change, often regardless of cost. To the media, Earth Day was "Day One of the Fix-It."

For Further Reading

A continuing flood of books on ecology as the primary environmental science and on NGOs quickly outdates any attempt at a bibliography. Peter J. Bowler's *The Norton History of the Environmental Sciences* (1992) is a lucid and comprehensive analysis that puts the environmental sciences in an excellent historical perspective. By far the best detailed analysis of the nature of ecology, and its forebears, is the new edition of Donald Worster's classic *Nature's Economy: The Roots of Ecology* (1977, 1994). A solid philosophical and methodological history can be found in Robert P. McIntosh's *The Background of Ecology: Concept and Theory* (1985). A candid and entertaining insider's history is by Frank Benjamin Golley, *A History of the Ecosystem Concept in Ecology* (1993). Eugene P. Odum's textbook is still definitive. For a powerful statement on the human nature condition from Odum as a leader in the field, see his *Ecology and Our Endangered Life-Support Systems* (1989). A good environmental science textbook can also be a rewarding introduction to the field, such as Daniel D. Chiras's *Environmental Science: Action for a Sustainable Future* (3rd ed., 1991). Most such textbooks are unexpectedly aggressive in their advocacy of ecology as a subversive and corrective science. Rachel Carson, *Silent Spring* (1962; still available in several editions) is required reading, together with Frank Graham, Jr.'s influential analysis of its immediate impact, *Since Silent Spring* (1970). See also Thomas Dunlap, *DDT: Scientists, Citizens, and Public Policy* (1988), and James Whorton, *Before Silent Spring* (1974). The best assessment of the emergence of America's environmental problems remains William Ophul's 1977 *Ecology and the Politics of Scarcity: The Unraveling of the American Dream,* which was extensively updated in 1992. For the rise of the environmental movement in general, and especially the role of NGOs, the best brief review is by Riley E. Dunlap and Angela G. Mertig, *American Environmentalism: The U.S. Environmental Movement, 1970–1990* (1992); Kirkpatrick Sale's brief history, *The Green Revolution: The American Environmental Movement 1962–1992* (1993), is disappointing in its vague generalities and lack of detail. The best longer historical analysis by far is by an important activist, Robert Gottlieb, who makes his own insightful analysis in *Forcing the Spring: The Transformation of the American Environmental Movement* (1993). Gottlieb's book overshadows the still excellent *A Fierce Green Fire: The American Environmental Movement* (1993) by former *New York Times* environmental writer Philip Shabecoff. The radical group Earth First! receives a vivid blow-by-blow history in Susan Zakin's *Coyotes and Town Dogs: Earth First! and the Environmental Movement* (1993). The current (1990) state of environmental science, economics, and policy is explored extensively in B.L. Turner II et al., *The Earth as Transformed by Human Action* (1990).

CHAPTER FOURTEEN

RISK AND REGULATION: ENVIRONMENTALISM ENTERS THE MODERN ERA

If the voice of reform comes, it will come from the people, not the agencies. Only an active, enlightened citizenry can keep the bureaucracy energized and on the straight and narrow path.

—WILLIAM O. DOUGLAS, 1972

Don't kill all the lawyers until they undo what gives you cause to kill them.

—ENVIRONMENTAL LAW PROFESSOR WILLIAM H. RODGERS, JR., 1994

The Impossible Dream:
Making a Risk-Free Environment

Ralph Waldo Emerson once wrote, "As soon as there is life there is danger." Americans of an earlier era were more resigned than we are to injury, disease, and early death. They were also willing to take higher risks for the sake of large rewards. In the first ten years on the Mississippi and Ohio rivers, 300 steamboats blew up with the loss of 3,000 lives. Americans nevertheless stayed with steamboats. The same would be true of pioneering railroads, automobiles, and airplanes. It was a proud tradition. Americans had been taking chances since independence and a war of rebellion. They risked a new form of government based on open disagreement and controversy and filled the land with immigrants willing to cross thousands of miles of stormy ocean for the sake of unknown opportunities. Similarly, most Americans believed that if they were willing to risk money, time, skill, and energy, they could become successful entrepreneurs and business leaders. No one who looked at the American character in the nineteenth century and the first half of the twentieth century said that Americans were cautious.

American society had also been built on the belief that technological innovation would improve the American way of life. Technology offered a substitute for hard physical labor. It also produced goods more rapidly, at lower prices, with higher quality. Technological "fixes" were also believed to solve social problems—city water systems improved cleanliness and electric street lighting reduced crime rates. By the 1950s technology was expected to be (1) safe, with no risk or inherent problems, (2) efficient in its use of energy, (3) of high quality and trouble free, (4) clean and not significantly harm the environment. These expectations were a tall order and also reflected the optimism of the American public that technology owed them a risk-free world. Americans were educated into a belief in overdesign, redundancy, and substitution ability—so much technology was available that any problem could be solved several times over. In reality, the public was selectively choosing to accept hazards, such as 50,000 deaths a year on the highways, for perceived benefits and conveniences, such as the private automobile for everyone.

Industrial Breakdowns:
"The Big Technological Letdown"

In the second half of the twentieth century it became painfully clear that technological improvement had not overcome the classic four horsemen of the apocalypse: war, pestilence, famine, and death. Now, in the 1960s and 1970s, a fifth threat grabbed Americans by the throat—industrial pollution. Americans complained of local air and water pollution, garbage dumping, and abandoned industrial waste sites. At one time, raw nature was the source of risk, to be tamed by technology. Now the tables were turned: Once the source of safety, technology has become the source of risk. The shock of surprise could not have been greater.

Americans experienced "the big technological letdown." Each new technology often created new and different problems. In 1967 the Public Health Service released its pioneering survey of the health effects of sulfur oxides, which in turn was vigorously denounced by the coal industry. Americans began to feel a new burden: seemingly endless industrial breakdowns. Synthetic chemical compounds posed new health risks: PBBs in Michigan, Kepone in Virginia, PCBs in the Hudson River, and toxics in Love Canal and the "Valley of Drums" near Louisville, Kentucky. Americans were also shaken by the energy crisis during the winter of 1973–74, when oil prices skyrocketed from $3 a barrel to over $30 a barrel. As a result, Americans began to shift their thinking from energy consumption to energy conservation.

Battling the Chemical Industry

Much of America's postwar prosperity depended on synthetic organic chemicals, the production of which expanded from less than 10 billion pounds in 1940 to more than 350 billion pounds in 1980, when Superfund pollution regulations were passed. The industry employed more than 800,000 workers and its annual sales exceeded $260 billion. By 1980 a total of 70,000 synthetic chemicals had been introduced, with 1,500 additional compounds being added annually. The original advantage of synthetic chemicals, it was said, was that they resist biological deterioration. Such bioaccumulation, however, became a recognized problem in the 1960s and was one of the strongest arguments made in Rachel Carson's condemnation of DDT and other pesticides in *Silent Spring* in 1962. In 1964 the Velsicole Chemical Company plant in Memphis, Tennessee, discharged the pesticide endrin into the lower Mississippi River, leading to a massive fish kill. DDT levels were so high in Lake Michigan perch that their consumption was restricted. Herbicides like 2,4,5-T and 2,4-D gained notoriety as Agent Orange defoliates during the Vietnam War. The Federal Insecticide, Fungicide, and Rodenticide Act (FIFRA) was extensively revised in 1972 for the first time in 25 years. By the 1970s the public's attention expanded from its specific worries over pesticides to a broad-based concern for hazardous waste contamination of air, water, and land. Although the petrochemical industry was acknowledged as essential to modern life, it took most of the blame for toxic dumps, air pollution, contaminated water supplies, and farm soils loaded with pesticides and herbicides. In 1976 Congress expanded the pollution control agenda when it passed the Toxic Substances Control Act (TOSCA) that sought to control not just pesticides and herbicides but all toxic chemicals. EPA reported that more than 90 percent of all Americans have measurable quantities of hazardous substances such as styrene, ethyl phenol, ethyl benzene, and toluene in their bodies. Historian Samuel Hays concluded, "Toxic threats seemed to be as widely dispersed as the environment itself."

Regulating the Risks: America's "Environmental Era"

The general public, nongovernmental organizations, and the media looked to the federal government for intervention and cleanup. Americans had learned from public welfare programs during the Depression of the 1930s and the national mobilization during World

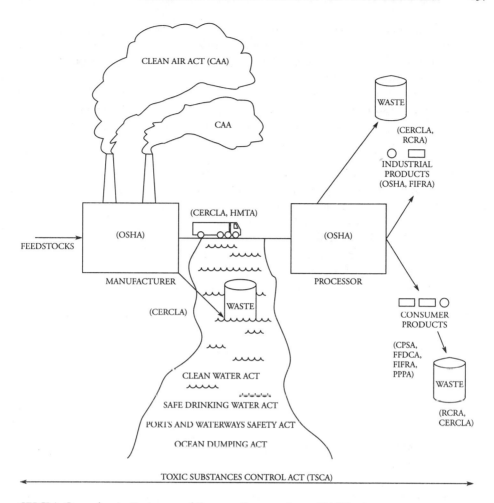

CLEAN AIR ACT (CAA)

CAA

(CERCLA, HMTA)

WASTE

(CERCLA, RCRA)

INDUSTRIAL PRODUCTS (OSHA, FIFRA)

(OSHA)

FEEDSTOCKS

(OSHA)

MANUFACTURER

PROCESSOR

(CERCLA)

WASTE

CONSUMER PRODUCTS

(CPSA, FFDCA, FIFRA, PPPA)

WASTE

(RCRA, CERCLA)

CLEAN WATER ACT

SAFE DRINKING WATER ACT

PORTS AND WATERWAYS SAFETY ACT

OCEAN DUMPING ACT

TOXIC SUBSTANCES CONTROL ACT (TSCA)

CERCLA: Comprehensive Environmental Response, Compensation, and Liability Act
FFDCA: Federal Food, Drug, and Cosmetic Act
RCRA: Resource Conservation and Recovery Act
FIFRA: Federal Insecticide, Fungicide, and Rodenticide Act
CPSA: Consumer Product Safety Act
OSHA: Occupational Safety and Health Act
HMTA: Hazardous Materials Transportation Act
PPPA: Poison Prevention Packaging Act

Diagram of Regulations Affecting the Lifecycle of a Potentially Hazardous Chemical. This shows the multiple and often-overlapping rules and regulations by which state and federal agencies attempt to limit environmental harm to humans and the environment.

War II that the federal government could take the lead in achieving a better society. Earlier in American history, government regulation was limited and selectively enforced: The Interstate Commerce Commission regulated the railroads, the Food and Drug Administration monitored food additives and drugs, the Federal Trade Commission administered antitrust laws, and the Securities and Exchange Commission was watchdog over stock and bond markets. Beginning in the 1960s, the federal government stepped into environmental protection. It became a permanent issue in national affairs, including new environmental planks in party platforms for presidential campaigns.

Beginning in 1970 with the passage of the National Environmental Protection Act (NEPA), we can justifiably speak of an American "environmental era" when the nation was galvanized into urgent action and when environmental issues were absorbed into the public mainstream. (A probusiness backlash may have closed the era with the election of a conservative Republican Congress in 1994.) The primary changes were brought on by the passage of NEPA, the creation of the all-inclusive Environmental Protection Agency (EPA) in 1970, and the strict measures, technology-forcing procedures, and tight deadlines of the 1970 Clean Air Act and the 1972 Clean Water Act. These were the centerpieces of a blitzkrieg of legislation dedicated to protecting air, water, wetlands, wilderness, and endangered species, as well as setting limits on industrial pollution and waste. Although the Clean Air Act of December 1970 established rigorous expectations, it was anticipated by clean air acts in 1963 and 1967. The specific regulations that came out of the Clean Water Act of 1972 were preceded by the clean water laws of 1960 and 1965. The unyielding standards of the 1974 Endangered Species Act were anticipated by congressional legislation in 1964 and 1968. Roadless wilderness regions were designated by means of the Wilderness Act of 1964. Additional laws in 1968 defined and created wild and scenic rivers, national hiking trails, and two new national parks, Redwoods in northern California and North Cascades in Washington state.

Old-line conservation organizations such as the Sierra Club and the Wilderness Society began their rapid growth in membership in the 1960s. President John F. Kennedy's secretary of the interior, Stewart Udall, put the blessing of the federal government on environmental protection, and President Lyndon B. Johnson said he gave environmental recovery high priority. Such legislation was cheered by environmentalists as the nation's answer to an industrial indifference that was tolerated by city and state governments. The public urged the federal government to declare war on pollution to protect public health and the environment. Not all went well, however. Superfund, launched in 1980 by Congress as the biggest environmental effort in American history to identify and clean up tens of thousands of toxic waste dumps, was by 1990 reviled for interminable delays bordering on gridlock, its dense bureaucracy, its boondoggle for lawyers and consultants, and its trillion dollar cost, of which only 12 cents of every dollar is used for actual cleanups. After a decade of investigation, EPA estimated in 1989 that there remained between 130,000 and 425,000 contaminated waste sites across the country.

Example: Low-Level Chronic Toxicity of Lead

Poisoning from lead has been known since ancient times: When the human body is exposed to lead, it can experience convulsions, comas, and other brain and nervous system disorders, as well as anemia, colic, kidney and heart disease, hypertension, and sterility. Indeed, lead pipe plumbing has been used to explain the fall of the Roman Empire. In America lead has been a widely used metal in households since colonial times, including lead pigments in paints, glazes, and enamels, lead solder, lead pipe, leaded glass, tableware, cookware, inks, and lead bullets. These uses increased significantly with industrialization. Between 1940 and 1977 the yearly use of lead doubled to more than 1.5 million tons, particularly in leaded gasoline, but also in lead-acid batteries, lead solder in food cans, lead in plastics, and in the glass in televisions.

Part of the problem is that lead is an element that doesn't break down: When introduced into the environment, it remains toxic indefinitely. In Robert Gottlieb's words, "an epidemic of low-level lead exposure" spread across most of American society and especially hit urban housing of low-income children and industrial workers. The first public warnings on the toxicity of lead came in the 1920s from the public health pioneer Alice Hamilton (see Chapter 9). During the Depression some families burned battery casings for fuel. Public outrage took hold in the 1930s and 1940s when medical studies linked lead poisoning in children to peeling windows, walls, furniture, and baby equipment. Only after 1940 did paint companies reluctantly replace lead with other pigments, but already as many as a third of all housing in eastern working-class cities like Pittsburgh had high concentrations of lead on walls, doors, moldings, and window frames. By the 1960s Dr. James Mason, of the federal Centers for Disease Control, called lead poisoning "the most common societally devastating environmental disease of young children in the United States."

Leaded gasoline was the source of over 90 percent of the lead in the ambient air. Here the 1970 Clean Air Act came into play and forced the installation of catalytic converters on auto exhausts and soon a ban on leaded gasoline. These two actions did much to clean up the air and was called a major success, but the lead paint in urban housing continued to flake and peel. A national campaign emerged from the efforts in minority neighborhoods in Chicago by the Citizens Committee to End Lead Poisoning (CCELP). Public anger induced lead cleanup efforts in Philadelphia, Washington, New York, and Baltimore. The debate led to a lawsuit against a reluctant federal Housing and Urban Development agency (HUD) to force inspection of property and removal of lead. The U.S. surgeon general issued a statement about identification of the widespread presence of lead in urban homes, the dangers of exposure, and the need for removal. This momentum led to passage in 1971 of the Lead-Based Paint Poisoning Prevention Act that limited the lead content of paint and created paint removal programs. Peeling paint would be scraped away, removed by chemical means, or enclosed (encapsulated) by covering. Typical costs ran $5,500 to $8,900 per home, with lows at $2,500 but as high as $25,000 for 15 percent of the homes. As late as 1991, 1 in 6 American children remained in danger of significant neurological and behavioral impairment from lead exposure, as well as 400,000 newborns annually with toxic lead levels. Society continues to pay a high price for having used lead extravagantly in the past, both in health damages to people and costs of cleanup of toxic sites.

Public Perception of Risk and Scientific Evidence: The Dilemma

One of two broad categories of environmental risk is the potential of *harm to human health* by contact with polluted air, contaminated water resources, and disposal of waste materials on tracts of land. These risks usually take the shape of frightening cancers, disabling lung diseases, and harsh irritations to eyes and skin. Most attention by federal and state regulatory agencies was given to public health. A second category is *harm to ecological resources:* clean rivers, living wetlands, rare species safe in their ecosystems, unlittered beaches, and clear air to enjoy mountains and canyons. These are judged ecological resources worth protecting. Before the 1960s the conservation and preservation movements focused primarily on such wilderness protection and opportunities for pleasant recreation. The two categories of public health and ecological risk began to overlap when ecological science identified the connections between human well-being and the health of individual organisms and species populations in ecosystems.

An important distinction must be made between *risk of harm* and the *certainty of harm.* If asbestos is released into the air, some people will develop cancer, but others will remain unharmed. Asbestos poses a risk, but not a certainty, that cancer will develop. Americans also make distinctions between *acute risk,* such as the threat of cancer from smoking or asbestos, and *chronic risk,* such as urban pollution. These are not quite the same as *catastrophic risk,* such as a nuclear power plant accident, compared to *low-level risk,* such as household radon. Overall, risk assessors also distinguish between *human-made (anthropogenic) hazards* and *natural hazards,* such as landslides, floods, tornadoes, hurricanes, and earthquakes. Even in natural hazards, people often choose to put themselves at risk by building on unstable hillsides or floodplains or allowing questionable building practices in earthquake zones. Society responds quickly to acute risk (chemical spill in a river) and catastrophic risk (nuclear accident) because causes and effects are fairly easy to establish. Most of the debate about environmental regulation is over chronic risks. Relationships between causes and effects are harder to establish. This was even true in the connections finally made between lead-based paint and childhood development or between exposure to asbestos fibers and lung cancer.

Public perception of risk, particularly in a democratic society, has shaped attitudes more than formal evaluations by scientific experts. One poll revealed that Americans thought that botulism kills 500 people a year when the real number is 5. Sometimes Americans' behavior toward environmental risks is bizarre. They worry about dental X-rays, yet more than 20,000 are at risk each year of contracting cancer from excessive radon in their household basements. The public underestimates the risks of death from voluntary causes, such as driving a car. The risk in the United States of someone dying in a car accident in any year is 1 in 5,000, a risk most have decided is worth taking. Once a hazard has been identified, and its probability and severity established, the next step is to establish risk acceptability. This is one of the trickiest issues facing modern society. A science-based health risk is one thing; knowing the public acceptability of that risk is another. How safe is safe enough? Some environmentalists insist, "Only no risk is safe enough," whereas industry insists that "the most feasible alternative is safe enough." The public, sensitized by the environmental movement, insists on zero-risk levels for most pollutants, which is an impossible goal for an industry-dependent society. For some pollutants such as carbon monoxide, we can tolerate an uncertain small level, but vinyl chloride is a nonthreshold pollutant. A major conflict also arises between "quality-based standards" (pristine air) and "available-technology standards" (air from a smokestack with a scrubber). Environmentalists worried that all the risks which actually existed were not being revealed, and industry believed the risks were being exaggerated. Public debate also swirls around perceived fairness in distribution of risk: When an incineration plant is built in a poor or minority community, is it being punished for wastes produced by more affluent people? Acceptable risk is also tied to perceived benefit, whether it is the convenience of the personal automobile or nuclear-generated electricity without smokestack pollution. In 1985 William

Ruckelshaus defined risk management, in its broadest sense, as "adjusting our environmental policies to obtain the array of social goods—environmental, health-related, social, economic, and psychological—that forms our vision of how we want the world to be." A safe world, like a risky environment, remains a public choice.

Fear of Cancer Shapes Two Decades of Environmental Debate

Cancer has persistently been one of history's most frightening diseases. Since ancient times, humans have feared the invasion of cancer into their bodies because it was relentless in the wracking pain it caused and the undignified death that seemed inevitable. For modern Americans, the realization that industrial society significantly increased the risk of cancer from toxic chemicals was particularly threatening. Obviously, there are noncancer environmental threats such as lead or ozone, but cancer is particularly frightening. This fear and anger against an irreversible illness (remission is not a cure) led public demands for instant and wholesale controls. Agencies such as EPA could justify regulatory activism, even when extreme and costly, if they could base their case on cancer. This was aided by improved research techniques and increased data (from parts per million to parts per billion and parts per trillion) that established clearer links between toxic materials and cancer. The debate over the connection between toxic pollution and cancer often centered on thresholds. Humans can absorb low levels of many substances without ill effects, including common elements like sodium that are dangerous at higher levels. But in dealing with cancer, the policy of government agencies has been to assume that there is no threshold for carcinogens, that any level of exposure may be harmful. In order to serve public interest despite scientific uncertainty, environmental agencies tended to use "worst case scenarios." In effect, the threshold became zero. The actual risk was probably less.

In 1958, when Congress passed an amendment to the 1938 Pure Food, Drug, and Cosmetic Act, it included a zero-risk provision—the controversial Delaney Clause—that any food additive found to induce cancer when ingested by animals was absolutely prohibited in processed foods, regardless whether it posed any demonstrable risk of harm to humans. This zero-threshold viewpoint has been challenged for its rigidity (e.g., components of food change their carcinogenic potential when they are cooked). There are differences between tests on animals and human vulnerability. Defenders of the Delaney Clause argued that society should adhere to the better-safe-than-sorry rule. The courts often ruled, as in a 1981 Supreme Court decision concerning the textile industry, that the health of employees outweighs all other considerations. During the shifting political climate of the 1990s, critics complained about the "perils of prudence" by EPA. One estimate in 1990 reported that total annual cancer deaths from stratospheric ozone depletion, indoor radon, lead in drinking water, hazard waste sites, and other threats might range from 17,000 to 44,000 deaths out of the 485,000 annual cancer deaths in the United States. Advocates of tight controls complained that many cancer-producing substances were not regulated by the EPA, skewing the statistics. In addition, if there are dangers from a single substance, called single-medium risk, this may not account for the cumulative effects of multiple sources of exposure, which is likely in modern society, so that a school-age child could be exposed to lead in old paint, asbestos residues in old school buildings, as well as risk from industrial smog and widely applied pesticides. Different pollutants can also have synergistic effects, meaning that interactions among them can enlarge the overall risks. Such cumulative effects had been one of Rachel Carson's concerns back in 1962.

Example: Asbestos and Cancer

Asbestos has long been known as one of nature's most useful substances, and it is now also known to be one of the most lethal. It is a silicate mineral fiber found in veins of metamorphic rock and has been mined and used at least since the days of the ancient Egyptians and Romans. Highly resistant to heat, friction, and acid, asbestos is flexible, mold free, and has great tensile strength. When combined with cement, it is weather resistant. Because it is fire resistant and strong, modern industrial societies found it an extremely versatile and economical substance, and it was used widely in building insulation, roof shingles, floor tiles, fireproof linings, hair dryers, patching plaster, theater curtains, car clutch and brake pads and linings, and shipbuilding. Most Americans came daily into contact with asbestos at home, at school, and in the workplace.

The problem arose when it became clear that asbestos fibers, which are easily dislodged, loosed in the atmosphere, and inhaled, cause lung tissue irritation and scarring. This is for life, since the fibers neither break down nor are expelled. Asbestosis, or pulmonary fibrosis, is a gradual buildup of scar tissue over 10 or 20 years. Lung cancer among asbestos insulation workers is four times the expected rate, even after only low-level exposure for a short time. If such workers smoke, the incidence is 92 times greater. Asbestos is the only known cause of mesothelioma, a highly malignant cancer that kills victims within a year. Health risk from asbestos has been known for a long time; some life insurance companies stopped selling policies to asbestos workers as early as 1918. During World War II, 5 million factory and shipyard workers had some exposure to asbestos. Since World War II, between 11 million and 13 million American workers have been exposed, of which 8 percent are expected to die from asbestos-related diseases. The use of asbestos was banned in the United States in 1978 for insulation, fireproofing, and building finishing, with all asbestos products to be phased out by 1996. World production has held steady, but American production has dropped to less than 1 percent of global use.

Public recognition of the harm from asbestos also raised questions of blame and responsibility. One major corporation, Johns-Manville, the leading producer of commercial asbestos, received the lion's share of 11,000 lawsuits out of more than 30,000 claiming $2 billion of damages. The company filed for bankruptcy in 1983. Apparently, according to the case before the Supreme Court of New Jersey in 1986, Johns-Manville knew of serious hazards to asbestos workers as early as the mid-1930s, but had "knowingly and deliberately" failed to protect workers from "serious health hazards with utter and reckless disregard for safety and well-being," and withheld its information from the public. A company memo written in 1949 by its medical director suggests a 40-year-long "conspiracy of silence." The doctor wrote that, even when 704 out of 708 asbestos workers examined had X-ray evidence of asbestosis, as long as the men felt well, they should be kept ignorant of their condition until they became disabled and sick. Then they should be informed and go on disability. One attorney said that Johns-Manville could even have anticipated the legal damages in a cost-benefit analysis to decide whether to market its products. The corporation was "a knowing wrongdoer."

Because asbestos remained a widespread material in school buildings, in 1979 the EPA began assisting school districts in removing asbestos that was beginning to crumble from pipes and ceilings. Ironically, the removal process itself, by releasing sealed fibers into the atmosphere, created an immediate large-scale risk over a lesser long-term risk. Actual exposure in school buildings was on the average less than a thousandth of the limit that OSHA has placed on workplace exposure. But the level of public concern was so high that Americans are spending over a billion dollars to save each life by removing asbestos from buildings, although asbestos in good condition can be left alone. Many schools and businesses are removing old asbestos more out of fear of lawsuits than for health reasons.

Environmentalism's Newfound Weapons: Law and Regulation

Law and the Making of Environmental Policy

Environmental law, like all law, is not an end in itself. It is an instrument by which the goals of society can be accomplished. Environmental law became a means for Americans to put teeth into their overall environmental desires to clean up the air and water, to remove solid wastes and toxic chemicals, and to protect wilderness and endangered species. In other words, environmental law turns abstract ideas and generalized goals into functional results, such as the Clean Water Act or the Endangered Species Act. Environmental law can occur as common law, public statutes, agency regulations, police power, litigation, and the procedures of the courts. The United States, with its English heritage, is a common law country. Common law is the body of legal rules based on the traditional customs of a society. Trash burning, for example, is a punishable "nuisance" because it is outside normal community standards. An oil company can be judged negligent when it pollutes neighborhood wells. These cases then can become precedents for similar cases in the future. But often the common law cannot account for social change, such as the heightened environmental awareness that emerged in the 1960s. To recognize social change, a legislature can pass public statutes to bring about needed changes and supersede common law. In a democratic society, public statutes, such as the 1970 National Environmental Protection Act (NEPA), the 1970 Clean Air Act, and the 1972 Clean Water Act, come from a popularly elected legislature after open debate.

The "Public Trust" Is a Precedent for Environmental Protection

America's historic commitment to the absolute right of private property has been freshly challenged by the concept of public trust. If you cannot build a profitable gasoline station or convenience store on your suburban property because it violates environmental and zoning regulations, your argument that the law keeps you from making a better living cannot take precedence over public trust. Public trust can be traced back at least to the Code of Justinian in A.D. 529: "By the law of nature, these things are common to mankind: the air, running water, the sea, and consequently the shores of the sea." These are for the free and unimpeded use of the general public. Especially they are not susceptible to exclusive ownership; they belong to no one.

One example of public trust is access to shorelines and control of navigable rivers. The Northwest Ordinance of 1787 stated, "The navigable rivers leading into the Mississippi shall be common highways and forever free to the citizens of the United States." In 1810 a Pennsylvania court judged that no one could own the rights to fish in a Pennsylvania river. In 1821 the New Jersey Supreme Court concluded that no one could own shellfishing beds. The decisive case took place in Illinois in 1892, when the state "repented of its excessive generosity" in an earlier grant to the Illinois Central Railroad of extremely valuable Lake Michigan shoreline along downtown Chicago and recovered the shoreline for public use. The first environmental law, according to many lists, was the 1899 Rivers and Harbors Act, which made dumping in America's waterways a criminal act leading to stiff fines and imprisonment. When it was rediscovered in the 1960s, it was used effectively against companies and individuals who dumped liquid wastes. Confusion over the 1899 act helped move the nation toward the 1972 Clean Water Act.

Public trust was strongly reaffirmed in the modern environmental era. A 1966 Massachusetts court case that denied the construction of a ski resort on public land concluded that the potential for abuse by "improvement" for private commercial profit was too high. In 1970 the courts rejected the application by a developer to build a road and excavate for homesites on top of Colorado's 6,000-acre Florissant Fossil Beds, the world's most crowded and diverse collection of insect fossils embedded in fragile paper-thin shale formations. A 1983 California decision considered whether Los Angeles, which owned water rights from Mono Lake 180 miles to the north, could deplete the environmentally unique lake, possibly to its destruction, leading to the disappearance of brine shrimp and large California gull populations. In 1989 the court set a minimum lake level to protect the Mono Lake ecosystem.

Limits to Protection through the Marketplace

Example: The Reserve Mining Case

One case, which pitted federal regulatory agencies against the Reserve Mining Company, reveals how difficult environmental enforcement can be in the United States. Since the 1950s the company's iron ore operation at Silver Bay, Minnesota, mined and processed up to 50,000 tons of taconite ore a day, employed 3,000 people with a payroll of $31.7 million in 1969, with a capital investment exceeding $350 million, and which for a time supplied over 15 percent of the nation's iron ore. The operation was highly profitable, since the 50,000 tons produced a very high rate of about 15,000 tons of concentrated ore pellets each day. But 35,000 tons of solid waste went into the atmosphere and poured into Lake Superior. The waste contained chrysotile, a type of asbestos. Scientific research, as we saw in Chapter 13, cannot be certain that inhalation of asbestos fibers will in every case cause cancer, but the risk is significant enough to require that the pollution be stopped. Delays, such as Reserve Mining would seek, were serious, since asbestos-related disease pathology emphasizes the problem of "initial exposure": There were significant increases in the incidence of cancer even among asbestos manufacturing workers employed for less than three months, and longer exposure raised the risk even higher. The federal government first went to court in 1969 to force Reserve Mining to stop the pollution. In 1971 the new EPA began a 15-year-long battle with the company over pollution control.

In 1974 a federal district court judge ordered the plant to shut down, in part because of the "intransigence" of the company in refusing to control its air and water discharge. Another judge fined Reserve nearly a million dollars for violating its discharge permit and an extra $200,000 for withholding evidence. Reserve did not begin to correct its problems and instead went to a higher appellate court, which said that more time was needed to review the case. Local feelings against Reserve Mining ran high because the plant was allowed to resume operations and continued to produce asbestos wastes. In 1976 the court ordered that all water pollution must cease by July 7, 1977. The company agreed to construct a water pollution control facility, under the condition that it could continue operations. Infractions of pollution control ordinances continued into 1985. By then the local population had lived in a polluted and perhaps poisonous environment for 35 years. In the summer of 1986 Reserve Mining went bankrupt, not because of its pollution problems, but because taconite mining was no longer profitable. The solid waste tailings in the lake and the maintenance of the control facility belonged to no one after 1986, and the primary question became who would be responsible. The legal system was powerful enough to take the company to court, cost it money, and force correction of pollution. The legal system was slow and cumbersome to the extent that while the company violated the law, Reserve Mining Corporation nevertheless could be said to be the overall winner because it delayed corrective measures and continued profitable operations until taconite mining itself became uneconomical.

Example: The Kepone Case

Environmental law, among its several biases, is based on doubts that private industry can handle environmental problems by itself. The manufacturing of the pesticide Kepone during the 1950s and 1960s by Allied Chemical Corporation shows how corporate decision-making typically attempted to internalize as much profit and externalize as much cost as possible, even after a life-threatening danger was uncovered.

Kepone was an effective pesticide because contact with it induced loss of control over muscular coordination, convulsions, DDT-like tremors, and eventually death. But Kepone's effects went far beyond its intended use: It caused cancer, liver damage, reproductive system failure, inhibition of growth, and muscular failure in fish, birds, and mammals. Although Kepone was insoluble in water, it was fat soluble, capable of being absorbed and accumulated by contact through the skin. These dangers were well known. Nevertheless, since 1966 Allied Chemical had been discharging untreated wastes containing Kepone into a tributary of the James River, near its plant in Hopewell in southern Virginia. The river itself emptied into Chesapeake Bay. With the collaboration of a subcontractor, Life Science Products Company, Allied Chemical saw production rise to 2.5 million pounds per year while the waste ran into the public sewers. Inside the plant, 70 percent of the employees, "virtually swimming in the stuff" with no protective equipment or warning signs in accordance with OSHA regulations, began to show "the shakes"—tremors, quickened pulse rates, unusual eye movements, together with weight loss and tender enlarged livers. After a foreign-born doctor in the plant blew the whistle on the violations, the state forced the operation to close in the summer of 1975, but not until there was massive contamination of air, soil, and water in the area. The James River was closed to fishing for 100 miles around because of the threat of accumulated

Kepone in fish bodies. Allied Chemical and Life Science faced a combined maximum fine of over $20 million and imprisonment of responsible individuals for up to five years. The Kepone defendants waived their constitutional right to a jury trial, where they might have had to face an outraged public. Ultimately only one case came before a civil court, and most legal claims by injured employees or government bodies were settled out of court with no details made public. Was it cheaper for Allied Chemical and Life Sciences to settle out of court years later than to control the waste from the first?

The Kepone case raised larger issues of environmental law, responsibility, and ethics. To what extent were decision makers (including attorneys) at Allied Chemical and Life Science, who were aware of the dangers of Kepone poisoning, obliged to reveal the problem and its dumping onto public waters? Would a whistleblower be ostracized and possibly lose his or her job because Allied Chemical and Life Science would be required to make expensive operational changes? Did the company and subcontractor have final responsibility? At what point were federal, state, and community agencies obligated to take over to protect public health and the environment? Environmental lawyer Zygmunt Plater called the Kepone case "an example of antisocial, but economically rational, behavior that relied on externalizing the cost of controlling the release of hazardous chemical wastes." But was the criminal case remedy, which required fines and threatened imprisonment, more beneficial to a clean environment than a civil remedy including cleanup by the polluters?

EPA: The Environmental Protection Agency

Historic Regulatory Agencies and "Big Government"

The first regulatory agencies emerged in the late nineteenth century to correct abuses in child labor, railroad company gouging of farmers, and industrial workers' health. Most federal natural resource agencies were more involved in management than in conservation. The U.S. Forest Service opened public forests to the highly profitable forest industry, particularly in the Pacific Northwest. The Bureau of Land Management, which managed a quarter of the land of the lower 48 states, leased its western grazing and mining lands to private interests at costs established in the 1870s and 1880s. As for environmental protection, only the U.S. Fish and Wildlife Service identified threats to wild species. It challenged the U.S. Department of Agriculture over the wholesale use of so-called safe synthetic pesticides (one of FWS's employees was Rachel Carson). Only one other agency, the U.S. Public Health Service, was troubled about the negative impacts of industrial development. In 1963, armed with new powers by the Clean Air Act, the PHS began to assess health effects of air pollution. So little had been done in the past that it needed to create "criteria documents" to establish air quality standards. Americans continued to have faith in the ability of regulatory agencies to find ways to make life safer. Other agencies involved in environmental regulation are the Occupational Safety and Health Administration (OSHA), the National Institutes of Health (NIH), the Centers for Disease Control (CDC), and the National Oceanic and Atmospheric Administration (NOAA).

The Politics of Environmental Regulation, 1970 to 1996

How did the Environmental Protection Agency (EPA) become the superagency that it is today? EPA turned environmental protection into one of the most powerful and visible functions of the national government. The proenvironment momentum of the 1960s led to passage at the end of 1969 of the broad-based National Environmental Protection Act. It was largely the work of Sen. Henry Jackson (D-Wash.) and Lynton Caldwell, an inventive policy analyst and scholar. In Caldwell's astonished words, passage of NEPA was a "political anomaly," a statement of national policy that was not the product of any specific legislative agenda or battle. There was little debate in Congress, little input from proenvironment lobbyists among the NGOs, and few immediate complaints from the polluters. In fact, Jackson and Caldwell had hoped for a highly publicized national debate that would induce the United States to become the leader of a global environmental cleanup. They wanted environmental cleanup and protection to be defined primarily in technical terms and environmental policy to be grounded in scientific research. This hope was far too optimistic.

NEPA did not create the Environmental Protection Agency (EPA), despite the similar initials. Rather, NEPA created the president's Council on Environmental Quality (CEQ). CEQ by the end of 1970 proposed a separate agency—EPA—to consolidate the nation's environmental response, to treat "air pollution, water pollution, and solid wastes as different forms of a single problem." The concept behind EPA had an ecosystem ring to it, and hopes ran high for a major national changeover. EPA began operations on December 12, 1970, with a large ready-made bureaucracy of 6,000 government personnel patched together from the air quality, solid waste, and drinking water units of the Department of Health, Education and Welfare, the water quality and pesticides research arms of the Department of the Interior, and the pesticides regulation unit of the Department of Agriculture, together with people from the Food and Drug Administration and the Atomic Energy Commission. Most important, EPA is the only regulatory agency whose administrator reports directly to the president. It was independent, not part of a larger department, such as the Department of the Interior, where many said it belonged. This profoundly influenced American environmental policy, since pollution regulation functioned independently and not from inside a traditional federal department. EPA opened its doors with extraordinary regulatory powers and has consistently enjoyed remarkable freedom of action. This autonomy would be regularly tested by contrary forces such as the energy crisis, high inflation, and wide swings in the economy.

EPA was given the responsibility for the protection of natural resources, for pollution control, and for public health and quality of life. EPA's tools were the Clean Air Act and the Occupational Health and Safety Act, both passed in 1970, the Federal Water Pollution Control Act (Clean Water Act) of 1972, and the Endangered Species Act in 1973. EPA also accepted limits on its jurisdiction. If impacts on quality of life and standard of living had human origins, such as economic or social effects, they were not EPA-covered activities. For example, citizens approached EPA for assistance over the psychological effects of the radiation release during the 1979 Three Mile Island nuclear accident in Pennsylvania. EPA was not authorized to respond to such human impacts.

EPA's first administrator, William Ruckelshaus, made EPA a high-profile and deliberately activist agency that immediately went to court. In its first 60 days, it brought five times as many enforcement actions as the agencies it inherited collectively had brought during any similar period. The cities of Atlanta, Cleveland, and Detroit were sued for illegal sewage discharges. The Reserve Mining Corporation was sued for dumping taconite into Lake Superior. Armco Steel was sued for polluting the Houston Ship Channel, I.S. Plywood-Champion Papers for polluting the Ohio River, ITT Rayonier for dumping pulp waste products into Washington's Puget Sound, and Union Carbide for throwing particulate matter in the air around Parkersburg, West Virginia, and Marietta, Ohio.

EPA's activism highlighted inherent problems that constantly bedeviled its mission to bring environmental change. It ran into major debates over the uncertainty or incompleteness of scientific data. There were complaints from environmental groups that industry used this uncertainty to delay or counter the creation of national standards for air and water quality, and prevented the enforcement of EPA rulings. Too often, it appeared, EPA's bureaucracy moved toward regulatory gridlock as it tried to appease the conflicting interests of environmentalists, industry, technological viability, and scientific certainty. Public suspicion arose when highly technical political battles were fought far from public scrutiny or even its knowledge. On the other hand, the business community, hit hard by EPA's environmental clampdown, complained that the agency was nothing more than an environmental advocate with unfair government muscle behind it. Its defenders insisted that one of EPA's key roles was to act as a counterforce against long-standing and powerful industrial lobbies.

The Nixon White House attempted to mollify angry complaints from polluting industries by creating a Quality of Life Review committee in the spring of 1971. The committee was to rein in EPA by requiring that economic development and fiscal concerns (e.g., business interests) receive due consideration in the process of writing regulations. In addition, all proposed EPA regulations were to be submitted for scrutiny by other relevant agencies. This process was to be coordinated by Nixon's Office of Management and Budget (OMB). Environmentalists complained that this meant OMB and not EPA was making final decisions. EPA, with public support behind its aggressive proenvironment enforcement, was largely able to ignore or bypass Nixon's restrictions. Russell Train, a moderate proenvironment Republican like Ruckelshaus, moved to be EPA administrator in 1974 from his position as chair of the Council on Environmental Quality. EPA's power continued to expand. The passage of toxic waste acts TOSCA and RCRA in 1976 gave EPA authority over chemical land dumps, which became the most controversial and costly environmental agenda for the next 20 years. Douglas M. Costle, Jimmy Carter's EPA administrator in 1977, sharpened the focus on hazardous waste. Costle, in his words, wanted to make EPA more than only a "guardian of birds and bunnies." It should be, he said, "a preventive health agency" that would move against suspected carcinogens in toxic substances, pesticides, and drinking water. Costle told the American Chemical Society in late 1978 that EPA "cannot wait for [scientific] proof positive in the form of dead bodies." By the late 1970s the EPA could cast itself as a cancer protection agency. At the same time, EPA's active intervention was contradicted and confused by Carter's EO 12044 that created Regulatory Analysis Review Groups (RARG). This reintroduced economic and cost-benefit analysis to reduce regulatory burdens on business and government. Carter revived the power of the Office of Management and Budget (OMB) to act as a watchdog over EPA.

The Reagan-Bush administrations (1980–92) marked a turning point in the fortunes of the EPA as both presidents insisted that the agency redirect its priorities from advocacy to a "neutral broker" position. Candidate Reagan, never friendly toward environmentalism ("When you've seen one redwood, you've seen them all"), had claimed in 1980 that trees and plants, not private industry, were the chief cause of air pollution. He said that environmental protection must not be "a cover for a 'no-growth' policy and a shrinking economy." As president, Reagan became the leading spokesman to reduce regulatory controls over private industry with EPA as his primary target. He advanced his proindustry and antiregulation policies by installing three Colorado promoters of mining and energy development, James Watt as secretary of the interior, Anne Gorsuch as EPA director, and Robert Burford as head of the Bureau of Land Management. Gorsuch, a little-known Colorado legislator with no environmental credentials, was ordered to shrink the agency. EPA's budget had risen from $701 million in 1980 to $1.35 billion in 1981 before it fell to $515 million in 1982. Personnel were cut by 23 percent from a high of nearly 13,000 people. Professional staff were demoralized by the openly hostile administrations, bringing a high turnover of 40 percent. EPA's effectiveness declined significantly. Between 1980 and the end of 1982, the number of cases it brought to court was cut in half, from 200 to 100, and enforcement orders dropped by one-third. This meant a large number of cases remained pending, and many environmental violations were ignored. Reagan's EO 12291 in 1981 required that all major regulatory rules were to be submitted to OMB for rigorous cost-benefit analysis. Only rules where benefits clearly exceeded costs could be enacted, or the next least costly option. EPA's activities were also to be channeled through a new White House Task Force on Regulatory Relief, a new Regulatory Analysis Review Group, and a Cabinet Council on Natural Resources. These steps deliberately caused major delays, encouraged objections, and created a cautious and nervous EPA. Reagan also ordered that many EPA responsibilities for enforcement of the Clean Air Act, the Clean Water Act, and the Safe Drinking Water Act be turned over to the states, where industrial development often took priority over environmental protection.

A new political factor was that Congress (and the public) began to distrust the White House and government agencies for speedy environmental cleanup. Public opinion favoring environmental protection emboldened Congress to resist Reagan's attempts to dismantle the regulatory process. It began enacting highly prescriptive laws that went into specific details, technologies, and rigorous timetables for fulfillment, regardless of economic cost. Nevertheless, EPA administrator Anne Gorsuch said her assignment at EPA was to turn the agency around to support "industrial revitalization" and to lighten the regulatory "overburden" that EPA had placed on industry. Regulations restricting hazardous liquid wastes in landfills were suspended. In 1983, however, Gorsuch resigned because of her mismanagement of toxic waste site cleanup enforcement, especially laxness at the dioxin-ridden Times Beach site in Missouri. A congressional investigation also revealed her cronyism with industry, particularly in Colorado, illegal private meetings with representatives of regulated companies, and light penalties for violators. No one was paying for cleanups. She was replaced by a reluctant William Ruckelshaus, who nevertheless restored some credibility to EPA. Ruckelshaus emphasized to the public the difference between risk assessment, a matter of science, and risk management, a matter of politics. Once an objective scientific assessment of risk had been arrived at, he said, the public needed to decide how much risk it wanted to live with and make a conscious choice between danger and cost. After rebuilding EPA's credibility, and bridging the gap between industry and environmentalism, Ruckelshaus resigned in 1984. He was replaced by Lewis Thomas, a criminal justice lawyer who had headed EPA's Times Beach toxic waste task force. Thomas tried to avoid the further politicization of EPA's personnel and policies. He also shifted EPA back from the public health strategy of Douglas Costle toward an overall environmental approach. This shift was reflected by a revised Clean Water Act, which was mostly devoted to nonhealth issues, passage of the Resource Conservation and Recovery Act (RCRA), which dealt with reduction of pollution at its source, and higher priority given to recycling of waste materials. He emphasized that the Clean Air Act required protection of long-distance visibility as an essential quality of the national parks and wilderness regions. Such visibility was threatened by air pollution from industrial operations and coal-fired power plants, particularly in the Southwest.

In 1989 William Reilly of the World Wildlife Fund became George Bush's EPA administrator and found himself often at odds with his disinterested boss, who found more virtue in free economic growth. The United States found itself increasingly isolated (as we see in Chapter 15) on the international scene because of its environmental foot-dragging even while it continued as the world's major source of pollution and resource consumption. Public disbelief when Bush sought reelection as the "environmental president" helped the Democrats and Bill Clinton recapture the administration after 12 years of Reagan-Bush Republicanism. The public believed that Clinton would encourage his vice president, Al Gore, to institute broad environmental policies based on his best-selling book, *Earth in the Balance.* Clinton named as EPA administrator Carol Browner, former head of the Florida Department of Environmental Regulation. Browner promoted new themes that sought to bring business and environmentalists together, such as pollution prevention, industrial ecology, and partnerships with states. She also gave higher priority to environmental justice following pressure from grassroots groups and other NGOs over the siting of waste facilities in minority and low-income neighborhoods. However, Clinton seemed disinterested in major environmental steps, and innovations such as whole ecosystem protection that Gore and Browner sought languished from the beginning of the Clinton presidency.

Despite the tensions, state-federal collaboration did emerge on hazardous waste, industrial air quality, and industrial water. According to the Clean Air Act, for example, all the states were directed to prepare State Implementation Plans (SIPs) describing how they would reduce emissions from existing sources in designated air quality districts that exceeded the ambient air quality goals. Any district not meeting air quality standards was classed as in a state of "nonattainment." The states took on larger roles to reduce water pollution from agricultural and community uses, to maintain groundwater quality, and to manage municipal waste. The strongest state programs emerged in California, New Jersey, New York, Massachusetts, Illinois, Minnesota, and Wisconsin, often exceeding federal requirements. Between 1969 and 1980 California, Delaware, Minnesota, Ohio, and Vermont spent the most per capita on environmental programs; Texas, South Carolina, Michigan, Oklahoma, and Utah spent the least. In the mid-1990s, several states, including Pennsylvania, Ohio, Rhode Island, and Colorado, were cited by EPA for nonfullfillment of their designated responsibilities.

A fresh conservative backlash against the power of federal environmental agencies began to be heard after the 1994 elections that gave Republicans dominance in both the House and the Senate. The public's anger and frustration at a bloated, self-serving, and indifferent federal bureaucracy brought on a vigorous critique in Congress of the wide authority of the EPA, as well as land management policies by the Forest Service, the Bureau of Land Management, and the National Park Service, and of health and safety agencies. Major environmental laws that required reauthorization, like the Clean Air Act, the Clean Water Act, Superfund, and the Endangered Species Act, came under attack. One particularly effective strategy by Congress was not to change environmental regulations (because of fears of public outcry) but to remove most or all funding for their enforcement. Another strategy, revived from the Reagan-

Bush years, was to require detailed risk-benefit assessment involving lengthy delays and specific price tags for each health and environmental goal. One move involved America's long-standing belief in the inviolability of private property: Government "takings," or the reduction of the value of private property because of environmental regulations, would have to be compensated at market value. Landowners were to be compensated if trees could not be cut down to protect an endangered species or if a privately owned wetland could not be filled. The government would have to pay industries to limit their discharge of chemical wastes into waterways or their emission of hazardous air pollutants into the air because such limits would reduce company profits. One of the most important objectives of the 1994–95 Congress was to turn many environmental protection laws and procedures over to the states, which claimed to be much closer to the realities of local environmental problems.

The outcry from environmental organizations was loud but largely ineffective because of the overwhelmingly conservative majorities in both houses of Congress. Critics complained that lobbyists from chemical polluting industries and natural resource companies (forests, oil, natural gas, mining) were in control behind the scenes to "sell out" 30 years of environmental protection. A revised Clean Water Act, it was said, would allow industry to increase toxic discharges to waters and sewers. Environmentally critical wetlands would be unprotected and disappear. Enforcement funds for the Clean Air Act were reduced. Funding was severely cut for enforcement of the Endangered Species Act, a moratorium sought on new listings, and the law itself threatened with extinction. Sales of trees on federal land was to be accelerated and all federal safeguards removed for "salvage" timber, which was not limited to fallen trees but included any "damaged" trees and surrounding healthy trees. One of the strongest moves in Congress was to shut down lobbying by environmental organizations that received federal funding for any reason. Public fears about the removal of many environmental safeguards forced some pullback by the congressional conservatives and aided in Bill Clinton's 1996 reelection as president. Advocates of environmental protection noted that over the previous 20 years the nation's waters and air had become cleaner, health threats from toxic substances were reduced, and that ecosystem science had created a better informed nation about its environmental heritage. They admitted that many government agencies were indifferent to costs of protection, created a burdensome ganglia of regulations, and sometimes failed to meet their objectives, one of the most notorious cases being Superfund's inability to clean up more than a few of thousands of toxic waste sites. They also noted that the United States still had far to go, pointing to 30 regions across the country that did not meet air quality standards, that toxic substances endangered the population, that polluting industries were not likely to police themselves, and that wilderness regions continued to diminish.

The Power of Administrative Law

Advocates for environmental protection discovered that administrative law, by which federal agencies functioned on a day-to-day basis, was one of their most effective tools. Early in the history of the nation, Congress learned that it could not pass laws covering every aspect of the national life, particularly the fine details. It made sweeping federal laws, but delegated authority to federal agencies. Federal agencies like the Forest Service and the Food and Drug

Administration made rules, codes, and regulations that have the force of law. Administrative law became a critically important political battleground inside government agencies. During the New Deal of the 1930s, government bureaucracies became active shapers of society in the new "administrative state." This form of direct action spread widely during the national mobilization of World War II, and "big government" became a permanent feature of postwar American society. In 1946 Congress passed the Administrative Procedure Act to confirm agency rule making and its authority. At their worst, government bureaucracies (with over 2 million employees by 1968) fostered procedures of "numbing complexity and detail." Critics complained that Americans were victimized because there was no separation of powers in a federal agency. It made rules like a legislature. It investigated infractions as a prosecutor. It conducted hearings like a judge. It enforced its rules like a cop. At its best, administrative law was the direct enactment of public policy. Most agency regulations were preventative, to keep a nuisance or pollution from taking place at all. The sweeping administrative authority enjoyed by the EPA came from NEPA-based regulatory powers it had received from the Council on Environmental Quality. For example, the RCRA (the Resource Conservation and Recovery Act) statute from Congress is 96 pages long. Its administrative law is articulated by EPA in 128 pages of regulations. Such rule making has sometimes been called "secondary legislation." One important section of the 1946 law requires opportunity for public comments on rules before they are issued as final. This public participation has involved not only concerned citizens, but also brought responses from legislative oversight committees, state and local agencies, and environmental groups or trade associations. Such public input brings into EPA the multiple values and ambiguities of the American political process.

A Powerful Tool: The Environmental Impact Statement (EIS)

The most significant provision of the NEPA statute was its requirement for broad and detailed Environmental Impact Statements (EISs) covering a wide range of government activities, particularly public works projects that modify the physical world. A provision in the 1972 Clean Air Act gave EPA the power to evaluate all EISs. More than 12,000 EISs were prepared in the first decade of operations. In the 1980s and 1990s EPA reviewed about 450 EISs a year and, according to one early survey, discovered that about 8 percent contained "serious abuses," 30 percent more had "major substantive shortcomings," and a total of 65 percent contained "substantial informational deficiencies." This unusually broad power over virtually all federal, state, and local government activities that might affect the environment made EPA, in one lawyer's words, into a "general environmental busybody, gossip, and gadfly." The EIS process guaranteed EPA review of any changes on land, water, or air resulting from a federally funded project. This was not only federal activity, but any changes where a federal license was required, such as building a new nuclear reactor. EISs were defined as "action-forcing" procedures. They were to pursue a cost-benefit analysis but emphasize "maximum mitigation." Each EIS was required to offer alternatives if EPA judged the project was environmentally harmful. EPA also had the draconian authority to shut a project down if it judged the action, or the alternatives, environmentally unacceptable. In many cases, the necessity of filing an EIS for most federal projects also opened the door to citizen participation in the environmental protection process. EIS procedures required public notice and public hearings. Citizens had the right to ask for clear explanations about the technical particulars of projects, where major problems were often hidden. They acquired a legal opportunity to hold up projects in court by putting the merits of an EIS before a judge for scrutiny.

EPA reviewed logging of national forests, management of water resources, development of minerals and mining, highway and airport construction, urban redevelopment, oil development (including offshore), and related interventions into the natural environment. Environmental impacts included not only the natural environment of wilderness areas, rivers, shorelines, and other unique geographical features, but also impacts on public health, and to assure "safe, healthful, productive, and esthetically and culturally pleasing surroundings" for all Americans. Simple physical assessment was insufficient. The EIS process deliberately included social, historical, cultural, and archeological impacts, such as potential flooding of Native American sites. The Department of the Interior wrote EISs for projects in its national parks, wilderness areas, wildlife refuges, and mining. The Army Corps of Engineers filed EISs on watershed protection, flood control, and navigation. The Department of Agriculture reported on matters like forestry and range management and pesticide use. When the Soil Conservation Service (SCS) was taken to task by EPA for radical stream channelization (dredging) in Florida that stripped away trees and shrubs, changed water flows dramatically, and ignored the threat of fish decline, it told the court, "Conservation is our middle name" and that the project vastly improved agriculture for poor people (which it did). EPA retorted that its mission was to prevent adverse environmental effects and that "benefits" are not environmentally beneficial when a place is disturbed. Major federal units, like Agriculture, Department of Defense, and Department of Energy, sought exemptions from the EIS requirement, but failed. EISs were criticized as mechanical exercises, excessive paperwork, improper rationalizations of scientific or management disputes, or political quarrels. Congress

The Shortest Environmental Impact Statement Ever Written

EISs are supposed to be "concise, clear, and to the point" but are usually masterpieces of bureaucratic obfuscation. The 101 words by the Bureau of Reclamation for the Palmetto Bend Project "makes up in candor what it lacks in detail":

Palmetto Bend Project, Jackson County, Tex. Proposed construction of a 12.3-mile long, 64-foot high earth fill dam on the Navidad River. The purpose of the project is the supply of industrial and municipal water. Approximately 18,400 acres [11,300 of which will be inundated] will be committed to the project; 40 miles of free-flowing stream will be inundated; nine families will be displaced; fresh water inflow to the Metagorda estuary will be altered; fish and shellfish nursery areas will be impaired; habitat for such endangered species as the Texas red wolf, the American alligator, the Southern bald eagle, the Peregrine falcon, and the Atwater prairie chicken will be lost.

Needless to say, the bureau later "improved" on this effort.

has legislated exemptions for environmental impact statements, most notably the Alaska oil pipeline, logging in Alaska's Siuslaw National Forest, Tennessee's Tellico Dam (of snail darter fame), and a controversial highway in Hawaii.

During the Reagan-Bush administrations, EISs were widely criticized by conservatives for focusing on adverse environmental effects without including economic benefits. In fact, EISs became the best example of an overall cost-benefit rule found in the American legal system. They created an integrated decision-making policy instead of fragmented and single-issue approaches to pollution problems. They took environmental protection away from just the end-of-pipeline symptoms of pollution to primary causes that encouraged "pollution prevention" and "industrial ecology" (see Chapter 15). EISs depended on rational science that emphasized the quantification of consequences, the use of controls, and the importance of monitoring. The EIS created new sophisticated approaches based on ecological science, such as the evaluation of nonlinear effects (phase change, changes in baseline conditions, magnification, feedback), of secondary and tertiary effects, of multiple exposure and cumulative effects. By 1990 environmental impact statements were thoroughly integrated into decision making at all levels of government, with a formalized decision-making process. Other nations, following the American example, began their own EIS reviews. Its attractions included early warning of an environmental problem. It was intended to look at the future consequences of highways, airports, sewage treatment plants, and other human interventions. Although aimed at government decision makers, EISs vastly improved overall gathering of information in the federal government and its access by the citizenry. The EIS became a particularly powerful weapon for citizen lobbies to delay or to halt numerous projects, notably nuclear power plants and radioactive waste storage sites.

The Clean Air Act of 1970 Sets Rigorous Standards and Procedures

Smoke troubles have a long history. Thirteenth-century London suffered from killing smogs from countless wood-burning fireplaces and forges. In the eighteenth century, French visitors to England's factory towns were incredulous over the smoke, dust, grit, filthiness, and overall darkness. We have seen in Chapter 9 the first struggles with air pollution in America's industrial centers like Pittsburgh. For the 100 years before 1970, most Americans living in Pittsburgh, Buffalo, Cleveland, Cincinnati, or Chicago accepted chronic scratchy throats that turned into lung disease as a price of steady jobs. Patriotic World War II production winked at trivialities like a smoky neighborhood. Postwar prosperity brought high industrial production with heavier still smokestack pollution and industrial grit. It became clear that the airsheds around sprawling industrial cities could not absorb more debris. In 1948 at Donora near Pittsburgh, an extended temperature inversion (a warm air layer above a heavier cool air layer that can concentrate pollution) killed 20 people and hospitalized hundreds. Donora was a turning point that turned public opinion against air pollution. Similar "accidents waiting to happen" were expected at other industrial centers like Youngstown in Ohio and Gary outside Chicago.

Early attempts were made to measure the dangers of air pollution. Nineteenth-century city public health laws based their smoke control on the color and density of high-sulfur coal. The city smoke pollution inspector, overworked, underpaid, and easily intimidated, would compare the smoke coming out of a stack with the different shadings from gray to black on his "Ringelmann" chart. A factory owner often got off free by arguing that the visual readings were arbitrary and there was no direct proof his smokestack was an immediate health problem. City authorities acquiesced to his complaints about costs. By the 1950s some sources of pollution were being reduced. Backyard burning of trash and burning in city dumps came to an end. Coal-fired steam locomotives were replaced by diesel railroad equipment. Residential heating in northeastern cities from Boston to Pittsburgh changed from smog-producing coal to imported Arabian oil or natural gas supplied by pipelines from Texas. Air pollution emerged in the 1960s as a potent political issue, including the passage of federal legislation in 1963 and 1967. In Pittsburgh, the Group Against Smog and Pollution (GASP) became a vocal advocate of clean air, as did Chicago's Campaign Against Pollution (CAP). Lobbying by the Coalition for Clean Air moved the debate to Congress, where it was urged on by a persuasive report, *Vanishing Air*, from Ralph Nader's "Raiders," and by presidential hopeful Edmund Muskie, who chaired the Senate Committee on Air and Water Pollution.

When the new Clean Air Act (CAA) was signed into law in December 1970, it was the first nationwide step in which the federal presence became the dominant force for cleanup. CAA set National Ambient Air Quality Standards (NAAQS) based solely on the protection of public health and not on economic factors. Ambient standards set the maximum concentrations of air pollutants, including "an adequate margin of safety" for the elderly or people with respiratory conditions. The CAA directed EPA to reduce pollution from "mobile sources"— cars and later trucks—by 90 percent for carbon monoxide and hydrocarbons and 82 percent for nitrogen oxide. As for "stationary sources" of emissions, such as factories, refineries, and utilities, CAA gave EPA authority to set national standards. Six "criteria pollutants"—suspended particulates, sulfur dioxide, hydrocarbons, carbon monoxide, nitrogen oxides, and photochemical oxidants (and later lead as a seventh)—were used by EPA to set nationwide pollution standards. Severely hazardous air pollutants, such as benzene and asbestos, were separately regulated. "Nonattainment" areas were mostly urban regions like Los Angeles or metropolitan New York. The enforcement of CAA introduced the concepts of "thresholds" above which exposure to pollution would not be permitted, as well as "margins of safety" to compensate for long-term, low-level exposure, or where effects were suspected but not scientifically established. The act did much to establish the policy of "forcing" regulations to require pollution reduction to a given level regardless of economic cost or technological limitations. It set ambitious target dates for control of emissions. CAA also reinforced the existing policy, soon to be vigorously criticized, that pollution problems could be solved through "back-end" or "end-of-the-pipe" engineering controls. The alternative—"pollution prevention"—did not become part of EPA's agenda until the 1980s, and the Pollution Prevention Act was not passed until 1990.

The Clean Air Act of 1970 allowed low levels of pollution. EPA recognized that eastern factory airsheds could never be entirely restored to natural purity, but in many unpopulated and scenic western areas, it pressed hard to prevent "significant deterioration" of high-quality air. The 1977 amendments to the Clean Air Act mandated three air classifications: Class I created special visibility protection requirements for international and national parks and wilderness areas beyond a certain acreage. No downward classification was allowed. By the 1970s pollution began to cloud the pristine air (sight lines had historically extended to

60 miles or more) at the Grand Canyon and the national parks, monuments, and wilderness areas of southern Utah. Some of the pollution was traced to the controversial coal-fired Four Corners power plant, which was required to limit power generation and retrofit smokestack cleaners. Pollution also came, environmentalists argued, from as far as Los Angeles. Class II was in effect all remaining areas, except for zones already heavily polluted by industry and/or automobiles, which were Class III.

Despite uneven and inconsistent policies and results, and complaints from both industry and environmentalists (for opposite reasons), the Clean Air Act was reauthorized in 1977. After bitter political struggle, the CAA was again reauthorized in 1990 to include more rigorous antipollution amendments on ozone, particulates, and carbon monoxide. Nearly 100 areas in the country had not met their NAAQS, especially on ozone, with eight "severe" areas and one "extreme" area (Los Angeles). The 1990 amended act tightened the limits on motor vehicle tailpipe emissions and pushed the development and use of clean fuels. Lead emissions from autos had dropped from 156,000 pounds in 1970 to less than 3,000 pounds in 1987. Yet the goal of eliminating health problems from auto pollution was still far away. Between 1954 and 1982, the number of motor vehicles in the United States increased 320 percent. Los Angeles's pollution, mostly from autos, was still monumental—its air quality violated federal standards 143 times between 1985 and 1987. Fifty-nine other American cities still did not meet carbon monoxide standards, and it was said that fully a third would never meet the standards. Congress, in a direct slap at EPA inaction during the Reagan-Bush administrations, set rigorous standards for hydrocarbons, carbon monoxide, nitrogen oxide, and particulates. Congress acted directly to control acid rain pollution by reducing maximum allowances for smokestack emissions of sulfur oxide and nitrogen oxide. It directed EPA to achieve stringent controls over air pollution control by the year 2000.

Example: Automobile Emissions

Americans' long-term love affair with the privately owned automobile brought on the collapse of a highly successful public transportation infrastructure. Railroad and trolley transportation had virtually disappeared by 1960; bus lines were stigmatized as for the lower class. Autos, often carrying a single commuter, became elephantine in the 1950s and 1960s—over 20 feet long and weighing more than 2 tons. The world's cheapest gasoline, a tenth of European prices, fed the habit. As we saw in Chapter 8, tens of millions of automobiles, and the highways and parking they required, had become the dominant feature of America's metropolitan regions since the 1920s. By the early 1960s auto emissions in major urban areas contributed 30 to 60 percent of three main air pollutants—hydrocarbons, carbon monoxide, and nitrogen oxides—that were directly linked to cancer, bronchitis, pneumonia, emphysema, asthma, and the common cold. A polluted atmosphere also impaired perception and thinking, slowed reflexes, and threatened unborn children's growth and mental development. By 1960 the health effects of auto emissions were estimated to cost the nation $680 million annually in health care, lost productivity, and premature death. The automobile industry steadfastly denied that motor vehicles contributed to the obvious air pollution in the cities. California, with the highest concentration of cars, was burdened with the most serious auto-based urban smog. In 1960 it imposed its own strict emission standards, but did not require pollution control equipment on all new cars until 1966. The auto industry protested its inability to meet the deadline. It also claimed that the high cost of control would be passed on to angry car buyers. In fact, the four major American manufacturers had already developed exhaust control devices and patented them, but agreed among themselves not to install them voluntarily because they would be "an economic and maintenance burden on motorists." The industry privately agreed not to compete with each other on pollution controls and to discourage independent development outside the industry. When the Justice Department got hold of these insider agreements in the summer of 1968, it filed a major antitrust suit against GM, Ford, Chrysler, and the now defunct AMC. The proindustry Nixon administration settled the antitrust suit in 1970, but the industry's strategy infuriated Congress enough to bring quick passage of the 1970 Clean Air Act.

The highly specific statutory tactics of the Clean Air Act (a "harm-based" statute) was a "crude blunt instrument" that forced technological innovation and installation of pollution controls. The automobile industry continued to claim that such low levels of hydrocarbons, carbon monoxide, and nitrogen oxide were impossible to attain with current technological know-how. One result was that they tinkered to upgrade pre-1970 engines "with a jungle of little pipes and sensors piled on to try to clean up the old baby's emissions" rather than develop cleaner-burning engines. The catalytic converter was an add-on device rather than a technological revolution. One benefit was that the converter in turn forced fuel companies to produce lead-free gas on a massive scale, since leaded fuel "poisons" the converter and destroys its effectiveness. Pollution control technologies did not stand still. American, Japanese, and European manufacturers explored stratified charge engines, fuel reactor systems, flywheel storage motors, and hybrid gasoline-electric propulsion units. Nonpetroleum-based fuels included methanol, which dramatically reduced hydrocarbons but produced two to five times more carcinogenic formaldehyde than unleaded gasoline. Natural gas was temptingly efficient but released more nitrogen oxide. Hydrogen as a fuel was a third more efficient, produced no carbon monoxide or unburnt hydrocarbons, and very little nitrogen oxide, but it was scarce and would have required a major costly retooling in the energy industry. The temptation to turn to electric cars was hampered by the old problem of pollution from coal-fired or oil-fired electric generation plants. Electric cars had to be plugged in for recharge somewhere. Radical control measures, such as suggested by former EPA administrator Lewis Thomas, to reduce the number of cars on the road and restrict the miles Americans may drive, had been rejected as un-American. Environmental lawyer Zygmunt Plater wondered about pragmatic tradeoffs: "How heavily should concern for the national economy weigh against concern for the environment? Are we perhaps, however, reaching a point in our nation's and planet's history where the social costs of our automobility outweigh its social benefits?" At what point in terms of cost and convenience Americans would shift to public transportation or other alternatives is not clear. One alternative, already in place for decades in Europe, was to raise the price of gasoline to over $10 a gallon in 1990 dollars.

The 1972 Clean Water Act Pushes Technological Innovation

In the United States, the ability of water to wash away, thin out, and distribute most substances made it the universal solvent for the removal of human and industrial wastes. For decades, Americans assumed that their majestic rivers and the Great Lakes could be used for waste dumping, regardless of impacts on local swimming, fishing, or health. Not until after World War II, with the great acceleration of industrial development, was public attention drawn to industrial chemical discharges as well as household pollution. Rivers that ran through cities like Pittsburgh, Cleveland, Chicago, Boston, and New York City became cesspools of decay with little or no fish life and disgustingly unattractive for public swimming or boating. Beginning in the 1960s government agencies began to collect water pollution data about the extent of industrial wastes. Treatment beyond chlorinating or aeration was unknown.

As with other environmental problems in the 1960s and 1970s, public outrage forced federal action. Limited clean water legislation was passed in 1960 and 1965. The major "technology-forcing" legislation was the 1972 Water Pollution Control Act Amendments, better known as the Clean Water Act. It was revised and strengthened in 1977. The 1972 legislation revolutionized public responsibility for the nation's water supplies and waterways. Waste disposal was no longer a legitimate use of a river or lake. Discharge of raw pollutants became illegal. The act's goal was to "restore and maintain the chemical, biological and physical integrity of the nation's waters." The introduction of complex synthetic chemicals into water systems required new methods of control beyond biodegradation, since they did not undergo biological changes into harmless substances. This required industrial procedures that cut water use, reduced the level of discharge of wastes, and encouraged recovery and reuse of materials. Some major corporations, such as 3M, DuPont, and Dow Chemical, shifted company strategies toward pollution prevention, life-cycle engineering, and industrial ecology that promised reduction, recovery, and reuse of waste. The Clean Water Act had positive results. Around the city of Cleveland, the water quality of Lake Erie and the Cuyahoga River improved dramatically. Fish returned to the lower Hudson River. Industrial pollution of the Ohio River system from above Pittsburgh to the Mississippi dropped significantly. Groundwater systems in eastern industrial states received protection in the nick of time.

Superfund and the Controversial Control of Dangerous Land Sites

Potentially dangerous substances help produce the material benefits of modern life. Some are manufactured, like PCBs and petroleum distillates; others are in nature, such as mercury, arsenic, and lead. They become dangerous when artificially concentrated for industrial or domestic use. When properly contained, these materials cause little mischief. However, when released into the environment as solid waste they threaten serious harm to humans, plants, animals, and entire natural systems. Some always were obvious dangers—solid wastes stored in 55-gallon drums along a factory's back fence, raw residues dumped into an industrial landfill, or containers of chemical gunk carried by garbage trucks onto the town dump. One general estimate in the 1970s was that every year America's factories produced 40 million metric tons of potentially dangerous substances. There was virtually no control over their dumping, spilling, or burning.

The environmental protection revolution in the 1960s and the 1970s largely overlooked these dangerous substances. Most solid wastes, no matter how toxic, were treated as problems of "materials handling, routing garbage trucks, and bulldozing landfills," to be regulated by local governments. Most states, under enormous pressure to offer favorable economic conditions to keep industry at home, looked the other way. As late as 1975 Congress and the EPA hoped the states would regulate solid wastes since they were not "fugitive" gases, particulates, or liquids that crossed state borders which were already controlled by the clean air and water acts. A Solid Waste Disposal Act had been passed in 1965. A small federal Office of Solid Waste anticipated future policy when it urged a national "cradle-to-grave" manifest system to cover each batch of a dangerous substance from its generation to its eventual destruction or permanent disposal. In 1972 California established the nation's first hazardous waste program. But there was little state or federal experience to guide the regulation writers. Hazardous wastes had never been inventoried or listed. No one inside or outside EPA even knew what the hazards were, their location, who was responsible, let alone how or where they were being disposed of. Toxic wastes were like a series of time bombs set to detonate tomorrow, in the near future, or in the next generation.

The first significant national law to deal with hazardous and solid wastes was the Resource Conservation and Recovery Act (RCRA) of 1976. Before RCRA, most waste producers kept hazardous waste on local sites in slag piles, pits, ponds, and lagoons, or shipped it away to unknown sites where it was carelessly dumped. RCRA's task was formidable. It was responsible not only for hazardous wastes, but also solid wastes generally, including non-hazardous industrial waste, municipal waste, and medical waste. RCRA set a framework for regulating the cradle-to-grave system: the generation, transportation, treatment, and disposal of hazardous wastes. EPA defined hazardous wastes according to irritability, corrosivity, reactivity, toxicity, flammability, persistence and degradability, and potential of the material to bioaccumulate in plants and animals. EPA also had to make specific decisions concerning levels of risk to public health—"The dose makes the poison." Not until mid-May of 1980, prodded by the public uproar in the summer of 1978 over the leaking of toxic materials at Love Canal, did EPA publish a large segment (520 pages in the Federal Register) of RCRA regulations. EPA chose a New Jersey chemical waste dump for the press conference. Shortly before the press conference, the dump exploded. EPA's report also caused an explosion that rattled American industry when it cut acceptable limits for "hazardous" concentrations of 14 major industrial chemicals from one-tenth to one-hundredth of the existing national drinking water standard. It set limits on chemical concentrations in sewage sludge, many paper mill wastes, mining slag, and wastes from flue gas smokestack scrubbers. EPA estimated that by 1980 enough hazardous waste continued to be produced daily to fill the New Orleans Superdome from floor to ceiling. Ninety percent was disposed of improperly and there were thousands of abandoned dumps scattered across the country.

By 1982 EPA reported that it had already located more than 180,000 places, mostly illegal and unmonitored, where hazardous waste was being dumped. In 1984 the public was shocked to learn that new studies showed the annual production of hazardous waste that RCRA was supposed to control was not 40 million metric tons, but 150 million metric tons. Another 150 million metric tons were not regulated at all, and less than a quarter of the 60,000 hazardous waste-producing firms were subject to RCRA regulations. Citizen lawsuits induced Congress to reauthorize RCRA, now including the Hazardous and Solid Waste Amendments (HSWA). The result was a very prescriptive law with many provisions that looked more like regulations than legislation. EPA began to categorize types of hazardous waste: toxic, corrosive, ignitable, reactive, and what was transmittable through all environmental media—air, water, biota, and land. It identified cleanup technologies: chemical neutralization, physical stripping, biological (aerobic) systems, thermal (incineration), and also landfilling and removal. Congress also wrote "hammers" into HSWA. Its statutory requirements forced EPA to act by a certain date and severely limited EPA's discretion. HSWA rules became among the most expensive that EPA has issued. Cleanup of a medium-size hazardous waste facility typically cost tens of millions of dollars that were passed on to users. The cost of depositing 1 cubic yard of gasoline-contaminated soil in a RCRA landfill facility ranged between $100 and $200. PCB-contaminated soil was the most expensive for land disposal at $470 per ton. By 1985 RCRA regulated 247 million metric tons and exempted 322 million metric tons. It also allowed states, such as California and New Jersey, to adopt programs that are more stringent than the federal minimum. One negative side effect of the high costs of RCRA disposal was dangerous illegal dumping. One illegal dump under a New Jersey interstate highway overpass caused a fire in the late 1980s that damaged and closed the highway for several months.

The aim of RCRA and HSWA was to prevent future Love Canals, not clean up the existing ones. The problem of tens of thousands of inactive but hazardous waste sites led to the 1980 law, called CERCLA, the Comprehensive Environmental Response, Compensation, and Liability Act, best known as Superfund. CERCLA was the first environmental law designed to remedy past problems. CERCLA directed EPA to identify sites, rank them according to the hazards they present, and maintain a National Priority List (NPL) for cleanups. The nation entered unknown territory, particularly over who was liable for abandoned hazardous dumps. Current owners were often not the original dumpers. Nevertheless, they were liable for expensive cleanups. One EPA official said: "RCRA says how you should handle wastes properly, and if you don't, I've got penalties of $25,000 per day. But what really gets your attention is not the $25,000 per day penalty, it's the fact that you might end up inadvertently creating a $50 million Superfund cleanup."

According to political scientist Susan Buck, at the cost of $1.6 billion over five years, "The main accomplishment of Superfund was to develop an understanding of the magnitude of the problem." A conservative estimate by the Office of Technology Assessment figured that cleanup costs would be $100 billion over 50 years for less than a fifth of 31,000 sites. OTA's more aggressive estimate was up to $500 billion with 425,000 sites to clean up. The price would be higher taxes for public costs, higher product prices as industry paid, reduced industrial output because capital was diverted, and possible unemployment. Superfund became its own toxic quagmire. The original Superfund policy was idealistic: "shovels first, lawyers later," which became "lunch now, lawyers maybe, but shovels never" in sweetheart deals between EPA and industry, particularly during the early 1980s. OTA and GAO (General Accounting Office) both damned Superfund management for its foot-dragging. There were allegations that the entire program was ill conceived, merely excessive federal response to Love Canal. Even EPA admitted the citizenry ran less risk from toxic substances than from indoor radon. Superfund was vulnerable to industrial lobbying to modify national minimum cleanup standards, to change the nature of "acceptable risk," and to redefine "permanent cleanup" to reduce costs.

More than half of the nation's hazardous waste was still outside EPA review. Exclusions included domestic sewage, household waste, agricultural wastes used as fertilizers, and a growing number of special industrial wastes such as cement kiln dust, fly ash from coal, waste crankcase oil, oil drilling brines and muds, and mine overburden. There were complaints that much industrial waste with high toxicity had been wrongly ignored by federal regulations. EPA's long-term policy was to phase out most methods of land disposal of hazardous waste by means of incineration and physical-chemical treatment, each with their own environmental threats. Waste management became a new growth industry in the 1980s; its largest firms had sales in the hundreds of millions of dollars. CERCLA was significantly modified in 1986 by the Superfund Amendment and Reauthorization Act (SARA), provided with $9 billion in funding. SARA's Title III included community "right-to-know" provisions that also clamped down on industry. Polluters were required to maintain and make available records about harmful chemicals that were used or stored on the site and to record and report annual emissions of such chemicals. This became the Toxics Inventory List (TRI) that forces industry to provide local communities with information on potential threats to local health as part of the "process of informed consent." Thomas Jefferson would have cheered. In fact, many major polluting corporations had simply never bothered to assemble such information. Once collected, one of the world's leading chemical companies, DuPont, was so horrified at its total data that it initiated a nationwide chemical reduction program. SARA moved away from the concept of environmental protection at any cost to use technology-based controls. But SARA also tightened operating permits and put teeth into enforcement: Fines ranged from $5,000 for a first-time citation to $500,000 for a corporation "knowingly endangering" the public through a deliberate, illegal release, and a possible prison term for the perpetrators. States followed suit, with New Jersey and California exceeding federal standards.

Despite the muddle over excessive costs, perpetual litigation, and relatively few complete cleanups, Superfund did have some accomplishments. EPA identified over 30,000 sites potentially requiring Superfund action. More than 1,200 sites were placed on the National Priorities list, and EPA undertook 1,300 emergency actions. EPA reported in the 1990s that "No site today poses an immediate health threat to the public." The scope of hazardous waste became clearer to the public, as well as the nation's incapacity to solve a grave environmental problem. On average, 12 years passed from the time EPA becomes aware of a site to a final site cleanup. Americans learned that environmental cleanup involves politics, economics, public interest, and technical innovation.

Conclusion: Three Cultures—Science, Law, and Economics

The laws Congress passed and the regulations EPA enforced beginning in 1970 were the outcome of a widespread belief that the American environment and public health were in jeopardy. Environmental law is a way to change hostile behavior by, in the words of an environmental law textbook, "presenting the bill" to the responsible parties. Whoever is to blame for an environmental problem deserves the blame and has probably been a willful violator of the law. The threat of legal action, because it is so specific, is extremely effective. The case of long-term asbestos harm to thousands of people, for example, became so costly in hundreds of millions of dollars as to put the producer, the large Johns-Manville corporation, out of business. The cost to Exxon for the Alaska oil spill ran several billion dollars. The arena of law is extremely powerful because it comes down heavily on specific events that do harm, on private corporations that are responsible, and it names individual persons who cannot hide behind anonymity.

Science and law belong to different cultures: Scientists are not troubled by the idea that a question may simply not have an answer, but judges and lawyers are. The pace of scientific proof is sometimes glacial; guilty polluters can take advantage of the delays and uncertainty. Environmental law searches for clear cause-and-effect relationships in a world that science sees full of many constantly changing and interdependent elements full of ambiguous probability. Laying blame for lung cancer on specific factory smokestacks in an atmosphere swirling with constantly changing chemicals involves high levels of scientific doubt. When people die of cancer is it because they were exposed to asbestos or other pollutants, or were habitual smokers, or did they fall victim to "just bad luck"? Scientific data are not an end in themselves; they establish standards—levels of acceptable or unacceptable risk to health— that allow public debate to be better informed about social, ethical, and environmental issues. Informed debate, as Thomas Jefferson repeatedly stated, is an essential ingredient of a democratic society. EPA also came under criticism for little sense of balance between health risks and economic costs. Most regulatory agencies were forbidden to factor the social and economic costs of risk reduction. Even its friends wondered whether EPA's rigid deadlines for high environmental standards, to be fulfilled regardless of economic and technological obstacles, were appropriate. There are economic incentives. The economic alternative to regulation is to put a price on the use of resources or on the pollution that harms society. Regulations originally arose in response to failures in private markets because they treated air, water, and land as free goods. Direct regulation by government compels companies to internalize (have to account for) the social costs of their actions. By the 1990s market incentives included pollution fees, marketable permits, deposit-refund systems, and the elimination of government subsidies to environmental threats, such as coal, oil, and natural gas. After the passage of NEPA in 1970, the Securities and Exchange Commission (SEC) attempted to include environmental disclosure in company financial reports to stockholders. If a company had to make substantial outlays for environmental compliance, cleanup, or go to court, its market value and future ability to do business would be materially affected. Legal action by the National Resources Defense Council (NRDC) in 1977 pushed SEC to establish rigorous requirements of publicly owned companies. SEC acted against U.S. Steel in 1979 for failing to disclose pending environmental control costs, and it required an environmental audit. In 1980 the SEC charged Occidental Petroleum Corporation for failing to disclose costs of pending litigation ($942 million in claims), environmental compliance, and liabilities from waste sites like Love Canal.

Most Americans concluded that in its first two decades, EPA was an overall success. Some early tensions in EPA have continued into the 1990s, notable whether its mission was to find a balance between environmental protection, industrial expansion, and resource development. Or should EPA be the primary champion of environmental values against counterpressures from elsewhere in government and from industry? Modern environmentalism is still characterized by a pattern of reacting to individual problems ("catastrophic" events) rather than a comprehensive and long-term strategy.

For Further Reading

For entry into the complex and fascinating world of the politics, the science, and the economics of environmental regulation, there is no better place to start than Daniel J. Fiorino's

Making Environmental Policy (1995). Environmental law itself is a moving point on a moving line and controlled by the immediacy of contemporary politics. Law case books, infamous in the memory of all law students, nevertheless help the researcher to penetrate the notoriously dense thickets of legislation, regulation and litigation. Two very different but complementary case books are by Zygmunt J. B. Plater et al., *Environmental Law and Policy: Nature, Law, and Society* (1992), and William H. Rodgers, Jr., *Environmental Law* (2nd ed., 1994). Particularly useful, brief, and lucid is the overview by Susan J. Buck, *Understanding Environmental Administration and Law* (1991). See also Morton Horwitz, *The Transformation of American Law* (1977). There is no coherent and comprehensive study of the EPA, but readers will find a useful study of its early years by Alfred A. Marcus in *Promise and Performance: Choosing and Implementing an Environmental Policy* (1980); a book by Marc K. Landy et al., *The Environmental Protection Agency: Asking the Wrong Questions* (1990), offers an informative one-sided analysis. For a solid and outspoken analysis of Superfund as probably the most controversial and costly piece of environmental legislation, see John A. Hird's excellent *Superfund: The Political Economy of Environmental Risk* (1994). Balanced studies of environmental risk are harder to find. See the doubts raised by Mary Douglas and Aaron Wildavsky in *Risk and Culture: An Essay on the Selection of Technologies and Environmental Dangers* (1983), which are updated in Kenneth R. Foster, David E. Bernstein, and Peter W. Huber, *Phantom Risk: Scientific Inference and the Law* (1993). One useful overview of risk issues is Theodore S. Glickman and Michael Gough (eds) *Readings in Risk* (1990). Fundamental studies include Baruch Fischhoff et al., *Acceptable Risk* (1981), and the landmark discussion of risk, acceptability, and perception by William W. Lowrance, *Of Acceptable Risk: Science and the Determination of Safety* (1976). On the fear of cancer from environmental pollution, see John D. Graham et al., *In Search of Safety* (1988). The historical and social context for both risk and regulation are well served by Robert Gottlieb, *Forcing the Spring: The Transformation of the American Environmental Movement* (1993), Philip Shabecoff, *A Fierce Green Fire: The American Environmental Movement* (1993), Riley E. Dunlap and Angela G. Mertig (eds.), *American Environmentalism: The U.S. Environmental Movement, 1970–1990* (1992), and the now classic Samuel P. Hays, *Beauty, Health, and Permanence: Environmental Politics in the United States, 1955–1985* (1987). A clear, brief, and somewhat outdated survey is Joseph M. Petulla, *Environmental Protection in the United States: Industry, Agencies, Environmentalists* (1987). All of the topics in this chapter are quickly dated and the issues made obsolete by technological change and political currents, so readers need to search for recent and updated materials.

CHAPTER FIFTEEN

INTO THE TWENTY-FIRST CENTURY: THE UNITED STATES AND THE GLOBAL ENVIRONMENT

One of the penalties of an ecological education is that one lives alone in a world of wounds.

—ALDO LEOPOLD, 1949

Over the last hundred years, life on earth was dominated by growth. Growth of population, of production, of income and capital formation, of exhaustion and pollution. This growth is going to stop and must stop, and the only question is by what means? Voluntarily, by government and free will, or through natural processes, which means collapse and disaster?

—JAY FORRESTER, *THE LIMITS TO GROWTH* (1972)

Human survival hinges on a host of environmental services provided by natural systems—from forests' regulation of the hydrological cycle to wetlands' filtering of pollutants. As we destroy, alter, or appropriate more of these natural systems for ourselves, these environmental services are compromised. At some point, the likely result is a chain reaction of environmental decline—widespread flooding and erosion brought on by deforestation, for example; or worsened drought and crop losses from desertification; or pervasive aquatic pollution and fisheries losses from wetlands destruction. The simultaneous unfolding of several such scenarios could cause unprecedented human hardship, famine, and disease.

—WOUTER VAN DIEREN FOR THE CLUB OF ROME, 1995

The Tragedy of the Commons

Nothing comparable to the blue-green-brown earth has yet been found anywhere else in the universe. Biologist Garrett Hardin took up the challenge of its preservation. In a 1968 essay, "The Tragedy of the Commons," he described how exponential human population growth, which was running out of control, was a remorseless and futile eating away at the planet. Hardin put the problem in a parable about a village commons, a publicly owned pasture which would inevitably be destroyed by its users motivated by greed that was very rational. Any individual user of the pasture stood to profit by grazing as many of his cattle as possible because the grass was free. But if all members of the community did the same thing, the commons would quickly be overgrazed, eroded, and useless for feeding animals (and humans) in the future. Hardin found his answer in the concept of sustainable yield: no more cattle than the carrying capacity of the commons. Hardin then turned to industrial pollution: "Here it is not a question of taking something out of the commons, but of putting something in—sewage, or chemical, radioactive, and heat wastes into water; noxious and dangerous fumes into the air; and distracting and unpleasant advertising signs into the line of sight." Like the cattle put to pasture, production costs were reduced by dumping wastes onto the commons while profits belonged to the individual producer. The problem arose when dumping overflowed the carrying capacity of air, water, and the land. Such problems, he concluded, did not have technical solutions, but demanded "change in human values or ideas of morality." Hardin added, "Consider bank-robbing. The man who takes money from a bank acts as if the bank were a commons. . . . When men mutually agreed to pass laws against robbing, mankind became more free, not less so." Yet, he observed, if population grows exponentially, our individual shares of the world's goods would decrease and our freedom would wither away.

Some of Hardin's critics among neoclassical economists said an upward spiral of prices on the marketplace would reduce demand for the admittedly scarce resources of the commons. When oil prices shot up tenfold during the 1973 crisis, for example, Americans began to drive smaller and more efficient cars. Other critics emphasized continuous human inventiveness to make better use of scarce resources, or simply to find new resources. They noted that the Industrial Revolution was jump-started in England by the shift from scarce trees to

UNDOUBTEDLY THE GREATEST environmental photograph of the twentieth century is of the earth's sphere taken from space. Seen for the first time as a whole, Earth was alluring: blue oceans, green and sandy continents, swirls of white clouds. The picture became one of the modern world's icons. An alternative photo, even more impressive, was called "Earthrise" and showed the beautiful globe rising above a desolate moonscape. The first human landing on the moon on July 20, 1969, and the view of Earth from there, made many people realize that their global environment had many of the characteristics of a closed system. "Spaceship Earth" became a metaphor for environmental awareness. Biologist Lewis Thomas reverently wrote of the magical realization: "Aloft, floating free beneath the moist gleaming membrane of bright blue sky, is the rising earth, the only exuberant thing in this part of the cosmos. It has the organized, self-contained look of a live creature, full of information, marvelously skilled in handling the sun." Commentators repeatedly compared the barrenness of space with the colorful vitality of Earth. The pictures were ironic because they cost tens of billions of dollars and diverted immense technological resources from global environmental needs to boost equipment and men in space to the moon and offer the new image of the lonely, life-filled, endangered planet Earth.

plentiful coal. Still other critics, drawing on the eighteenth- and nineteenth-century philosophies of John Locke, Jeremy Bentham, and Adam Smith, saw the answer in even wider privatization of the commons. This included the right to exclude others and the right to capture the full value of one's property. On this basis, Americans sold off their public domain between 1785 and 1935. However, some parts of the commons are not readily converted into private property, such as air, oceans, and wildlife. Other natural systems have the features of commons but are more easily reduced to ownership—forests, prairies, wetlands, and underground hydrocarbons. With his discussion of the commons, Hardin opened the modern environmental debate between private self-interest and public well-being. Protection of private self-interest became the linchpin of U.S. international policy, contrary to a global trend toward public well-being.

America's Environmental Isolationism

Some environmental problems have always crossed national borders, such as acid rain, nuclear radiation, and atmospheric ozone depletion. One substance in particular, petroleum, which fueled and heated human societies during most of the twentieth century, became a major source of global pollution, industrial profiteering, and regional warfare. Alternative concepts to industrial growth received increased attention, such as sustainable development and appropriate technologies. Between 1972 and 1992 environmentalism itself became a preeminent factor in shaping international relations, national economics, and daily life. The United States only belatedly, and reluctantly, began to join in international accords to deal with global environmental issues.

The Lost Opportunity

In 1944 Gifford Pinchot was the grand old man of the conservation movement. He had outlived his great adversary John Muir by 30 years. Earlier, in May 1940, as England suffered the Luftwaffe's blitz and war clouds darkened America's perspective, Pinchot told a scientific congress that war could only be avoided if every nation had fair access to natural resources. This was "an indispensable condition of permanent peace." A seed had been planted by Pinchot that was fertilized by the war. Obviously World War II had strained the resources of the Allies, and resource loss, such as petroleum, helped defeat the Axis powers. In June 1944 Pinchot proposed an international conference on conservation of natural resources to his old friend, President Franklin D. Roosevelt. The president said to Pinchot, "I am surprised that the world knows so little about itself" and agreed to the need for dedicated study of nature. Nevertheless, in July 1944 when the Bretton Woods Conference, held in New Hampshire, established a $9 billion plan for postwar reconstruction, the natural world was still treated as simply the global commons to be consumed by the victor nations, a hoard to be sacrificed for postwar economic recovery. Food and forest production would be expanded by the new Food and Agriculture Organization (FAO), petroleum exploitation would be efficiently channeled through the Anglo-American Petroleum Agreement, and the new World Bank would create international policies and financing to encourage consumption of goods. Disappointed, Pinchot again pressed President Roosevelt to convene a conference, which, according to one account, would "consider the setting up of an international organization to promote the conservation of natural resources, fair access to necessary raw materials by all countries, information exchange, and the drawing up of an inventory of natural resources and a set of principles on their conservation." But Roosevelt died in April 1945 and Pinchot in October 1946, and the conference and proposed organization died with them. The United States became wary of international conferences on conservation and environment during the Cold War with the Soviet Union; they might become showcases for communist propaganda by attacking capitalist economic development. Nor were they necessary, American officials argued, because of an abundance of undeveloped (and probably still undiscovered) resources, together with continuously advancing technological "fixes" whenever a resource problem might arise, such as nuclear-generated electricity, processed foods, and synthetic fabrics.

The most pressing postwar issue was restoration of food production to reduce the imminent starvation of millions of people, a crisis that was predicted to last through several postwar years. One of Roosevelt's famous Four Freedoms had been "Freedom from Want." An Englishman, Sir John Boyd Orr, the first director-general of the FAO, wrote in 1953, "The present world food shortage has raised again the specter of Malthus." About 150 years earlier, the English economist Thomas Malthus wrote a shocking, controversial, and persuasive essay of impending disaster to humanity because human populations grew geometrically but their food arithmetically, meaning inevitable starvation and widespread death on a global basis. Under such demands for postwar recovery, no international environmental organization of the kind that Pinchot proposed to Roosevelt seemed possible. A minuscule prewar International Office for the Protection of Nature (IOPN), headquartered in the Low Countries, became the IUPN (International Union for the Protection of Nature) in 1948 with a new home in Basel, Switzerland, but it remained understaffed and underfinanced. It did urge in 1949 that environmental impacts be reviewed in Third World development projects sponsored by international aid agencies. "Protection" became "conservation" in 1956 when the name changed to IUCN (International Union for Conservation of Nature and Natural Resources). IUPN/IUCN had an uneasy relationship with the UN Educational, Scientific, and Cultural Organization (UNESCO), which had been founded in November 1946 to further international cooperation in its fields. But UNESCO was woefully weak in science, and even indifferent to it, and used the word *conservation* to mean the preservation of cultural artifacts like works of art, historic buildings, and libraries. Natural resource conservation, except for a small project on the Amazon rain forest, was beyond UNESCO's thinking in a postwar world bent on rebuilding its industrial foundations. Greater ecological understanding did not emerge until the fall of 1968 when UNESCO sponsored the Biosphere Conference in Paris. The conference addressed the human impact on the biosphere, including air and water pollution, overgrazing and deforestation, and the drainage of wetlands. It emphasized that many natural resources were reaching a critical threshold of scarcity that would make them less supportive of human society. It emphasized that further economic development had not taken environmental degradation into account. The conference also called for environmental inventories, monitoring of resources, and environmental training on a worldwide basis. But the conference had no means to put its recommendations into effect.

Postwar American Indifference to Global Environmental Scarcity

Environmental doomsaying was not popular in the United States, which had emerged from World War II as the most powerful nation on earth, the only major power not to have suffered direct physical damage to its land and resources. Incomes continued to rise, consumer spending reached new heights, an explosion in home building and auto production created record energy consumption. By 1955 the United States, with one-twentieth of the world's population, was consuming over one-third of the world's resources. Population scientists Paul and Ann Ehrlich reported in 1989 that "A baby born in the U.S. represents twice the impact on the Earth as one born in Sweden, three times one born in Italy, 13 times one born in Brazil, 35 times one in India, 140 times one born in Bangladesh or Kenya, and 280 times one born in Chad, Rwanda, Haiti, or Nepal." Contrary to an emerging ecological view on the global scene, Americans believed that talk of scarce resources and limits to growth was premature and probably irrelevant. New scientific discoveries and technological inventions would compensate for any real problems, they concluded, just as the once starved Dust Bowl region had now become "the breadbasket of the world." Americans looked on their prosperity as achievable worldwide in a short time (as long as the United States prevailed and not the Soviet Union); the postwar world was on a permanent, long-term economic upswing. The irony of America's long-term global environmental indifference was that the United States had long been the world's innovator to create national wilderness parks and to establish programs for soil and water conservation. Two decisive events in the United States, the publication of Rachel Carson's *Silent Spring* in 1962 and Earth Day on April 22, 1970, greatly increased America's internal environmental awareness (as we saw in Chapters 13 and 14), but did little to break its international isolationism. In the 1970s the United States refused to sign the Law of the Seas treaty. In 1972, when the United States banned domestic use and production of DDT, the chemical industry continued to promote its use and production overseas. Presidential administrations seemed determined to apply 1950s Cold War industrial competition to an environmentally sensitive world that was increasingly vulnerable to population growth, resource scarcity, and pollution.

Oil Makes the World Go Round . . . for a Time

The dominant substance of the industrial world during most of the twentieth century has been a dark brown, heavy, smelly viscous liquid called petroleum. Supplies are not infinite. Petroleum is an underground fossil fuel unevenly distributed around the world, with a glut of supply in the underpopulated Middle East, and heavily consumed where no native supplies exist, such as Japan, Germany, China, and India. Since approximately 1920 the world has consumed a total of 575 billion barrels of oil, at first slowly but after World War II at a greedy rate. Proven reserves are 900 billion barrels, which our energy-hungry world will consume at its current pace in 40 years. An additional 525 billion barrels that were estimated as undiscovered would carry current consumers another 24 years. Global oil production will reach its high point no later than 2010 and probably will run out in the lifetime of some people reading this book. If a person is 20 years old today, it is very likely that his or her teenage children will not be able to drive gasoline-powered cars. Reduced use and better conservation can extend the modern world's "oil bubble," but if developing countries continue to expand their populations and demand their "moral right" to industrialization and consumerism equal to the developed nations, then oil consumption will accelerate and cut the era of access to oil in half.

Risky Dependency on Oil

Briefly, what is the nature and history of this risky dependence on a single substance in limited supply? The first major energy revolution took place 10,000 years ago, with the use of fuels, mostly wood and animal dung, for fire for cooking and heating, together with the muscle power of newly domesticated animals. For most of the rest of human history, even as trade and manufacturing grew, most energy was still human and animal muscle supplemented by windmills and waterwheels. Wood and charcoal were burned to produce small amounts of iron, copper, tin, and glass. The first serious fuel shortage came with the decline of Britain's forests through overcutting. The English learned to shift to coal for fuel, despite its dirtiness and foul smoke, which, together with steam engines and textile machinery, introduced the second major energy revolution, the Industrial Revolution. The replacement of coal by oil early in the twentieth century can be called a third major energy revolution. The gasoline-powered internal combustion engine and oil-fired electric power offered labor-saving efficiency.

In a marketplace world, the opportunity for great wealth from petroleum was enormous. Since the early 1900s the major U.S. oil companies, with the direct intervention of the State Department, enjoyed exclusive petroleum concessions over large geographical areas of suspected oil reserves in foreign countries. The Arab-American Oil Company (ARAMCO) consortium in Saudi Arabia pumped its first successful wells in 1938, although the size of the Saudi Arabian reserve was not appreciated until after World War II. ARAMCO was one of several consortia that had complete control over production and pricing and paid the host nation a fixed low price. However, Middle Eastern nationalism and worldwide inflation induced the formation in 1960 of the Organization of Petroleum Exporting Countries (OPEC). Decision-making power began to shift in favor of the host nations. The so-called oil crisis of October 1973 unexpectedly hit industrial nations when the Persian Gulf members of OPEC unilaterally raised prices by 70 percent. The Arab states also began a series of production cutbacks and embargoed all exports to the United States, Canada, the Netherlands, and several Caribbean islands, all of which had taken Israel's side in several Arab-Israeli disputes. All of western Europe was threatened with similar embargoes. Two months later, in December 1973, OPEC escalated prices again, this time by 130 percent. Prices continued to rise from an artificially low $3 a barrel to $30 a barrel, which shook world economies. The embargo against the United States and other nations was lifted in March 1974. Oil-based economic turmoil was repeated in 1979, resulting in inflation, economic stagnation, and widespread unemployment. Despite what seemed to be ransom prices, oil remained the world's fuel of choice.

Under the pressure of scarce oil and high prices, Americans worked energetically at conservation (storm windows, smaller automobiles) and oil substitutes (coal gasification, shale oil, enhanced oil field recovery), but did not take drastic measures to cut back on overall oil consumption. The nation remained dependent on the automobile and oil-based plastics and chemicals. There was little movement toward alternatives: public transportation, solar and other renewable forms of energy, mandated recycling, and shifts from oil-based industrial and consumer goods. Following several years of international efforts, world oil consumption was reduced enough to cut OPEC's share of world production from approximately 50 percent in 1979 to approximately 30 percent in 1986. But by the early 1980s the United States again depended on foreign supplies for more than half its petroleum. American leadership in the costly and controversial 1991 Gulf War to recover Kuwait (5 percent of the world's oil) from Iraq's (5 percent of the world's oil) grasp is not surprising. Americans are still so dependent on oil that they are willing to risk the harm of severe international trade deficits that largely result from oil imports. At best, future consumption of oil will be more difficult as reserves are depleted and oil is harder to reach and prices rise.

Is Oil a Major Source of Environmental Harm?

A large proportion of the environmental problems that we face today have their origin in fossil fuels, especially petroleum. (Admittedly, coal was even a worse polluter and killer when it was the dominant fuel between approximately 1850 and 1950.) Oil pollution ranges from spills from offshore drilling rigs to pipeline fractures in wilderness regions to supertanker accidents to air pollution from smokestacks and auto exhausts to long-lived petroleum-based plastic wastes. The first major oil transportation disaster was the wreck of the tanker *Torrey Canyon* in March 1967. It spilled 875,000 barrels off England's Cornish Coast, where hundreds of miles of coastline were polluted. Crude oil "floats," or slicks washed ashore. Oil density can also cause it to sink and cover life on the sea bottom. So little was known about oil removal that attempts to use detergents only added to the biological damage. Cleanup alone cost £6 million. In March 1978 the small oil tanker *Amoco Cadiz* lost its steering off the coast of Brittany in France and broke up when blown ashore. The tanker's entire cargo of about 1.6 million barrels of crude oil spilled into the water and onto the beaches of southern England and northern France. The combination of the spill and chemical detergents introduced for cleanup killed thousands of seabirds, commercial-value fish, and shellfish, destroyed fish hatcheries, shellfish beds, and livelihoods of local workers, and disrupted important resort and tourism businesses. History's most notorious and dangerous tanker spill took place when the *Exxon Valdez* ran negligently aground in April 1989, and 11 million gallons spread over Alaska's Prince William Sound, once one of the world's richest habitats for seabirds and sea otters. Commercial fishing may have been permanently destroyed, and Exxon became liable for $8.5 billion of cleanup and damages. Many supertankers now have double steel hulls, but this was not a mandated requirement until 1990. The largest spill from drilling released 3.1 million barrels in June 1979 into the Gulf of Mexico at Ixtoc from an offshore oil well owned by Pemex, the national Mexican oil company. The most publicized offshore oil rig release was the Union Oil Company leak beginning in 1969 off Santa Barbara, California, and not ending until mid-1970. A February 1976 barge accident dumped a million gallons into the Chesapeake Bay and killed 20,000 birds. In January 1988 an oil storage tank near Pittsburgh, Pennsylvania, collapsed and dumped a million gallons into the Monongahela River. A 20-mile-long oil slick flowed into the Ohio River. A million people in several cities along the way were for days without their normal drinking water facilities. While the well blowouts and wrecked tankers captured the headlines, between 1980 and 1986 there were almost 70,000 oil spills in U.S. waters, or an average of more than 27 a day. In addition, continuous oil pollution comes from oil sludges (also contaminated with lead) from automobile crankcases dumped into sewers, leaks at seaports and pipelines, and illegal seawater flushing of tanker holds. As long as oil consumption remained high, so did the spread of oil pollution.

Responses to the 1970s Oil Crisis

Alternatives to Oil Dependency

The answers thus far to the world's petroleum dependency are not reassuring. Over half the energy consumed in the United States is wasted by ordinary loss, incorrect applications, and inefficiency. Americans use oil-based energy faster than any other people in the world at any time in human history. Domestic U.S. oil production reached its absolute peak in 1975. In the United States in 1990, petroleum accounted for 45 percent of the nation's total energy consumption, double that of the other two nonrenewable fuels, coal and natural gas. So-called renewable energy sources—hydroelectric, solar, wind, and geothermal power—supplied 5 percent, and nuclear power provided 7 percent. With only 6 percent of the world's population, the United States consumed about 30 percent of the world's energy. Coal appeared to be the obvious primary alternative fuel, but it was recognized as a mixed blessing. The United States has the world's largest coal reserves that would last 200 years. Coal damages lungs and costs lives in underground mines. Strip mining pollutes and destroys the landscape. Coal combustion for power releases waste heat, particulates, sulfur oxides, nitrogen oxides, carbon monoxide, and carbon dioxide. Coal-fired power plants are the primary source of acid rain. Commonplace cleanup technologies such as smokestack scrubbers turn some of this into solid toxic wastes, such as fly ash sludge, adding to the landfill problem. Coal is the dirtiest major fossil fuel known.

Conservation

One important answer has been the conservation of energy in lighting, home heating, home air conditioning, appliances, packaging, industry, and agriculture. The simple expedient of changing lighting from incandescent to florescent bulbs cuts energy use two-thirds. Overall, in modern office buildings, electric consumption could be cut in half, and the output of 75 power plants could be conserved. California law in the early 1980s required new refrigerators to be 50 percent more efficient than units sold five years earlier and air conditioners, 20 percent more efficient. The 1987 federal National Appliance Conservation Act required that by 1992 all major household appliances, such as refrigerators, had to consume 20 percent less electricity, reducing demand for electricity at the equivalent of 20 large nuclear power plants. Another concept was cogeneration, by which waste heat, such as hot water from a power plant, is not released into the atmosphere but applied for office heating or food processing. Traditional power generation was 50 to 70 percent efficient of fuel use; cogeneration boosted this to 80 to 90 percent. A New Jersey YMCA, for example, purchased a cogeneration system for $130,000. It generated 70 percent of the Y's electricity and also heated its rooms, showers, and swimming pool at a net savings of $50,000 a year. Although home or office conservation can be brought on line rapidly, other conservation changes take place more slowly because of built-in lags. Auto models take five years to change. Public transportation systems, such as San Francisco's BART, may require decades to plan, fund, and construct. Nuclear power plant construction alone notoriously takes more than a decade. Conservation did not, as critics contended, mean "freezing in the dark." One estimate by the World Resources Institute in 1987 said that if the peoples of the world made more efficient use of their current energy use by the year 2020, although the population will have doubled, energy needs would only go up 10 percent.

Hard Paths versus Soft Paths

The physicist Amory Lovins in 1976 received widespread attention when he advocated a "soft energy path" for the future. A "hard energy path" depends on high technology, capital-intensive use of nonrenewable oil and coal resources, and nuclear power. Large does not necessarily mean efficient: 70 percent can be lost in electric power generation, long-distance transmission, and transfers onto distribution networks. Lovins's soft energy path applied energy conservation and turned to renewable energy sources using decentralized user-owned technologies: active and passive solar heating, biomass conversion, wind power generation, and small-scale hydroelectric plants. The soft energy path was not antitechnology; it sought to position technological innovations within the broader framework of social and economic systems. Emphasis was on "appropriate technology," such as solar energy for housing, that suited a sustainable quality of life. Lovins emphasized end uses as the proper measure of effective and efficient energy consumption. On this basis, only 8 percent of all energy needs in America, he claimed, actually require electricity; more than half of all uses could be satisfied by space heating or cooling. He concluded that the United States has an oversupply, not a shortage, of electricity. Lovins's prediction has largely come true. Regions such as the Pacific Northwest enjoy a large oversupply of electric power. A similar approach had been proposed in 1973 by the British economist E. F. Schumacher. "Small is beautiful" focused on "economics as if people mattered." Schumacher, in turn, quoted Aldo Leopold: "By and large, our present problem is one of attitudes and implements. We are remodeling the Alhambra with a steamshovel, and are proud of our yardage." According to Schumacher, the need is not to throw away the steamshovel, but to use it more appropriately to build a highway instead, to reconsider whether the Alhambra needs remodeling, and if it does, to use tools that suit its needs.

The Battle over Nuclear Power

Nuclear energy literally burst on the public in August 1945 when the United States used two fission bombs against Japan to hasten the end of World War II, at the cost of 200,000 immediate deaths and radioactive injury and death to tens of thousands more. Americans, and the rest of the world, immediately realized that a new kind of energy had been unleashed. Americans were also convinced from the first of the peaceful use of atomic energy, particularly generation of electrical power instead of burning limited resources of coal, oil, and natural gas. Nuclear energy that boiled water to produce steam to drive turbines was believed to be so efficient that it was "too cheap to meter." The first pilot nuclear power plant was at Shippingsport, Pennsylvania, using a water-cooled system based on U.S. Navy nuclear submarine technology. Soon nuclear power plants sprang up across the United States, Europe, the Soviet bloc, India, and the Pacific Rim of Asian nations, probably reaching a peak of 300 by 1990.

They now generate about 15 percent of electricity worldwide, including nearly 20 percent in the United States, over 60 percent of the power generated in France and Belgium, about 25 percent in Japan, and heavy use in many other European nations.

A series of accidents at nuclear power plants threatened high radiation levels inside the plants and release into the atmosphere to affect regional populations. The accidents at Browns Ferry in Alabama in 1975 and Three Mile Island in Pennsylvania in 1979 created a public up-roar but did not cause any deaths. Most devastating was the explosive release of radioactive materials from the large nuclear power complex at Chernobyl in Ukraine in 1986, where the top of the reactor blew off, spread radioactive material directly over an area of 30 kilometers around the plant, required the evacuation of about 135,000 people in the Kiev region, and af-fected livestock, crops, and people as far away as Britain and northern Sweden. Two people died in the initial explosion and 29 more in a few months from radiation illness; as many as a million other people acquired significantly higher risks of cancer. A federal report issued in 1982 predicted that the worst possible nuclear accident in the United States (a 2 percent probability before the year 2000) would cost more than 100,000 lives and $300 billion if it took place in a heavily populated region such as New Jersey. Following growing public protest that began in the 1960s, the construction of nuclear power plants came to an end in the United States, where it had reached a high of 40 in 1973 and fell to none by 1979. Already more than 20 plants have been decommissioned in the United States and western Europe. As the nuclear industry depended on increasingly old plants, tons of nuclear wastes were stored at lethal levels at power plants and many military installations and were also collected at less risky levels from medical and industrial uses. A national search for permanent sites in geologi-cally stable locations took place in the 1980s and 1990s. The Nuclear Waste Policy Act of 1982–83 found sites at the long-standing weapons site in Hanford, Washington, and at Yucca Mountain, Nevada, and Deaf Smith, Texas, but the program ran into deep political and legal trouble that effectively voided the 1998 target date. An underground salt formation near Carlsbad, New Mexico, may start to receive nuclear wastes for multimillennia storage. Most nuclear wastes remain temporarily stored at local facilities. The debate is more grave because of the need for absolute protection for as long as 13,000 years, much longer than the continu-ous existence of any known human institution.

Rethinking Industrialization

1972 Report to the Club of Rome: The Limits to Growth

In 1972 a slim 205-page volume sent a ripple through the worlds of government policy mak-ers, business interests, and environmentalists alike. *The Limits to Growth,* sponsored by the Club of Rome, had an impact on public environmental issues second only to Rachel Carson's *Silent Spring* a decade earlier. Within a decade, it had sold about 9 million copies in 29 lan-guages. The Club of Rome was an informal group of about 30 industrialists, scientists, and economists, mostly European, brought together in April 1968 by the Italian financier Aurelio Peccei to "discuss a subject of staggering scope—the present and future predicament of man." It soon grew to about 70 members of 25 nationalities, including Middle Eastern, Japanese, and American representatives. They were joined in the summer of 1970 by a computer team from the Massachusetts Institute of Technology, led by Jay Forrester and Dennis Meadows, pioneers in the new field of systems analysis. The combined efforts of the Club of Rome and the MIT team led to the first computer-based global modeling of a "world problematique" of the growth and expansion of human societies.

After two experimental starts, the team arrived at World3, a model containing five basic factors, they said, that "determine, and therefore, ultimately limit, growth on this planet— population, agricultural production, natural resources, industrial production, and pollution." The team insisted that the usual economic or political timetables of months and years must be extended into decades and centuries to understand the nature and movement of global environmental forces and their human implications. The team also included a disclaimer that their critics often ignored: "The model we have constructed is, like every other model, imperfect, oversimplified, and unfinished. We are well aware of its shortcomings, but we believe that it is the most useful model now available for dealing with problems far out on the space-time graph."

Many readers hoped, and their critics insisted, that the team's three primary conclusions were overwrought: (1) if present trends in the five factors continue unchanged, the absolute limits to economic growth on the planet will be reached within the next 100 years, resulting in a sudden and uncontrollable decline in both population and industrial capacity;

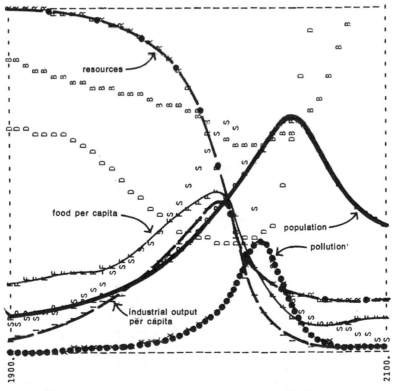

World Model Standard Run. This was the third attempt in 1972 by the MIT-Club of Rome team to establish a useful computer-based global model of the limits of continuous growth.

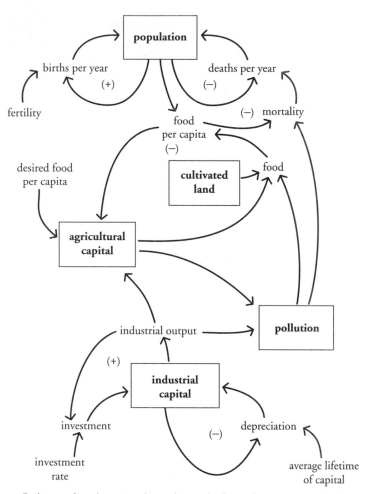

Feedback Loops of Population, Capital, Agriculture, and Pollution. This systems approach allowed a better understanding of the complexities and interactions of many environmental problems.

(2) these trends can be altered, but only if society is willing to shift from exploitive industrialization toward ecological and economic stability that is sustainable far into the future. The report insisted that such change must still satisfy basic human material needs as well as assure the fulfillment of human opportunity and potential; and (3) the sooner the world decides to make the change, despite the organizational difficulties, the greater will be its chance of success. Overall, the study said its model showed that growth will cease in one way or another; the issue is whether the new conditions will be congenial or hostile to human society.

The team emphasized "doubling time" as a mode of exponential growth. For example, the interest of a sum of money left in a bank at 7 percent interest will double in 10 years, or 7 years at 10 percent, or 70 years at 1 percent. This was the result of a positive feedback loop with continuous increase. The team noted that world population, for example, has been growing exponentially at an increasing rate since 1650, with a 2.1 percent increase per year in 1970, or a doubling time of 33 years. Exponential growth can also explain industrial output and food production, the consumption of raw materials and energy, and the capacity of the planet to absorb wastes and recycle basic chemical substances. The team admitted that upper limits were unknown, yet certainly they were finite. The team also emphasized the concepts of "natural delays" between the release of a pollutant into the environment and its negative effect on the ecosystem. When DDT was completely banned in 1972 in the United States, its levels still accumulated in fish and would not come back down to the 1970 level until 1995. Also problematic was "overshoot of carrying capacity," as when goats overgraze their range or auto pollution creates a health alert in the Los Angeles basin. In other words, humanity can induce uncontrollable overuse of the planet unless there is planning to control trends well before they reach their limits. Otherwise natural delays will lead inevitably into dangerous overshoots and inevitable environmental (and societal) collapse. Such concepts dominate contemporary policy making about large-scale climate threats such as atmospheric ozone depletion and global warming.

The concept of the limits to growth became the dominant theme in President Jimmy Carter's *Global 2000* state of the world report in 1980. Outraged criticism came from progrowth and protechnology advocates. Herman Kahn and the conservative Hudson Institute published a rebuttal, *The Next 200 Years,* in 1976. Kahn believed the course of human history offered an optimistic outlook: "Two hundred years ago almost everywhere human beings were comparatively few, poor and at the mercy of the forces of nature, and 200 years from now, we expect, almost everywhere they will be numerous, rich and in control of the forces of nature." Kahn's basic premise, not documented by any computerized model, was that when certain limits are reached, new technologies will remove the limit or buy time for future adjustments (called elasticity of substitution). Examples are highly efficient irrigation systems, nuclear power, coal gasification, and solar energy. Kahn and his team insisted that any tampering with highly successful current trends toward ever-greater industrialization and consumerism would be unethical because interference would condemn the peoples of the less developed nations to lives of hopeless poverty. The most expert critique, *Models of Doom* (1974), came from a University of Sussex (England) team that focused on weaknesses in the methodology of the MIT team, the way the model was limited to five topics, and the ideological values of the modelers. The Sussex critics concluded that the MIT team was far too bold in its conclusions based on limited and narrowly focused data, it made interconnections between the five topics deceptively far more precise than could be known, the model focused on purely physical limits to the neglect of the power of economics, social forces, and especially cultural values, and it ignored the potential for a continued rise in technological efficiency and further discovery of exploitable resources. The Sussex team also wondered whether MIT inordinately trusted computer modeling for long-term forecasts 130 years into the future. It noted that no one 100 years ago could have anticipated the world's dependence on oil or the appearance of nuclear power. Another critic, Wassily Leontief, in a 1977 study for the United Nations, made his forecast sensitive to rising prices: Demand would decline as prices rose (called the demand-dampening characteristic of prices) and allow society to stretch out scarce resources like petroleum, natural gas, copper, lead, mercury, gold, silver, and zinc. Whether it was praised or vilified, *The Limits to Growth* created a powerful policy tool— "macroenvironmentalism" using large-scale systems analysis. Over the years the Club of Rome/MIT team openly admitted the limitations of their modeling. They acknowledged several times in the 1970s and 1980s that proenvironment political and economic shifts had forced reconfiguration of their charting and delayed their doom-saying timetable.

Nevertheless, in their 1992 sequel, *Beyond the Limits: Confronting Global Collapse and Envisioning a Sustainable Future,* the team reaffirmed the reality of fundamental physical limits to growth. They claimed that by 1990 the world had already overshot some of its limits.

The International Agenda: Shift from Growth to Sustainability

The modern sustainability debate opened in 1972 at the UN-sponsored Stockholm Conference. It led to the establishment of the UN Environmental Programme (UNEP), which among other things stressed the importance for Third World nations to include environmental costs when they industrialize. Fifteen years later, in 1987, the UN-sponsored World Commission on Environment and Development (also titled the Brundtland Commission) published the widely read book *Our Common Future.* This report provided the classic definition of sustainable development as "development that meets the needs of the present without compromising the ability of future generations to meet their own needs." It emphasized that essential ecological processes must be maintained if economic development can be sustained over the long run. Sustainable development thus practices "biocentrism," the viewpoint that humanity is best understood as it is enclosed within nature. This turns on its head the historic Western belief that nature is simply raw material to serve human consumption.

The practice of sustainable development may go back to city-state regulations by the ancient Greeks, whose laws avoided exploitation of resources and sought environmental balance to sustain the *polis* indefinitely. Overall, however, the historic record is not reassuring. Once the eastern Mediterranean was covered with large forests before civilization produced today's rugged treeless badlands. The decline of the Roman Empire has been attributed to a deadly combination of agricultural erosion of Italy's soils together with poisoning from lead-piped plumbing. Spain's rapid descent from its sixteenth-century greatness came in large part because its sheepherders overgrazed its once lush central highlands. Nor is the recent record of resource management around the world any better. The cutting of the last trees for firewood in east Africa's Sahel has only made starvation more extreme and ungovernable. Russia's Aral Sea contains only 10 percent of its historic water because of exaggerated irrigation of a nearby desert. Nepal's deforestation for firewood created dust storms that obscured the Himalaya Mountains. The reduction of the Amazon rain forest ("the lungs of the world") continues almost unabated. Agriculture is probably the most challenging aspect of sustainable development in the face of constantly growing world food needs that can only be drawn from depleted soils and shrinking water supplies. Farming in much of the developing countries is highly exploitive. Small family or tribal operations, with limited access to equipment, fertilizers, and pesticides, suffer from low productivity, intensive hand labor, and heavy environmental degradation. Sustainable agriculture seeks to balance food production, environmental conservation, and profitability. This is a tall order. In modern countries, it is also a sharp turn away from industrial farming that measures success by short-term profits. The leading question is what degree of environmental degradation is a necessary price for a healthy farm society, or whether a clean, safe natural environmental is compatible with profitable agriculture. It is clear that in the United States and Canada, vast food surpluses—temporarily so large that they can be used for nonfood purposes like ethanol fuel—are being created at great environmental cost not passed on to the consumer. One objective of agricultural sustainable development is to track soil and water consumption as costs instead of a free commons. Critics of the sustainability approach argue that its production levels would not match global population growth.

The debate that swirls around sustainable development is whether the concept is self-contradictory, an oxymoron, because the term *development* means economic growth that consumes natural resources. The term *sustainability* has often been used in its place. A 1994 analysis offered a distinction between "weak" and "strong" sustainability. Weak sustainability affirms that any weakening of today's environment that is likely to leave tomorrow's world worse off should be corrected. It uses a "constant capital" approach that sees the environment as an exchangeable form of capital. "We can consume or destroy environmental resources as long as we compensate for the loss by increasing the stock of man-made assets, like roads, buildings, and machinery." A human-made infrastructure can be substituted for a natural infrastructure. In contrast, strong sustainability grounds itself in the concept that not all capital is exchangeable. "Critical natural capital"—the ozone layer, the carbon cycle, genetic biodiversity—cannot be traded because it has primary ecological functions—global life support—as well as secondary service to humanity. Human-made capital is flexible, but natural capital must be protected.

The New Economics: Uncoupling Growth and Quality of Life

From a sustainability point of view, widely used post–World War II methods to measure economic growth are misleading. They fail to account properly for the costs created by consumption of natural resources. The natural world contributes to industrial production through raw materials that become food, fuels, metals, and timber. Equally important are the negative costs that nature absorbs. Despite the warning signals, most nations today practice depletion of natural resources, partly because they treat it not as loss but as income. The dumping of waste onto the commons is not defined as a doubled cost both in the creation of waste and the defiling of the commons. According to the sustainability argument, humanity has outgrown the era of traditional or "frontier" economics with no limits to growth or pollution. Herman Daly at the World Bank wrote in 1992 that attention must be given to "sink limits," the capacity of the environment to absorb the wastes we produce. Sink limits are being widely violated and overreached. Sustainable development is not a repudiation of growth, but the recognition of its costs. In 1986, 17 percent of the U.S. GNP went unrecognized as the costs of air and water pollution, together with long-term degradation. Seven percent involved the costs of the depletion of nonrenewable resources and the loss of farmland and wetlands. Looked at in another way, between 1980 and 1986, even if long-term degradation was taken out of the picture, environmental costs took 7 percent out of the GNP that was otherwise claimed to rise by 11.6 percent. A similar environmental depletion cost would reduce Mexico's annual GNP by 6 percent, Costa Rica's by 10 percent, Indonesia's by 3 percent, and Zimbabwe's by 3 percent. In the words of a 1995 report to the Club of Rome, "We have not become richer by having a machine to destroy garbage, as compared to when we had no garbage to get rid of. Yet according to the economics of the Industrial Revolution, our wealth has increased [when we acquire a machine to destroy garbage]." Nor have other declines been factored into such costs. Few inhabitants of the modern world will deny that overall public services have declined, public transportation is bad, the inner cities are decrepit and unsafe, many senior citizens are impoverished, medical care is costly and unavailable to larger populations, education is collapsing, high culture is becoming invisible, scientific research is deemphasized, and the environment has been neglected. Greater industrial productivity did not guarantee better health care, education, and justice. In 1989, after the economist Herman

Daly and the ethicist John Cobb reviewed the previous 20 years, they concluded that the link between the growth of industrial production and the increase in human welfare had become progressively weaker. National GNPs had risen significantly, but they did not increase standard of living and quality of life, except for a small elite. Canadians Scott Slocombe and Caroline Van Bers say, "We should be thinking in terms of sustainable societies, not sustainable development." A sustainable society, they argue, is attentive to personal rights, family stability, health and safety, as well as a respect for nature.

Global Environmentalism and the Demonizing of the United States

It Took 20 Years to Get from Stockholm to Rio (via Nairobi)

Long-standing global environmental problems became visible in the 1970s. When scientists discovered DDT in the fatty tissue of arctic fish and Antarctic penguins, hundreds of miles from any place where the pesticide was used, they realized that a local environmental problem had quickly became global. Air and water moved in global currents; birds and porpoises traveled tens of thousands of miles. In the early 1970s the useful synthetic PCBs (polychlorinated biphenyls), used for electric insulators, plastic food containers, epoxy resins, caulking compounds, wall and upholstery coverings, and contained in soap, paint, paper, waxes, and cosmetics, were found worldwide in cows' milk, fish meat, and human bodies. PCB production was banned in the United States in 1977, but 1.2 billion pounds had already been released into the world environment. Evidence said that its decomposition products were even more toxic than the original material. Other widespread risks that received attention in the 1980s and 1990s were the chemical depletion of the earth's life-saving ozone layer in the upper atmosphere, the tree-killing and lake-destroying acid rain from industrial pollution, and the gradual but ominous temperature rise in the earth's overall climate.

An international milestone was the UN Conference on the Human Environment held in June 1972 in Stockholm, Sweden. The conference was remarkable in the respectful attention it gave to nongovernmental organizations (NGOs; mostly citizens' groups) and to less developed countries (LDCs; sometimes also called developing nations, the Third World or South). The conference noted that the environmental issues debated by the more developed countries (MDCs; sometimes also called developed countries, or North) were limits to growth, the population explosion, pollution control, and protection of natural resources. But these were irrelevant to the LDCs who experienced "daily realities of poverty, hunger, disease and survival," requiring adequate shelter, clean drinking water, adequate sanitation, and food and jobs for burgeoning populations. Hence the LDCs insisted on economic development through industrialization and the green revolution (high-yield, genetically improved crops requiring large doses of chemical pesticides); resulting environmental problems would have to wait. The Stockholm Conference was the turning point when "environmental issues had broken through" into international politics. A delegation from the United States did attend, but it was seen as obstructionist when it opposed many LDC principles, it attempted to water down a proposed accord on toxic substances, and abstained from voting on a resolution condemning nuclear weapons testing. Americans were also embarrassed by widespread criticism for the human and environmental costs of the Vietnam War. The United States received praise only for sponsoring a proposed ten-year moratorium on commercial whaling.

One of the conference's most important outcomes was the creation of the UN Environment Programme (UNEP). It would be headquartered in Nairobi, Kenya, as a commitment to LDCs. From the first, much was expected from UNEP, but it was underfunded, understaffed, and lacked centralized authority (to avoid competing with other UN agencies). It depended excessively on the style and interests of its respective directors (Maurice Strong until 1976, and until recently Mostafa Tolba). Its location in Nairobi kept it from useful interaction with other UN agencies that were mostly located in Europe and the United States. One of UNEPs first priorities was to overcome a major deficiency in modern environmental research—lack of significant ecological data. Its Earthwatch network, designed to monitor environmental processes and trends and provide early warning of environmental hazards, included environmental data surveys through its Global Environmental Monitoring System (GEMS) and the International Register of Potentially Toxic Chemicals (IRPTC). INFOTERRA was its International Referral System for the exchange of information. American policy makers seemed largely indifferent to UNEP's activities, which concentrated on ocean pollution, ozone layer protection, and control of desertification that were not high American priorities.

International recognition of human-made pollution gradually brought nations together. The likelihood of disastrous global warming from high levels of CO_2 emissions from fossil fuel burning led to numerous conferences but no significant controls. The same was true of acid rain from polluting smokestacks that deadened lakes and destroyed forests in Europe and America. International agencies came under criticism for their ponderous bureaucratic operations, the lack of any sense of urgency, indifference to Third World needs for development, and close associations with polluting industries. Alternative actions came from grassroots activism by NGOs who advocated alternative technologies and antipollution programs. In 1981 the United States was the only nation to vote against UN Resolution 37/137, Protection Against Products Harmful to Health and Environment, specifically intended to aid Third World countries to protect themselves from international profiteering. In 1987 the Montreal Protocol was signed by 24 nations, including the United States, to reduce CFC production (freons or chlorofluorocarbons used in refrigeration and cleaning) to prevent further thinning of the protective atmospheric layer of ozone gas that screens out 99 percent of the sun's harmful ultraviolet light. Without ozone screening, ultraviolet light causes serious skin burning and cancer in humans and animals, impacts crop growth, and promotes lethal mutations. Critics wondered whether the goal to reduce CFCs by 50 percent by 1999 was sufficient, when the ozone layer was thinning by 5 percent each year. In 1989 the United States was only one of four nations that did not sign the Convention on the Control of Transboundary Movements of Hazardous Wastes and Their Disposal, despite the fact that the convention resulted in part from the failed 6,000-mile journey in 1987 of an American barge laden with 3,168 tons of garbage from Long Island to find a dumping ground. U.S. government policy has also been less forthcoming on global climate change, monetary strategies for environmental protection in the Third World, biodiversity, and pollution from offshore oil drilling.

The dramatic end of the Cold War in the late 1980s, when eastern European nations abruptly abandoned their Soviet-style communist governments, offered a short-lived regional opportunity for environmental recovery. The eastern bloc nations (East Germany, Poland, Czechoslovakia, Hungary, Rumania, Bulgaria, Yugoslavia, and Albania) had paid no attention to industrial pollution in their 40 or more years of communist rule. Their rivers, soil, and air became astonishingly deadly. In one East German factory town, entire families would retreat regularly down the shafts of salt mines to breathe clean air. Acid rain and pollution from the smokestacks of outmoded industry continued to ravage the countryside and workers' towns. Green political parties and environmental activist groups appeared quickly across eastern Europe to seek Western cleanup assistance. They also sought to establish "middle-ground" industrial societies that integrated more rigorous environmental controls than had historic capitalism. But the large cleanup was soon sacrificed on the altar of rapid acceptance of Western consumerism. Russia, for example, gives highest priority to modernizing its obsolete oil production facilities (15 percent of the world's petroleum) with little regard to the environmental problems that will arise. As Soviet power faded and China focused on internal improvements, American power created the greatest hegemony known to human history. American military intervention to rescue oil-important Kuwait from Iraqi conquest and to secure Saudi Arabia went unchallenged. Dark and acrid smoke from hundreds of Kuwaiti oil field fires set by retreating Iraqi troops clouded thousands of square miles in the Persian Gulf, but fortunately did not affect global climates, such as was feared for the Indian Ocean. In the early 1990s American foot-dragging to control CO_2 industrial emissions dominated the global debate; there was no counterforce. American refusal to join in an international treaty to prohibit exploitation of Antarctic resources effectively killed an important agreement.

June 1992 Earth Summit at Rio:
UN Conference on Environment and Development

Twenty years after the Stockholm Conference, the UN held a second major world environmental conference in June 1992 at Rio de Janeiro, Brazil. The UNCED (UN Conference on Environment and Development) was an extraordinary event, attended by the world's political leaders, delegates from 113 nations, native peoples from North and South America, representatives of 7,900 NGOs, women's organizations, world religious figures, corporate CEOs and officials, 9,000 journalists, as well as a large general public. This time, America's official stance was downright hostile. At first, President George Bush refused to attend, despite the fact that over 100 heads of government at the conference would make it the largest such gathering ever in history. U.S. officials were particularly suspicious that they might be forced by public opinion, here and abroad, into signing proclamations and protocols about climate CO_2 control, biodiversity, endangered species, and forest protection that would be repellent to the probusiness and antienvironment Bush administration. The Bush administration felt that species protection was overwrought, although many biologists judged that the current loss of species was 1,000 times the normal rate. Only on deforestation would the United States exercise leadership. A few weeks before the conference, public opinion and the persistence of Bush's EPA secretary William K. Reilly compelled a reluctant president to attend and make a formal address.

At Rio, the United States was accused of replacing the old Soviet Union as the new international outlaw. It was tarred as the world's environmental naysayer, the globe's "Uncle Filthy," the enemy of world pollution controls, and the president was labeled "Mr. Smoke." It seemed America could do nothing right. The United States was accused of an evasive tropical forest proposal because it had few tropical forests and had sold off its own national forests at a loss. The United States offered $150 million in aid for overseas forest protection, but this was shown up as a puny amount compared to $10 billion that Japan provides each year to help poor countries pay for environmental programs. At Rio, the world's other nations called on the United States, as the single remaining superpower, to exercise energetic leadership through an environmental version of the 1940s Marshall Plan.

There was a good deal of truth to the Bush administration's fears. Preconference planning resulted in Agenda 21, a hotly debated 800-page document with 115 items, which was eventually signed by 134 nations but not the United States. It contained strong language about the growing risk to the entire globe's web of life, called for a second industrial revolution to undo the negative consequences of the first, and demanded immediate corrective actions worldwide to stabilize the environment (described as both a race against time and a 100-year commitment). The major industrial nations were called on to contribute as much as $125 billion a year and provide technical expertise to allow less developed nations to establish a balance between sorely needed economic development and environmental protection. One oft-repeated statement was, "If the West could spend that kind of money to rescue Kuwait [during the Gulf War] it can spend as much to rescue the world." Third World nations spoke of an "ecological debt" owed to less developed countries. The United States, they said, owed money for the excessive environmental damage it already had done. Maneka Gandhi, India's environmental minister, said, "We are the victims. Our responsibility is to ourselves." India's environmental activist Anil Agarwal feared "green imperialism" by which the West would force a dubious ecological order on the Third World, using tools like the prodevelopment World Bank and the environmentally controversial GATT trade negotiations: "No Bangladeshi peasant can influence policies in developed countries, even if global warming—caused largely by Northern emissions—may submerge half their country." Maurice Strong, UNCED's organizer, said, "The trading system is the method by which we all do our business. It can transfer its problems and its costs to the environment." The thinly veined threat from the Third World was that they would create the same heavily polluting and resource-wasteful industries as the West had long enjoyed. Such enterprise would overwhelm the earth's air and water, deplete global resources, and force drastic limitations worldwide. The United States replied that such demands were unacceptable redistribution of wealth and improper interference in its foreign policy. G-77, the loose association of "nonaligned" Third World countries (at first 77 nations, now 128 nations) retorted that they were heading off efforts by the rich nations to manipulate and exploit the nonrich nations. With their large and growing populations, the threat was not an idle one.

The United States was reviled for not sharing its wealth as the world's single biggest economy, and for resisting controls as the world's biggest polluter. The issues were real: The United States produced about one-fourth of the world's carbon dioxide and was the only industrialized nation to oppose limits on emissions. Americans emitted 4 to 5 metric tons of carbon per person per year, compared to 0.2 metric tons for India and 0.6 for China. It was noted that each American had a planetary impact 70 times greater than the average person in Uganda or Laos, 20 times that of India, 10 times that of China, and twice that of Japan, England, France, Sweden, or Australia. The Americans tended to analyze environmental issues differently, to see them as possible entrepreneurial opportunities for the development of clean technologies that could be adopted in the world marketplace. Maurice Strong worried about American intransigence and the need for world leadership in environmental improvement. "We cannot do it without the U.S. If the U.S. cannot lead, it still has an inherent veto over what happens." One Bush administration official worried, "If Rio is judged a failure, no one will be shy about whom to blame." The aggressive and detailed plans of other nations for self-improvement and global assistance, such as Japan's New Earth 21, also isolated America's intransigence. The Japanese saw the agendas of UNCED as issues that might dominate world politics for decades. According to one Japanese industrialist, their New Earth 21 "aims, over the next hundred years, at restoring the earth's functions to its state prior to the industrial revolution." The Japanese also realized they might also get the jump on new worldwide markets in pollution control devices and environmentally benign equipment. In this they were joined by European industrialists, especially from Germany. Particularly outspoken was the influential Swiss businessman, Stephan Schmidheiny, who chaired the Business Council for Sustainable Development (including ALCOA, DuPont, 3M, and Chevron). The council released a report in May 1992 that declared, "Economic growth and environmental protection are inextricably linked. The bottom line is that the human species is living more off the planet's capital and less off the interest. This is bad business." Virtually everyone agreed that economic issues are a dominant theme in environmental protection.

The UNCED conference at Rio was not judged a failure; neither was it an outstanding success, and many laid blame on the United States. Sustainable development was the dominating theme at the conference despite its being damned by industry for slowing economic development and by environmentalists for rationalizing continued environmental damage. At the close of the conference, the Bush administration joined the other participants to sign an agreement on climate change (20 percent fewer carbon emissions by 2000) but only after it had been watered down. The United States was the only major nation not to sign the convention on biological diversity on the grounds that it interfered with profitable genetic engineering opportunities. A statement on forest policy was also widely accepted. Complaints ranged from limited funding for the Rio declaration, lack of practical ways to enforce the Rio agreements, and lack of future targets or timetables. Critics also said that the conference failed to address the inherent contradictions of sustainable development, the threat of global population overload, and specific issues like militarism, fossil fuel pollution, and nuclear wastes.

Response: The "Greening" of Corporate America and the Rise of Industrial Ecology

In the last decade of the twentieth century, only the wildest optimists insisted that the global environment can continue to absorb increased levels of industrial pollution. A growing number of scientists, engineers, business leaders, economists, and policy makers describe present conditions as a risky state of "transitional instability" that has already done near-fatal global harm. No one could ignore the environmental insults forced on society by industrial failures—thousands of local people sickened or killed by the chemical outburst at Bhopal in India, the temporary but profound destruction of the Rhine River ecosystem by the waste spill from the Sandoz company, or the notorious *Exxon Valdez* petroleum coating of an Alaska coastline equal in scale on the East Coast from Long Island to the Carolinas. China's leap forward during the 1980s and 1990s, for example, to become a major industrial power depended largely on the burning of its enormous supplies of highly polluting brown coal that has created health-crisis levels of air pollution. On the other hand, the concepts of limits to growth

PRODUCT MANUFACTURING COST STATEMENT

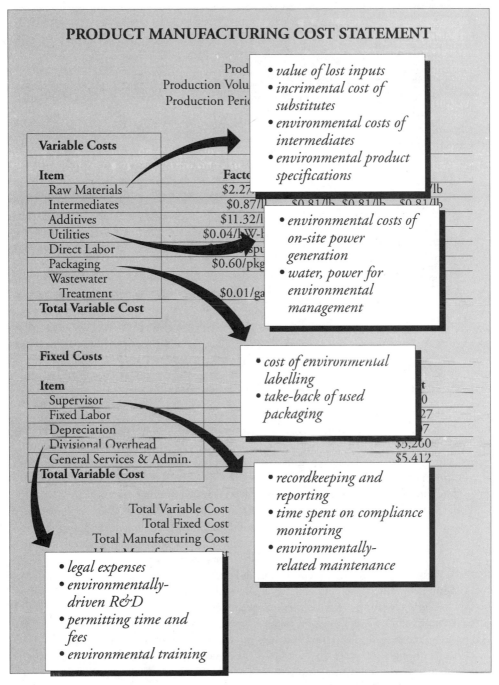

Some Environmental Costs Hidden in a Typical Corporate Cost Statement. New industrial planning—often described as lifecycle engineering or industrial ecology—is beginning to incorporate environmental costs and devise new means to turn a former "waste stream" into a new "product stream."

The Life Cycle of Steel

One answer, first urged in the 1950s, has been to treat a material like steel in its complete "life cycle." According to this view, it is not enough to transform the natural resources such as iron ore, coke, and limestone in steel production, but also to track the fabrication and final disposal of the steel. For example, in manufacturing, a substantial fraction of the steel ends up as scrap, which should be recycled rather than thrown to rust on a dump site. Manufactured steel articles—automobile bodies, refrigerators, stoves, typewriters—have finite lifetimes before they wear out, corrode, break, or simply become obsolete. It usually takes about 20 years between the time the steel is first made and when it is scrapped to be recycled or simply to disintegrate in a landfill. It has been estimated that the amount of steel that absolutely cannot be recovered is about 1 percent of the amount in use. Looking at between 1870 and 1950 alone, it has been estimated that nearly 40 percent was lost either through the production process or disintegration of 2 billion tons of pig iron that were produced in the United States. Policy analyst Harrison Brown said this loss corresponded to about 6 tons of steel per person, and the steel still in use was about 8 tons per person. He estimated that in 1951 alone 25 million tons of new pig iron production (of a total of 75 million tons) was required to replace the losses, most of which were unnecessary. Other critical substances, such as lead, a quarter of which is consumed each year, need life-cycle study, as well as a host of chemicals.

(and pollution) and sustainability have been institutionalized in some government and industrial collaborations, such as the Netherlands. The developed world of Europe, the United States, and Japan has established environmental controls. Industrial growth across Asia, Africa, and Latin America is being rethought.

The numbers of active industrial innovators included familiar chemical producers like DuPont, 3M, and Dow Chemical, energy companies like Amoco and Mobil, manufacturers of consumer goods like Johnson & Johnson, and basic industries such as AT&T and Allied-Signal. They have proposed industrial restructuring through appropriate technologies, new types of internal management, and long-term strategic planning under a variety of approaches that first appeared in print in the late 1980s: industrial ecology, industrial metabolism, life-cycle engineering, re-engineering, parallel engineering, and full-cost accounting. The terminology is very revealing because these approaches employ a near organic, ecological, whole-systems, and holistic viewpoint that has long been advocated in ecological science. Several regulatory strategies also drove businesses to reduce potential environmental impacts: strict limits on physical waste discharge, emissions taxes, product-take-back requirements, pollution control technologies, permitting fees, and the hiring and training of environmental personnel. Industrial ecology offered several important shifts from traditional American business practices. Industry often had the mistaken belief that environmental costs were already well known. Conventional accounting practices, for example, looked at raw materials, manufacturing processes, and product design, but not at environmental costs that are now recognized to account for up to 20 percent of total costs. These costs were distorted or invisible if a business looked only at the purchase of a particular chemical and ignored its storage, the treatment of contaminated rinse water, management of the resulting sludge, getting the necessary permits, monitoring compliance, subsequent reporting, and additional worker training. The new thinking emphasized reduced waste and pollution more than waste management. It required attention to a product's entire life cycle from raw material extraction to product disposal—production, use, recycling, disposal.

The environmental challenge to an industrial society that promotes consumerism is daunting. According to a 1995 update to the Club of Rome, "It is no longer enough simply to consider the environmental performance of a product from cradle to grave, but, even more fundamentally, we will have to ask whether the likely impacts are balanced by the meeting of real needs." It added, "Our industrialized societies will have to re-invent themselves, just as agricultural societies re-invented themselves during the Industrial Revolution." And, "The transition to sustainability is urgent because the deterioration of global life-support systems, that is, the environment, imposes a time limit. We do not have time to dream of creating more living space or more environment, such as colonizing the moon or building cities beneath the sea; we must save the remnants of the only environment we have, and allow time for, and invest in, the regeneration of what we have already damaged."

An Environmental Worldview: The Gaia Hypothesis

As we have seen, environmentalism spawned several fresh ideological challenges to the global hegemony of Western industrialization, technological hubris, resource exploitation, and consumerism. For example, the biologist Garrett Hardin spoke of "the tragedy of the commons" in *Science* in 1968; the Club of Rome espoused "the limits to growth" in 1972; economist E. F. Schumacher proposed "small is beautiful—economics as if people mattered" in 1973, and the concept of "sustainable development" received focused attention in the 1980s by the World Commission on Environment and Development.

The most comprehensive, and most hotly debated, environmental theory was James E. Lovelock's "Gaia" hypothesis. In his 1979 book *Gaia, a New Look at Life on Earth*, Lovelock wrote that *Gaia*—the Greek name for the earth as goddess—was shorthand for the concept that "the physical and chemical condition of the surface of the Earth, of the atmosphere, and of the oceans has been and is actively made fit and comfortable by the presence of life itself." Lovelock is a widely published atmospheric scientist, member of the Royal Society, consultant to NASA's first lunar survey and to California's Jet Propulsion Laboratory, and inventor of the electron capture detector that first demonstrated chlorofluorocarbons (CFCs) were accumulating in the atmosphere. (Lovelock's detector had already provided hard data on DDT accumulation for Rachel Carson's *Silent Spring*.) For almost three decades, he has worked independently—a "rogue researcher"—out of his own laboratory in southern England. Lovelock's description of the life-based earth system stood in sharp contrast to conventional wisdom of Western science and industrial society that life itself was in a continuous one-way adaptive response to the relatively immutable material world. Instead, Lovelock used the new research tools of ecological science, systems analysis, Norbert Weiner's cybernetics (self-regulating systems), and more recently, Ilya Prigogyne's chaos-to-order theory, to identify life on Earth (all living things, not just humans) as an active force that shapes and changes the material world in order to make the planet a better place for itself. A friendly review in *Co-Evolution Quarterly* called the Gaia hypothesis "one of the epochal insights of the 20th century." A more cautious review in *Scientific American* described Gaia as "a daring hypothesis, a kind of geochemical myth for our time." Lovelock thought Gaia might be damned from church pulpits as Darwin's theory of evolution had been a century earlier, but instead he was mostly vilified by fellow scientists and largely ignored by the two major English-language science journals, *Science* in the United States and *Nature* in the United Kingdom. Even freewheeling and respected scientists like Nobel laureate George Wald, biologist Stephen Jay Gould, and cosmologist Carl Sagan disdained a living earth theory. Wald said, "Gaia is a buzzword for bringing in the customers. I teach my students that the stars are alive. Planets are dead ashes, hangers-on of the sun." Gould found Gaia a captivating notion, but scientifically unproven and dead wrong. Sagan saw not enough science and too much religious appeal in the Earth as a life force. Lovelock responded that "Gaia may turn out to be the first religion to have a testable scientific theory embedded within it." When Gaia acquired nonscientific, pantheistic, and spiritual overtones—even as a secular alternative to humanism—it did not help its scientific credibility.

Lovelock insisted that "the Earth's living matter, air, oceans, and land surface form a complex system which can be seen as a single organism." He coined the word *geophysiology* to explain the process. He continued, "Gaia sees a tightly coupled process where the evolution of life and the evolution of the rocks, oceans, and atmosphere are so tightly joined together that they are really one single process." Living things do not simply evolve to suit a changing environment; they continuously interact with their inorganic surroundings in ways that specifically keep the planet a fit place for life. Lovelock asked, "If you were sitting on Mars, how could you tell that there was life on Earth? What would give it away?" The answer, he said, was the utterly bizarre earth atmosphere, which did not fit physical and chemical expectations. The atmospheres of both Mars and Venus, for example, had settled into a textbook chemical equilibrium, in which everything that can react has formed stable compounds, in both cases at least 95 percent carbon dioxide. On early earth, CO_2 had ranged between an infinitesimal 0.028 percent to 0.034 percent. Unlike Mars or Venus, the mature earth's atmosphere continues in constant ferment between oxidizing gases such as oxygen and carbon dioxide, neutral gases such as nitrogen and carbon monoxide, and reducing gases such as hydrogen, methane, and ammonia. "Quite anomalous. Ours is a really strange planet." Lynn Margulis entered the picture by pinpointing the influence of the basic building blocks of life—microbes, particularly bacteria—on the life-material world linkage. She is a microbiologist at the University of Massachusetts and member of the National Academy of Sciences. "Without the few pounds of anerobic bacteria in each of our guts," she said, "no one would ever digest food, and without the nitrogen-fixing bacteria in the soil, no food would ever grow in the first place." She focused on dynamic processes such as fermentation, photosynthesis, and respiration. Here she found an answer to the question, why is there so much free oxygen floating around—approximately 21 percent of the air—when it is a volatile gas that should be combining with methane or carbon? At the end of the proterozoic era 2.5 billion years ago, oxygen soared from virtually nothing to 21 percent through the global spread of microbial communities. Lovelock added, "It must take a lot of work to keep up such a wild disequilibrium." He concluded that the work came from another highly interactive phenomenon on earth—life. Life is very opportunistic. The most recent geological wrinkle is human intervention—"the deadly convulsive impact of man." Could the Gaian mechanism adjust to the high-level challenge of industrialization and population growth? On the other hand, says Gaia's friendly journalist Lawrence E. Joseph, the Gaian hypothesis means that humanity's power is trifling when compared to the "unfathomable resiliency" of life on earth. Humans' "ability to vandalize is not at all the same as the ability to control or conquer." Life cannot be stopped. Lovelock was so optimistic that he insisted, against all evidence, that the human-made threats of CFCs and ozone depletion would be corrected by natural processes. He later regretted this assertion.

Whatever the scientific opinion about the Gaian hypothesis, it satisfied a long-standing public need. Back in 1971 historian of religion in America Sidney Mead wrote, "We can find a stable identity only through an imaginative grasp that we are one with all of life in time and space, and, recognizing that there is no marked boundary between what we call organic or inorganic, that human life *is* the planet becoming conscious of itself." The work of Lovelock and Margulis has been advocated, with a rigorous constructive criticism, by the outspoken climate scientist Steven Schneider, formerly at the National Center for Atmospheric Research (NCAR) in Boulder, Colorado, and currently at Stanford University. Schneider also warned, "Thus far, the case for Gaia is way overstated, and now Lovelock and Margulis have to back it all up." All three scientists were considered mavericks for their cross-disciplinary research, and even possibly scientifically irresponsible for their interest in the Gaia hypothesis.

Environmentalism Enters the Mainstream

Beginning in the 1970s big business and big government in the United States began to find competition from, dare we say, "big environmentalism." Big environmentalism first attained critical mass when the public, the media, government, and industry simultaneously began to pay attention to Carson's 1962 attack on DDT. By 1969–70 big environmentalism began to compete, with the passage of the National Environmental Protection Act (NEPA), with big business, big military, and big government. NEPA was the centerpiece of a blitzkrieg of legislation that followed, dedicated to protecting air, water, wetlands, wilderness, endangered species, and a myriad of other natural phenomena, as well as setting limits on industrial pollution and waste. The role of the government shifted, like an earthquake, from economic developer to environmental watchdog and regulator. Today big environmentalism touches every part of American life, from the workplace and school to home and recreation. For Superfund cleanups alone, every American will pay $2,000. Big environmentalism has reshaped the automobile industry with higher gasoline mileage goals, agriculture with lower chemical use, industry with health, pollution, and waste controls, and influenced most Americans to reduce waste and enter recycling programs. The power of big environmentalism did not come from government alone. Acting in the name of environmental protection, public interest groups (NGOs) proliferated in the 1980s and became more confrontational. These private organizations went after industry with the tenacity of a pit bull, and they mastered legal tactics and regulatory leverage. They brought the American nuclear industry to its knees. A major national corporation, Johns-Manville, decided to file for bankruptcy rather than go through the ordeal of decades of lawsuits from thousands of citizens affected by widespread asbestos use in schools, offices, and homes. Exxon acquired a permanent black name, not to mention decades of costs running into billions of dollars, because of the Alaska *Exxon Valdez* oil spill. A company like Dow Chemical, caught in the controversy over Agent Orange (the chemical defoliant widely used during the Vietnam War), has its innovative responses to ozone depletion go unnoticed.

This mainstreaming meant that environmental issues such as wilderness preservation, outdoor recreation, public health, and ecological balance became connected to nonenvironmental concerns such as distributive justice for underrepresented groups and minorities. Urban ghettos or rural black-belt communities had long been targeted for noxious facilities: hazardous waste landfills, incinerators, paper mills, and garbage dumps. A 1983 General Accounting Office study showed a strong relationship between the locations of off-site hazardous waste landfills and the racial and socioeconomic status of surrounding communities. Another study in 1987 concluded, "Race was the most potent variable in predicting the location of uncontrolled (abandoned) and commercial toxic waste sites in the United States." Specific cases cited were Houston and Dallas in Texas, the town of Institute in West Virginia and Emelle in Alabama, the latter the largest toxic waste dump in the United States. Blacks were discovered to have higher blood levels of carbon monoxide and pesticides. Black children had a rate of lead poisoning six times that of white children, leading to charges of "environmental racism." Minority communities were asking whether they bore environmental costs to spare the larger community. There were complaints that the South was an environmental dumping ground.

Unlike other historic forms of institutional giantism, big environmentalism is not necessarily a bad outcome because environmental problems are real, large scale, and universal, affecting all humanity in personal ways and threatening a forbidding future if the problems are uncorrected. Environmental problems cross political and economic boundaries, the classic cases being the Chernyobl nuclear accident, the ozone hole, climate warming, and above all, uncontrolled population growth. It is tempting to call the environmental revolution a turning point in history. Fifty years of the Cold War is over. Instead of East versus West, as the Rio Conference showed, the debate centers now on North versus South, developed countries versus the developing. Environmental debates and actions could replace the Cold War as the organizing principle in public affairs. Yet environmentalism is far from achieving important strategic goals: stabilizing world population, installing environmentally appropriate technologies, guaranteeing that economic accounting includes environmental consequences, fostering enforceable international agreements, focusing global education on environmentalism, and promoting social and political conditions that are conducive to the emergence of sustainable societies.

A Final Word

Environmentalism in America cannot be seen in isolation. It is in continuous feedback with other forces in American history and culture. We have seen how it went through numerous transformations, from the time when Europeans first arrived to wonder at a luxuriant and teeming wilderness and transform it into the world's most envied farmland. They drove off and exterminated the alternative viewpoints based on 10,000 years of Native American experience. An Enlightenment gridiron geometry, with rationality as its guide, transformed two-thirds of the domesticated landscape (west of the Pennsylvania line, north of the Ohio River, and everything west of the Mississippi River until the Spanish landscape of the Southwest) into a mathematical grid. Alternatively, the romantic Transcendentalists looked at the same landscape and found God under every rock and in the eyes of raccoons, and told of visionary spiritual renewal in wild places. Capitalism found its own path by putting dollar value on rich rocky beds of iron ore, coal, limestone, copper ore, bauxite, oil, natural gas, and other basic materials for the engines of industry. The Progressives were dedicated to the most efficient and utilitarian consumption of nature's bounty, even of the forests and national parks. The counterculture of the 1960s turned the world upside down toward a neoromantic back-to-the-land simplicity. Rachel Carson's *Silent Spring* helped create a popular public climate that insisted on government intervention for environmental protection and pollution cleanup, a viewpoint that has continued into the 1990s.

The perspective of the French *Annales* historian Fernand Braudel is particularly useful to environmental historians. Braudel argues it is long-term forces—geographical or economic directions that take as long as a century or a millennium to take shape—that ultimately dominate human well-being and the irreversible arrow of time called history. Presidential and congressional terms come and go, but the interaction between a people and their geography is an enduring fact. The difference in American history, with the dizzying speed of its development, is that the pace of change has been accelerated. On the North American continent, Braudel's millennia may have become decades. Sociologist Riley Dunlap identified distinctive eras of modern environmentalism:

1.   The Progressive era was represented by the philosophy of wise management of natural resources for continued human use.
2.   The New Deal emphasized the mitigation of resource problems—flood control and soil conservation—as well as the development of resources—energy through the TVA—to stimulate economic recovery.
3.   The 1950s focused on preservation of areas of natural beauty and wilderness for public enjoyment, led by the Sierra Club, including debates over the Grand Canyon and Echo Park in Dinosaur National Monument.
4.   By the 1960s these older issues coalesced and were combined into environmental concerns with a new scientific sophistication: the impact of new technologies, delayed complex and difficult-to-detect effects, and consequences for human health and well-being as well as for the natural environment.

To Dunlap's list, we can add:

5.   The oil crisis of 1973.
6.   The Reagan-Bush backsliding years.
7.   Environmental revival by 1990 when toxic wastes, beach contamination, the *Exxon Valdez* oil spill, ozone destruction, and global warming became public issues.
8.   The return to political power of a conservative backlash in the Congress of 1994.

Each generation of Americans creates its own environmental prison that shapes how we perceive the world around us. The great environmental essayist Loren Eiseley tells of a stroll through some woods while his dog Beau raced around in excitement: "I looked on, interested and sympathetic, but aware that the big black animal lived in a smell prison as I, in my way, lived in a sight prison." No generation can be said to have done a better job at perception than any other generation; each generation simply had its own toolbox by which to pry open the American environment in its own way.

The United States still persists as nature's nation. There is more than a touch of environmental determinism in American history. No one would repudiate the consumption of a national treasury of soil, water, and underground minerals to serve the health and safety and well-being of a prosperous society. For many Americans, the technological fix is still on. They believe they can depend on a seemingly infinite technological creativity that reliably solves environmental and human problems. The modern social critic Victor Ferkiss suggested that technology is now so absolute worldwide that "running and hiding become increasingly difficult." Once it was said that the environment was everlasting while humanity was changeable. Our technological hubris has made the environment into something changeable as well. Eiseley emphasized "the deepening shell of technology" that is a barrier between humanity and the environment. We have lost, he argued, a sense of a "wider nature" to which we still inevitably belong. There is still some truth to the notion that humanity is a chip in the stream of history from which we cannot escape. Technological agility is deceptive when it offers the notion that humans can be aloof from several billion years of biological experience. Nature gives humanity instructions; we choose to regard or disregard them. Or more accurately, we are still trying to learn how to read nature's instructions. And we are still trying to teach ourselves that it is essential not to disregard them. The difference today, compared to 200 years ago, and compared to humanity's 3-million-year past, is that the initiative now lies with humanity. Loren Eiseley reminded us that human technology can only plagiarize nature, never replace it. Our task, and it has been the task of this book, is to avoid obtuseness and indifference toward the only environment we will ever have.

We need to recognize some environmental successes that are promising. In public health we can point to the virtual elimination of a lead-filled atmosphere as Americans adopted lead-free gasoline for automobiles. There are positive results generally from the adoption of clean air and water acts. Fishing has returned to Ohio's Cuyahoga River and the Hudson River. Toxic landfills are being identified and the cleanup has begun. More realistic pictures of the economic costs, and benefits, of a cleaner and sustainable environment are now far better integrated into the balance sheets of American industry. Manufacturers have begun the process of tracking raw materials and chemical compounds through their entire life cycles. Sustainable agriculture is no longer an invisible agenda. It has become far more difficult for the American government to sidestep global environmental expectations. Household recycling has become a lifetime crusade for many Americans. Concepts like the protection of entire ecosystems—endangered species in endangered landscapes—have captured the American imagination. Above all, the American public has become much more scientifically sophisticated in its constant support of environmental protection. Long ago, when Europeans first invaded the future United States, they looked upon the landscape as a raw material to be tamed and consumed. Today many Americans, descendants of those Europeans, look upon their natural surroundings as a treasure.

For Further Reading

There is no suitable or comprehensive global environmental history, although the worldwide historical implications were provocatively set out in 1991 by Clive Ponting's *A Green History of the World: The Environment and the Collapse of Great Civilizations,* and in 1993 by I.G. Simmon's *Environmental History: New Perspectives on the Past.* The current status of global environmental problems such as population, land, water, biota, tropical regions, and theoretical and scientific debates are covered in the invaluable 1990 book, *The Earth as Transformed by Human Action: Global and Regional Changes in the Biosphere over the Past 300 Years,* edited by a team of researchers led by B.L. Turner, II, which in turn is an major update of the classic 1956 study edited by William L. Thomas, Jr., *Man's Role in Changing the Face of the Earth. Annual State of the World* reports come from Lester Brown's Worldwatch Institute, as well as its new annual series *Vital Signs: The Trends That Are Shaping Our Future.* More comprehensive, and filled with useful data, are the semiannual reviews from the World Resources Institute (WRI). The international environmental scene and its implications since World War II, and particularly since 1972, is critically renewed by John McCormick in *Reclaiming Paradise: The Global Environmental Movement* (1989). Global decision making is best explored by Lynton Keith Caldwell in *International Environmental Policy* (2nd ed., 1990); the environmental implications of growth, wealth, and quality of life are explored in a 1995 report to the Club of Rome, *Taking Nature into Account* (1995), edited by Wouter Van Dieren. Readers should also find their way to the original sources, notably the original Club of Rome report, Donella H. Meadows et al., *The Limits to Growth* (1972), and the useful update, Donella H. Meadows et al., *Beyond the Limits: Confronting Global Collapse and Envisioning a Sustainable Future* (1992). See also Garrett Hardin's classic essay, "The Tragedy of the Commons," *Science* 162 (December 13, 1968): 1243–1248. The most effective critiques of the limits to growth come from Herman Kahn et al., *The Next 200 Years* (1976) and Julian L. Simon and Herman Kahn, *The Resourceful Earth* (1984). For the original concept of sustainable development, see the quasi-official World Commission on Environment and Development, *Our Common Future* (1987), also called the Bruntland Report. The tentative policies of the Clinton administration have been set out in Al Gore, *Earth in the Balance* (1992), and *Technology for a Sustainable Future* (1993), a report by the President's Council on Sustainable Development. For the 1992 Rio Conference on Environment and Development, see the querulous and vivid report, Adam Rogers, *The Earth Summit: A Planetary Reckoning* (1993), the controversial draft statements made by the UN in 1992, *Agenda 21, Rio Declaration, Forest Principles,* and the final declaration published in 1992 as *Earth Summit '92: The United Nations Conference on Environment and Development.* The new concept of industry-centered sustainability has developed its own literature. See especially Robert U. Ayres and Udo E. Simonis, *Industrial Metabolism: Restructuring for Sustainable Development* (1994), and Daryl Ditz et al., *Green Ledgers: Case Studies in Corporate Environmental Accounting* (1995). Finally, the controversial Gaia hypothesis by James Lovelock can be assessed by digging into two of his books, *The Ages of Gaia* (1988) and *Gaia: A New Look at Life on Earth* (1979); see also Lawrence E. Joseph, *Gaia, the Growth of an Idea* (1990).

INDEX

Abbey, Edward, 421, 426
Aberdeen, Lord, 165
Aboriginal California, 22
acceptable risk, 440
acute risk, 440
Adams, Ansel, 421
Adams, Henry, 57–58, 117, 119, 172
Adams, John, 137
Addams, Jane, 270, 273, 277
administrative law, 451–454
Administrative Procedure Act of 1946, 452
Agarwal, Anil, 483
Agassiz, Louis, 192–193
Agee, James, 247
Agent Orange, 436, 490
Age of Wood, 141, 144
agriculture
    in the Appalachians, 348
    challenges of early American, 57–61
    of colonial Virginia, 78–79
    Department of Agriculture and, 232
    evidence of early Native American, 19–22
    farm industrialization and, 237–239
    frontier abundance of, 79–80
    Hispanic culture and, 314
    industrialization and, 151
    Jefferson/Hamilton debate and, 120–121
    lack of water and western, 309–310
    maps of colonial, 74
    natural resources of American, 17
    out of frontier wilderness, 61–69
    of Pennsylvania colony, 75–76
    prosperity and production of, 138–140
    railroad transportation and, 182–183
    of southern English colonies, 76–77
    tobacco and corn, 68–69
    U.S. tradition of, 55–57
    See also farming; land; water networks
Alaska, 394–396
Alaska Coalition, 395
Alaska National Interest Lands Conservation Act of
    1980, 395
Alaska Native Claims Settlement Act (ANCSA), 395
Albanese, Cathy, 195, 196, 205

Albany Plan of Union, 95
alcohol consumption, 140
Alexander, Sir William, 71
Allen, Ethan, 88
Allied Chemical Corporation, 445–446
Allyn, Henry, 168
Amana Community, 206
Ambler Realty Company v. Village of Euclid, Ohio, 252
American Association for the Advancement of Science
    (AAAS), 417
American Association for Labor Legislation, 278
American Chemical Society, 448
American cities
    built across the U.S., 243–244
    as built environment, 244
    infrastructure flaws of, 266–267
    infrastructure system of, 244–245
    mobility and, 253–255
    mobility between suburbs and, 255–260
    pollution/waste of, 270–272
    preindustrial infrastructures of, 123–125
    private land-ownership in, 125–126
    public parks of, 279–281, 374
    public works/utilities for, 250–251
    railroad transportation and, 251, 253
    restrictive zoning in, 252
    Russell Sage Foundation report on one, 277–284
    safety, convenience, and health in, 126–128
    toxic chemical dumping and, 296–301
    urban decay and failed renewal of, 264–266
    See also United States
American Civic Association, 278
American continent
    biological exchange of Old World to, 46–47
    confusing climate of, 18–19
    early people of, 18–25
    European discovery of, 10–11
    European exploration of, 14–15, 25–35
    European impact on, 48–49
    European invention of, 11–13
    great forests of, 15–16
    natural agricultural resources of, 17
    pre-European environment of, 13–14
    pre-European wildlife of, 16–17

American continent *(continued)*
  reality behind myths of, 13–17
  vulnerability to European conquest, 45–46
  See also American frontier; United States
American discovery debate (18th century), 51–54
American Economic Association, 278
"American Environmental History:" (White), 7
"American Environmental History" (Jamieson), 7
American frontier
  animal management in, 66–68
  constructing farmland out of, 61–65
  development of, 62–63
  domestic lifestyle in, 140–141
  early land privatization of, 71–73
  geography and European spread in, 73–79
  isolation of, 59
  National Parks to preserve last of, 371–374
  natural wonders of, 375
  quitrent system of, 72
  settlement of Appalachian, 347–348
  survey of, 102–105
  tobacco and corn agriculture in, 68–69
  utopian communities of the, 205–209
  See also American continent; land speculation;
    United States
American Philosophical Society, 190
"The American Scholar" (Emerson), 195
American Sociological Society, 278
"American System" (Clay), 319
American transcendentalism, 193–197
Amoco Cadiz oil spill, 471
Anaconda Copper Mining Company, 297
Anaconda mine, 225
Anasazi people, 23, 311
Anderson, "Andy," 294
animal management, 66–68
Annales (Braudel), 491
antienvironmentalist movement, 429–431
Antiquities Act of 1906, 379, 381
Anzaldúa, Gloria, 185
Appalachian Development Corporation, 354
Appalachian forest, 348–349
Appalachian mining industry, 349–353
Appalachian Mountain Club, 388
Appalachian Mountains, 134–135
Appalachian region
  demolition of, 346–355
  environmental challenges of, 345–346
  forest of, 14, 348–349
  reclamation in, 338–342
Appalachian Regional Commission, 354
Appalachian Trail, 401
Arab-American Oil Company (ARAMCO), 470
The Arcadian or Pastoral State (Cole), 203
ARCO, 297–298

Arctic National Wildlife Range, 395
Armour, Philip D., 291
Arnold, Matthew, 372
Arnold, Ron, 431
asbestos, 440, 442–443, 444–445, 489
asbestosis, 442
Ashby, Daniel, 111
Ashley, William Henry, 159
Aspinall, Wayne, 333
Astor, John Jacob, 159, 165
Aub, Joseph, 287
Audubon, John James, 192, 372, 419
Audubon Society, 389, 395, 419
automobile emissions, 456–457
available-technology standards, 440

Babbitt, Bruce, 383
Baca, George, 420
"Back to Nature? Never! Forward to the Machine!"
    (Slossen), 236
Bacon, Francis, 10
Ballinger, Richard A., 389
balloon frame house, 144
Baltimore, 124, 125
Bancroft, Herbert Howe, 157
Bari, Judi, 428
Baritz, Loren, 228–229
BART (Bay Area Rapid Transit System), 264, 473
Bartlett, Richard A., 159, 297
Barton, Benjamin Smith, 33
Bartram, John, 189
Bartram, William, 78, 189–190
Batteau, Allen, 346, 354
Bazelon, David T., 240
Beard, Charles, 96
beaver fur trade, 32–33, 158–159, 161, 188–189
Bellamy, Edward, 209, 260
Benedict, Ruth, 184
Benson, Ezra Taft, 414
Bentham, Jeremy, 467
Benton, Thomas Hart, 165, 178
Berkeley, Sir William, 71
Bessemer blow, 222
Bethlehem Steel Corporation, 299
Beyond the Limits (Club of Rome/MIT team), 478
Bierstadt, Albert, 198, 376, 400
big environmentalism, 489–490
"the big technological letdown," 435–436
Big Thompson Project (Colorado), 322
Billington, Ray, 97
Bill of Rights (1798), 116
Bingham Copper mine, 225
biocentric farming, 365–366

biocentrism, 478
Biosphere Conference of 1968 (Paris), 468
Bird, Elizabeth Ann R., 6
Birkbeck, Morris, 134
black slavery population, 77
Black Swamp, 135
Blackwelder, Brent, 340–341
Blanchard, Thomas, 143
Blizzard of 1888, 256
Board of Water Commissioners (California), 325
Bohlen, Jim, 428
Boles, Chester, 247
Bonus Bill of 1817, 131
Bookchin, Murray, 301, 405
Boone, Daniel, 136
Boone, Joel T., 353
"Boone Report" (1947), 353
Boorstin, Daniel, 265
Borchert, John, 361
Boston, 124, 126, 127, 128
Boston Manufacturing Company, 147
Boulder (Hoover) Dam, 322, 324, 334–335
Bowler, Peter J., 405, 411
Bowman, Isaiah, 266
Braudel, Fernand, 149, 491
Bretton Woods Conference (1944), 467
Bridger, Jim, 159, 378
British North America, 86
    See also American continent
Brodsky, Joseph, 1–2
Brookhaven National Laboratory, 423
Brooks Range, 394, 395
Brower, David R., 391, 392, 401, 414, 420, 421
Brown, Capability, 201
Browner, Carol, 450
Brown, Harrison, 486
Brown, Richard D., 119
Browns Ferry nuclear power plant, 339, 474
Brundtland Commission, 478
Buck, Susan, 460
Buffalo Bill Dam, 315
Buffalo Commons, 366
buffalo extermination, 38–39
Buffon, Comte de (Georges-Louis Leclerc), 52, 54, 188–189
built environment
    cities as, 244–245
    engineering profession and, 248–249
Bureau of Land Management (BLM), 390, 392, 420, 430, 446
Bureau of Public Roads, 261
Bureau of Reclamation (Reclamation Service)
    Central Valley Project and, 328–329
    Colombia Basin Project and, 334–335
    creation of, 320–322

Echo Park dam of, 324, 390–391, 420, 421
    exclusion of wilderness protection by, 379
    on Palmetto Bend Project, 453
    Reclamation Act of 1902 and, 319–320
    wilderness movement and, 391, 392, 393–394
Burford, Robert, 449
Burke, Edmund, 201
Burnaby, Andrew, 65
Burnham, John, 238
Burnt-Over District (New York), 206, 208, 209
Burr, Aaron, 163
Burroughs, John, 388, 407
Burton, William, 227
Bush, George, 450, 482
Business Council for Sustainable Development report (1992), 484
Butcher, Devereaux, 420
Butte Miner newspaper, 297
Butte, Montana case study, 296–298
Butterfield Overland Mail, 173

Cabet, Etienne, 207
Cabot, John, 71
Caldwell, Lynton, 447
California
    Aboriginal, 22
    Central Valley Project of, 322, 328–329
    end of hydraulic empires of, 330
    gold rush of, 166–167, 314
    State Water Project of, 329–330
    water needs of, 324–325
    water wars of, 325–328
California geological survey (1860s), 164–165
California's gold rush, 166–167
California water projects, 324, 326
Callender, James T., 112
Callicott, Baird, 398
Campaign Against Pollution (CAP), 455
canal transportation, 131–132
cancer fears, 441–443
Candide (Voltaire), 207
Cape Cod (Thoreau), 196
Carey Act of 1894, 310, 317
Carlyle, Thomas, 195, 206, 207, 272–273
Carnegie, Andrew, 220, 221, 230, 235, 273
Carnegie Steel works, 220, 231, 276, 283
Carson, Rachel, 6, 391, 413–415, 423, 432, 442, 469, 474, 487, 491
Carter, Jimmy, 323, 381, 395, 448, 477
Cartier, Jacques, 16–17, 28–29
Casey, Jim, 344
Cassidy, Sean D., 428
Cass, Lewis, 225
Caterpillar Tractor Corporation, 352

Catlin, George, 370–371
cattle industry, 66–67
Caudill, Harry, 339, 346, 347, 348, 352, 354, 355
Cavelier, René-Robert, Sieur de La Salle, 30
Cedar Bog Lake food cycle, 409–410
Center for the Defense of Free Enterprise (CDFE), 430–431
Centers for Disease Control (CDC), 446
Central Arizona Project (CAP), 324, 336–338, 393, 394
Central Pacific Railroad, 179–183
Central Park (New York City), 374
Central Valley Project (California), 322, 328–329
certainty of harm, 440
Chadwick, Edwin, 128
Challenger disaster, 212, 323
Champlain, Samuel de, 17, 29
Chandler, Harry, 327
Channing, William E., 206
chaos-to-order theory (Prigogyne), 488
Charles I (England), 71
Charles II (England), 71
Charles River Bridge case (1837), 232
Charlevoix, Pierre François Xavier de, 30
Chastellux, Marquis de, 52–53, 58, 65, 190
Chavez, Cesar, 330
chemical industry, 436
chemical life cycle, 437
chemical pesticides, 413–415, 436, 445–446, 480
    See also DDT
Cherney, Darryl, 428
Chernobyl nuclear accident, 474, 490
Cherokee Nation, 40, 44
Cherokee "Trail of Tears," 40
Chicago
    fire/rebuilding of, 127
    meat industry of, 290–295
    railroad system and, 179, 254–255
    Sanitary District system of, 285, 307
Chicago Union Stock Yards, 291–293, 294
Chicago World's Fairs (1893 and 1933), 212, 217, 270
Chief Joseph, 22
China, 484
chlorofluorocarbons (CFCs), 429, 481, 487, 489
Choice 32, 7
chronic risk, 440
Chudacoff, Howard P., 265, 267–268
Church, Frederick, 400
cities. *See* American cities
Citizen Oversight Councils, 425
Citizen's Clearinghouse for Hazardous Waste (CCHW), 424–425
Citizens Committee to End Lead Poisoning (CCELP), 439

city parks, 279–281, 374
Civic Club (Pittsburgh), 279
"Civil Disobedience" (Thoreau), 196
Civilized Tribes of the Southeast, 40
Civil Works Administration (CWA), 264
claims clubs, 110
Clark, Andrew H., 356, 367
Clark, George Rogers, 87
Clark, Victor S., 176
Clark, William Andrews, 17, 297
Claude, George, 201
Claude glass, 201
Clawson, Marion, 390
Clay, Henry, 131, 146, 319
Clean Air Act of 1970
    administrative process through, 425
    environmental politics and, 446, 447, 449–451
    on evaluating EISs, 452
    on leaded gasoline, 439
    passage of, 422, 424, 438, 443
    standards/procedures of, 454–457
Clean Water Act of 1970, 424, 425, 438, 443, 444, 447, 449, 450–451, 457–458
Clements, Frederic, 407–408, 409, 411
climate
    confusing state of American, 18–19
    early Native farming and, 18–22
    environmental challenge of High Plains, 355–356
    High Plains miracle (1878–1887), 358–359
    irrigation for High Plains, 361–366
    natural history and, 191
    Shay's rebellion and, 89
Clinton, Bill, 450, 451
Clinton, De Witt, 205
Club of Rome, 474–475, 477–478, 479, 487
CO_2 emissions, 481, 482
coal auger, 351
Cobb, John, 480
Cochrane, Willard W., 364–365
Cody, William F. "Buffalo Bill," 315
Cody, Wyoming, 315
Coe, Ernest F., 384
Co-Evolution Quarterly, 488
coffee consumption, 140
Cold War, 481–482, 490
Coleridge, Samuel Taylor, 189, 195
Cole, Thomas, 198–199, 202–204, 373
Colliers magazine, 212
colonialism, 25–27
Colorado Basin Project, 333–336
Colorado River, 305, 322, 324, 331–333
Colorado River Compact, 332–333
Colorado River Company, 337
Colorado River Storage Project, 390–391
Colorado River Storage Project Act of 1956, 333

Colter, John, 378
Columbian Exposition (1893), 156, 203, 209
Columbia River, 305
Columbia River Basin Project, 332–333
Columbus, Christopher, 5, 12
Commoner, Barry, 405, 414
common law, 443
Community Development Act of 1974, 266
Comprehensive Environmental Response, Compensation, and Liability Act (CERCLA), 300, 460–461
Condorcet, Marquis de (Marie-Jean-Antoine-Nicholas de Caritat), 53
Confederation Congress, 101–102
Congressional Land Act of 1796, 106
Connecticut, 88–89, 107
The Conquest of Arid America (Smythe), 317
Conrad, Joseph, 51
conservation, 305–306, 472–473
Conservation Foundation, 422–423
The Conservation of Natural Resources in the United State (Van Hise), 305
Constitutional Convention, 94–96, 105, 231
The Consummation of Empire (Cole), 203
Continental Congress, 85
Continental Divide, 168
Conwell, Russell, 273
Cook, Captain, 207
Cooke, Jay, 378
Cook, Kenneth A., 365
Coolidge, Calvin, 216, 379
cooperative irrigation communities, 314–316
Cooper, James Fenimore, 79, 194, 372
Cooper, W. S., 408
Corliss, George H., 211
corn agriculture, 68–69
corporate structure, 229–234
"Corporation Pudding," 128
Corps of Volunteers for Northwestern Discovery, 161–162
Costle, Douglas M., 448, 449
Cosway, Maria, 201
Coulter, John, 159
Council on Environmental Quality (CEQ), 447, 452
The Course of Empire (Cole), 203
Cowles Bog, 299, 408
Cowles, Henry, 299, 408
Coxe, Tench, 121, 137
craft technology, 145
Crèvecoeur, Hector St. John de, 61, 133, 145, 190, 191, 204
Cronon, William, 7, 65, 70, 179, 184–185, 190, 221, 244, 294–295
Crosby, Albert, 67–68
Crosby, Alfred, 11, 43, 45, 46

Crowe, Frank, 334
Crowell, F. Elisabeth, 269, 270
Cumberland Gap, 136, 165
Cumberland Road, 135–136
Curry Company, 384
Curtis, John T., 356
Custer, George Armstrong, 167
Cutler, Rev. Manasseh, 97

D-9 bulldozer, 352
Daly, Herman, 479, 479–480
Daly, Marcus, 297
Dana, Charles A., 206
Daniel Boone's Wilderness Road, 60
Danly, Susan, 211
Dartmouth College v. Woodward, 232
Darwin, Charles, 46, 193, 406
Davis, Arthur Powell, 334
DDT, 413, 414, 415, 423, 436, 469, 477, 480
Death Valley, 175
The Decline of the West (Spenger), 209
deep ecology, 402
Deere, John, 224, 359
deforestation
    of Appalachian, 348–349
    farming and, 61–65
    Marsh's warnings on, 372–373
    See also forest
Delaney Clause, 441
Democracy in America (Tocqueville), 375
democracy of consumption, 237
Department of Agriculture, 232
de Pauw, Abbé, 52
Desert Land Act of 1877, 105, 310, 358
Desolation (Cole), 203
De Soto, Hernando, 17, 27–28
Destruction (Cole), 203
Devall, William, 426
DeVoto, Bernard, 391, 405
Dial magazine, 195
Dickens, Charles, 199, 201
Didion, Joan, 324
Dilg, Will H., 419
Dingell, John, 414
Dinosaur National Monument, 324
Division of the Biological Survey, 409
Division of Economic Ornithology and Mammology, 409
Dodge, Grenville M., 176
domestic lifestyle, 140–141
Dominy, Floyd, 322
Donora accident (1948), 454
Douglas, Marjorie Stoneman, 384
Douglas, William O., 405, 434

Dow Chemical, 490
Drake, E. L., 226
Drake, Sir Francis, 31
drinking water supply, 127–128
Driver, Harold, 20, 45
Drouillard, George, 159
Dubos, René, 405
Duggan, Stephen, 424
"dumbbell" tenement apartment, 281
Dunlap, Riley, 491
Dupuy, Gabriel, 268
Durand, Asher Brown, 198
Dust Bowl, 239, 359–361
"duty of water" ethics, 317
Duvall, William, 402
Dwight, Timothy, 399

Earl of Dunraven, 399
Earth in the Balance (Gore), 450
Earth Day 1970, 425, 432–433, 469
Earth First!, 6, 392, 402, 418, 426, 427–428, 431
Earth Island Institute, 421, 426
Earth (photographed from space), 466
"Earthrise" (photograph), 466
Earth Summit at Rio (1992), 429, 482–484, 490
Eastham, E. L., 154
Eaton, Fred, 327
Eccles, W. J., 30–31, 33
Echo Park reclamation project, 324, 390–391, 420, 421
Ecodefense (Foreman), 427
Ecological Society of America, 406–407
ecology
    becomes "big science," 416–417
    development of, 396–398, 406–417
    as modern science, 412–413
    as new integrative discipline, 431–432
    rise of industrial, 484–487
    wilderness philosophy and deep, 401–402
"Ecology and Development as Narrative Themes of World History" (Hughes), 7
Ecology journal, 409
economy
    environmental challenge of space and, 122–133
    environmentalism and, 461–462
    Jefferson/Hamilton debate over, 120–121
    material progress and, 136–141
    status of 1790 U.S., 116–118
    status of 1840 U.S., 148–152
    U.S. advantageous conditions and, 119, 122
ecosystem
    of Cedar Bog Lake, 409–410
    of Mono Lake, 444
    Rhine River, 484

scientific definition of, 412
ecosystem secession theory (Cowles), 299
Eddy, Mary Baker, 206
The Edge of the Sea (Carson), 413
"egotistical sublime," 213
Ehrlich, Paul R., 405, 469
Einstein, Albert, 193
Eiseley, Loren, 301, 421, 491, 492
Eisenhower, Dwight, 263
electrification, 335–336
El lines, 254, 257
Emerson, Harrington, 236
Emerson, Ralph Waldo
    as advocate for railroads, 198
    compared to Muir, 386
    environmentalism of, 407
    on industrial determinism, 148
    on nature, 193, 204
    on risk, 435
    Transcendentalism of, 194, 195–196
    "transparent eyeball" of, 201, 236
    on utopias, 206
Emmons, David, 173, 184, 185
Endangered Species Act of 1973, 340, 425, 429, 438, 443, 447, 450
The Ends of the Earth: (Worster), 7
energy conservation, 472–473
energy crisis (1973–74), 227–228, 436
    See also oil production
"engineered West," 173
engineering profession, 248–249
engineering urban water systems, 306–308
English exploration, 31–35
Enlarged Homestead Act of 1909, 105
Enlightenment, 187–190
entail, 72
environment
    Buffon on human intervention and, 188–189
    cities as built, 244–245
    contemporary issues of, 5
    Cowles's ecosystem secession theory on, 299
    historical/geographical perspective on, 4–5
    horses and, 272
    impact of 20th century industry on, 237
    impact of beaver trade on, 32–33
    impact of chemical pesticides on, 413–415, 436, 445–446, 480
    impact of colonialism/mercantilism on, 25–27
    impact of European plantings on, 68–69
    land ethic and, 396–398, 408
    oil spills and, 471–472
    polluted cities and, 270–276
    of pre-European American continent, 13–14
    redefined as natural resource, 221
    risk-free, 435

Spanish vs. American view of, 164–165
toxic chemical dumping and, 296–301, 438,
    458–461, 490
See also urban cleanup
environmental costs/typical cost statement, 485
Environmental Defense Fund (1967), 6, 422,
    423–424
"environmental era," 436–439
environmental government regulation
    new premise underlining, 234
    politics of, 447–451
    public expectations of, 436–438
    public trust and, 443–444
    Reserve Mining Company and, 444–445
    "secondary legislation" and, 452
    See also Environmental Protection Agency (EPA);
        United States
environmental history, 1–4
Environmental History Review, 7
Environmental Impact Statements (EIS), 299, 324,
    452–454
environmentalism
    cultural blend of science, law, economics and,
        461–462
    enters the mainstream, 489–490
    eras of modern, 491
    fear of cancer and, 441–443
    Gaia hypothesis and, 426, 487–489
    NGOs role in, 417–422
    public trust and, 443–444
    radical, 426
    Sagebrush Rebellion and, 429–430
    science as savior of the, 417
    shift from growth to sustainability, 478–479
    use of administrative law by, 451–454
    U.S. and global, 480–484
    Wise Use Movement and, 430–431
    See also nongovernmental organizations (NGOs);
        wilderness preservation
environmentalism isolationism, 467–469
environmental organizations, 418–422
Environmental Protection Agency (EPA)
    creation of, 416, 438
    history prior to, 446
    HSWA and, 459–460
    Lake Berkeley monitored by, 298
    Love Canal and, 300
    politics of (1970–1996), 447–451
    polluting industry allowed into clean air states by,
        422
    Reserve Mining Company and, 445
    response to fear of cancer by, 441–443
    Tenn-Tom project and, 341–342
    on toxic chemicals, 436
    See also environmental government regulation

Environmental Review, 6
environmental risk, 439–441
Erie Canal, 131–132, 150, 206, 210, 211, 243, 244
"ethical sabotage," 427
Ethyl Gasoline Corporation, 227
European culture
    conflict between Native American and, 24–25,
        40–41, 70
    Industrial Revolution and, 217–218
European society
    aggressive mentality of, 41–42
    disease of, 43
    ecological advantages to, 41
    overwhelming population of, 43–45
    use of technology by, 42–43
    use of *vacuum domicilium* principle by, 70
Evans, Oliver, 230
Evans, Walker, 247
Everett, Edward, 210
Everglades National Park, 384–385, 420
Excursions (Thoreau), 196
Exxon Valdez oil spill, 421, 425, 471, 484, 489, 491

factory system
    daily life/work and, 270
    human nature and, 217–218
    immigrant labor supply and, 228–229
    See also American cities; industrialization
Fairbanks, Morse & Company, 238
Farb, Peter, 385
Farmer's Home Administration, 361
farming
    Appalachian, 348
    by the Mormons, 170–171
    constructed out of American Frontier, 61–65
    government aid to, 365–366
    industrialization of, 237–239
    promotion of High Plains biocentric, 365–366
    See also agriculture; water networks
Federal Highway Act of 1921, 261
Federal Housing Authority (FHA), 265
Federal Insecticide, Fungicide, and Rodenticide Act
    (FIFRA), 436
Federal Land Policy and Management Act (FLPMA)
    of 1976, 390, 392, 429
Federal Roads Aid Act of 1916, 261
Federal Water Pollution Control Act. *See* Clean Water
    Act of 1970
feedback loops, 476
Ferkiss, Victor, 492
Findley, William, 92–93
Finger, Charles, 400
Finney, Charles Grandison, 206
Finn, Huckleberry (fictional), 158

Fisher, Marvin, 120
Fish and Wildlife Service (FWS), 413, 420
Fitzgerald, F. Scott, 10
Five Civilized Tribes of the South, 24
Fletcher, Colin, 205
Flint, Charles, 275
Flores, Dan, 7
Florida, 27–28
Florissant Fossil Beds (Colorado), 444
Fontenelle Dam (Wyoming), 322
Food and Agriculture Organization (FAO), 467
food cycle in a lake (Lindeman), 410
Food and Drug Administration, 451–452
food production, 138–140
    See also agriculture
Forbes, Stephen A., 407–408, 411
Ford Foundation, 423, 424
Ford, Henry, 227, 234, 235, 237, 400
Ford, John, 360
Foreman, David, 427–428
forest
    Appalachian, 14, 348–349
    European obsession with America's, 15–16
    farmland constructed out of, 61–65
    Marsh's warnings for protection of, 372–373
    of precolonial Virginia, 77–78
    wood and waste of, 65–66
    See also deforestation
Forest Reserve Act of 1891, 379
Forest Service, 379, 383, 390, 391, 392, 396, 451
Forrester, Jay, 464, 475
Fortune magazine, 236, 247
"Forty Million Forty-Acre Farms" slogan, 318
Fourier, Charles, 207, 314
Fourteenth Amendment, 232
Fox, Stephen, 421
Fradkin, Philip L., 332, 335
Frampton, George, 420
Franklin, Benjamin, 18–19, 53, 95, 124, 187, 188, 190
"free-market environmentalism," 424
Frémont, John C., 165, 174, 178
Fremont route, 160
French atmospheric nuclear testing, 428
French exploration, 27–28, 28–31
Freud, Sigmund, 405
Friends of the Earth, 395, 421
"frontier thesis" (Turner), 61, 156, 195, 243
Ft. Bridger, 168
Ft. Laramie, 168
Fulton, Robert, 147
Fundamentals of Ecology (Odum), 412
fur trade, 32–33

Gaia hypothesis, 426, 487–489
Gaia, a New Look at Life on Earth (Lovelock), 487

Gallatin, Albert, 59, 84, 111, 118, 130, 135
Game Management (Leopold), 397, 408
Gandhi, Maneka, 483
Gannett, Henry, 395
Garden of Eden, 207
Garden of Eden (Cole), 205
gasoline prices, 227–228
Gates, Paul W., 94
Gauley Bridge (West Virginia), 290
General Accounting Office studies (1983, 1987), 490
General Land Office, 109–110
General Land Office Survey (1860), 164
General Motors Futurama exhibit (New York World's
    Fair), 261
General Survey Act of 1824, 131
"Genesee country" plan, 89–90
Genet, Citizen Edmond Charles, 91
geographical information systems (GIS), 411–412
geography
    of Constitutional Convention, 94–96
    of English colonies, 73–79
    foreign threats to federal, 90–91
    ideology of material progress and, 136–137
    of revolution/independence, 85–98
    water supply and western, 313
Geological Survey, 313
geophysiology, 488
George, Henry, 373
Gibbons v. Ogden, 131
Gibbs, Lois, 300
Giedion, Siegfried, 292–293
Gila Wilderness Area, 396
Gilbert, Humphrey, 32–33, 71
Gilpin, William, 201
Glacier Bay National Monument, 395
Glacier Point (Yosemite), 377, 385
Glacken, Clarence, 415
Glen Canyon Dam, 427
Glidden, Joseph F., 238, 359
Global 2000 report of 1980 (Carter), 477
global environmentalism, 480–484
Global Environmental Monitoring System (GEMS),
    481
global warming, 18–19, 481
    See also climate
Goetzmann, William H., 162, 182, 193
gold rush (California), 166–167, 314
Golley, Frank, 410–411, 412
Gompers, Samuel, 275, 288, 353
Good Roads Movement, 261
Gore, Al, 450
Gorges, Sir Ferdinand, 71
Gorsuch, Anne, 449
Gottlieb, Robert, 425, 439
Gould, Jay, 230, 232
Gould, Stephen Jay, 488

Graduation Act of 1854, 104
Graham, Sylvester, 206
Grand Canyon, 383, 384, 386, 393–394
Grand Coulee Dam, 336
Grant, U. S., 371, 378
The Grapes of Wrath (Steinbeck), 239, 276, 360
Gray, L. C., 354
Gray Ranch (New Mexico), 422
Great American Desert, 357
Great American Land Grant Giveaway, 179
Great Basin region, 23
Great Depression, 264–266
Great Salt Lake, 315
Great Society (1960s), 354
Greeley, Horace, 157, 206, 314, 373
Greene, Nathanael, 85
Greenpeace, 418, 426, 428–429
Greenpeace (fishing boat), 428
Greenpeace III (ketch), 428
Greenpeace Two (converted minesweeper), 428
Grinnell, George Bird, 419
Group Against Smog and Pollution (GASP), 455
growth limits, 477–478
Gudger, George, 247
Gulf War (1991), 471, 482
Guthrie, Woody, 334, 360
Guymon-Hugoton natural gas field, 363

Haeckel, Ernst, 406
Hakluyt, Richard, 25
Halladay, Daniel, 238, 359
Hall, Eleanor, 410
Hamilton, Alexander, 96, 99, 100, 109, 120–121,
    146
Hamilton, Alice, 227, 286–288, 439
Hammond, George Henry, 291
Hancock, John, 87
hard energy path, 473
Hardin, Garrett, 405, 465, 467, 487
Hardy v. Holden, 289–290
harm to ecological resources, 439–440
harm to human health, 439
Harriman, E. H., 327, 395
Harvey, Fred, 384
Hayden, Ferdinand Vandiveer, 174, 193, 378
Hayes, Denis, 432
Haymarket Square riot, 276
Hays, Samuel P., 417, 431, 436
Hazardous and Solid Waste Amendments (HSWA),
    459–460
Heart of Darkness (Conrad), 51
Henderson, Richard, 136
Henry, Joseph, 357
Hering, Rudolph, 249
Hetch Hetchy Valley, 389–390

Hewitt, Abram, 216, 221
Higginson, Francis, 70
High Plains
    Dust Bowl disaster of, 239, 359–361
    early history of, 357–361
    environmental challenges of, 345–346, 355–356
    irrigation for climate of, 361–366
    miracle climate (1878–1887) of, 358–359
Highway Beautification Act of 1965, 263
Hindle, Brooke, 141, 151
Hinton, Richard J., 318
Hiroshima, 212
Histoire Naturelle (Buffon), 189
Hofstadter, Richard, 137
hog-killing, 67
Hohokam people, 23
Holcomb meatpacking plant, 294–295
Holden v. Hardy, 289–290
Holley, Alexander Lyman, 222
Hollon, W. Eugene, 171
Holmes, Oliver Wendell, 193
Homestead Act of 1862, 61, 105, 232, 238, 310, 358
Homestead Steel Strike (1892), 276
Hood, Clifton, 256, 257
Hooker Chemical Company, 299
Hoover Dam (Nevada), 322, 324, 334–335
Hoover, Herbert, 419
Hopi ideal man, 25
horses, 272
House Committee on Public Lands, 111–112
Housing and Urban Development (HUD), 439
Huckleberry Finn (Twain), 274
Hudson Bay Company, 165
Hudson, Henry, 122
Hudson Institute, 477
Hughes, J. Donald, 7
Hughes, Thomas, 235
human-made (anthropogenic) hazards, 440
Humboldt, Alexander, 190
Hundley, Norris, Jr., 329
hunting (Native American), 20
Huntington, Henry, 327
Hunt, Walter, 206
Hutchins, Thomas, 102

IBP (Iowa Beef Processors), 294–295
Ickes, Harold L., 391–392
"ideology of domesticity," 140
Illinois Central Railroad, 444
Illinois Commission on Occupational Diseases, 287
immigrant labor supply, 228–229
Independence Rock, 168
Indiana Dunes, 298–299
Indiana Dunes National Lakeshore, 299
Indian kinship property division, 71

IND (Independent) line, 258
industrial ecology, 484–487
industrial growth, 479–480
industrialization
    agriculture and, 151
    American corporations and, 229–234
    disillusionment about, 275–276
    of the farm, 237–239
    government and, 231–233
    immigrant labor supply and, 228–229
    of the Indiana Dunes, 298–299
    as inherently flawed, 272–276
    of iron and steel production, 220–221, 222
    labor-saving technology and, 145–146
    lead poisoning and, 438–439
    limits to, 147–148
    of meat processing, 290–295
    nonrenewable resources and, 221
    occupational diseases and, 286–290
    Pacific Northwest electrification and, 336
    petroleum and, 226–228
    pollution/waste due to, 270–272
    Progressive ideology and, 234–236
    public health issues and, 353
    rethinking, 474–480
    robber barons of, 230, 233
    Social Darwinism on, 273–275
    textile industry, 146–147
    in the twentieth century, 236–237
    use of lumber by, 348–349
    See also technology
Industrial Revolution
    cultural values and, 217–218
    environment price of, 465, 467
    impact on America by, 218–220, 245
    second Industrial Revolution vs., 234
Industrial Workers of the World ("Wobblies"), 297
INFOTERRA (International Referral System), 481
infrastructure system
    building of city, 244–245
    flaws in city, 266–267
    pollution/waste of, 270–272
    water network as, 304–306
    within environmental context, 6
    See also American cities
Insull, Samuel, 236, 250
International Biological Program (IBP), 416
International Geophysical Year, 415
International Harvester Company, 239
International Office for the Protection of Nature
    (IOPN), 468
International Register of Potentially Toxic Chemicals
    (IRPTC), 481
"Interpretation and Causal Analysis:" (Leibhardt), 7
Interstate Highway Act of 1956, 263

Interstate Oil Compact, 227
iron production, 220–221
"iron triangle," 425
Iroquois, 24
The Irrigation Age (Smythe), 317
irrigation communities, 314–316
Irrigation Crusade, 313, 316–318
    See also reclamation; water network
irrigation (High Plains), 361–366
"Irrigation in the United States" report (Hinton), 318
IRT (Interior Rapid Transit), 257–258
Irving, Washington, 372–373, 373
isolation psychology, 59
IUCH (International Union for Conservation of
    Nature and Natural Resources), 468
IUPN (International Union for the Protection of
    Nature), 468
Izaak Walton League, 389, 419

Jackson, Andrew, 61, 210
Jackson, Henry, 447
Jackson, John Brinkerhoff, 199
Jackson, William H., 378
James, Edwin, 357
Jamestown, 76
James, William, 273
Jamieson, Duncan R., 7
Japan, 484
Jarvis, William Charles, 404
Jay, John, 97
Jay's Treaty of 1794, 90–91
Jefferson, Thomas
    Constitutional debate position of, 95
    debate between Hamilton and, 120–121
    embargo against English trade by, 146
    enlightened view of nature by, 187–188
    on evils of cities, 271
    on free markets, 113
    on impact of intensive farming, 68
    instructions to Lewis and Clark by, 191–192
    interest in natural history by, 190–191
    on labor-saving technology, 209–210
    on land squatters, 110–112
    Louisiana Purchase by, 31
    on man's impact on climate, 19
    on material progress ideology, 137
    on measuring material well-being, 138–139
    on potential of Americans, 53–54
    public domain land plan by, 100–101
    on rule by the people, 404
    scientific expeditions sent by, 161–162
    on settlement across America, 80
    on transportation development, 130–131
    on U.S. economic development, 117

on wonders of nature, 375
Jennings, Francis, 20, 35, 36, 37, 48, 70
Jensen, Merrill, 93
Johns-Manville Corporation, 442, 461, 489
Johnson, Edward, 73
Johnson and Graham's Lessee v. William McIntosh, 70
Johnson, Lyndon B., 354, 394, 438
Johnson, Robert Underwood, 388
Johnson, Sir William Samuel, 70
Johnson, Willard D., 359
Joseph, Lawrence E., 489
Journal of American History, 7
Judah, Theodore, 174
Juday, Chancey, 409
The Jungle (Sinclair), 276, 293

Kahn, Herman, 405, 477
"the Kaintuck Hawg Road," 60
Kallet, Arthur, 290
Kalm, Peter, 16, 189, 191
Kansas Rural Center, 295
Kasson, John, 219
Kauffmann, John, 395
Kellogg, Paul U., 277, 278
Kennecott Copper Company, 225
Kentucky, 93–94
Kepone, 445–446
Kettering, Charles, 227
Kewennaw copper, 225
King, Clarence, 174–175, 193, 202
King, Martin Luther, 426
King, Thomas Starr, 376
Kipling, Rudyard, 292
Kirschenmann, Fred, 366
Kodachrome photography, 400
Krech, Shepard, 39
Krutch, Joseph Wood, 240, 421

labor-saving technology, 145–146, 209–210, 219
labor supply
    immigrant, 228–229
    occupational diseases and, 286–290
    strikes by, 275–276
LacLeod, William Christie, 184
LaGuardia, Fiorello, 259
Lake Berkeley, 298
land
    creating public domain, 91–93
    Indian kinship and, 71
    privatization of American, 106–108
    quitrents, primogeniture, entail and, 72
    reclamation of, 316, 318–319
    restrictive zoning of, 252

selling public domain, 98–105
toxic chemical dumping on, 296–301, 438,
    458–461
used as soldier payment, 87
Virginia cession (1784) of western, 93–94
See also land speculation; property rights; public
    domain land
Land Act of 1796, 109
Land Act of 1800, 109
Land Act of 1804, 111
Land Act of 1812, 109–110
Land Act of 1820, 111
Lander Cutoff (South Pass), 163
land ethic, 396–398, 408
"The Land Ethic" (Leopold), 396, 397
"Land Grab Act" of 1783, 100
Land Institute (Kansas), 366
landscape painting, 198–201, 202–204
land speculation
    claims clubs to discourage, 110
    Constitutional Convention on, 95–96
    federal efforts to curb, 108–112
    Land Survey Ordinance (1785) and, 98–99
    privatization through, 106–108
    public domain land and, 91–93
    in Vermont, 89–90
    See also American frontier; public domain land
Land Survey Ordinance of 1785, 96, 99–102, 110,
    313
Land Survey Ordinance of 1787, 346
Langenberg, Donald N., 417
Langford, Nathaniel Pitt, 378
Larkin, Jack, 114
Latrobe, Benjamin H., 143, 306
Lavender, David, 157
Lawrence, D. H., 212
Law of the Seas treaty, 469
The Laws of Railways (Redfield), 179
Lead-Based Paint Poisoning Prevention Act of 1971,
    439
leaded gasoline, 439
lead poisoning, 287, 438–439
Lear, Linda, 415
Leaves of Grass (Whitman), 195
Leclerc, Georges-Louis (Comte de Buffon), 52, 54,
    188–189
Leibhardt, Barbara, 7
Leonard, Zenas, 162
Leontief, Wassily, 477
Leopold, Aldo, 194, 386, 391, 396–398, 408, 415,
    420, 464, 473, 492
Leopold, A. Starker, 383
less developed countries (LDCs), 480, 481
Letters from an American Farmer (Crèvecoeur), 190
Let Us Now Praise Famous Men (Agee and Evans), 247

Lewis, Chris H., 7, 159, 161
Lewis and Clark expedition, 159–161, 191–193
Lewis, Meriwether, 17, 38, 39, 159, 161
Lewis, Peirce F., 266
Lewontin, R. C., 409
Licht, Walter, 145, 150, 152, 219–220
Life on the Mississippi (Twain), 213
Life Science Products Company, 445
Lillienthal, David E., 339
limited liability, 231
Limits of the Earth (Osborn), 405
The Limits to Growth (Club of Rome), 474, 477
Lincoln, Abraham, 61, 179, 228, 232, 248
Lindeman, E. C., 415
Lindeman, Raymond, 409–411
Linnaeus, Carolus, 188, 406
Lippincott, J. B., 327
Lisa, Manuel, 159
Lochner v. State of New York, 290
Locke, John, 11, 53, 70, 467
Long, Stephen H., 357
Looking Backward (Bellamy), 209
Lopez de Gomara, Francisco, 11
Los Angeles, 325–328, 330
    See also California
Los Angeles Basin, 164
Louisiana Purchase of 1803, 31, 40, 163
Love Canal, 299–301, 436, 459, 460, 462
Lovell, James, 97
Lovelock, James E., 487–489
Love, William T., 299
Lovins, Amory, 473
Lowell, Francis Cabot, 147
Lowenthal, David, 373
low-level risk, 440
Lubar, Steven, 151
LULU (locally unwanted land uses), 424
Luzerne County (Pennsylvania), 88

McCormick, Cyrus, 239, 359
McCormick Reaper Works, 276
McDonald, Forrest, 112
McFarland, J. H., 381
McHarg, Ian, 301
Macomb, Alexander, 90
McTaggart, David, 428
Madison, James, 65, 96
The Maine Woods (Thoreau), 196
Malthus, Thomas, 56, 468
Manes, Christopher, 426
Manhattan Island, 122–123, 124
Manifest Destiny, 61, 210, 313, 357, 358
Man and Nature (Marsh), 372–373
Mansfield, Jared, 107, 108

maps
    of colonial agriculture, 74
    main roads, canals, rivers, and lake transportation, 129
    showing American West explorations (1803–1879), 160
Marble Canyon dam, 393
Margulis, Lynn, 488, 489
Mariposa Big Tree Grove (Yosemite), 376–377
Marquette, Father Jacques, 29–30
Marshall, John, 70, 131
Marshall, R. B., 381
Marshall, Robert, 374, 391, 395, 420
Marsh, George Perkins, 372–373, 402, 407
Martineau, Harriet, 130
Martin, John, 104
Marx, Karl, 53
Mason, James, 439
material progress ideology, 136–137
material well-being measurements, 138–139
Mather, Stephen T., 377, 381–382, 384–385
Meadows, Dennis, 475
Mead, Sidney E., 156, 489
meat processing industry, 290–295
mechanical skills, 119, 122
Mechanization Takes Command (Giedion), 292
Meeker, Nathan Cook, 314
Meigs, Joseph, 192
Meigs, Josiah, 110, 111
Meining, Donald, 36–37, 99, 112, 155, 158, 267
Melosi, Martin V., 245, 267
Melville, Herman, 194, 197, 241
mercantilism, 25–27
Merchant, Carolyn, 6, 69
Meriam Survey (1928), 40
Merriam, C. Hart, 409
Mexican War of 1846, 157, 164, 178
Michaux, André, 59, 190
Midgley, Thomas, 227
Miele, Stefano, 229
Miller, Angela, 197, 200, 201, 204
Millerites, 206
Miller, Perry, 3, 212
Mills, Enos, 381
Mills, Robert, 178
Mineral King Valley, 393
mineral resources, 223–224
mining industry (Appalachian), 349–353
mining machinery, 353
Minuit, Peter, 122
MIT team, 475, 477
mobility
    between suburbs and cities, 255–260
    in the industrial city, 253–255
    See also transportation

Moby Dick (Melville), 194, 241
Model Cities program (1966), 266
Models of Doom (University of Sussex), 477
The Modern Temper (Krutch), 240
moneywrenching, 427–428
Mongollan culture, 23
The Monkey Wrench Gang (Abbey), 426
Mono Lake (California), 327–328, 444
Monroe, James, 96
Montgomery, Alice B., 277
Moran, Thomas, 198, 378, 400
More, Thomas, 207
Morgan, Dale, 156
Morgan, J. P., 232
Morill Act of 1862, 248
Mormons, 170–171, 206, 315–316
Mormon War of 1857–58, 171
Morrill Land Grant College Act of 1862, 232
Morrill Tariff of 1861, 232
Morris, Robert, 100
Morris, Wright, 197, 212
Morton, Thomas, 71
Moses, Robert, 258, 259
Mount St. Helens, 212
Moynihan, Daniel Patrick, 229
Muir, John
    alternative tourism practiced by, 400–401
    childhood memory of homesteading by, 80
    environmentalism of, 407
    on Glacier Bay (Alaska), 395
    Hetch Hetchy Valley and, 389
    on need to preserve wilderness, 379, 396
    Sierra Club founded by, 386
    wilderness movement and, 301, 374, 377
    wilderness philosophy of, 402
    Yosemite and, 387–388
Mulholland, William, 325–327
Müller, Paul, 413
multiple use strategy conference (1988), 430
Mumford, Lewis, 240, 245, 266, 301
Murie, Olaus J., 420
Murray, John, 88
Mushet, Robert, 222
Music Corporation of America (MCA), 385
Muskie, Edmund, 432

Nader, Ralph, 302, 414
Naess, Arne, 402
Nagasaki, 212
Narvaez, Captain Panfile de, 27
Nash, Gerald D., 226
Nash, Roderick, 395, 401
National Academy of Sciences, 232, 333
National Association of Audubon Societies, 419

National Audubon Society, 389, 395, 419
National Audubon Society v. Superior Court of Alpine County, 328
National Banking Act, 232
National Biological Survey, 416
National Center for Atmospheric Research (NCAR), 489
National Environmental Policy Act of 1970, 324
National Environmental Protection Act (NEPA) of 1970, 299, 333, 340, 390, 432, 438, 443, 447, 489
National Forest Management Act of 1976, 429
National Housing Association, 277
National Institutes of Health (NIH), 446
National Lead Company, 287
National Municipal League, 278
National Oceanic and Atmospheric Administration (NOAA), 446
National Park and Recreation Act of 1978, 392
National Parks
    Catlin's proposal for, 370–371
    commercial concessions of, 376–377, 383–386
    creation of additional, 379–383
    Everglades, 384–385, 420
    impact of tourism on, 398–401
    to preserve American wilderness, 371–374
    Yellowstone, 371, 378–379, 398, 400–401
    Yosemite, 376–377, 388
National Parks Association, 420
National Parks and Conservation Association, 395
National Park Service, 379–383, 390, 391, 401, 420
National Priority List (NPL), 460
National Resources Defense Council (NRDC), 462
National Road (U.S. 40), 135–136, 243
National Science Foundation (NSF), 416
National Toxic Campaign, 424–425
national triumphalism, 2–3
National Water Commission, 324
National Wilderness Preservation System, 392
National Wildlife Federation, 414
National Wild and Scenic Rivers Act, 394
National Wild and Scenic Rivers System, 395
Native Americans
    along the Oregon Trail, 168
    buffalo extermination and, 38–39
    Catlin's book on, 370
    conflict between European culture and, 24–25, 40–41, 70
    corn agriculture of, 69
    dismissed by white land-grabbers, 108
    during the western migration, 157–158
    European disease and, 43
    European legal alienation of, 70
    Europeans and, 35–38
    historic relations of whites and, 39–40

Native Americans *(continued)*
  kinship and property rights of, 71
  migration origins of, 18–19
  relationship between French traders and, 29–31, 33
  successful farming by, 19–22
  U.S. geographical regions of, 22–24
natural beauty, 398
Natural Bridge (Virginia), 199, 205, 210, 375, 399
"natural delays," 477
natural hazards, 440
natural history
  applied to western exploration, 191–193
  new world/old world, 188–189
  as utilitarian science, 189–190
natural resources
  environment redefined as, 221
  extracted minerals, 223–224
  mining the West's, 224–225
  U.S. as nation of, 221–228
Natural Resources Defense Council (NRDC), 422, 424
Nature, 488
nature
  American changing view of, 187–188
  artistic sublime representation of, 201–202
  civilization as conquest of, 405
  European view of, 187
  impact of tourism on, 398–401
  industrialization as control over, 219
  landscape painting as medium to, 198–201, 202–204
  Linneaus's system for cataloging, 188–189
  transcendentalist vision of, 193–197, 212–213
  U.S. as nation of, 204–205
  See also wilderness preservation
Nature Conservancy, 421–422
"Nature and the Disorder of History" (Worster), 7
"Nature" (Emerson), 195, 196
Neel, Susan Rhoades, 183–184
"Negro removal," 265–266
Nelson, Gaylord, 420, 432
Nettles, Curtis, 118
New Deal, 264, 334, 360, 452, 491
New Earth 19 (Japan), 484
Newell, Frederick, 320
New England, 31–35, 73–75
New France, 28–31
New Harmony, 206
Newlands Act of 1902, 319–320
Newlands, Francis G., 319
"New Military Tract" (Finger Lakes country), 89–90
New York City, 128, 306–308
New York City subway system, 257–259
The New Yorker magazine, 414
New York State, 89–90

New York Tenement House Department, 277
New York Times, 347, 354, 428
New York World's Fair (1939), 212, 261
The Next 200 Years (Kahn), 477
Nez Perce, 22
NIABY (not in any backyard), 424
Niagara Falls, 205, 210, 375, 399
Niagara Falls (city), 299
Niagara Falls State Reservation, 375
NIMBYs (not in my backyard), 418, 424
Nixon, Richard, 341, 432
nongovernmental organizations (NGOs)
  access to environmental policy through, 425–426
  at the Stockholm conference (1972), 480
  examples of, 417–422
  growing power/involvement of, 6, 489
  professionalization of, 422–426
  radical environmental, 426
  See also environmentalism
nonviolent civil disobedience, 426
Norris, Frank, 183, 276
Northern Pacific Railroad, 378–379
Northwest Ordinance of 1787, 40, 96–98, 444
Northwest Passage, 28–29
Notes on the State of Virginia (Jefferson), 53, 117, 161, 190–191
Novak, Barbara, 201
nuclear facilities, 339
nuclear power debate, 473–474
nuclear testing, 428
Nuclear Waste Policy Act of 1982–83, 474
Nye, David E., 205, 210, 211, 213
Nye, Russel Blaine, 119

occupational diseases, 286–290
The Octopus (Norris), 183, 276
Odum, Eugene P., 405, 412–413, 415, 416, 431
Oelschlaeger, Max, 402
Office of Management and Budget (OMB), 448
Ogallala aquifer (High Plains), 361–364
Ogden v. Gibbons, 131
Ohio, 106–109
Ohio Company, 95, 97, 106, 108
Ohio Valley, 134–135
oil price crisis (1973–74), 227–228, 436, 472–474, 491
oil production
  alternatives to dependency on, 472–474
  environmental harm and, 471–472
  reduced levels of, 469–470
  risky dependency on, 470–471
  See also energy crisis (1973–74)
oil spills
  Amoco Cadiz, 471

Exxon Valdez, 421, 425, 471, 484, 489, 491
  impact on environment by, 471–472
Okefenokee Swamp (Great Dismal Swamp), 76
Old Economy, 206
Old Northwest (1785–1787), 103
Olmstead, Frederick Law, 280, 290–291, 374, 376
Olsen, Sigurd, 420
Omnibus Park Bill of 1978, 392
100,000,000 Guinea Pigs (Kallet and Schlink), 290
Oneida Community, 206
Onuf, Peter, 90
OPEC (Organization of Petroleum Exporting Coun-
  tries), 470, 471
Oregon migration, 157, 168–169
  See also the West
Oregon Trail, 168–169
The Origin of Species (Darwin), 406
Oroville Dam (California), 329
Orr, Sir John Boyd, 468
Osborn, Fairfield, 405, 422
OSHA (Occupational Safety and Health Administra-
  tion), 288, 443, 446, 447
Otis, Harrison Gray, 327
Our Common future (Brundtland Commission), 478
Our Plundered Planet (Osborn), 405, 422
Outdoor America (Izaac Walton League), 419
Overland Telegraph Company, 173
overland travel, 133–134
Owen, Robert, 207, 209
Owens Valley (California), 327
Owens Valley project, 327
The Oxbow (Cole), 203, 204

Pacific Historical Review 54, 7
Pacific Northwest, 165–173
Pacific Northwest Regional Planning Commission
  (PNWRPC), 336
Pacific Telegraphy Company, 173
Paige, Timothy, 317
Palmetto Bend Project, 453
Panama Canal, 340
Pangaea period, 46
Parker, Arthur C., 37
Parkes, Henry Bamford, 233, 274
Parkman, Francis, 168, 372
Pasteur, Louis, 277
patent system, 230
Paulding, James K., 234
Paul, Rodman W., 297
Peace of Paris (1763), 31
Peale, Charles Willson, 190
Peccei, Aurelio, 474
Penn, Admiral Sir William, 71
Pennsylvania, 75–76, 87–89

Pennsylvania Steel Company, 222
Pennsylvania tenement house law of 1903, 280–281
Penn, William, 71, 124
Permain Period, 46
Persons, Stow, 186
Peterson, Russell, 419
petroleum industry, 226–228
Petulla, Joseph M., 272
Philadelphia, 124–125, 127, 306, 308
Philadelphia Centennial Exposition of 1876, 211
Philbrick, Francis, 135
phosphorus necrosis ("phossy jaw"), 285
PHS (Public Health Service), 287–288, 289
Physical Geography as Modified by Human Action
  (Marsh), 372
Pickering, Timothy, 100
pigs, 67–68
Pike, Zebulon, 357
Pilcher, Joshua, 357
Pinchot, Gifford, 235, 249, 373, 381, 389, 396, 402,
  430, 467–468
Pinckney's Treaty of 1795, 91
PIRGs, 418, 425
Pisani, Donald J., 314, 315
Pittsburgh Civic Commission, 284
Pittsburgh Renaissance, 284
Pittsburgh (Russell Sage Foundation Report),
  276–284
Pittsburgh Survey, 277–278
"Place: An Argument for Bioregional History"
  (Flores), 7
The Place No One Knew: (Porter), 394
"A Place for Stories:" (Cronon), 7
Plains Indians, 23–24, 38–39, 44
Plateau region Native Americans, 22
Plater, Zygmunt, 446, 457
Plumb, J. H., 97
podzol soil, 73
Poe, Edgar Allen, 194, 197
Polanyi, Karl, 233
pollution
  of American cities, 270–272
  of automobile emissions, 456–457
  of chemical pesticides, 413–415, 436, 445–446, 480
  of DDT, 413, 414, 415, 423, 436, 469, 477, 480
  EPA lawsuits over, 448
  of factory cities, 270–272
  global warming and, 481
  natural delays of, 477
  racial aspects of, 490
  SARA's "right-to-know" provision on, 461
  under communist rule, 481–482
  of the United States, 483
  See also Clean Air Act of 1970; environmental gov-
    ernment regulation

Pony Express, 173
"poor-white" families, 247
Popper, Deborah, 365–366
Popper, Frank, 365–366
Porter, Eliot, 394, 421
Potter, David, 119
Powell, John Wesley, 172, 306, 313, 315, 318, 319,
    320
Prairie Indians, 24
"Precambrian Basement," 13–14
"preemptors" (squatters), 110–112
preindustrial infrastructures, 123–125
President's Council on Environmental Quality
    (1971), 341
Price, Edward T., 72
Priestly, Joseph, 136, 190, 335
Prigogyne, Ilya, 488
primogeniture, 72
prior appropriation principle, 310–311
Pritchard, Paul, 420
Proclamation Line and Quebec Act of 1763, 98, 116
Progressive Era (1900), 354
Progressive ideology
    on conservation, 305–306
    "duty of water" ethics of, 317
    environmentalism and, 491
    of multiple use, 299
    on social efficiency/technology, 234–236, 309
property rights
    American dream defined by, 98–99
    European establishment of, 71
    quitrents, primogeniture, entail and, 72
    restrictive zoning and, 252
    struggle over Pennsylvania, 87–89
    U.S. Supreme Court (1834) on, 87
    vacuum domicilium principle and, 70
    within American cities, 125–126
    See also land
Proposition 65 (California), 425
prosperity
    during age of wood, 141–143
    food as symbol of, 138–140
Protection Against Products Harmful to Health and
    Environment (UN Resolution), 481
public city parks, 279–281, 374
public domain land
    Constitutional Convention on, 95–96
    creation of, 91–93
    federal efforts to curb speculation of, 108–112
    lack of water in, 310–311
    Northwest Ordinance of 1787 on, 96–98
    selling experiment of, 98–105
    speculation over, 106–108
    survey of, 102–105
    timeline on, 104–105
    See also land; land speculation

public health issues, 353
Public Health Service Act, 285
Public Health Service survey (1967), 436
Public Interest Research Groups (PIRGs), 418, 425
public perception of risk, 439–441
public trust doctrine, 328, 443–444
Public Works Administration, 264
public works/utilities, 250–251
Pullman Railway Car Company, 276
Pulteney, Sir William, 89–90
Pure Food, Drug, and Cosmetic Act of 1958, 441
Pursell, Carroll, 220, 235, 240
Putnam, Rufus, 108

quality-based standards, 440
quality of life, 479–480
Quebec Act of 1784, 116
quitrents, 72

radical environmentalism, 426
railroad system
    Chicago and, 291–292
    as engineering feat, 175–183
    impact on the West by, 173
    as technical sublime, 210–212
    transformation of America by, 251, 253
Rainbow Warrior (Greenpeace vessel), 428
Raleigh, Walter, 32–33
Ramparts Dam proposal, 395
Rauschenbusch, Walter, 274
Raynal, Abbé de (Guillaume-Thomas), 51–52, 53,
    191
RCRA (Resource Conservation and Recovery Act),
    452
Reagan, Ronald, 429, 448–449
reclamation
    in California, 324–330
    defining, 316
    reconstructing Appalachia, 338–342
    using the Colorado River, 331–333
    the West and federal, 318–319
    See also Irrigation Crusade; water networks
Reclamation Act of 1902, 319–320, 392
Reclamation Service. *See* Bureau of Reclamation
    (Reclamation Service)
Redfield, Isaac F., 179
Regulatory Analysis Review Groups (RARG), 448
Reid, Alastaire, 48
Reilly, William K., 450, 482
Reisner, Marc, 318, 323, 327
Renaissance Two (Pittsburgh), 284
Reorganization Act of 1933, 382
Report on the Arid Region of the United States (Powell),
    172, 313

Report on Manufacturers (Hamilton), 121
Report of the Secretary of the Treasury on the Subject of Public Roads and Canals (Gallatin), 130
Republican Virtue, 219–220
Reserve Mining Company, 444–445, 448
The Reshaping of Everyday Life (Larkin), 114
Resource Conservation and Recovery Act (RCRA) of 1976, 450, 459
Resources for the Future (RFF), 423
restrictive zoning, 252
Revolutionary War geography, 85–87
Rhine River ecosystem, 484
Ribicoff, Abraham, 414
rice agriculture, 77
Rickey, Thomas, 327
Riebsame, William, 356
Riis, Jacob, 273
Rio de Janeiro Conference (1992), 429, 482–484, 490
riparian rights doctrine, 310
risk-free environment, 435
risk of harm, 440
risk management, 441
Rivers and Harbors Act of 1899, 444
road/highway system, 260–264
Roadless Area Review and Evaluation (RARE, RARE II), 392
Road to Survival (Vogt), 405
robber barons, 230, 233
Robbins, William G., 155
Robinson, Michael C., 308, 320
Rockefeller, John D., Jr., 232, 504, 379
Rock Mountain National Park, 399
Rocky Mountains, 202, 225
Rodgers, William H., Jr., 434
Rohrbough, Malcolm J., 110, 112
Romanticism, 193–197
Romantic landscape painting, 198–201, 202–204
Roosevelt, Franklin Delano, 264, 321–322, 334, 336, 360, 381, 392, 467, 468
Roosevelt, Theodore, 235, 249, 319, 325–327, 354, 379, 388, 389, 400, 402
Rostow, Walter, 150
Rothenberg, David, 402
Rousseau, Jean-Jacques, 207, 217
Rowley, Peter, 431
Royal Swedish Academy of Sciences, 189
Royko, Mike, 242
Ruckelshaus, William, 440–441, 447, 449
Rush, Benjamin, 19, 118, 127, 191
Ruskin, John, 204
Russell Sage Foundation report of 1914, 277–284

Sacajawea, 159
Sacramento River Valley, 164
Safe Drinking Water Act, 425, 449

Sagan, Carl, 488
"Sagebrush Rebellion," 429–430
Sahara Club, 431
St. Lawrence River, 28–29, 30–31
St. Louis, 254–255
salinity, 337
Salisbury, Harrison E., 347
Salt River Project (Arizona), 321
San Bernadino, 164
A Sand County Almanac (Leopold), 396, 397, 408, 492
San Fernando Valley, 165
Sanitary District of Chicago, 285, 307
San Joaquin Valley (California), 164, 317, 328–329, 330
Santa Clara County v. Southern Pacific Railroad, 232
Santa Fe Trail, 163
Sauer, Carl Ortwin, 366
Saunders, Glenn, 323
The Savage State (Cole), 203
Sax, Joseph L., 386, 391, 393, 401
Schereschewsky, Joseph, 289
Schlink, F. J., 290
Schmidheiny, Stephan, 484
Schneider, Steven, 489
Schumacher, E. F., 473, 487
Science, 431, 487, 488
Scientific American, 211, 363, 488
Scioto Company, 97
Scott, Thomas, 232
The Sea Around Us (Carson), 413
Sears, John F., 399, 401
Sears, Paul, 356
Sea Shepherd Conservation Society, 426
Second Industrial Revolution, 234–236
Second Treatise on Government (Locke), 70
Securities and Exchange Commission (SEC), 462
Segal, Howard P., 219
Sellers, Christopher, 270, 285, 288, 289
Sequoia National Park, 398
Sequoyah nuclear power plant, 339
Sessions, George, 402
Seven Ranges survey, 102–105, 108
Seymour, Whitney North, Jr., 424
Shakespeare, William, 10
Shawn, William, 414
Shaw, Ronald E., 211
Shays, Daniel, 89
Shay's Rebellion, 88, 89
Sherman Anti-Trust Act of 1890, 233
Sherman, William Tecumseh, 357
"shoeleather epidemiology," 286
Shosone Land and Irrigation Company, 315
Siemens, William, 222
Sierra Club, 6, 323, 386–388, 389, 392, 394, 395, 419, 421, 428, 438

Sierra Club Legal Defense Fund, 392, 421, 427
Sierra giant sequoias, 376
Silent Spring (Carson), 6, 391, 413–415, 423, 432, 436, 469, 474, 487, 491
Simon, Julian, 405
Sinclair, Upton, 276, 293
sink limits, 479
Siuslaw National Forest (Alaska), 454
Slater, Samuel, 146
slavery, 77, 78, 126
Slocombe, Scott, 480
Slossen, Edwin P., 236
smallpox, 43, 127
Smith, Adam, 118, 137, 148, 467
Smith, Anthony Wayne, 420
Smith, Jedediah, 159
Smith, John, 13, 34, 188
Smith, Joseph, 206
Smith route, 160
Smythe, William E., 313, 317, 318, 319
snail darter fish, 340, 411
"The Social Construction of Nature:" (Bird), 6
Social Darwinism, 273–275
social efficiency, 234–236
"Social Gospel," 274
Sociobiology: The New Synthesis (Wilson), 415
soft energy path, 473
Soil Conservation Service (SCS), 313, 346, 453
Solid Waste Disposal Act of 1965, 425, 459
"So Long, It's Been Good to Know Ya" (Guthrie), 360
the South
    between post-Civil War and W.W. II, 246
    as environmental dumping ground, 490
    European spread in, 76–77
    "poor-white" families of, 247
    slavery in, 77, 78
    urbanization development in, 126
Southern Pacific Railroad, 388
Southern Pacific Railroad v. Santa Clara County, 232
South Pass, 165, 168, 178
Southwest Desert Native Americans, 23
Soviet Union, 482
"Spaceship Earth" (photograph), 466
Spanish exploration, 27–28
Spanish Florida, 27–28
Spanish settlements, 311, 314
Spenger, Oswald, 209
Sperry, Elmer, 235
Speth, Gus, 424
Sporting Arms and Ammunitions Manufacturers' Institute, 397
spotted owl, 426
squatters, 110–112
standard of living, 137–141
Standard Oil, 232, 233

Stanford, Leland, 182
State Implementation Plans (SIPs), 450
State of New York v. Lochner, 290
State Water Project (California), 329–330
steamboat transportation, 132–133
steel life-cycle, 486
steel production, 220–221, 222
Steffens, Lincoln, 289
Stegner, Wallace, 172
Steinbeck, John, 239, 276, 360
Stein, Jeffrey K., 341
Stilgoe, John R., 100, 199
Stockholm Conference (1972), 480–481
Stock-Raising Homestead Act of 1916, 105
Stoddard, Charles H., 390
Stowe, Harriet Beecher, 414
Stowe, Irving, 428
strikes, 275–276
strip mining, 350–353
Strong, Maurice, 483
subway systems, 257–259
Sullivan, John, 54, 90
Sumner, William Graham, 273
Superfund, 300, 432, 438, 450, 451, 458–461
Superfund Amendment and Reauthorization Act (SARA), 425, 436, 461
Superior Court of Alpine County v. National Audubon Society, 328
supersonic transport (SST), 424
Susquehanna Company, 88
Sutter's saw-mill, 166–167
Swdgwick, Theodore, II, 220
Swift, Gustavus F., 291
Symmes, John Cleves, 106
systems approach, 235–236
    See also industralization

Taar, Joel, 268
Taft, William Howard, 389
Tallmadge, John, 492
Tansley, Arthur George, 409
Tarr, Joel A., 272
Taylor, Bayard, 372
Taylor, Frederick Winslow, 236
Taylor Grazing Act of 1935, 110
Tea Water Pump (Lower Manhattan), 128
Technics and Civilization (Mumford), 240
technological hazards, 227
technological sublime, 209–212
technology
    aiding High Plains farming, 359
    craft, 145
    engineering profession and, 248–249
    labor-saving, 145–146, 209–210, 219

letdown of, 435–436
modern expectations of, 435
monopolization of profitable, 230
of railroad development, 175–183, 210–212
romancing of machine, 209–210
social construction of, 229–230
social efficiency through, 234–236
used by European society, 42–43
used by Pennsylvania Dutch farmers, 76
of water irrigation, 317
the West and engineering, 173
of wood industry, 142–143
See also industrialization
Tecumseh, 157
Tellico Dam project (Tennessee), 340, 454
"Telling Stories About the Future:" (Lewis), 7
"The Tempest" (Shakespeare), 10
Tennessee-Tombigbee Project ("Tenn-Tom"),
340–342
Tennessee Valley Authority Act of 1933, 338–339
Tennessee Valley Authority (TVA), 338–340,
345–346, 354
Teton Dam (Idaho), 322–323
textile industry, 146–147
"The Theoretical Structure of Ecological Revolutions"
(Merchant), 6
Thomas, Lewis, 449, 457, 466
Thompson, Laura, 25
Thoreau, Henry David, 155, 193, 194, 195–198,
199, 373, 386, 402, 407
Three Mile Island nuclear accident (1979), 447, 474
Three-Year Homestead Act of 1912, 358
Timber Culture Act of 1873, 105, 310, 358
Timber and Stone Act of 1878, 105
Times Beach, Missouri, 300
Tippecanoe, 157
tobacco agriculture, 68–69, 77
Tocqueville, Alexis de, 375
Tongass National Forest (Alaska), 420
Torrey Canyon disaster, 471
tourism, 398–401
"town pump" (Pittsburgh drinking water supply), 282
toxic chemical dumping, 296–301, 438, 458–461,
490
Toxics Inventory List (TRI), 461
Toxic Substances Control Act (TOSCA), 425, 436
Toynbee, Arnold, 277
"The Tragedy of the Commons" (Hardin), 465
"Trail of Tears," 40
Train, Russell, 448
transcendentalism, 193–197, 212–213
transcontinental railroads, 173, 175–183, 210–212,
251, 253
transportation
canal, 131–132

improvement of roads/highway, 260–264
infrastructure development for, 128–133
mobility of city, 253–255
overland, 133–136
railroad, 173, 175–183, 210–212, 251, 253
steamboat, 132–133
of the western migration, 166–167, 172–173
Transylvania, 93–94
Travels in New York and New England (Dwight), 399
Treaty of Greenville (1795), 108
tree spiking, 427
Trollope, Frances, 59, 199
"The Trophic Dynamic Aspect of Ecology" (Linde-
man), 409
Trueblood, Ted, 430
Tudor, Henry, 65
Turner, B. L., 406
Turner, Frederick Jackson, 61, 156, 195, 240, 243
Turner, Orasmus, 62
Turner, William, 317
Twain, Mark, 158, 213, 274
typhoid, 278–279, 285

Udall, Stewart, 406, 414, 438
Uhrlich, Ann, 469
"uncertainty principle," 417
Uncle Tom's Cabin (Stowe), 414
UN Conference on the Human Environment of 1972
(Stockholm), 480–481
Under the Sea Wind (Carson), 413
undeveloped country (UDC), 115–116
UN Educational, Scientific, and Cultural Organiza-
tion (UNESCO), 468
UN Environmental Programme (UNEP), 478, 481
UN Environment and Development Conference
(UNCED) conference (Rio de Janeiro), 429,
482–484, 490
Union Pacific Railroad, 179–183
United Company of Philadelphia for Promoting
American Manufactures, 118
United States
challenges of early agriculture in, 57–61
economic status (1790) of, 116–118
economic status (1840) of, 148–152
"environmental era" of, 436–439
environmental history of, 1–4
environmental isolationism of, 467–469
environmental issues related to, 5
environmental law/regulation in, 443–446
environmental/social advantages of, 119, 122–136
farming tradition of, 55–57
global environmentalism and demonizing of,
480–484
impact of Northwest Ordinance (1787) on, 96–98

United States *(continued)*
  Indian regions of future, 22–24
  industrialization of, 145–148
  Industrial Revolution impact on, 218–220
  material life within, 136–141
  as nation of natural resources, 221–228
  natural wonders of, 375
  as nature's nation, 204–205
  network of cities across the, 243–244
  preindustrial infrastructures of, 123–125
  rise of industrial ecology in the, 484–487
  status of corporations in, 231–234
  transportation development in, 128–136
  See also American continent; American frontier
Universal Oil Products Company, 227
UN Resolution 37/137, 481
Unruh, John, 166
urban cleanup
  beginnings of, 285
  of Love Canal, 299–301
  occupational diseases and, 286–288
  using water as flushing agent in, 285–286
urban water systems, 306–308
U.S. 40 (National Road), 135–136, 243
U.S. Army Corps of Engineers, 173, 178, 308–309,
    319, 335, 340–342, 385, 453
U.S. Atomic Energy Commission, 416
"The Use and Abuse of Vegetational Concepts and
    Terms" (Tansley), 409
U.S. environmental history, 1–4
"The Uses of Environmental History" (Cronon), 7
U.S. Geological Survey (USGS), 172, 174
U.S. Housing Authority, 265–266
U.S. Public Health Service (PHS), 287–288, 289
U.S. Steel Corporation, 298
Utah, 170–171
Utopia (More), 207
utopian communities, 205–209

Vaca, Alvar Núñez Cabeza de, 27–28
vacuum domicilium principle, 70
"Valley of Drums" (Kentucky), 436
Van Bers, Caroline, 480
Vandalia, 93
Vanderbilt, Cornelius, 230
Van Dieren, Wouter, 465
Van Hise, Charles R., 305–306, 310, 316–317
Vaux, Calvert, 374
Veblen, Thorstein, 274–275
Veiller, Lawrence, 277
Vérendrye, Pierre, 17
Vermont, 89–90
Verrazano, 122
Village of Euclid, Ohio v. Ambler Realty Company, 252

Virginia, 77–79, 93–94
Virginia Military Tract, 107
Vogt, William, 405
Voltaire, 207

Wade, Richard C., 253
Walden Pond, 195–196, 197, 373
Walden (Thoreau), 196
Wald, George, 488
Walker, Timothy, 242, 272–273
Wallace, Alfred Russel, 46
Walt Disney Enterprises, 393
Waring, George E., 286
Warner, Sam Bass, 126
Warren, Kemble, 174
Washington, George, 95, 97, 100, 106, 108, 137
Washington Park (Pittsburgh), 279–280
"water closets," 285
water networks
  of California, 324–330
  Chicago's, 285, 307
  drinking supply and, 127–128
  engineering urban, 306–308
  as infrastructure, 304–306
  of irrigation communities, 314–316
  reclamation and irrigation projects for, 316–324
  salinity and, 337
  U.S. Army Corps of Engineers and, 308–309
  western lack of water and, 309–311
  See also Clean Water Act of 1970; reclamation
water projects (California), 326
water wars, 325–328
Watson, James D., 193
Watt, James G., 383, 422, 429, 431, 449
Watts Bar nuclear facility, 339
Watts, May T., 14
Wayburn, Peggy, 396
Wayne, "Mad Anthony," 108
Wealth of Nations (Smith), 137, 148
The Wealth of Nature: (Worster), 7
Weart, Spencer, 212
Webster, Noah, 19, 87
A Week on the Concord and Merrimack Rivers
    (Thoreau), 196
Weiner, Norbert, 488
Weisberger, Bernard, 230
Weiser, Mark, 149
Weller, Jack, 354
Wells, David A., 219
Wentworth, John, 169
the West
  Anasazi Indians of, 23, 311
  cooperative irrigation communities of, 314–316
  during the beaver fur trade, 158–159, 161

environmental history of, 155–156
gold rush of, 166–167
government facilitates routes to, 162–163
lack of water in, 309–310
landgrabbing of, 156–158
migration transportation to, 166–167, 172–173
mining the, 224–225
the Mormon experiment in, 170–171, 315–316
older Spanish settlements of, 311, 314
Oregon migration of, 157, 168–169
reclamation and irrigation of the, 316–324
routes to Pacific Northwest, 165–173
survey and inventorying, 174–175
takeover of Spanish territory of, 163–165
Western Reserve (Connecticut), 107
Westlands Water District, 329
West, R. G., 408
Wheeler, George M., 174, 175
"whistleblowers," 288
White, C. Albert, 108
White, E. B., 414
Whitehead, Alfred North, 137, 205
White, Lynn, Jr., 249
White, Richard, 7, 305, 336, 342
White-Stevens, Robert, 414
"White Wings" sanitary employees, 286
Whitman, Walt, 195
Whitney, Asa, 178
Whitney, Eli, 230
Whitney, Josiah D., 174
Wilderness Act of 1964, 323, 383, 391–392, 395, 402, 420
wilderness philosophy, 401–402
wilderness preservation
of Alaska, 394–396
campaign for Grand Canyon, 393–394
Hetch Hetchy/Echo Park and, 389–391
impact of tourism on, 398–401
John Muir and, 386–388
modern wilderness movement and, 391–394
See also environmentalism; National Parks; nature
Wilderness Road, 136
Wilderness Society, 323, 391, 395, 397, 402, 420, 438
wildlife (pre-European American), 16–17

Wild and Scenic Rivers Act of 1968, 323
Wilkes, Commander, 165
Wilkinson, James, 163
Willamette Valley, 165
William McIntosh v. Johnson and Graham's Lessee, 70
Williamson, Hugh, 95
Williams, Roger, 71
Wilson, E. O., 415
Wilson, J. A., 291–292
Wilson, Woodrow, 389
Winthrop, Jonathan, 44, 70
Wisconsin Power and Light Company, 340
"wise-man's burden," 235
Wise Use Movement, 430–431
wood industry
balloon frame house of, 144
prosperity through, 141–143
See also forest; industralization
Woodward v. Dartmouth College, 232
Wordsworth, William, 189, 195
World Commission on Environment and Development, 478
World model standard run, 475
World Wildlife Fund, 450
Worster, Donald, 6–7, 7, 197, 315
Wounded Knee (1890), 40
WPA (Works Progress Administration), 265
Wright, Louis B., 67
Wyoming Valley (Pennsylvania), 87–89

Yannacone, Victor, 423
Yard, Robert Sterling, 382, 420
"Yazoo frauds" (Georgia), 91
Yellowstone National Park, 371, 378–379, 398, 400–401
Yosemite National Park, 376–378, 385–386, 388, 398
Young, Brigham, 170, 171, 315

Zahniser, Howard C., 391, 394, 420
Zakin, Susan, 427
zoning, 252
Zybach, Frank, 363

CREDITS

Chapter 2 p. 62 (a), Smithsonian Institution; p. 62 (b), Smithsonian Institution; p. 62 (c), Smithsonian Institution; p. 62 (d), Smithsonian Institution.

Chapter 4 p. 144, Charles Singer, et al., *A History of Technology* (London: Oxford University Press, 1954–58). By permission of Oxford University Press.

Chapter 5 p. 180–81, Redrawn by W. Matt Pinkney.

Chapter 6 p. 200, Corbis-Bettmann; p. 203, The Granger Collection, New York.

Chapter 7 p. 222, North Wind Picture Archives.

Chapter 8 p. 259, © New York City Transit Authority.

Chapter 9 p. 281, Science and Technology Research Center, New York Public Library; p. 282, Harvard College Library; p. 312, public domain.

Chapter 11 p. 351, diagram of contour strip mining of coal, from G. Tyler Miller, *Living in the Environment,* 10/e © 1998 by Wadsworth Publishing Company. Reprinted with permission.; p. 352, Permission to reproduce this photograph has been granted by Caterpillar Inc.; p. 363, Courtesy of Valmont Industries, Inc. Valley, Nebraska.

Chapter 13 p. 410, American Midland Naturalist.

Chapter 15 p. 466, Courtesy of NASA.